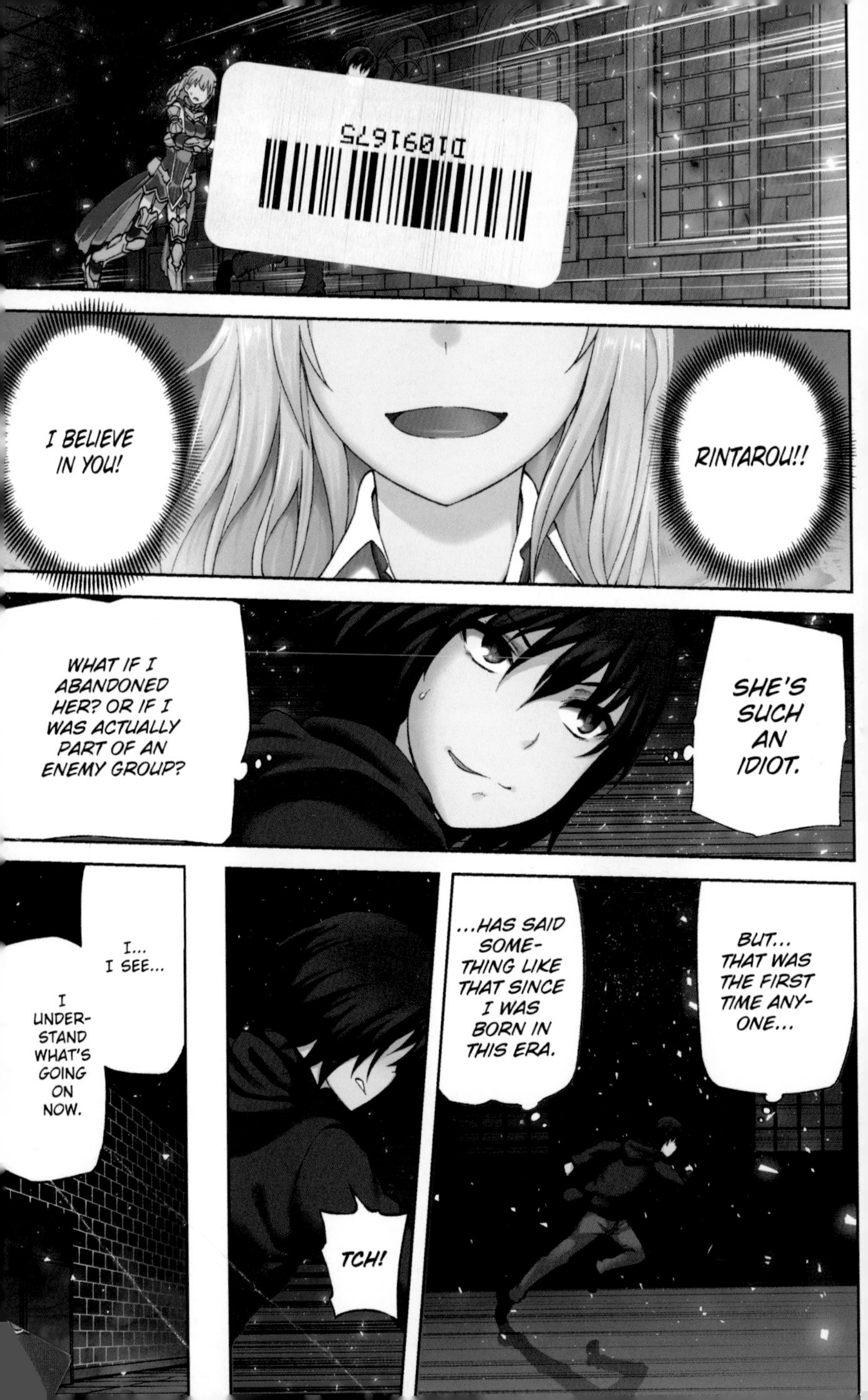
RINTAROU!!
I BELIEVE IN YOU!
SHE'S SUCH AN IDIOT.
WHAT IF I ABANDONED HER? OR IF I WAS ACTUALLY PART OF AN ENEMY GROUP?
BUT... THAT WAS THE FIRST TIME ANY-ONE...
...HAS SAID SOME-THING LIKE THAT SINCE I WAS BORN IN THIS ERA.
TCH!
I... I SEE...
I UNDER-STAND WHAT'S GOING ON NOW.

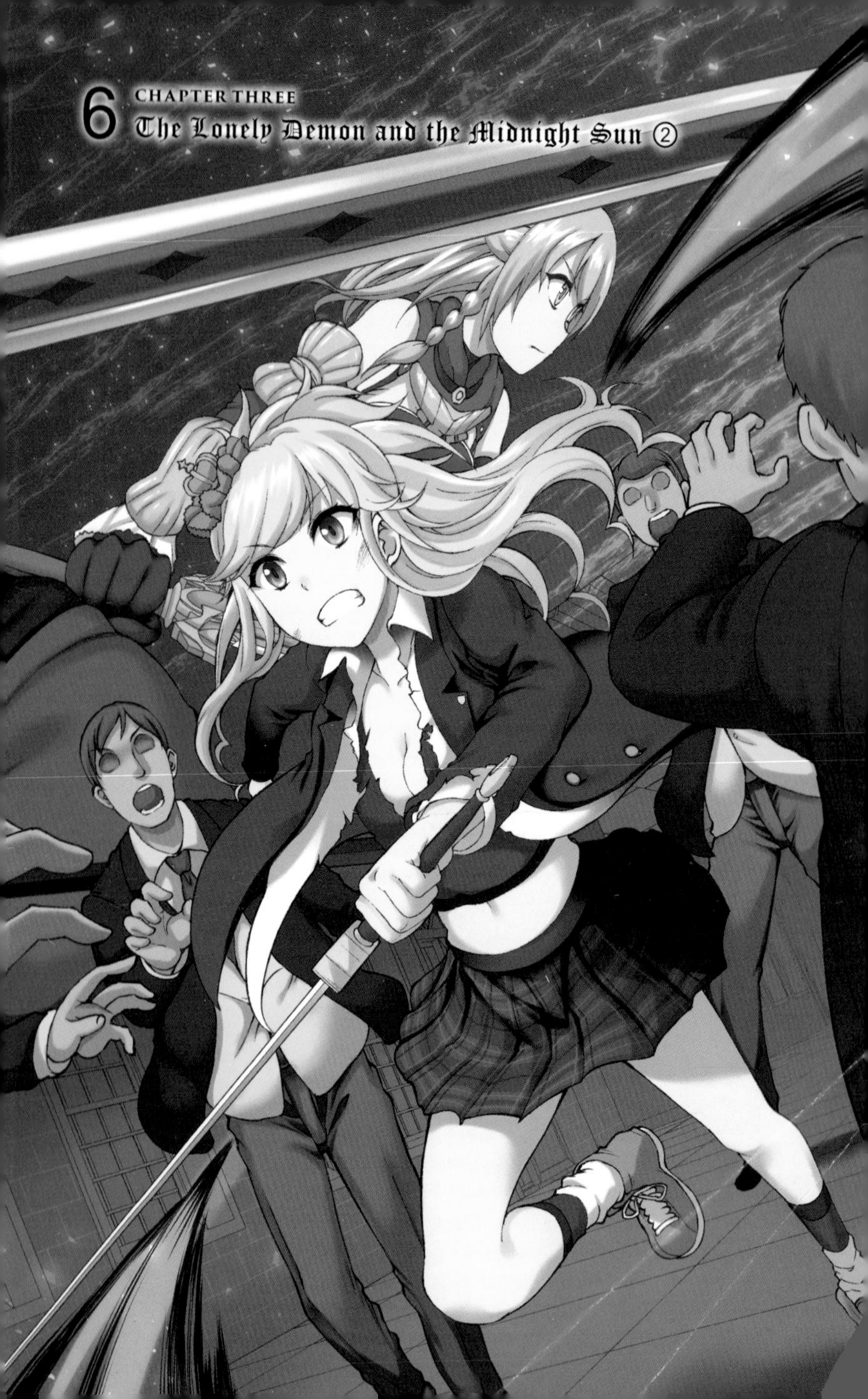
6
CHAPTER THREE
The Lonely Demon and the Midnight Sun ②

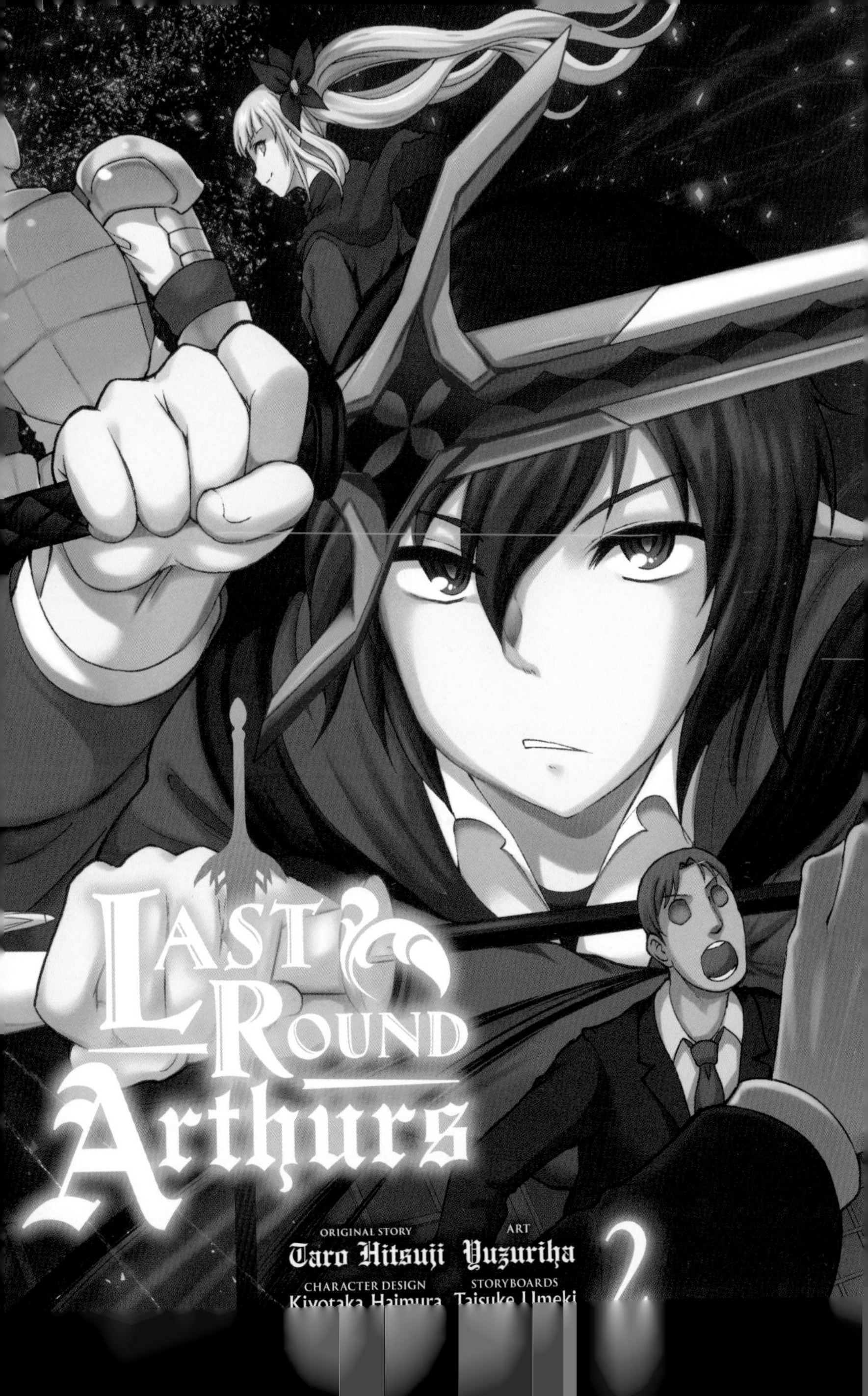
LAST ROUND Arthurs
ORIGINAL STORY
Taro Hitsuji
ART
Yuzuriha
CHARACTER DESIGN
Kiyotaka Haimura
STORYBOARDS
Taisuke Umeki
2

6

CHAPTER THREE

The Lonely
Demon and
the Midnight Sun
②

001

7

CHAPTER THREE

The Lonely
Demon and
the Midnight Sun
③

027

8

CHAPTER THREE

The Lonely
Demon and
the Midnight Sun
④

047

9

CHAPTER THREE

The Lonely
Demon and
the Midnight Sun
⑤

071

10

CHAPTER THREE

The Lonely
Demon and
the Midnight Sun
⑥

101

11

CHAPTER FOUR

The Leading Hand
①

131

12

CHAPTER FOUR

The Leading Hand
②

161

13

CHAPTER FIVE

Parting
Ways

191

14

FINAL CHAPTER

Luna's
Steel Sword

225

CONTENTS

LAST ROUND ARTHURS

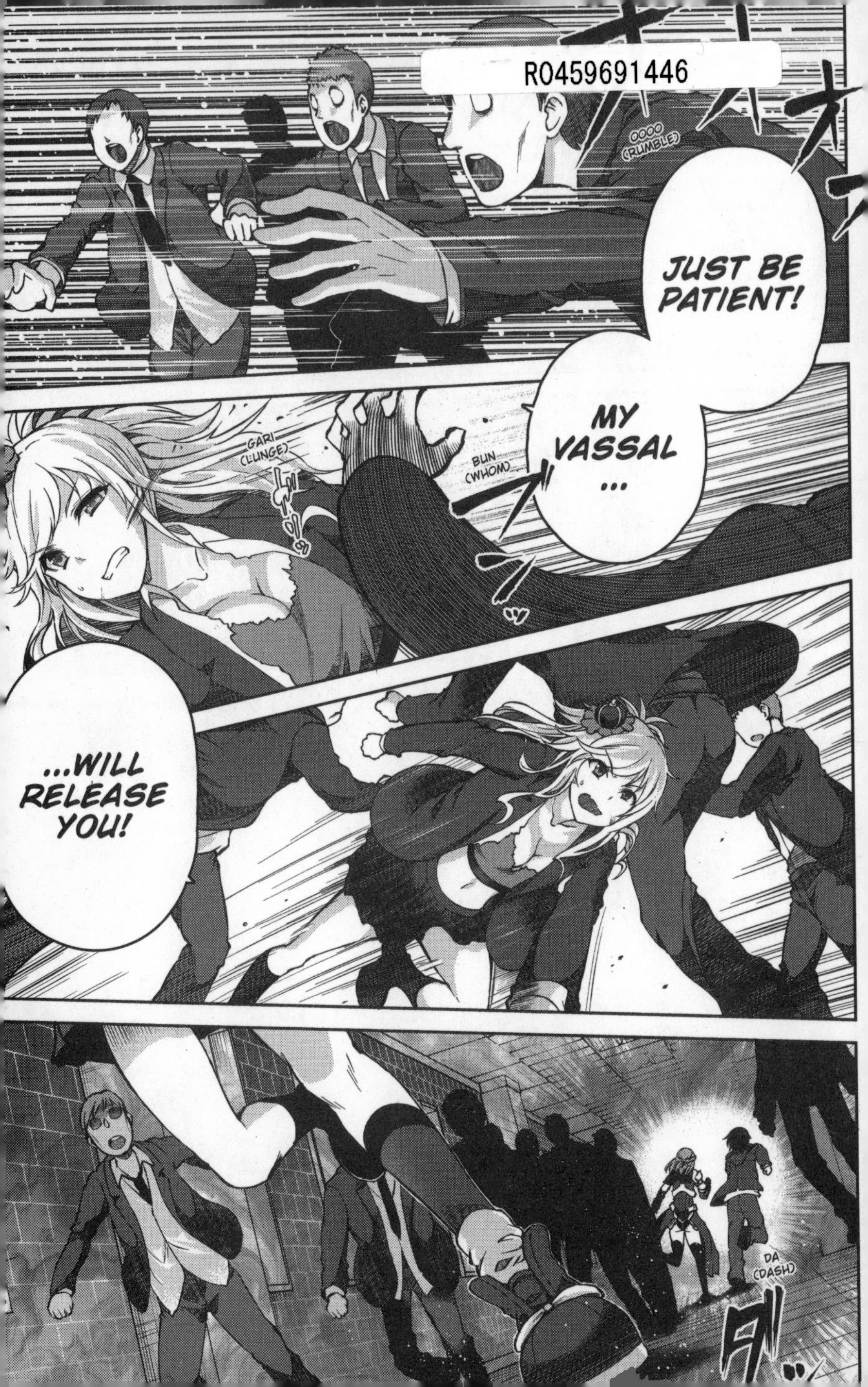
OOOO (RUMBLE)
JUST BE PATIENT!
MY VASSAL ...
BUN (WHOM)
GARI (LUNGE)
...WILL RELEASE YOU!
DA (DASH)

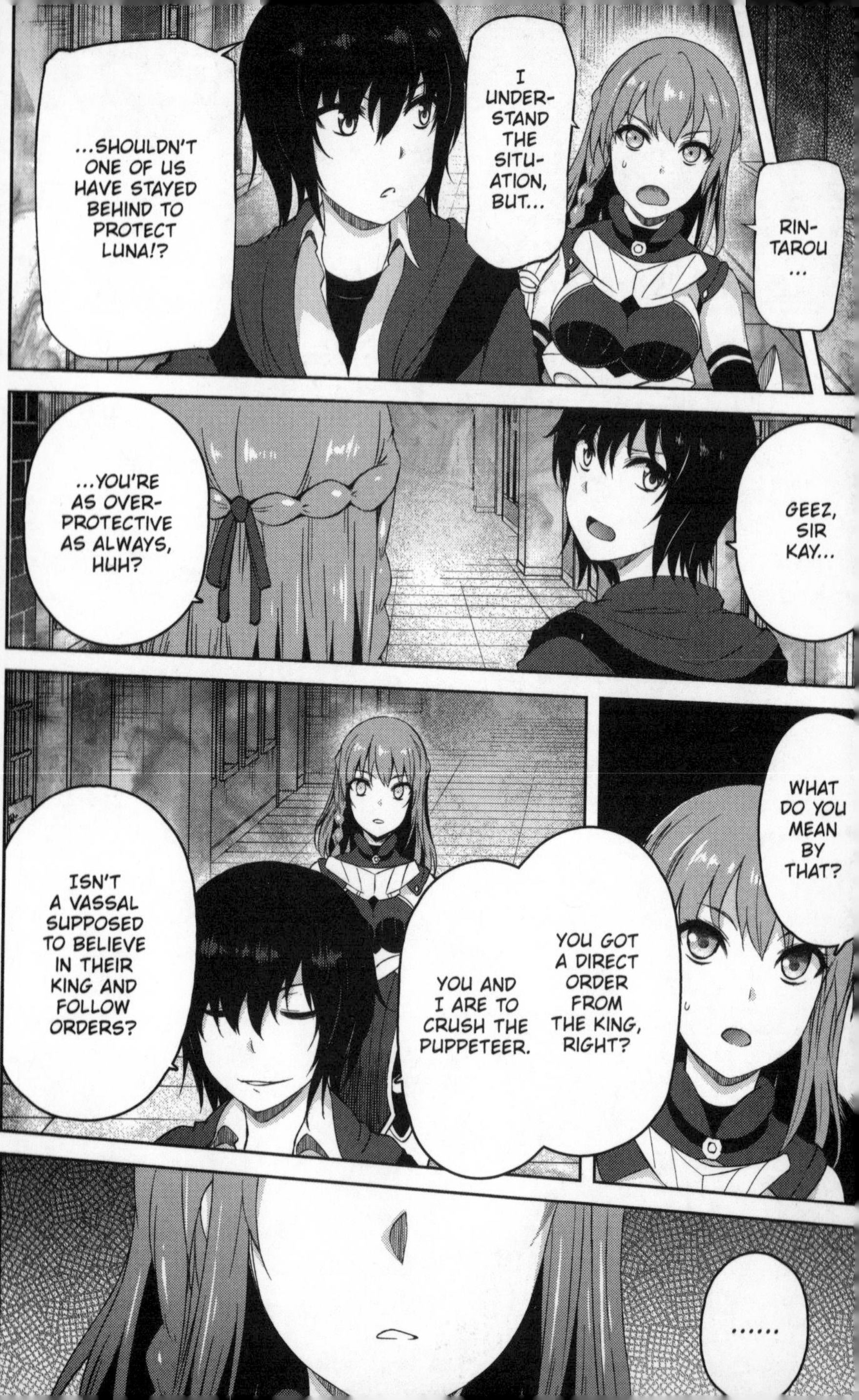
RIN-TAROU ...
I UNDER-STAND THE SITU-ATION, BUT...
...SHOULDN'T ONE OF US HAVE STAYED BEHIND TO PROTECT LUNA!?
GEEZ, SIR KAY...
...YOU'RE AS OVER-PROTECTIVE AS ALWAYS, HUH?
WHAT DO YOU MEAN BY THAT?
YOU GOT A DIRECT ORDER FROM THE KING, RIGHT?
YOU AND I ARE TO CRUSH THE PUPPETEER.
ISN'T A VASSAL SUPPOSED TO BELIEVE IN THEIR KING AND FOLLOW ORDERS?
......

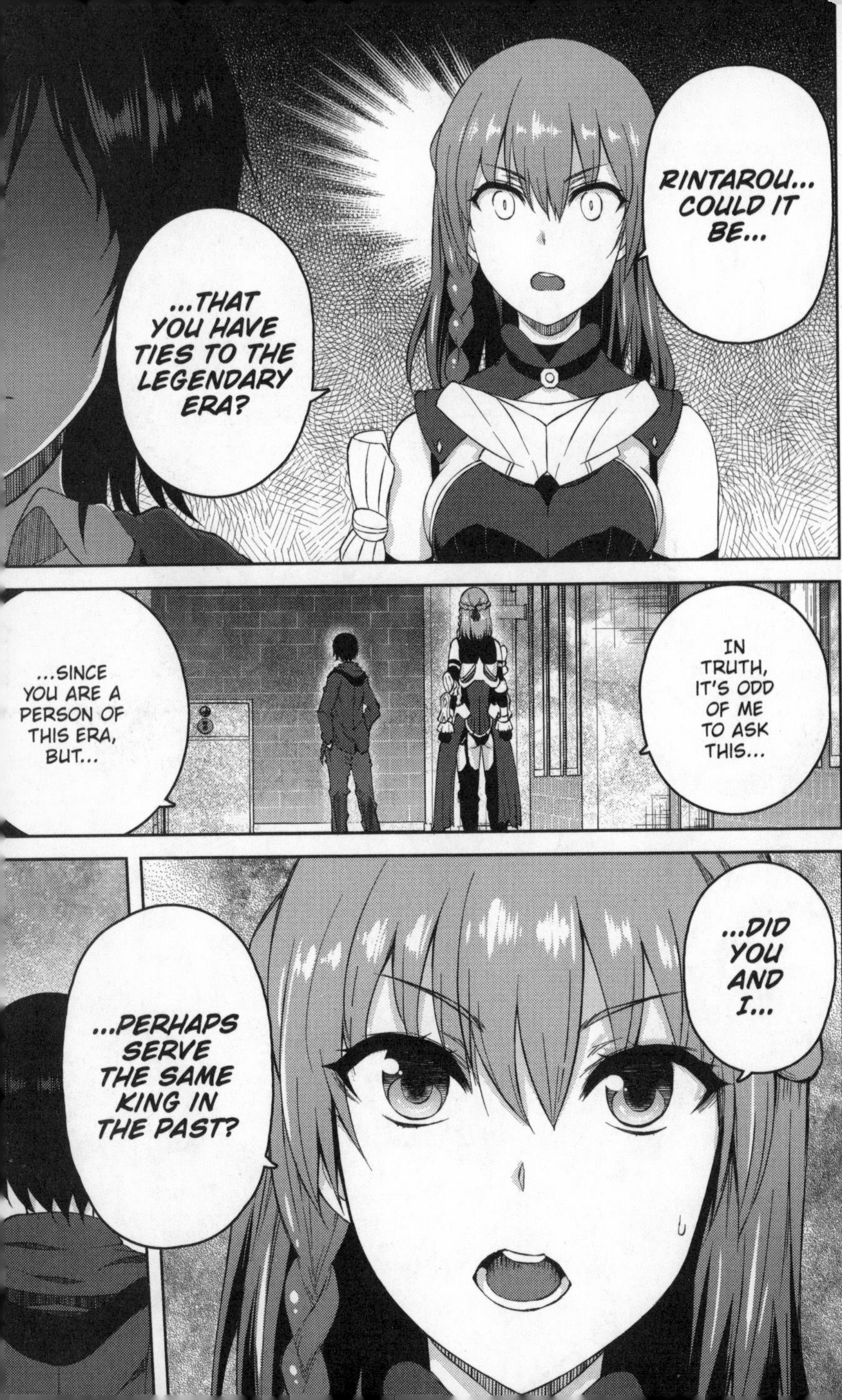
RINTAROU... COULD IT BE...
...THAT YOU HAVE TIES TO THE LEGENDARY ERA?
IN TRUTH, IT'S ODD OF ME TO ASK THIS...
...SINCE YOU ARE A PERSON OF THIS ERA, BUT...
...DID YOU AND I...
...PERHAPS SERVE THE SAME KING IN THE PAST?

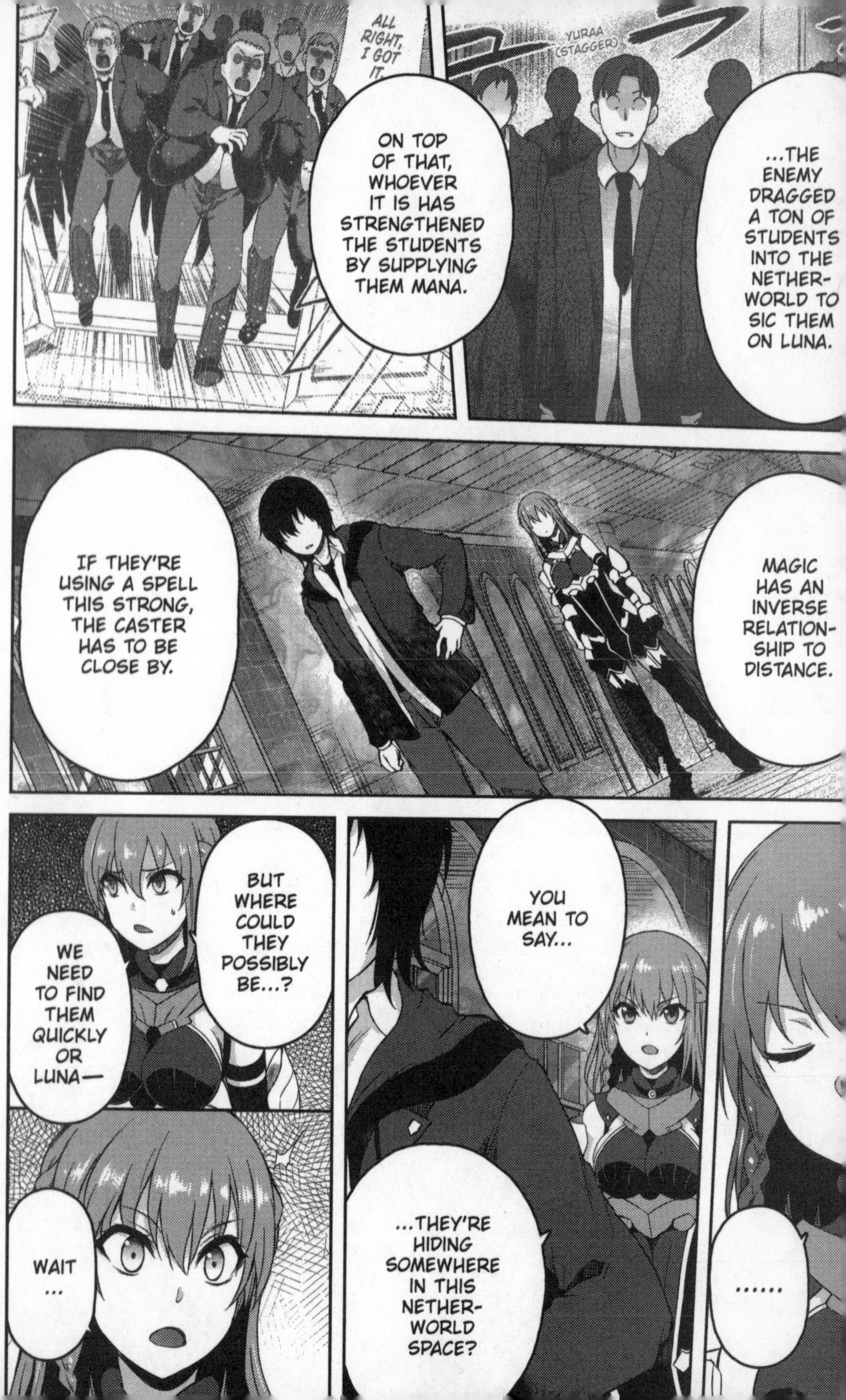
YURAA (STAGGER)
...THE ENEMY DRAGGED A TON OF STUDENTS INTO THE NETHER-WORLD TO SIC THEM ON LUNA.
ON TOP OF THAT, WHOEVER IT IS HAS STRENGTHENED THE STUDENTS BY SUPPLYING THEM MANA.
ALL RIGHT, I GOT IT.
MAGIC HAS AN INVERSE RELATION-SHIP TO DISTANCE.
IF THEY'RE USING A SPELL THIS STRONG, THE CASTER HAS TO BE CLOSE BY.
......
YOU MEAN TO SAY...
...THEY'RE HIDING SOMEWHERE IN THIS NETHER-WORLD SPACE?
BUT WHERE COULD THEY POSSIBLY BE...?
WE NEED TO FIND THEM QUICKLY OR LUNA—
WAIT ...

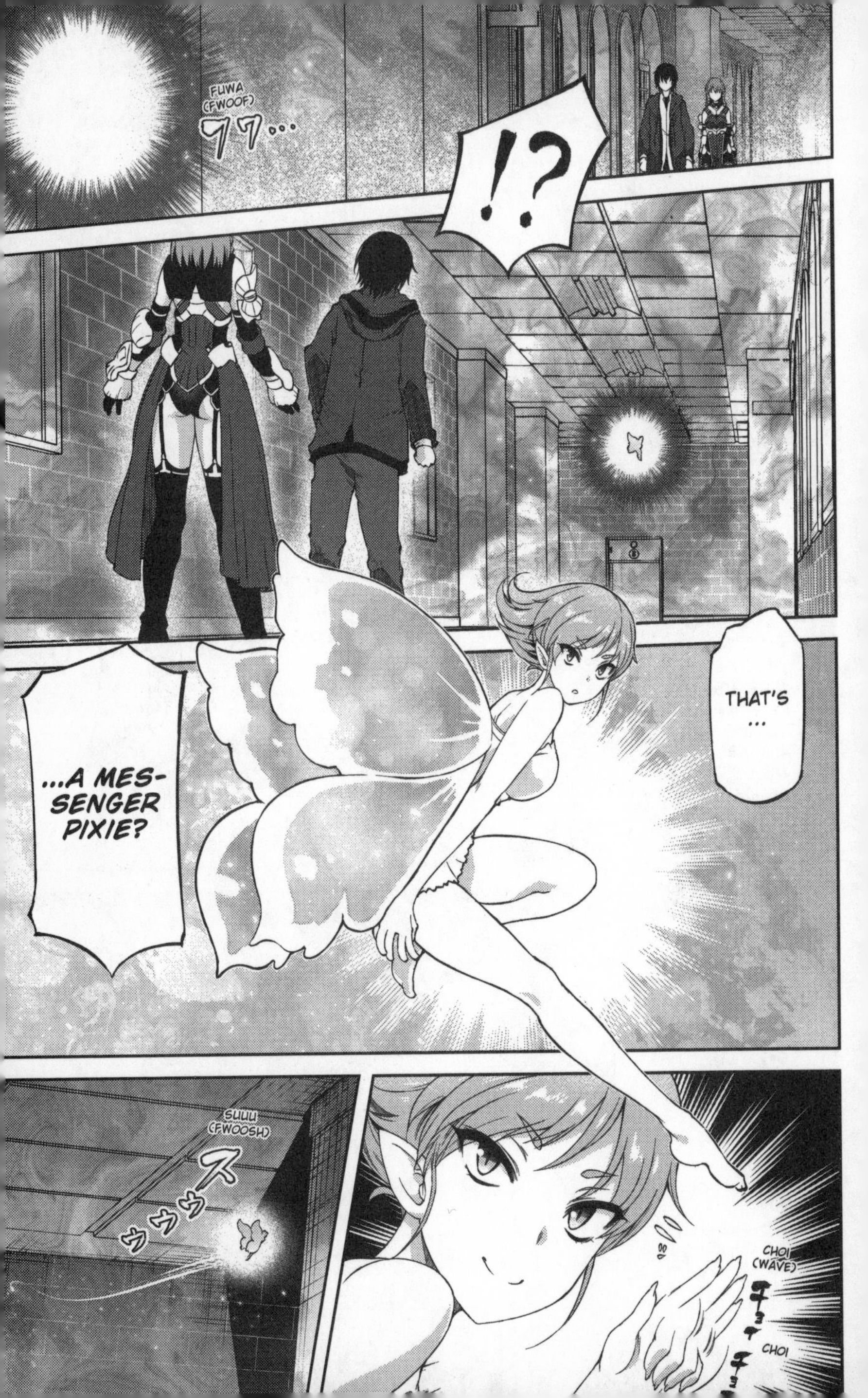

FUWA (FWOOF)
フワ…
!?
THAT'S ...
...A MES-SENGER PIXIE?
CHOI (WAVE)
チョイ
CHOI
チョイ
SUUU (FWOOSH)
スゥゥゥ

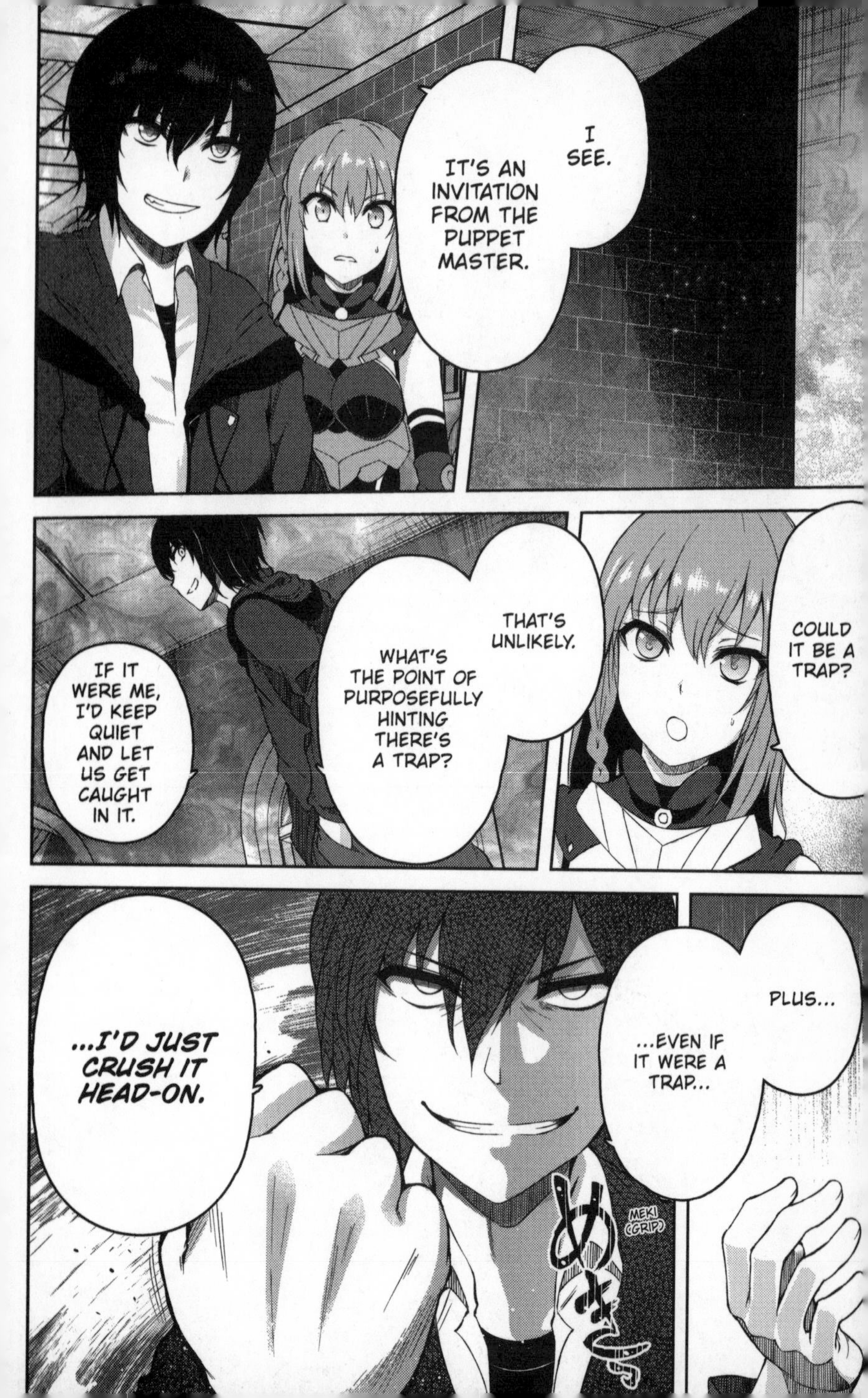
I SEE.
IT'S AN INVITATION FROM THE PUPPET MASTER.
COULD IT BE A TRAP?
THAT'S UNLIKELY.
WHAT'S THE POINT OF PURPOSEFULLY HINTING THERE'S A TRAP?
IF IT WERE ME, I'D KEEP QUIET AND LET US GET CAUGHT IN IT.
PLUS...
...EVEN IF IT WERE A TRAP...
MEKI (GRIP)
...I'D JUST CRUSH IT HEAD-ON.

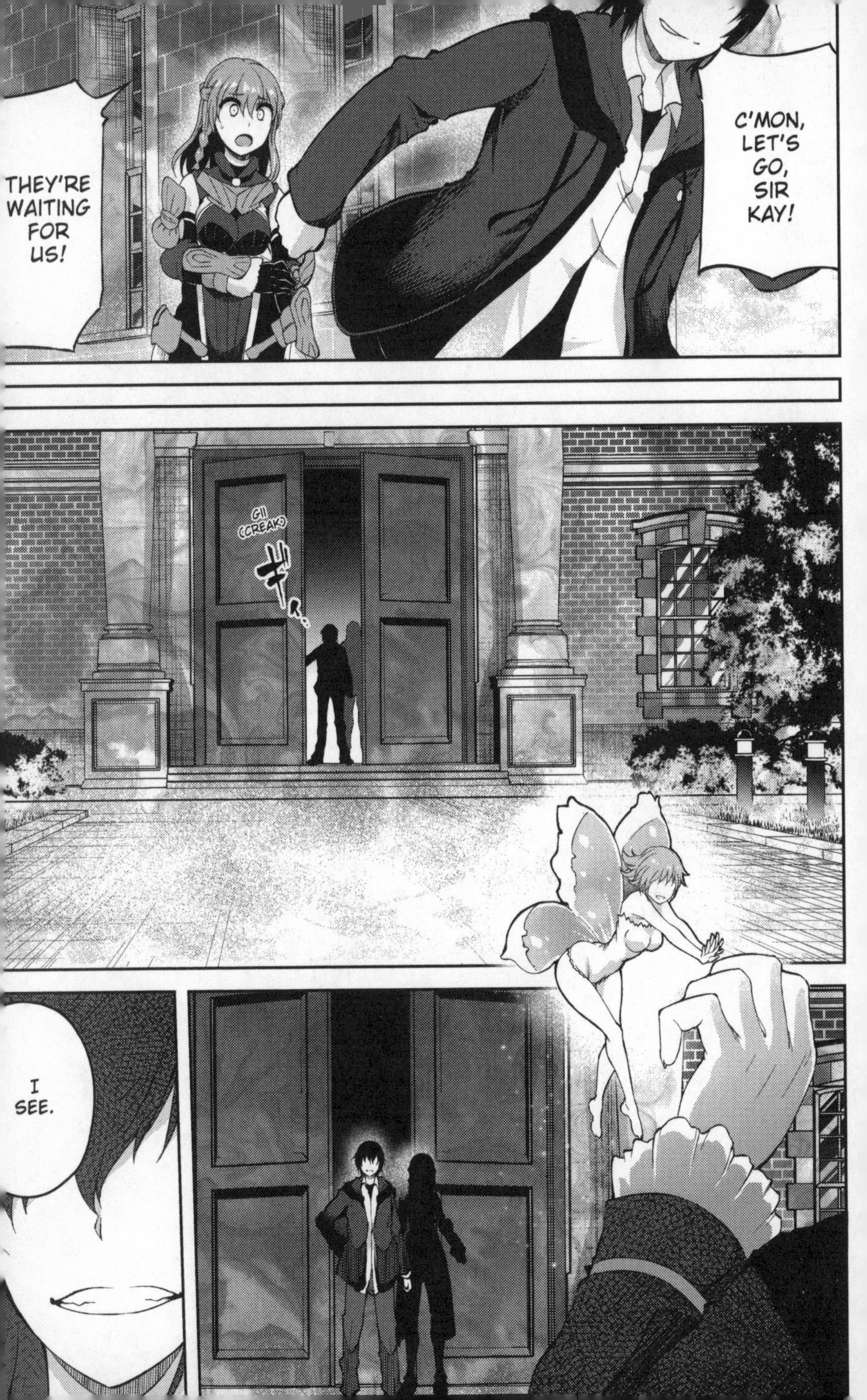
C'MON, LET'S GO, SIR KAY!
THEY'RE WAITING FOR US!
GII (CREAK)
I SEE.

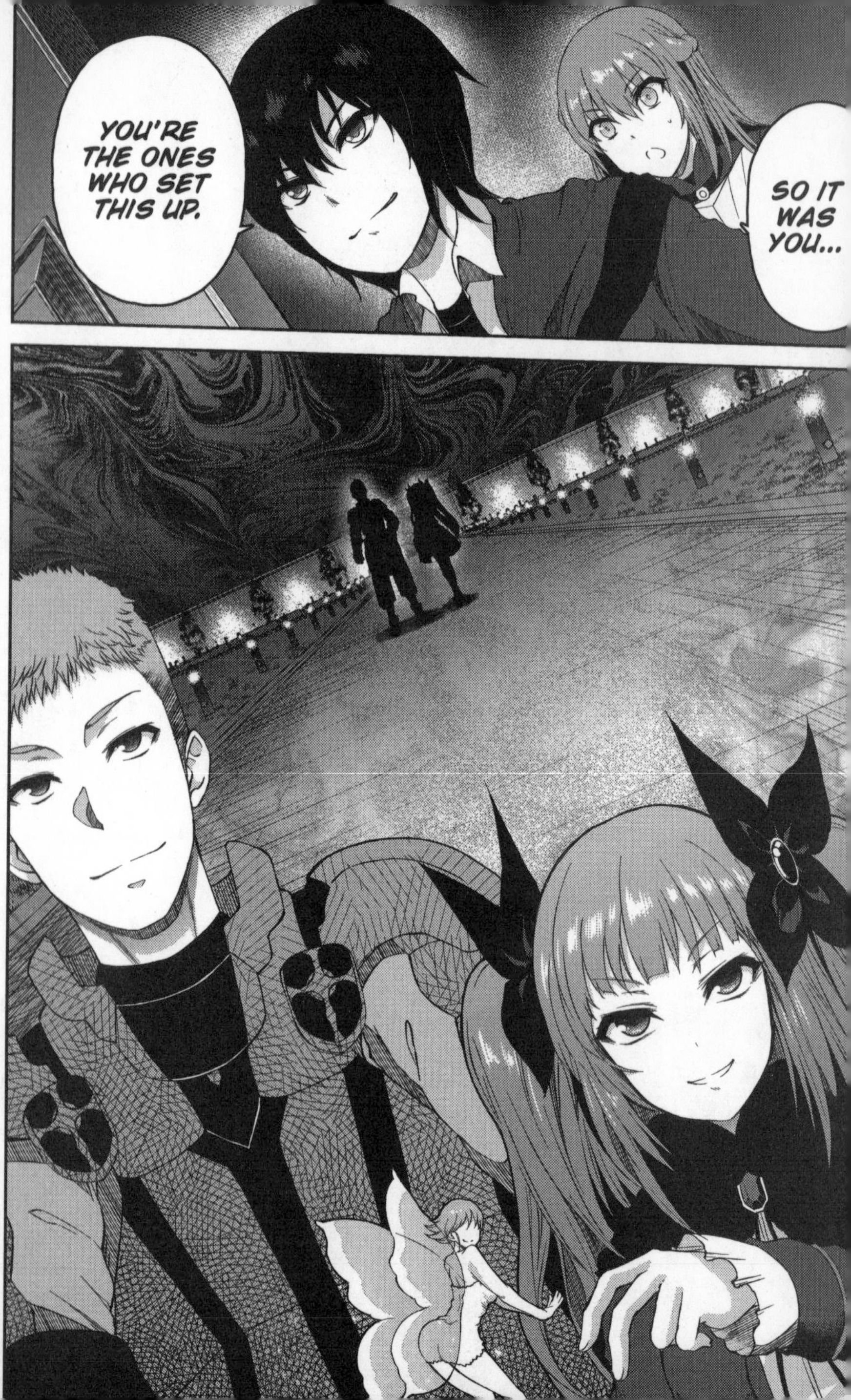
SO IT WAS YOU...
YOU'RE THE ONES WHO SET THIS UP.

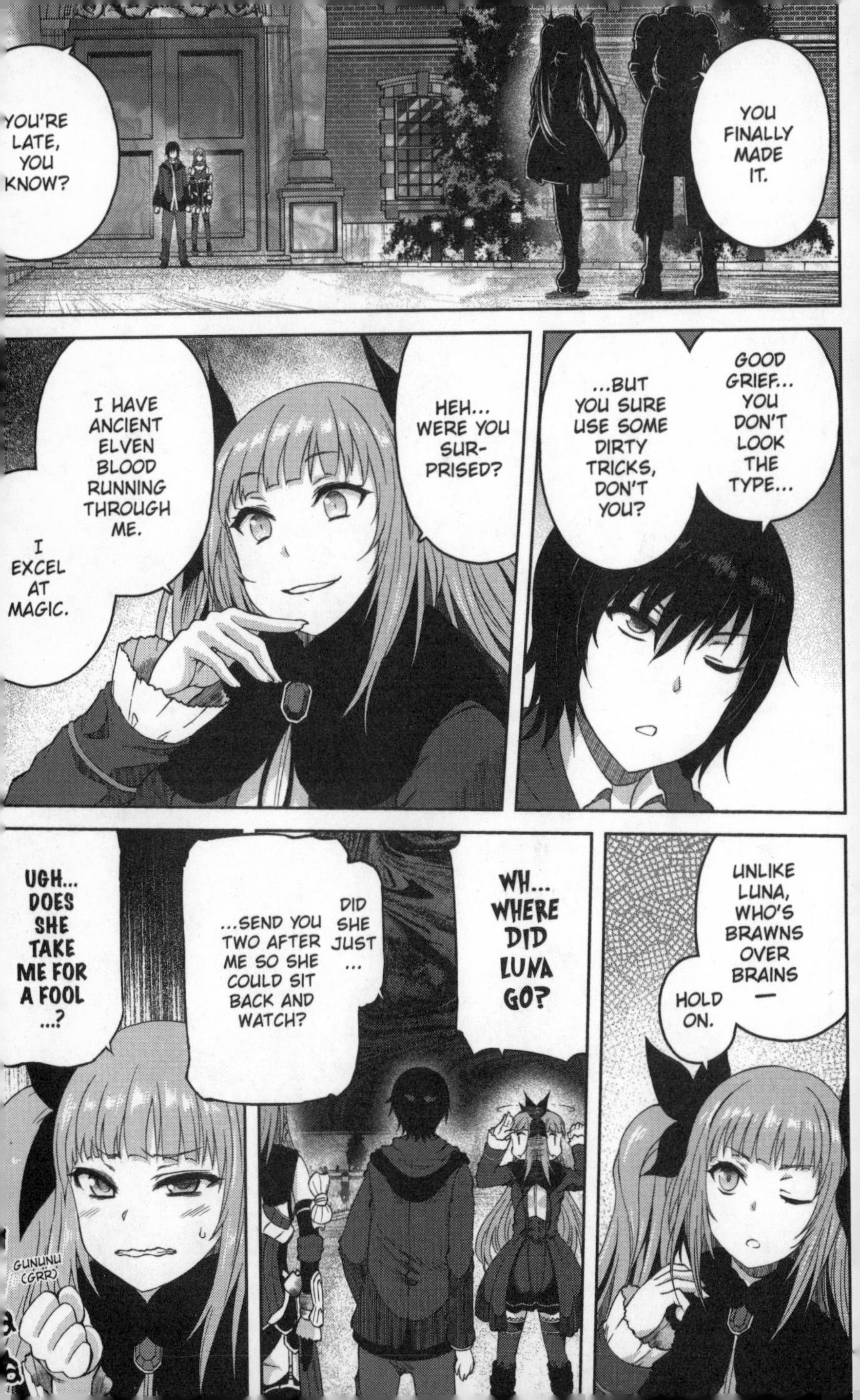
YOU FINALLY MADE IT.
YOU'RE LATE, YOU KNOW?
GOOD GRIEF... YOU DON'T LOOK THE TYPE...
...BUT YOU SURE USE SOME DIRTY TRICKS, DON'T YOU?
HEH... WERE YOU SUR-PRISED?
I HAVE ANCIENT ELVEN BLOOD RUNNING THROUGH ME.
I EXCEL AT MAGIC.
UNLIKE LUNA, WHO'S BRAWNS OVER BRAINS—
HOLD ON.
WH... WHERE DID LUNA GO?
DID SHE JUST...
...SEND YOU TWO AFTER ME SO SHE COULD SIT BACK AND WATCH?
UGH... DOES SHE TAKE ME FOR A FOOL...?
GUNUNU (GRR)

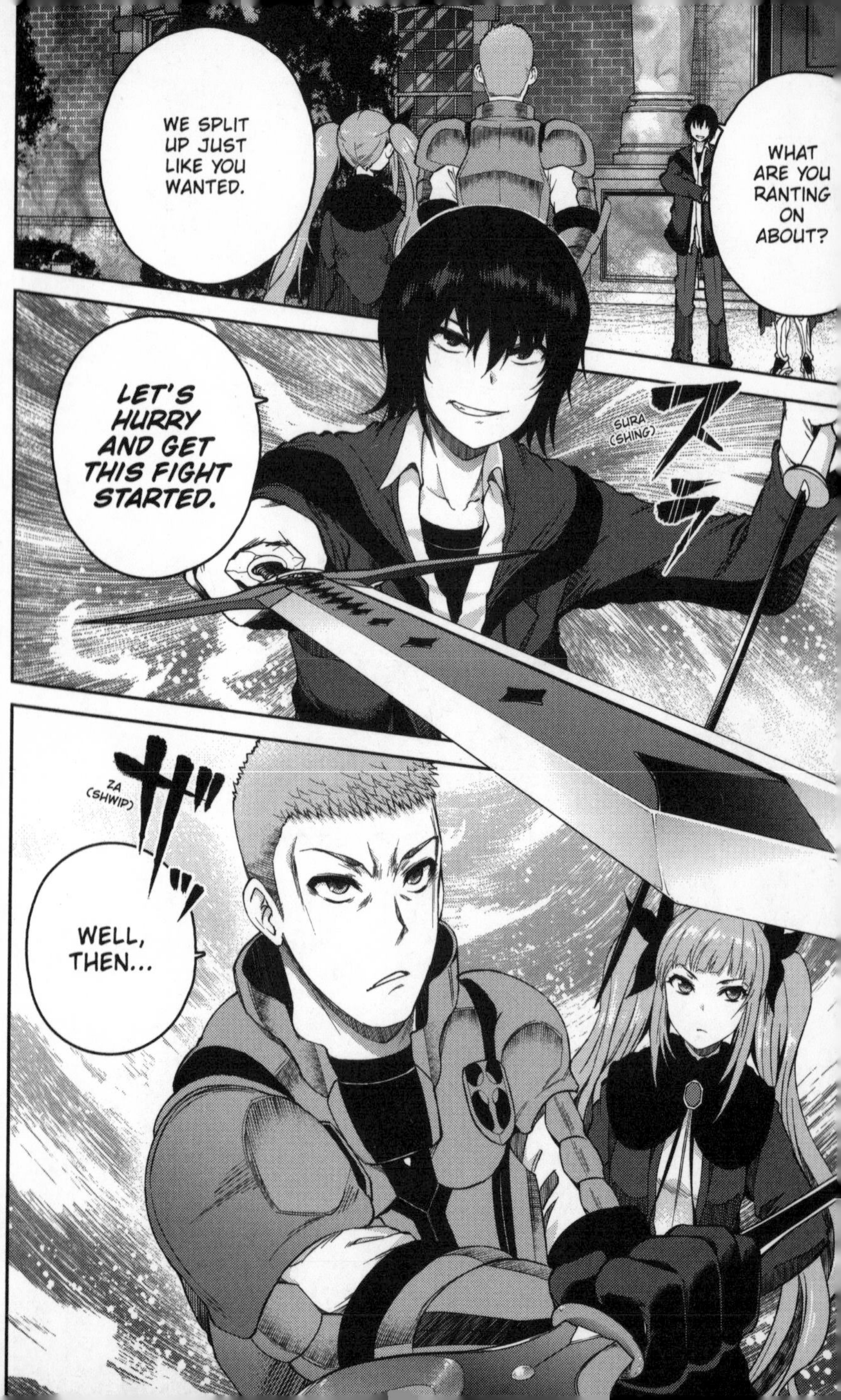
WHAT ARE YOU RANTING ON ABOUT?
WE SPLIT UP JUST LIKE YOU WANTED.
SURA (SHING)
LET'S HURRY AND GET THIS FIGHT STARTED.
ZA (SHWIP)
WELL, THEN...

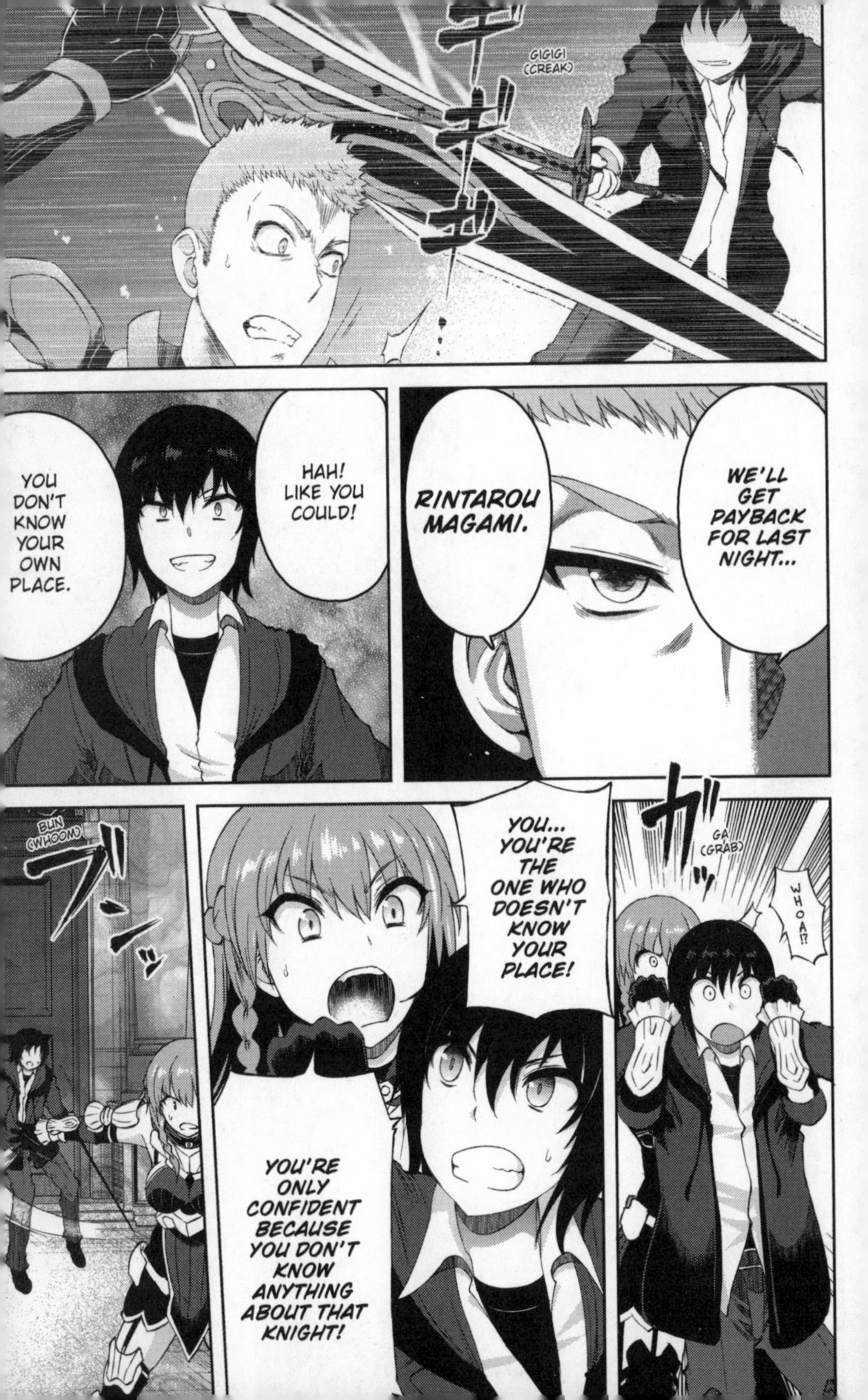
GIGIGI (CREAK)
WE'LL GET PAYBACK FOR LAST NIGHT...
RINTAROU MAGAMI.
HAH! LIKE YOU COULD!
YOU DON'T KNOW YOUR OWN PLACE.
GA (GRAB)
WHOA!?
YOU... YOU'RE THE ONE WHO DOESN'T KNOW YOUR PLACE!
YOU'RE ONLY CONFIDENT BECAUSE YOU DON'T KNOW ANYTHING ABOUT THAT KNIGHT!
BUN (WHOOM)

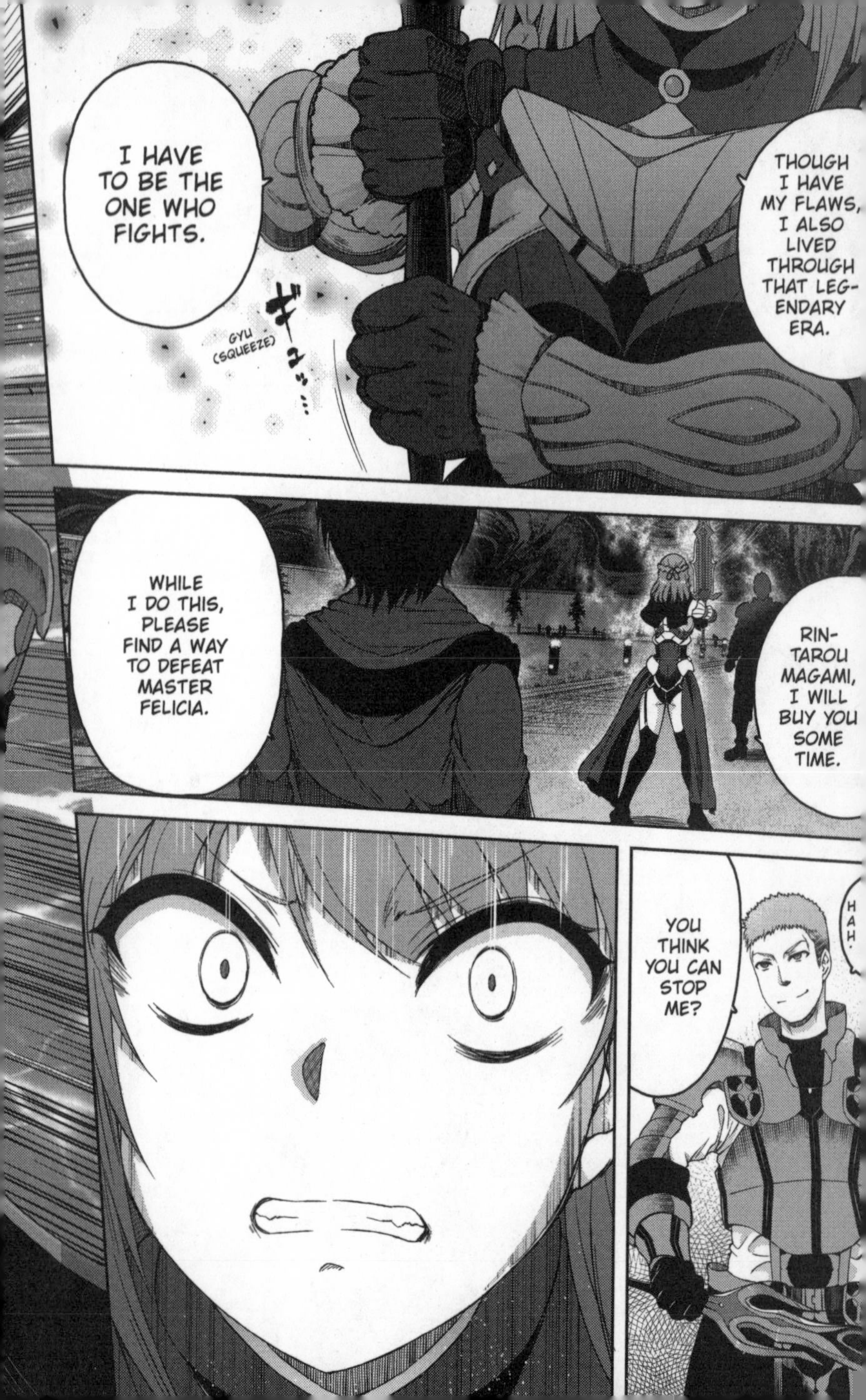
THOUGH I HAVE MY FLAWS, I ALSO LIVED THROUGH THAT LEGENDARY ERA.
I HAVE TO BE THE ONE WHO FIGHTS.
GYU (SQUEEZE)
RINTAROU MAGAMI, I WILL BUY YOU SOME TIME.
WHILE I DO THIS, PLEASE FIND A WAY TO DEFEAT MASTER FELICIA.
HAH.
YOU THINK YOU CAN STOP ME?

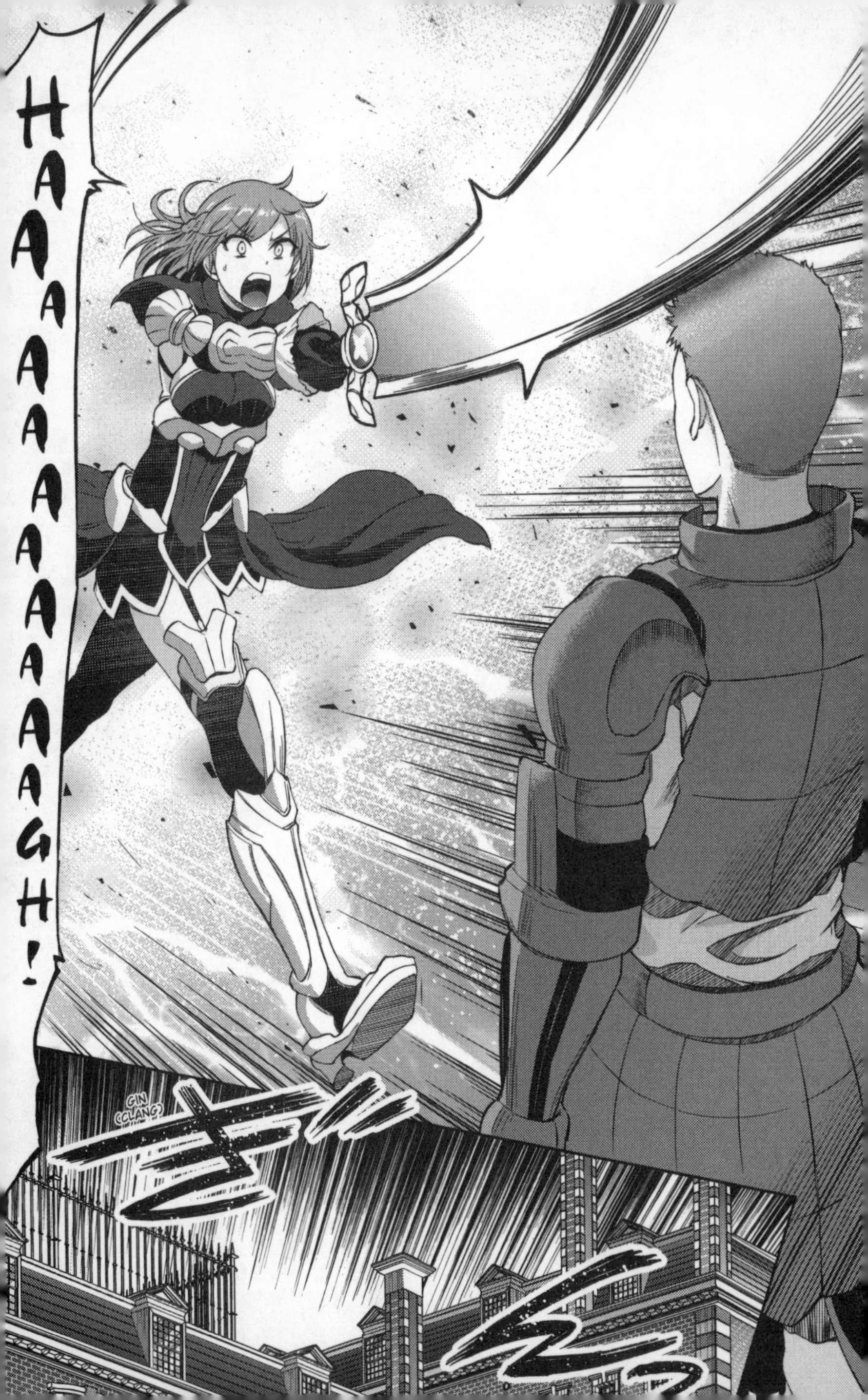
HAAAAAAAAAAAAAGH!
GIN (CLANG)

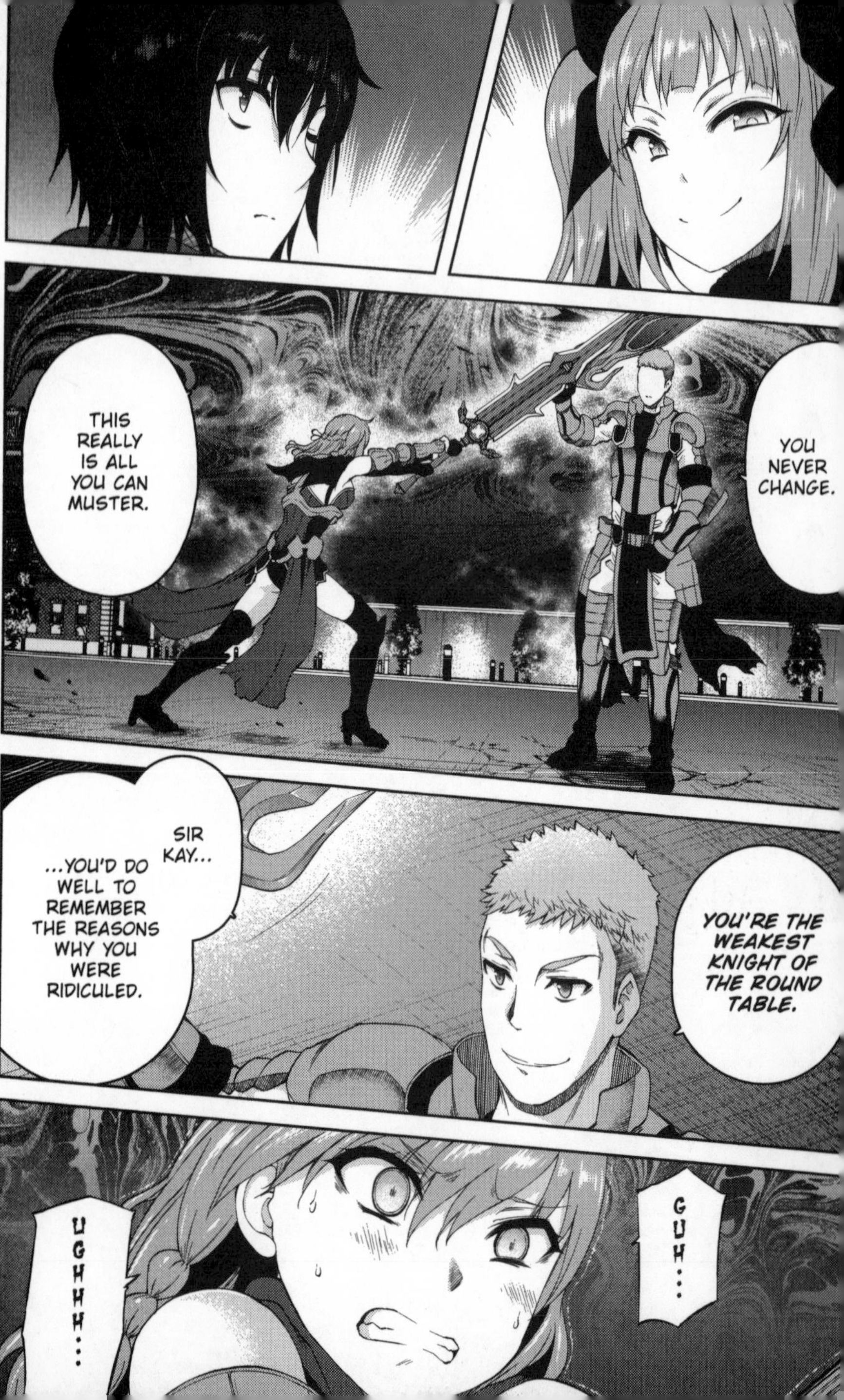
YOU NEVER CHANGE.
THIS REALLY IS ALL YOU CAN MUSTER.
YOU'RE THE WEAKEST KNIGHT OF THE ROUND TABLE.
SIR KAY...
...YOU'D DO WELL TO REMEMBER THE REASONS WHY YOU WERE RIDICULED.
GUH...
UGHHH...

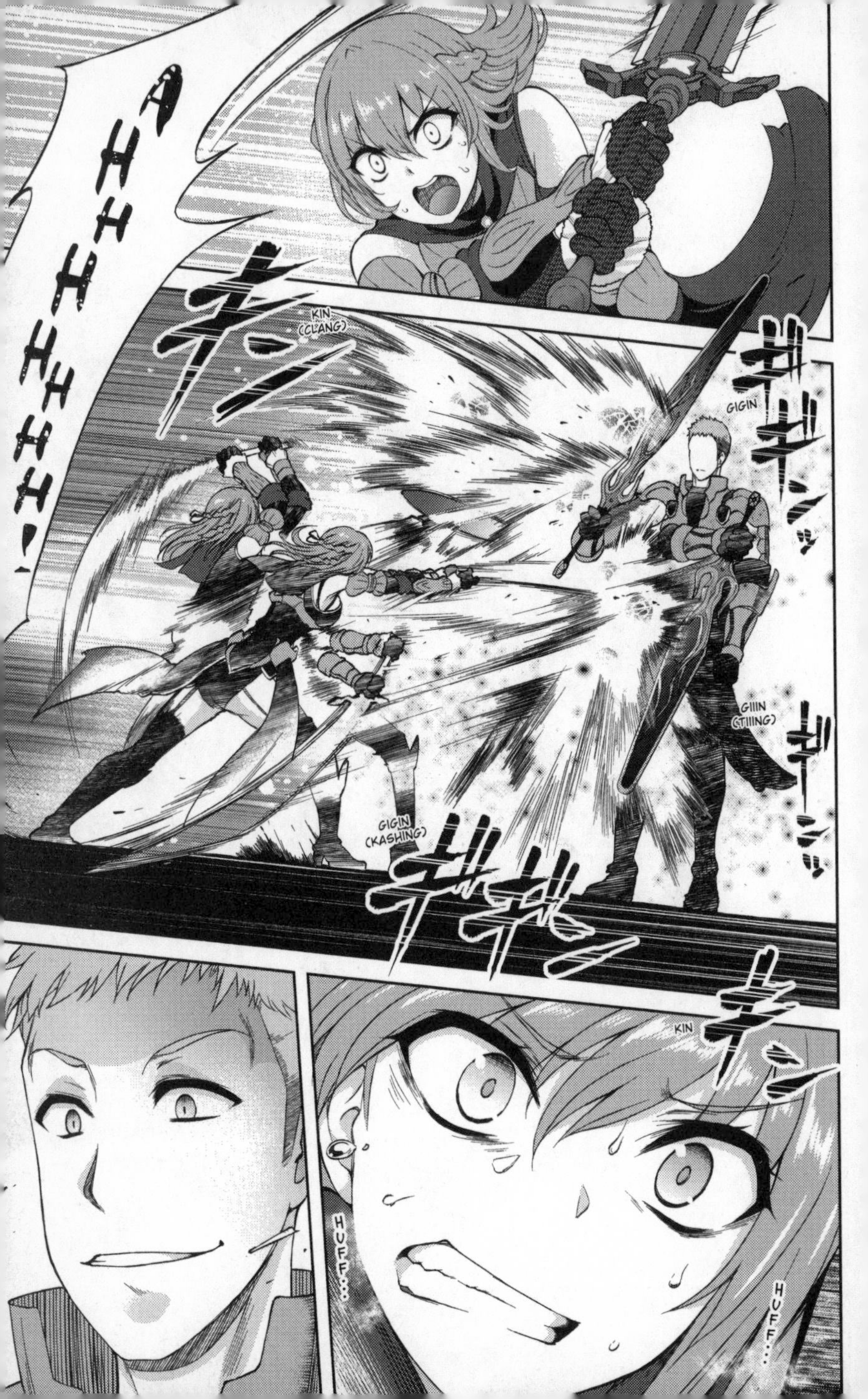
AHHHHHHHHH!
GIGIN
GIIIN (TIIING)
GIGIN (KASHING)
KIN (CLANG)
KIN
HUFF...
HUFF...

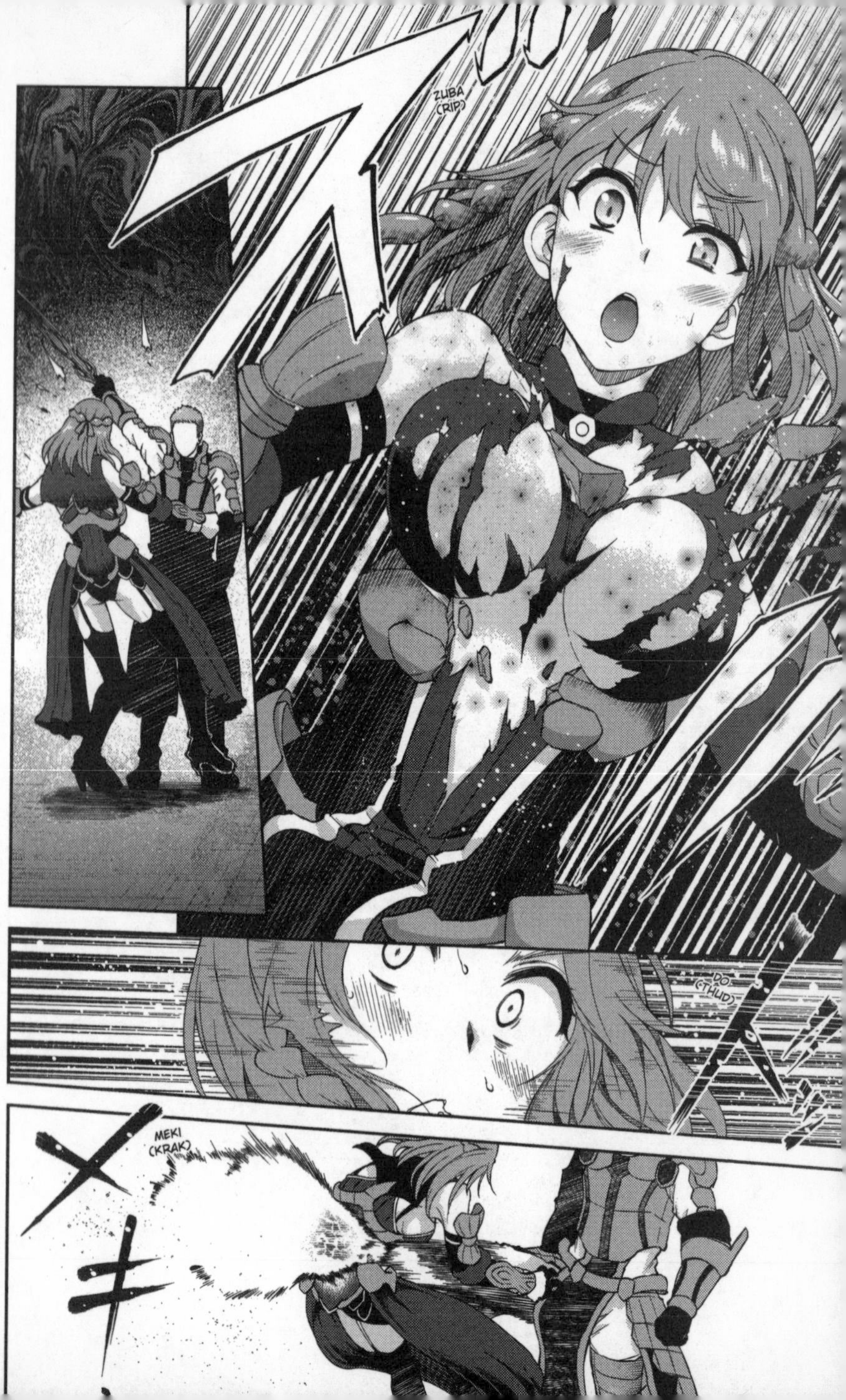
ZUBA
(RIP)
DO
(THUD)
MEKI
(KRAK)

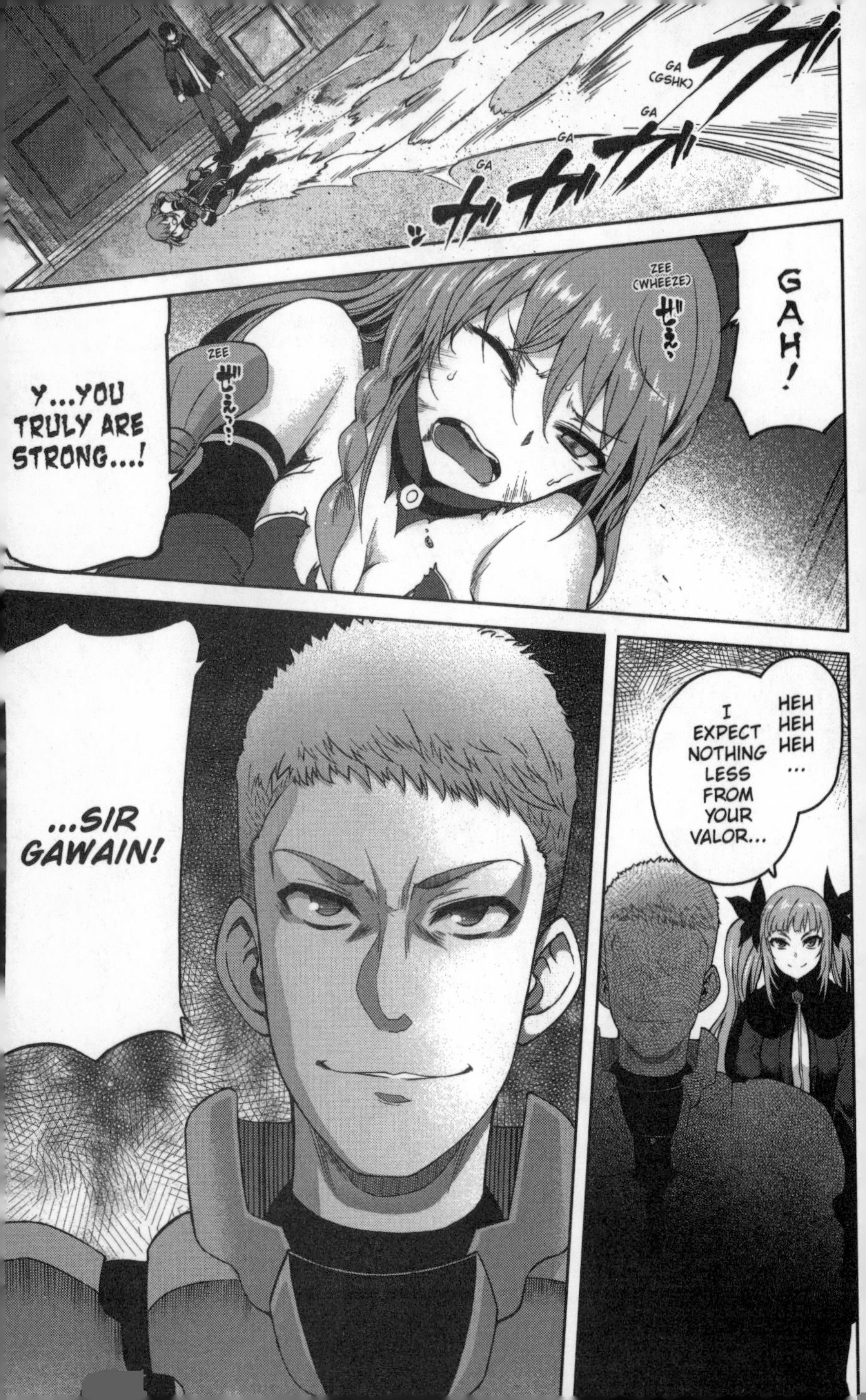
GA (GSHK)
GA
GA
GA
GAH!
ZEE (WHEEZE)
ZEE
Y...YOU TRULY ARE STRONG...!
HEH HEH HEH...
I EXPECT NOTHING LESS FROM YOUR VALOR...
...SIR GAWAIN!

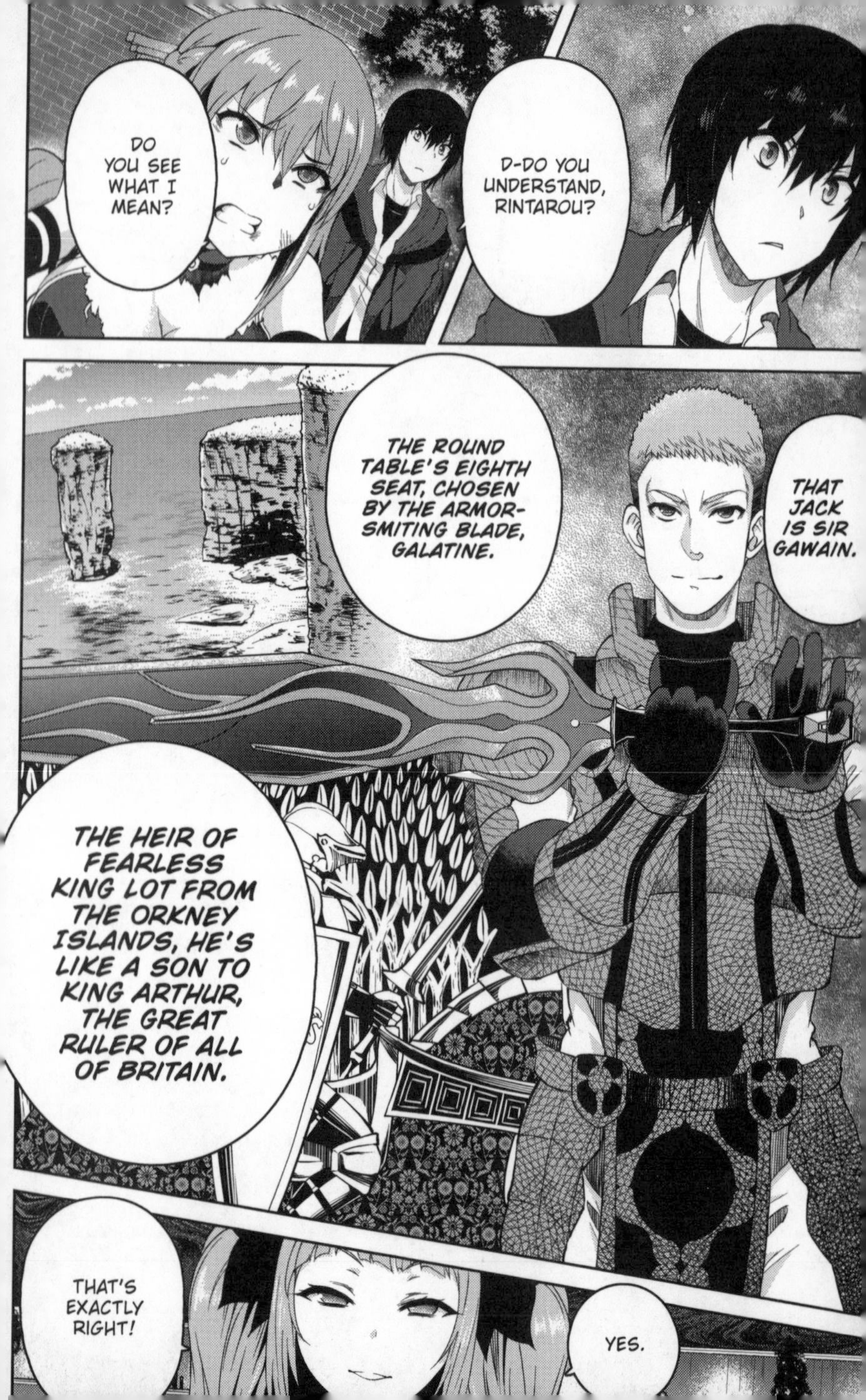

D-DO YOU UNDERSTAND, RINTAROU?
DO YOU SEE WHAT I MEAN?
THAT JACK IS SIR GAWAIN.
THE ROUND TABLE'S EIGHTH SEAT, CHOSEN BY THE ARMOR-SMITING BLADE, GALATINE.
THE HEIR OF FEARLESS KING LOT FROM THE ORKNEY ISLANDS, HE'S LIKE A SON TO KING ARTHUR, THE GREAT RULER OF ALL OF BRITAIN.
YES.
THAT'S EXACTLY RIGHT!

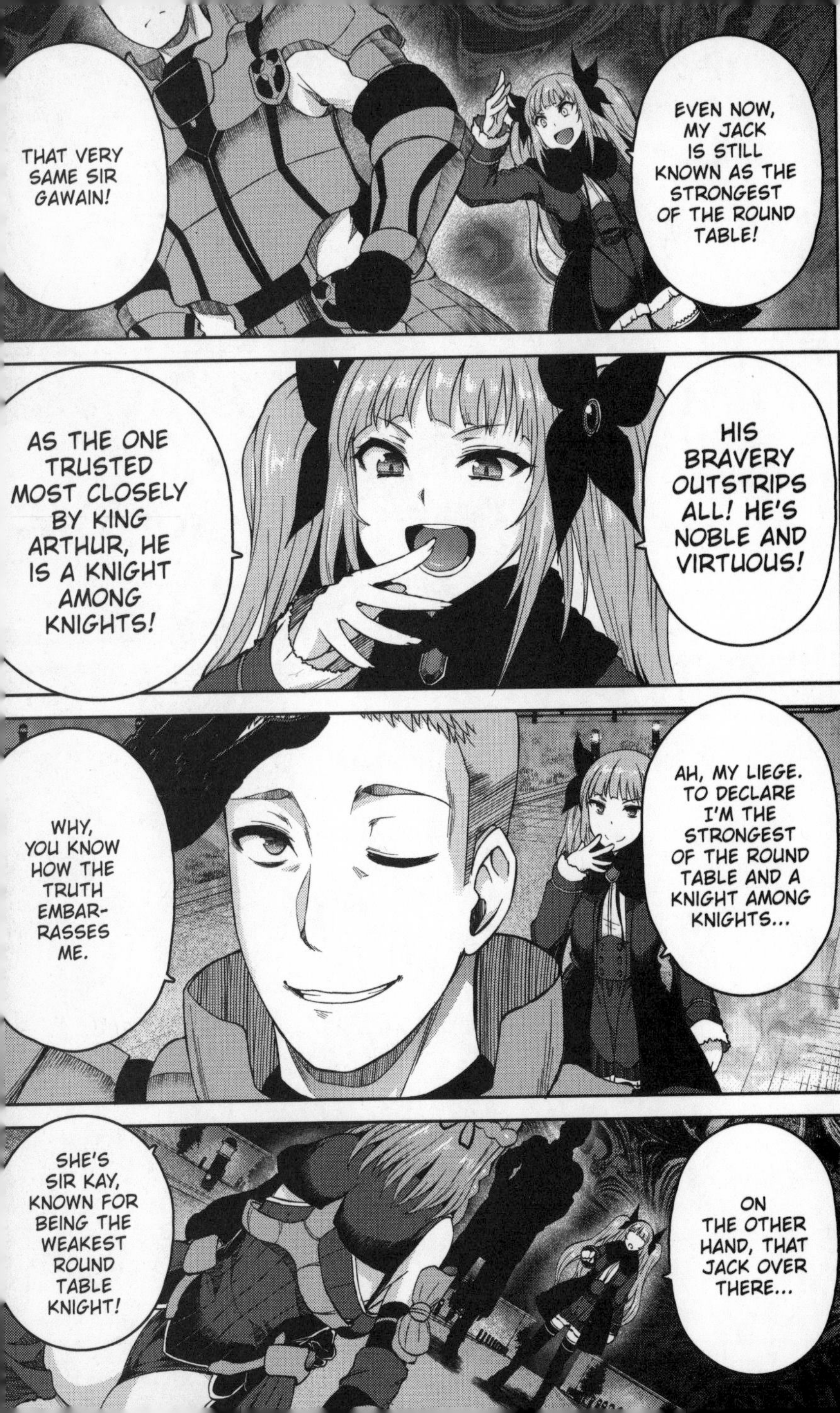
EVEN NOW, MY JACK IS STILL KNOWN AS THE STRONGEST OF THE ROUND TABLE!
THAT VERY SAME SIR GAWAIN!
HIS BRAVERY OUTSTRIPS ALL! HE'S NOBLE AND VIRTUOUS!
AS THE ONE TRUSTED MOST CLOSELY BY KING ARTHUR, HE IS A KNIGHT AMONG KNIGHTS!
AH, MY LIEGE. TO DECLARE I'M THE STRONGEST OF THE ROUND TABLE AND A KNIGHT AMONG KNIGHTS...
WHY, YOU KNOW HOW THE TRUTH EMBAR-RASSES ME.
ON THE OTHER HAND, THAT JACK OVER THERE...
SHE'S SIR KAY, KNOWN FOR BEING THE WEAKEST ROUND TABLE KNIGHT!

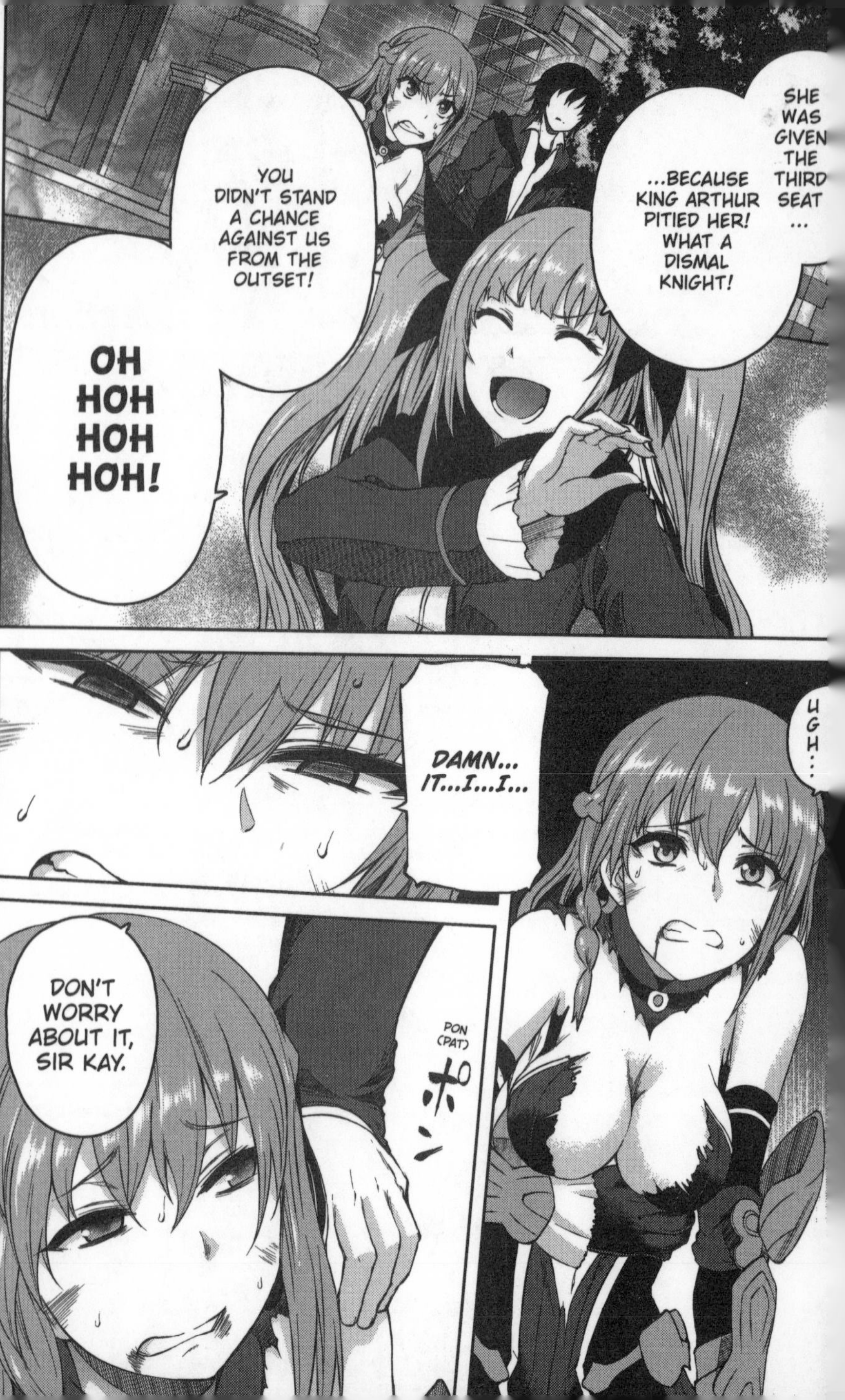
SHE WAS GIVEN THE THIRD SEAT ...
...BECAUSE KING ARTHUR PITIED HER! WHAT A DISMAL KNIGHT!
YOU DIDN'T STAND A CHANCE AGAINST US FROM THE OUTSET!
OH HOH HOH HOH!
UGH...
DAMN... IT...I...I...
PON (PAT)
DON'T WORRY ABOUT IT, SIR KAY.

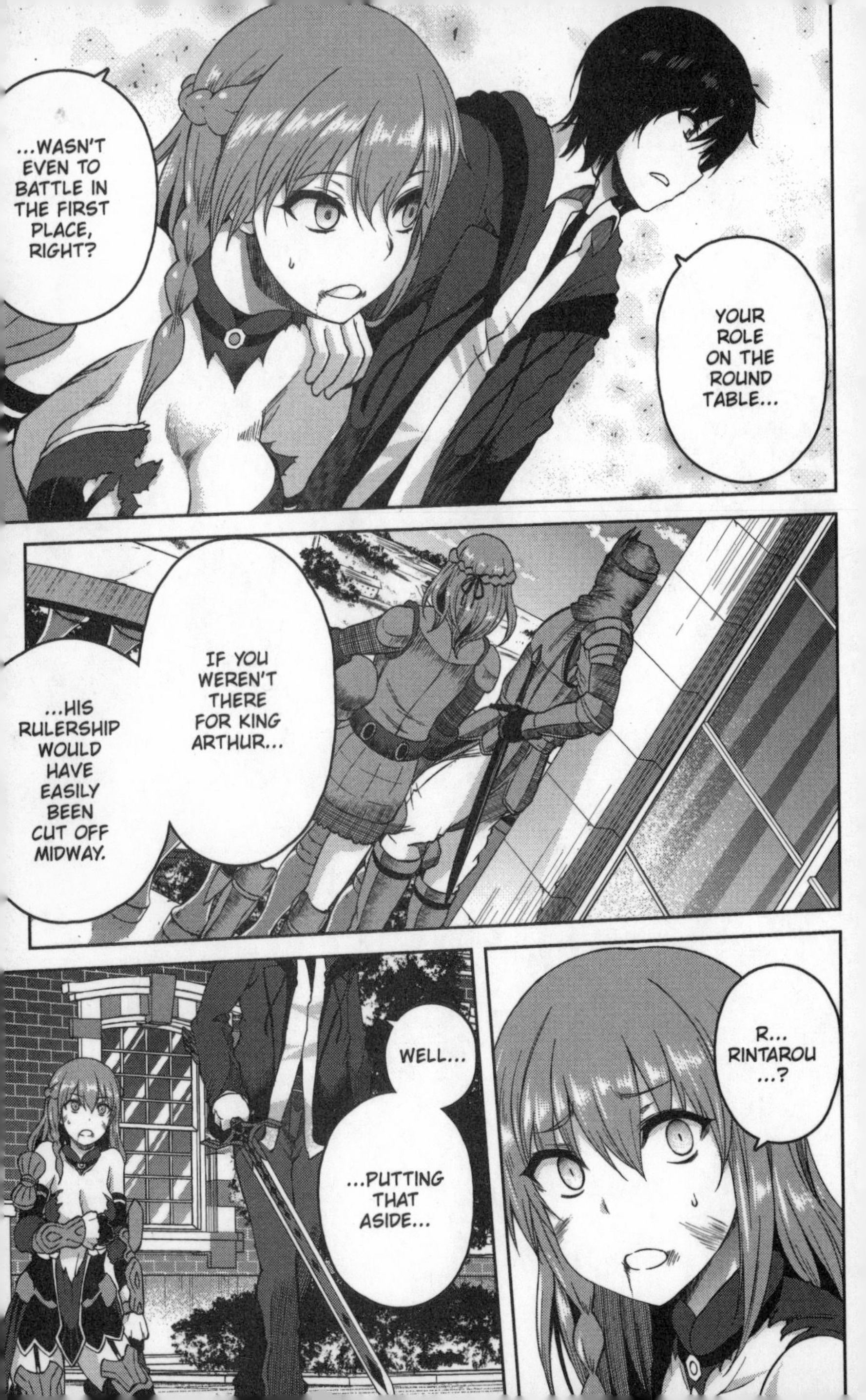
YOUR ROLE ON THE ROUND TABLE...
...WASN'T EVEN TO BATTLE IN THE FIRST PLACE, RIGHT?
IF YOU WEREN'T THERE FOR KING ARTHUR...
...HIS RULERSHIP WOULD HAVE EASILY BEEN CUT OFF MIDWAY.
R... RINTAROU ...?
WELL...
...PUTTING THAT ASIDE...

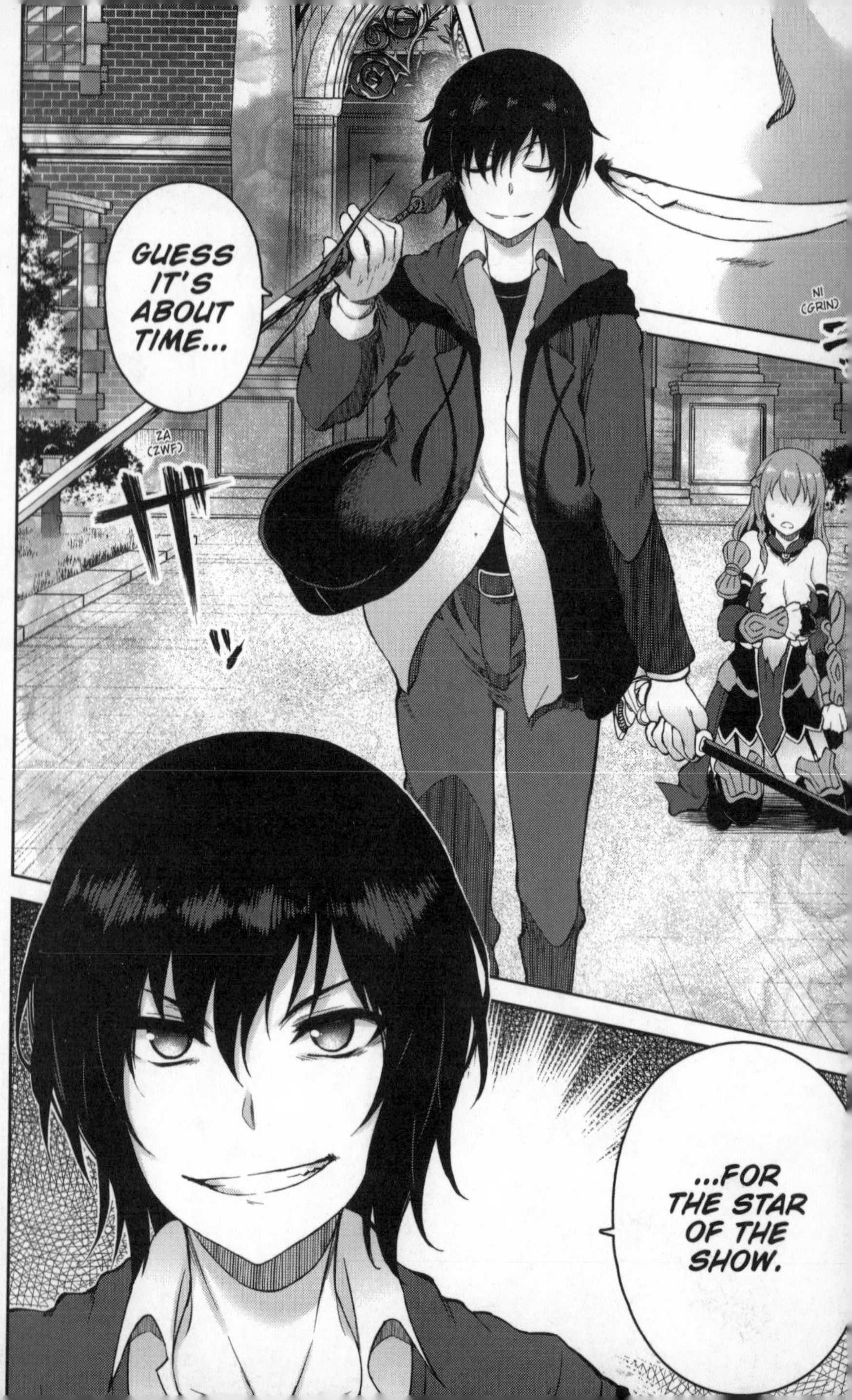
NI (GRIN)
GUESS IT'S ABOUT TIME...
ZA (ZWF)
...FOR THE STAR OF THE SHOW.

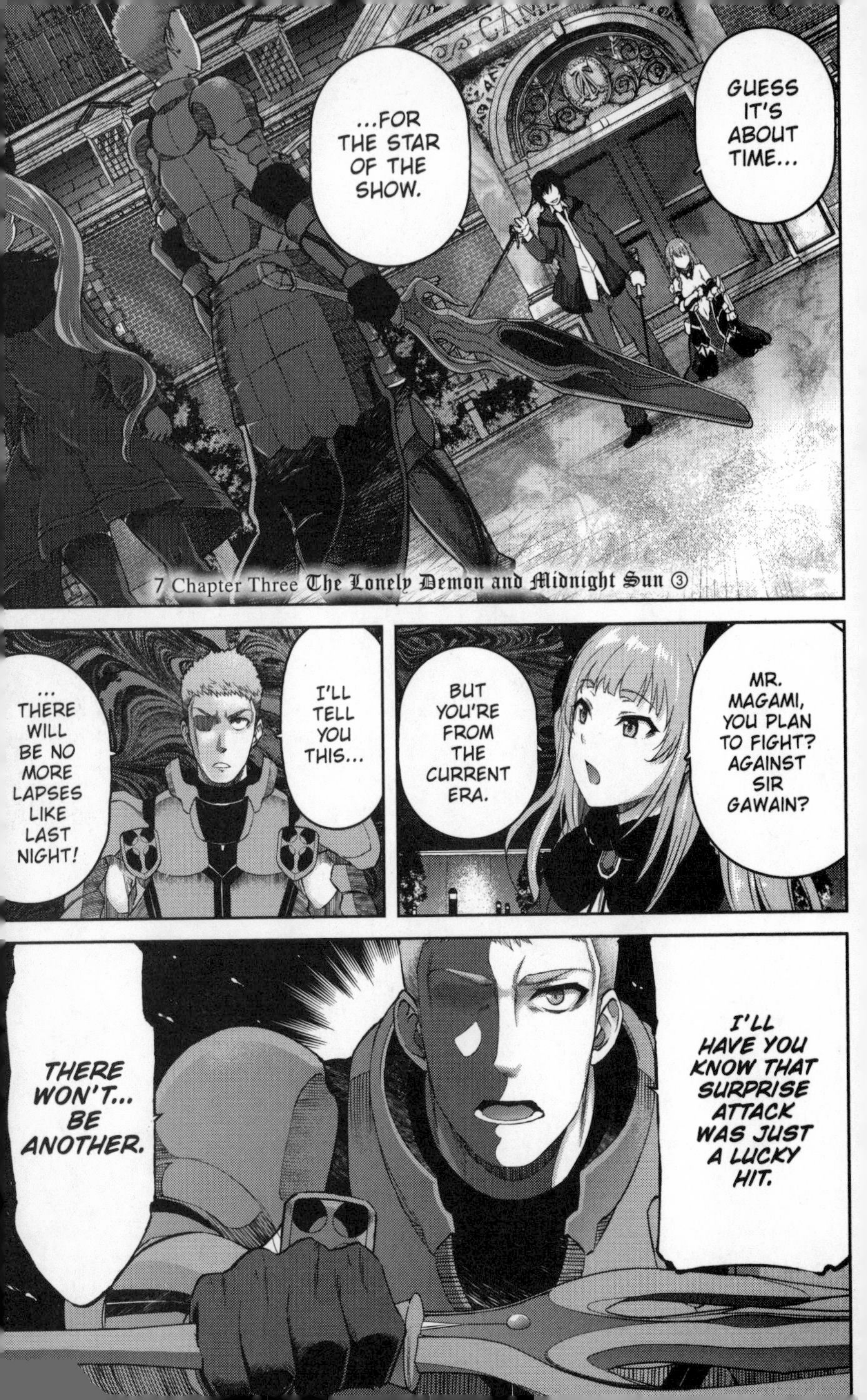
GUESS IT'S ABOUT TIME...
...FOR THE STAR OF THE SHOW.
7 Chapter Three The Lonely Demon and Midnight Sun ③
MR. MAGAMI, YOU PLAN TO FIGHT? AGAINST SIR GAWAIN?
BUT YOU'RE FROM THE CURRENT ERA.
I'LL TELL YOU THIS...
...THERE WILL BE NO MORE LAPSES LIKE LAST NIGHT!
I'LL HAVE YOU KNOW THAT SURPRISE ATTACK WAS JUST A LUCKY HIT.
THERE WON'T... BE ANOTHER.

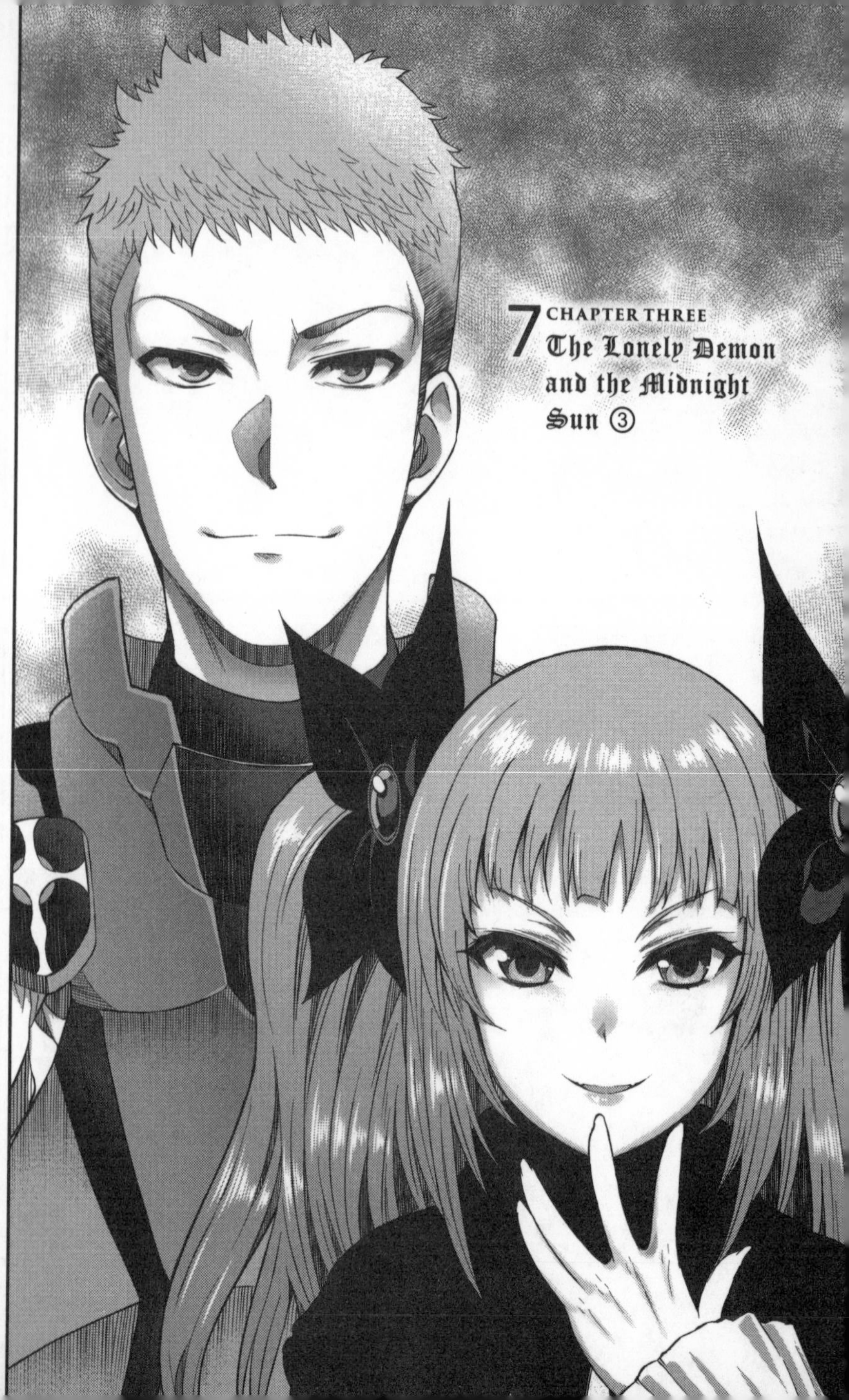
7 CHAPTER THREE
The Lonely Demon and the Midnight Sun ③

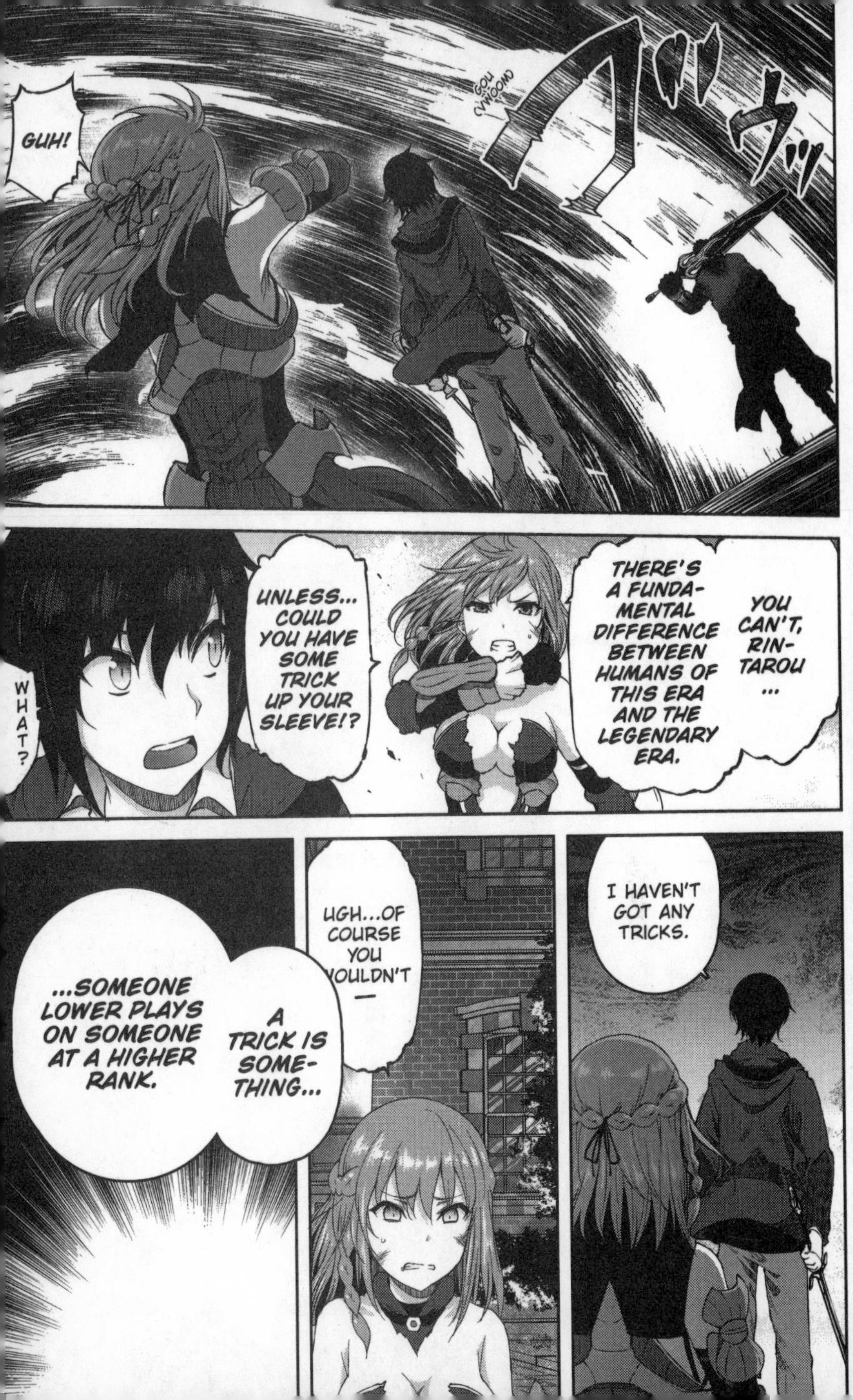
GOU (VWOOM)
GUH!
YOU CAN'T, RINTAROU...
THERE'S A FUNDAMENTAL DIFFERENCE BETWEEN HUMANS OF THIS ERA AND THE LEGENDARY ERA.
UNLESS... COULD YOU HAVE SOME TRICK UP YOUR SLEEVE!?
WHAT?
I HAVEN'T GOT ANY TRICKS.
UGH...OF COURSE YOU OULDN'T —
A TRICK IS SOMETHING...
...SOMEONE LOWER PLAYS ON SOMEONE AT A HIGHER RANK.

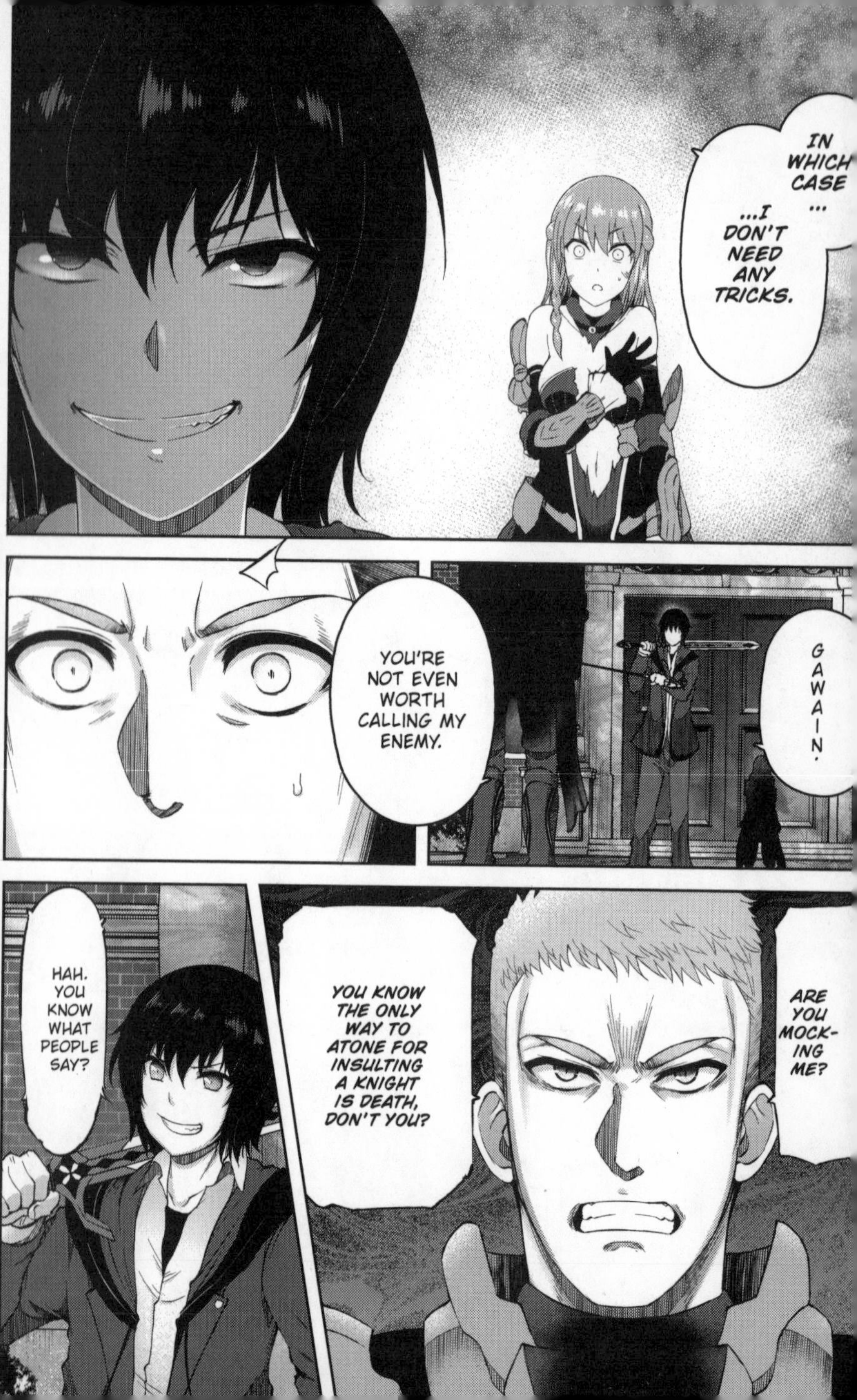
IN WHICH CASE ... ...I DON'T NEED ANY TRICKS.
GAWAIN.
YOU'RE NOT EVEN WORTH CALLING MY ENEMY.
ARE YOU MOCKING ME?
YOU KNOW THE ONLY WAY TO ATONE FOR INSULTING A KNIGHT IS DEATH, DON'T YOU?
HAH. YOU KNOW WHAT PEOPLE SAY?

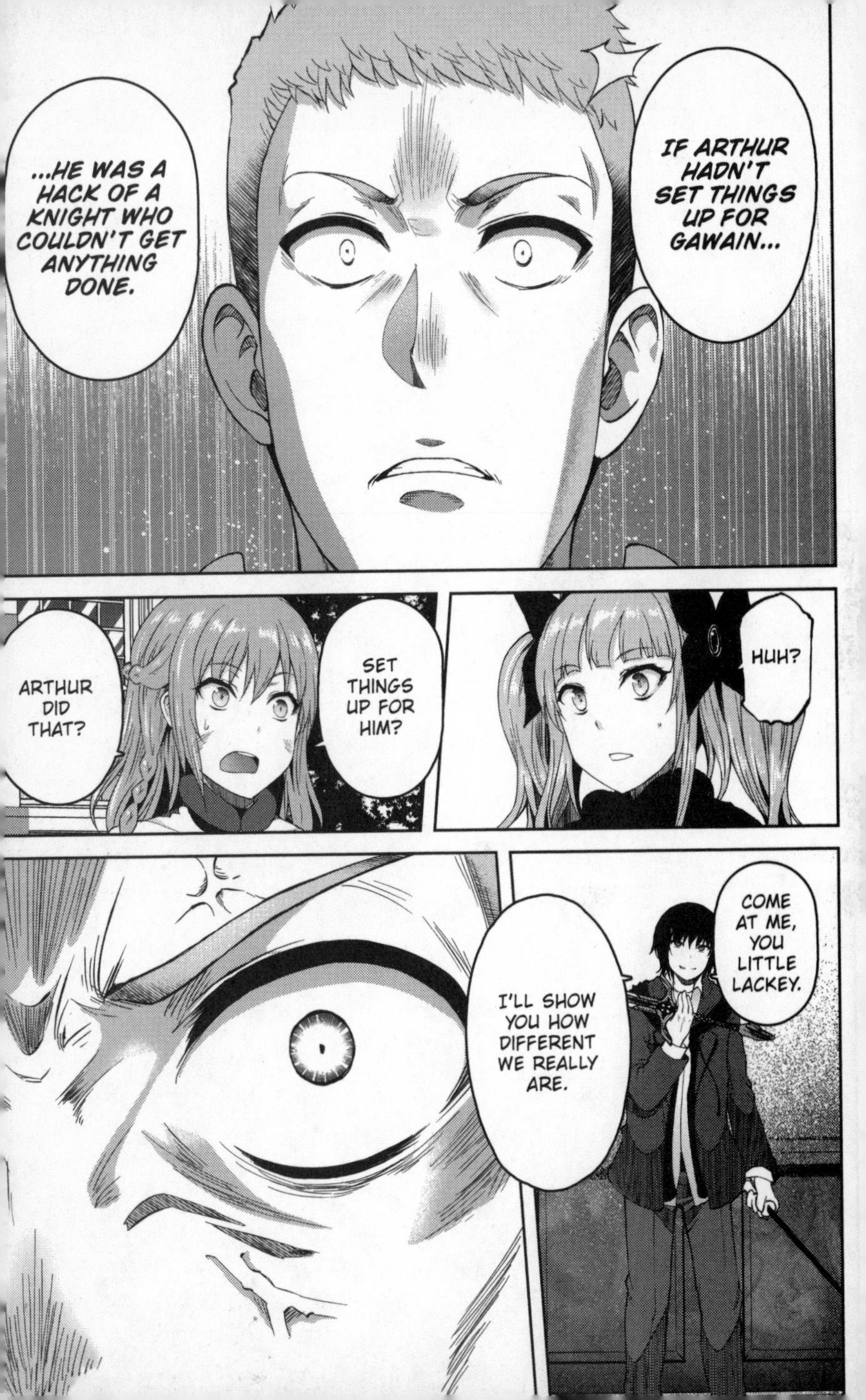
IF ARTHUR HADN'T SET THINGS UP FOR GAWAIN...
...HE WAS A HACK OF A KNIGHT WHO COULDN'T GET ANYTHING DONE.
HUH?
SET THINGS UP FOR HIM?
ARTHUR DID THAT?
COME AT ME, YOU LITTLE LACKEY.
I'LL SHOW YOU HOW DIFFERENT WE REALLY ARE.

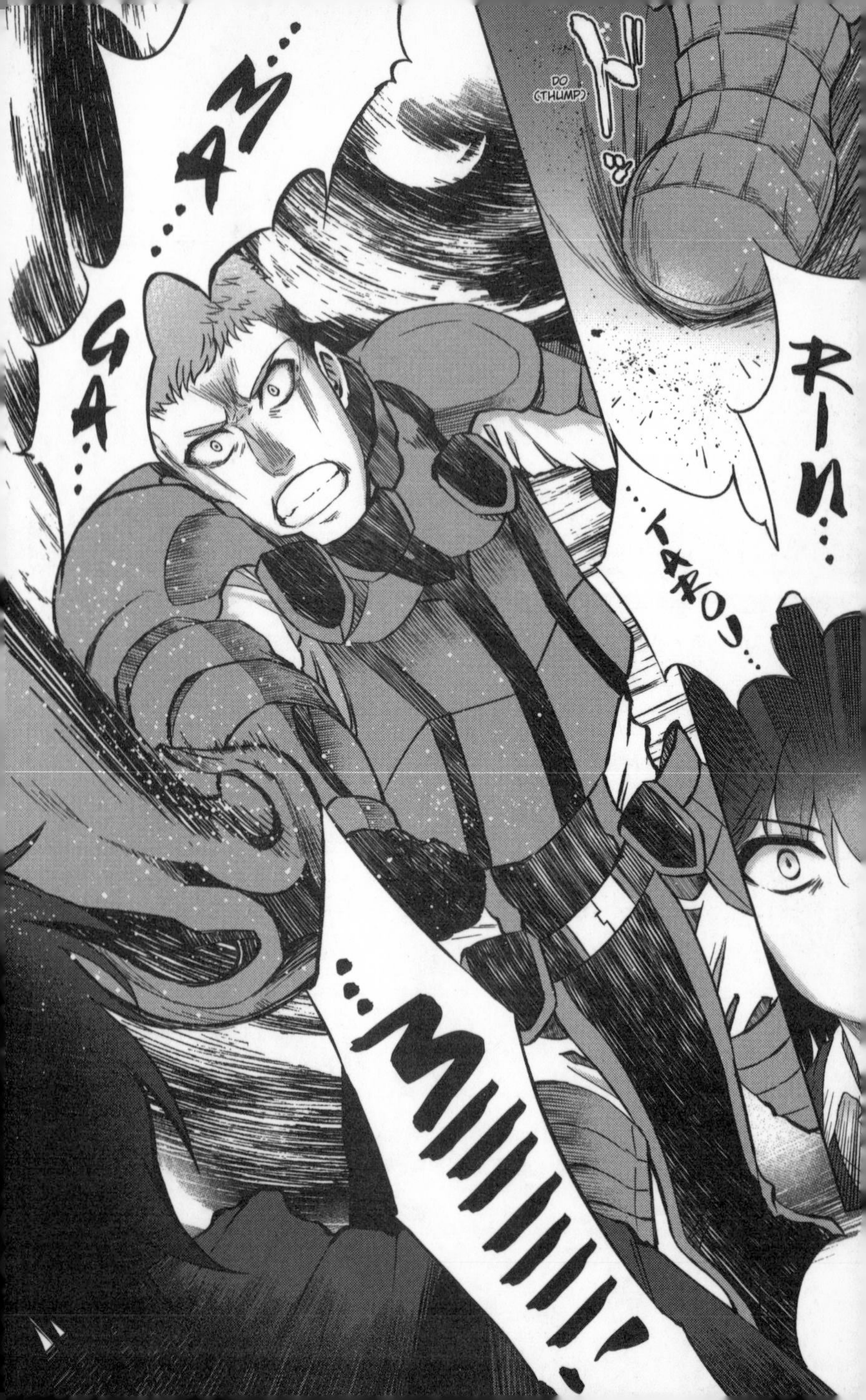
DO
(THUMP)
RIN...
...TAROU...
MA...
SA...
...MIIIII!

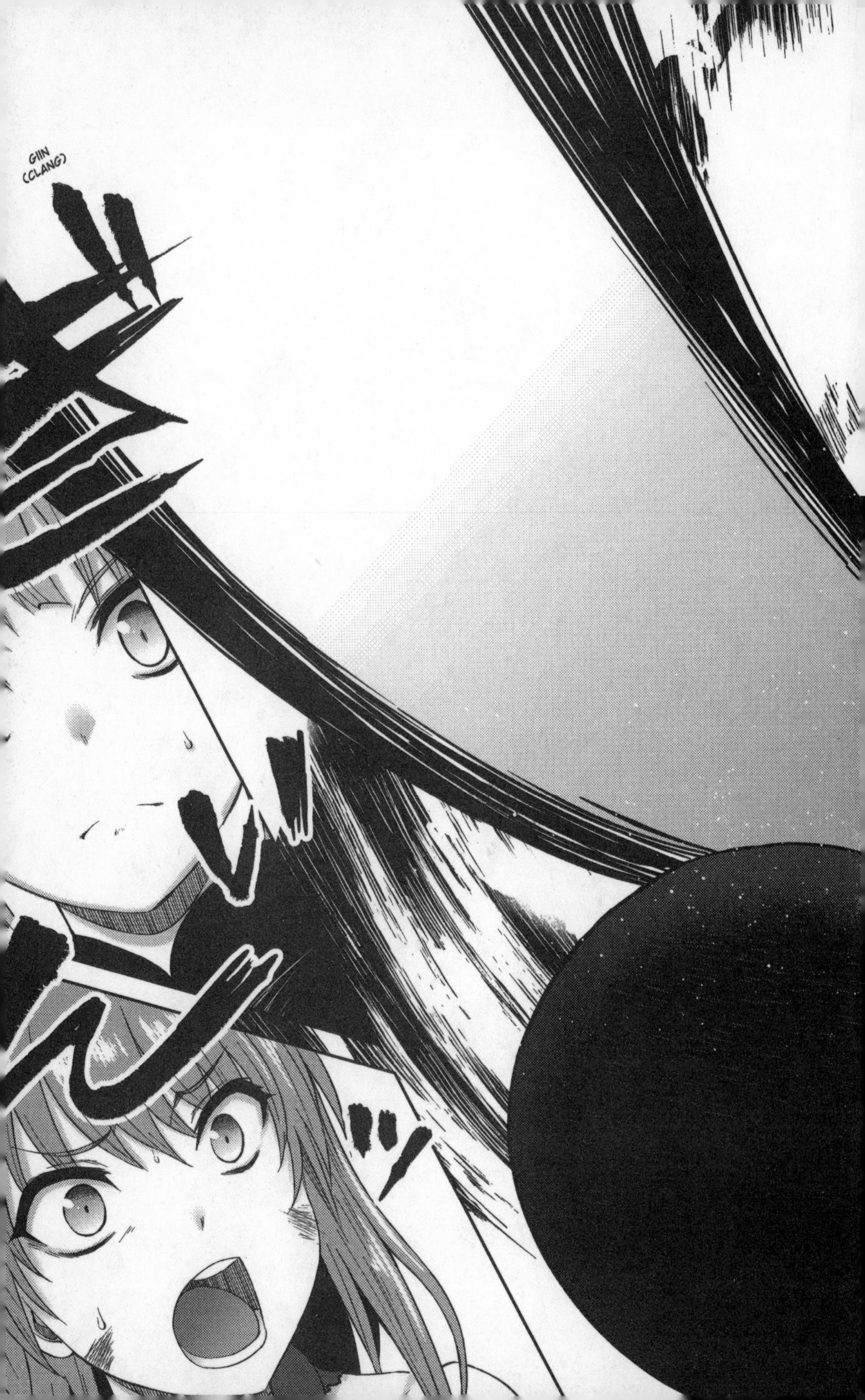
GIIN
(CLANG)

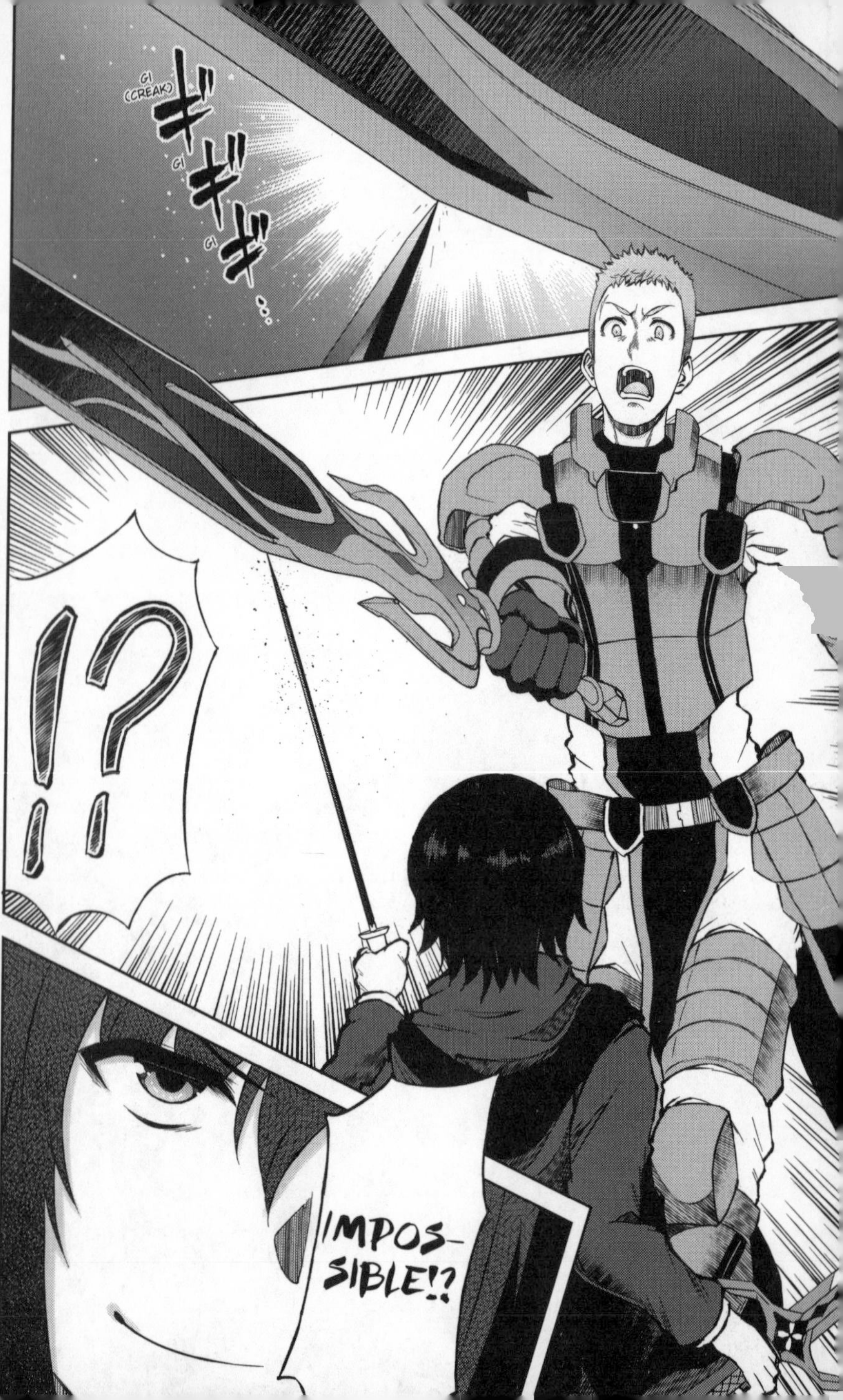
GI (CREAK)
ギ
GI
ギ
GI
ギ...
!?
IMPOS-
SIBLE!?

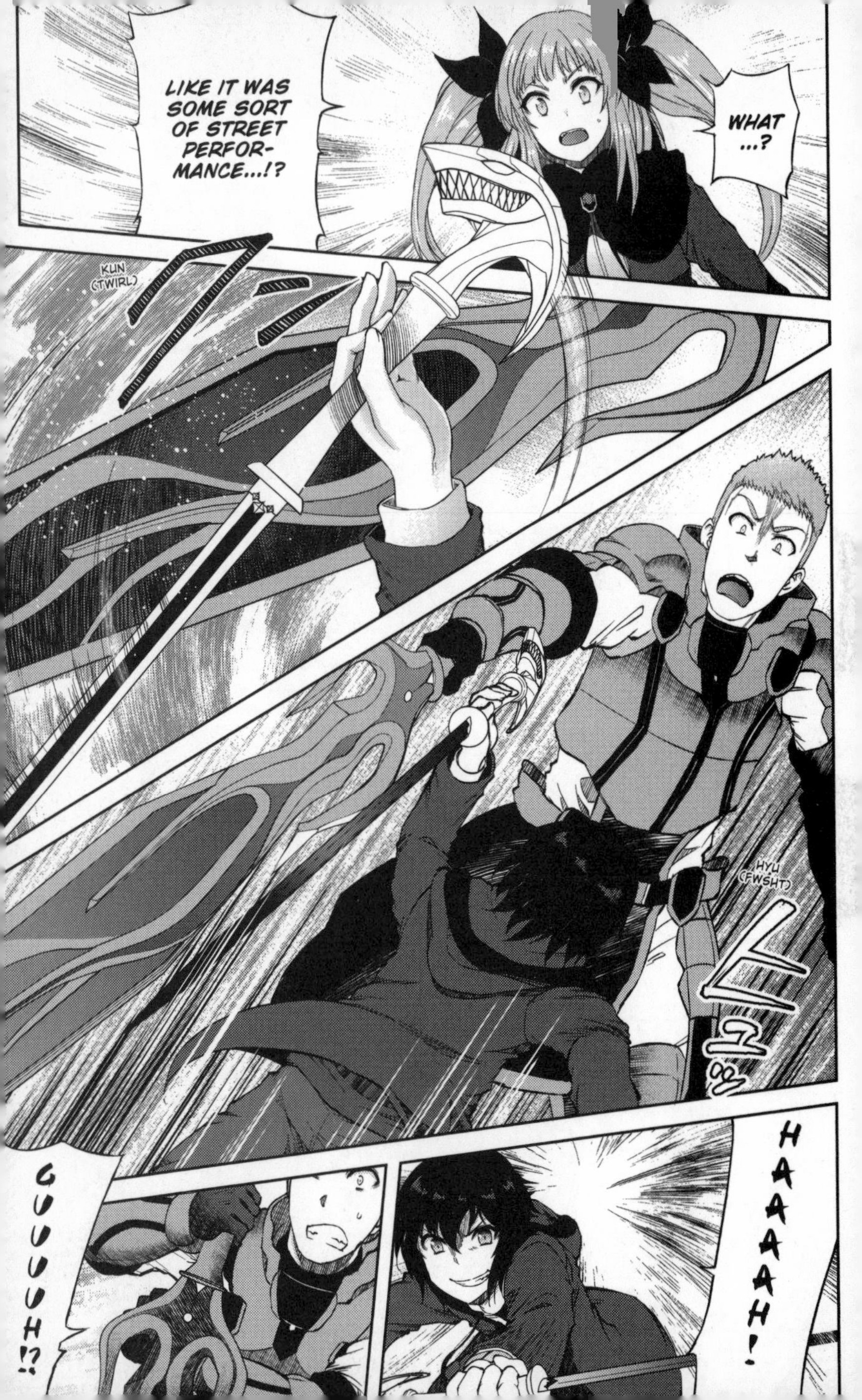
WHAT ...?
LIKE IT WAS SOME SORT OF STREET PERFORMANCE...!?
KUN (TWIRL)
HYU (FWSHT)
HAAAAAH!
GUUUUUH!?

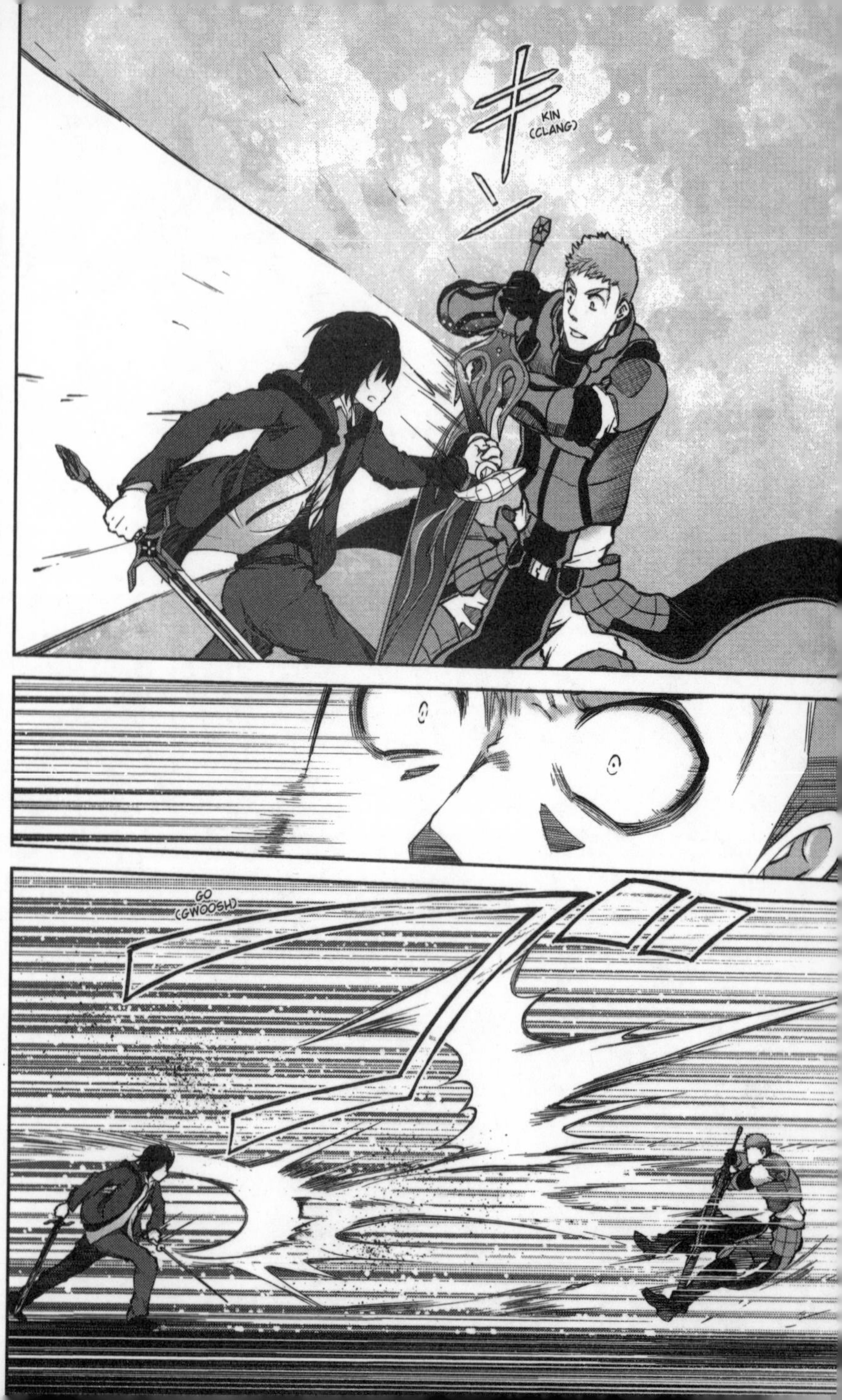
KIN
(CLANG)
GO
(GWOOSH)

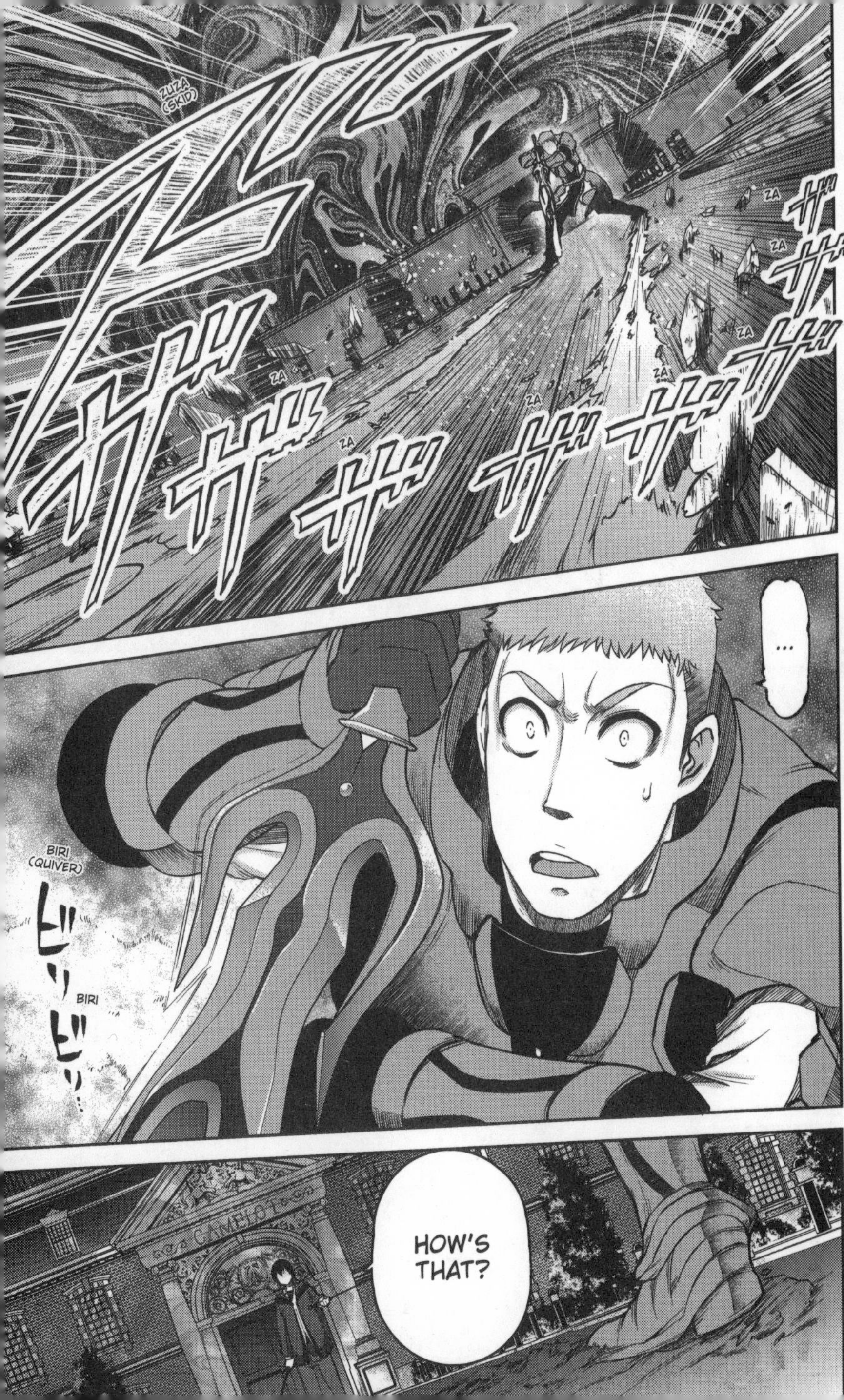
ZUZA (SKID)
ZA
ZA
ZA
ZA
ZA
ZA
...
BIRI (QUIVER)
BIRI
HOW'S THAT?

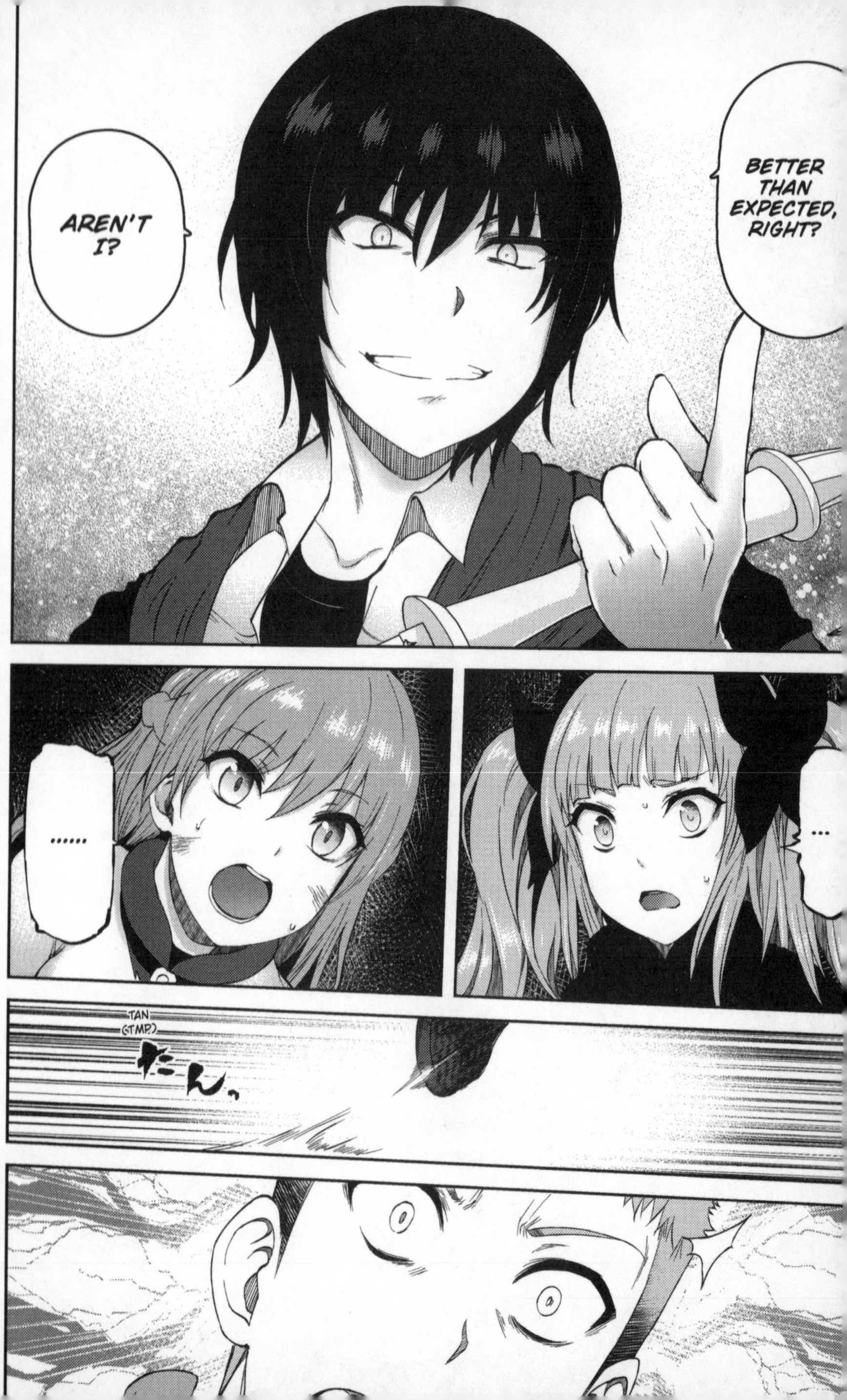
BETTER THAN EXPECTED, RIGHT?
AREN'T I?
...
......
TAN (TMP.)
たん

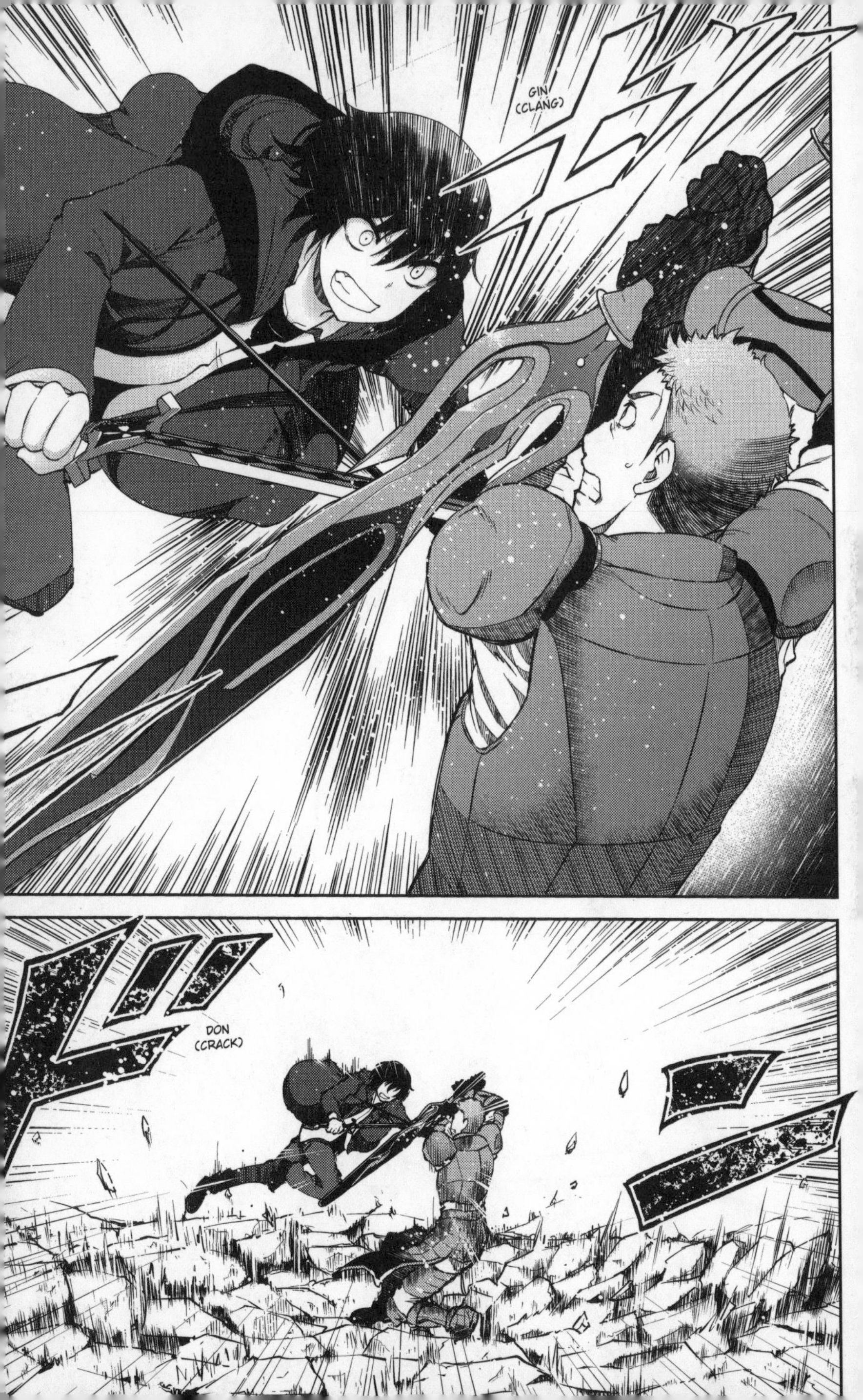
GIN
(CLANG)
DON
(CRACK)

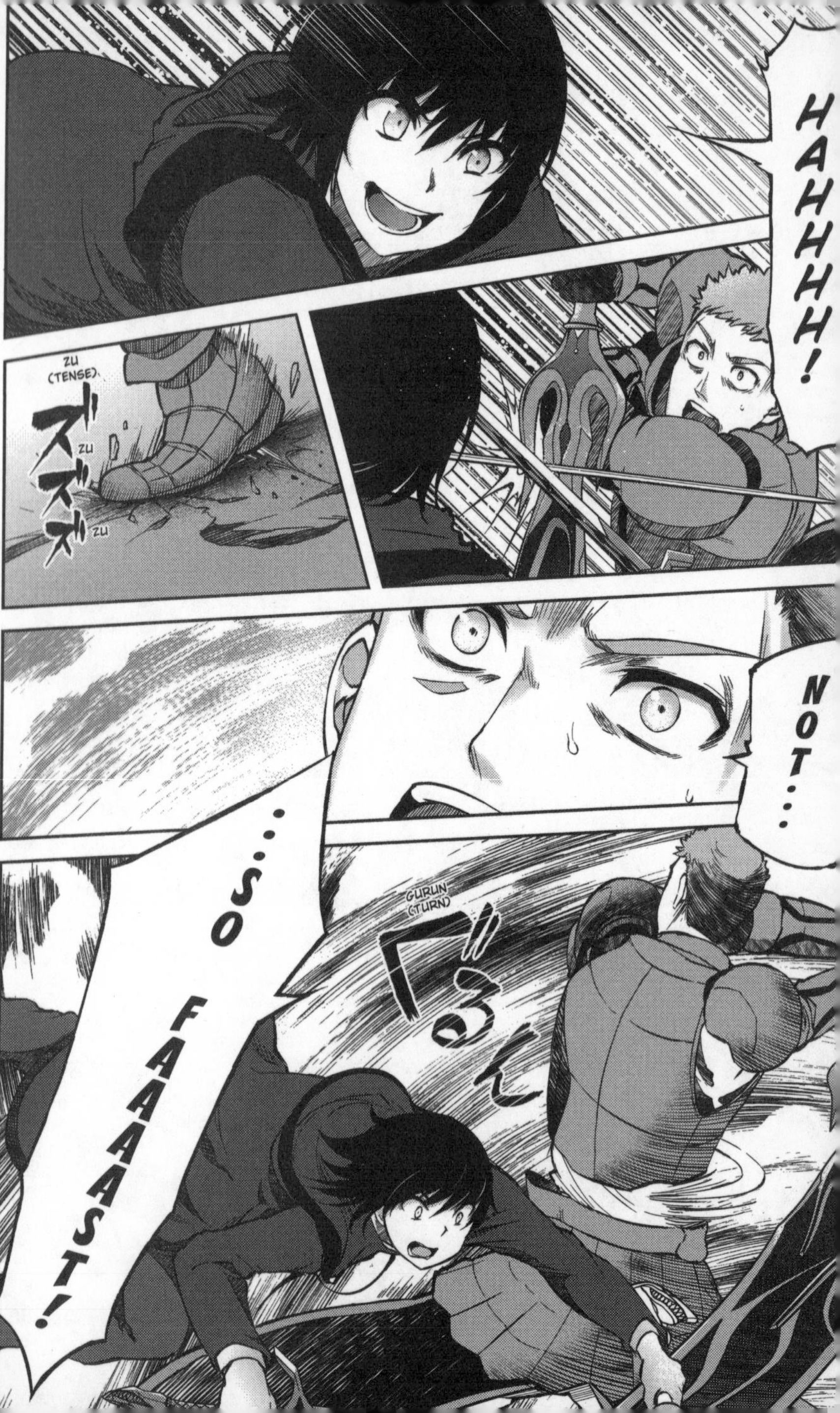
HAHHHHH!
ZU (TENSE)
ZU
ZU
NOT...
...SO FAAAAAST!
GURUN (TURN)

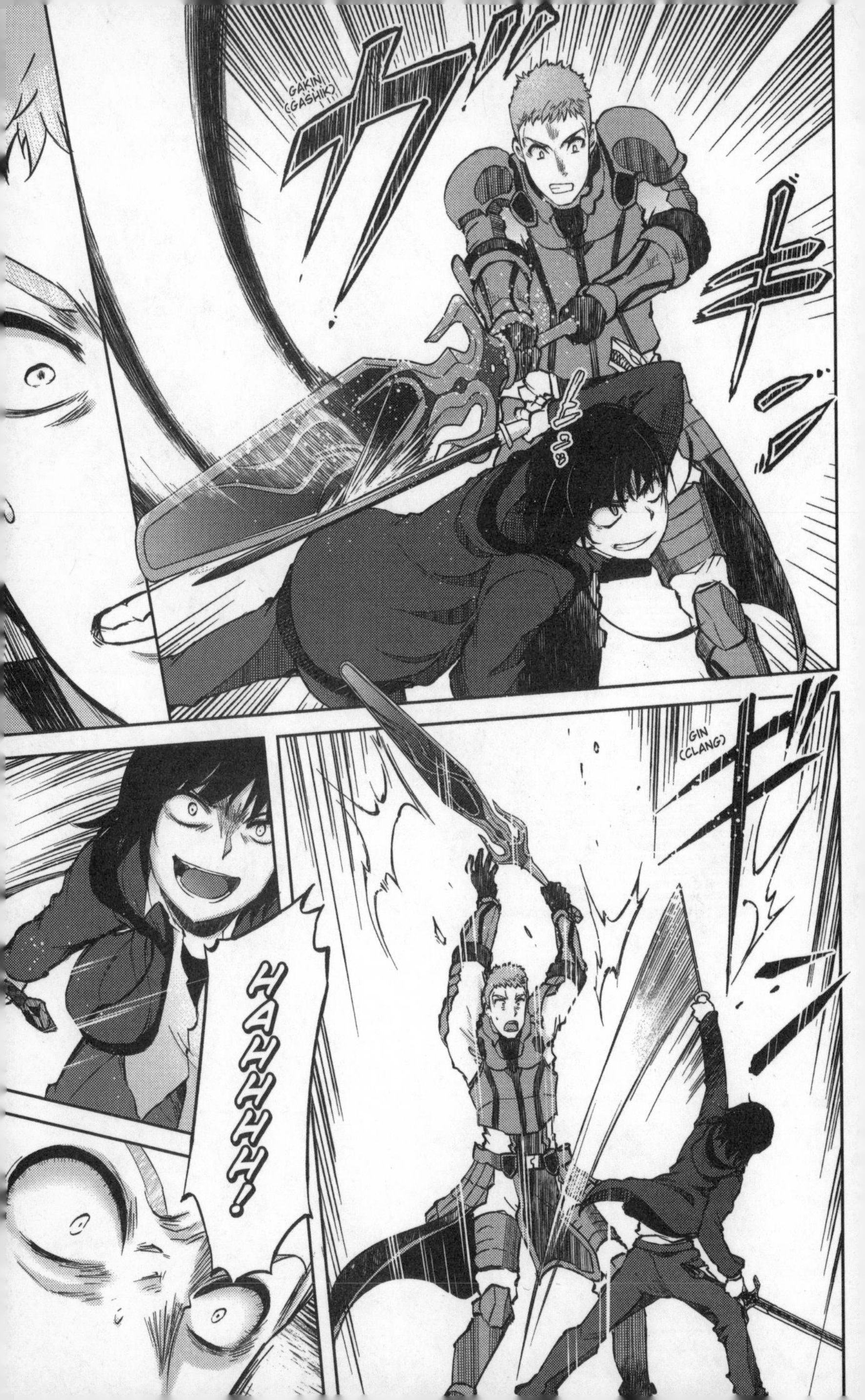
GAKIN (GASHIK)
GIN (CLANG)
HAHHHHH!

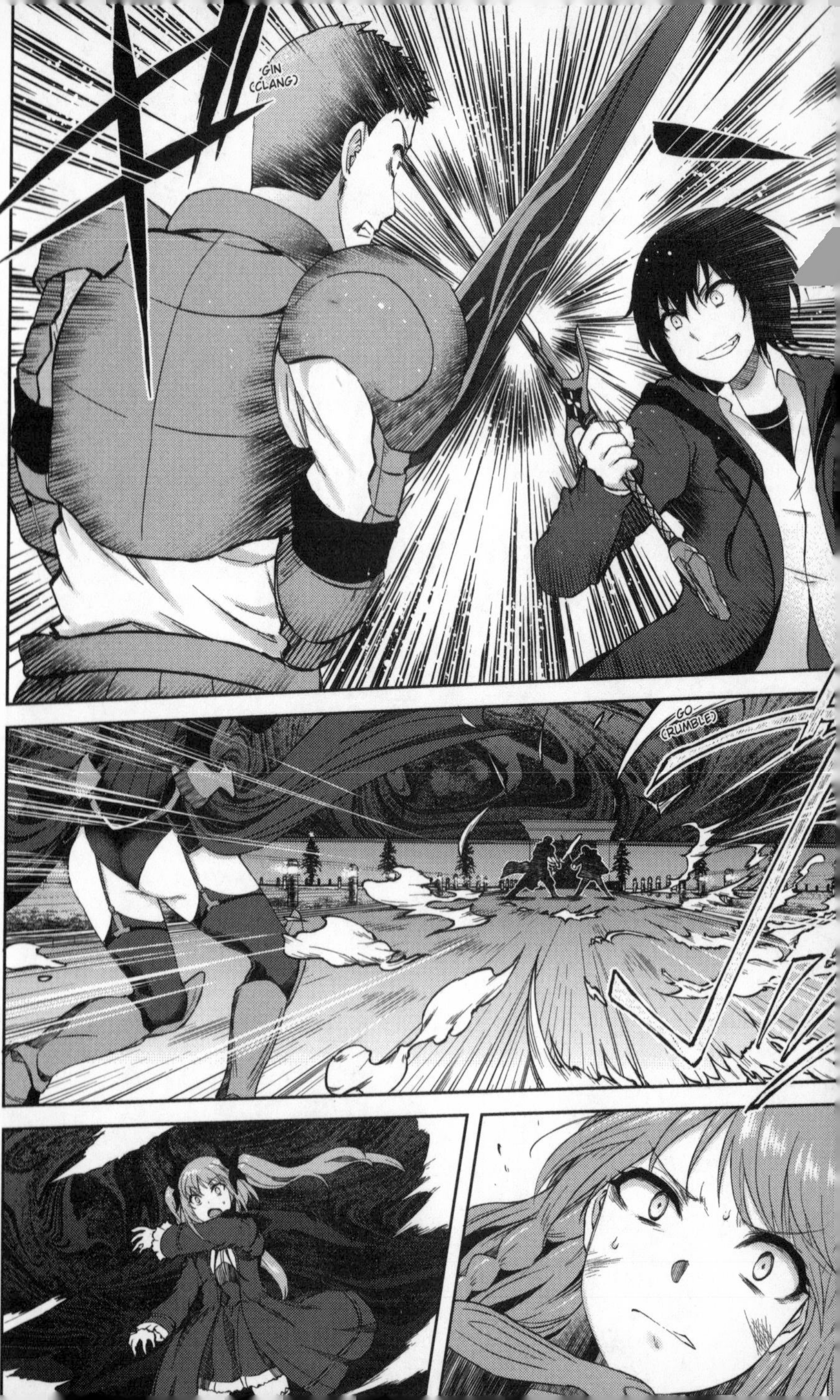
GIN
(CLANG)
GO
(RUMBLE)

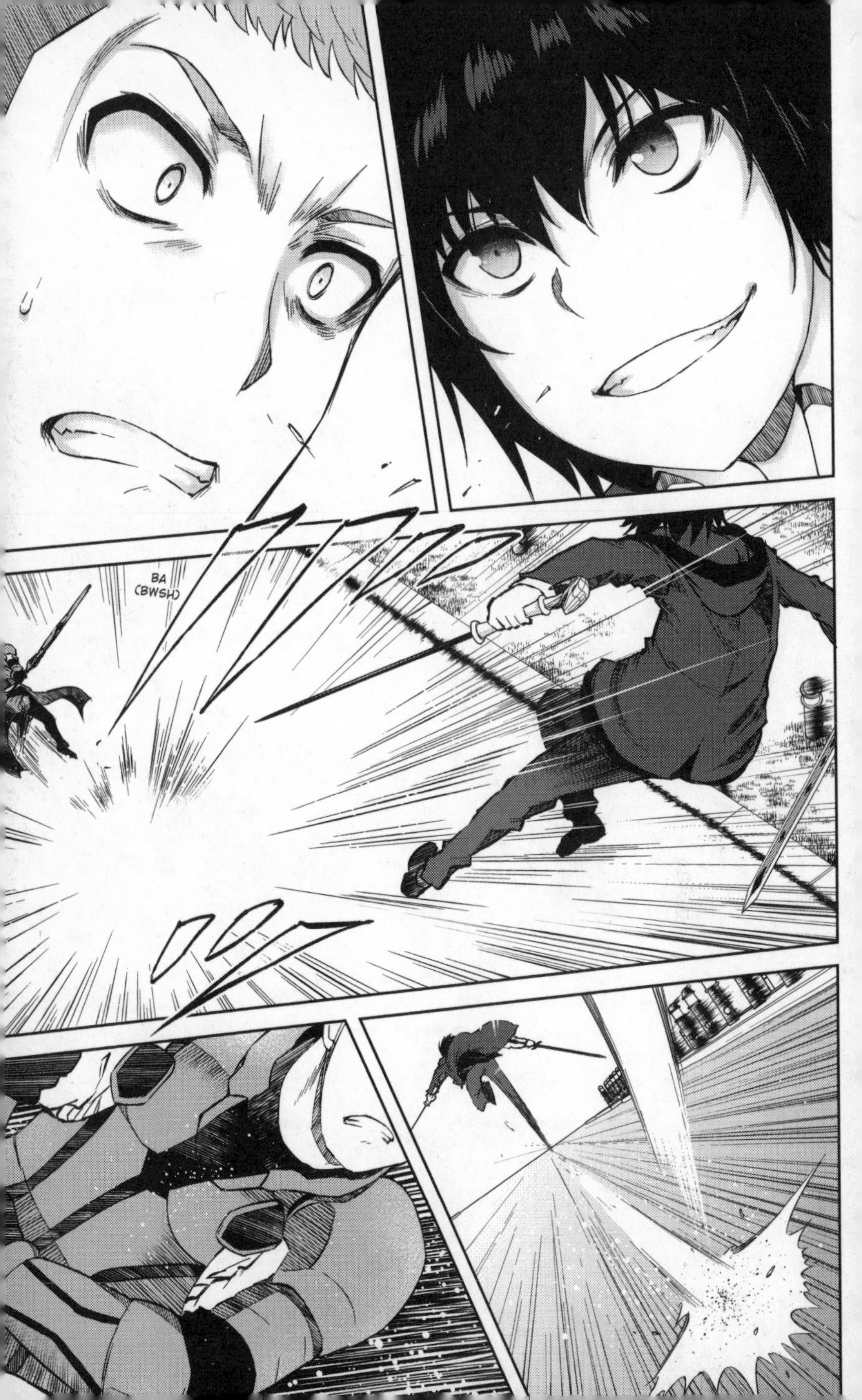
BA
(BWSH)

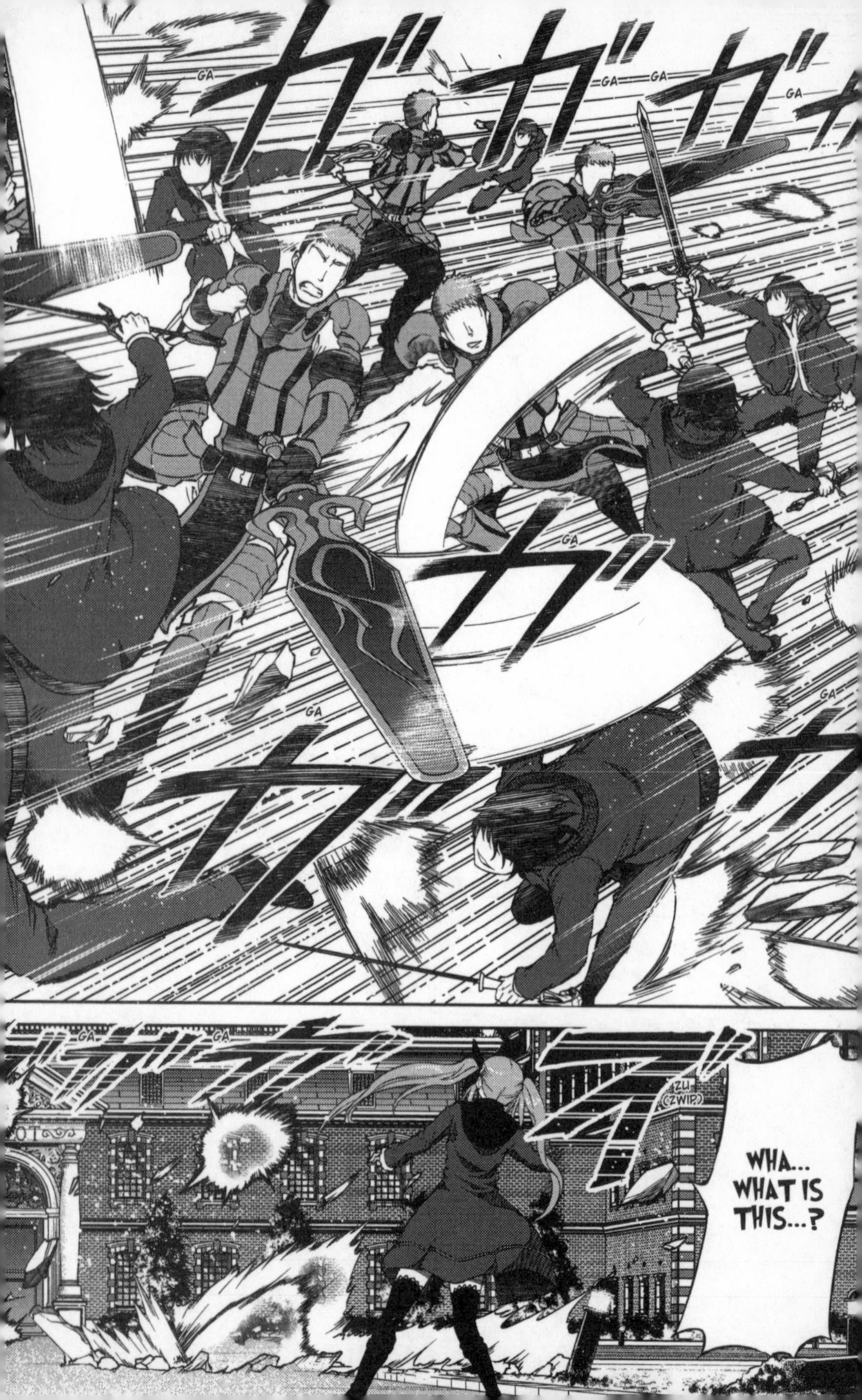
GA
GA
GA
GA
GA
GA
GA
ZU (ZWIP)
WHA... WHAT IS THIS...?
GA
GA

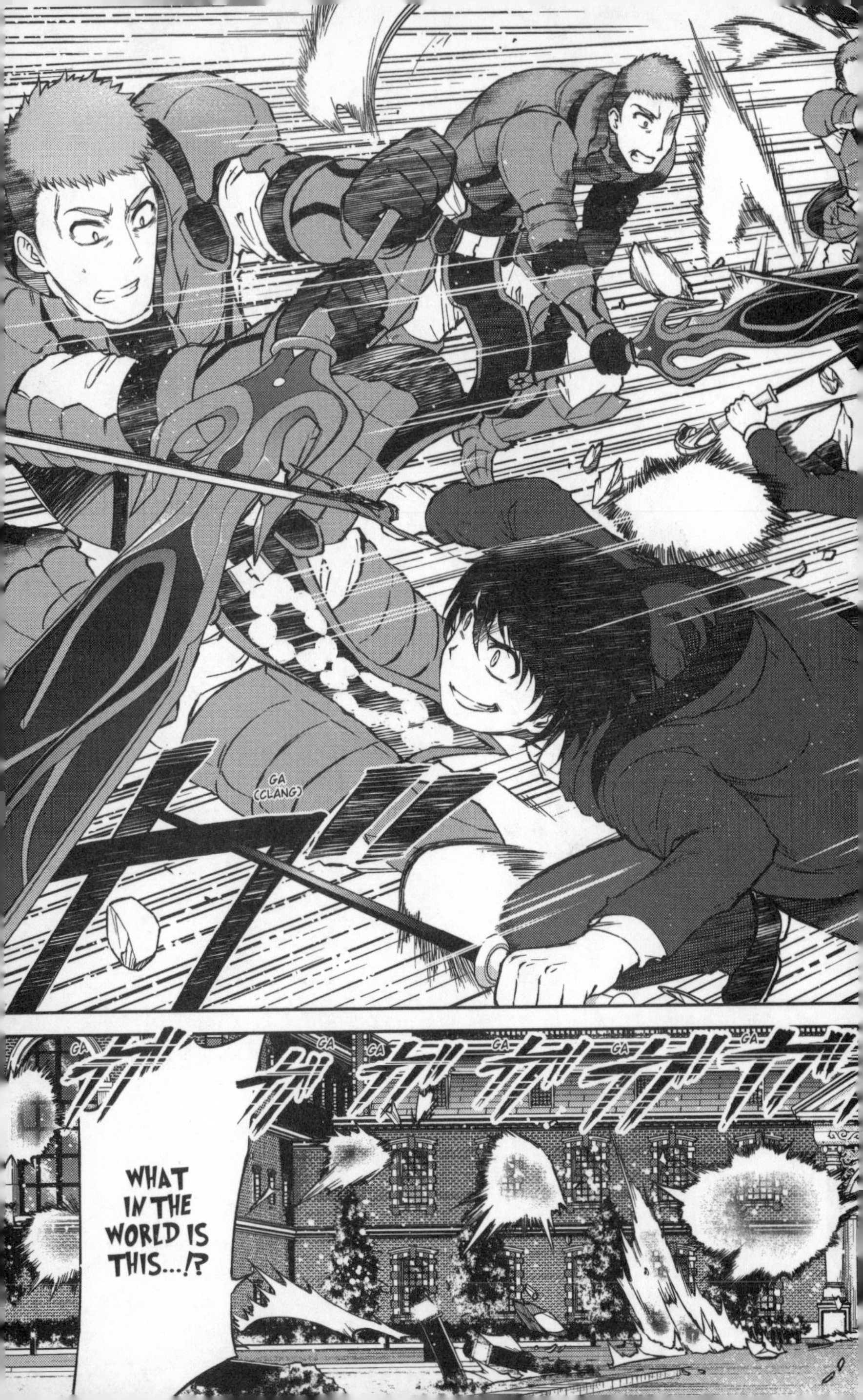
GA (CLANG)
GA GA GA GA GA GA
WHAT IN THE WORLD IS THIS...!?

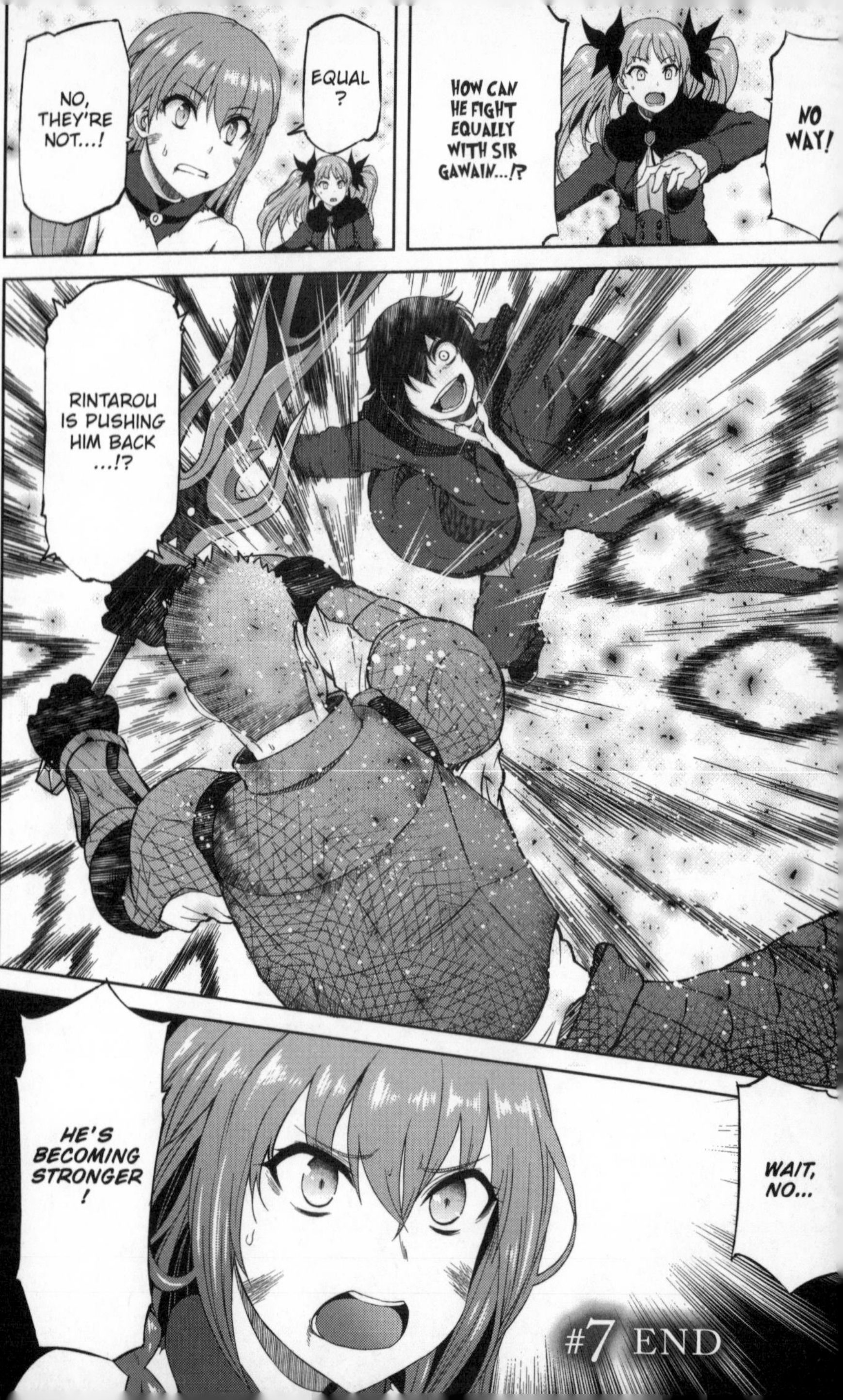
NO WAY!
HOW CAN HE FIGHT EQUALLY WITH SIR GAWAIN...!?
EQUAL?
NO, THEY'RE NOT...!
RINTAROU IS PUSHING HIM BACK...!?
WAIT, NO...
HE'S BECOMING STRONGER!
#7 END

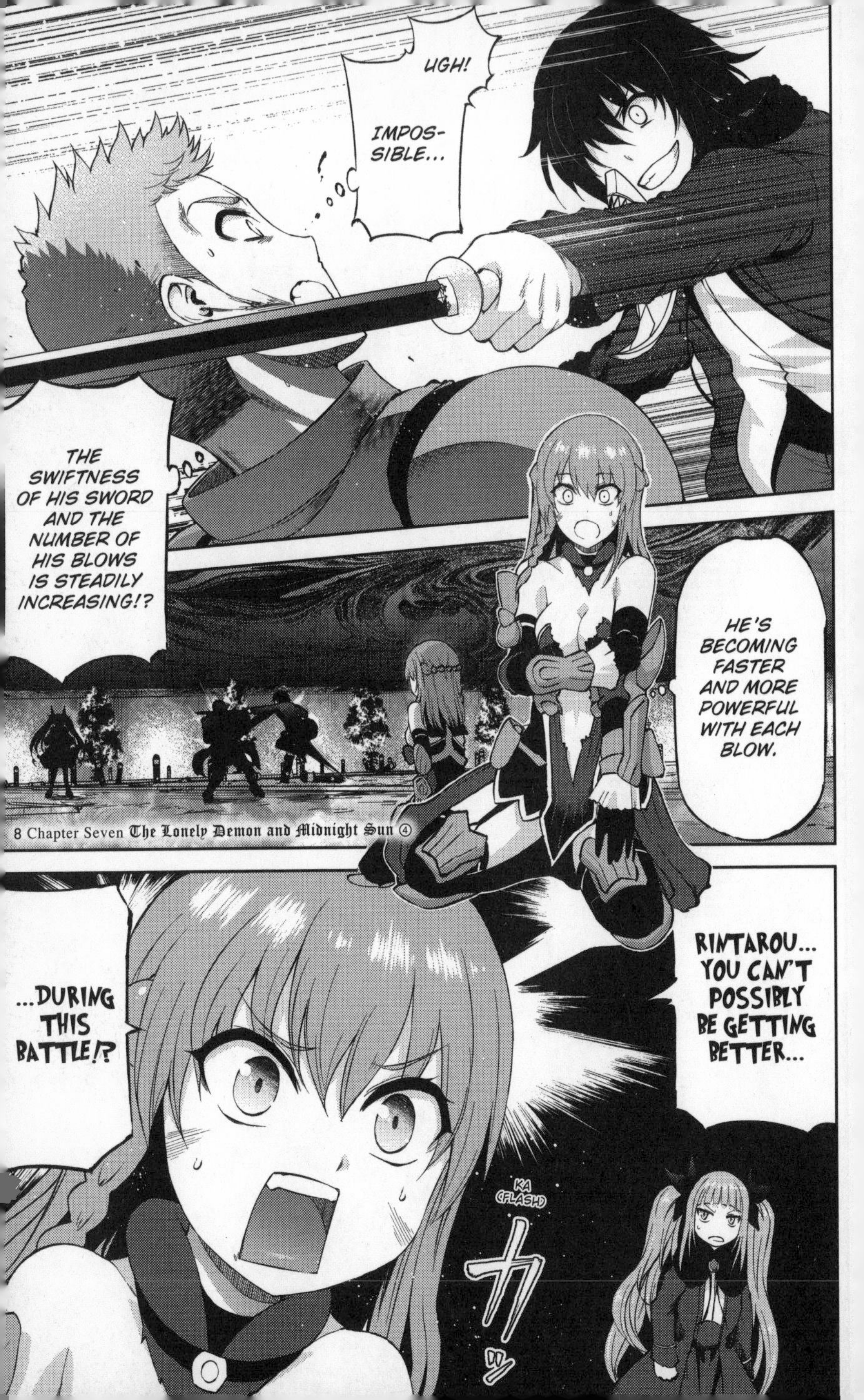
UGH!
IMPOS-SIBLE...
THE SWIFTNESS OF HIS SWORD AND THE NUMBER OF HIS BLOWS IS STEADILY INCREASING!?
HE'S BECOMING FASTER AND MORE POWERFUL WITH EACH BLOW.
RINTAROU... YOU CAN'T POSSIBLY BE GETTING BETTER...
...DURING THIS BATTLE!?
KA (FLASH)
カッ

8 CHAPTER THREE
The Lonely Demon and the Midnight Sun ④

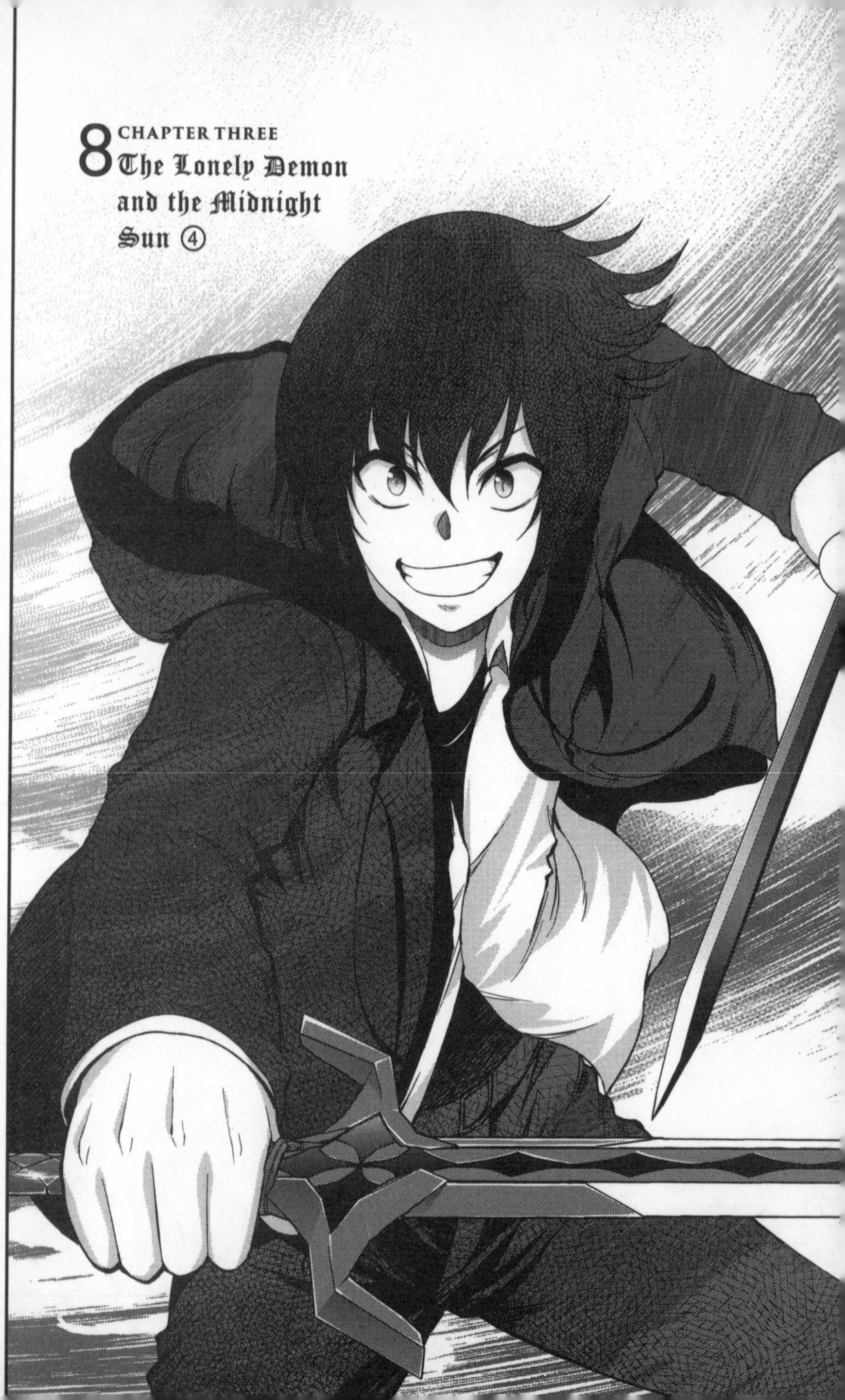

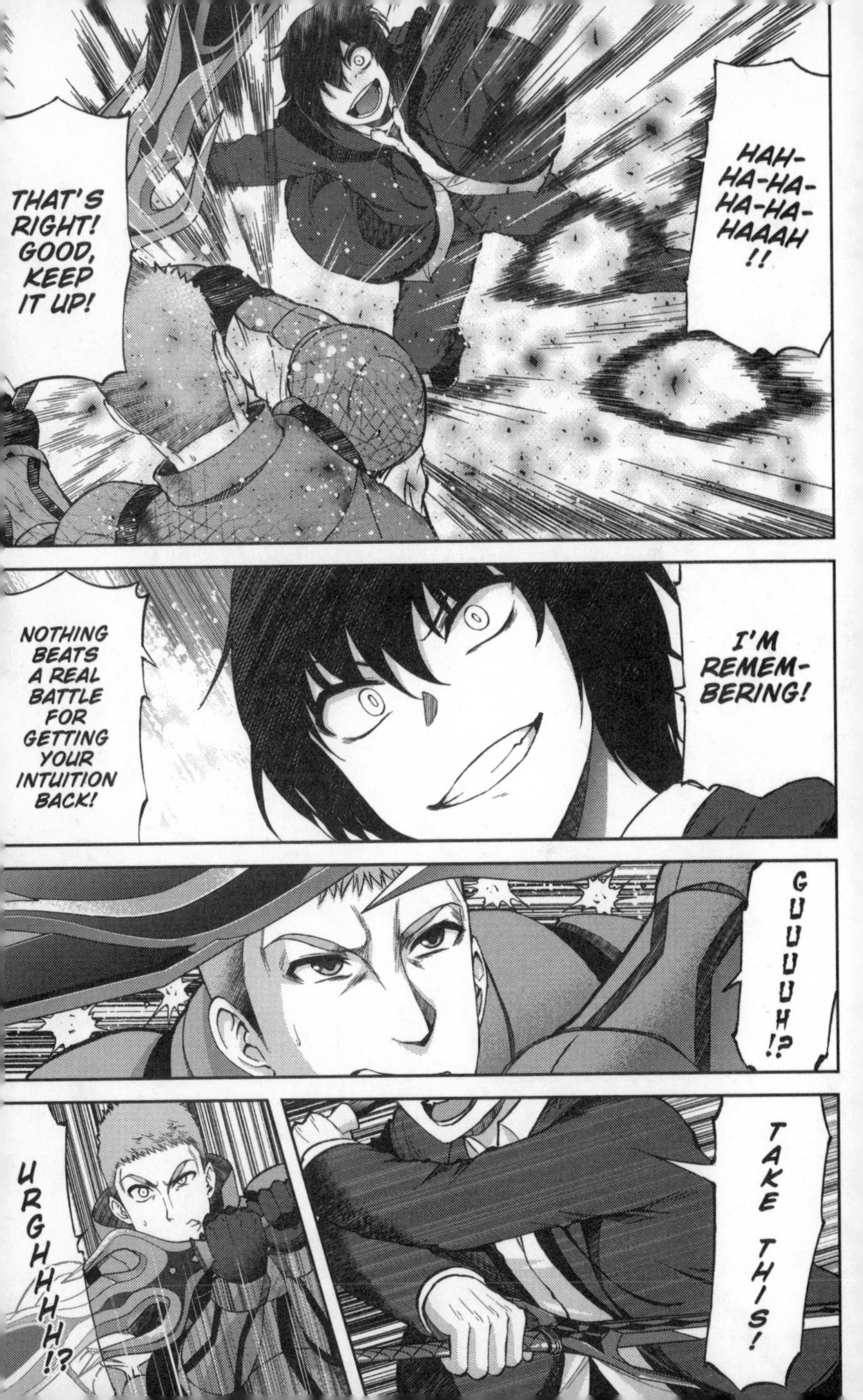
HAH-HA-HA-HA-HA-HAAAH!!
THAT'S RIGHT! GOOD, KEEP IT UP!
I'M REMEMBERING!
NOTHING BEATS A REAL BATTLE FOR GETTING YOUR INTUITION BACK!
GUUUUH!?
TAKE THIS!
URGHHHHH!?

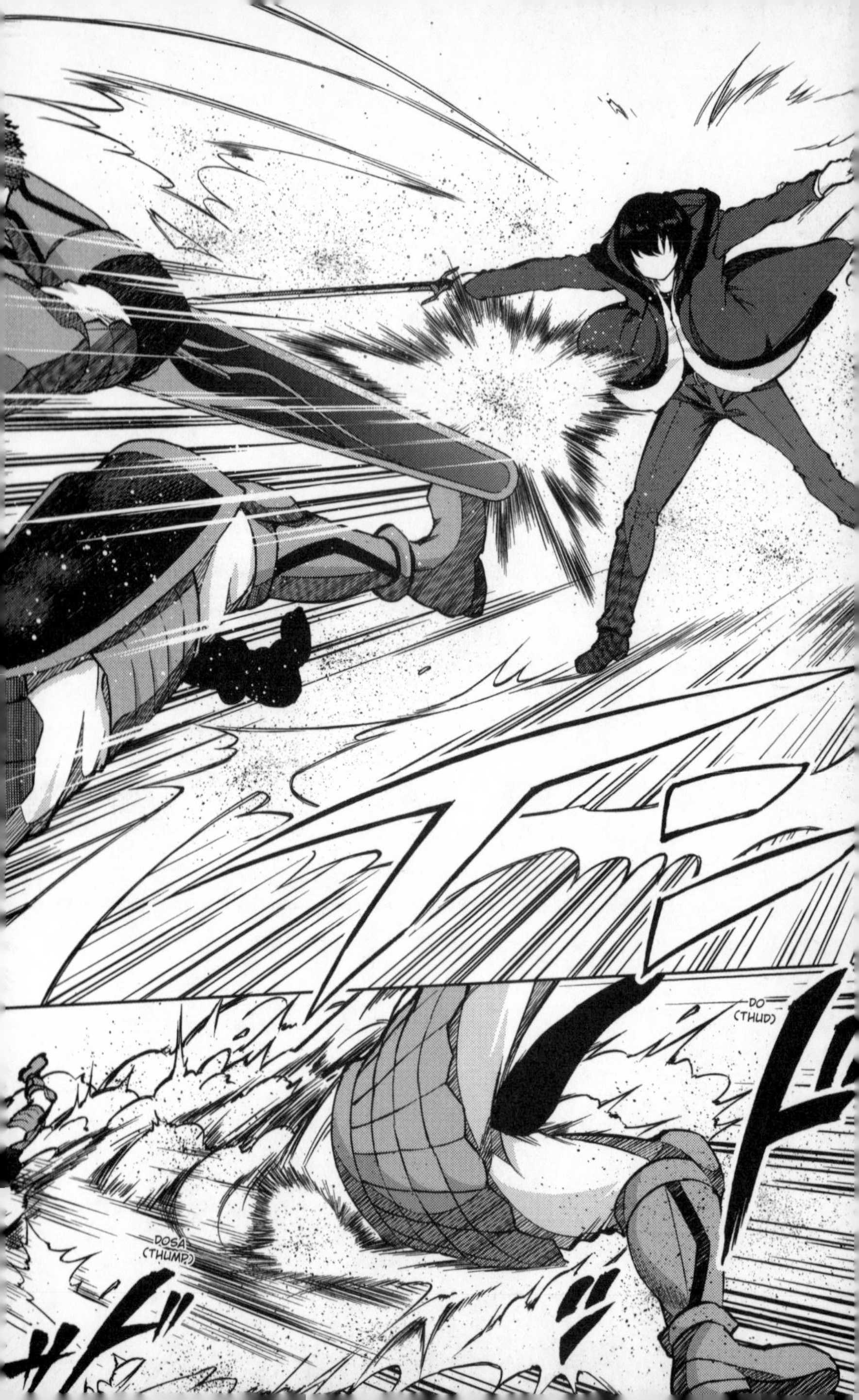
DO
(THUD)
DOSA
(THUMP)

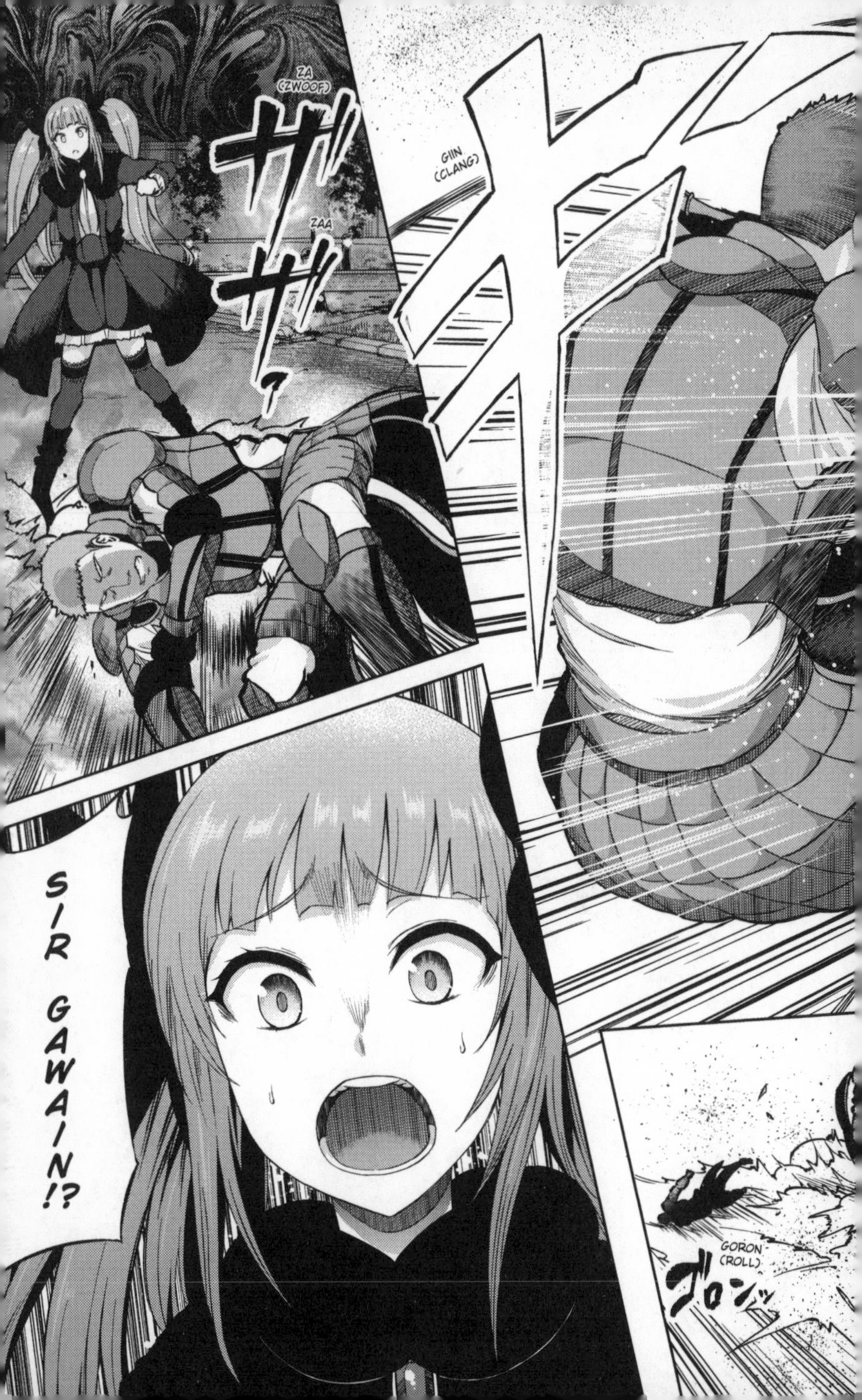
GIIN
(CLANG)
ZA
(ZWOOF)
ZAA
SIR GAWAIN!?
GORON
(ROLL)

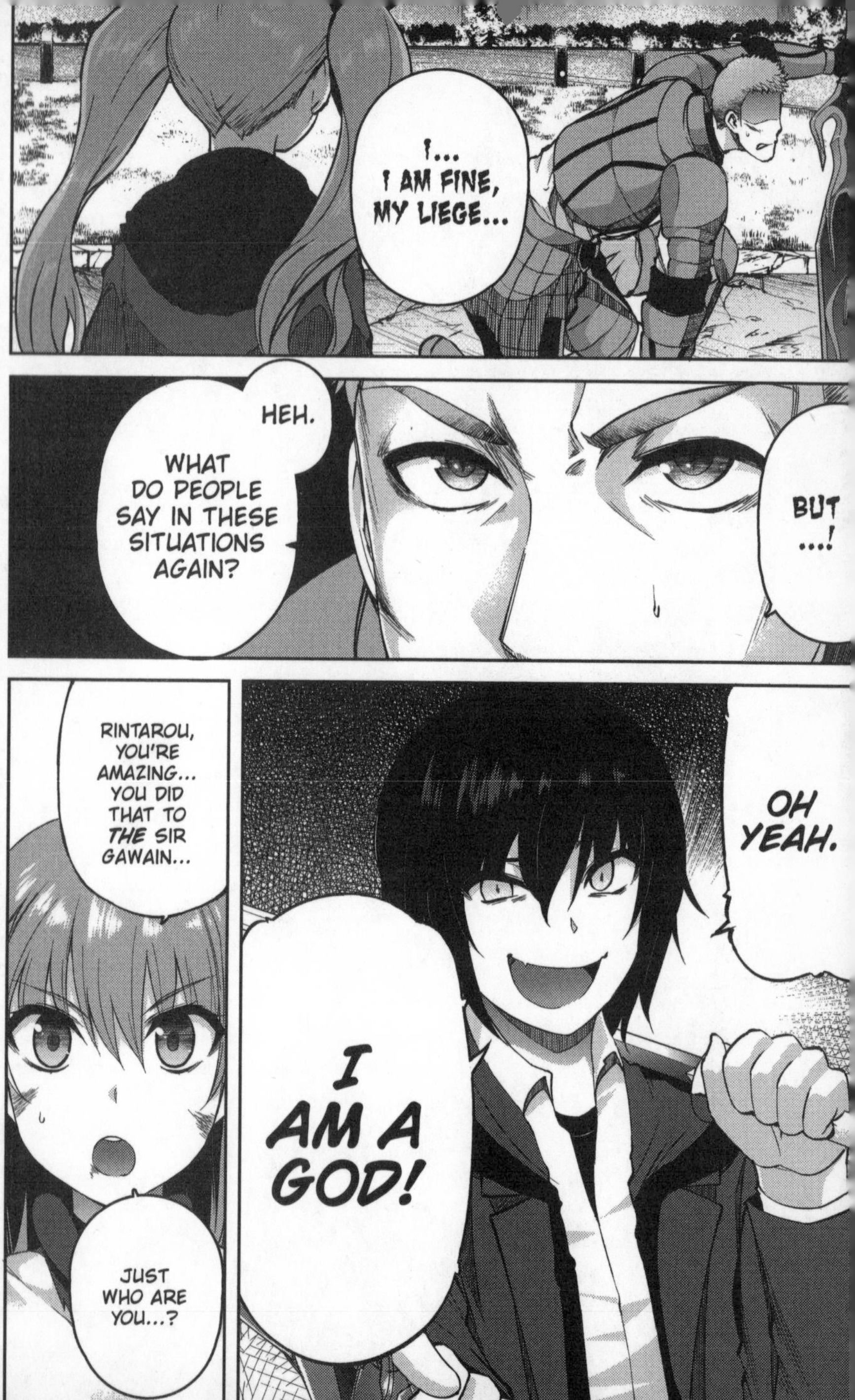
I... I AM FINE, MY LIEGE...
BUT ...!
HEH.
WHAT DO PEOPLE SAY IN THESE SITUATIONS AGAIN?
OH YEAH.
I AM A GOD!
RINTAROU, YOU'RE AMAZING... YOU DID THAT TO *THE* SIR GAWAIN...
JUST WHO ARE YOU...?

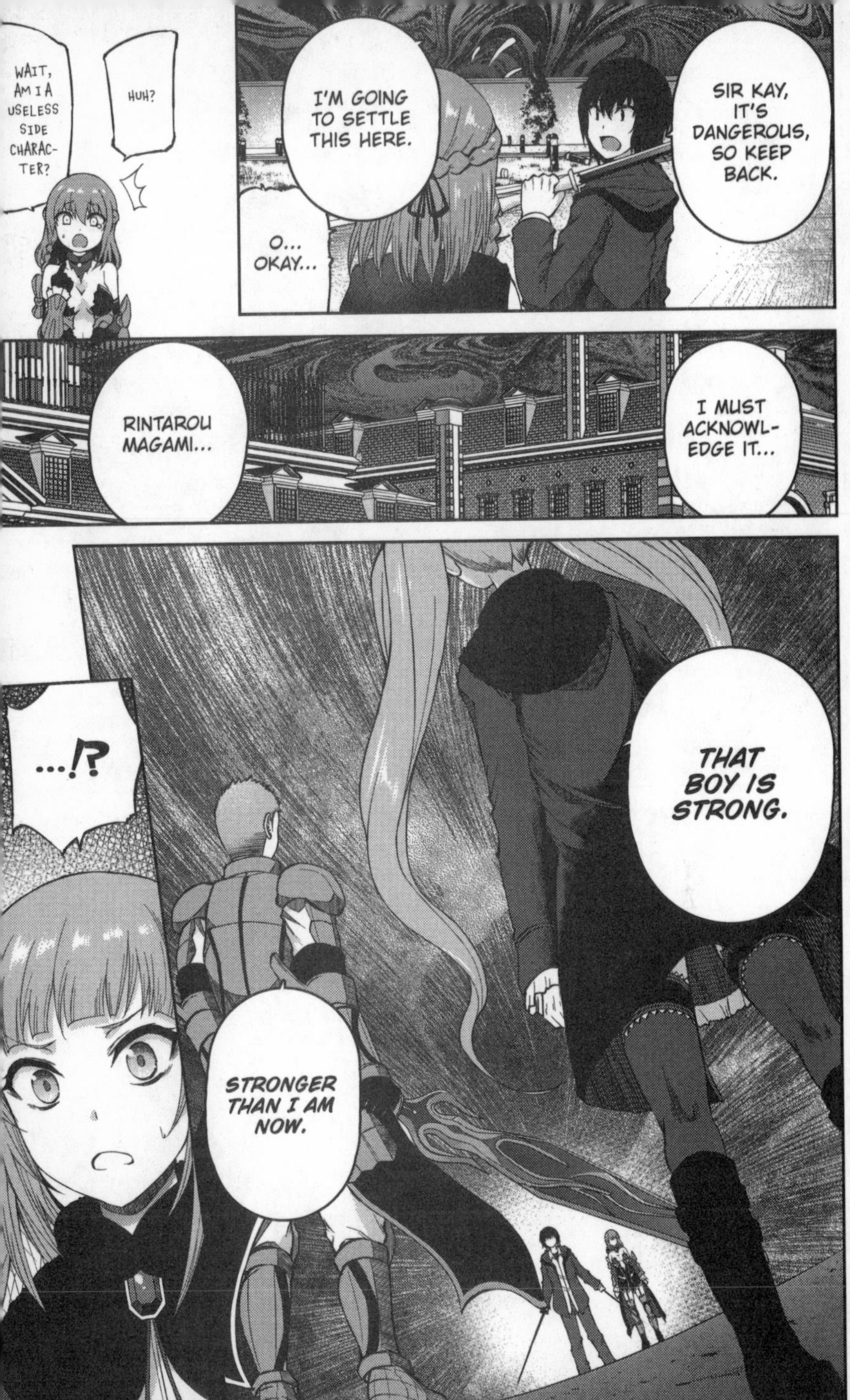
SIR KAY, IT'S DANGEROUS, SO KEEP BACK.
I'M GOING TO SETTLE THIS HERE.
O... OKAY...
HUH?
WAIT, AM I A USELESS SIDE CHARACTER?
I MUST ACKNOWLEDGE IT...
RINTAROU MAGAMI...
THAT BOY IS STRONG.
STRONGER THAN I AM NOW.
...!?

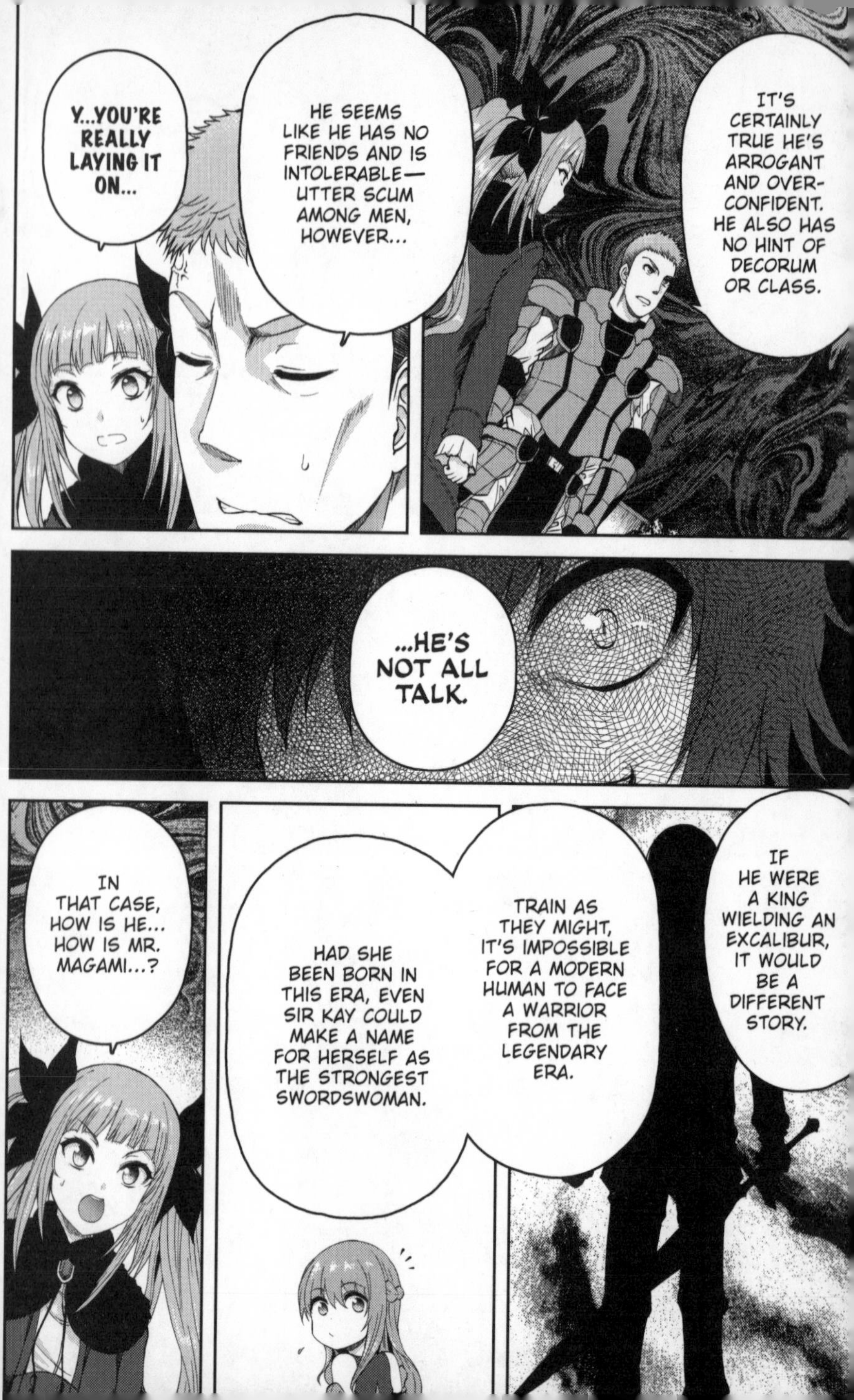
IT'S CERTAINLY TRUE HE'S ARROGANT AND OVER-CONFIDENT. HE ALSO HAS NO HINT OF DECORUM OR CLASS.
HE SEEMS LIKE HE HAS NO FRIENDS AND IS INTOLERABLE—UTTER SCUM AMONG MEN, HOWEVER...
Y...YOU'RE REALLY LAYING IT ON...
...HE'S NOT ALL TALK.
IF HE WERE A KING WIELDING AN EXCALIBUR, IT WOULD BE A DIFFERENT STORY.
TRAIN AS THEY MIGHT, IT'S IMPOSSIBLE FOR A MODERN HUMAN TO FACE A WARRIOR FROM THE LEGENDARY ERA.
HAD SHE BEEN BORN IN THIS ERA, EVEN SIR KAY COULD MAKE A NAME FOR HERSELF AS THE STRONGEST SWORDSWOMAN.
IN THAT CASE, HOW IS HE... HOW IS MR. MAGAMI...?

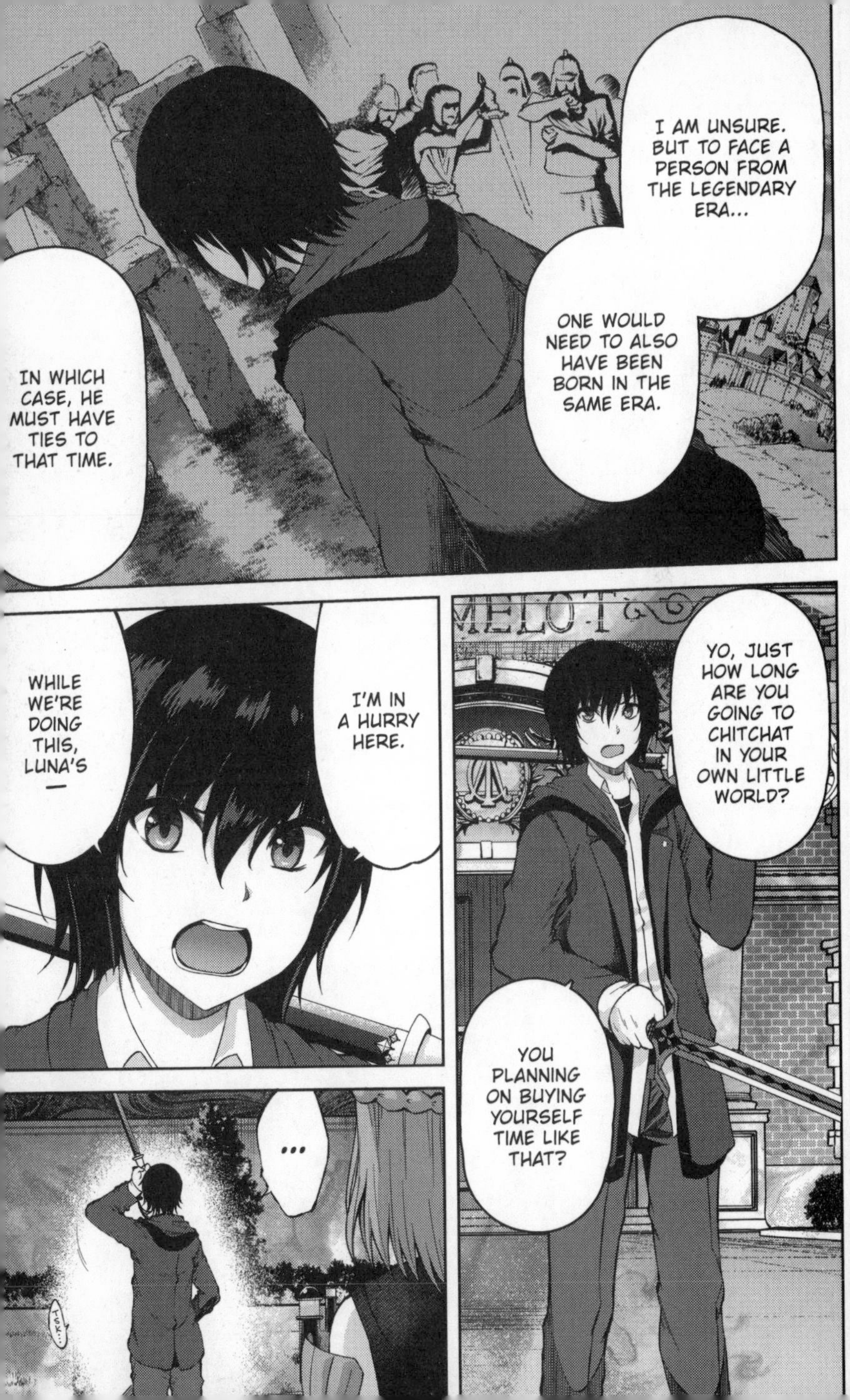
I AM UNSURE. BUT TO FACE A PERSON FROM THE LEGENDARY ERA...
ONE WOULD NEED TO ALSO HAVE BEEN BORN IN THE SAME ERA.
IN WHICH CASE, HE MUST HAVE TIES TO THAT TIME.
YO, JUST HOW LONG ARE YOU GOING TO CHITCHAT IN YOUR OWN LITTLE WORLD?
YOU PLANNING ON BUYING YOURSELF TIME LIKE THAT?
I'M IN A HURRY HERE.
WHILE WE'RE DOING THIS, LUNA'S —
...
TSK...

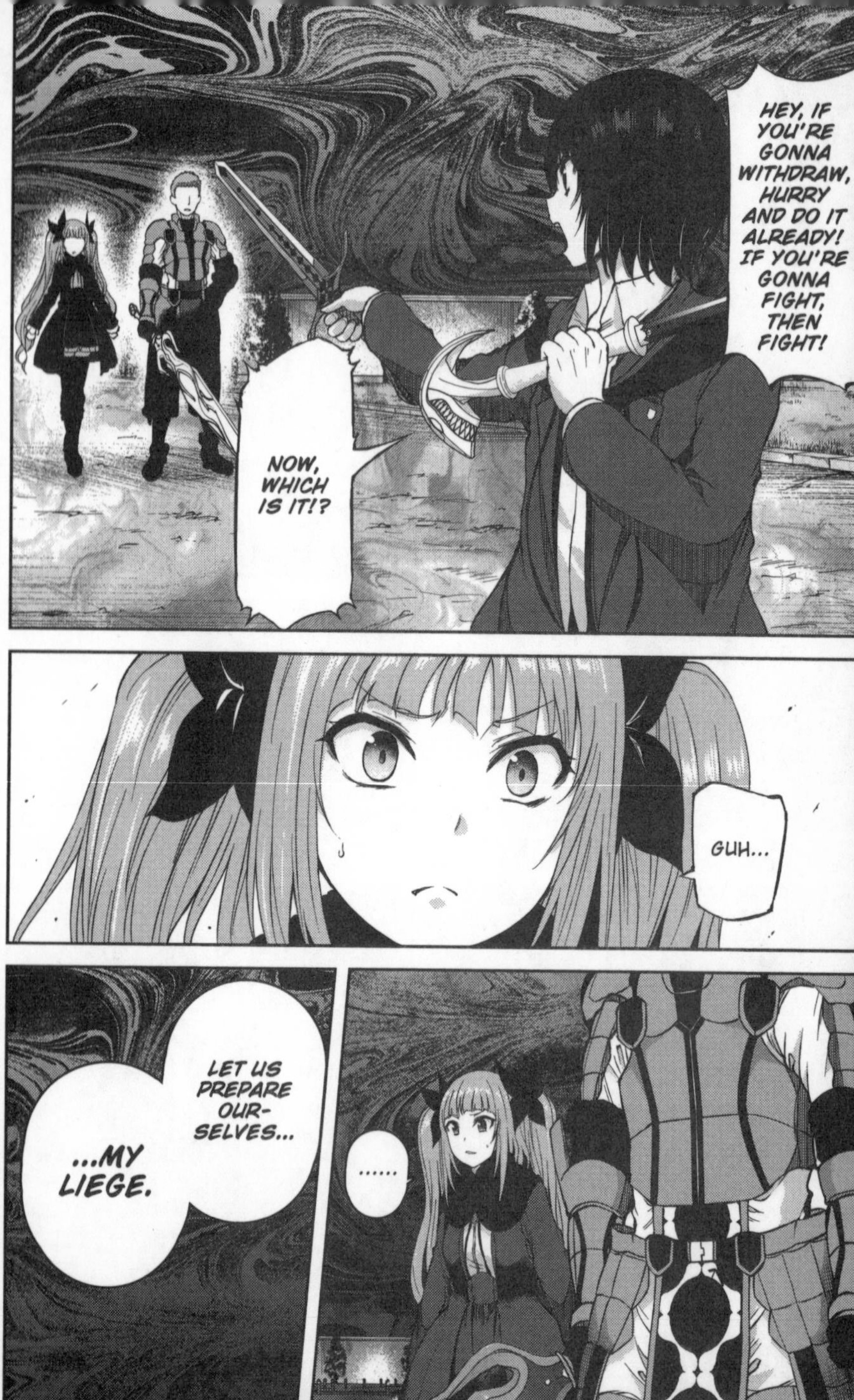
HEY, IF YOU'RE GONNA WITHDRAW, HURRY AND DO IT ALREADY! IF YOU'RE GONNA FIGHT, THEN FIGHT!
NOW, WHICH IS IT!?
GUH...
......
LET US PREPARE OUR-SELVES...
...MY LIEGE.

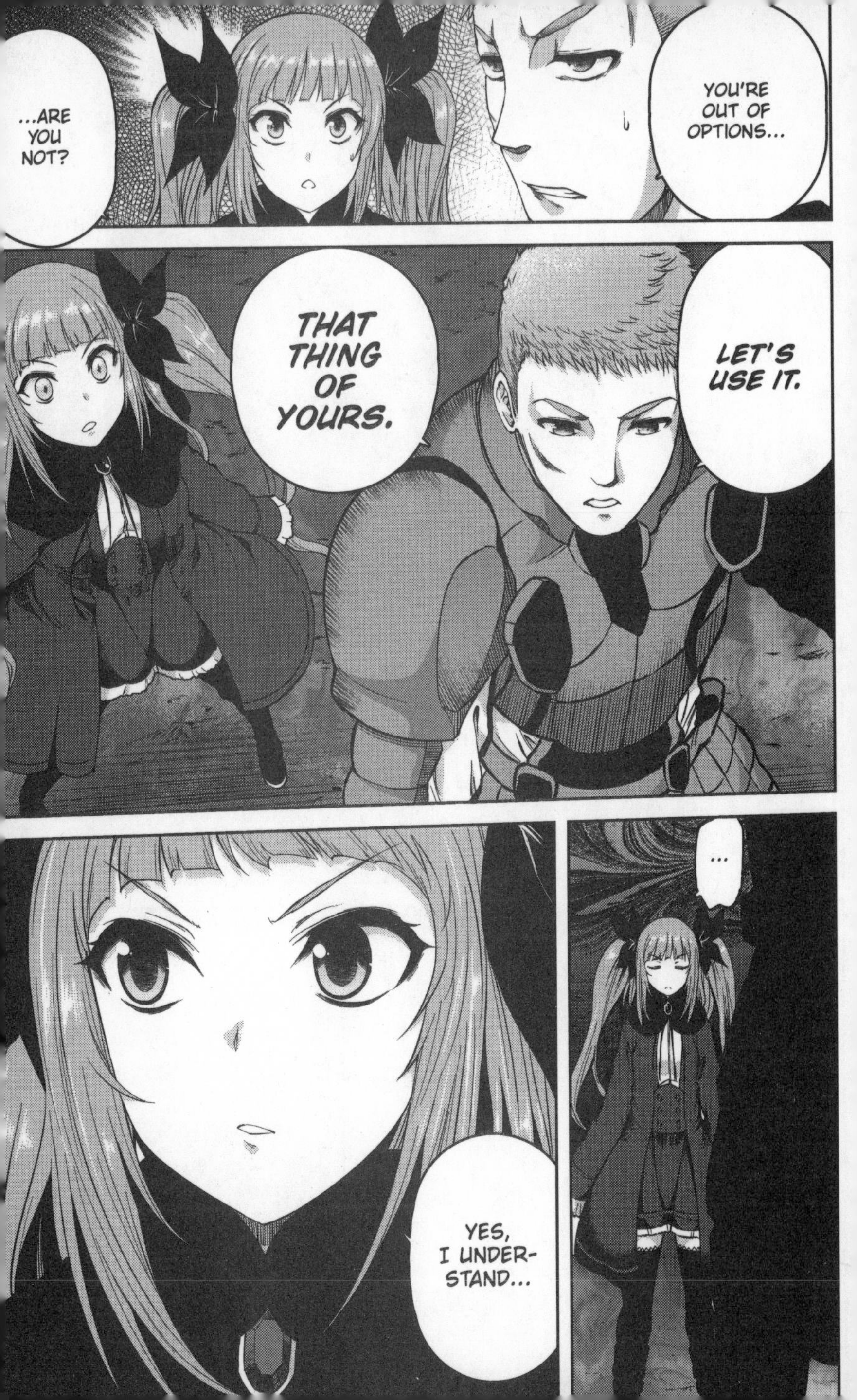
YOU'RE OUT OF OPTIONS...
...ARE YOU NOT?
LET'S USE IT.
THAT THING OF YOURS.
...
YES, I UNDER-STAND...

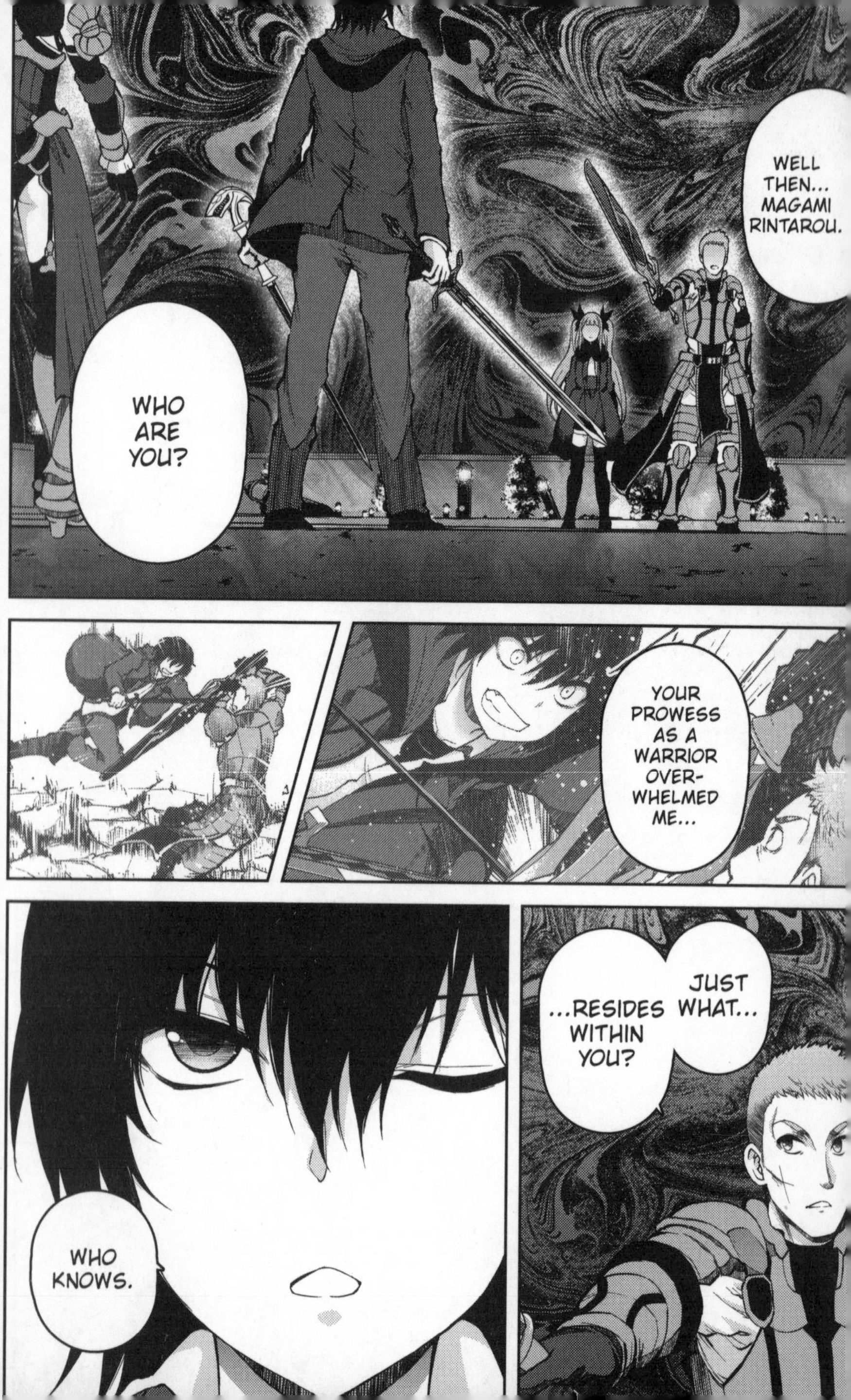
WELL THEN... MAGAMI RINTAROU.
WHO ARE YOU?
YOUR PROWESS AS A WARRIOR OVER-WHELMED ME...
JUST WHAT...
...RESIDES WITHIN YOU?
WHO KNOWS.

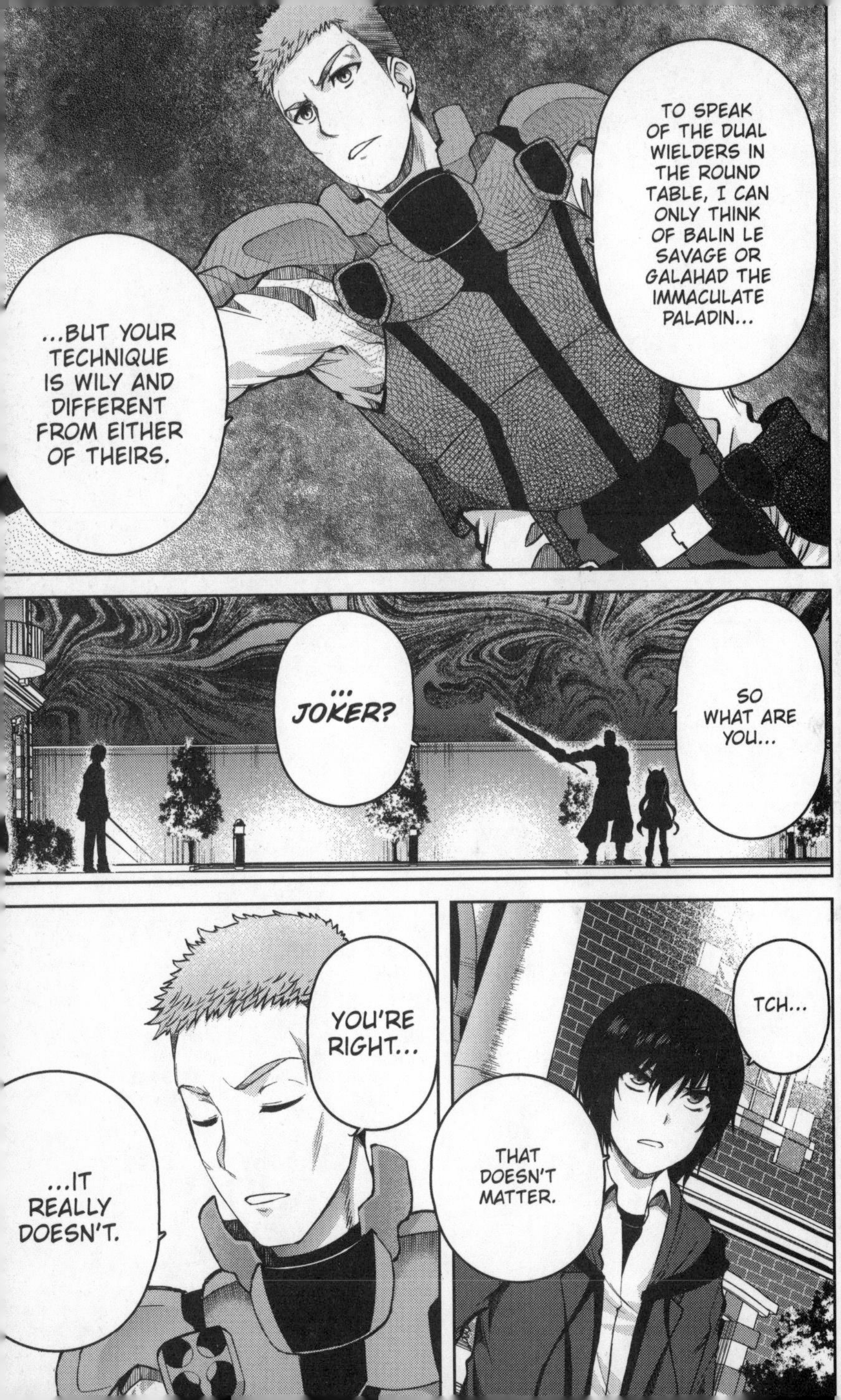
TO SPEAK OF THE DUAL WIELDERS IN THE ROUND TABLE, I CAN ONLY THINK OF BALIN LE SAVAGE OR GALAHAD THE IMMACULATE PALADIN...
...BUT YOUR TECHNIQUE IS WILY AND DIFFERENT FROM EITHER OF THEIRS.
SO WHAT ARE YOU...
...JOKER?
TCH...
THAT DOESN'T MATTER.
YOU'RE RIGHT...
...IT REALLY DOESN'T.

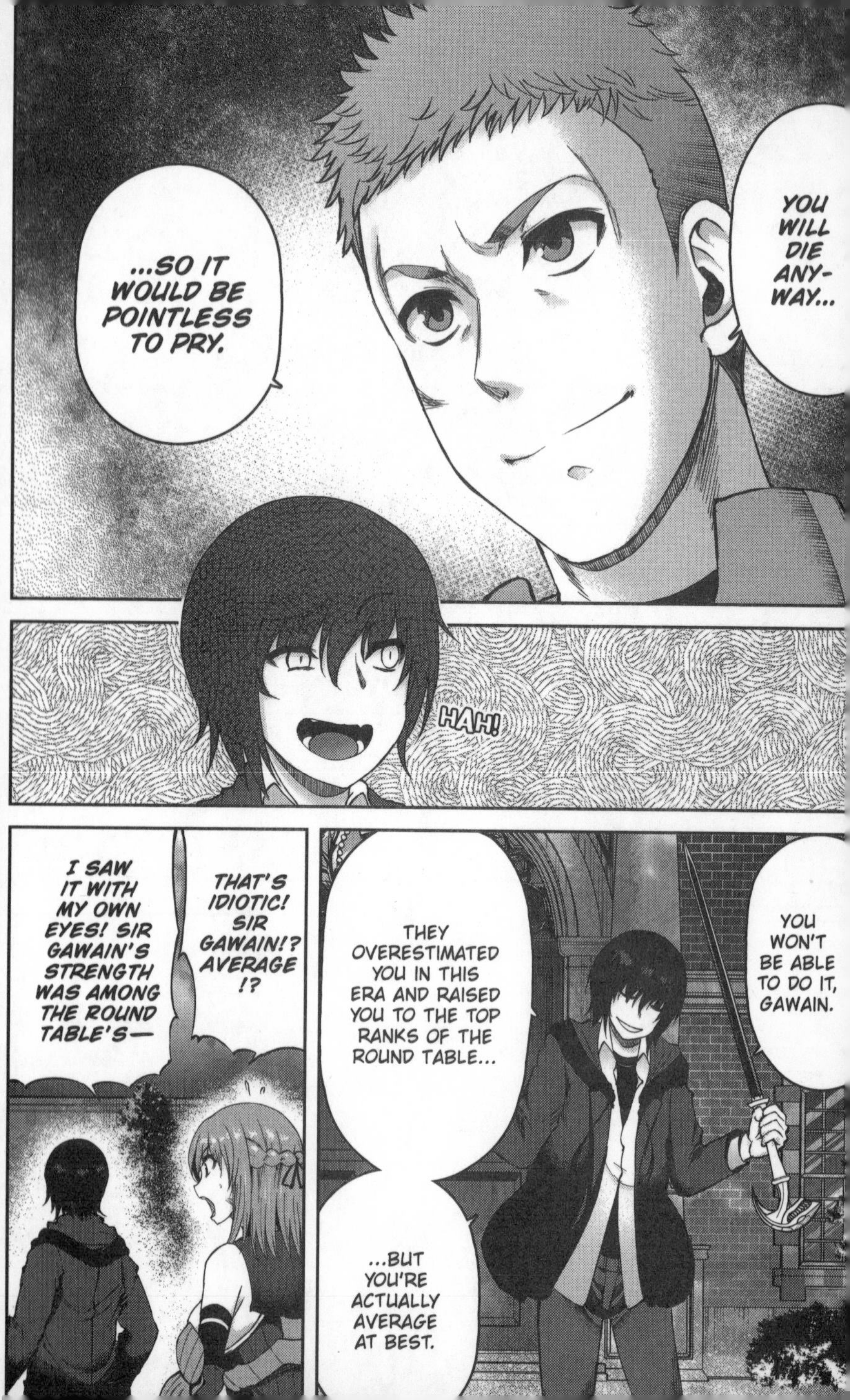
YOU WILL DIE ANYWAY...
...SO IT WOULD BE POINTLESS TO PRY.
HAH!
YOU WON'T BE ABLE TO DO IT, GAWAIN.
THEY OVERESTIMATED YOU IN THIS ERA AND RAISED YOU TO THE TOP RANKS OF THE ROUND TABLE...
...BUT YOU'RE ACTUALLY AVERAGE AT BEST.
THAT'S IDIOTIC! SIR GAWAIN!? AVERAGE!?
I SAW IT WITH MY OWN EYES! SIR GAWAIN'S STRENGTH WAS AMONG THE ROUND TABLE'S—

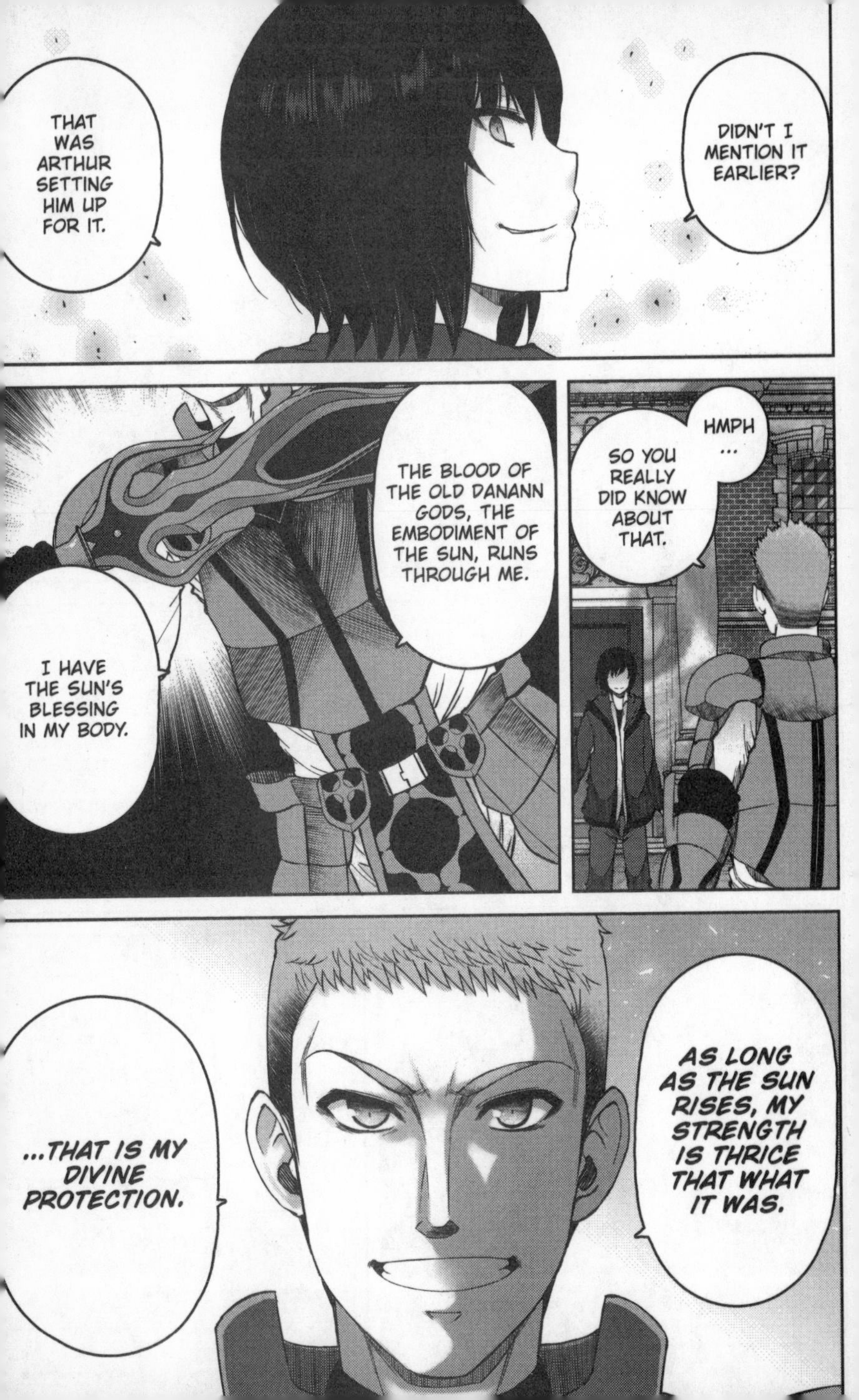
DIDN'T I MENTION IT EARLIER?
THAT WAS ARTHUR SETTING HIM UP FOR IT.
HMPH...
SO YOU REALLY DID KNOW ABOUT THAT.
THE BLOOD OF THE OLD DANANN GODS, THE EMBODIMENT OF THE SUN, RUNS THROUGH ME.
I HAVE THE SUN'S BLESSING IN MY BODY.
AS LONG AS THE SUN RISES, MY STRENGTH IS THRICE THAT WHAT IT WAS.
...THAT IS MY DIVINE PROTECTION.

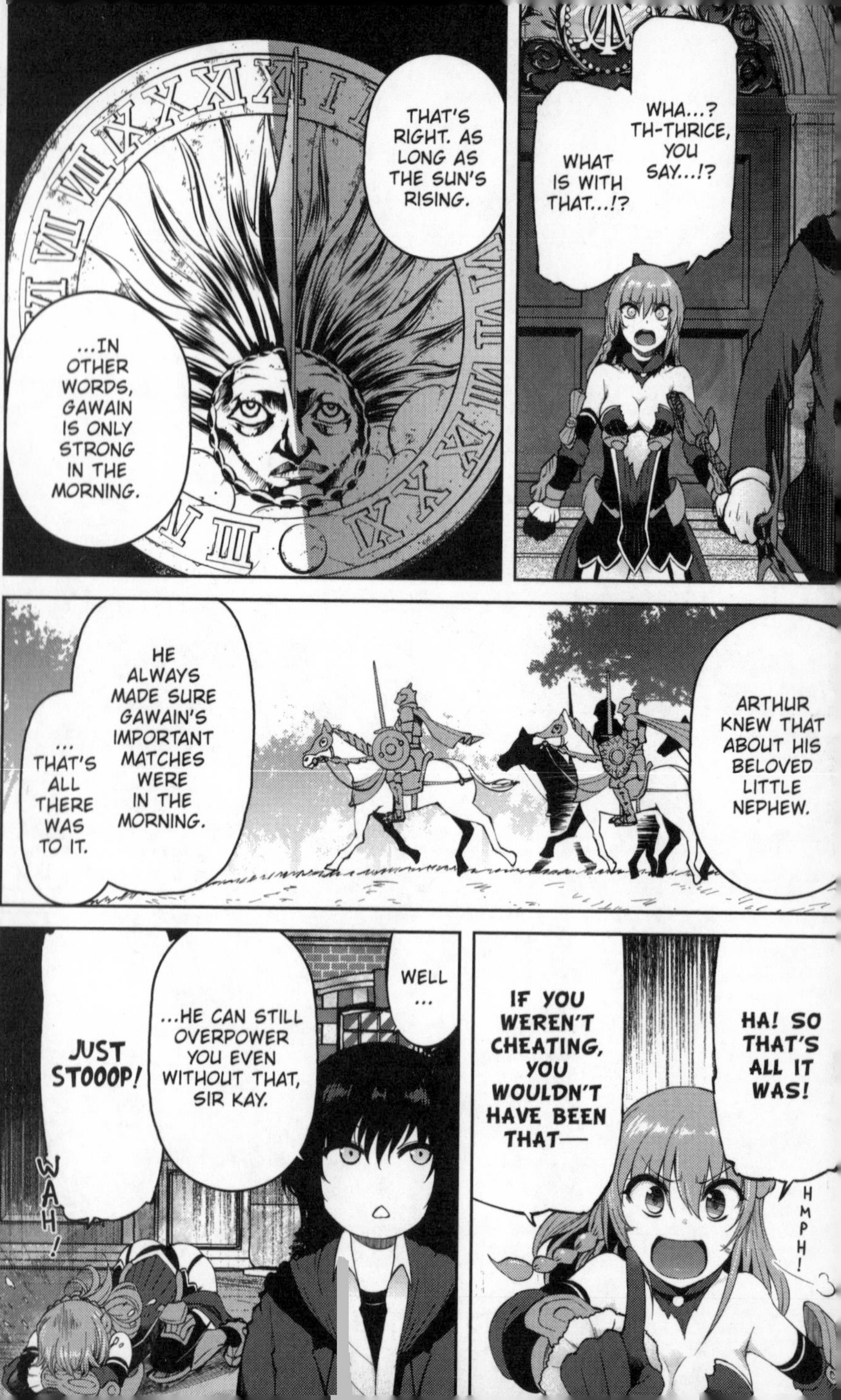
WHA...? TH-THRICE, YOU SAY...!?
WHAT IS WITH THAT...!?
THAT'S RIGHT. AS LONG AS THE SUN'S RISING.
...IN OTHER WORDS, GAWAIN IS ONLY STRONG IN THE MORNING.
ARTHUR KNEW THAT ABOUT HIS BELOVED LITTLE NEPHEW.
HE ALWAYS MADE SURE GAWAIN'S IMPORTANT MATCHES WERE IN THE MORNING.
...THAT'S ALL THERE WAS TO IT.
HA! SO THAT'S ALL IT WAS!
HMPH!
IF YOU WEREN'T CHEATING, YOU WOULDN'T HAVE BEEN THAT—
WELL...
...HE CAN STILL OVERPOWER YOU EVEN WITHOUT THAT, SIR KAY.
JUST STOOOP!
WAH!

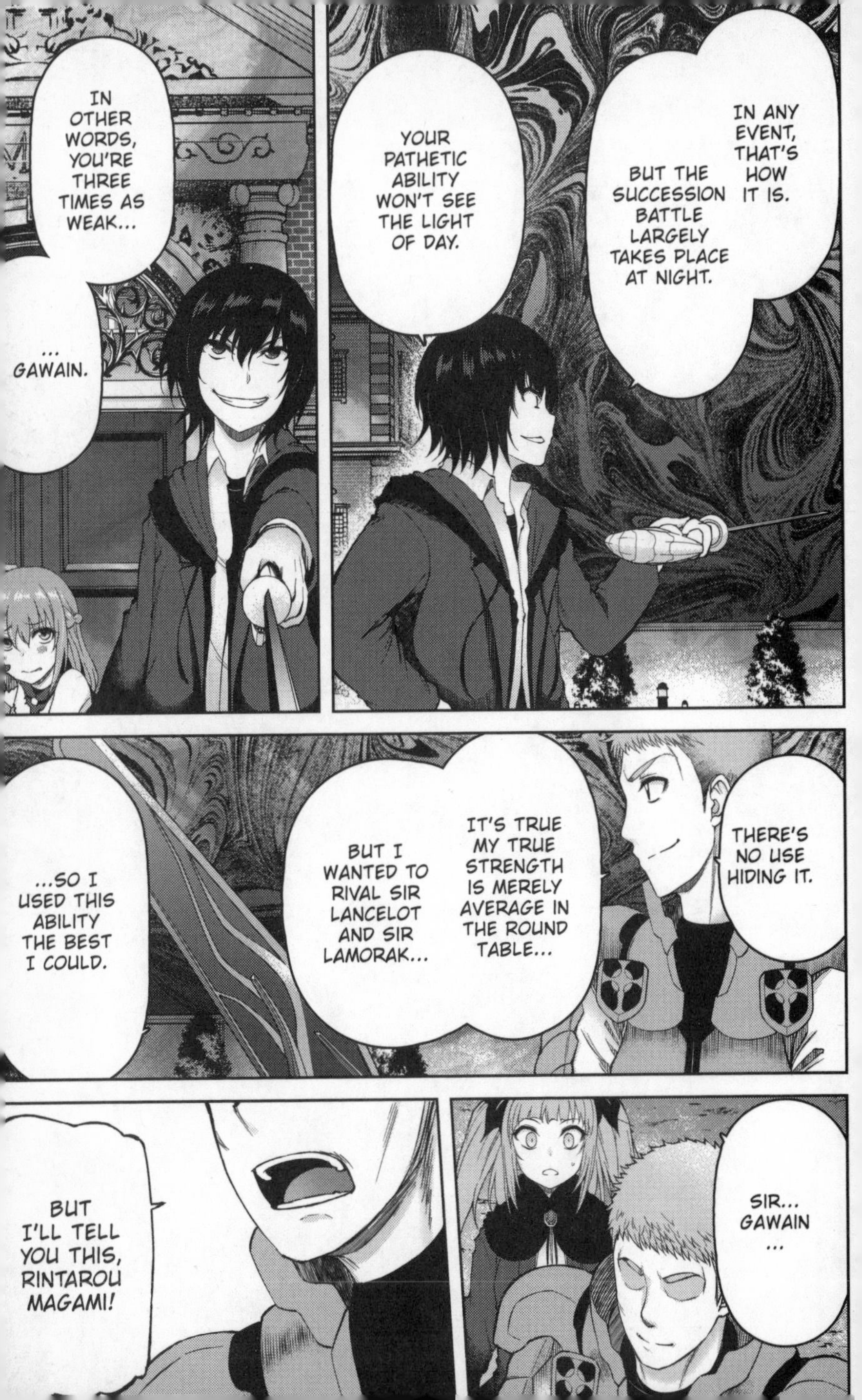
IN ANY EVENT, THAT'S HOW IT IS.
BUT THE SUCCESSION BATTLE LARGELY TAKES PLACE AT NIGHT.
YOUR PATHETIC ABILITY WON'T SEE THE LIGHT OF DAY.
IN OTHER WORDS, YOU'RE THREE TIMES AS WEAK...
...GAWAIN.
THERE'S NO USE HIDING IT.
IT'S TRUE MY TRUE STRENGTH IS MERELY AVERAGE IN THE ROUND TABLE...
BUT I WANTED TO RIVAL SIR LANCELOT AND SIR LAMORAK...
...SO I USED THIS ABILITY THE BEST I COULD.
SIR... GAWAIN...
BUT I'LL TELL YOU THIS, RINTAROU MAGAMI!

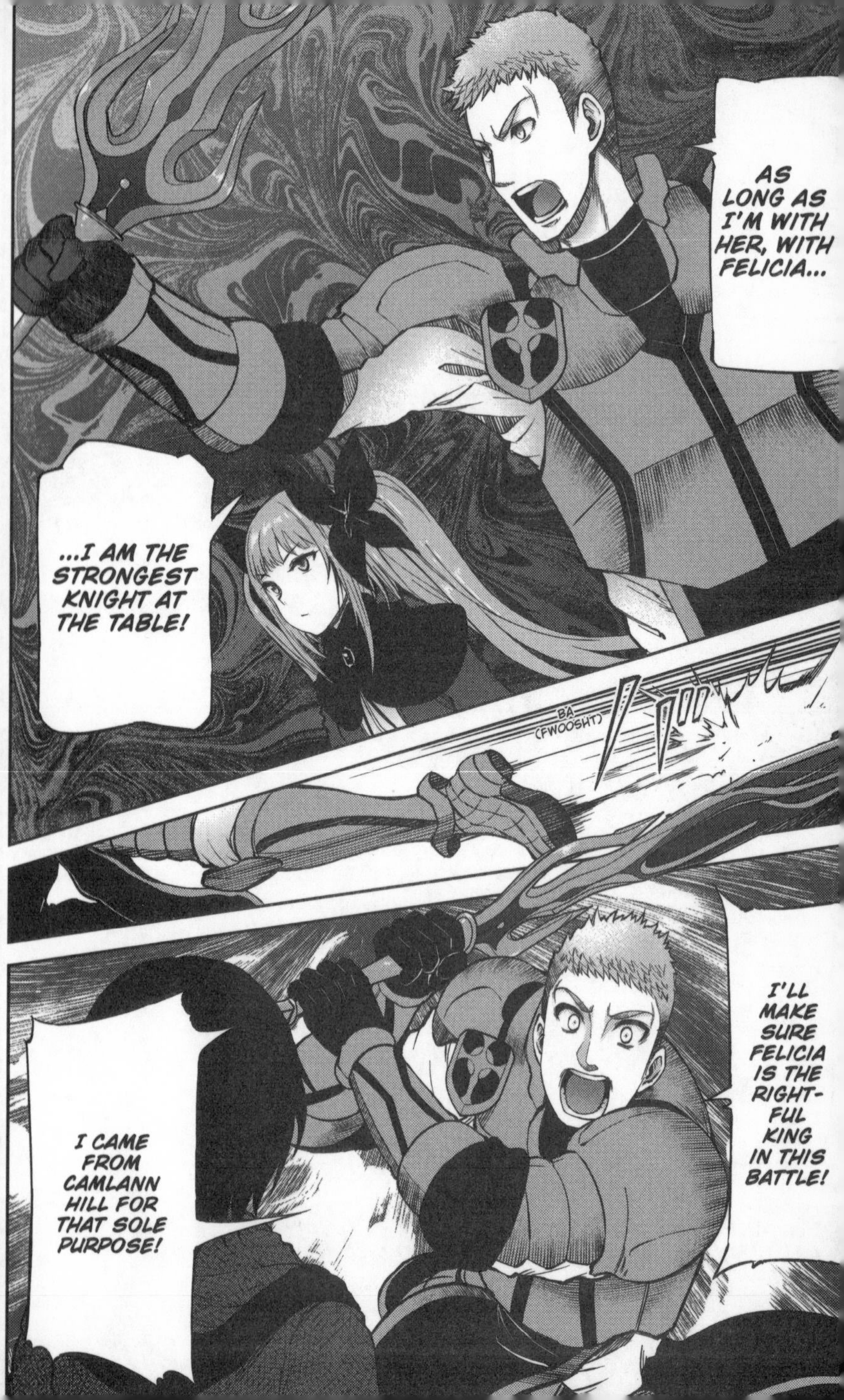
AS LONG AS I'M WITH HER, WITH FELICIA...
...I AM THE STRONGEST KNIGHT AT THE TABLE!
BA (FWOOSHT)
I'LL MAKE SURE FELICIA IS THE RIGHTFUL KING IN THIS BATTLE!
I CAME FROM CAMLANN HILL FOR THAT SOLE PURPOSE!

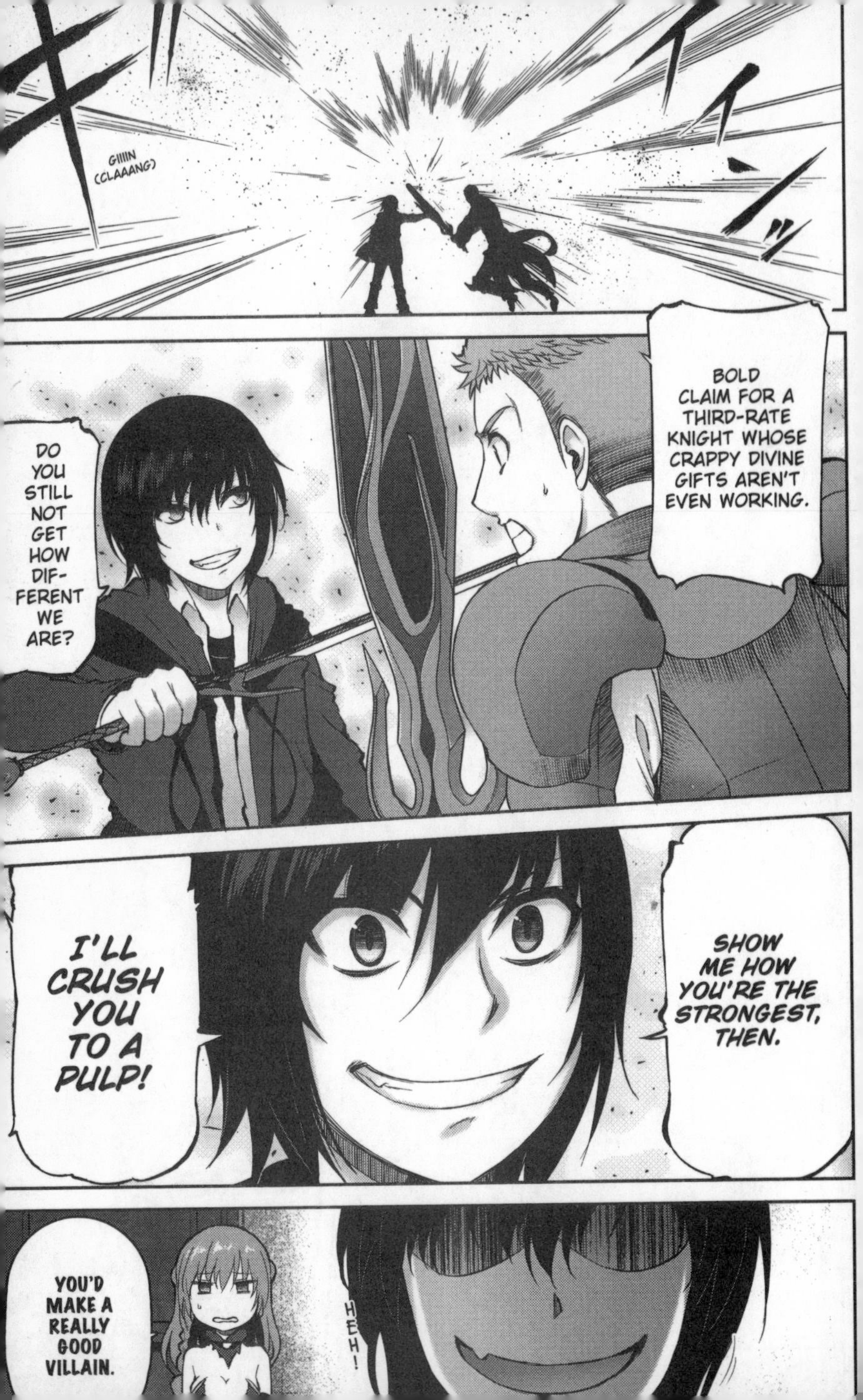
GIIIIN (CLAAANG)
BOLD CLAIM FOR A THIRD-RATE KNIGHT WHOSE CRAPPY DIVINE GIFTS AREN'T EVEN WORKING.
DO YOU STILL NOT GET HOW DIF-FERENT WE ARE?
SHOW ME HOW YOU'RE THE STRONGEST, THEN.
I'LL CRUSH YOU TO A PULP!
HEH!
YOU'D MAKE A REALLY GOOD VILLAIN.

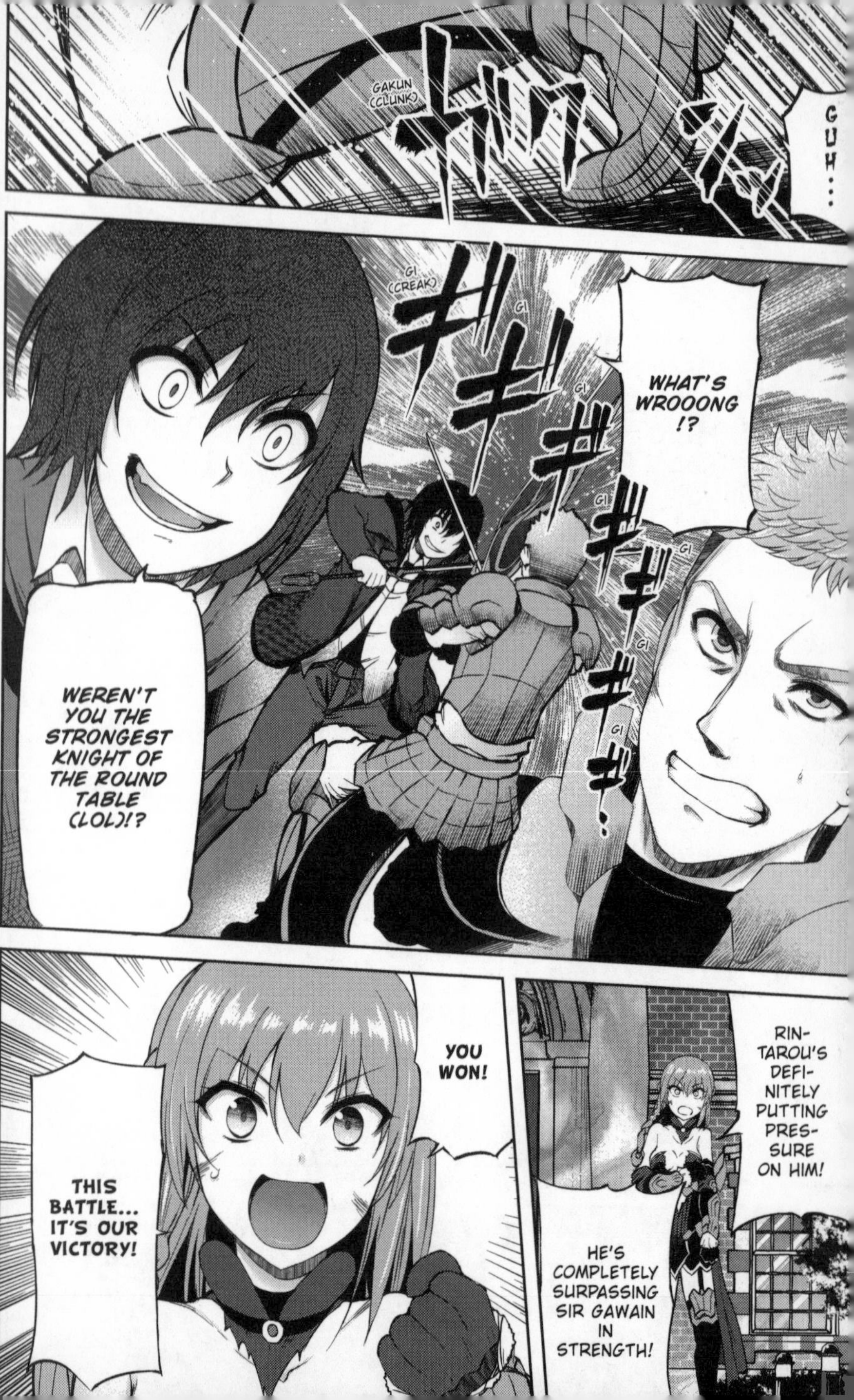
GUH...
GAKUN (CLUNK)
WHAT'S WROOONG!?
GI (CREAK)
GI GI GI GI GI GI GI
WEREN'T YOU THE STRONGEST KNIGHT OF THE ROUND TABLE (LOL)!?
RIN-TAROU'S DEFI-NITELY PUTTING PRES-SURE ON HIM!
HE'S COMPLETELY SURPASSING SIR GAWAIN IN STRENGTH!
YOU WON!
THIS BATTLE... IT'S OUR VICTORY!

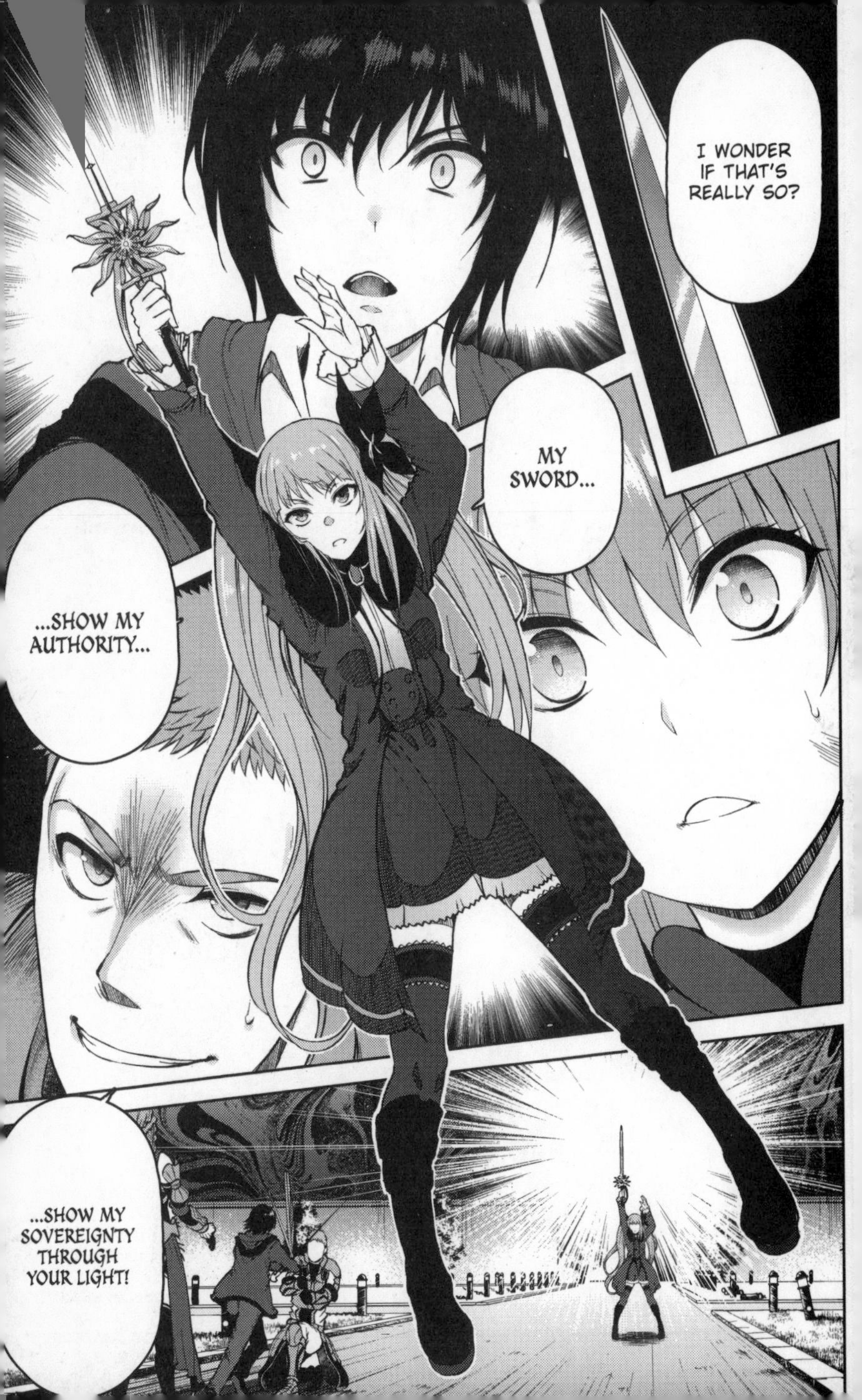
I WONDER IF THAT'S REALLY SO?
MY SWORD...
...SHOW MY AUTHORITY...
...SHOW MY SOVEREIGNTY THROUGH YOUR LIGHT!

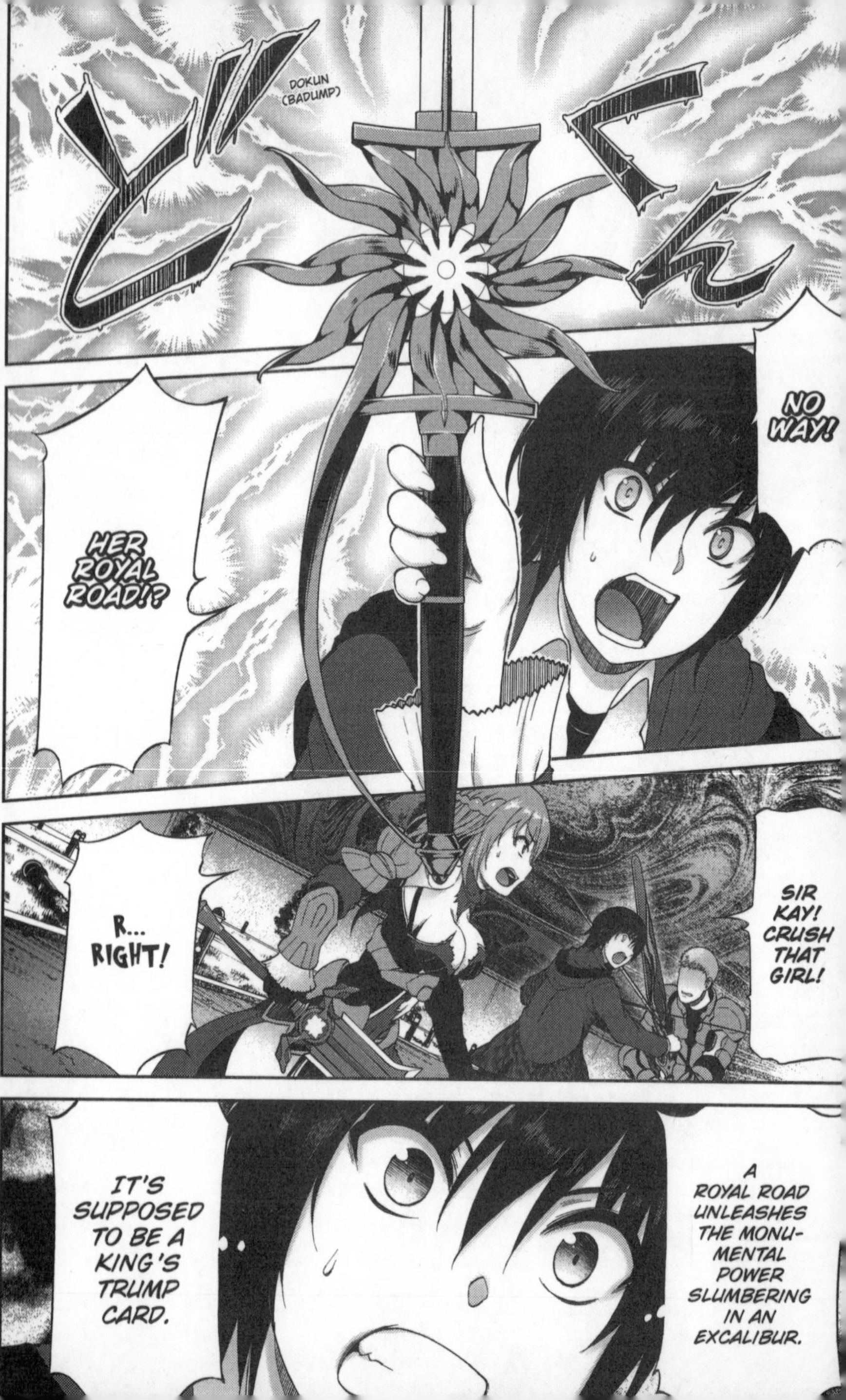
どくん
DOKUN (BADUMP)
NO WAY!
HER ROYAL ROAD!?
SIR KAY! CRUSH THAT GIRL!
R... RIGHT!
A ROYAL ROAD UNLEASHES THE MONU-MENTAL POWER SLUMBERING IN AN EXCALIBUR.
IT'S SUPPOSED TO BE A KING'S TRUMP CARD.

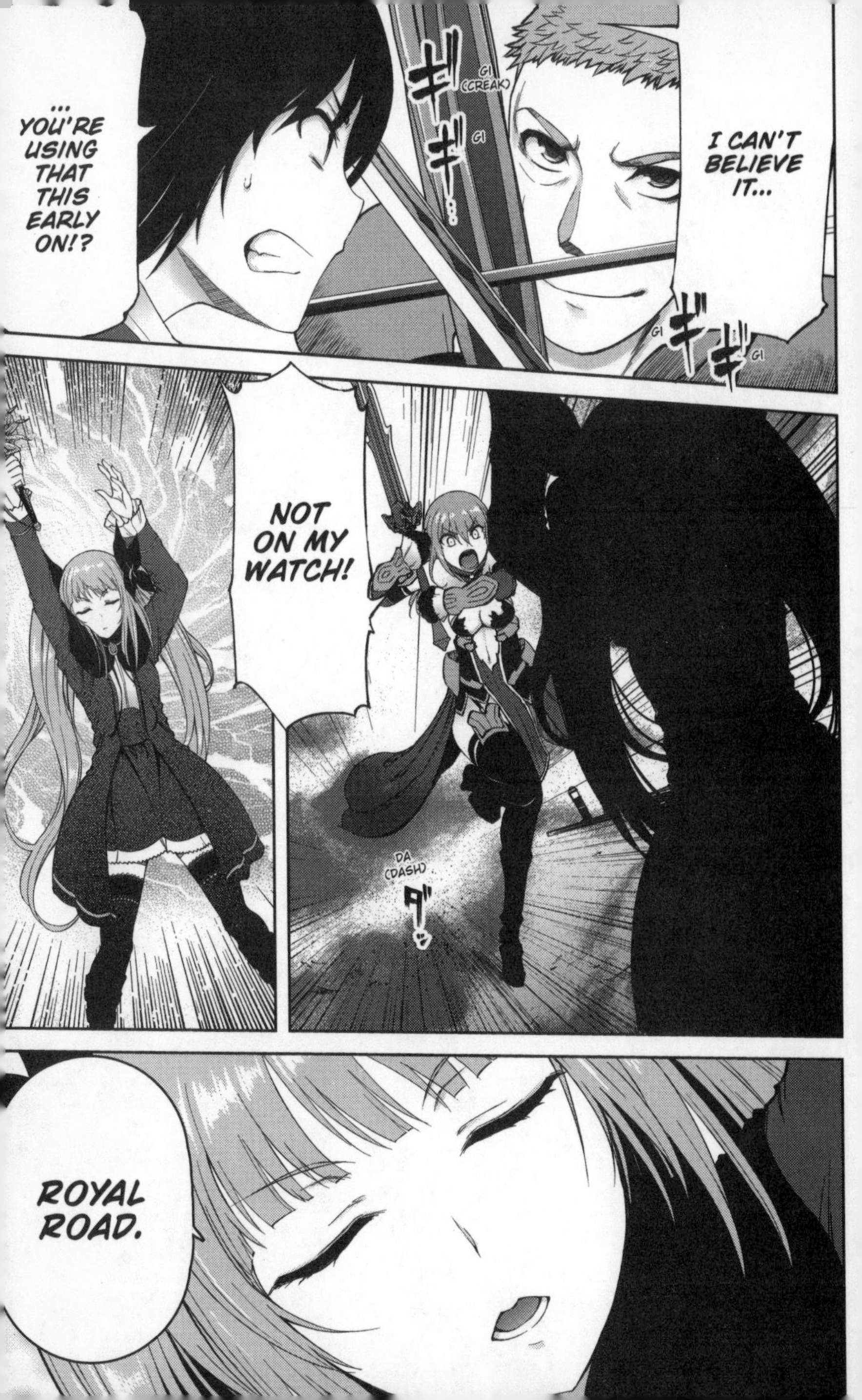

I CAN'T BELIEVE IT...
GI (CREAK)
GI
... YOU'RE USING THAT THIS EARLY ON!?
GI
GI
NOT ON MY WATCH!
DA (DASH)
ROYAL ROAD.

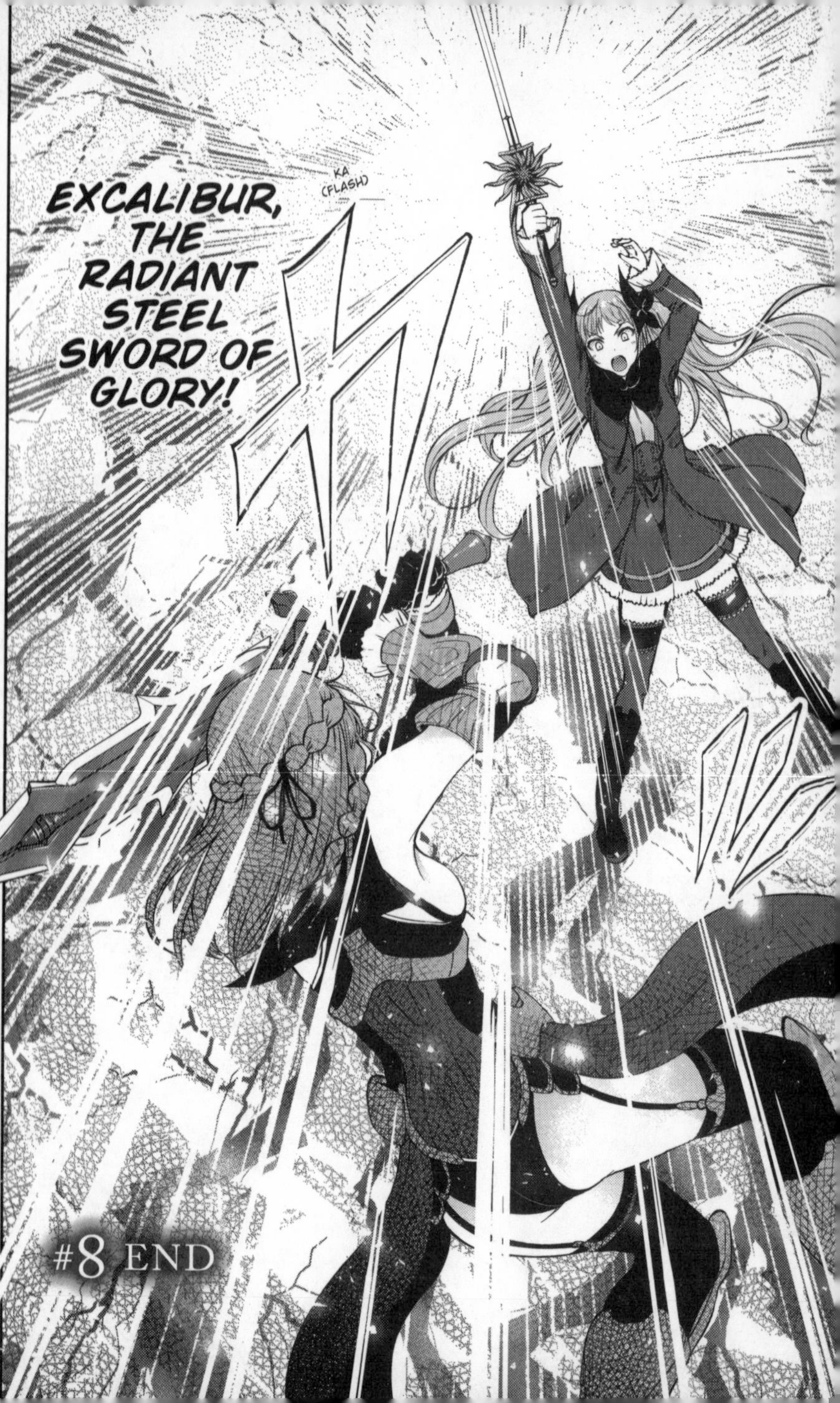
KA
(FLASH)
EXCALIBUR, THE RADIANT STEEL SWORD OF GLORY!
#8 END

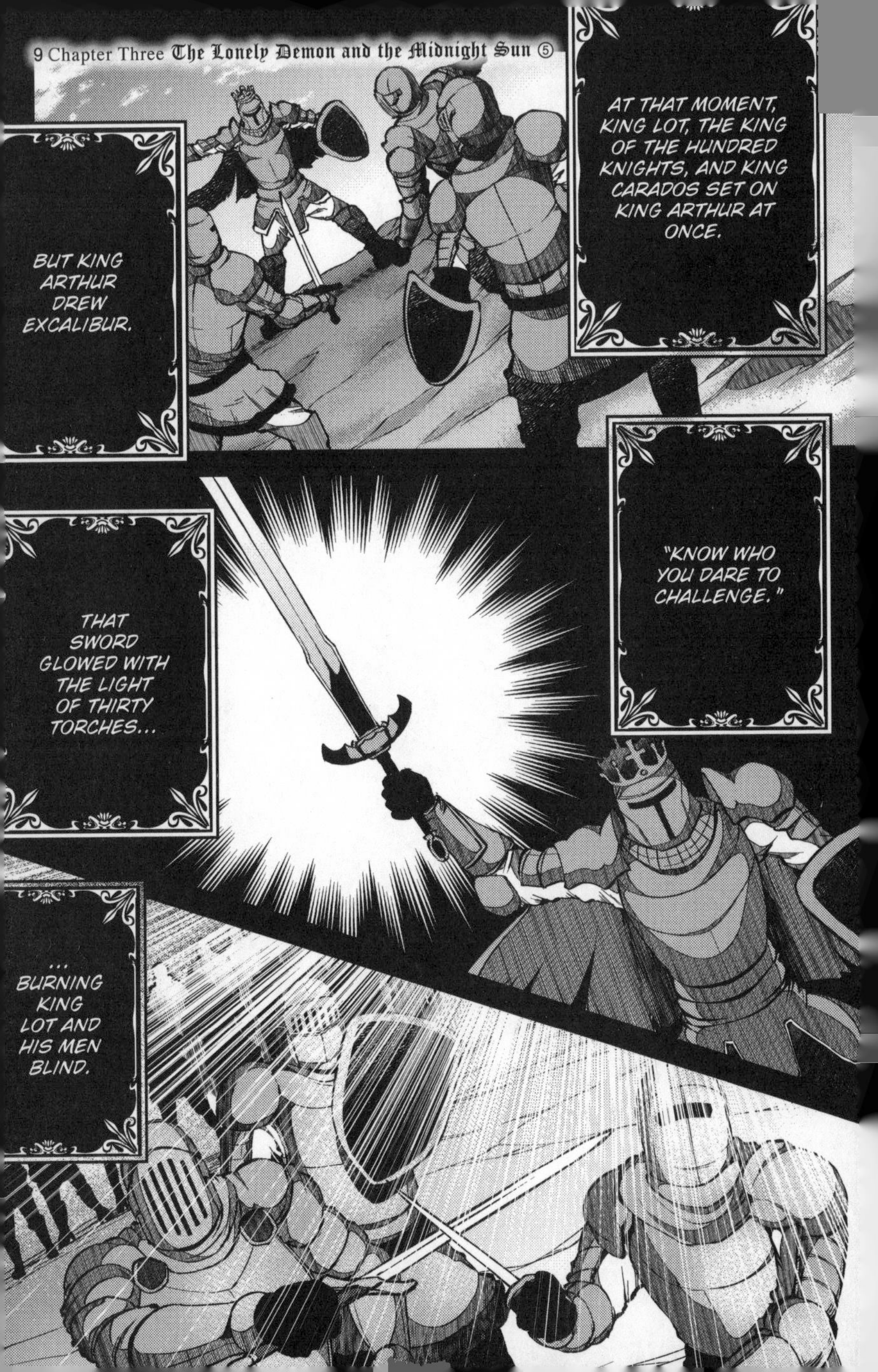
AT THAT MOMENT, KING LOT, THE KING OF THE HUNDRED KNIGHTS, AND KING CARADOS SET ON KING ARTHUR AT ONCE.
BUT KING ARTHUR DREW EXCALIBUR.
"KNOW WHO YOU DARE TO CHALLENGE."
THAT SWORD GLOWED WITH THE LIGHT OF THIRTY TORCHES...
... BURNING KING LOT AND HIS MEN BLIND.

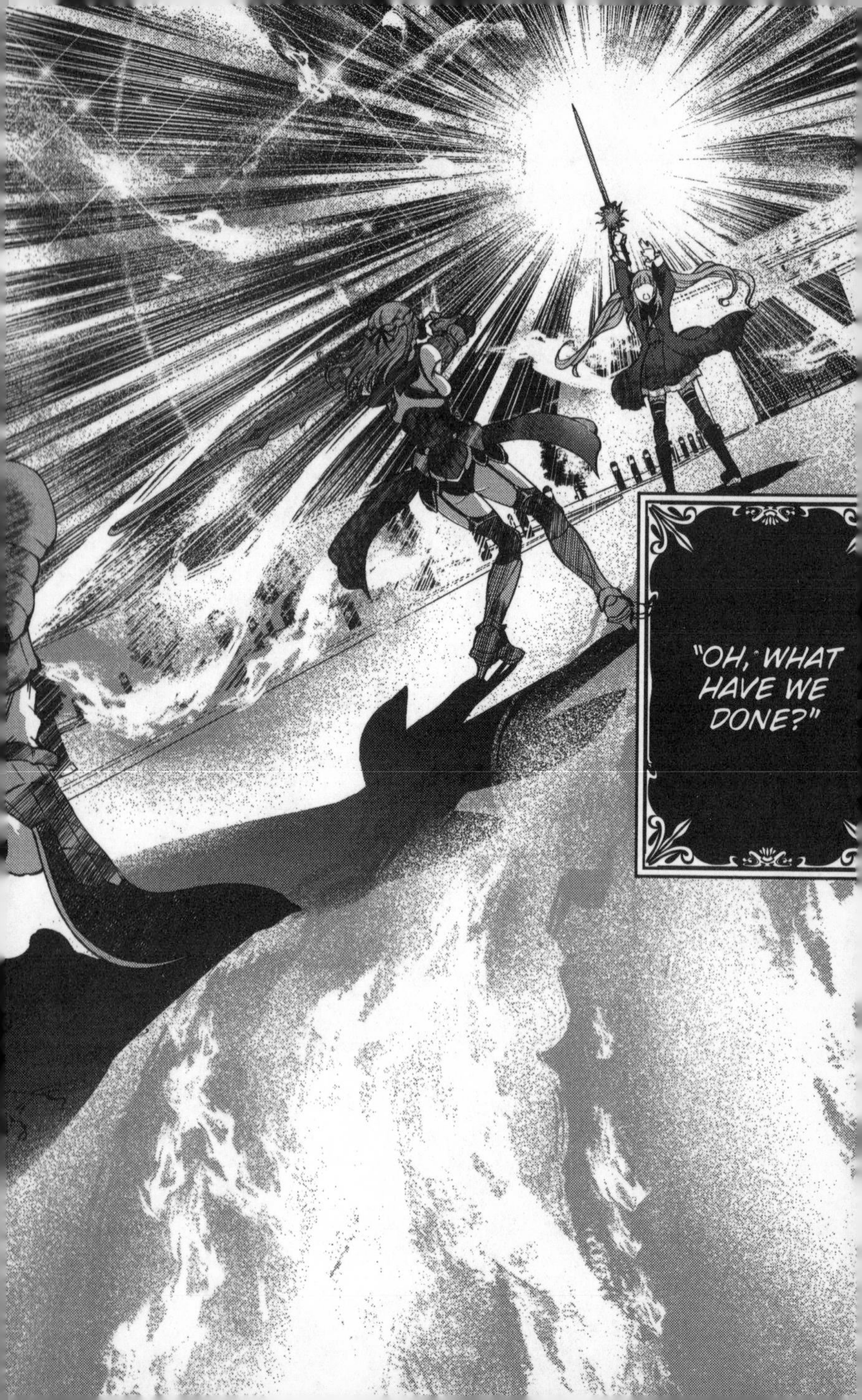
"OH," WHAT HAVE WE DONE?"

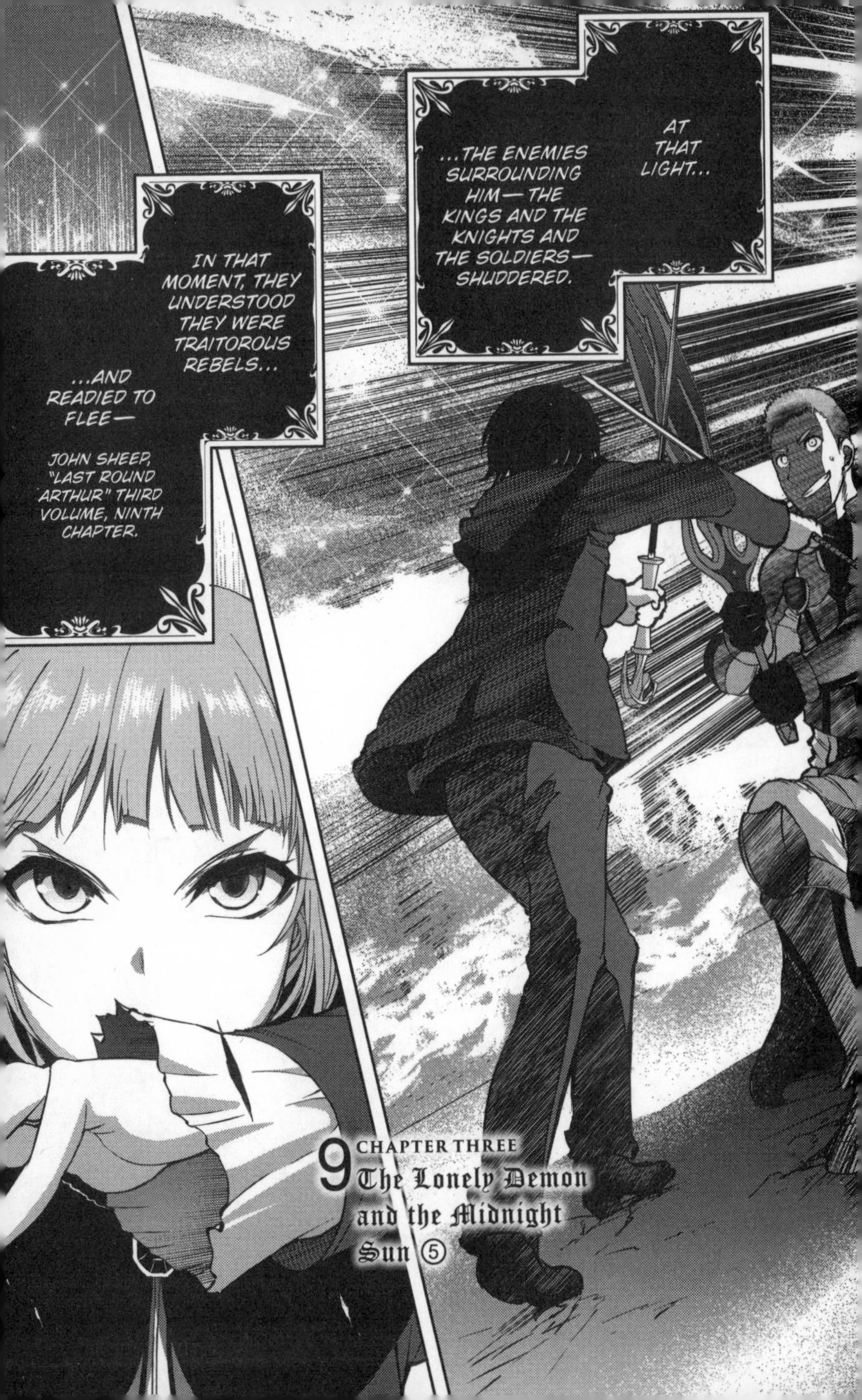
AT THAT LIGHT...
...THE ENEMIES SURROUNDING HIM—THE KINGS AND THE KNIGHTS AND THE SOLDIERS—SHUDDERED.
IN THAT MOMENT, THEY UNDERSTOOD THEY WERE TRAITOROUS REBELS...
...AND READIED TO FLEE—
JOHN SHEEP, "LAST ROUND ARTHUR" THIRD VOLUME, NINTH CHAPTER.
9 CHAPTER THREE
The Lonely Demon and the Midnight Sun ⑤

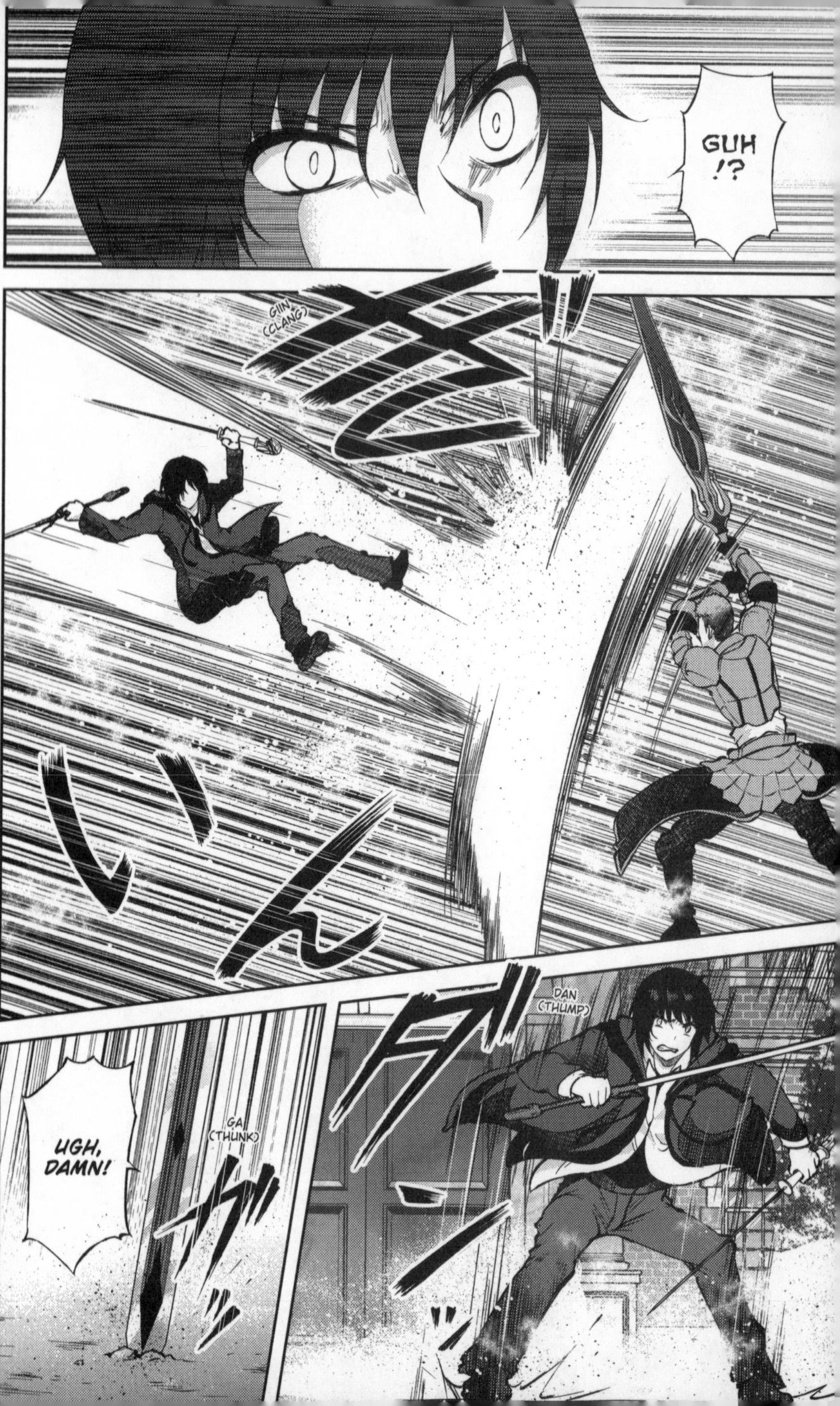
GUH !?
GIIN (CLANG)
DAN (THUMP)
GA (THUNK)
UGH, DAMN!

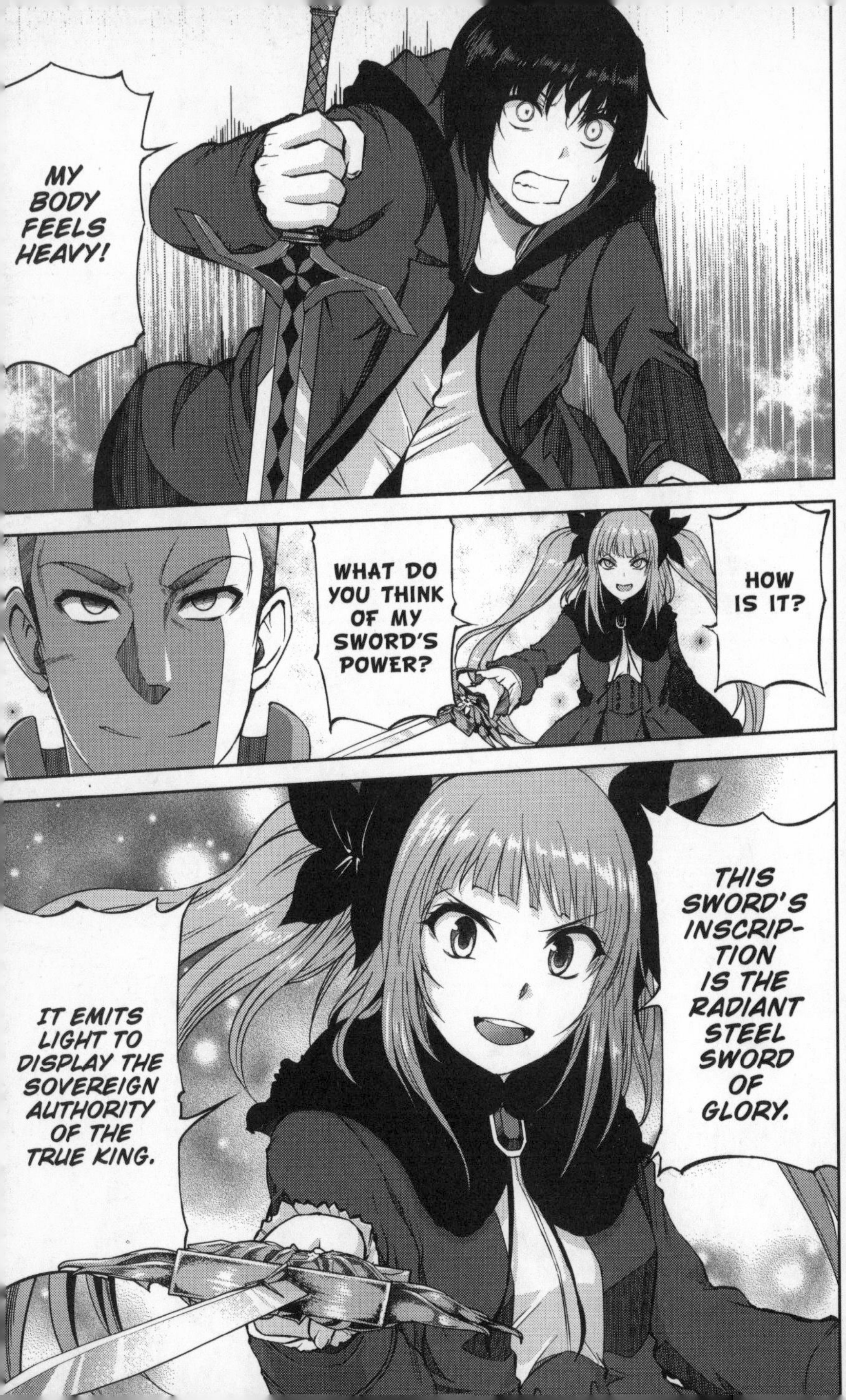
MY BODY FEELS HEAVY!
HOW IS IT?
WHAT DO YOU THINK OF MY SWORD'S POWER?
THIS SWORD'S INSCRIPTION IS THE RADIANT STEEL SWORD OF GLORY.
IT EMITS LIGHT TO DISPLAY THE SOVEREIGN AUTHORITY OF THE TRUE KING.

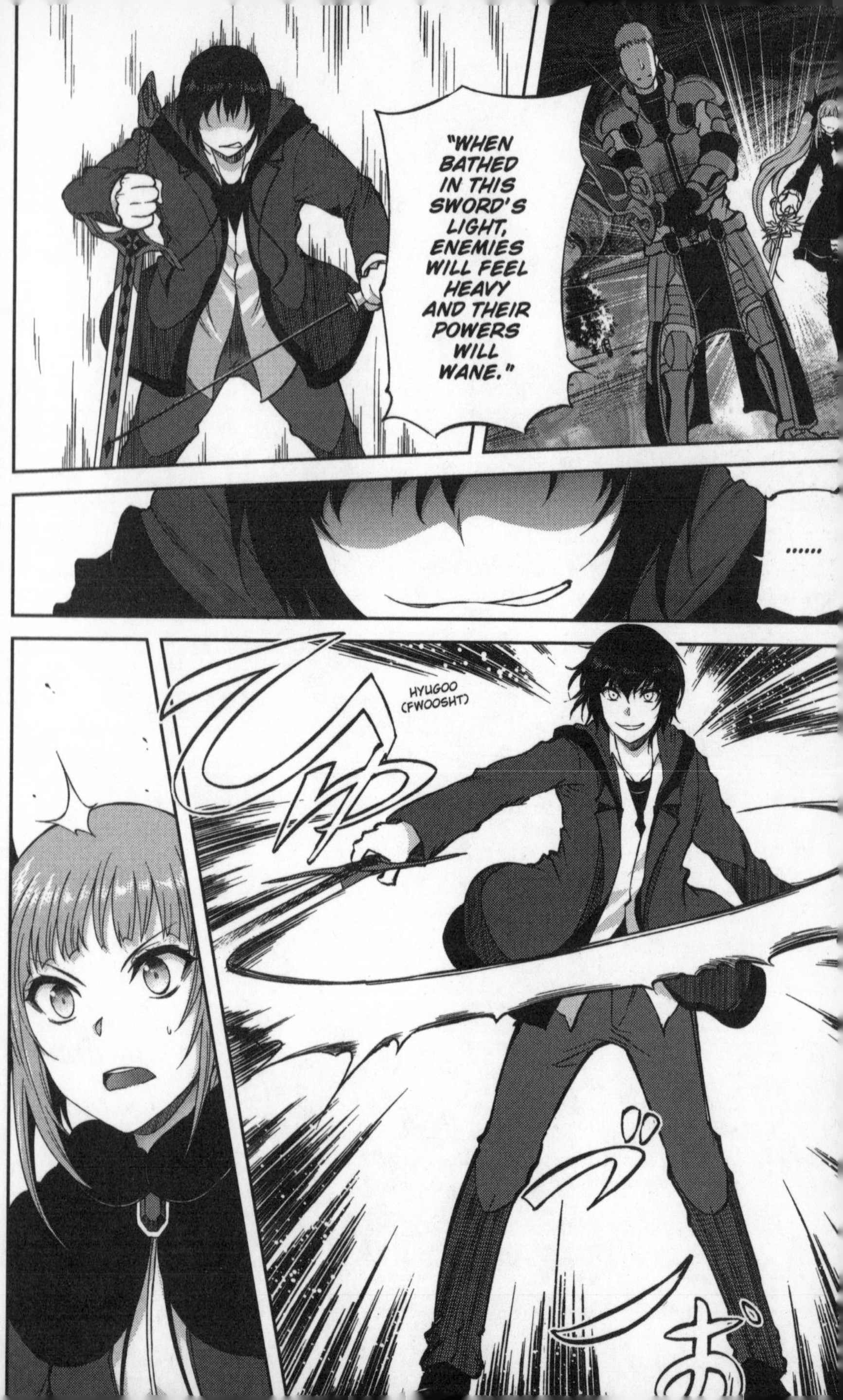
"WHEN BATHED IN THIS SWORD'S LIGHT, ENEMIES WILL FEEL HEAVY AND THEIR POWERS WILL WANE."
......
HYUGOO (FWOOSHT)

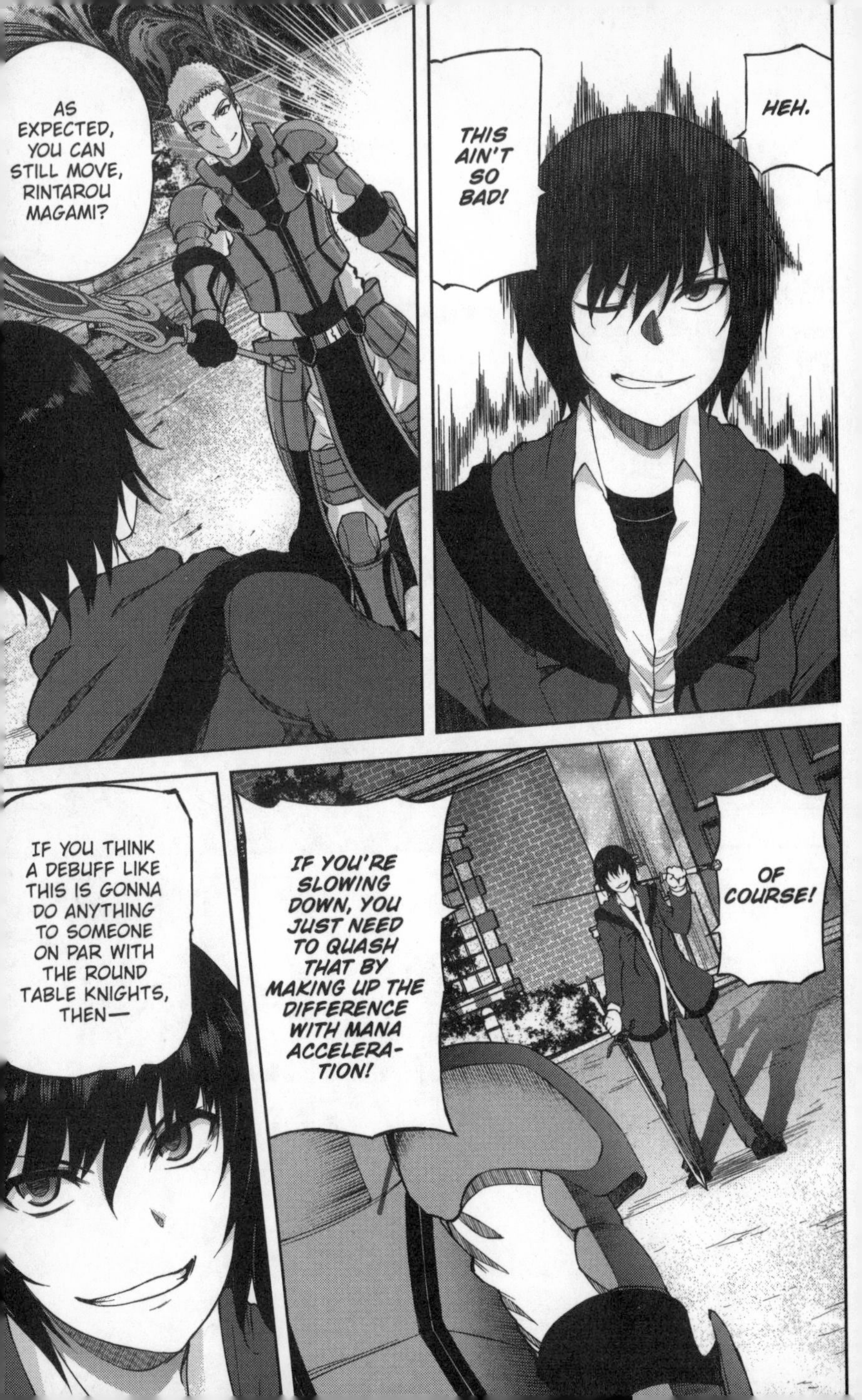
HEH.
THIS AIN'T SO BAD!
AS EXPECTED, YOU CAN STILL MOVE, RINTAROU MAGAMI?
OF COURSE!
IF YOU'RE SLOWING DOWN, YOU JUST NEED TO QUASH THAT BY MAKING UP THE DIFFERENCE WITH MANA ACCELERA-TION!
IF YOU THINK A DEBUFF LIKE THIS IS GONNA DO ANYTHING TO SOMEONE ON PAR WITH THE ROUND TABLE KNIGHTS, THEN—

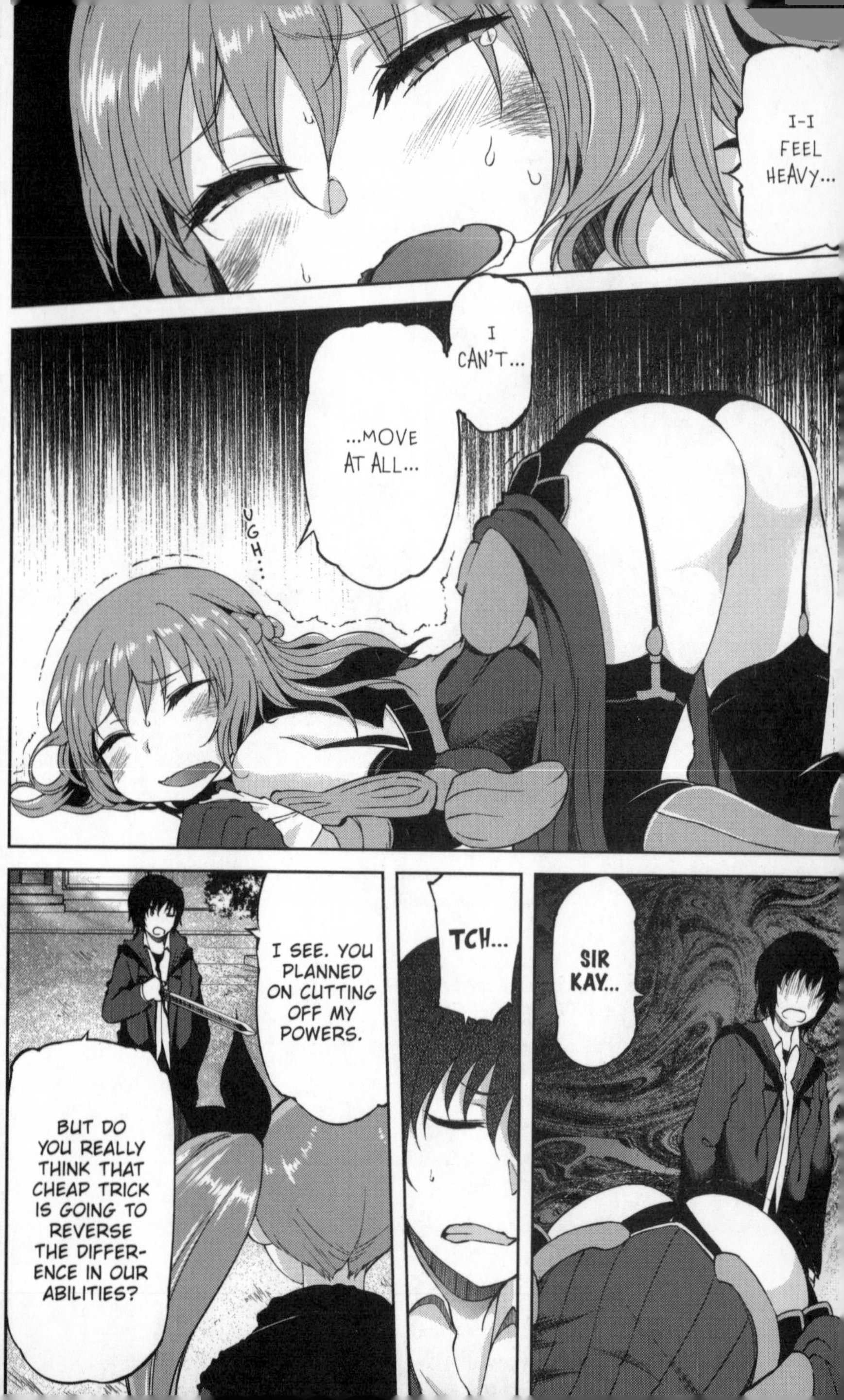
I-I FEEL HEAVY...
I CAN'T...
...MOVE AT ALL...
UGH...
SIR KAY...
TCH...
I SEE. YOU PLANNED ON CUTTING OFF MY POWERS.
BUT DO YOU REALLY THINK THAT CHEAP TRICK IS GOING TO REVERSE THE DIFFERENCE IN OUR ABILITIES?

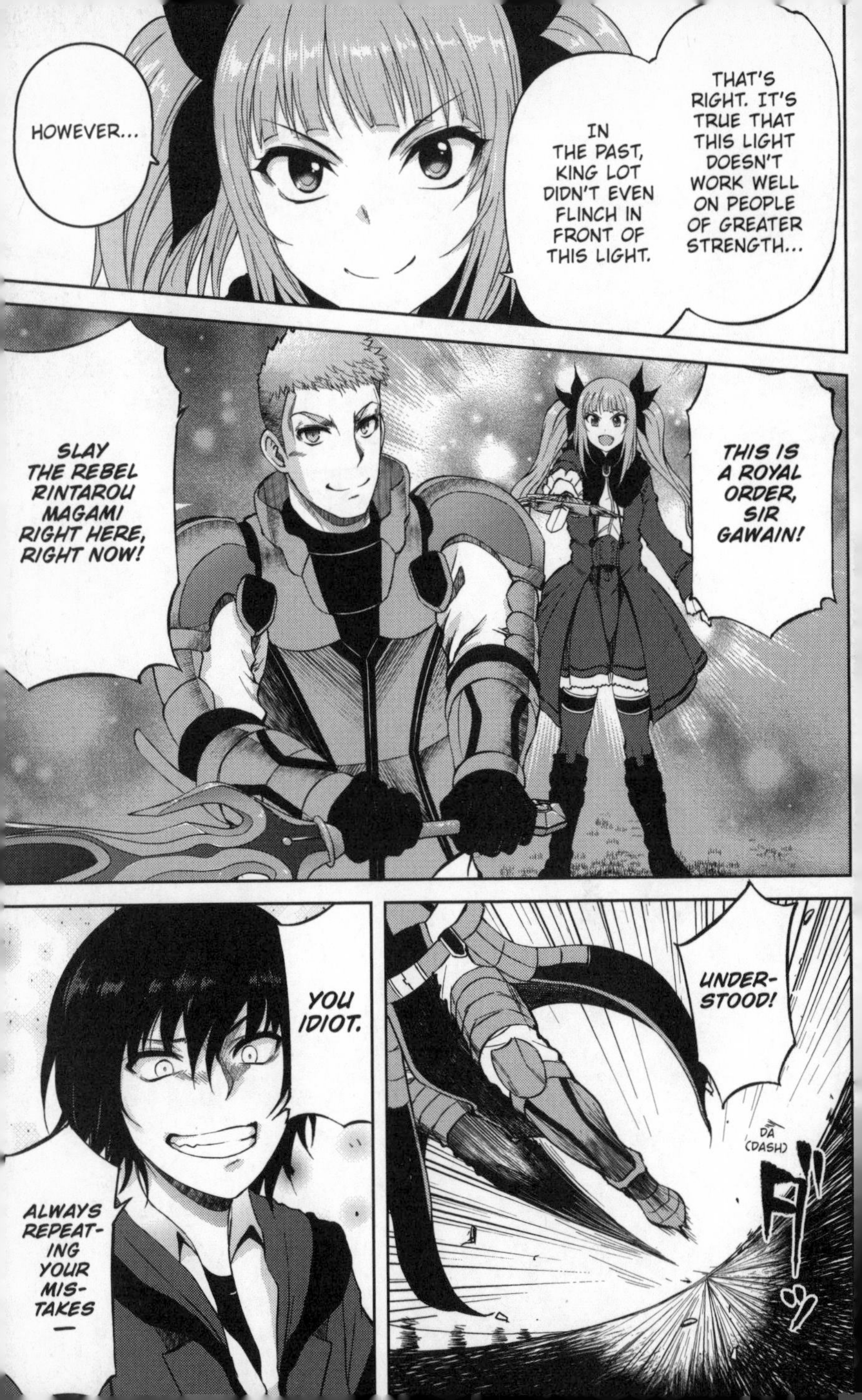
THAT'S RIGHT. IT'S TRUE THAT THIS LIGHT DOESN'T WORK WELL ON PEOPLE OF GREATER STRENGTH...
IN THE PAST, KING LOT DIDN'T EVEN FLINCH IN FRONT OF THIS LIGHT.
HOWEVER...
THIS IS A ROYAL ORDER, SIR GAWAIN!
SLAY THE REBEL RINTAROU MAGAMI RIGHT HERE, RIGHT NOW!
UNDERSTOOD!
DA (DASH)
YOU IDIOT.
ALWAYS REPEATING YOUR MISTAKES—

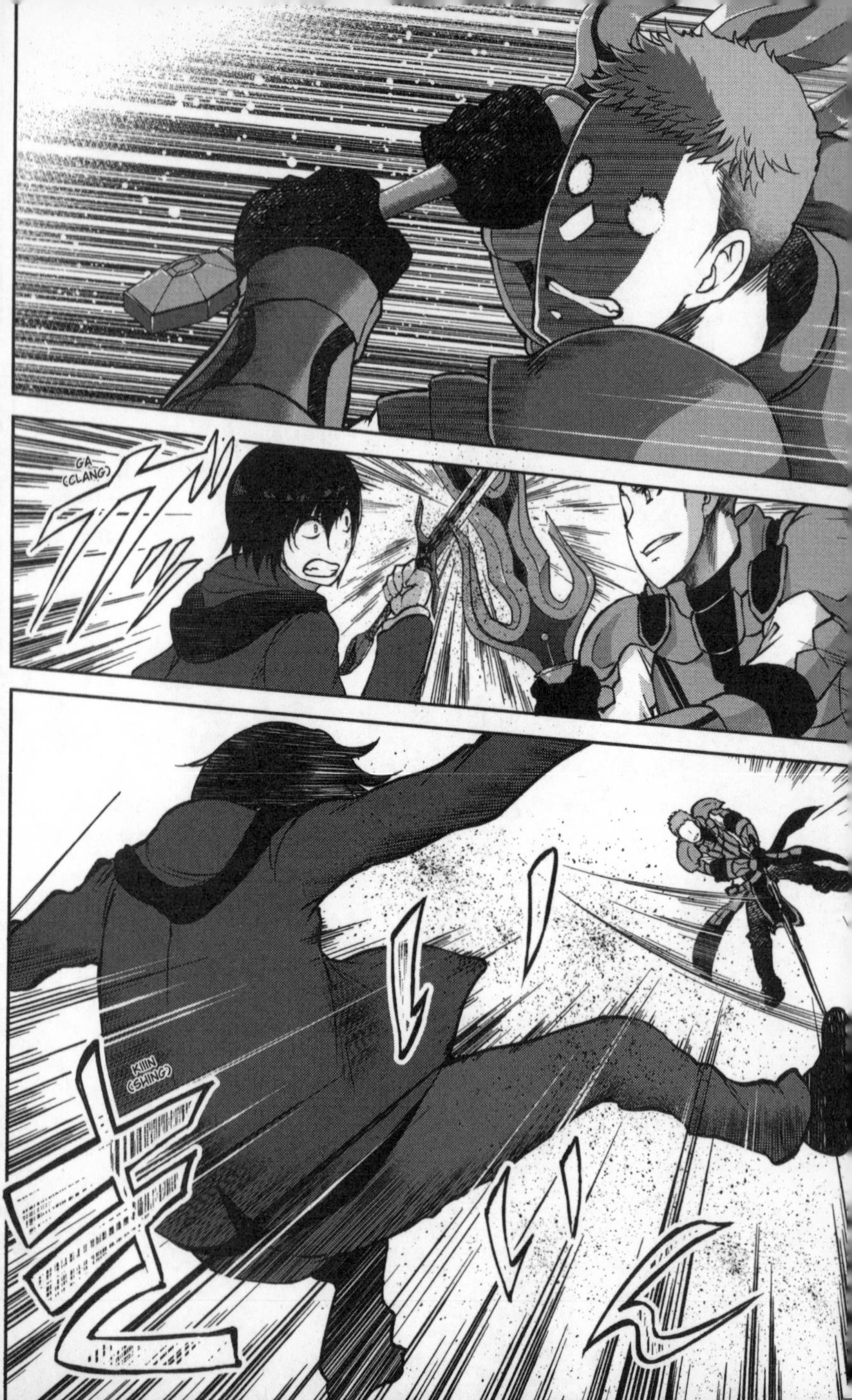
GA
(CLANG)
KIIIN
(SHING)

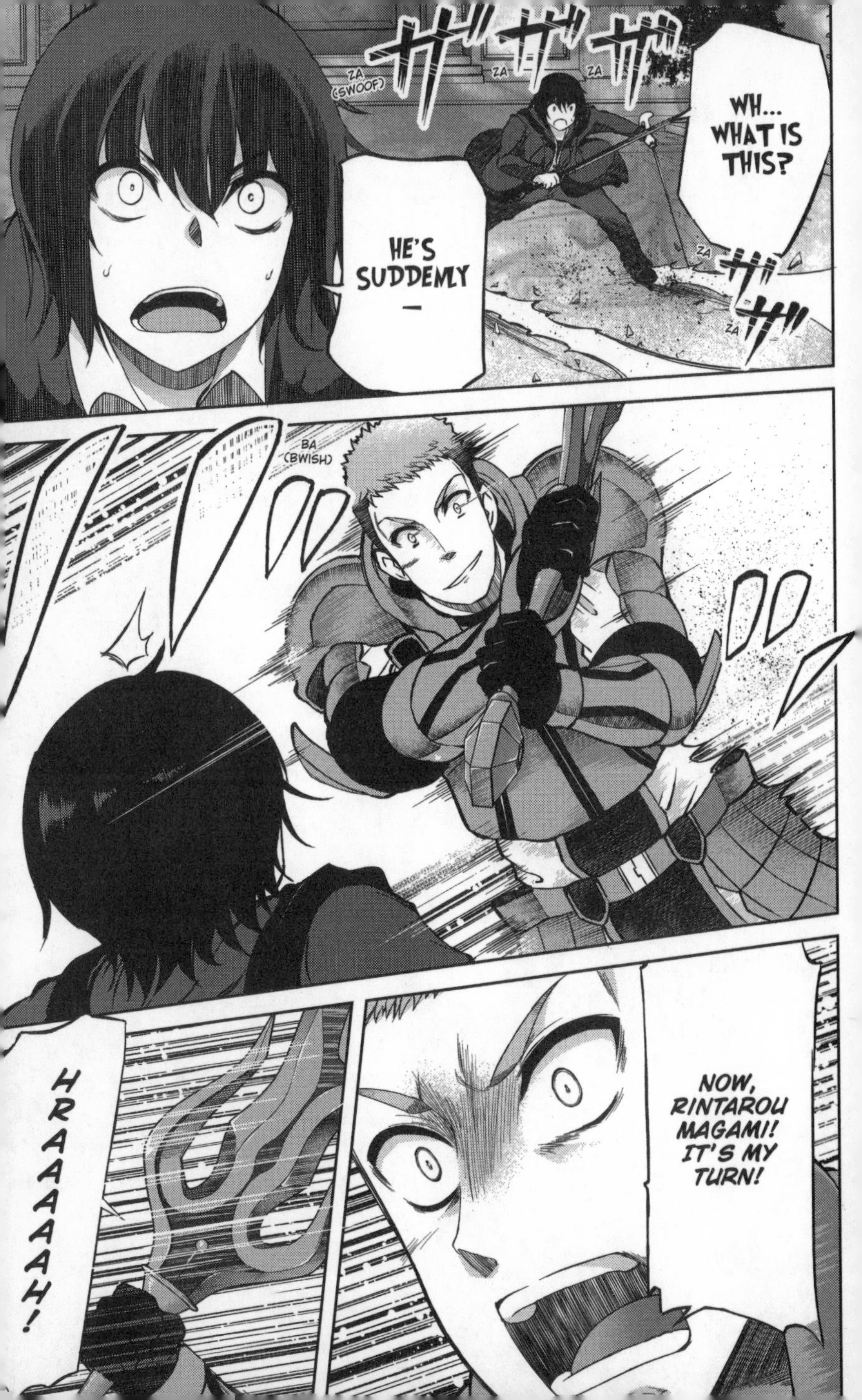
ZA (SWOOF)
ZA
ZA
WH... WHAT IS THIS?
ZA
ZA
HE'S SUDDENLY —
BA (BWISH)
NOW, RINTAROU MAGAMI! IT'S MY TURN!
HRAAAAAAH!

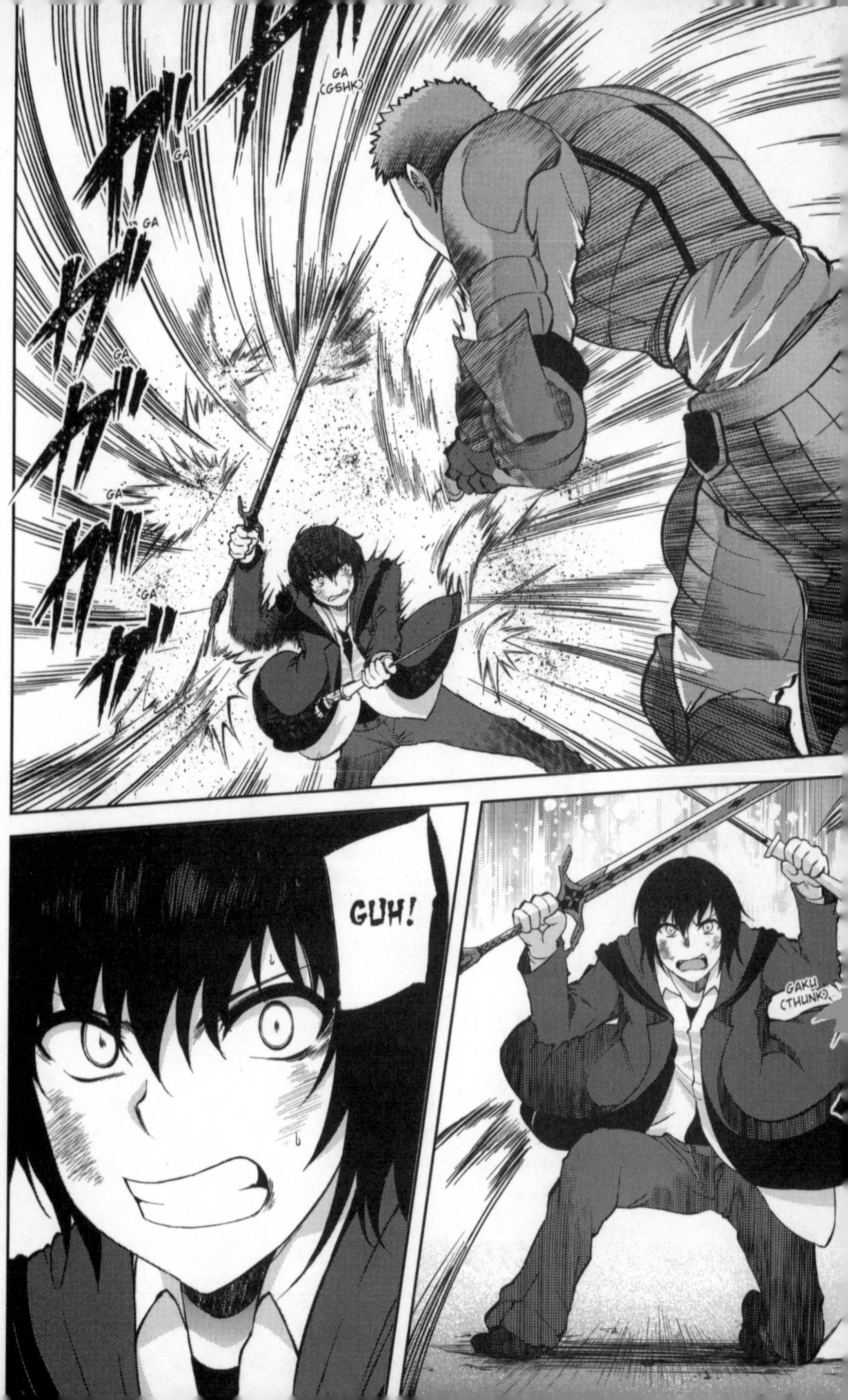
GA (GSHK)
GA
GA
GA
GA
GA
GAKU (THUNK)
GUH!

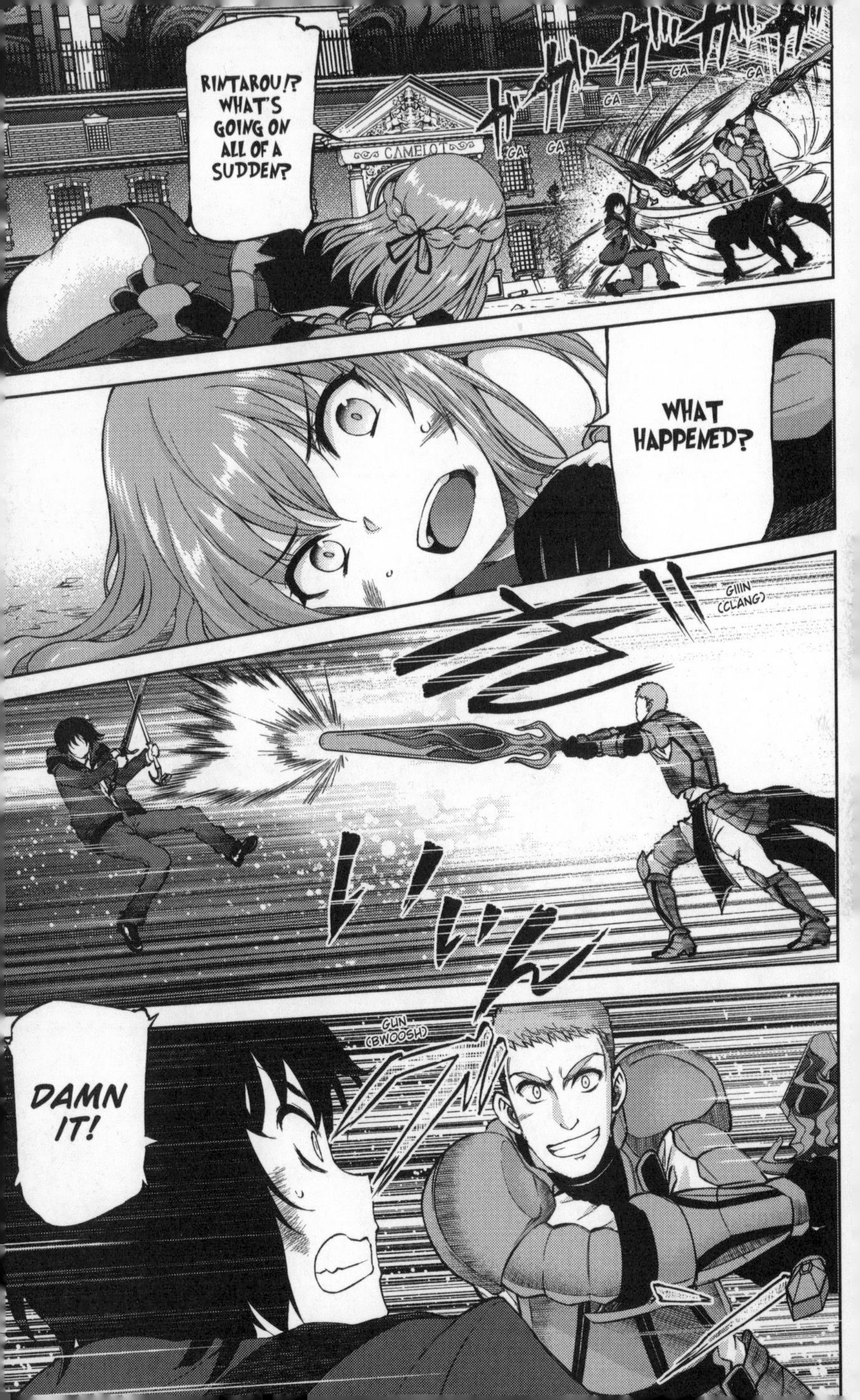
GA
GA
GA
GA
GA
RINTAROU!? WHAT'S GOING ON ALL OF A SUDDEN?
CAMELOT
WHAT HAPPENED?
GIIN (CLANG)
GUN (BWOOSH)
DAMN IT!

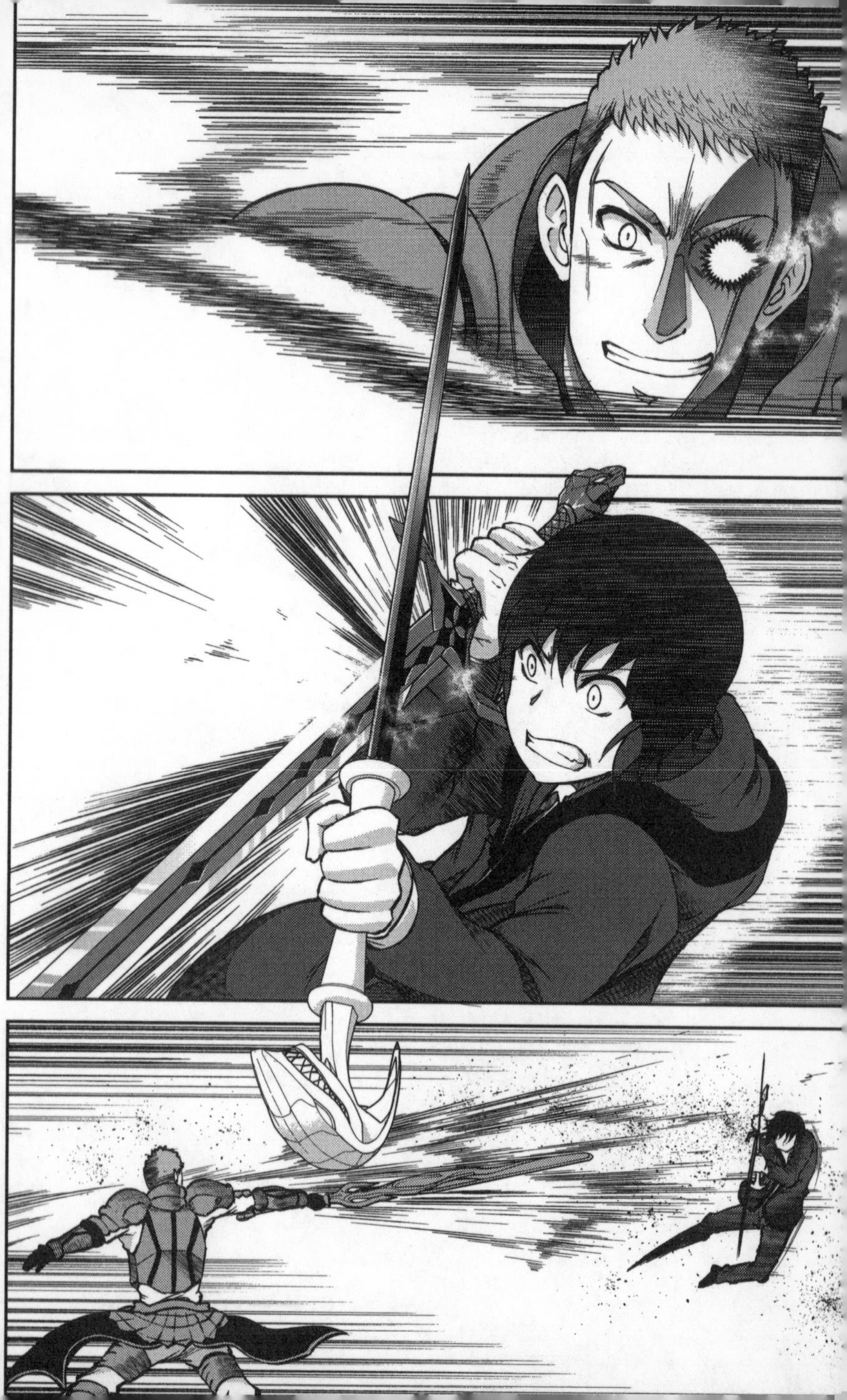

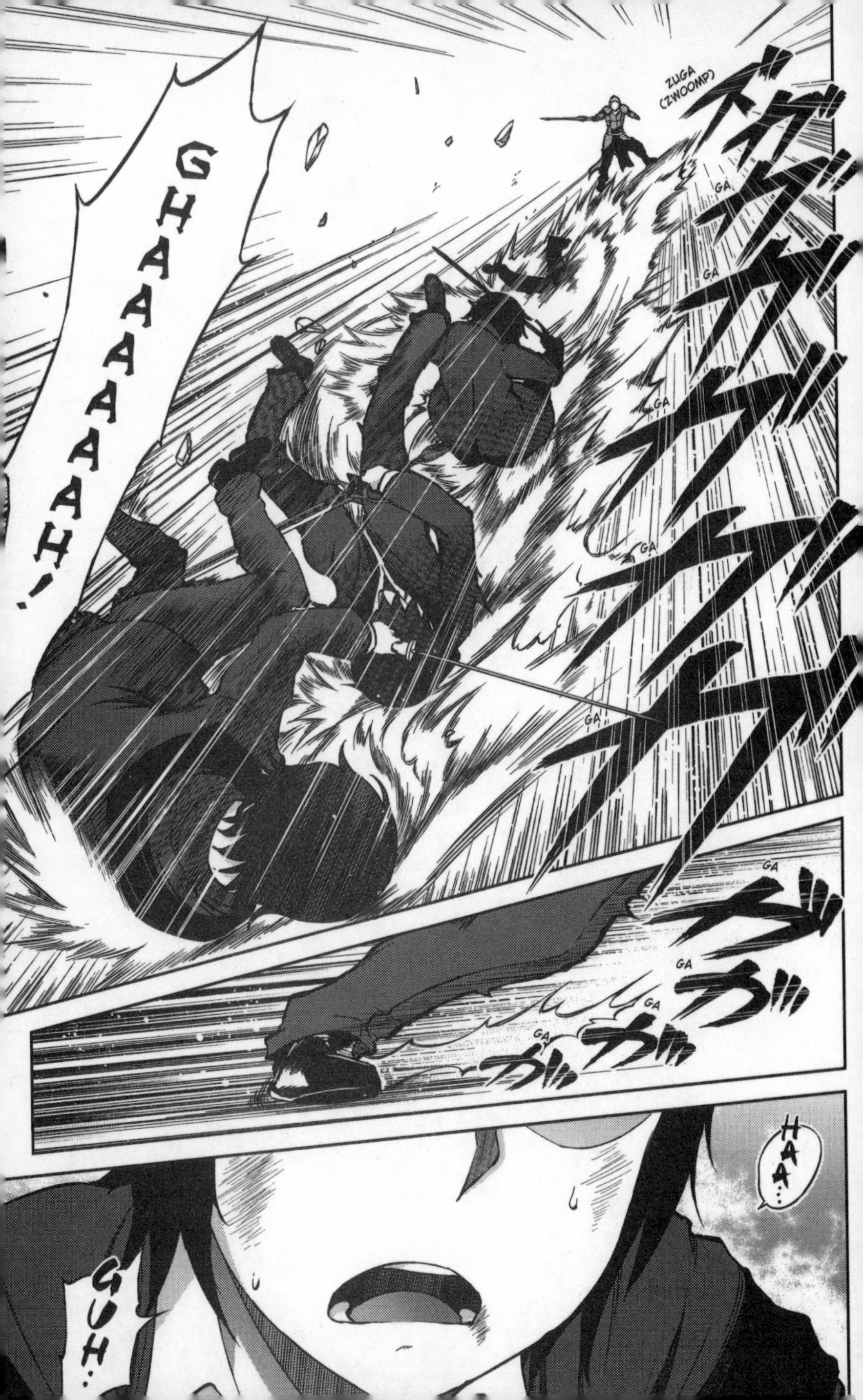
ZUGA (ZWOOMP)
GA
GA
GA
GA
GA
GHAAAAAAH!
GA
GA
GA
GA
HAA...
GUH...

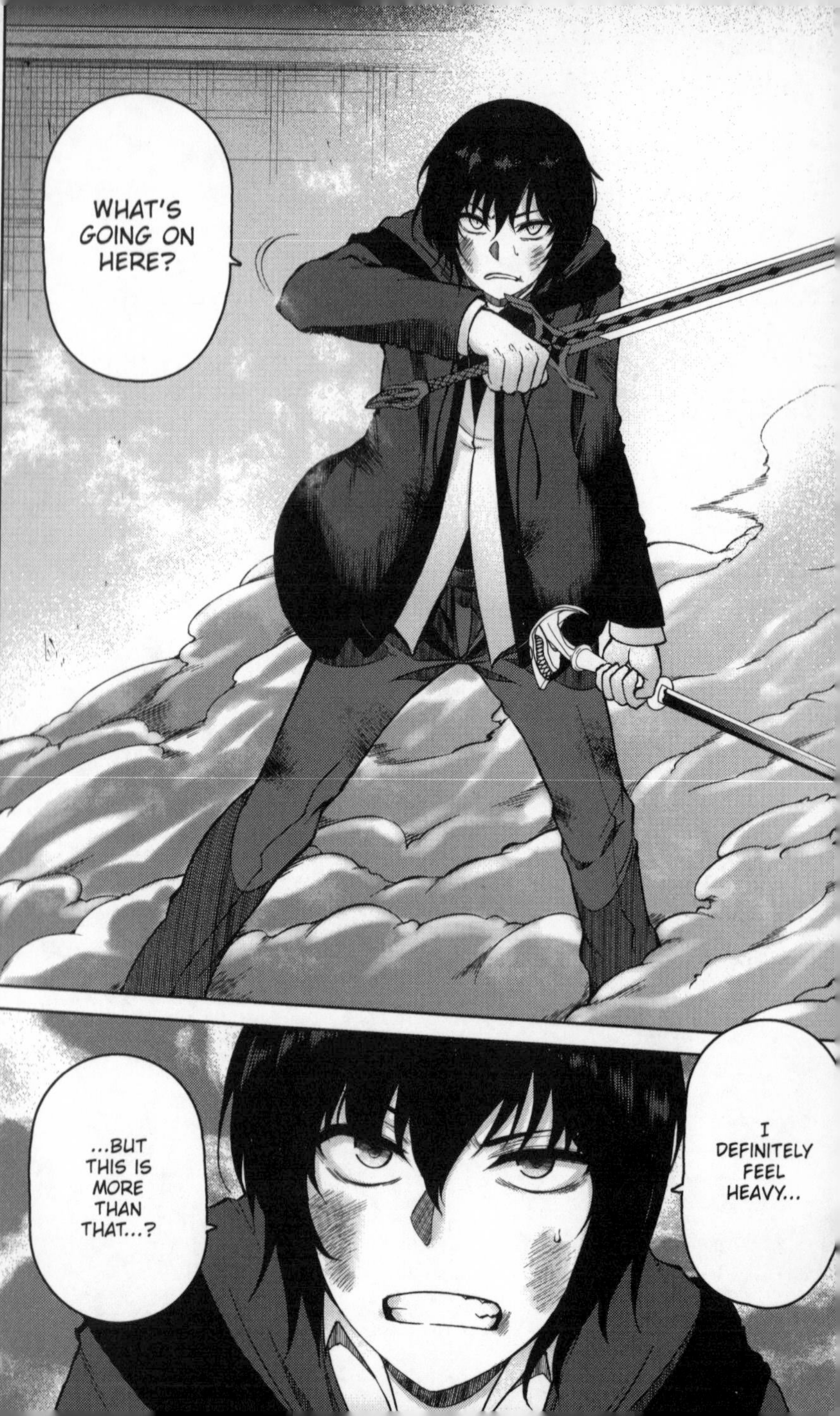
WHAT'S GOING ON HERE?
I DEFINITELY FEEL HEAVY...
...BUT THIS IS MORE THAN THAT...?

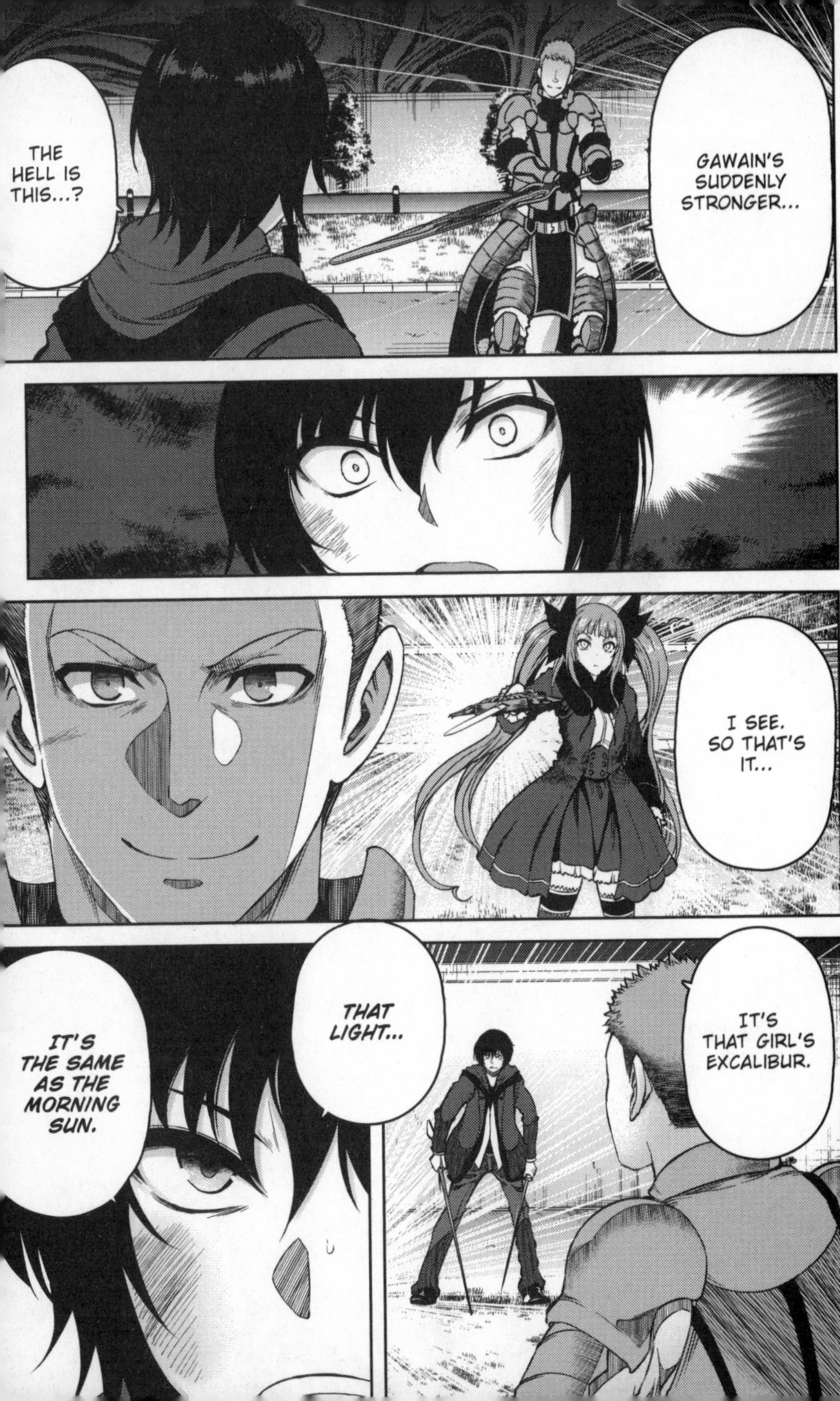
GAWAIN'S SUDDENLY STRONGER...
THE HELL IS THIS...?
I SEE. SO THAT'S IT...
IT'S THAT GIRL'S EXCALIBUR.
THAT LIGHT...
IT'S THE SAME AS THE MORNING SUN.

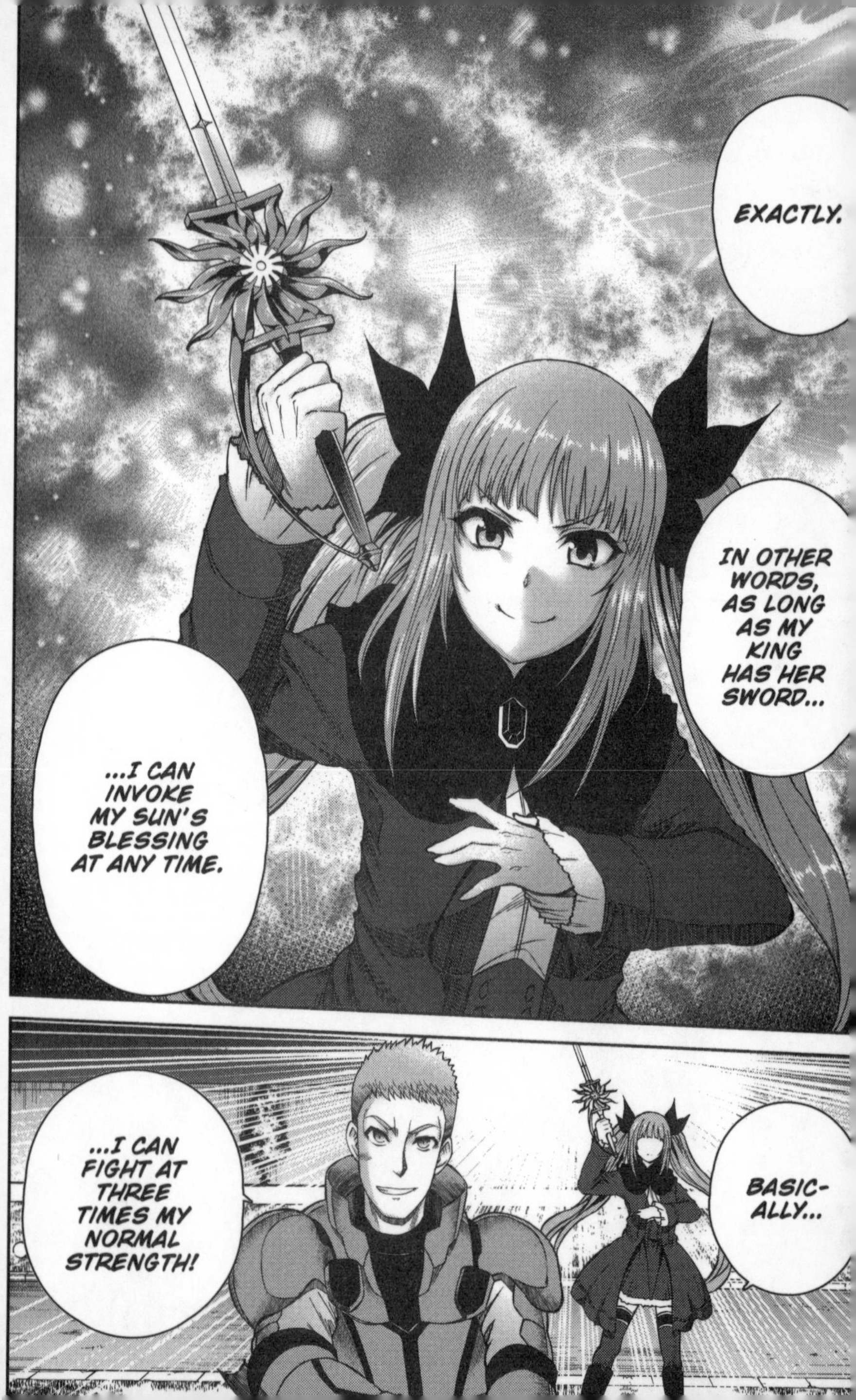
EXACTLY.
IN OTHER WORDS, AS LONG AS MY KING HAS HER SWORD...
...I CAN INVOKE MY SUN'S BLESSING AT ANY TIME.
BASIC-ALLY...
...I CAN FIGHT AT THREE TIMES MY NORMAL STRENGTH!

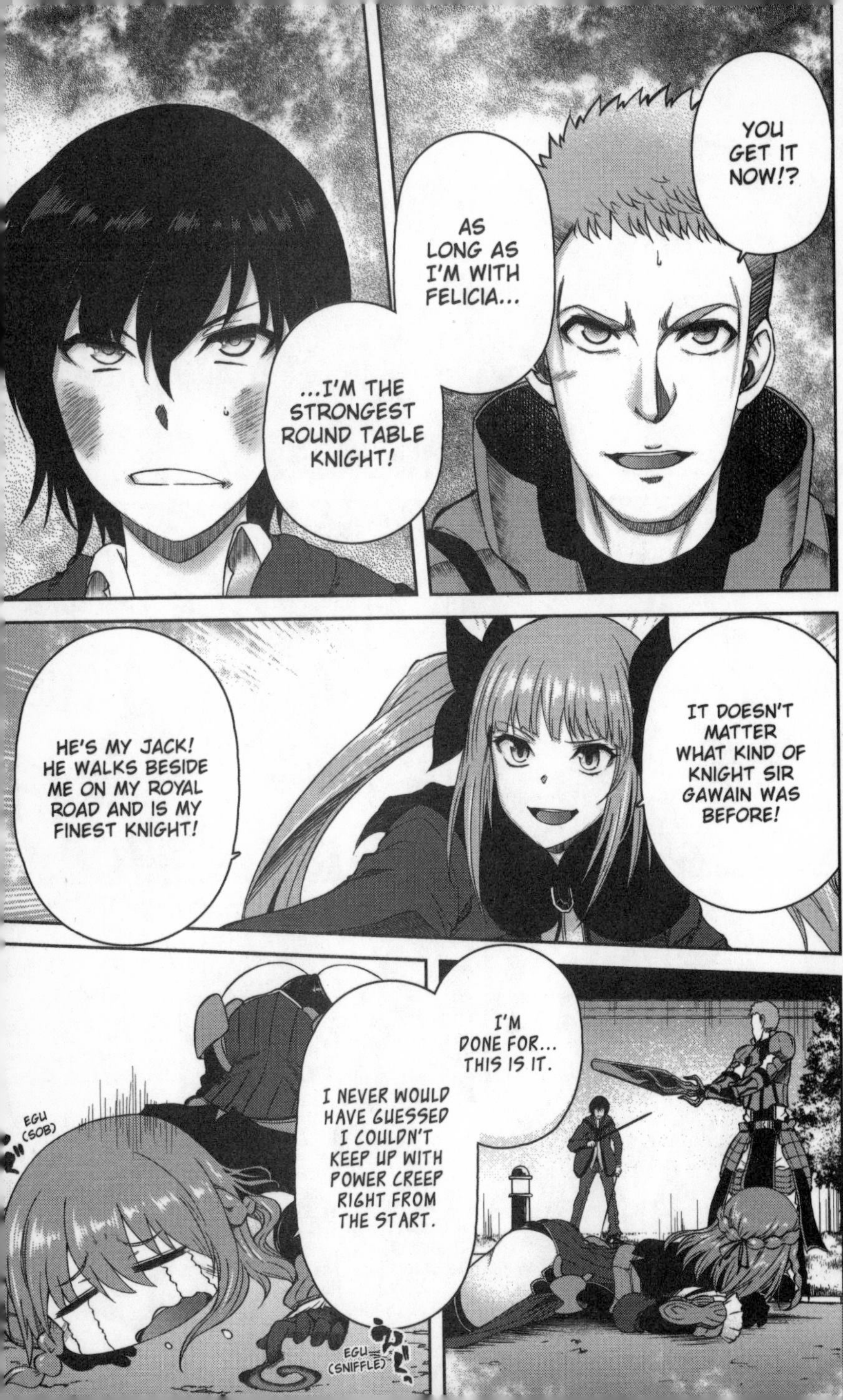
YOU GET IT NOW!?
AS LONG AS I'M WITH FELICIA...
...I'M THE STRONGEST ROUND TABLE KNIGHT!
IT DOESN'T MATTER WHAT KIND OF KNIGHT SIR GAWAIN WAS BEFORE!
HE'S MY JACK! HE WALKS BESIDE ME ON MY ROYAL ROAD AND IS MY FINEST KNIGHT!
I'M DONE FOR... THIS IS IT.
I NEVER WOULD HAVE GUESSED I COULDN'T KEEP UP WITH POWER CREEP RIGHT FROM THE START.
EGU (SOB)
EGU (SNIFFLE)

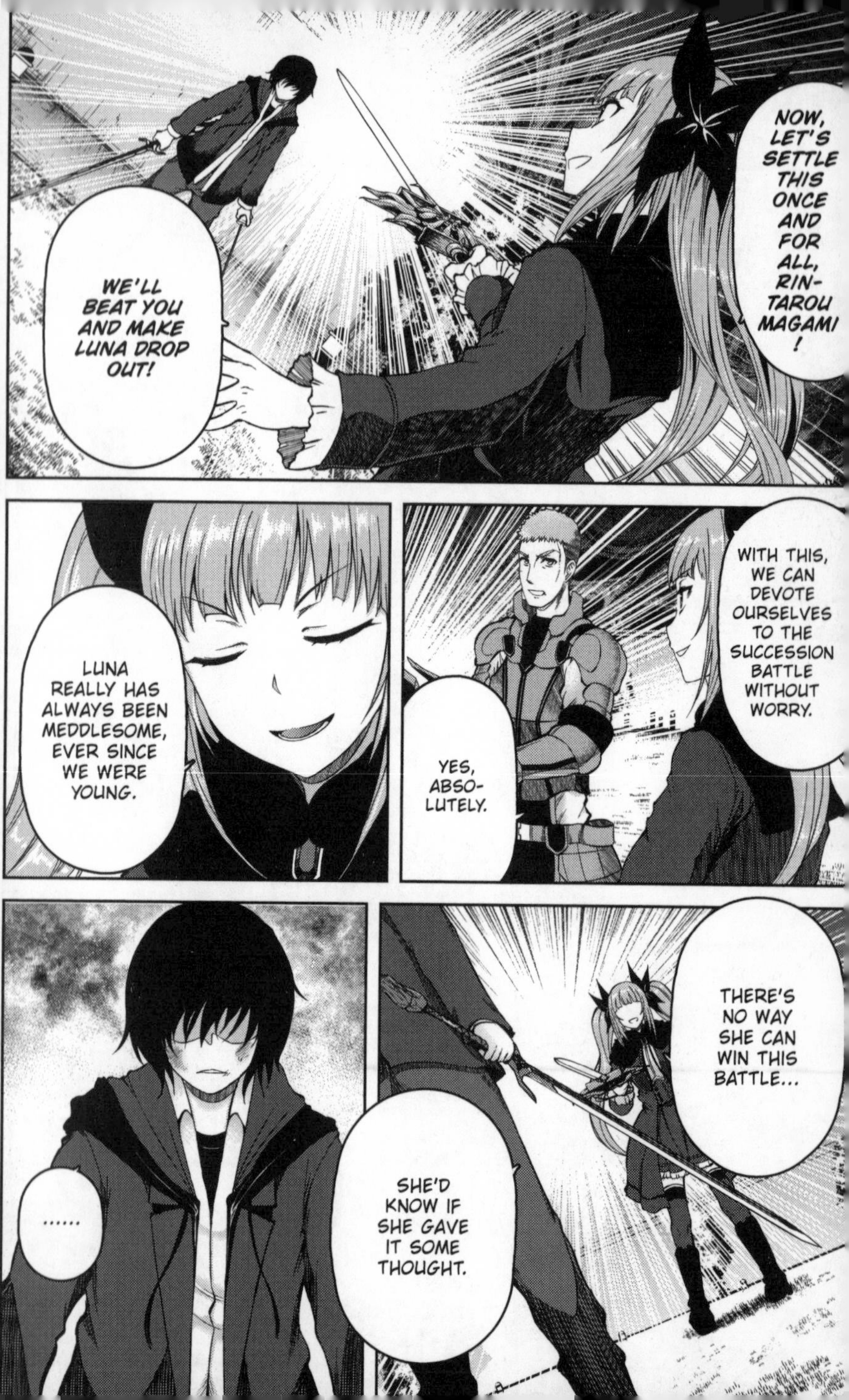
NOW, LET'S SETTLE THIS ONCE AND FOR ALL, RIN-TAROU MAGAMI!
WE'LL BEAT YOU AND MAKE LUNA DROP OUT!
WITH THIS, WE CAN DEVOTE OURSELVES TO THE SUCCESSION BATTLE WITHOUT WORRY.
YES, ABSO-LUTELY.
LUNA REALLY HAS ALWAYS BEEN MEDDLESOME, EVER SINCE WE WERE YOUNG.
THERE'S NO WAY SHE CAN WIN THIS BATTLE...
SHE'D KNOW IF SHE GAVE IT SOME THOUGHT.
......

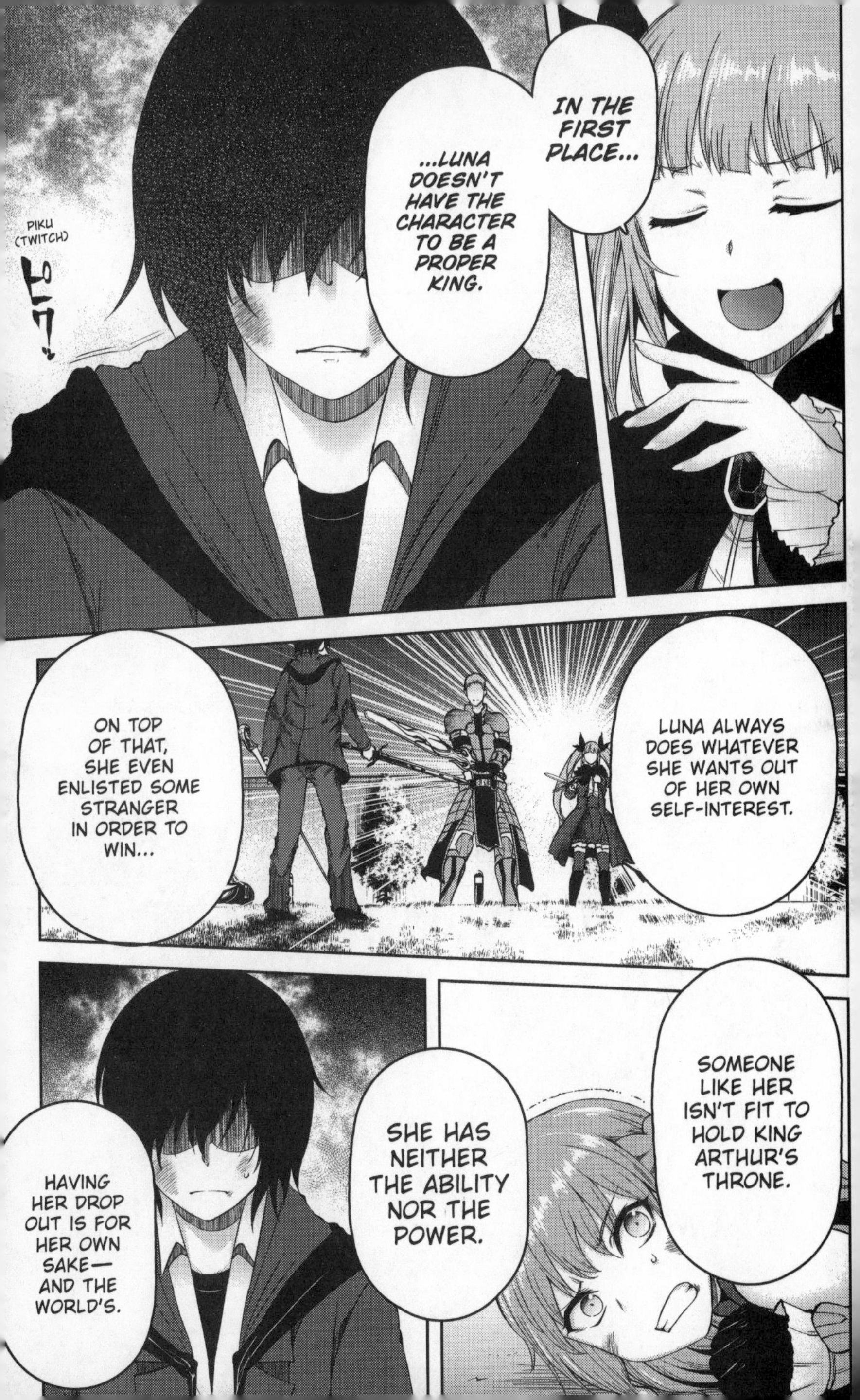
IN THE FIRST PLACE...
...LUNA DOESN'T HAVE THE CHARACTER TO BE A PROPER KING.
PIKU (TWITCH)
LUNA ALWAYS DOES WHATEVER SHE WANTS OUT OF HER OWN SELF-INTEREST.
ON TOP OF THAT, SHE EVEN ENLISTED SOME STRANGER IN ORDER TO WIN...
SOMEONE LIKE HER ISN'T FIT TO HOLD KING ARTHUR'S THRONE.
SHE HAS NEITHER THE ABILITY NOR THE POWER.
HAVING HER DROP OUT IS FOR HER OWN SAKE— AND THE WORLD'S.

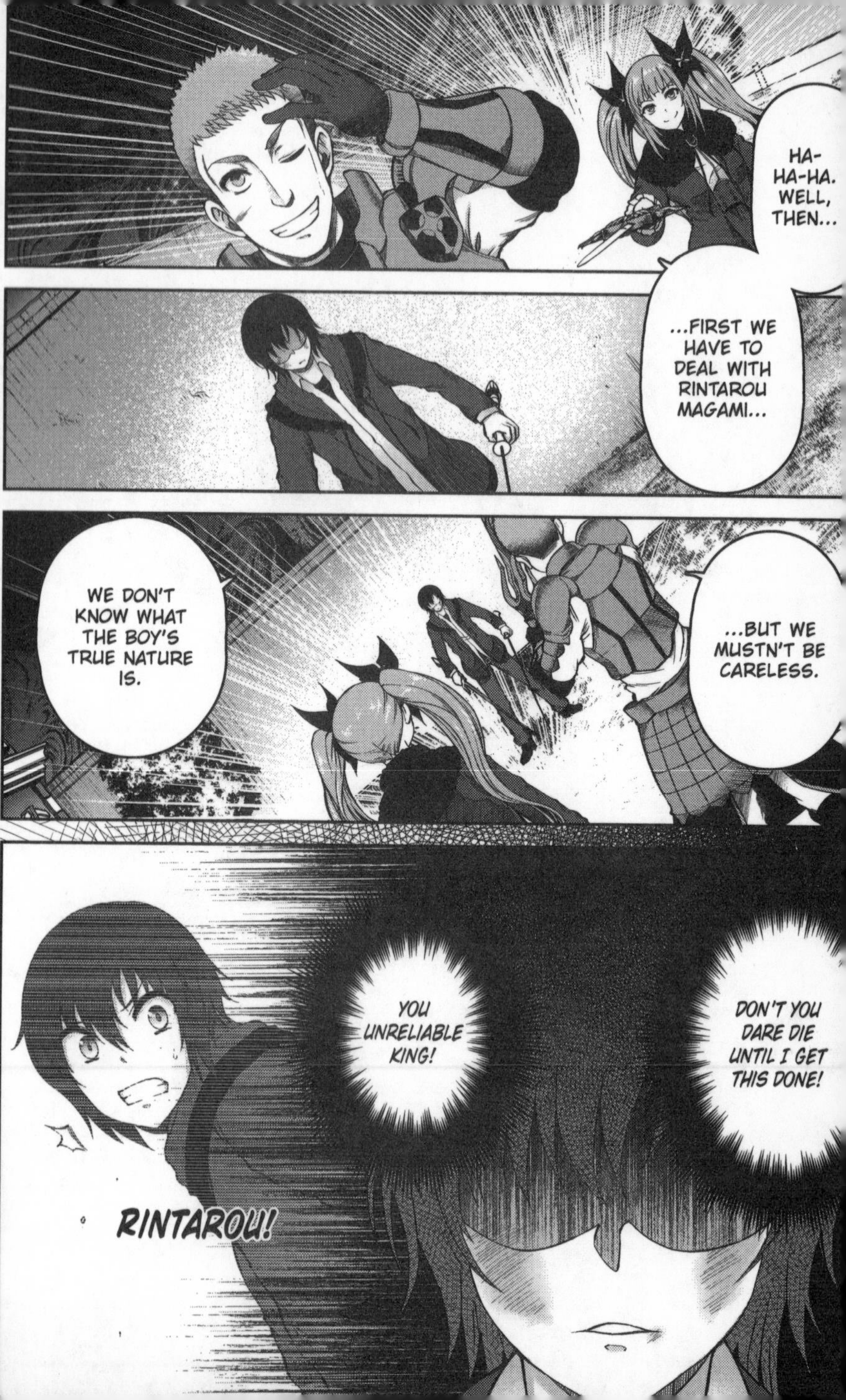
HA-HA-HA. WELL, THEN...
...FIRST WE HAVE TO DEAL WITH RINTAROU MAGAMI...
...BUT WE MUSTN'T BE CARELESS.
WE DON'T KNOW WHAT THE BOY'S TRUE NATURE IS.
DON'T YOU DARE DIE UNTIL I GET THIS DONE!
YOU UNRELIABLE KING!
RINTAROU!

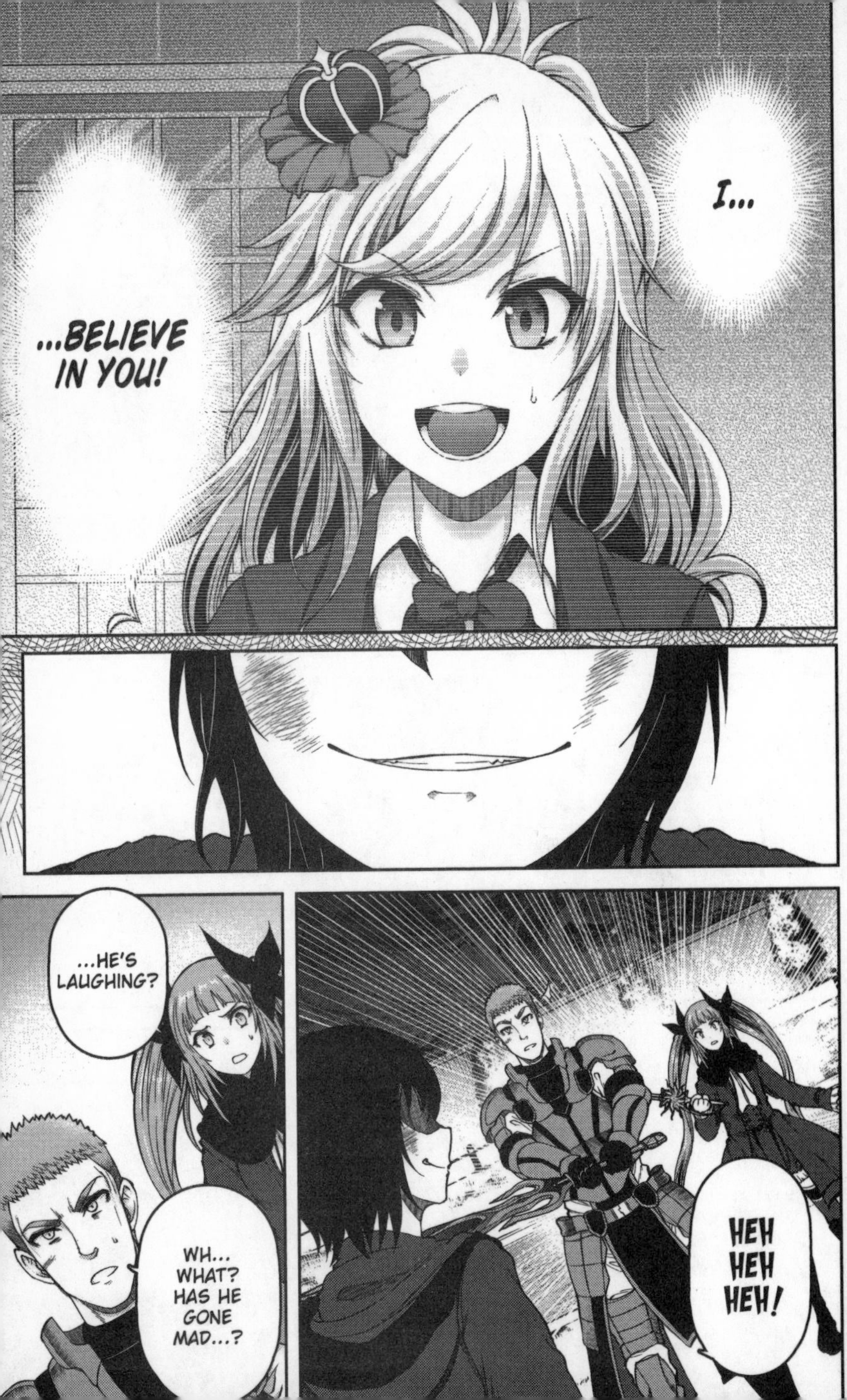
I...
...BELIEVE IN YOU!
HEH HEH HEH!
...HE'S LAUGHING?
WH... WHAT? HAS HE GONE MAD...?

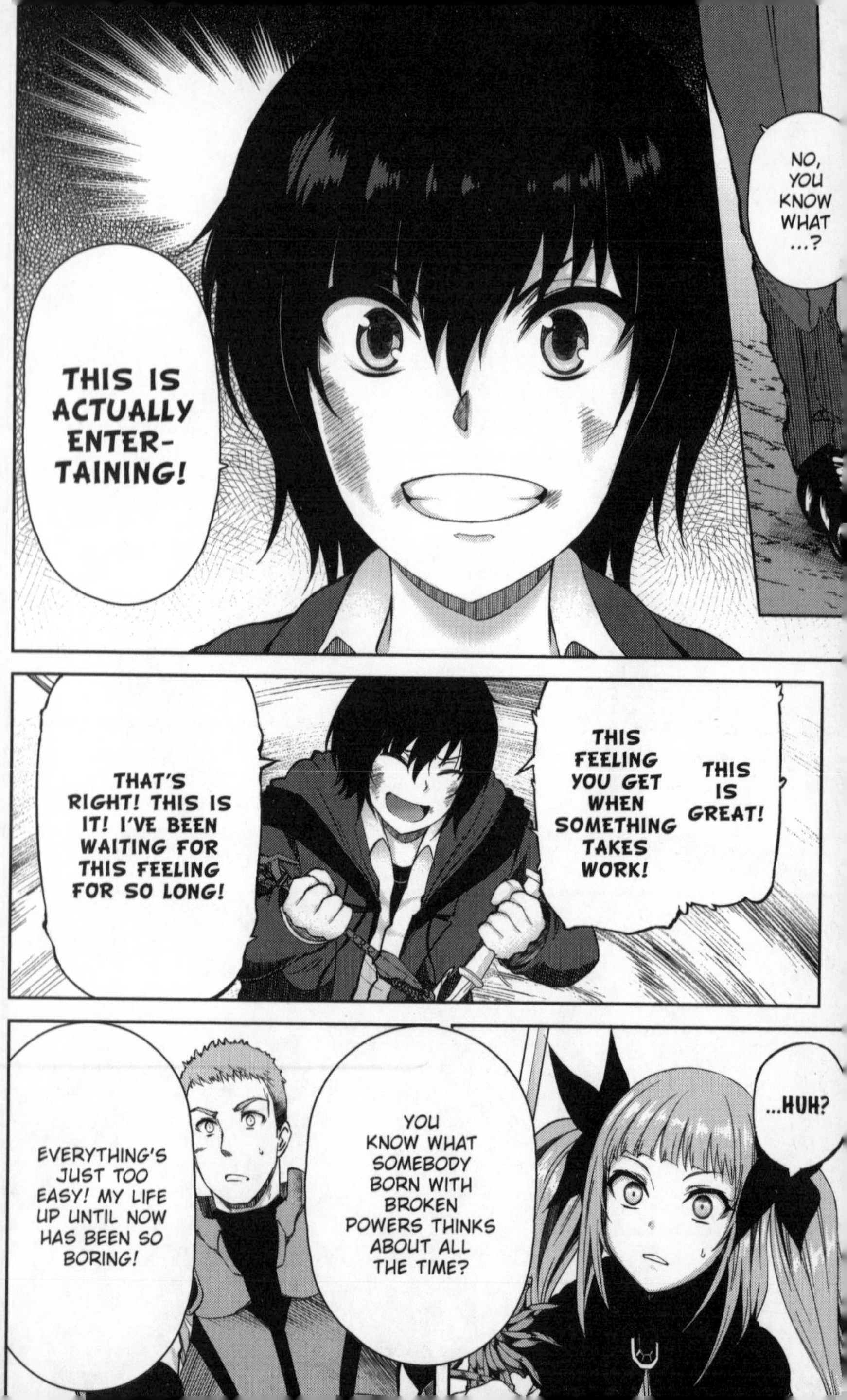
NO, YOU KNOW WHAT ...?
THIS IS ACTUALLY ENTER-TAINING!
THIS IS GREAT!
THIS FEELING YOU GET WHEN SOMETHING TAKES WORK!
THAT'S RIGHT! THIS IS IT! I'VE BEEN WAITING FOR THIS FEELING FOR SO LONG!
...HUH?
YOU KNOW WHAT SOMEBODY BORN WITH BROKEN POWERS THINKS ABOUT ALL THE TIME?
EVERYTHING'S JUST TOO EASY! MY LIFE UP UNTIL NOW HAS BEEN SO BORING!

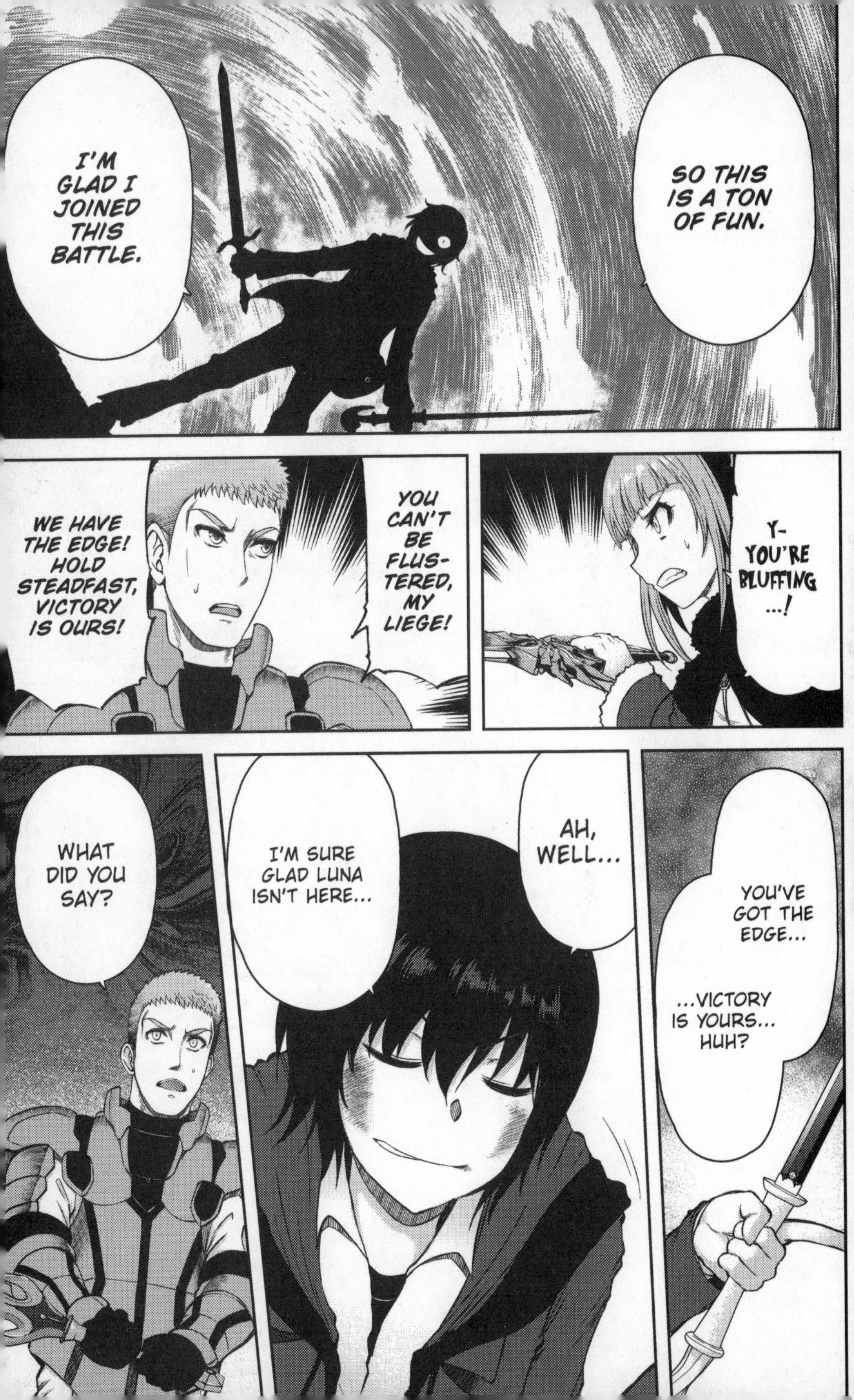
SO THIS IS A TON OF FUN.
I'M GLAD I JOINED THIS BATTLE.
Y- YOU'RE BLUFFING ...!
YOU CAN'T BE FLUS-TERED, MY LIEGE!
WE HAVE THE EDGE! HOLD STEADFAST, VICTORY IS OURS!
YOU'VE GOT THE EDGE...
...VICTORY IS YOURS... HUH?
AH, WELL...
I'M SURE GLAD LUNA ISN'T HERE...
WHAT DID YOU SAY?

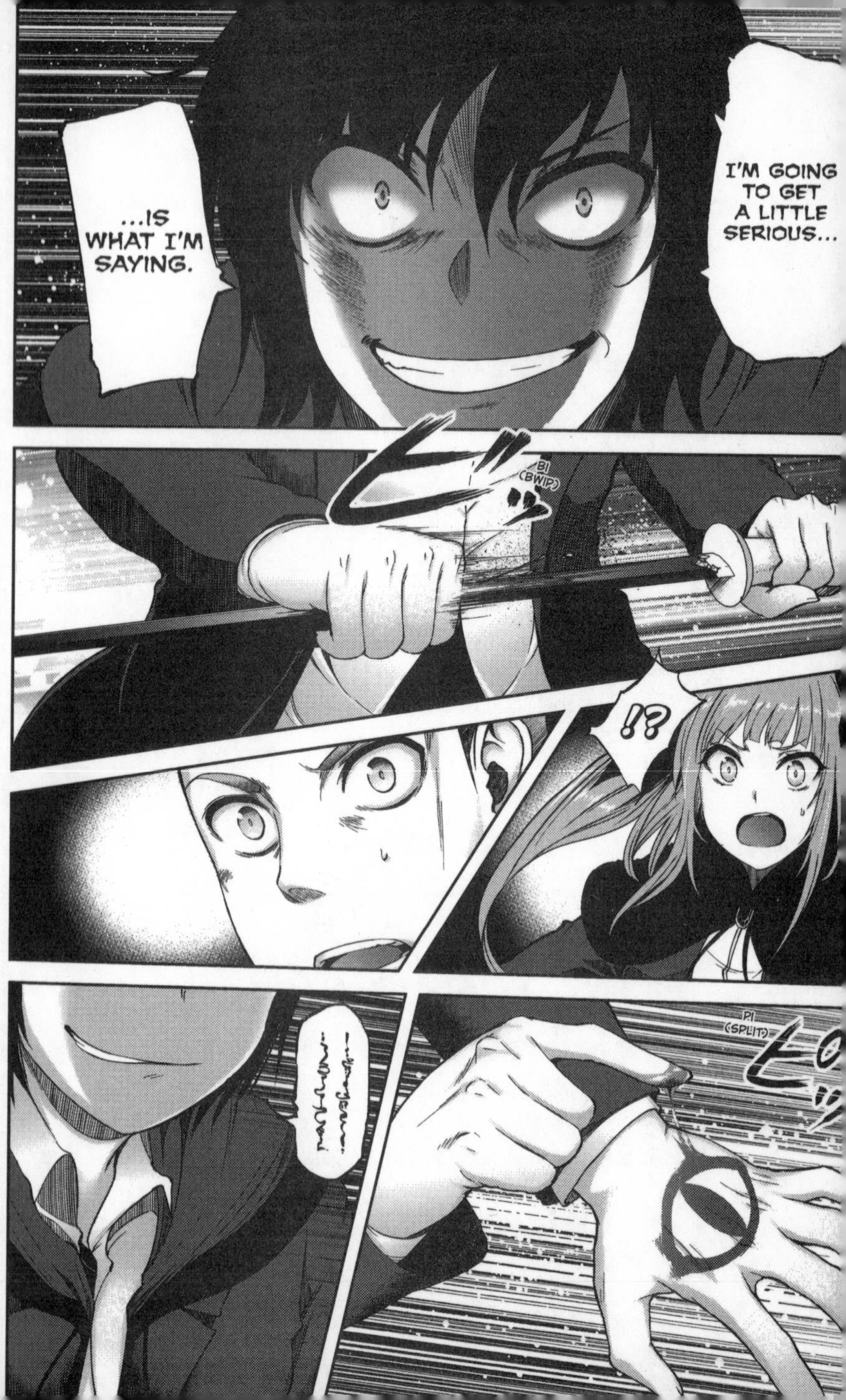
I'M GOING TO GET A LITTLE SERIOUS...
...IS WHAT I'M SAYING.
BI
(BWIP)
!?
PI
(SPLIT)

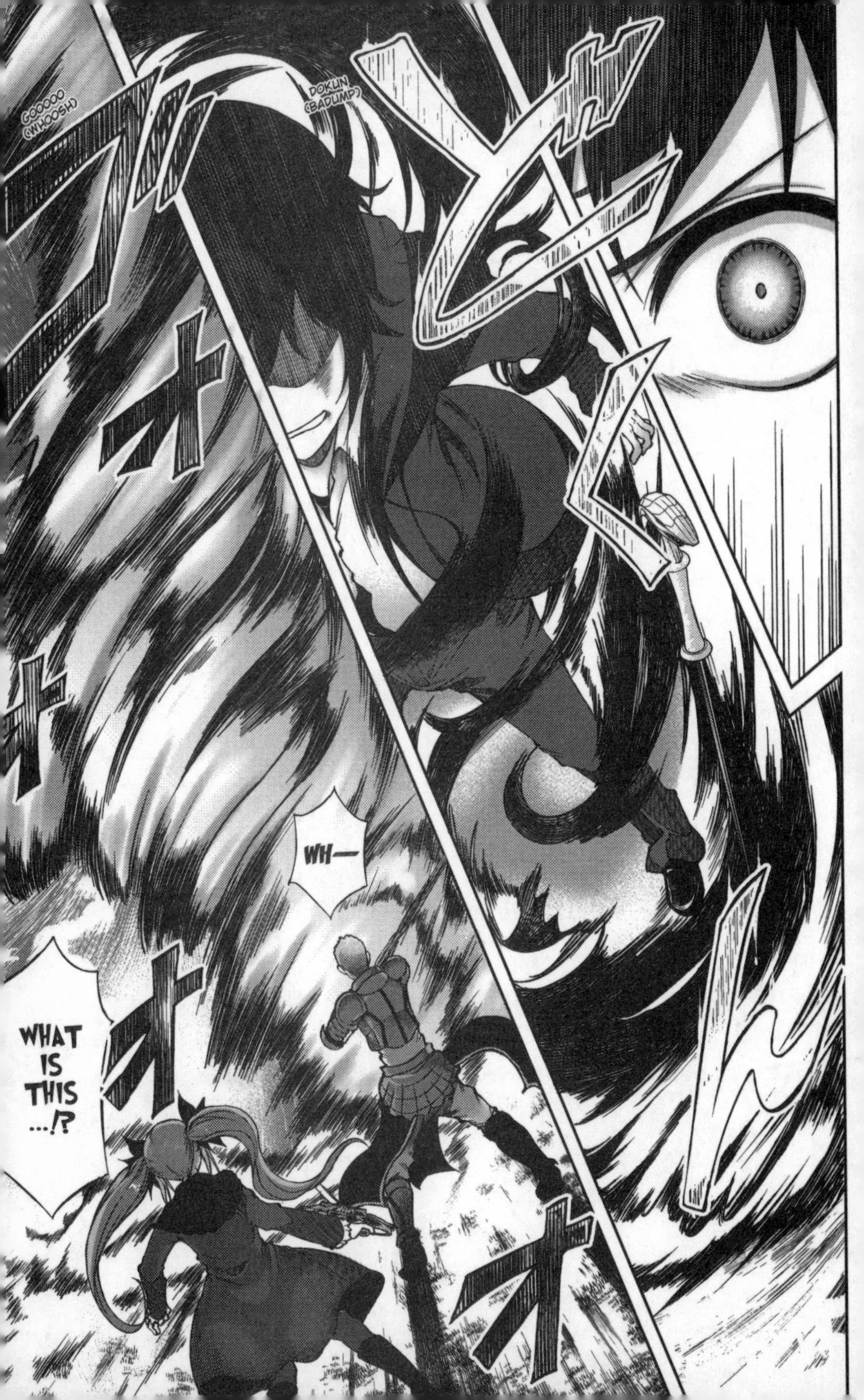
DOKUN (BADUMP)
GOOOOO (WHOOSH)
WH—
WHAT IS THIS ...!?

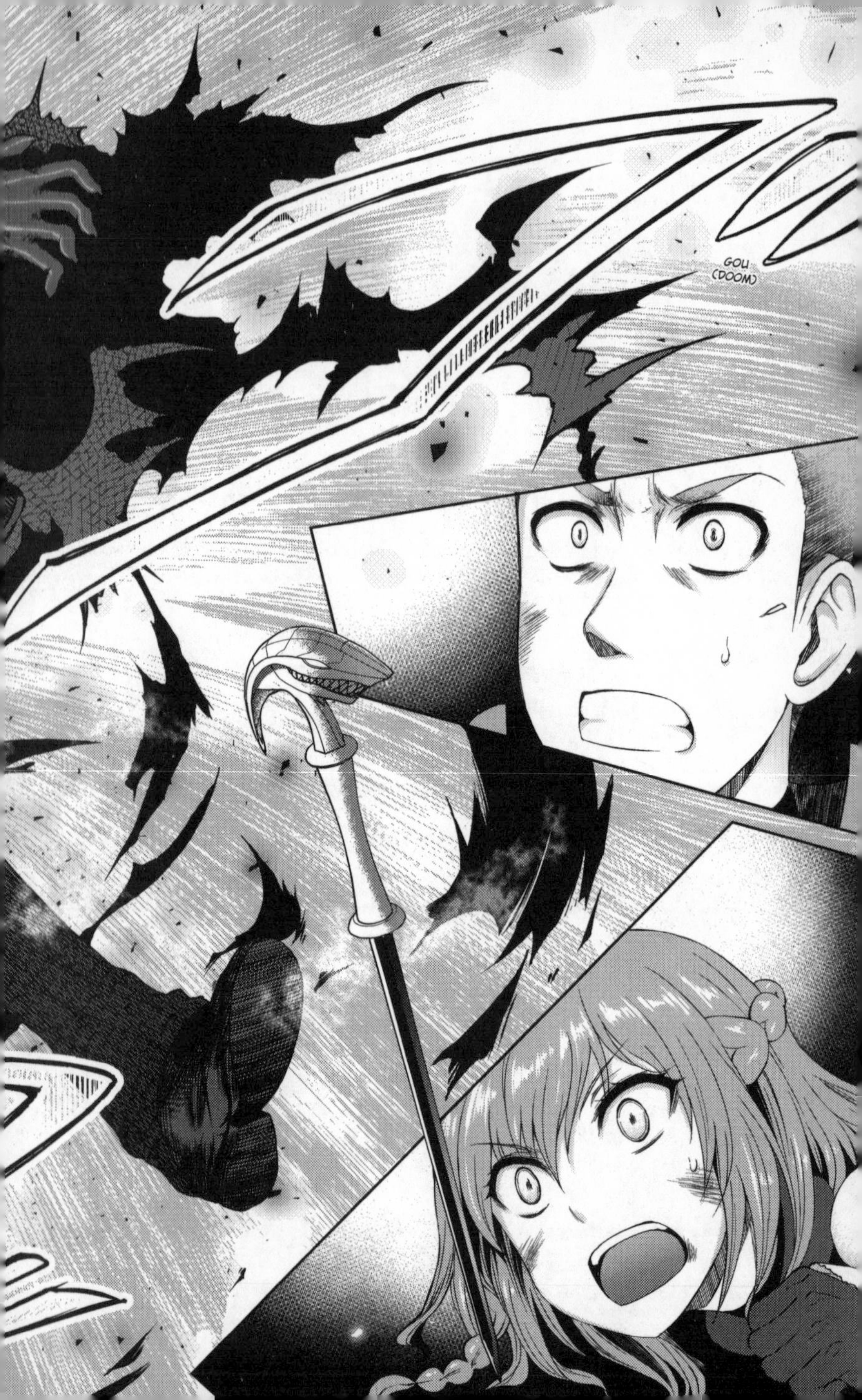
GOU
(DOOM)

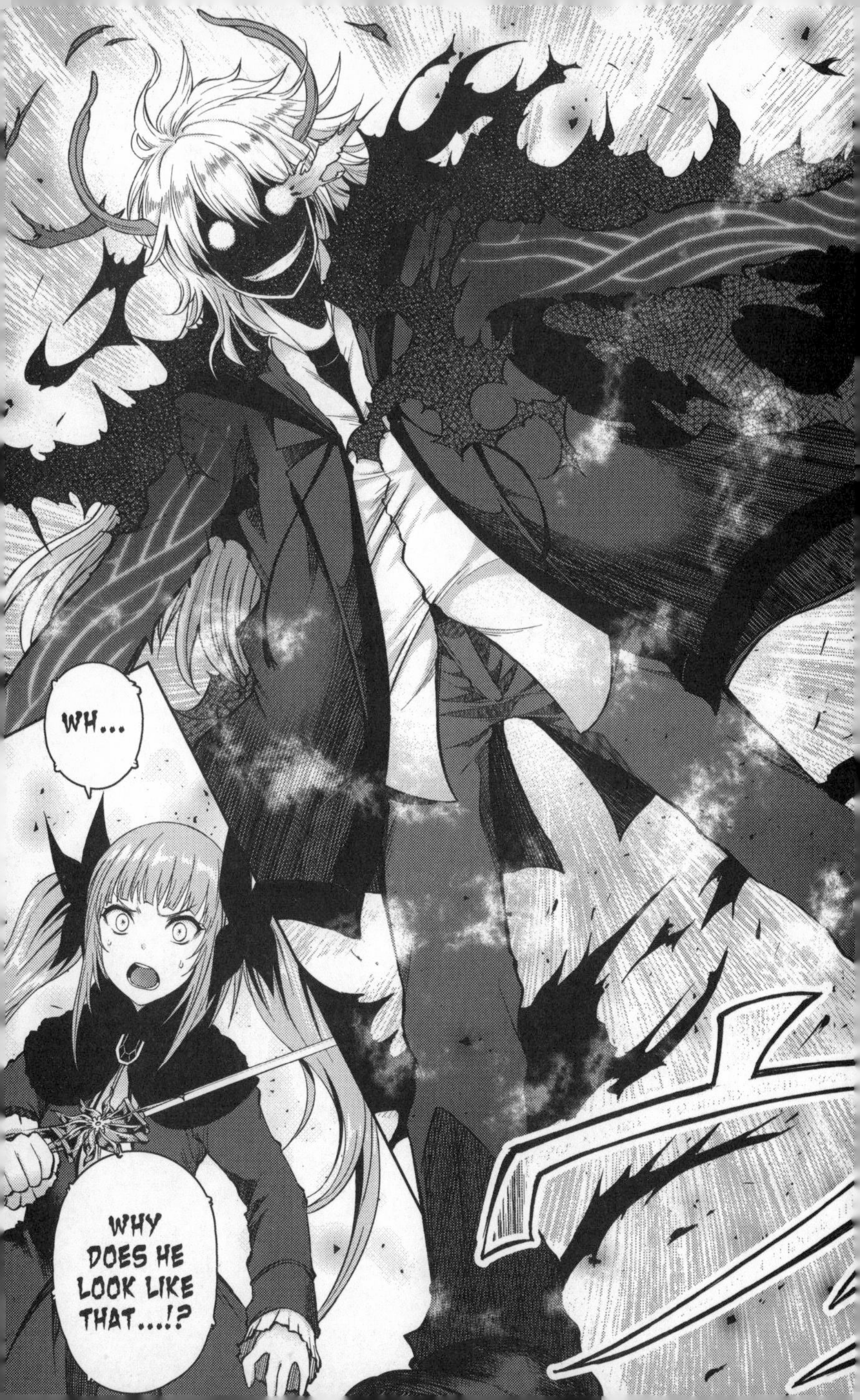
WH...
WHY DOES HE LOOK LIKE THAT...!?

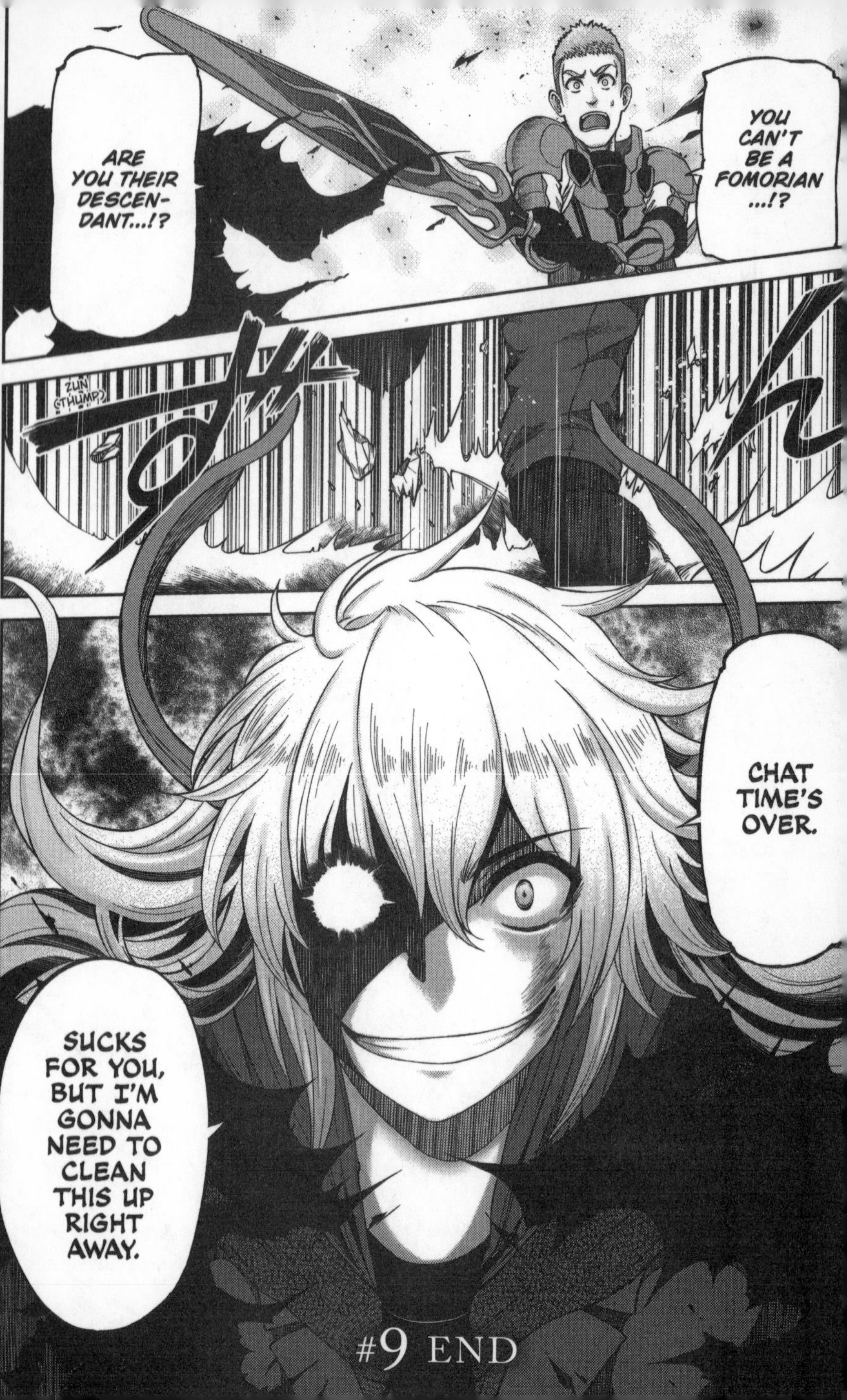
YOU CAN'T BE A FOMORIAN ...!?
ARE YOU THEIR DESCEN-DANT...!?
ZUN (THUMP)
CHAT TIME'S OVER.
SUCKS FOR YOU, BUT I'M GONNA NEED TO CLEAN THIS UP RIGHT AWAY.

#9 END

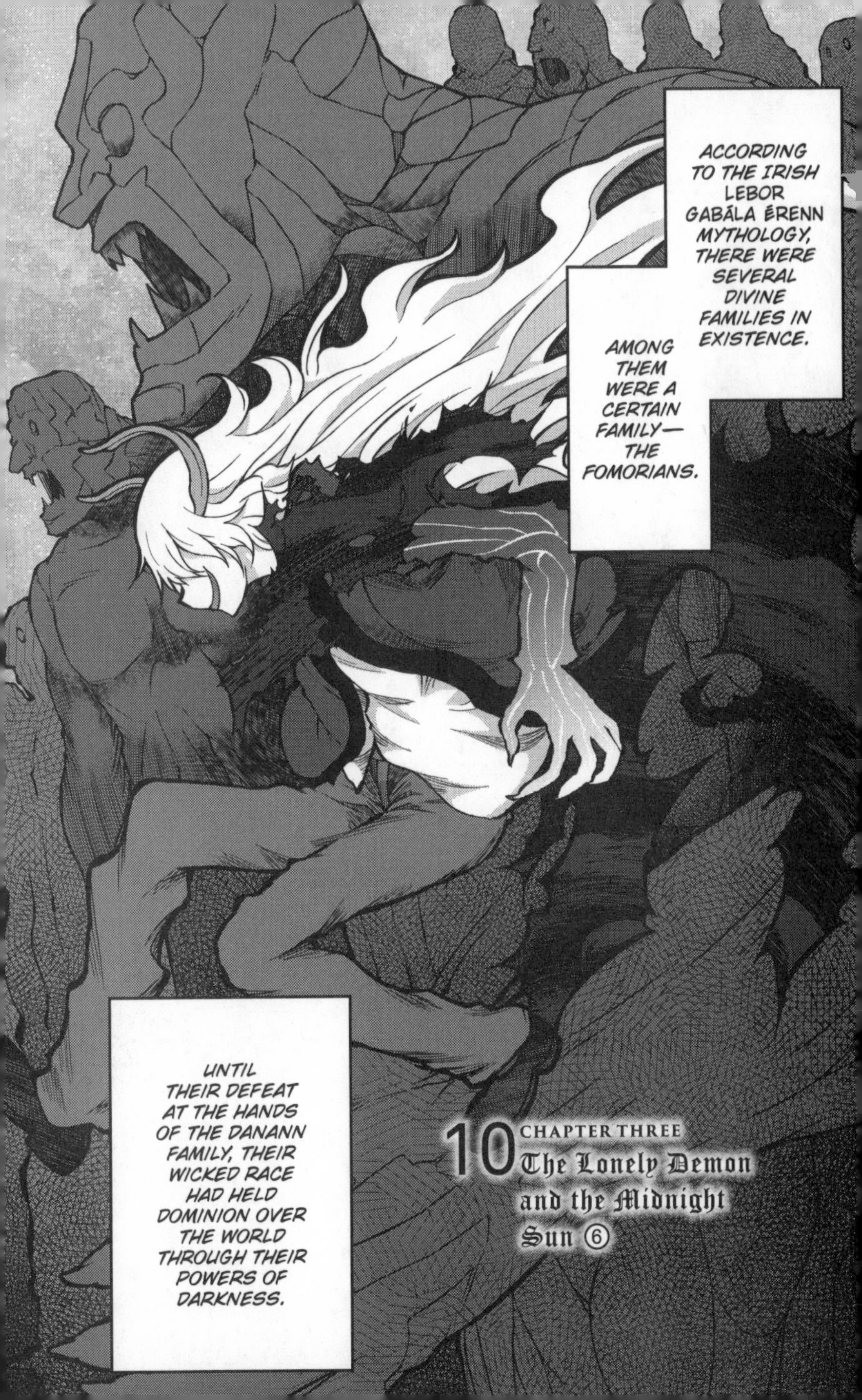
ACCORDING TO THE IRISH LEBOR GABÁLA ÉRENN MYTHOLOGY, THERE WERE SEVERAL DIVINE FAMILIES IN EXISTENCE.
AMONG THEM WERE A CERTAIN FAMILY— THE FOMORIANS.
UNTIL THEIR DEFEAT AT THE HANDS OF THE DANANN FAMILY, THEIR WICKED RACE HAD HELD DOMINION OVER THE WORLD THROUGH THEIR POWERS OF DARKNESS.
10 CHAPTER THREE
The Lonely Demon and the Midnight Sun ⑥

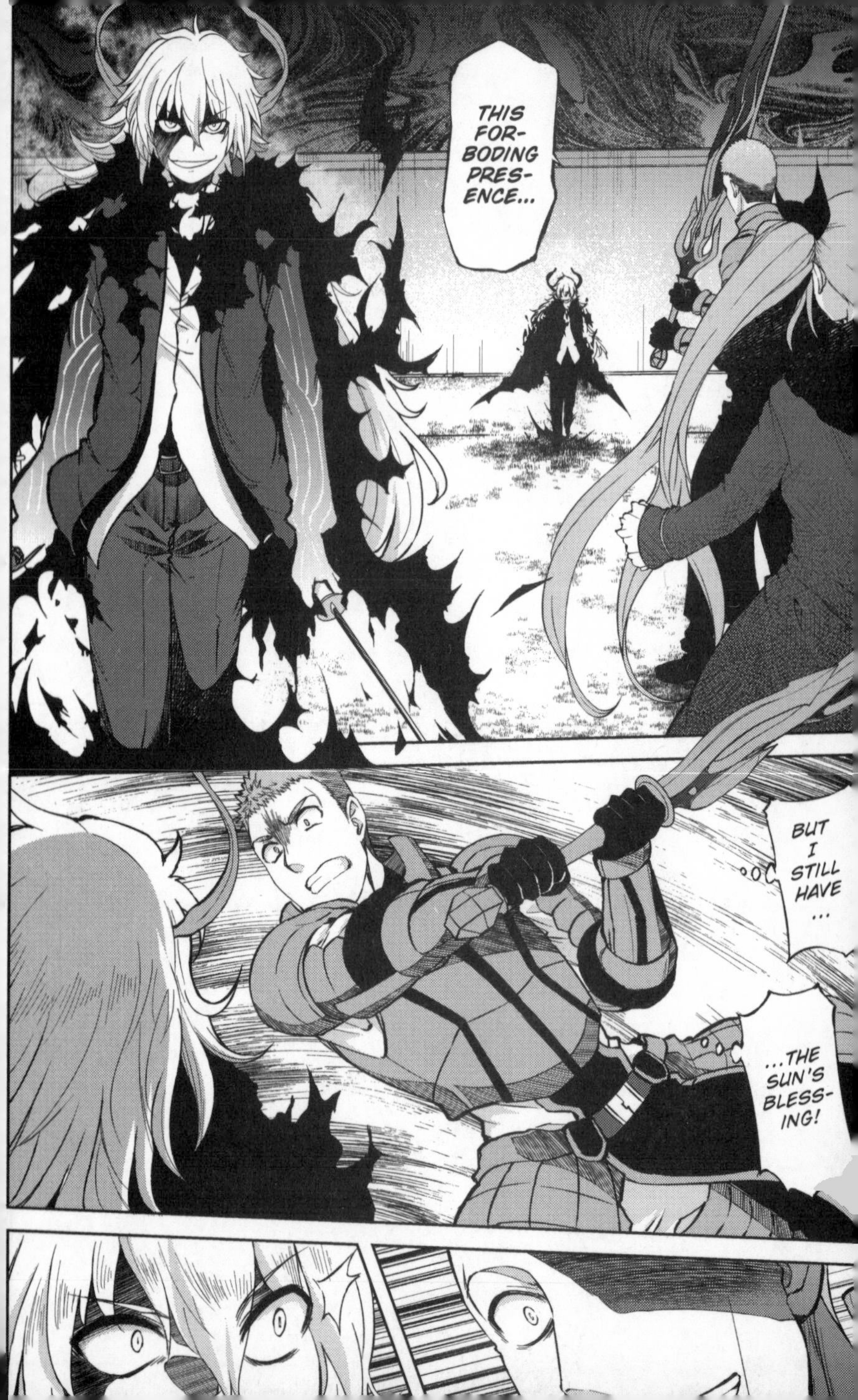
THIS FOR-BODING PRES-ENCE...
BUT I STILL HAVE ...
...THE SUN'S BLESS-ING!

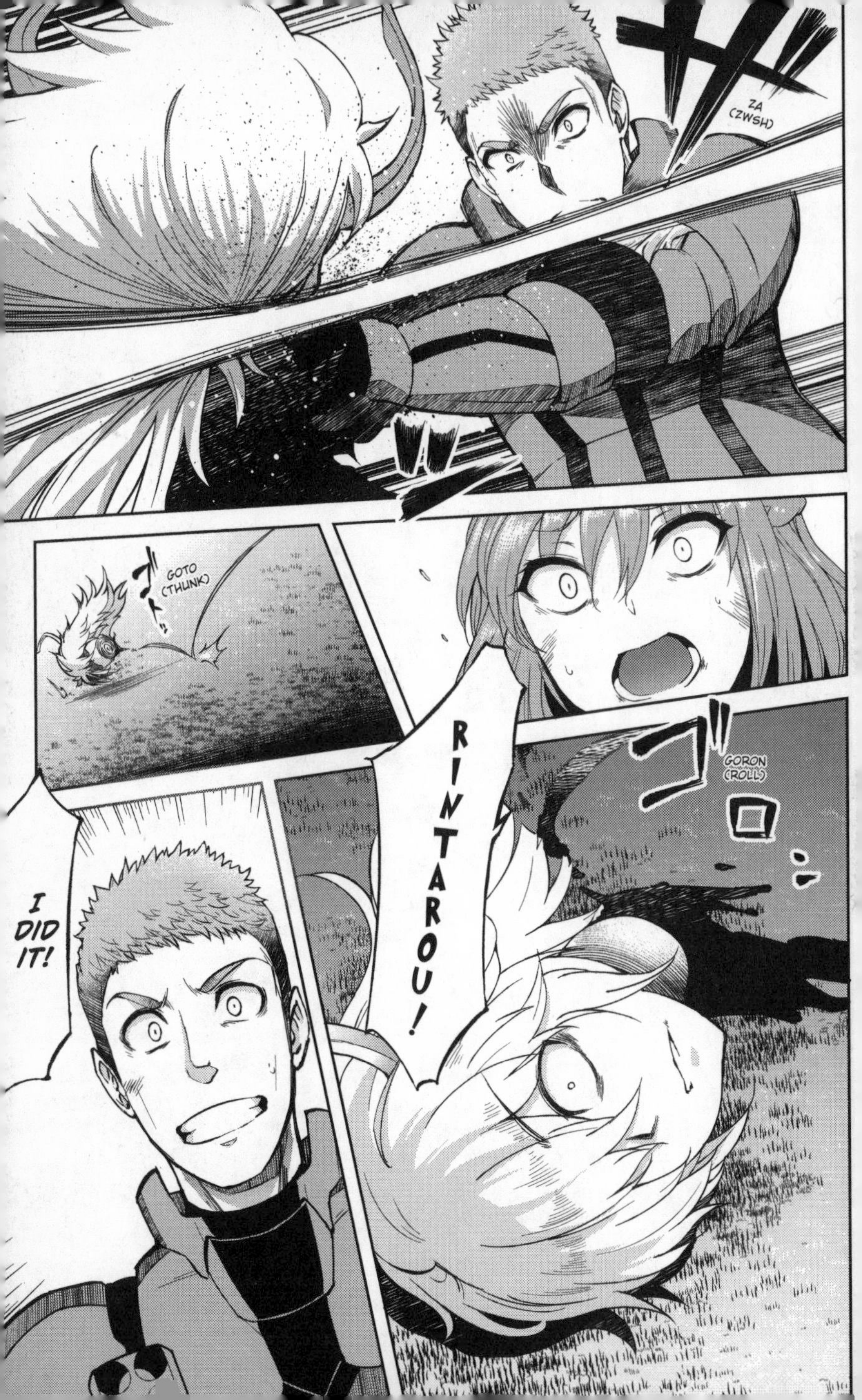
ZA (ZWSH)
RINTAROU!
GOTO (THUNK)
GORON (ROLL)
I DID IT!

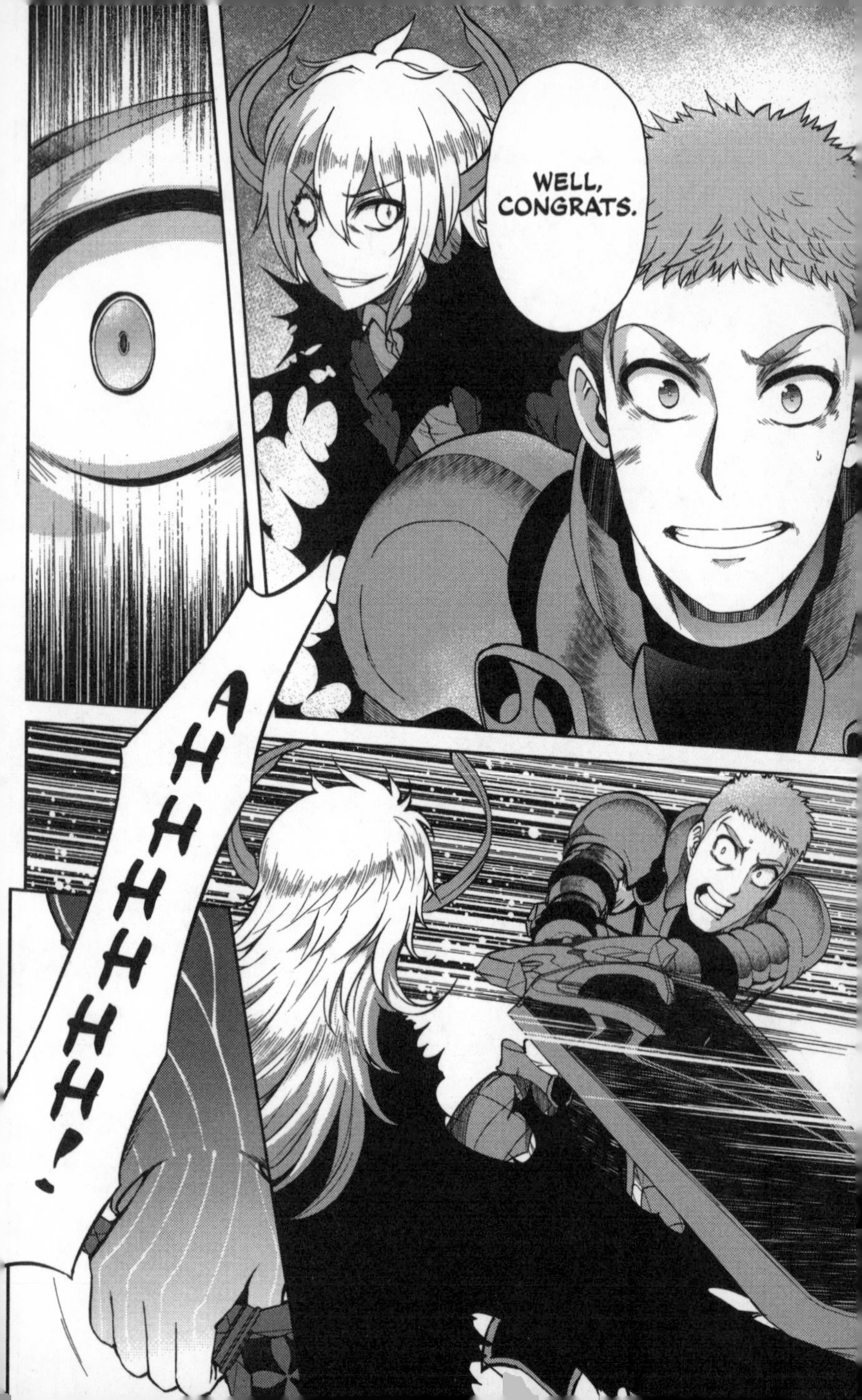
WELL, CONGRATS.
AHHHHHH!

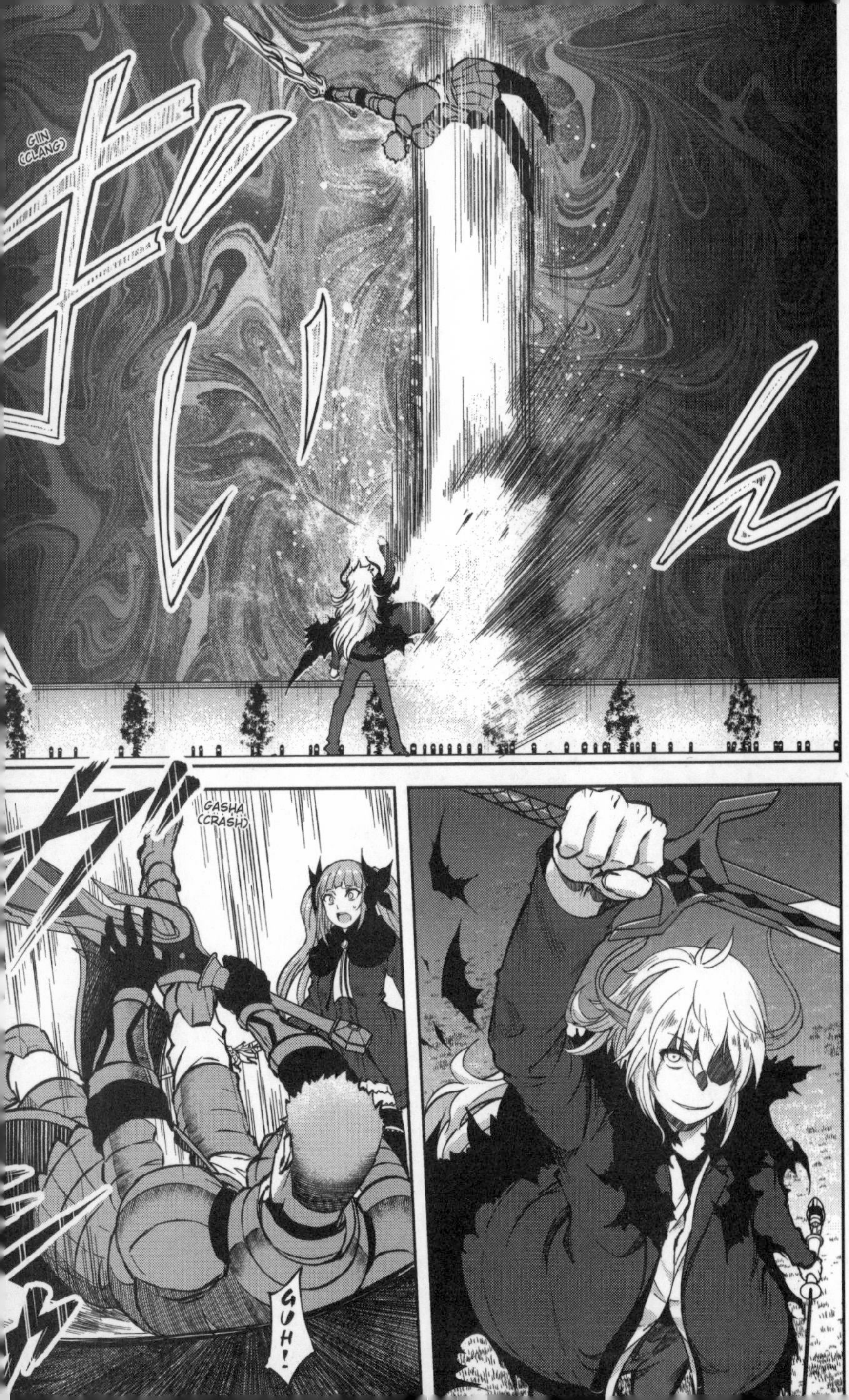
GIIN (CLANG)
GASHA (CRASH)
GUH!

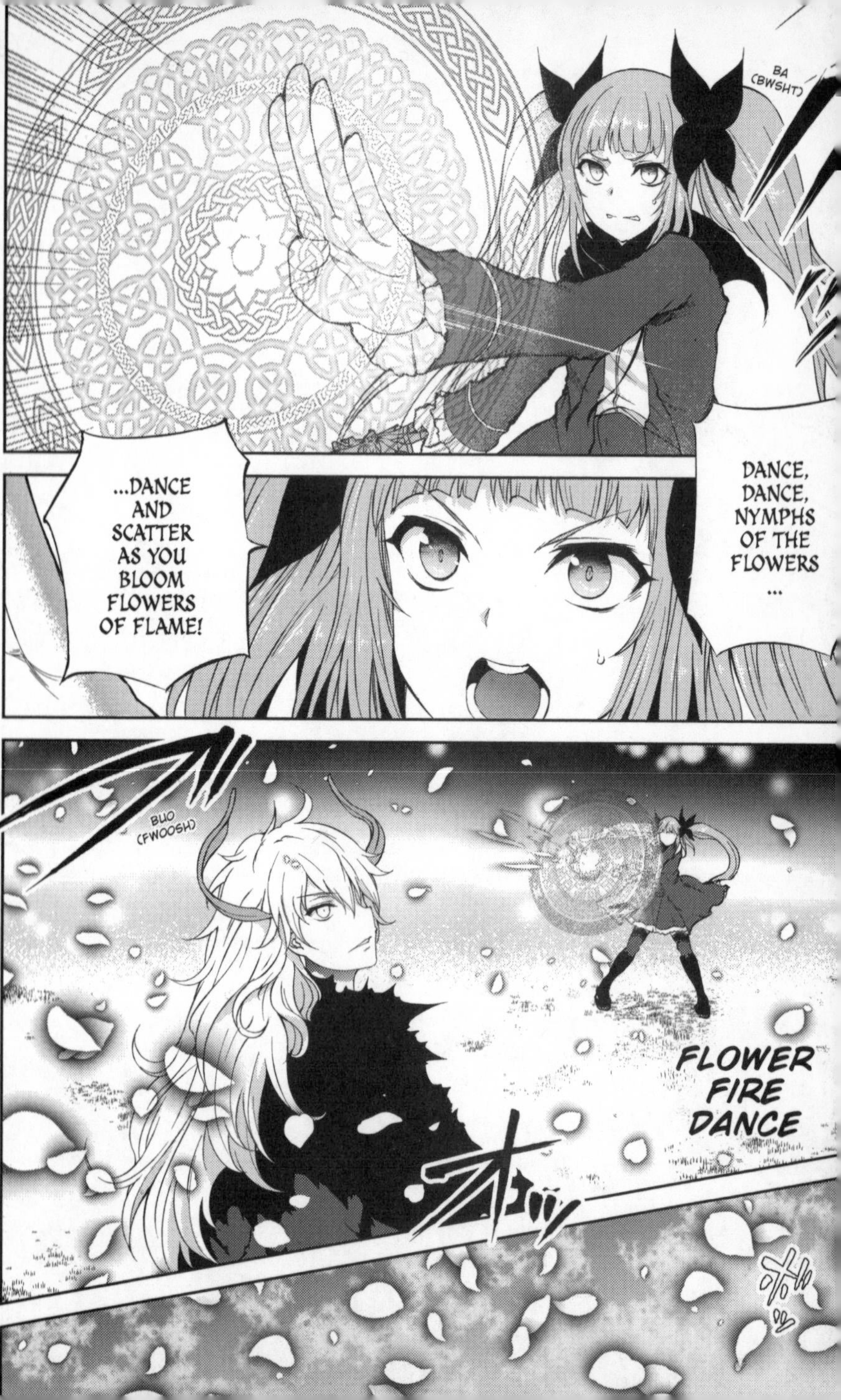
BA (BWSHT)
DANCE, DANCE, NYMPHS OF THE FLOWERS ...
...DANCE AND SCATTER AS YOU BLOOM FLOWERS OF FLAME!
BUO (FWOOSH)
FLOWER FIRE DANCE

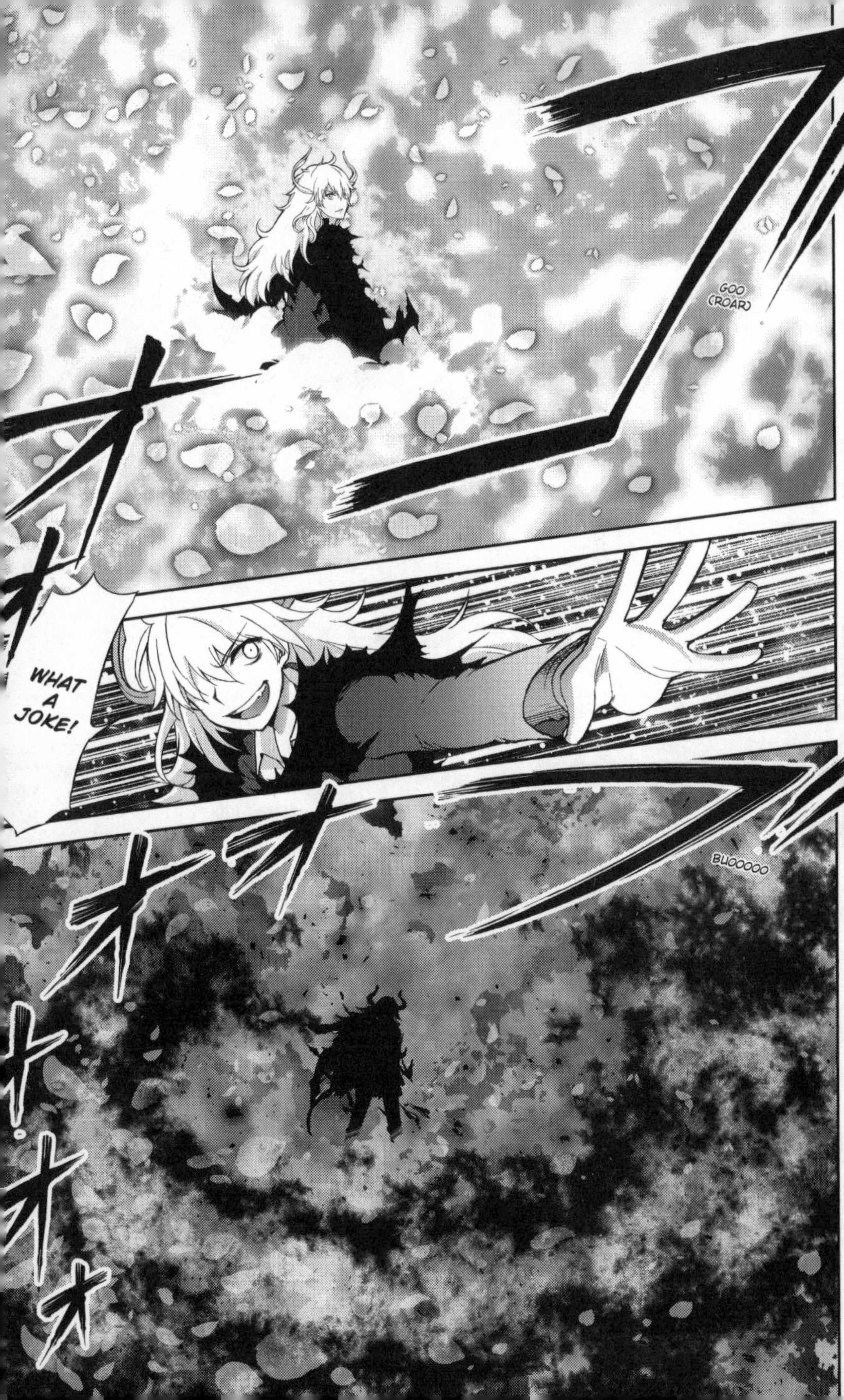
GOO
(ROAR)
WHAT A JOKE!
BUOOOOO

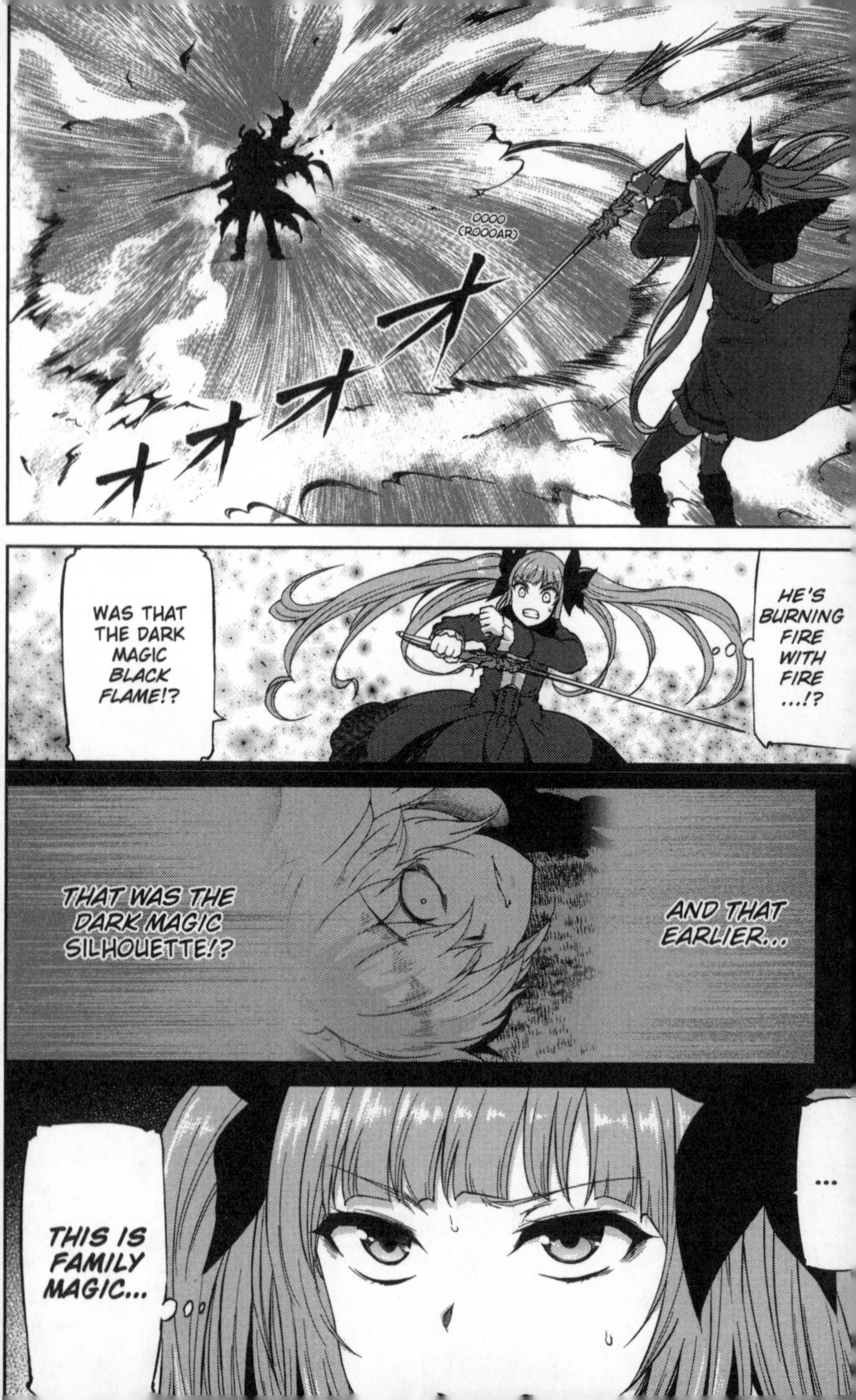

オオオオオ
OOOO (ROOOAR)
HE'S BURNING FIRE WITH FIRE ...!?
WAS THAT THE DARK MAGIC BLACK FLAME!?
AND THAT EARLIER...
THAT WAS THE DARK MAGIC SILHOUETTE!?
...
THIS IS FAMILY MAGIC...

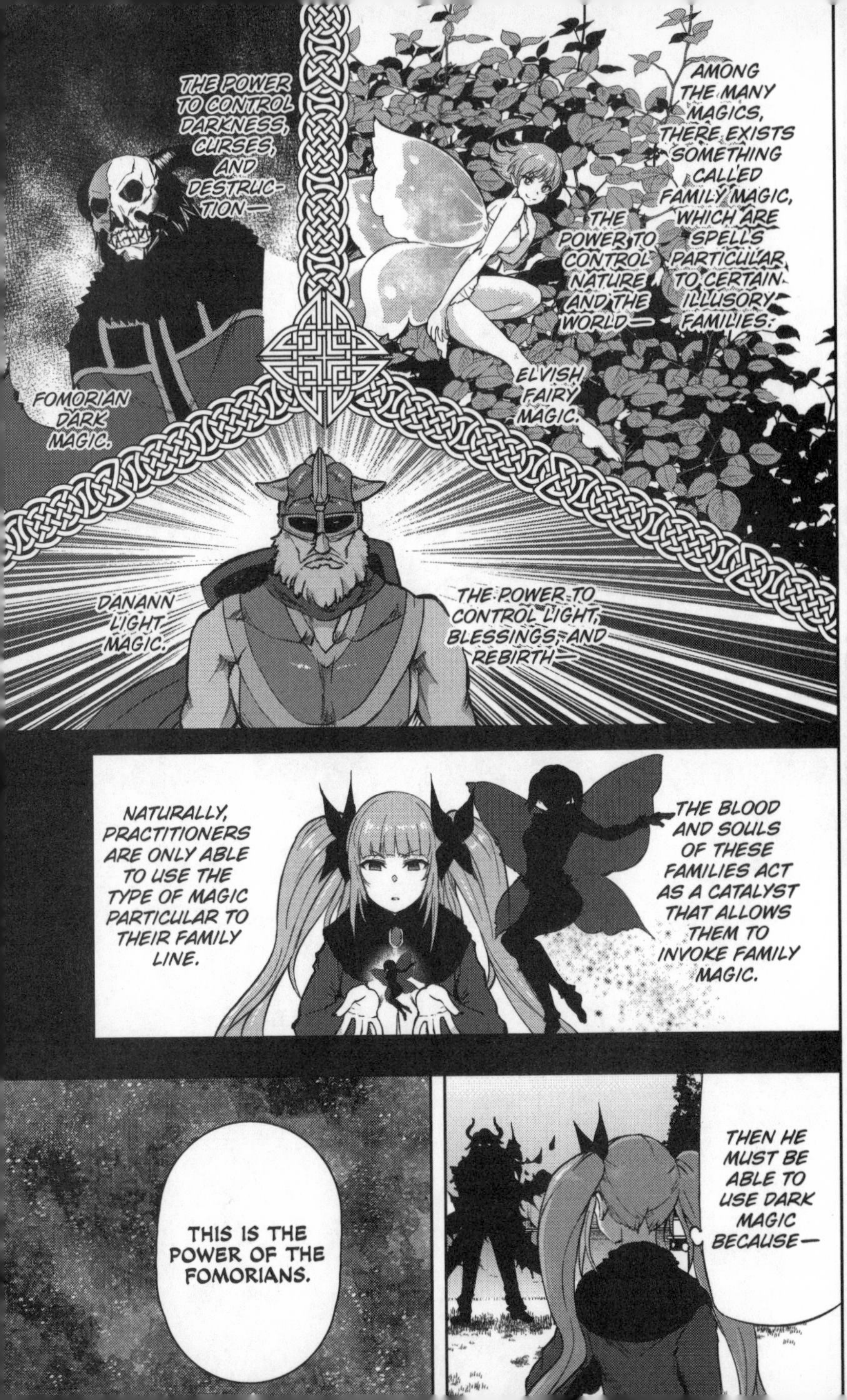
AMONG THE MANY MAGICS, THERE EXISTS SOMETHING CALLED FAMILY MAGIC, WHICH ARE SPELLS PARTICULAR TO CERTAIN ILLUSORY FAMILIES.
THE POWER TO CONTROL NATURE AND THE WORLD—
ELVISH FAIRY MAGIC.
THE POWER TO CONTROL DARKNESS, CURSES, AND DESTRUCTION—
FOMORIAN DARK MAGIC.
THE POWER TO CONTROL LIGHT, BLESSINGS, AND REBIRTH—
DANANN LIGHT MAGIC.
THE BLOOD AND SOULS OF THESE FAMILIES ACT AS A CATALYST THAT ALLOWS THEM TO INVOKE FAMILY MAGIC.
NATURALLY, PRACTITIONERS ARE ONLY ABLE TO USE THE TYPE OF MAGIC PARTICULAR TO THEIR FAMILY LINE.
THEN HE MUST BE ABLE TO USE DARK MAGIC BECAUSE—
THIS IS THE POWER OF THE FOMORIANS.

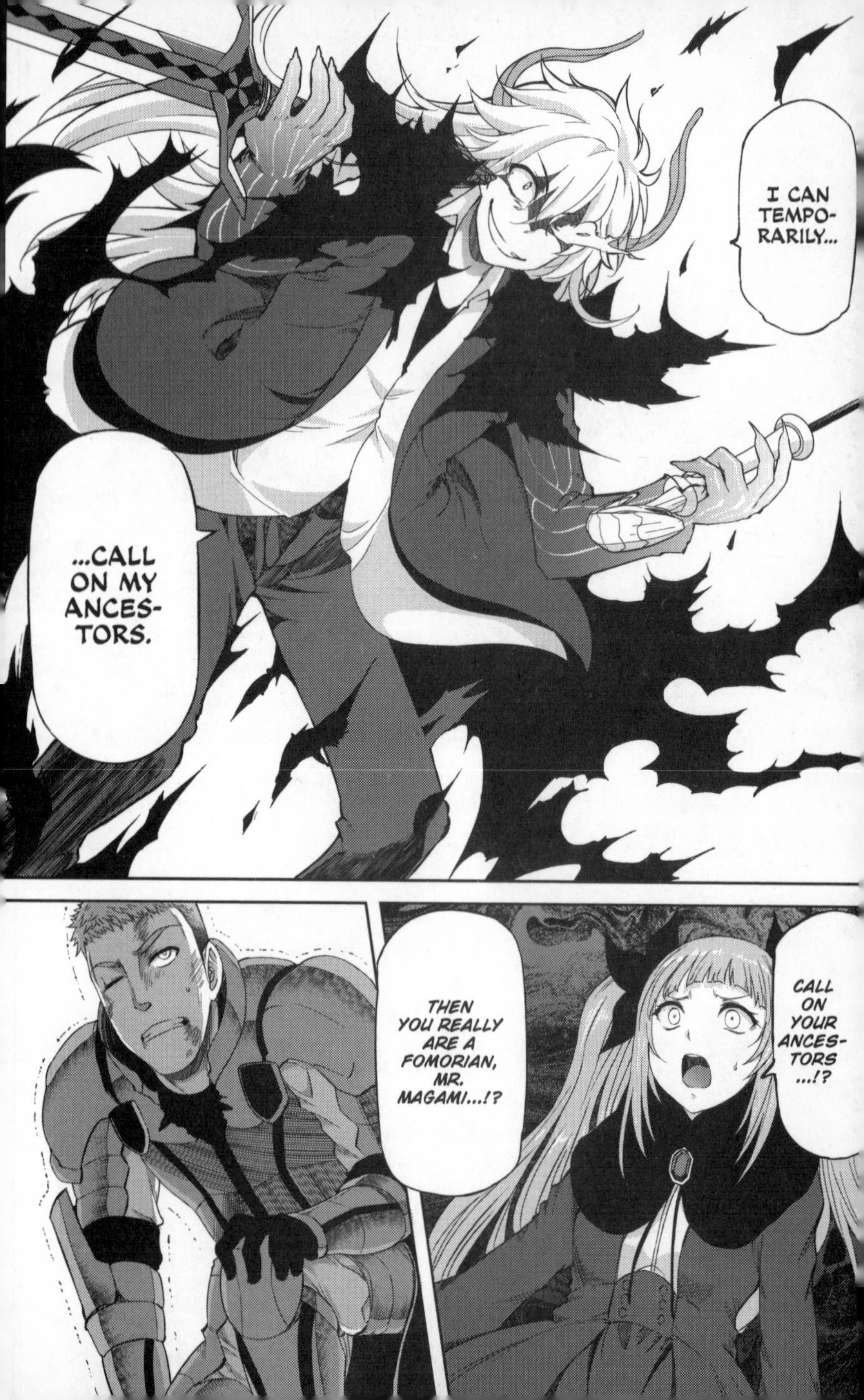
I CAN TEMPO-RARILY...
...CALL ON MY ANCES-TORS.
CALL ON YOUR ANCES-TORS ...!?
THEN YOU REALLY ARE A FOMORIAN, MR. MAGAMI...!?

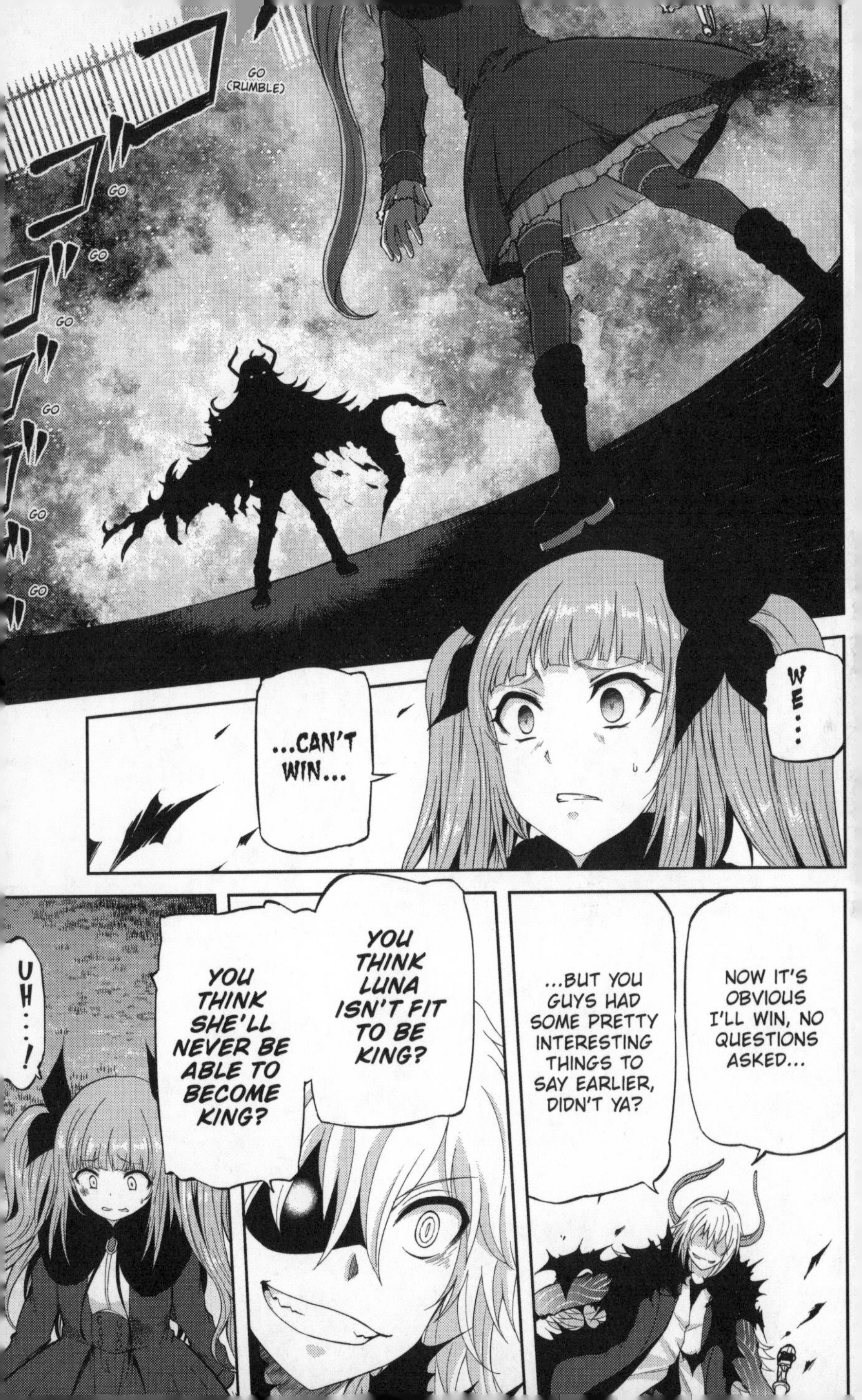
GO (RUMBLE)
GO
GO
GO
GO
GO
GO
WE...
...CAN'T WIN...
NOW IT'S OBVIOUS I'LL WIN, NO QUESTIONS ASKED...
...BUT YOU GUYS HAD SOME PRETTY INTERESTING THINGS TO SAY EARLIER, DIDN'T YA?
YOU THINK LUNA ISN'T FIT TO BE KING?
YOU THINK SHE'LL NEVER BE ABLE TO BECOME KING?
UH...!

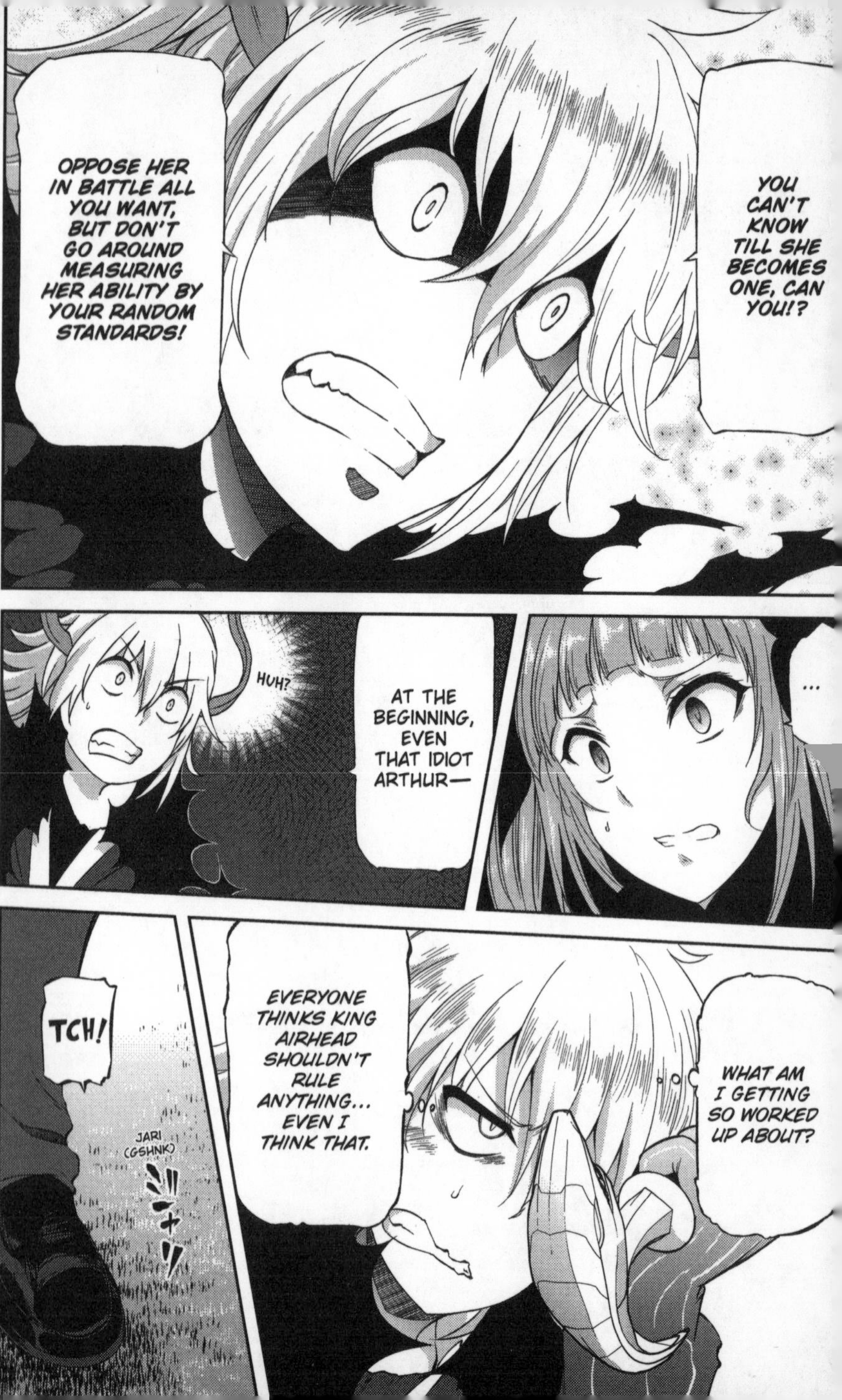
YOU CAN'T KNOW TILL SHE BECOMES ONE, CAN YOU!?
OPPOSE HER IN BATTLE ALL YOU WANT, BUT DON'T GO AROUND MEASURING HER ABILITY BY YOUR RANDOM STANDARDS!
...
AT THE BEGINNING, EVEN THAT IDIOT ARTHUR—
HUH?
WHAT AM I GETTING SO WORKED UP ABOUT?
EVERYONE THINKS KING AIRHEAD SHOULDN'T RULE ANYTHING... EVEN I THINK THAT.
TCH!
JARI (GSHNK)

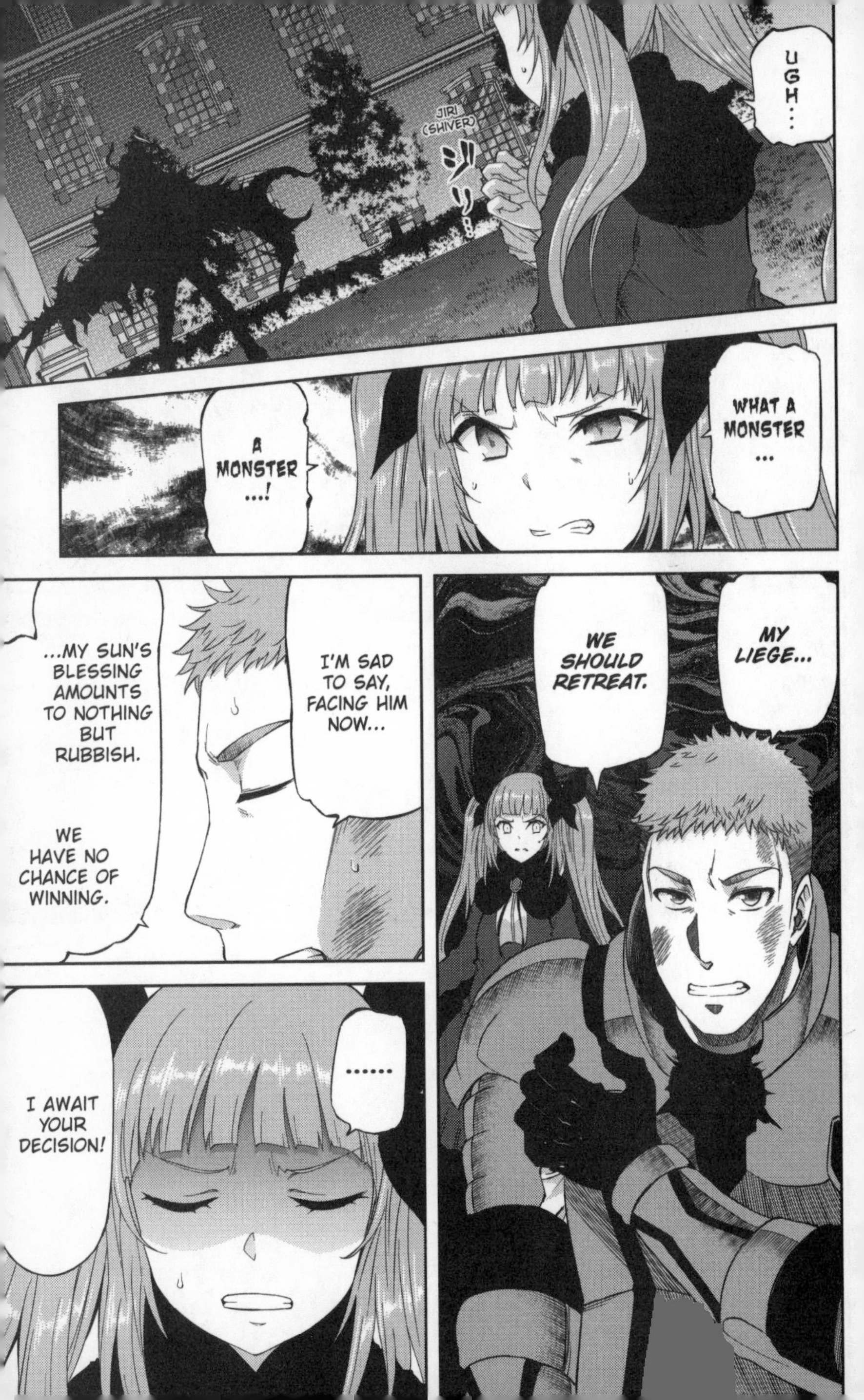
UGH...
JIRI (SHIVER)
WHAT A MONSTER ...
A MONSTER ...!
MY LIEGE...
WE SHOULD RETREAT.
I'M SAD TO SAY, FACING HIM NOW...
...MY SUN'S BLESSING AMOUNTS TO NOTHING BUT RUBBISH.
WE HAVE NO CHANCE OF WINNING.
......
I AWAIT YOUR DECISION!

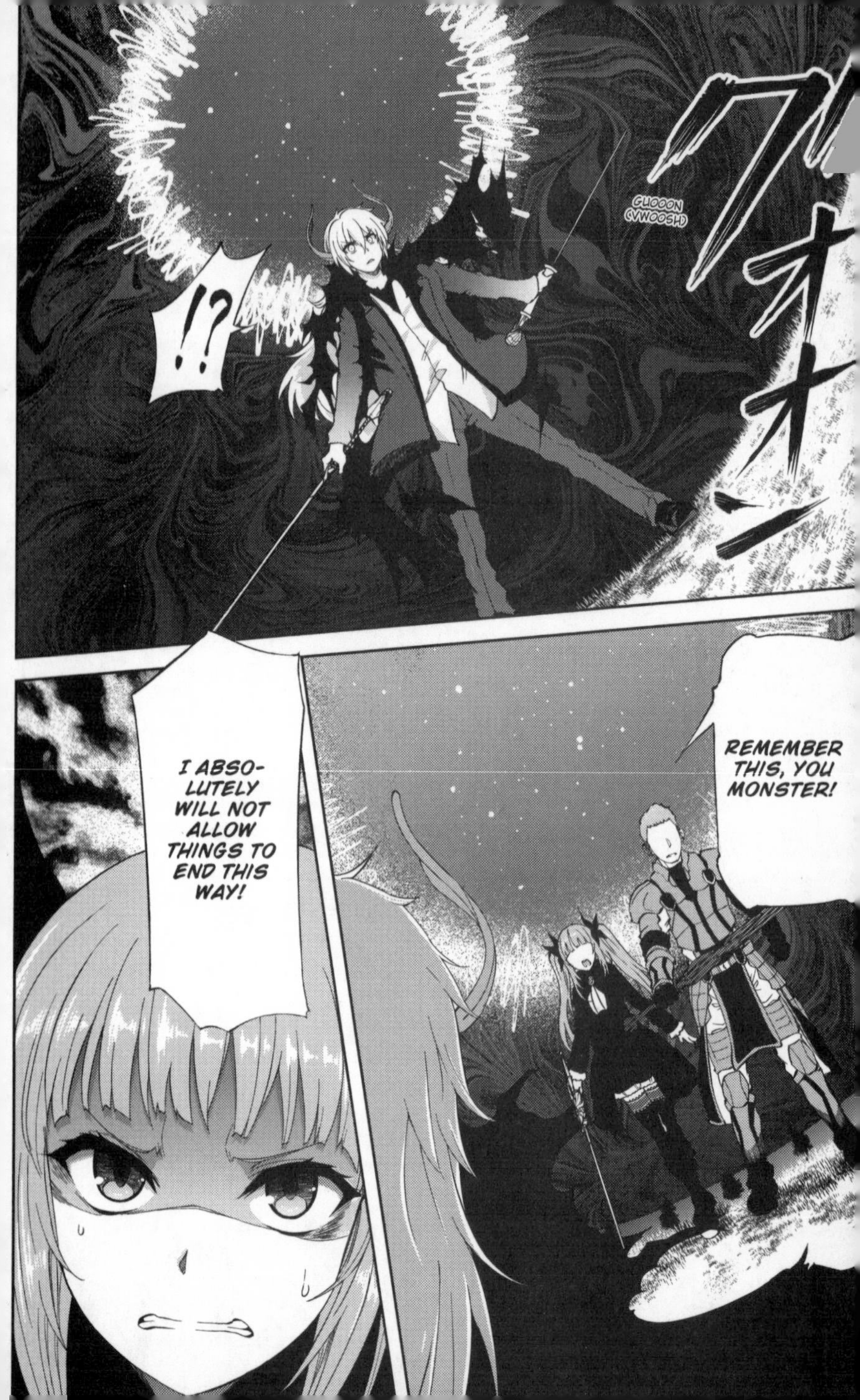
GUOOON (VWOOSH)
!?
REMEMBER THIS, YOU MONSTER!
I ABSO-LUTELY WILL NOT ALLOW THINGS TO END THIS WAY!

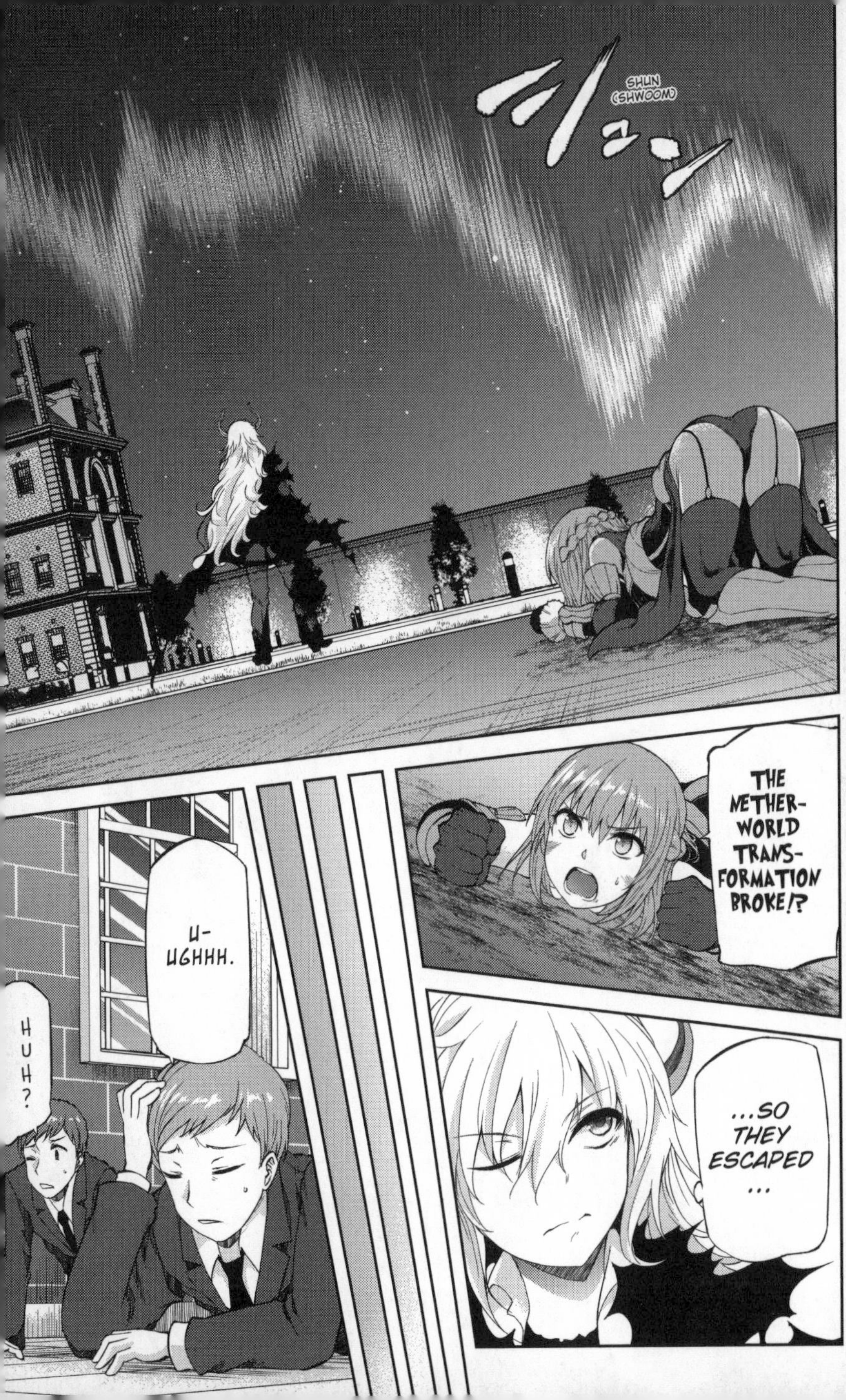
SHUN (SHWOOM)
THE NETHER-WORLD TRANS-FORMATION BROKE!?
...SO THEY ESCAPED...
U-UGHHH.
HUH?

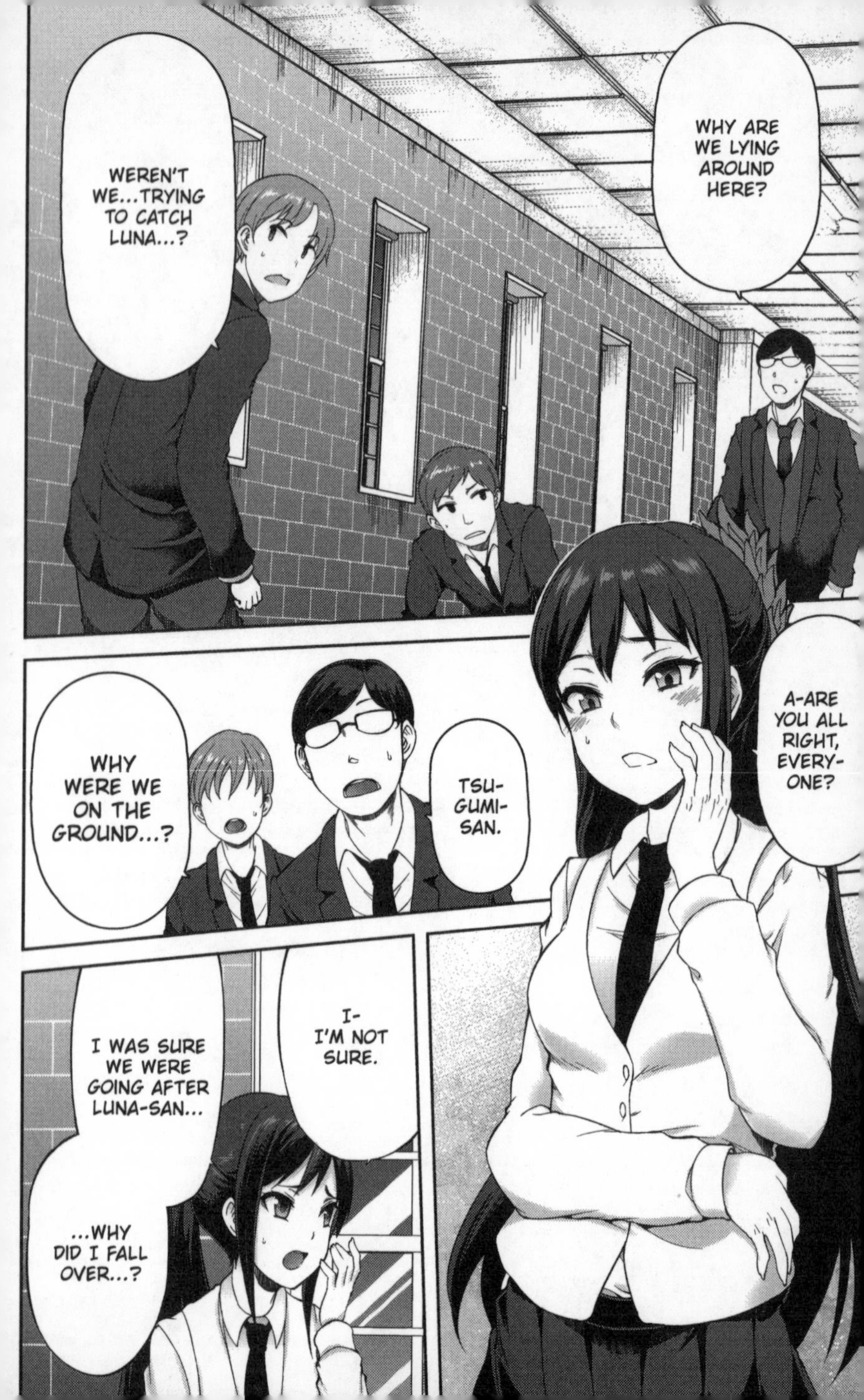

WHY ARE WE LYING AROUND HERE?
WEREN'T WE...TRYING TO CATCH LUNA...?
A-ARE YOU ALL RIGHT, EVERY-ONE?
TSU-GUMI-SAN.
WHY WERE WE ON THE GROUND...?
I- I'M NOT SURE.
I WAS SURE WE WERE GOING AFTER LUNA-SAN...
...WHY DID I FALL OVER...?

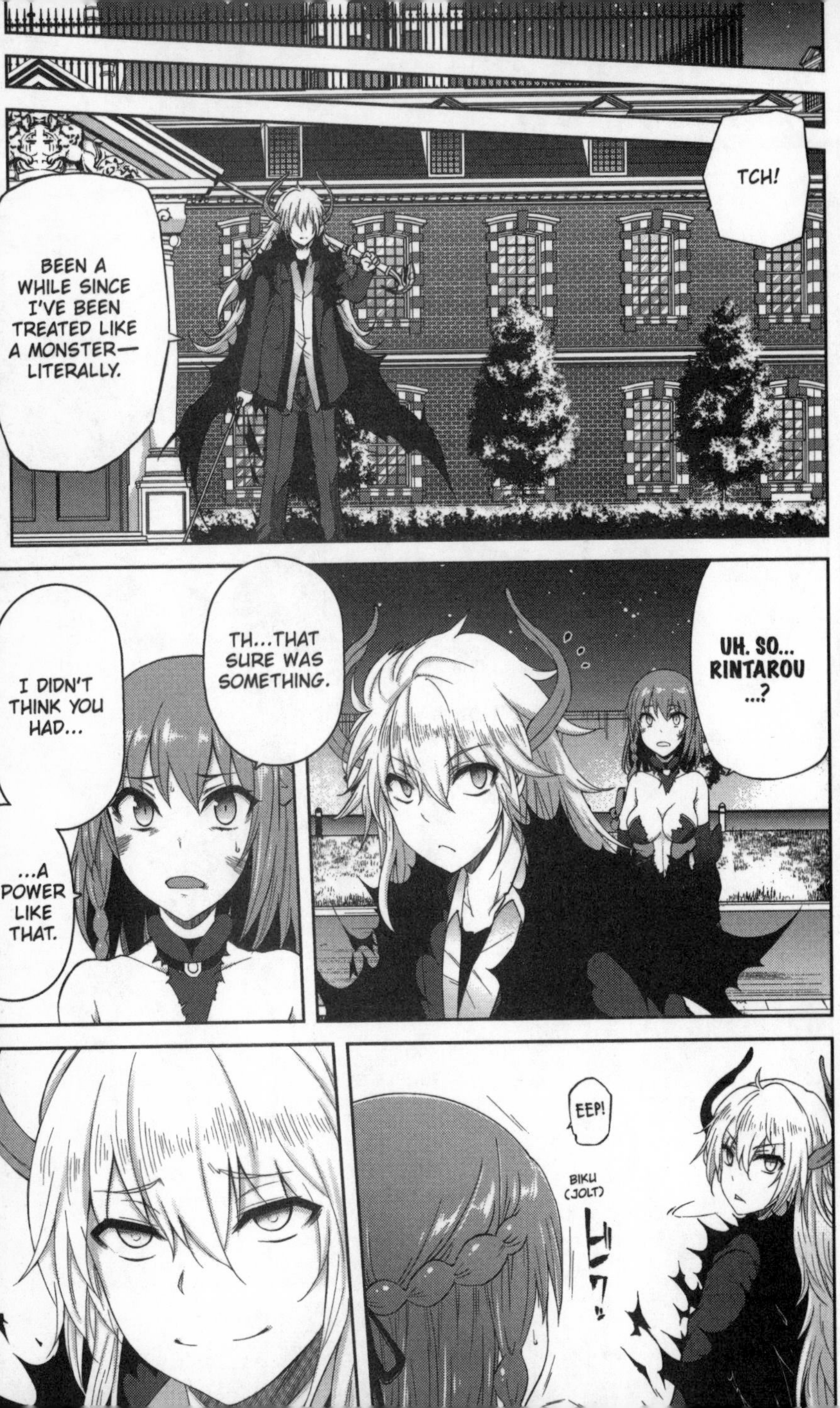
TCH!
BEEN A WHILE SINCE I'VE BEEN TREATED LIKE A MONSTER—LITERALLY.
UH. SO... RINTAROU ...?
TH...THAT SURE WAS SOMETHING.
I DIDN'T THINK YOU HAD...
...A POWER LIKE THAT.
EEP!
BIKU (JOLT)
ビクッ!!

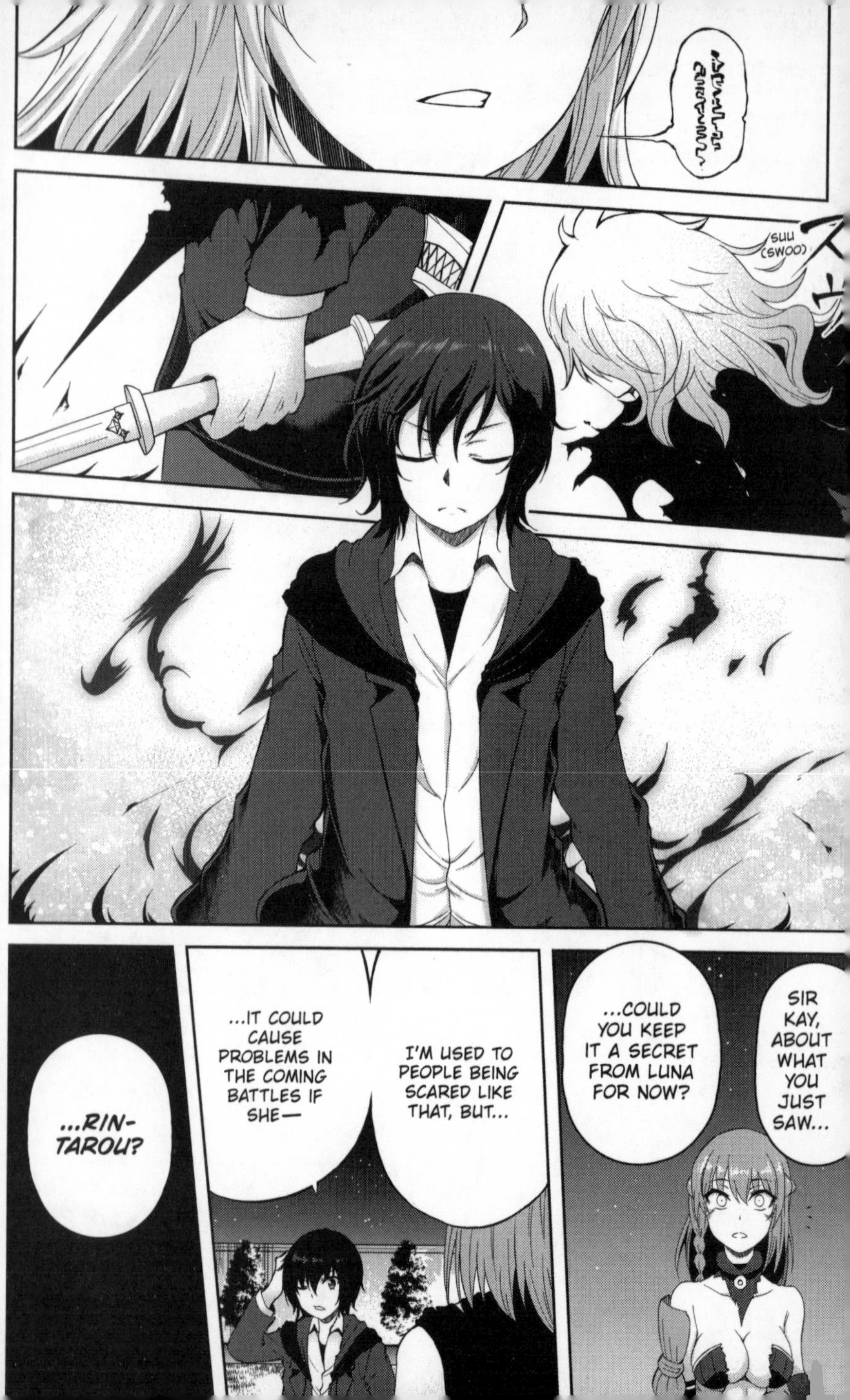
SUU (SWOO)
SIR KAY, ABOUT WHAT YOU JUST SAW...
...COULD YOU KEEP IT A SECRET FROM LUNA FOR NOW?
I'M USED TO PEOPLE BEING SCARED LIKE THAT, BUT...
...IT COULD CAUSE PROBLEMS IN THE COMING BATTLES IF SHE—
...RIN-TAROU?

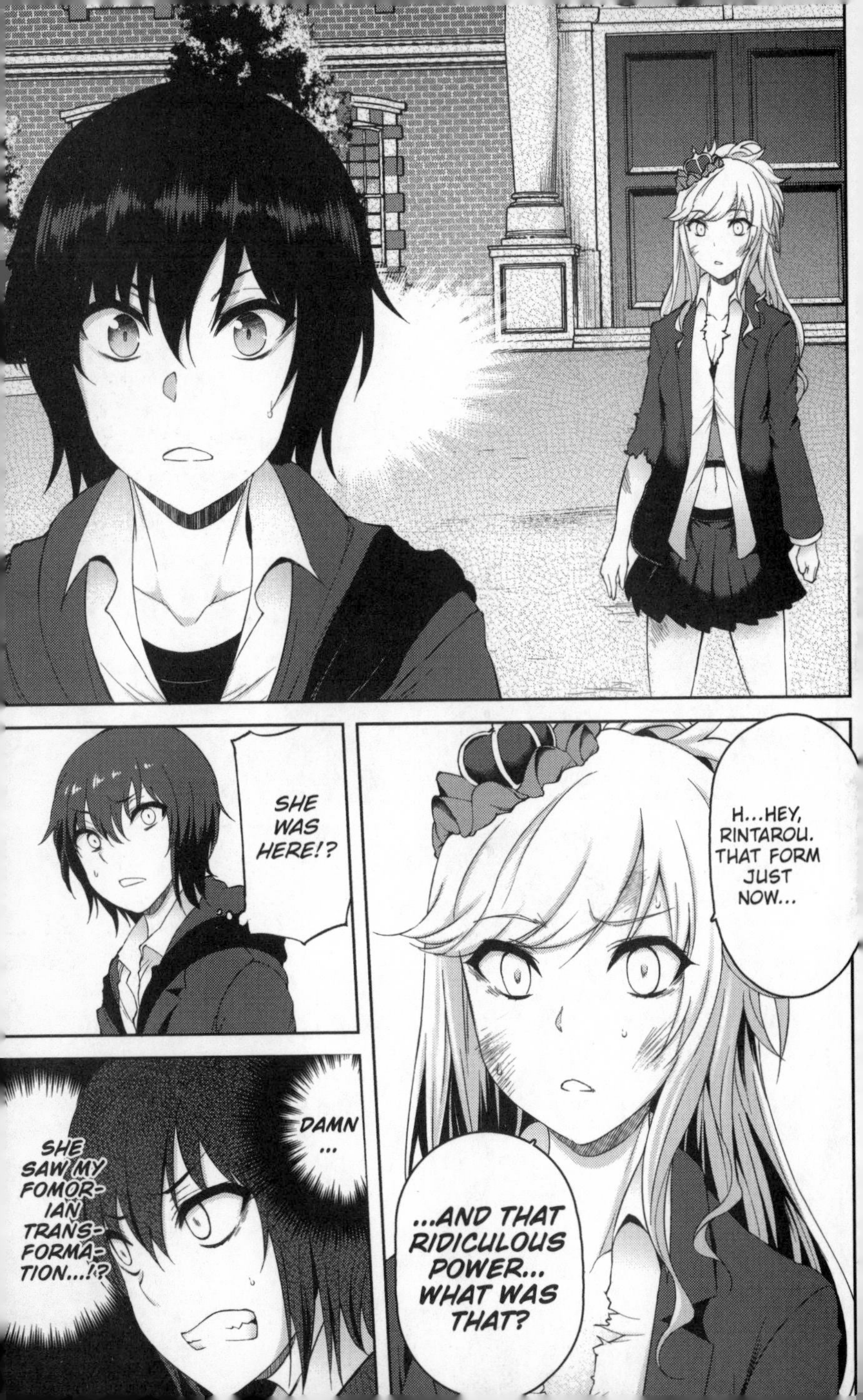
H...HEY, RINTAROU. THAT FORM JUST NOW...
...AND THAT RIDICULOUS POWER... WHAT WAS THAT?
SHE WAS HERE!?
DAMN...
SHE SAW MY FOMORIAN TRANSFORMATION...!?

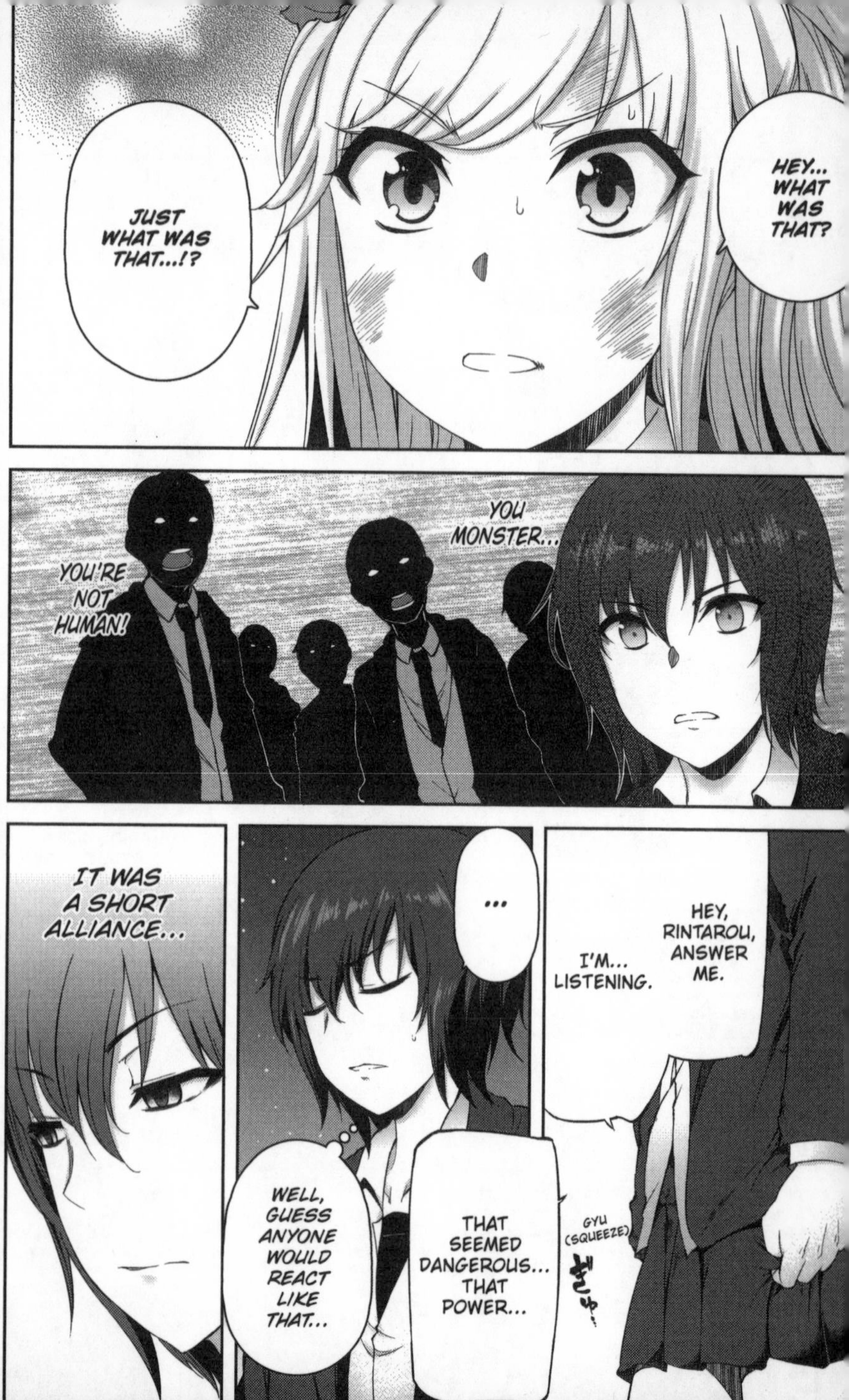
HEY... WHAT WAS THAT?
JUST WHAT WAS THAT...!?
YOU MONSTER...
YOU'RE NOT HUMAN!
HEY, RINTAROU, ANSWER ME.
I'M... LISTENING.
GYU (SQUEEZE)
THAT SEEMED DANGEROUS... THAT POWER...
...
WELL, GUESS ANYONE WOULD REACT LIKE THAT...
IT WAS A SHORT ALLIANCE...

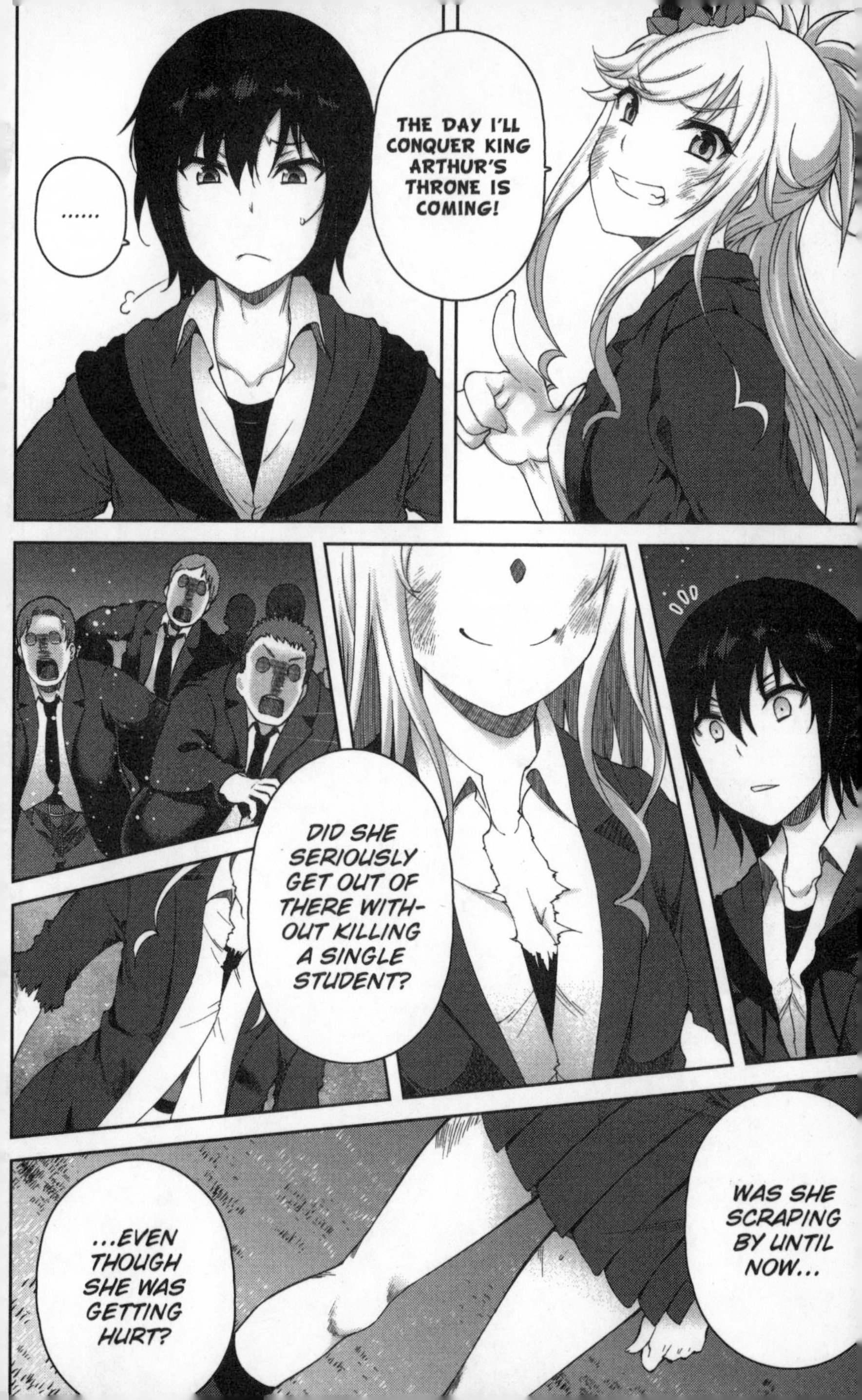
THE DAY I'LL CONQUER KING ARTHUR'S THRONE IS COMING!
......
DID SHE SERIOUSLY GET OUT OF THERE WITH-OUT KILLING A SINGLE STUDENT?
WAS SHE SCRAPING BY UNTIL NOW...
...EVEN THOUGH SHE WAS GETTING HURT?

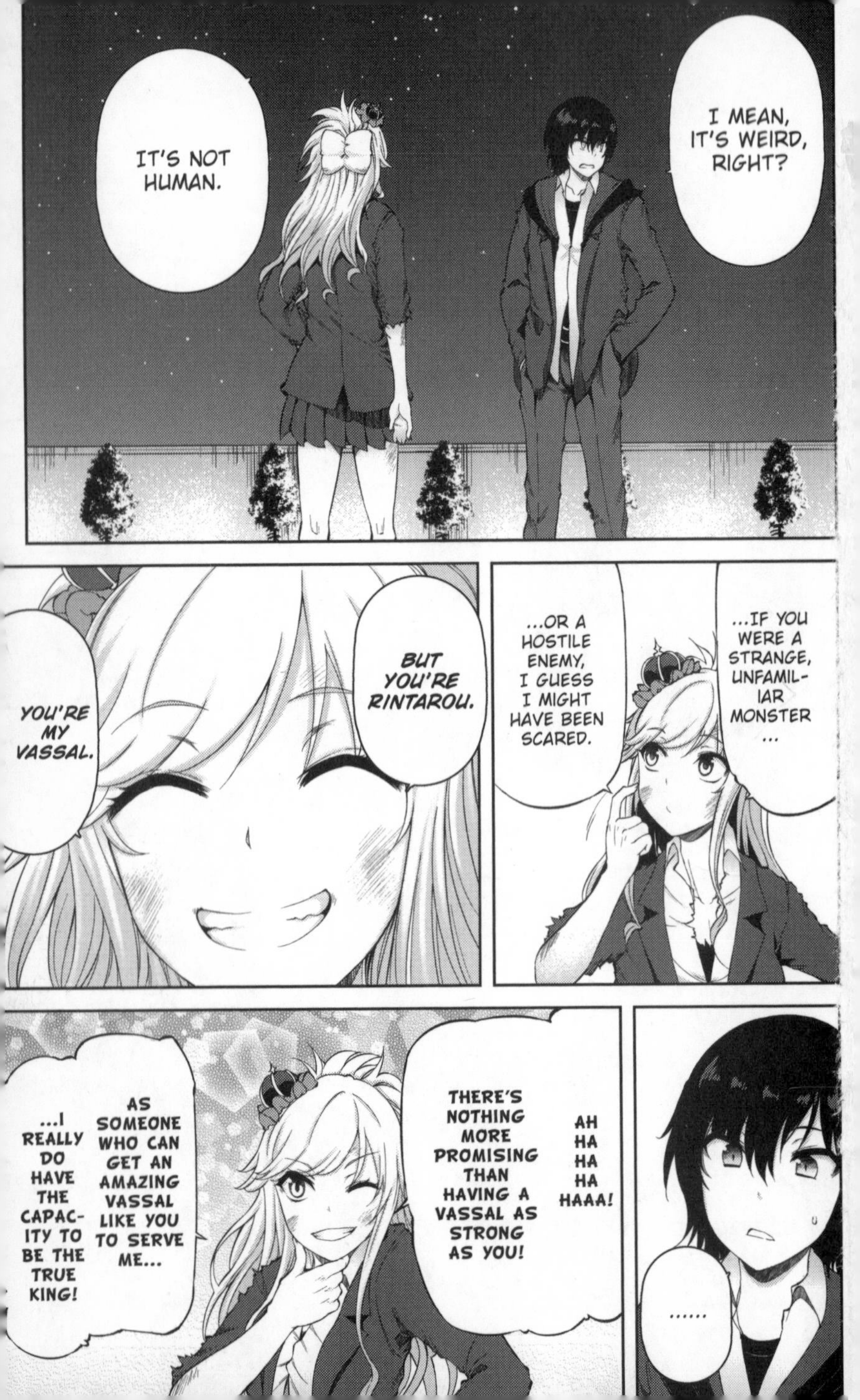
I MEAN, IT'S WEIRD, RIGHT?
IT'S NOT HUMAN.
...IF YOU WERE A STRANGE, UNFAMIL-IAR MONSTER...
...OR A HOSTILE ENEMY, I GUESS I MIGHT HAVE BEEN SCARED.
BUT YOU'RE RINTAROU.
YOU'RE MY VASSAL.
......
AH HA HA HA HAAA!
THERE'S NOTHING MORE PROMISING THAN HAVING A VASSAL AS STRONG AS YOU!
AS SOMEONE WHO CAN GET AN AMAZING VASSAL LIKE YOU TO SERVE ME...
...I REALLY DO HAVE THE CAPAC-ITY TO BE THE TRUE KING!

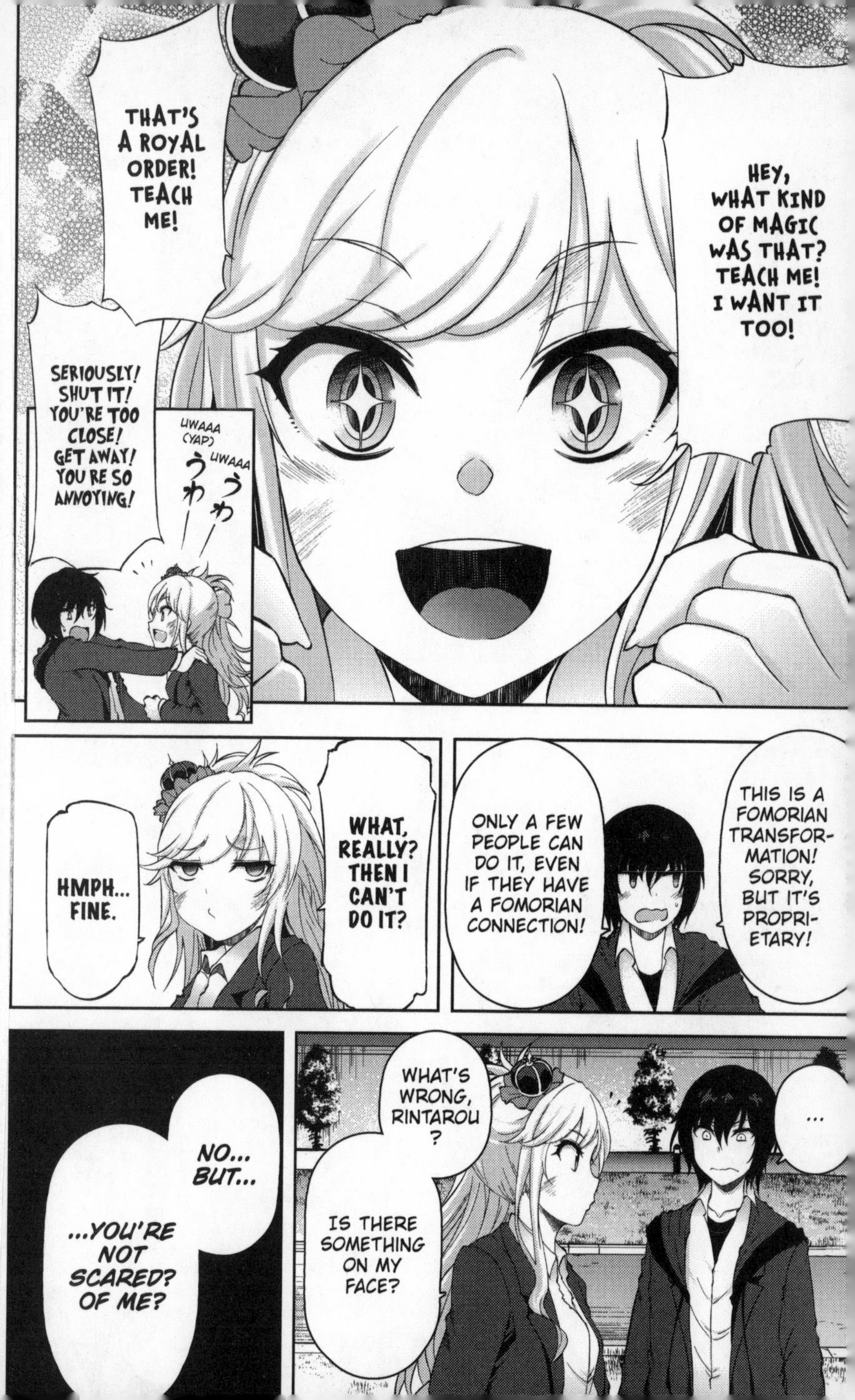
HEY, WHAT KIND OF MAGIC WAS THAT? TEACH ME! I WANT IT TOO!
THAT'S A ROYAL ORDER! TEACH ME!
UWAAA うわ
UWAAA (YAP) うわ
SERIOUSLY! SHUT IT! YOU'RE TOO CLOSE! GET AWAY! YOU'RE SO ANNOYING!
THIS IS A FOMORIAN TRANSFORMATION! SORRY, BUT IT'S PROPRIETARY!
ONLY A FEW PEOPLE CAN DO IT, EVEN IF THEY HAVE A FOMORIAN CONNECTION!
WHAT, REALLY? THEN I CAN'T DO IT?
HMPH... FINE.
...
WHAT'S WRONG, RINTAROU?
IS THERE SOMETHING ON MY FACE?
NO... BUT...
...YOU'RE NOT SCARED? OF ME?

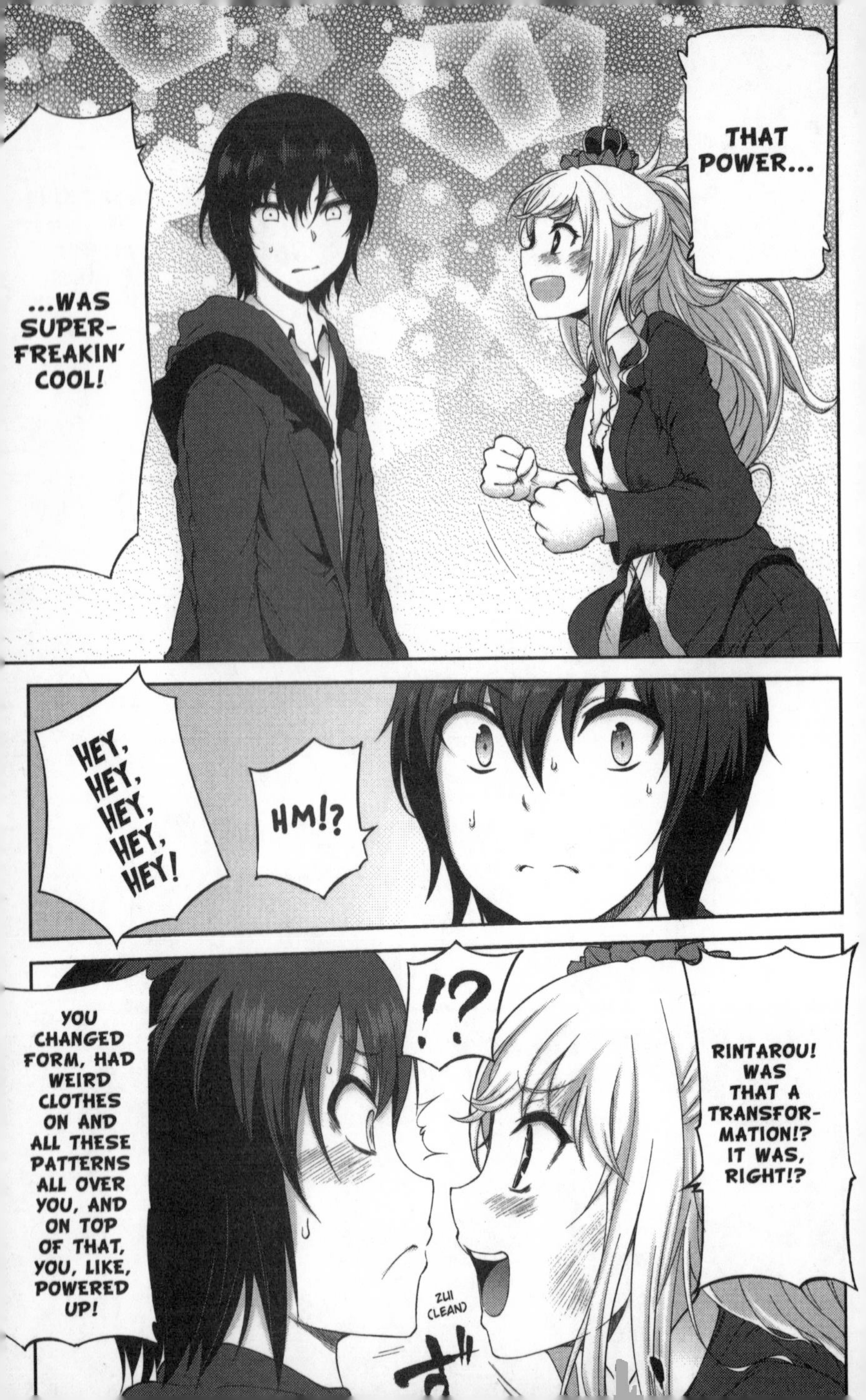
THAT POWER...
...WAS SUPER-FREAKIN' COOL!
HM!?
HEY, HEY, HEY, HEY, HEY!
RINTAROU! WAS THAT A TRANSFOR-MATION!? IT WAS, RIGHT!?
!?
YOU CHANGED FORM, HAD WEIRD CLOTHES ON AND ALL THESE PATTERNS ALL OVER YOU, AND ON TOP OF THAT, YOU, LIKE, POWERED UP!
ZUI (CLEAN)

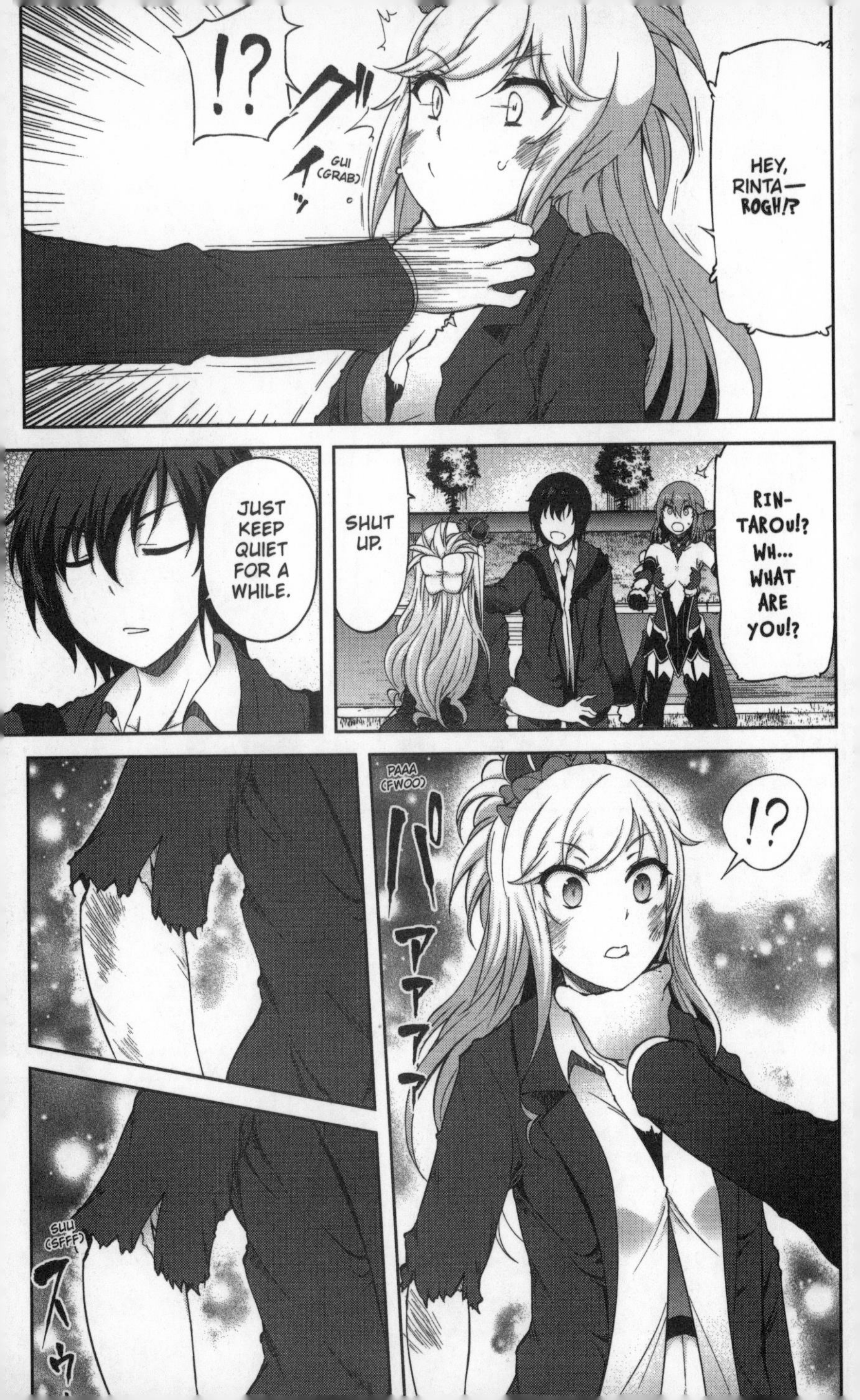
HEY, RINTA— ROGH!?
!?
GUI (GRAB)
RIN-TAROU!? WH... WHAT ARE YOU!?
SHUT UP.
JUST KEEP QUIET FOR A WHILE.
!?
PAAA (FWOO)
SUU (SFFF)

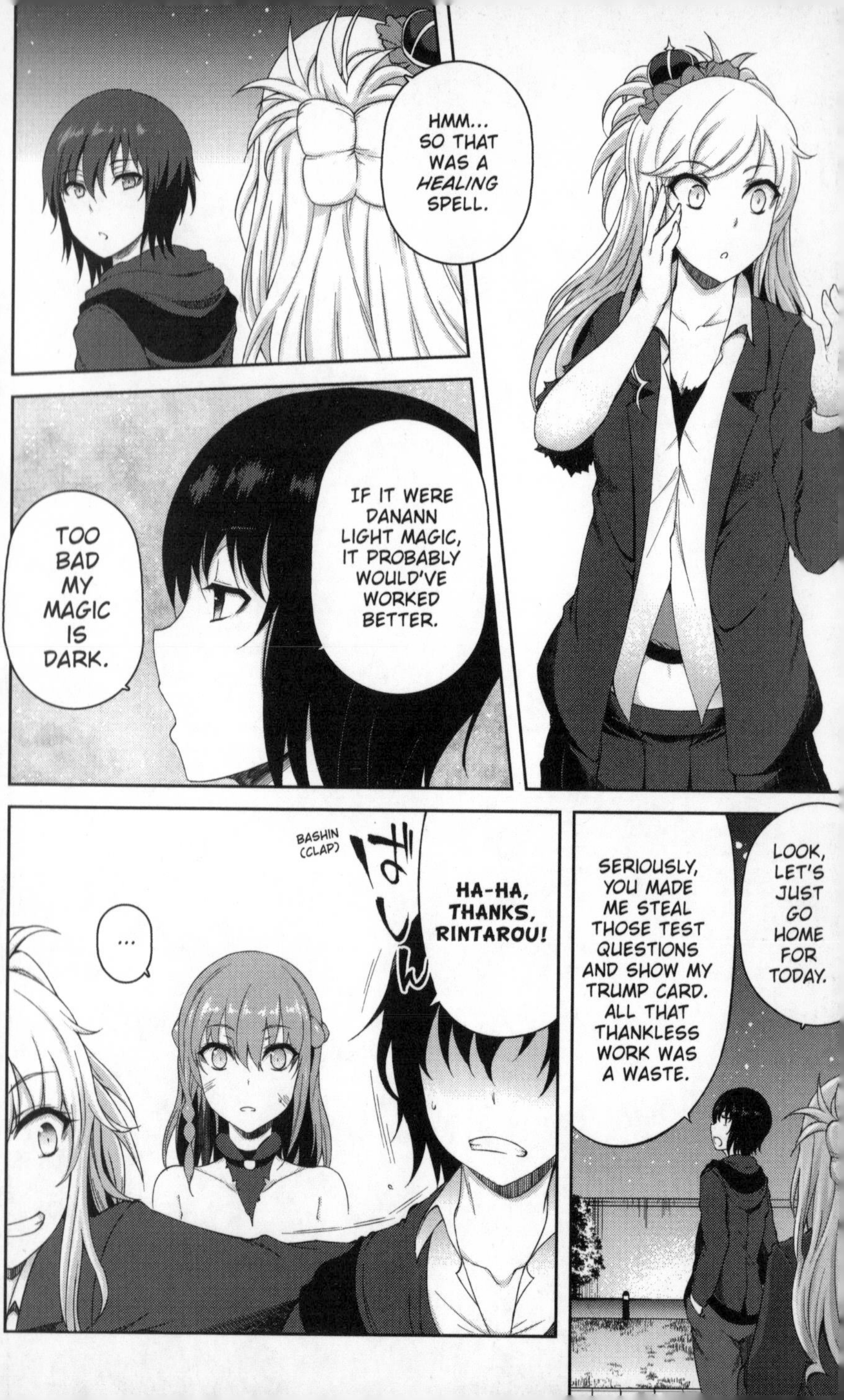
HMM... SO THAT WAS A *HEALING* SPELL.
IF IT WERE DANANN LIGHT MAGIC, IT PROBABLY WOULD'VE WORKED BETTER.
TOO BAD MY MAGIC IS DARK.
LOOK, LET'S JUST GO HOME FOR TODAY.
SERIOUSLY, YOU MADE ME STEAL THOSE TEST QUESTIONS AND SHOW MY TRUMP CARD. ALL THAT THANKLESS WORK WAS A WASTE.
HA-HA, THANKS, RINTAROU!
BASHIN (CLAP)
...

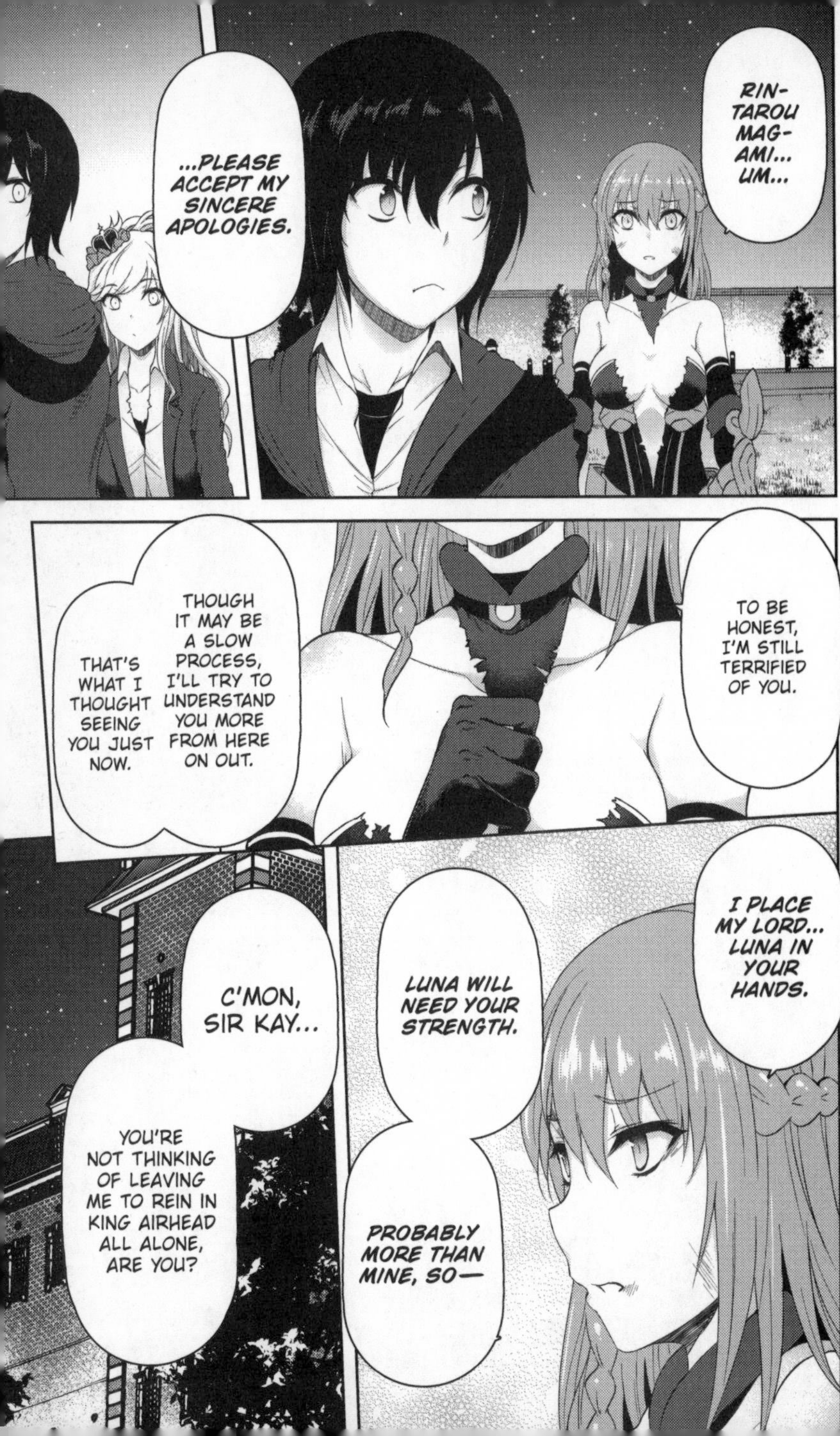
RIN-TAROU MAG-AMI... UM...
...PLEASE ACCEPT MY SINCERE APOLOGIES.
TO BE HONEST, I'M STILL TERRIFIED OF YOU.
THOUGH IT MAY BE A SLOW PROCESS, I'LL TRY TO UNDERSTAND YOU MORE FROM HERE ON OUT.
THAT'S WHAT I THOUGHT SEEING YOU JUST NOW.
I PLACE MY LORD... LUNA IN YOUR HANDS.
LUNA WILL NEED YOUR STRENGTH.
PROBABLY MORE THAN MINE, SO—
C'MON, SIR KAY...
YOU'RE NOT THINKING OF LEAVING ME TO REIN IN KING AIRHEAD ALL ALONE, ARE YOU?

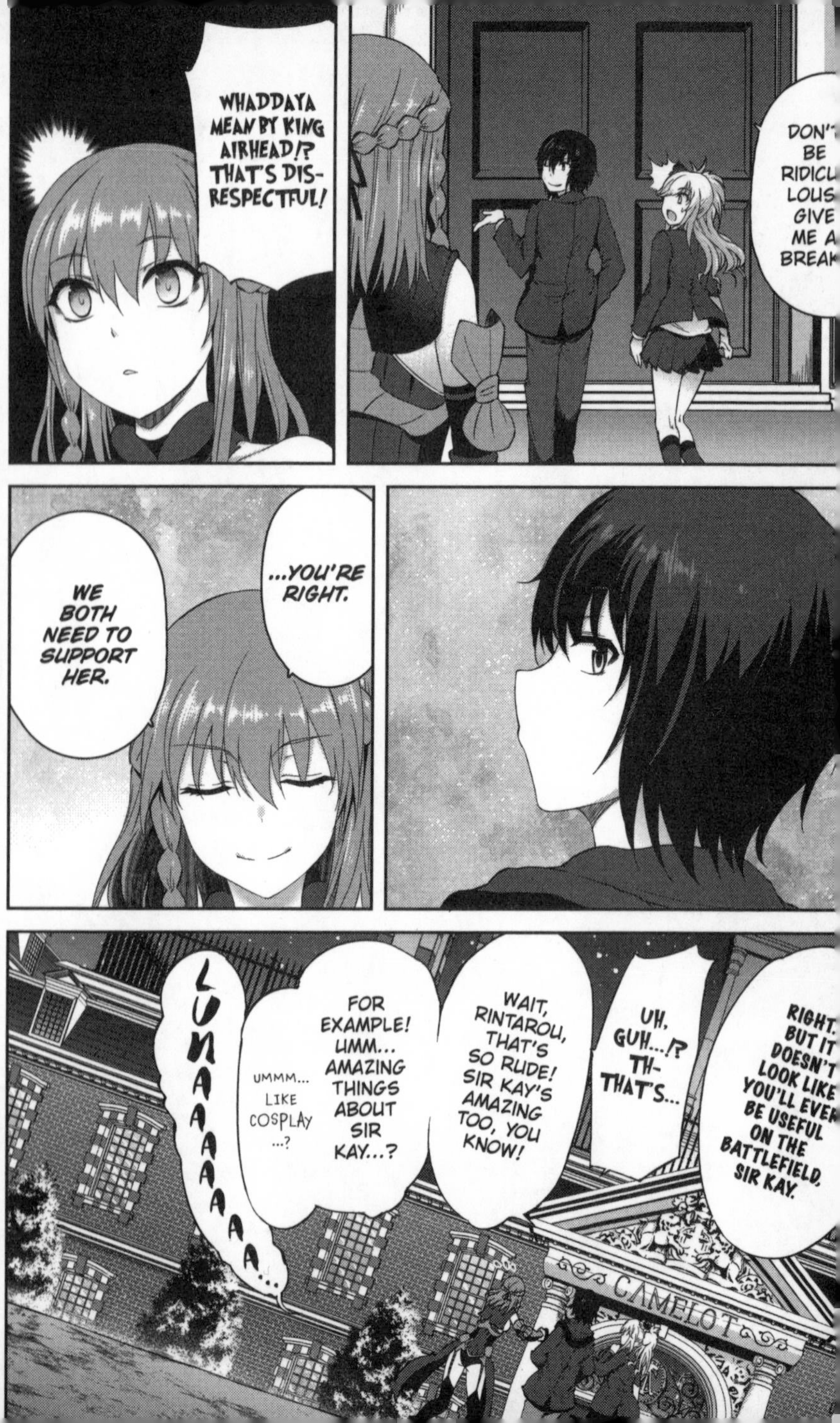
DON'T BE RIDICULOUS GIVE ME A BREAK
WHADDAYA MEAN BY KING AIRHEAD!? THAT'S DISRESPECTFUL!
...YOU'RE RIGHT.
WE BOTH NEED TO SUPPORT HER.
RIGHT. BUT IT DOESN'T LOOK LIKE YOU'LL EVER BE USEFUL ON THE BATTLEFIELD, SIR KAY.
UH, GUH...!? TH-THAT'S...
WAIT, RINTAROU, THAT'S SO RUDE! SIR KAY'S AMAZING TOO, YOU KNOW!
FOR EXAMPLE! UMM... AMAZING THINGS ABOUT SIR KAY...?
UMMM... LIKE COSPLAY...?
LUNAAAAAAAAA...
CAMELOT

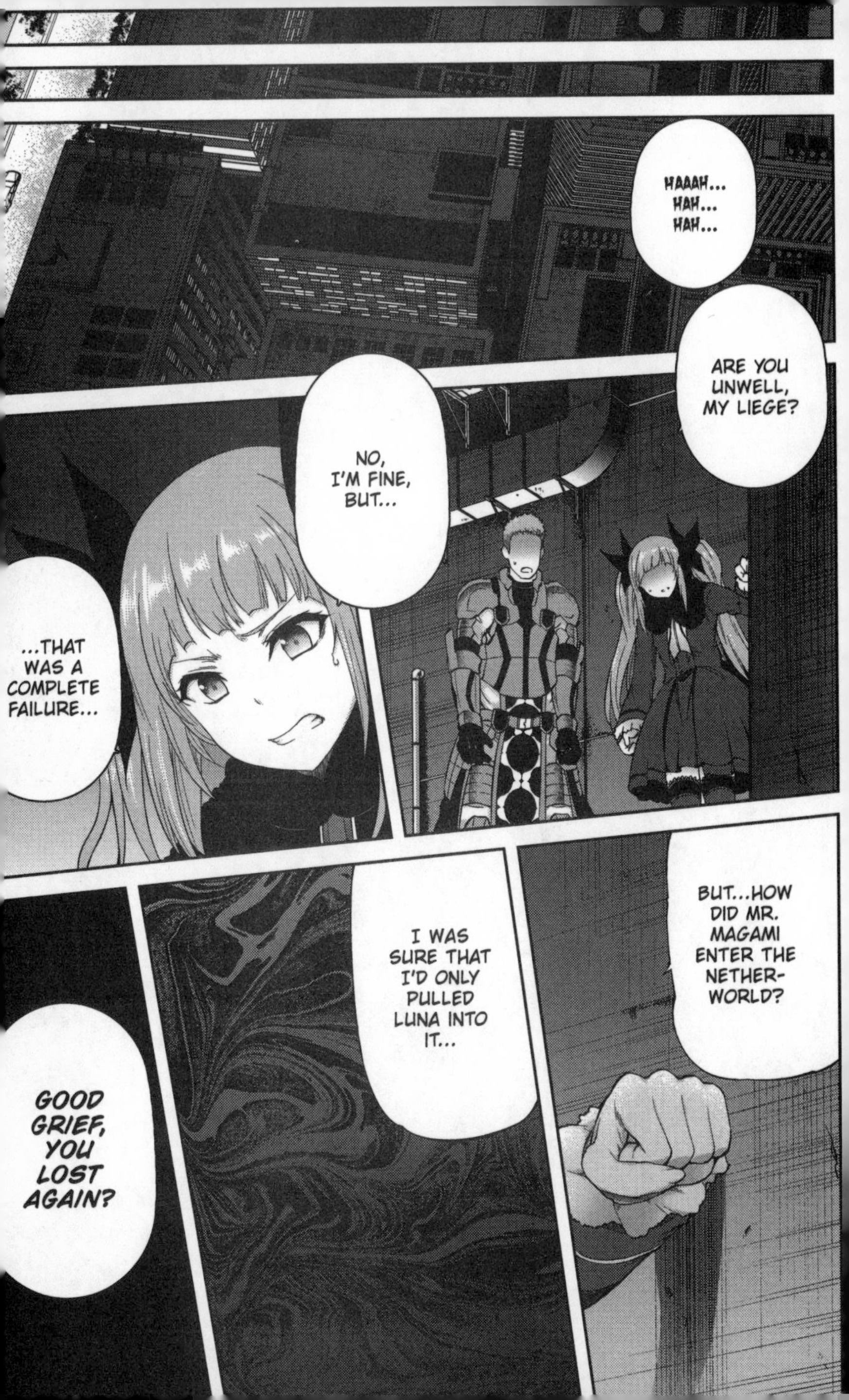
HAAAH... HAH... HAH...
ARE YOU UNWELL, MY LIEGE?
NO, I'M FINE, BUT...
...THAT WAS A COMPLETE FAILURE...
BUT...HOW DID MR. MAGAMI ENTER THE NETHER-WORLD?
I WAS SURE THAT I'D ONLY PULLED LUNA INTO IT...
GOOD GRIEF, YOU LOST AGAIN?

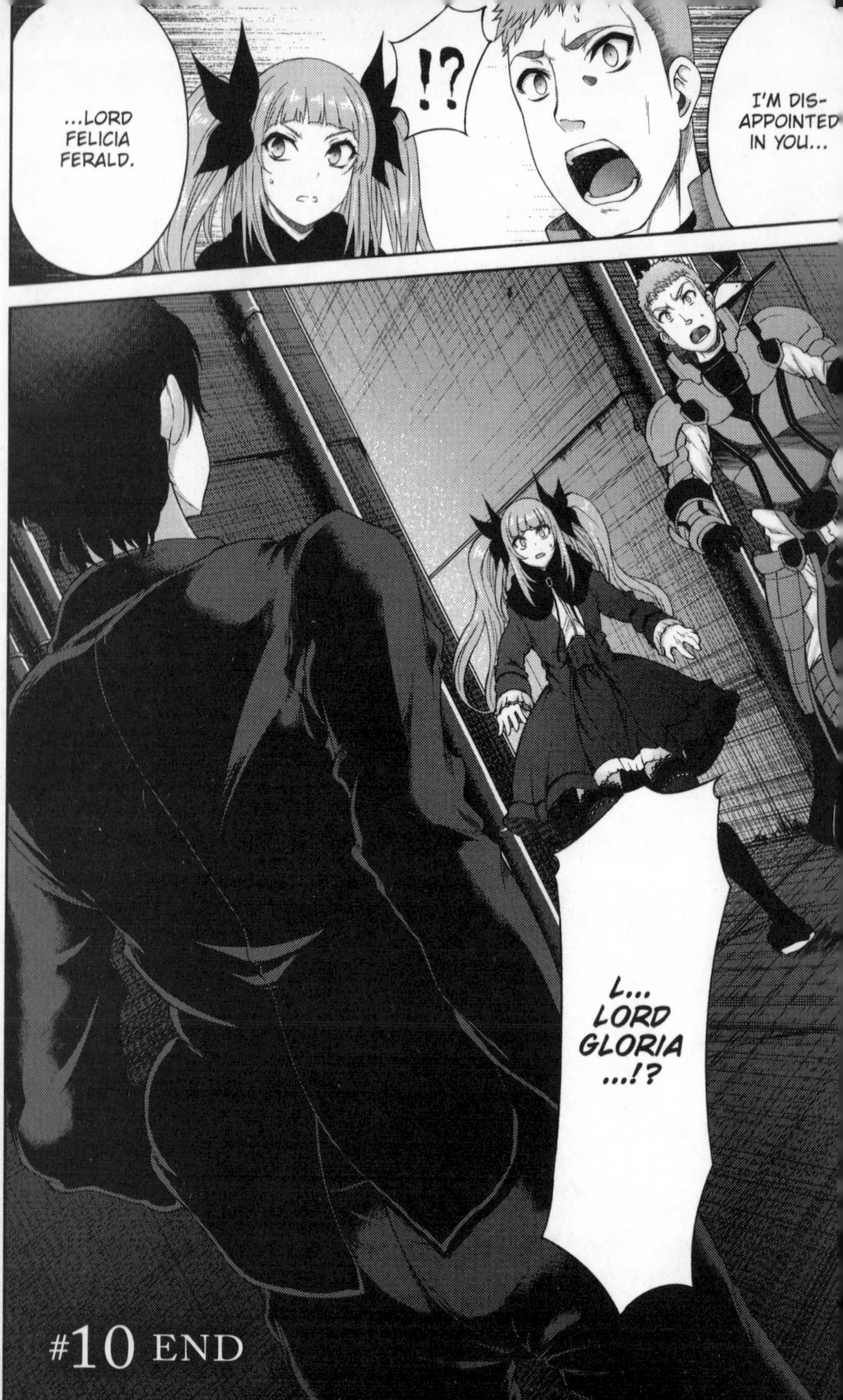
I'M DIS-APPOINTED IN YOU...
!?
...LORD FELICIA FERALD.
L... LORD GLORIA ...!?
#10 END

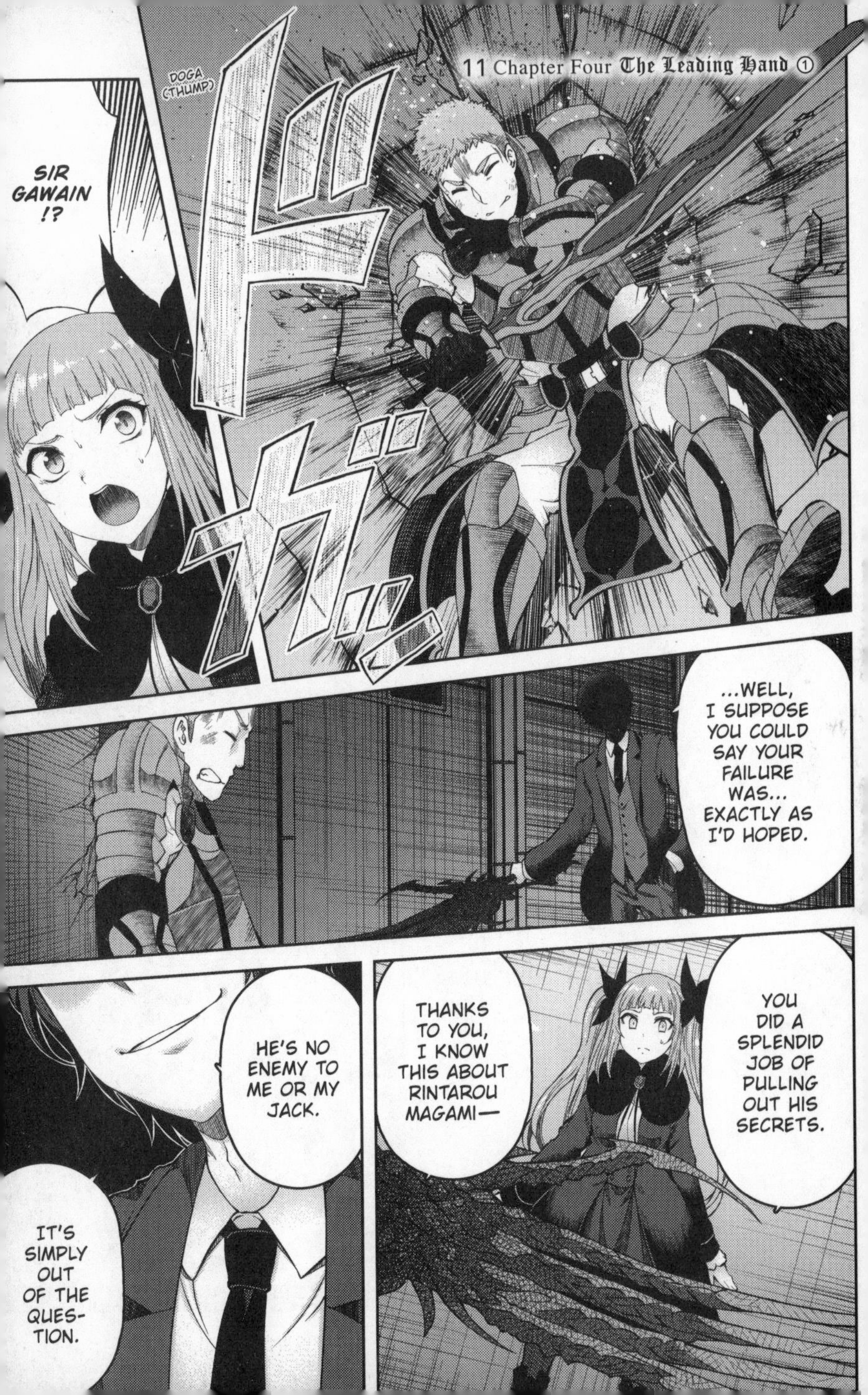
DOGA (THUMP)
SIR GAWAIN !?
...WELL, I SUPPOSE YOU COULD SAY YOUR FAILURE WAS... EXACTLY AS I'D HOPED.
YOU DID A SPLENDID JOB OF PULLING OUT HIS SECRETS.
THANKS TO YOU, I KNOW THIS ABOUT RINTAROU MAGAMI—
HE'S NO ENEMY TO ME OR MY JACK.
IT'S SIMPLY OUT OF THE QUES-TION.

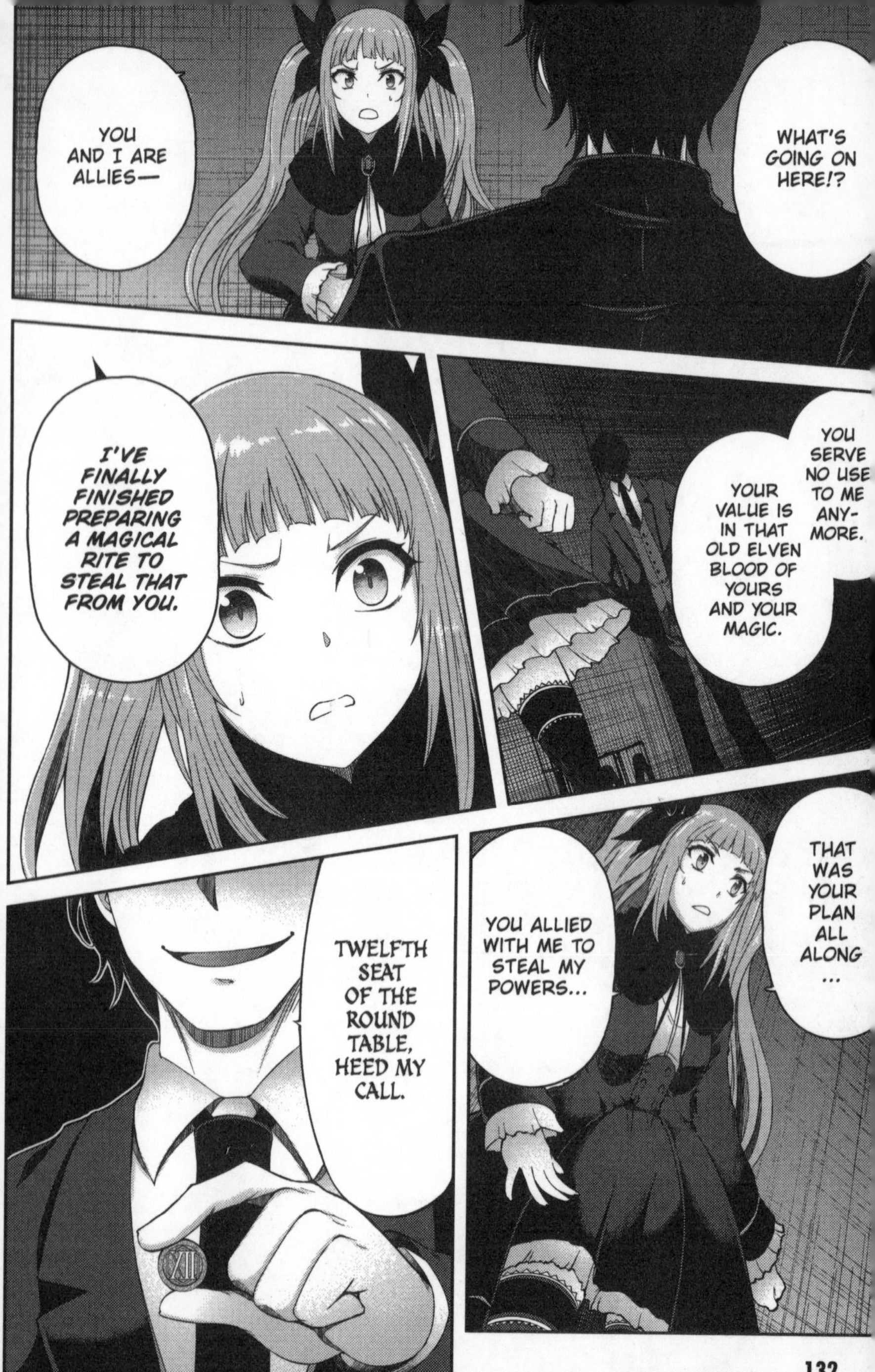
WHAT'S GOING ON HERE!?
YOU AND I ARE ALLIES—
YOU SERVE NO USE TO ME ANY-MORE.
YOUR VALUE IS IN THAT OLD ELVEN BLOOD OF YOURS AND YOUR MAGIC.
I'VE FINALLY FINISHED PREPARING A MAGICAL RITE TO STEAL THAT FROM YOU.
THAT WAS YOUR PLAN ALL ALONG...
YOU ALLIED WITH ME TO STEAL MY POWERS...
TWELFTH SEAT OF THE ROUND TABLE, HEED MY CALL.
XII

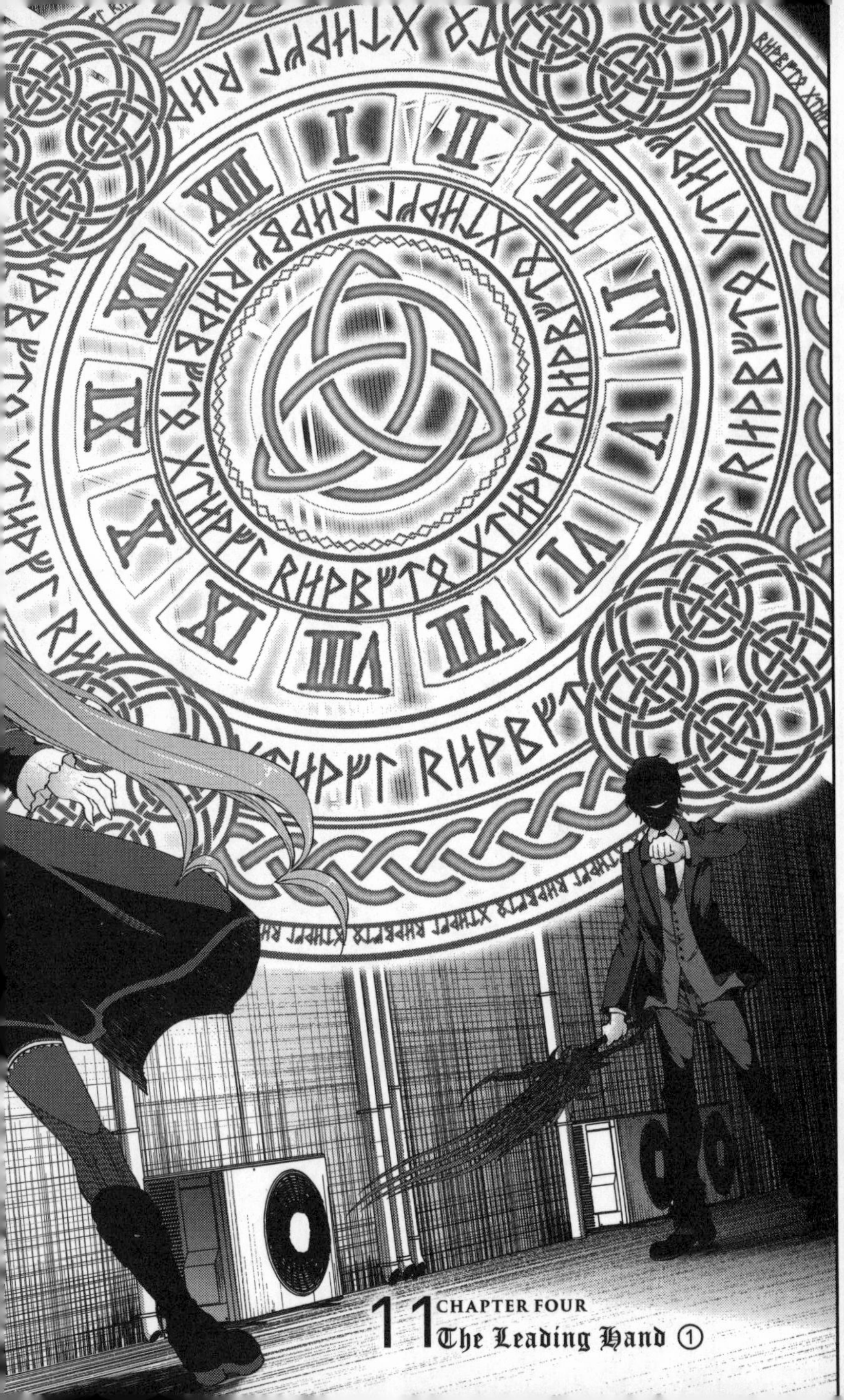
11 CHAPTER FOUR
The Leading Hand ①

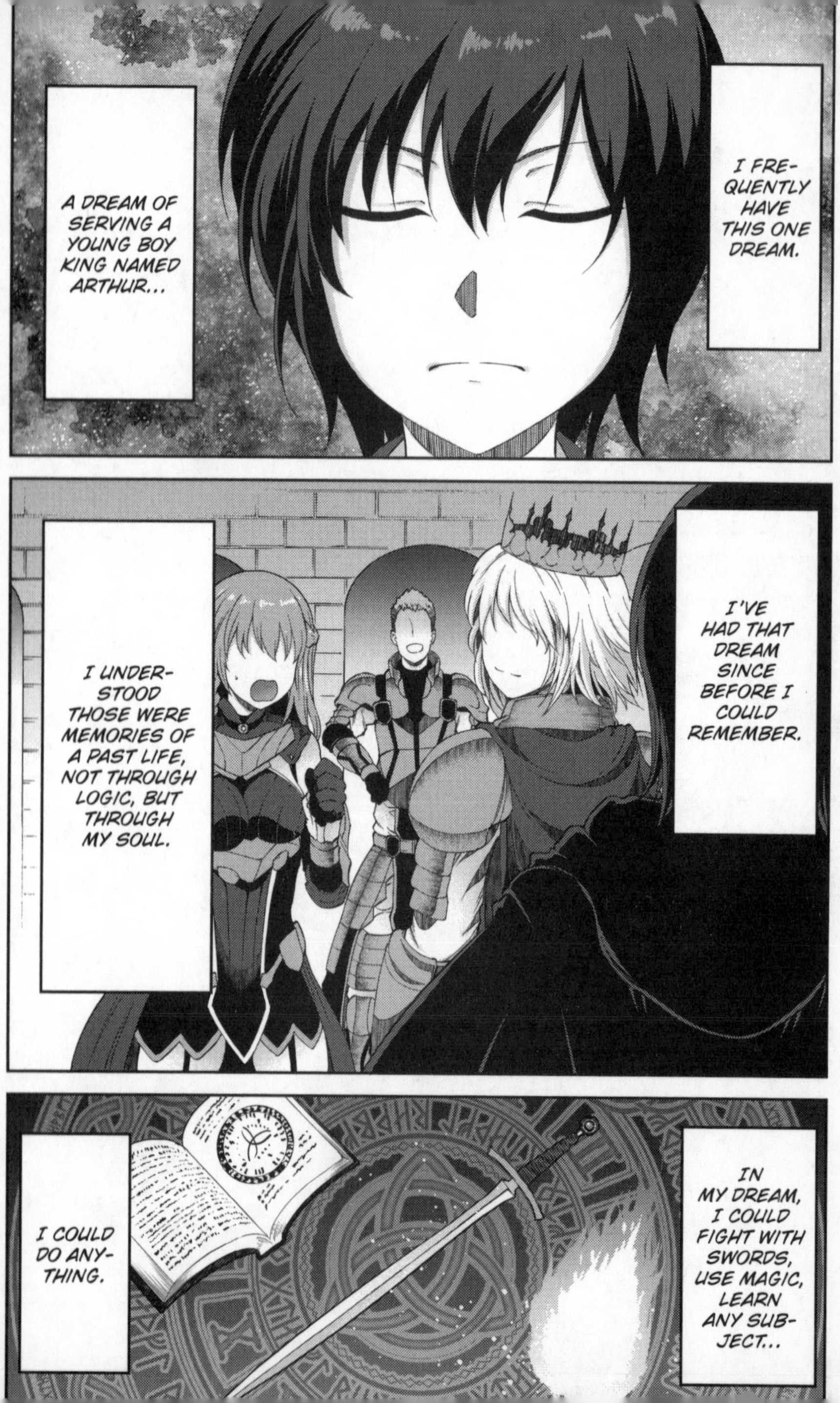
I FREQUENTLY HAVE THIS ONE DREAM.
A DREAM OF SERVING A YOUNG BOY KING NAMED ARTHUR...
I'VE HAD THAT DREAM SINCE BEFORE I COULD REMEMBER.
I UNDERSTOOD THOSE WERE MEMORIES OF A PAST LIFE, NOT THROUGH LOGIC, BUT THROUGH MY SOUL.
IN MY DREAM, I COULD FIGHT WITH SWORDS, USE MAGIC, LEARN ANY SUBJECT...
I COULD DO ANYTHING.

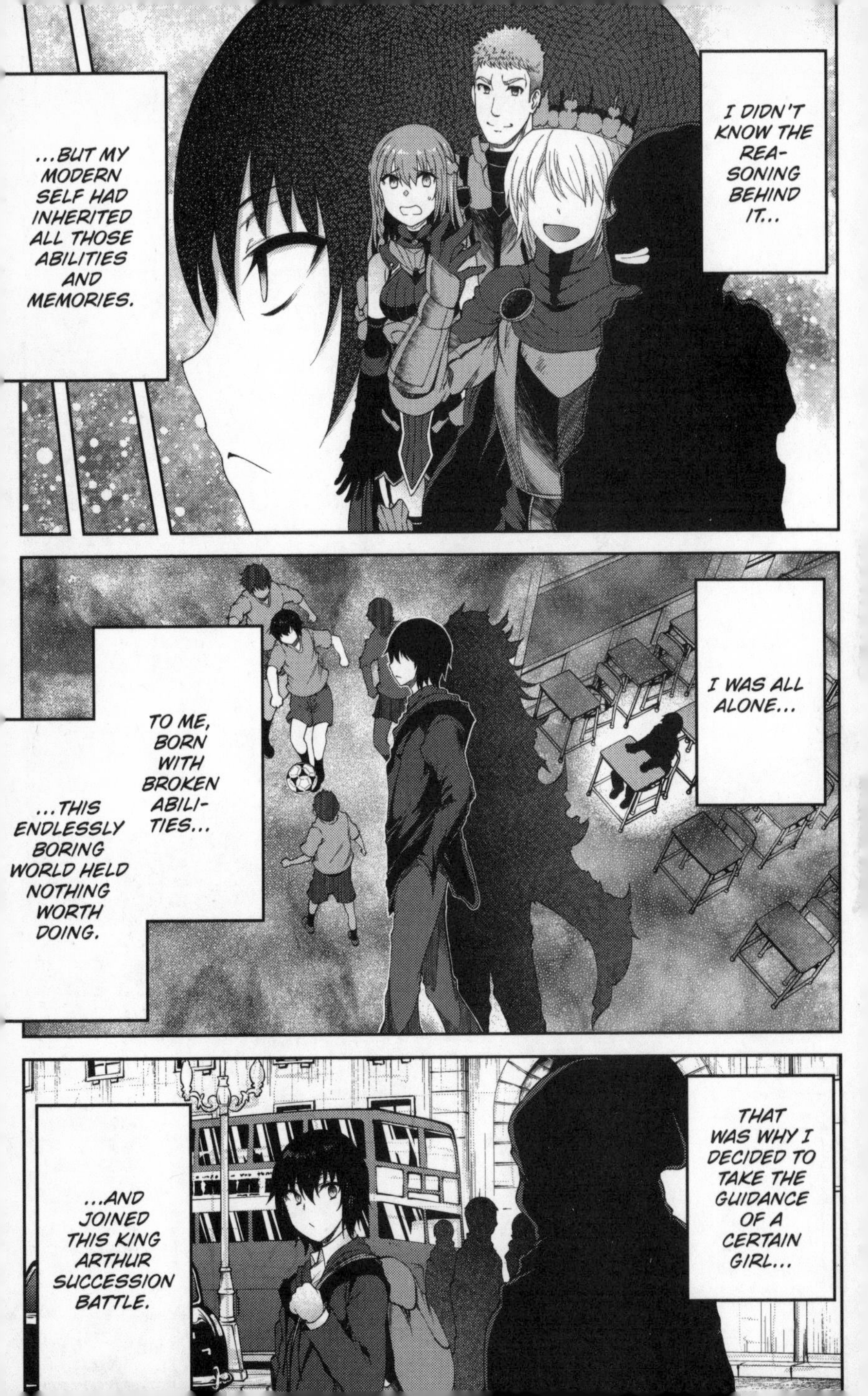
I DIDN'T KNOW THE REA-SONING BEHIND IT...
...BUT MY MODERN SELF HAD INHERITED ALL THOSE ABILITIES AND MEMORIES.
I WAS ALL ALONE...
TO ME, BORN WITH BROKEN ABILI-TIES...
...THIS ENDLESSLY BORING WORLD HELD NOTHING WORTH DOING.
THAT WAS WHY I DECIDED TO TAKE THE GUIDANCE OF A CERTAIN GIRL...
...AND JOINED THIS KING ARTHUR SUCCESSION BATTLE.

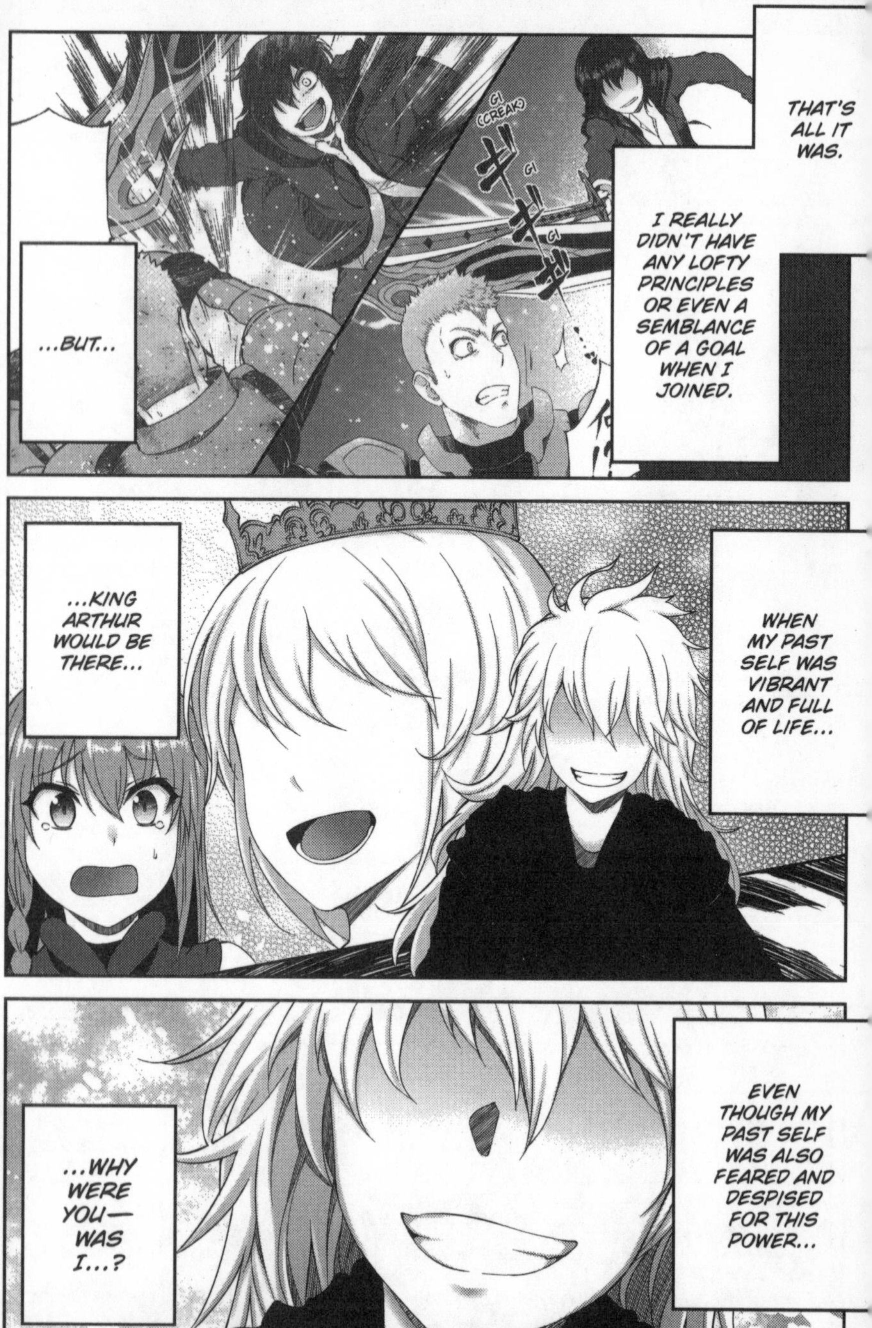
THAT'S ALL IT WAS.
I REALLY DIDN'T HAVE ANY LOFTY PRINCIPLES OR EVEN A SEMBLANCE OF A GOAL WHEN I JOINED.
GI (CREAK)
GI
GI
...BUT...
WHEN MY PAST SELF WAS VIBRANT AND FULL OF LIFE...
...KING ARTHUR WOULD BE THERE...
EVEN THOUGH MY PAST SELF WAS ALSO FEARED AND DESPISED FOR THIS POWER...
...WHY WERE YOU—WAS I...?

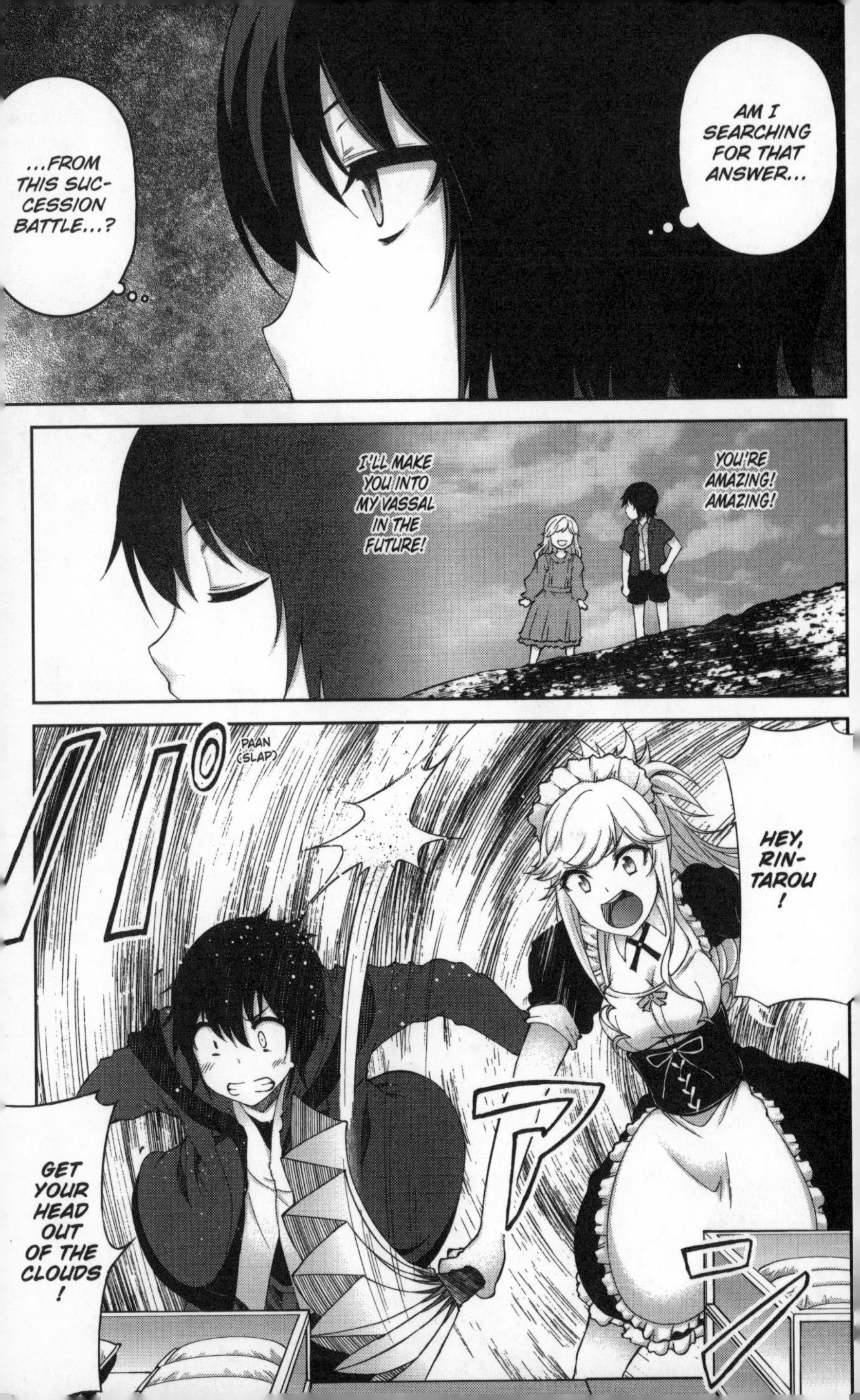
AM I SEARCHING FOR THAT ANSWER...
...FROM THIS SUCCESSION BATTLE...?
YOU'RE AMAZING! AMAZING!
I'LL MAKE YOU INTO MY VASSAL IN THE FUTURE!
HEY, RINTAROU!
PAAN (SLAP)
GET YOUR HEAD OUT OF THE CLOUDS!

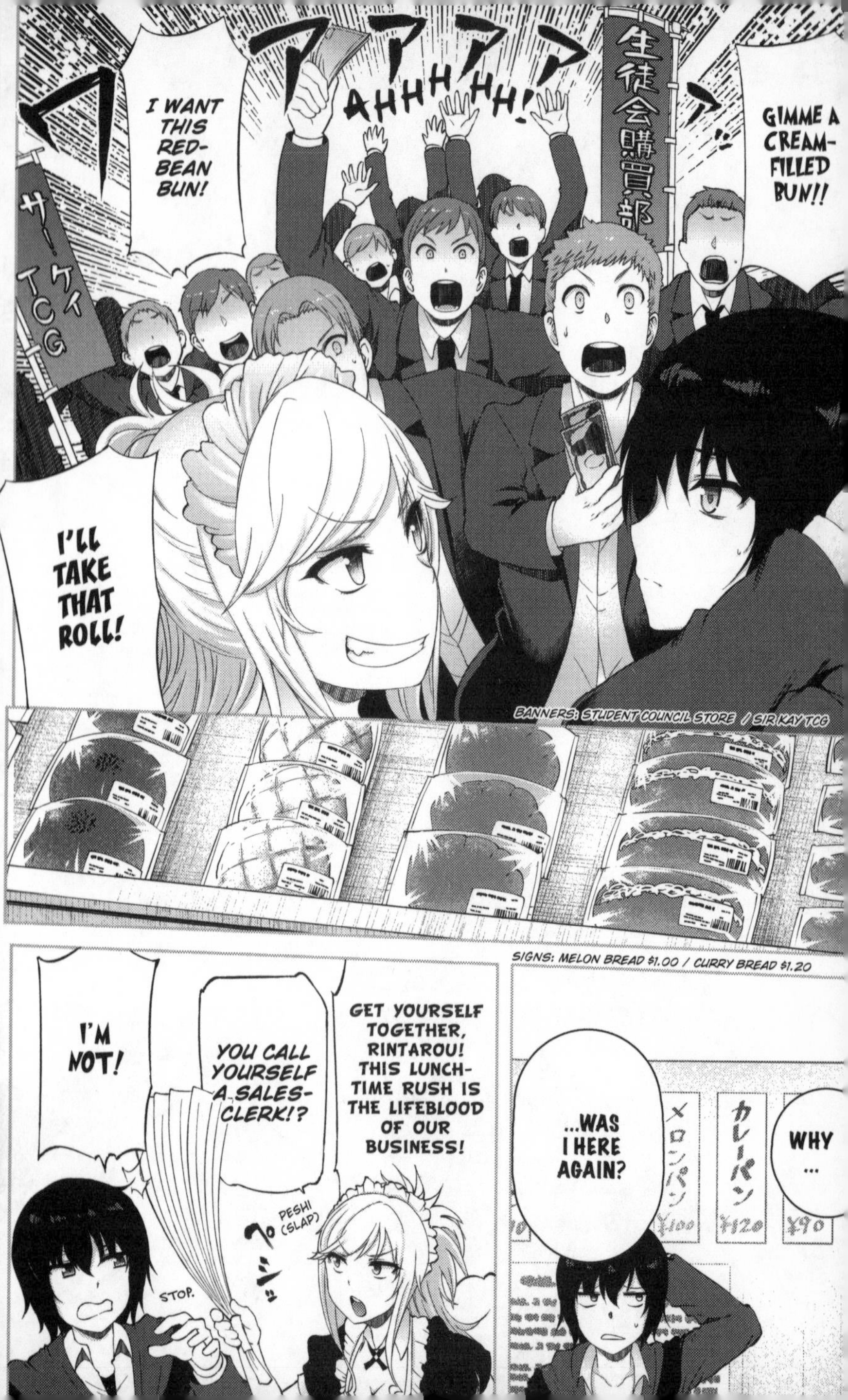
アアアアア
GIMME A CREAM-FILLED BUN!!
生徒会購買部
AHHHHHH!
I WANT THIS RED-BEAN BUN!
サー・ケイ TCG
I'LL TAKE THAT ROLL!
BANNERS: STUDENT COUNCIL STORE / SIR KAY TCG
SIGNS: MELON BREAD $1.00 / CURRY BREAD $1.20
WHY ...
...WAS I HERE AGAIN?
カレーパン ¥120
メロンパン ¥100
¥90
GET YOURSELF TOGETHER, RINTAROU! THIS LUNCH-TIME RUSH IS THE LIFEBLOOD OF OUR BUSINESS!
YOU CALL YOURSELF A SALES-CLERK!?
PESHI (SLAP)
I'M NOT!
STOP.

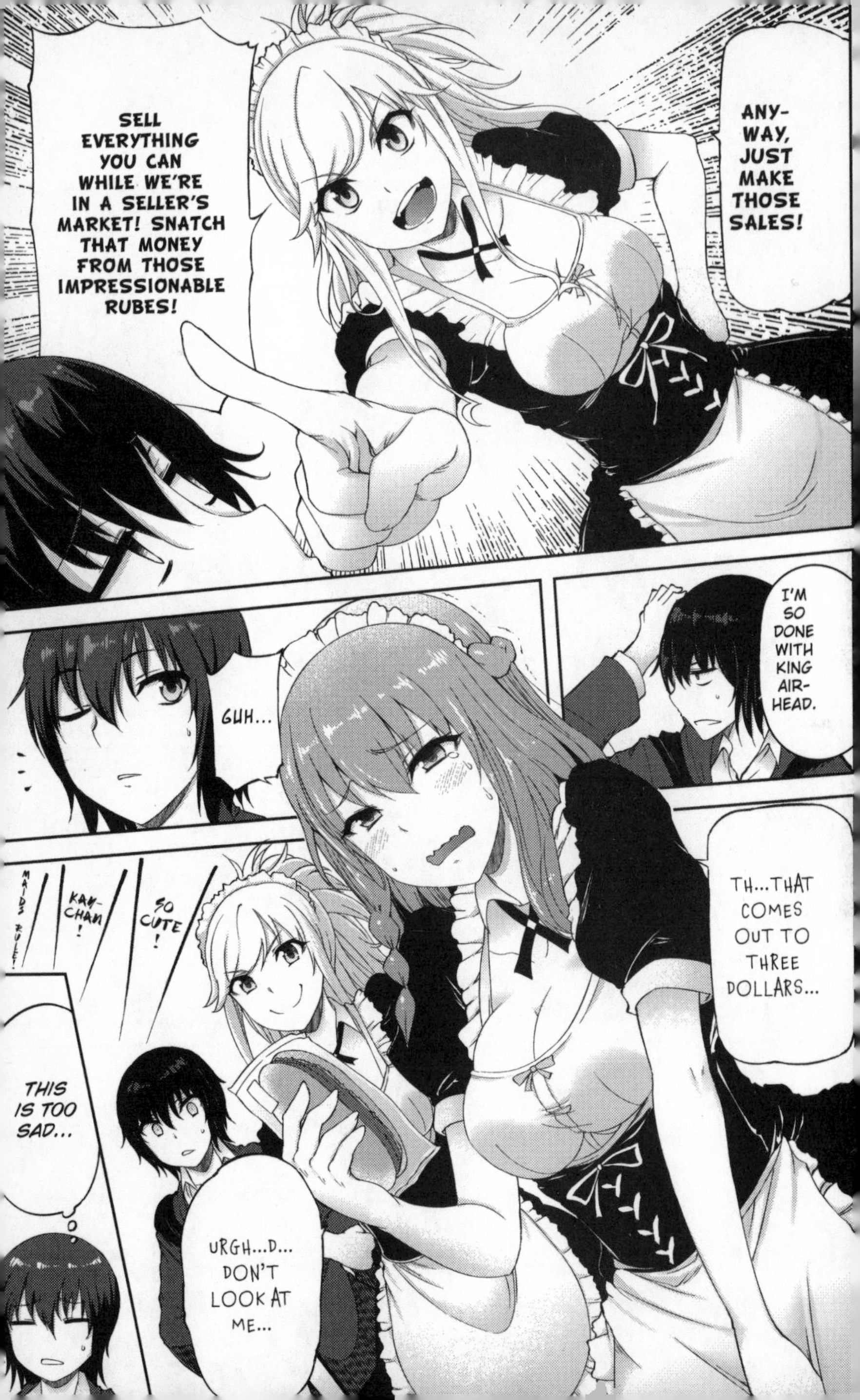
ANY-WAY, JUST MAKE THOSE SALES!
SELL EVERYTHING YOU CAN WHILE WE'RE IN A SELLER'S MARKET! SNATCH THAT MONEY FROM THOSE IMPRESSIONABLE RUBES!
I'M SO DONE WITH KING AIR-HEAD.
GUH...
TH...THAT COMES OUT TO THREE DOLLARS...
SO CUTE!
KAY-CHAN!
MAIDS RULE!
URGH...D... DON'T LOOK AT ME...
THIS IS TOO SAD...

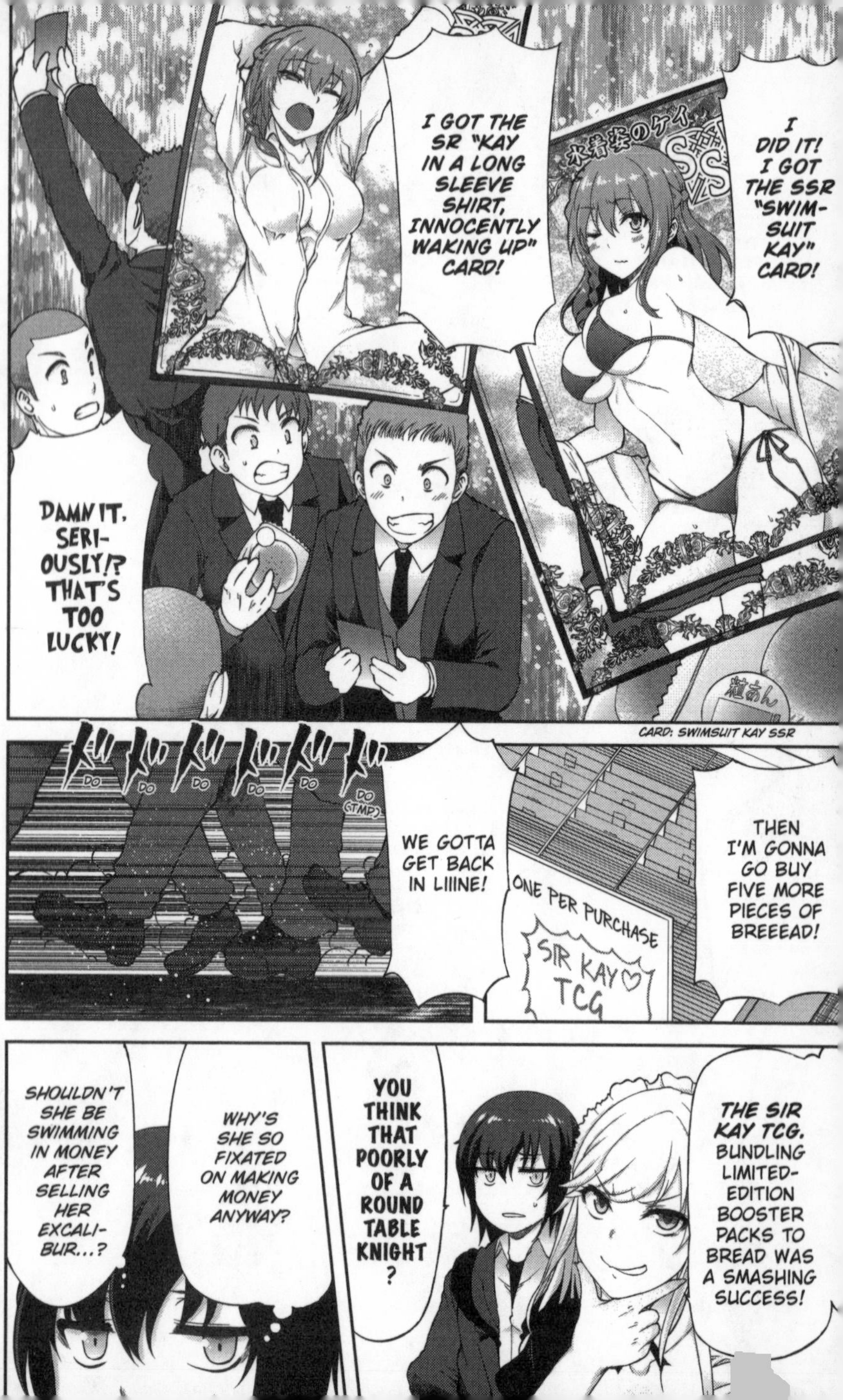
I DID IT! I GOT THE SSR "SWIMSUIT KAY" CARD!
水着姿のケイ
SSR
I GOT THE SR "KAY IN A LONG SLEEVE SHIRT, INNOCENTLY WAKING UP" CARD!
DAMN IT. SERIOUSLY!? THAT'S TOO LUCKY!
CARD: SWIMSUIT KAY SSR
THEN I'M GONNA GO BUY FIVE MORE PIECES OF BREEEAD!
ONE PER PURCHASE
SIR KAY♡ TCG
WE GOTTA GET BACK IN LIIINE!
DO DO DO DO DO DO (TMP)
THE SIR KAY TCG. BUNDLING LIMITED-EDITION BOOSTER PACKS TO BREAD WAS A SMASHING SUCCESS!
YOU THINK THAT POORLY OF A ROUND TABLE KNIGHT?
WHY'S SHE SO FIXATED ON MAKING MONEY ANYWAY?
SHOULDN'T SHE BE SWIMMING IN MONEY AFTER SELLING HER EXCALIBUR...?

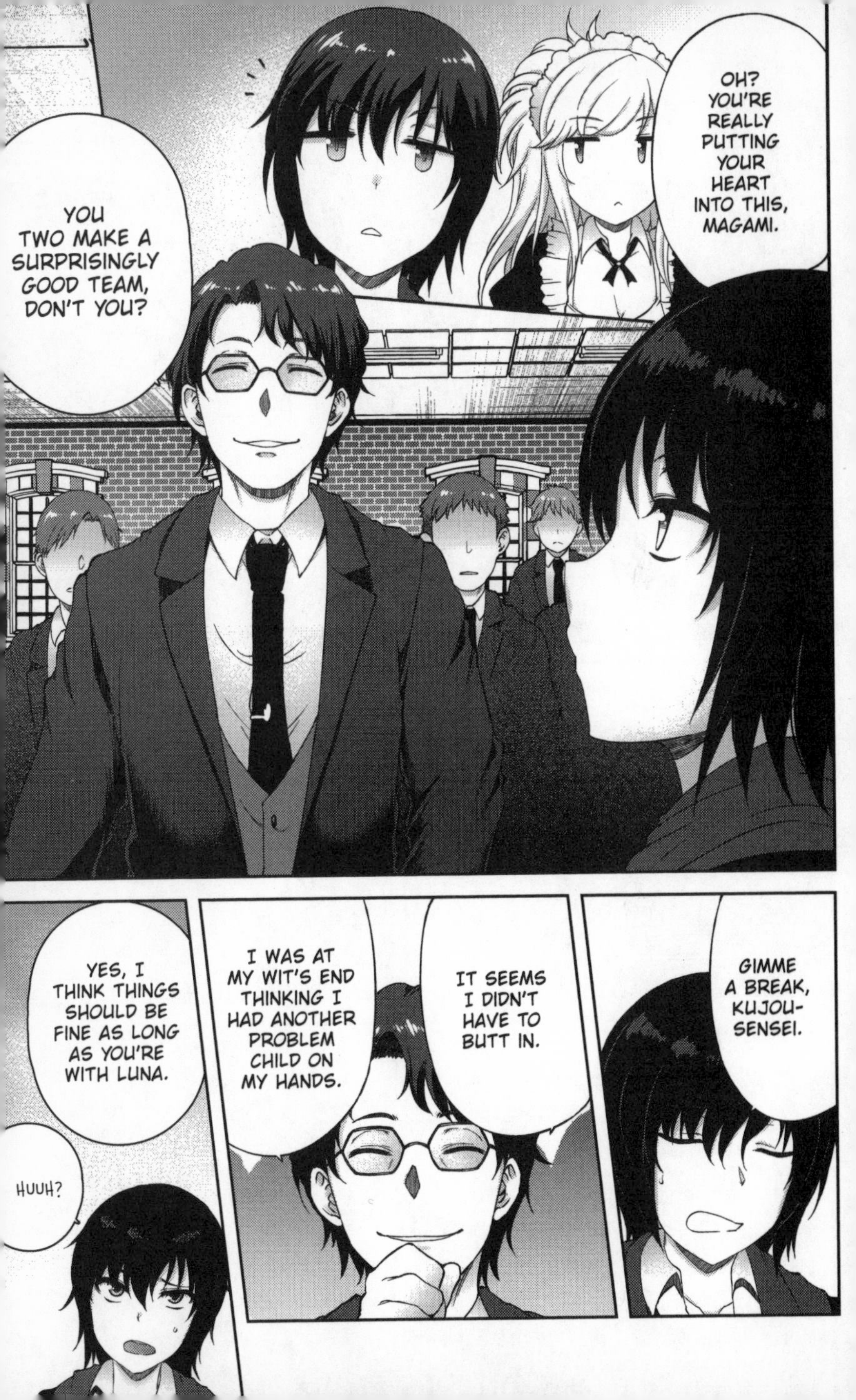
OH? YOU'RE REALLY PUTTING YOUR HEART INTO THIS, MAGAMI.
YOU TWO MAKE A SURPRISINGLY GOOD TEAM, DON'T YOU?
GIMME A BREAK, KUJOU-SENSEI.
IT SEEMS I DIDN'T HAVE TO BUTT IN.
I WAS AT MY WIT'S END THINKING I HAD ANOTHER PROBLEM CHILD ON MY HANDS.
YES, I THINK THINGS SHOULD BE FINE AS LONG AS YOU'RE WITH LUNA.
HUUH?

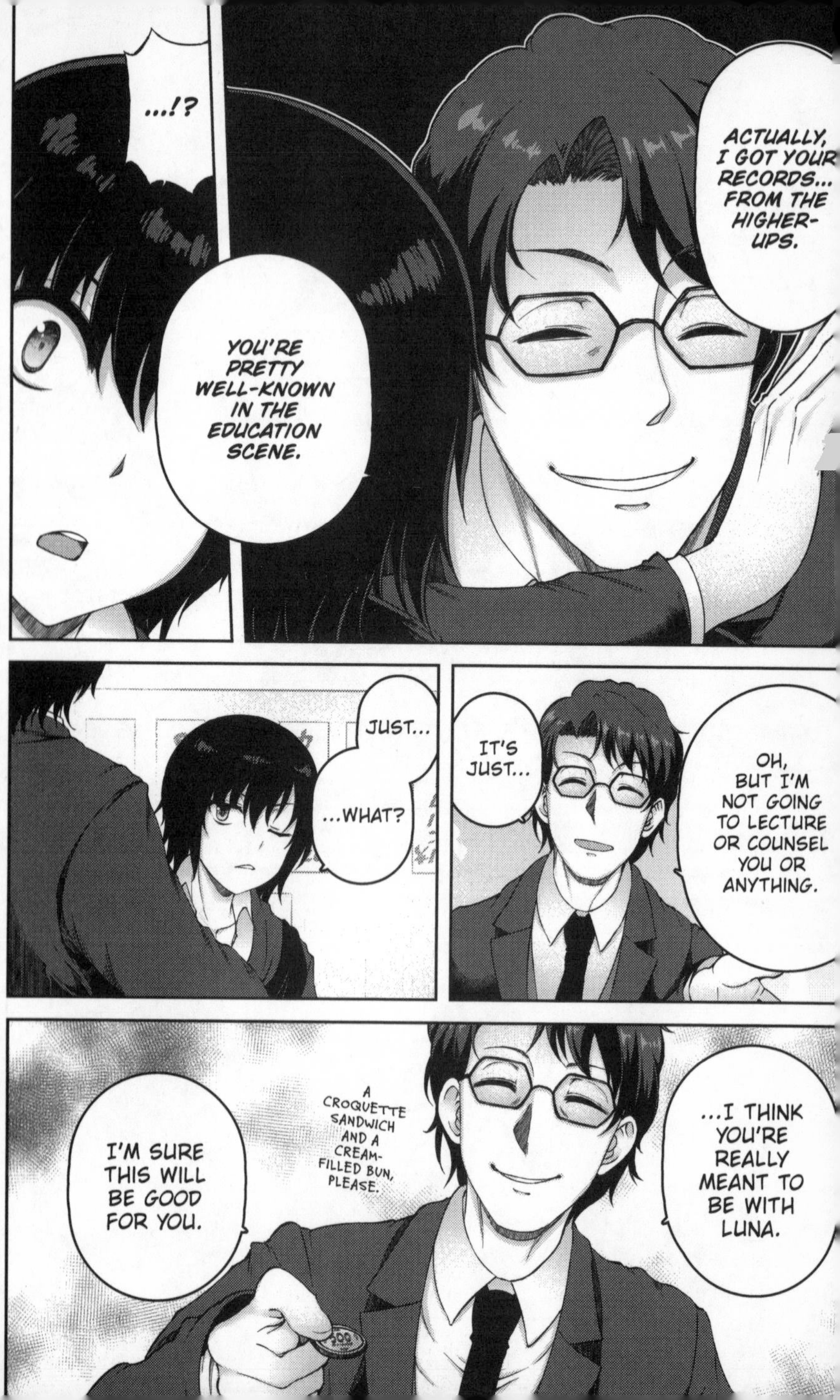
ACTUALLY, I GOT YOUR RECORDS... FROM THE HIGHER-UPS.
YOU'RE PRETTY WELL-KNOWN IN THE EDUCATION SCENE.
...!?
OH, BUT I'M NOT GOING TO LECTURE OR COUNSEL YOU OR ANYTHING.
IT'S JUST...
JUST...
...WHAT?
...I THINK YOU'RE REALLY MEANT TO BE WITH LUNA.
A CROQUETTE SANDWICH AND A CREAM-FILLED BUN, PLEASE.
I'M SURE THIS WILL BE GOOD FOR YOU.

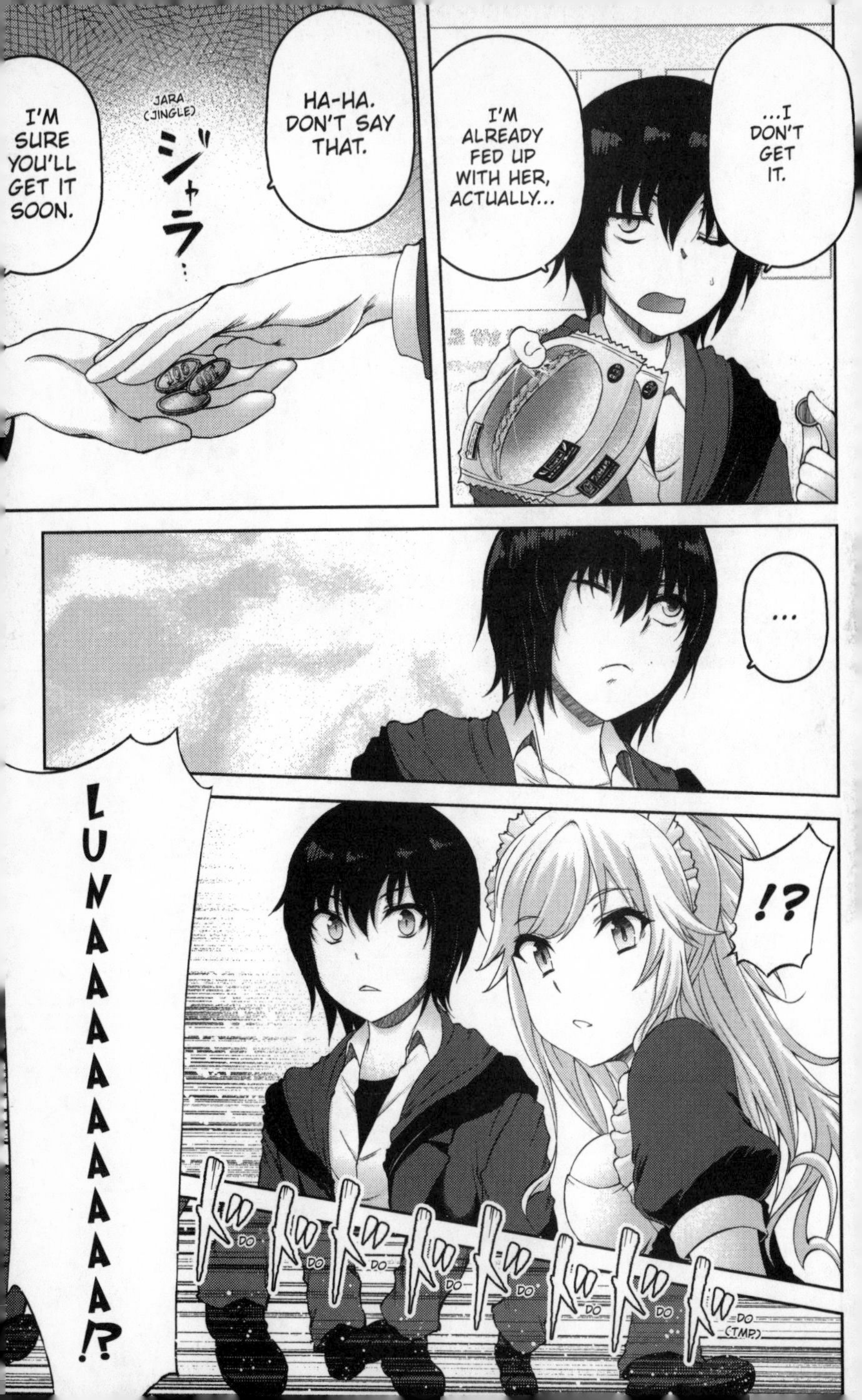
...I DON'T GET IT.
I'M ALREADY FED UP WITH HER, ACTUALLY...
HA-HA. DON'T SAY THAT.
ジャラ…
JARA (JINGLE)
I'M SURE YOU'LL GET IT SOON.
...
LUNAAAAAAAAAAAA!?
!?
ドッドッドッドッドッドッドッドッド
DO DO DO DO DO DO DO DO DO (TMP)

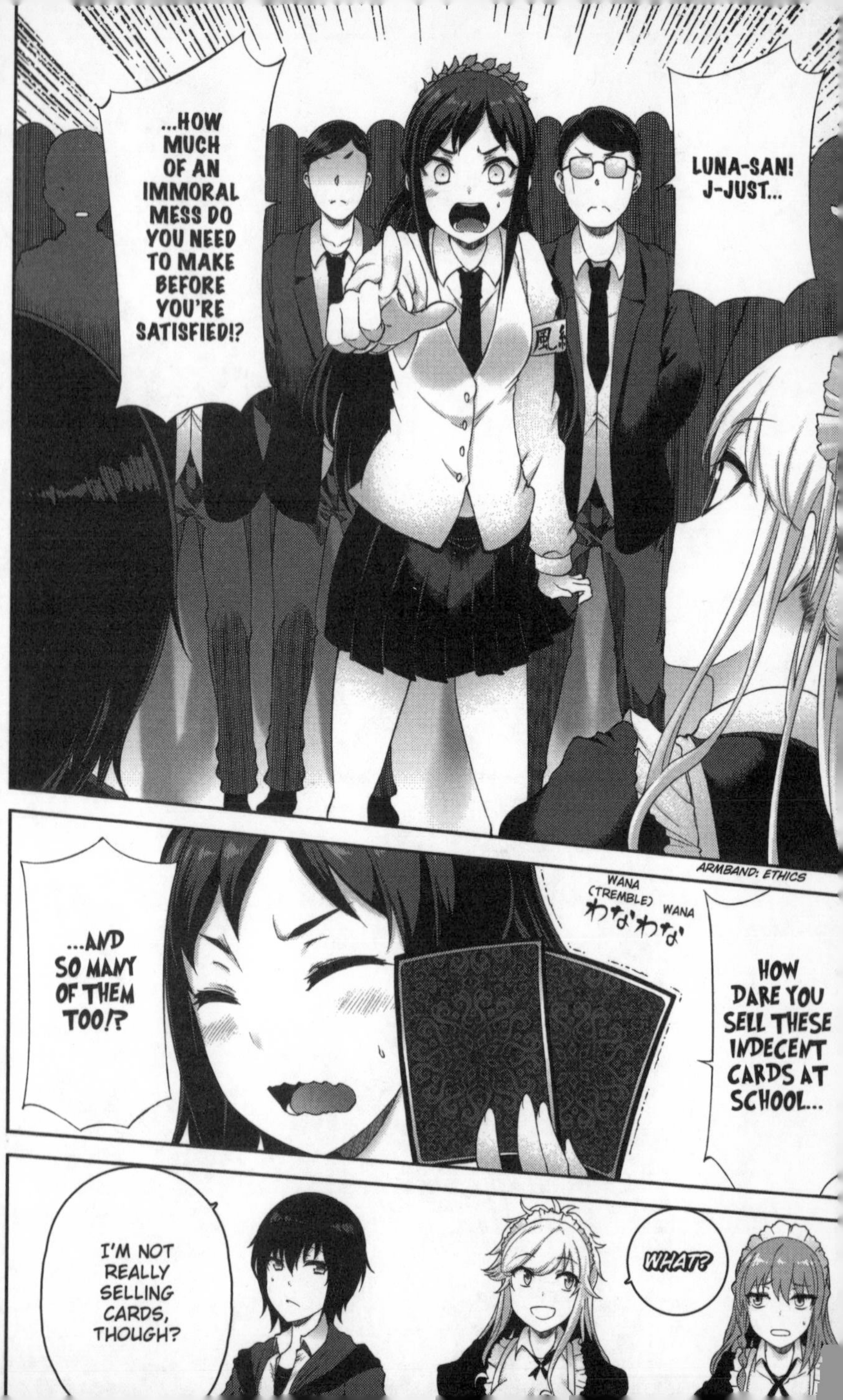
LUNA-SAN! J-JUST...
...HOW MUCH OF AN IMMORAL MESS DO YOU NEED TO MAKE BEFORE YOU'RE SATISFIED!?
ARMBAND: ETHICS
HOW DARE YOU SELL THESE INDECENT CARDS AT SCHOOL...
WANA (TREMBLE) WANA
わなわな
...AND SO MANY OF THEM TOO!?
WHAT?
I'M NOT REALLY SELLING CARDS, THOUGH?

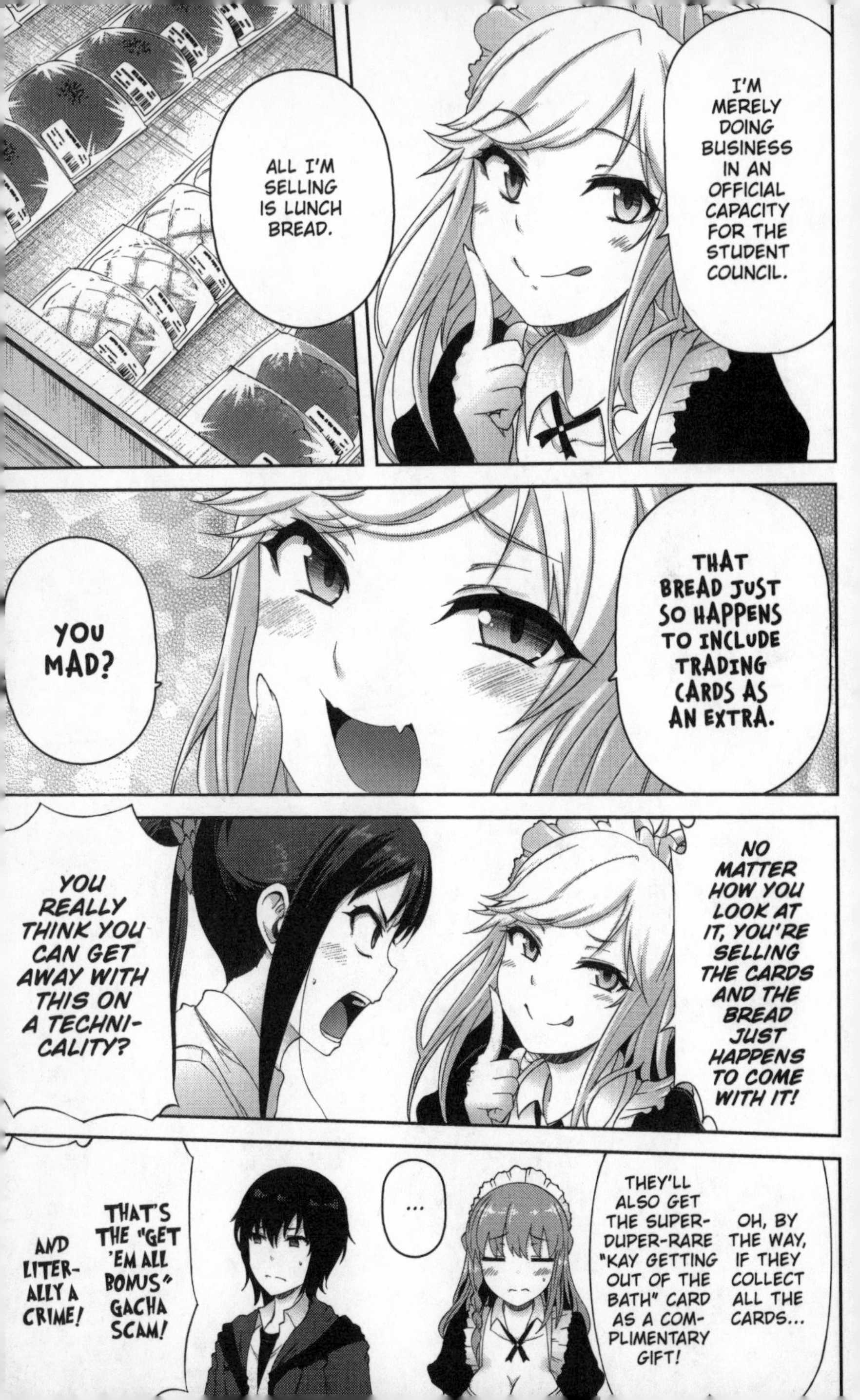
I'M MERELY DOING BUSINESS IN AN OFFICIAL CAPACITY FOR THE STUDENT COUNCIL.
ALL I'M SELLING IS LUNCH BREAD.
THAT BREAD JUST SO HAPPENS TO INCLUDE TRADING CARDS AS AN EXTRA.
YOU MAD?
NO MATTER HOW YOU LOOK AT IT, YOU'RE SELLING THE CARDS AND THE BREAD JUST HAPPENS TO COME WITH IT!
YOU REALLY THINK YOU CAN GET AWAY WITH THIS ON A TECHNI-CALITY?
OH, BY THE WAY, IF THEY COLLECT ALL THE CARDS...
THEY'LL ALSO GET THE SUPER-DUPER-RARE "KAY GETTING OUT OF THE BATH" CARD AS A COM-PLIMENTARY GIFT!
...
THAT'S THE "GET 'EM ALL BONUS" GACHA SCAM!
AND LITER-ALLY A CRIME!

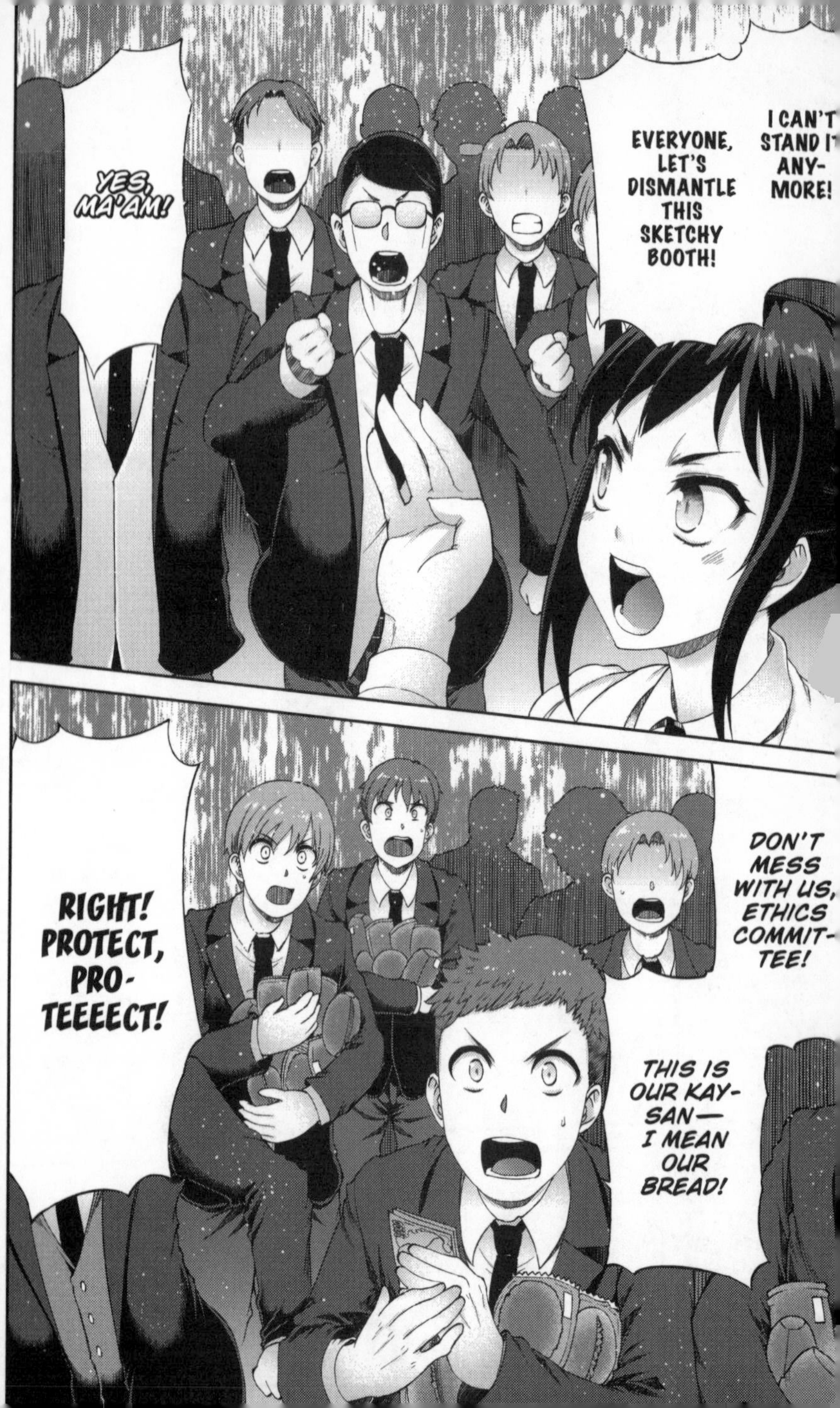
I CAN'T STAND IT ANY-MORE!
EVERYONE, LET'S DISMANTLE THIS SKETCHY BOOTH!
YES, MA'AM!
DON'T MESS WITH US, ETHICS COMMIT-TEE!
THIS IS OUR KAY-SAN— I MEAN OUR BREAD!
RIGHT! PROTECT, PRO-TEEEECT!

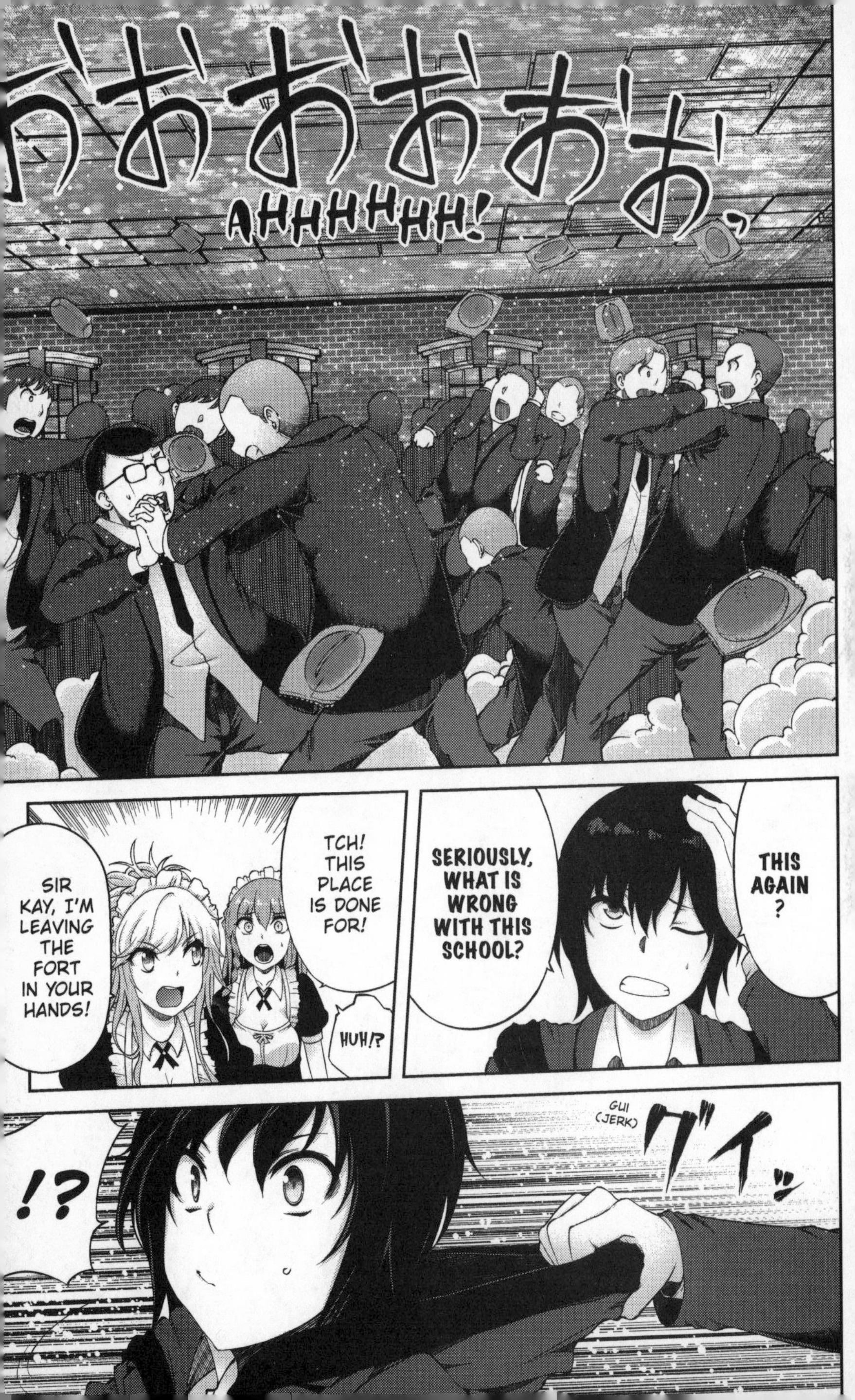
うおおおおおっ
AHHHHHHH!
THIS AGAIN ?
SERIOUSLY, WHAT IS WRONG WITH THIS SCHOOL?
TCH! THIS PLACE IS DONE FOR!
HUH!?
SIR KAY, I'M LEAVING THE FORT IN YOUR HANDS!
GUI (JERK)
グイッ
!?

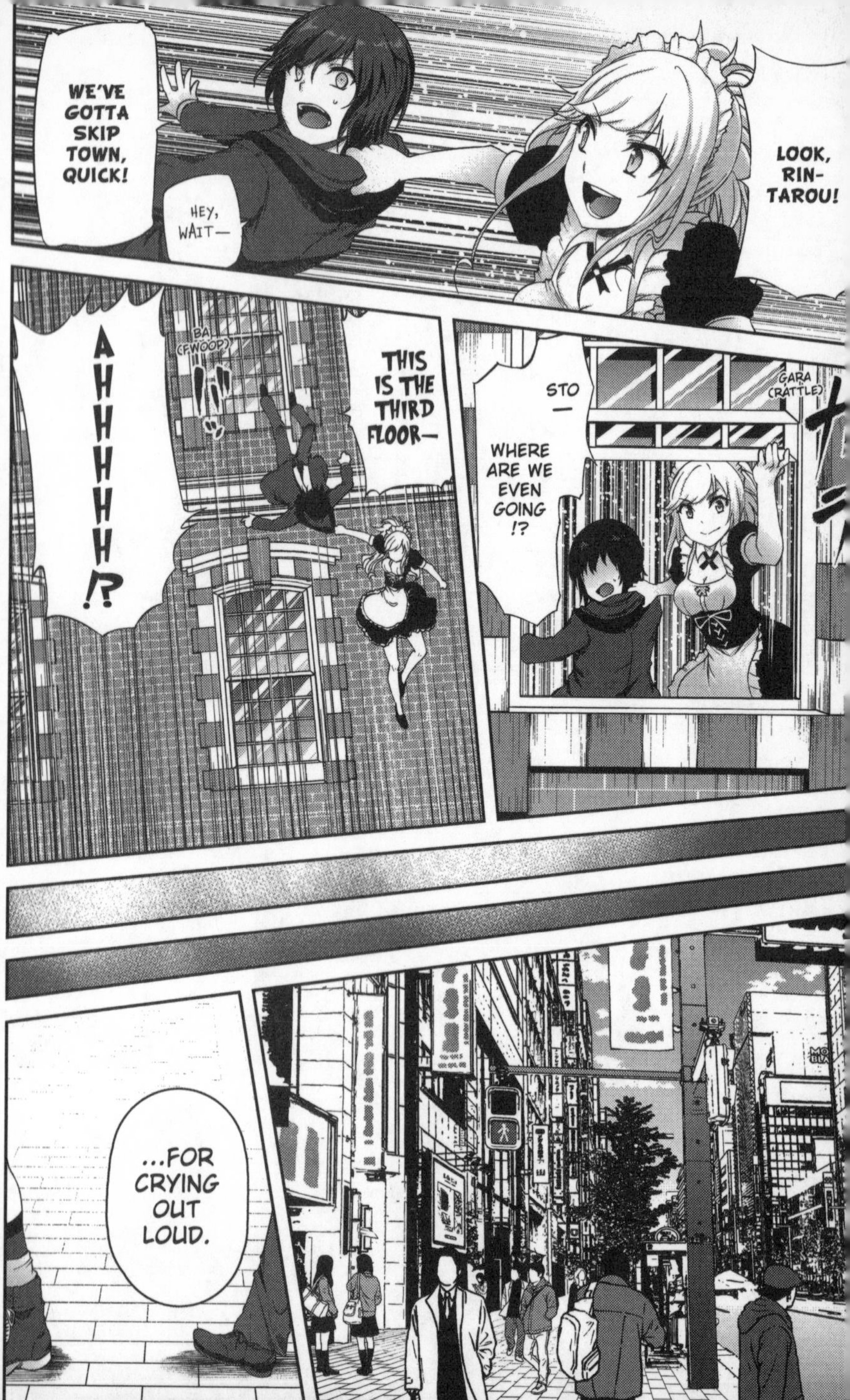
LOOK, RIN-TAROU!
WE'VE GOTTA SKIP TOWN, QUICK!
HEY, WAIT—
GARA (RATTLE)
STO—
WHERE ARE WE EVEN GOING!?
THIS IS THE THIRD FLOOR—
BA (FWOOP)
AHHHHHHH!?
...FOR CRYING OUT LOUD.

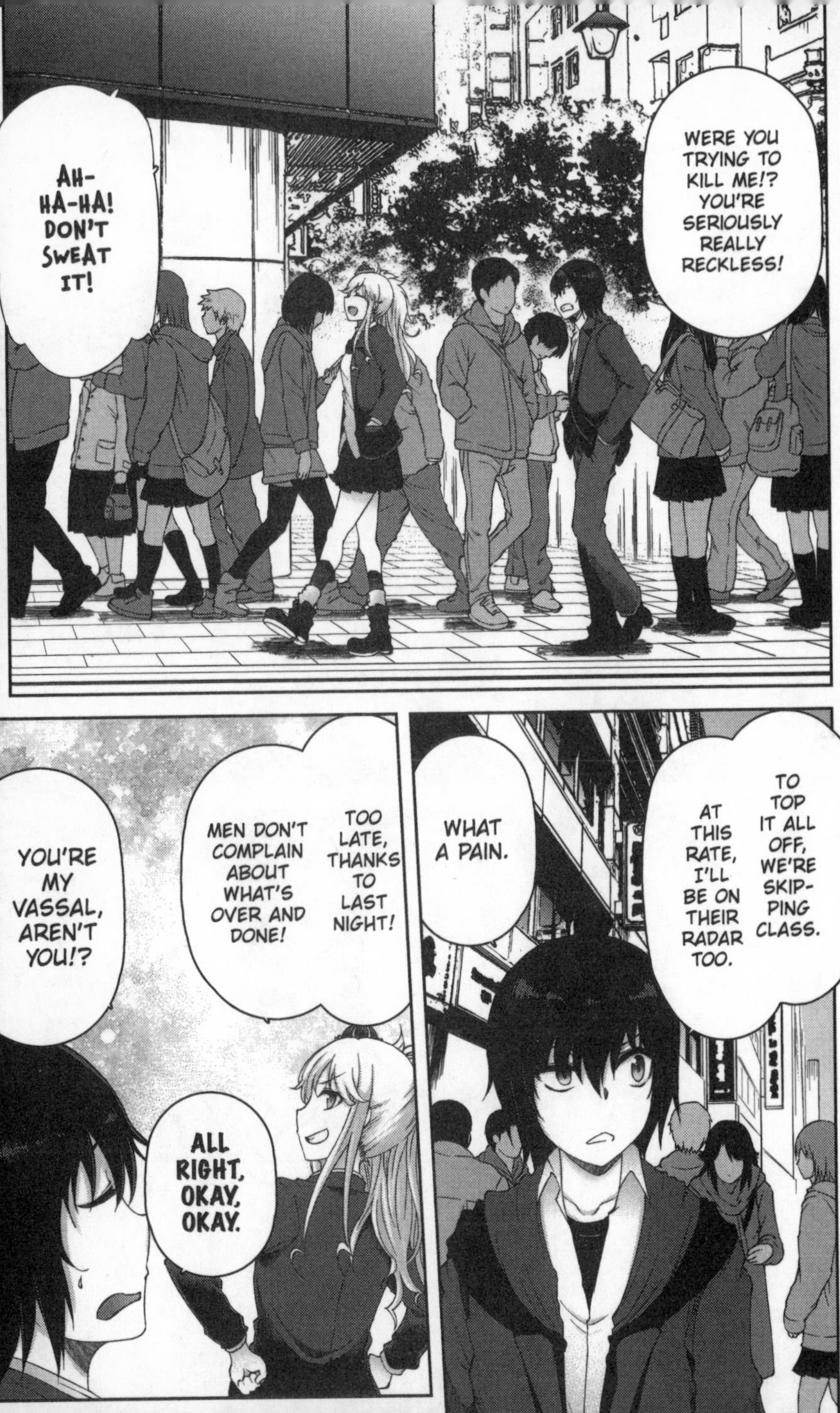
WERE YOU TRYING TO KILL ME!? YOU'RE SERIOUSLY REALLY RECKLESS!
AH-HA-HA! DON'T SWEAT IT!
TO TOP IT ALL OFF, WE'RE SKIP-PING CLASS.
AT THIS RATE, I'LL BE ON THEIR RADAR TOO.
WHAT A PAIN.
TOO LATE, THANKS TO LAST NIGHT!
MEN DON'T COMPLAIN ABOUT WHAT'S OVER AND DONE!
YOU'RE MY VASSAL, AREN'T YOU!?
ALL RIGHT, OKAY, OKAY.

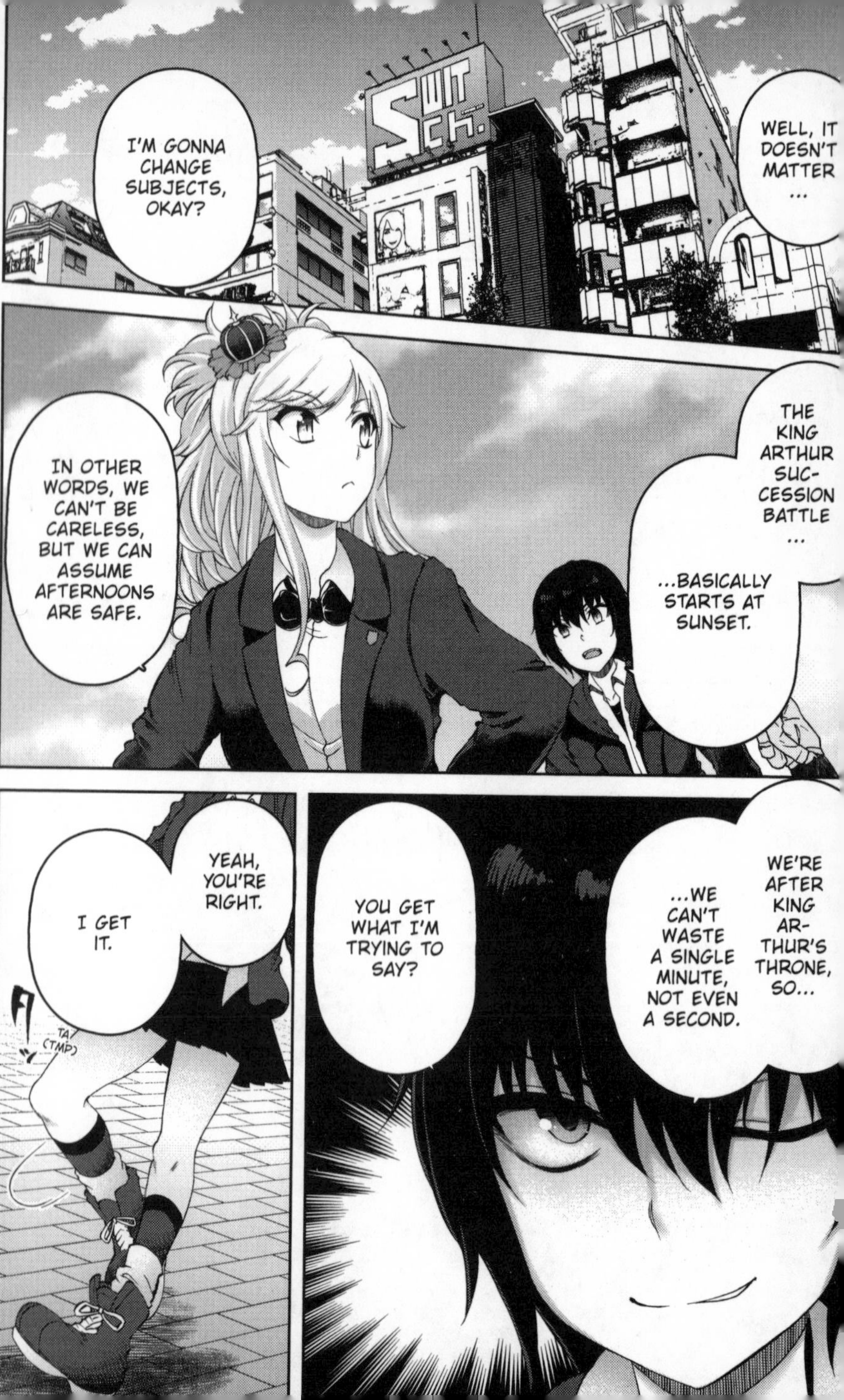
WELL, IT DOESN'T MATTER ...
I'M GONNA CHANGE SUBJECTS, OKAY?
THE KING ARTHUR SUC-CESSION BATTLE ...
...BASICALLY STARTS AT SUNSET.
IN OTHER WORDS, WE CAN'T BE CARELESS, BUT WE CAN ASSUME AFTERNOONS ARE SAFE.
WE'RE AFTER KING AR-THUR'S THRONE, SO...
...WE CAN'T WASTE A SINGLE MINUTE, NOT EVEN A SECOND.
YOU GET WHAT I'M TRYING TO SAY?
YEAH, YOU'RE RIGHT.
I GET IT.
TA (TMP)

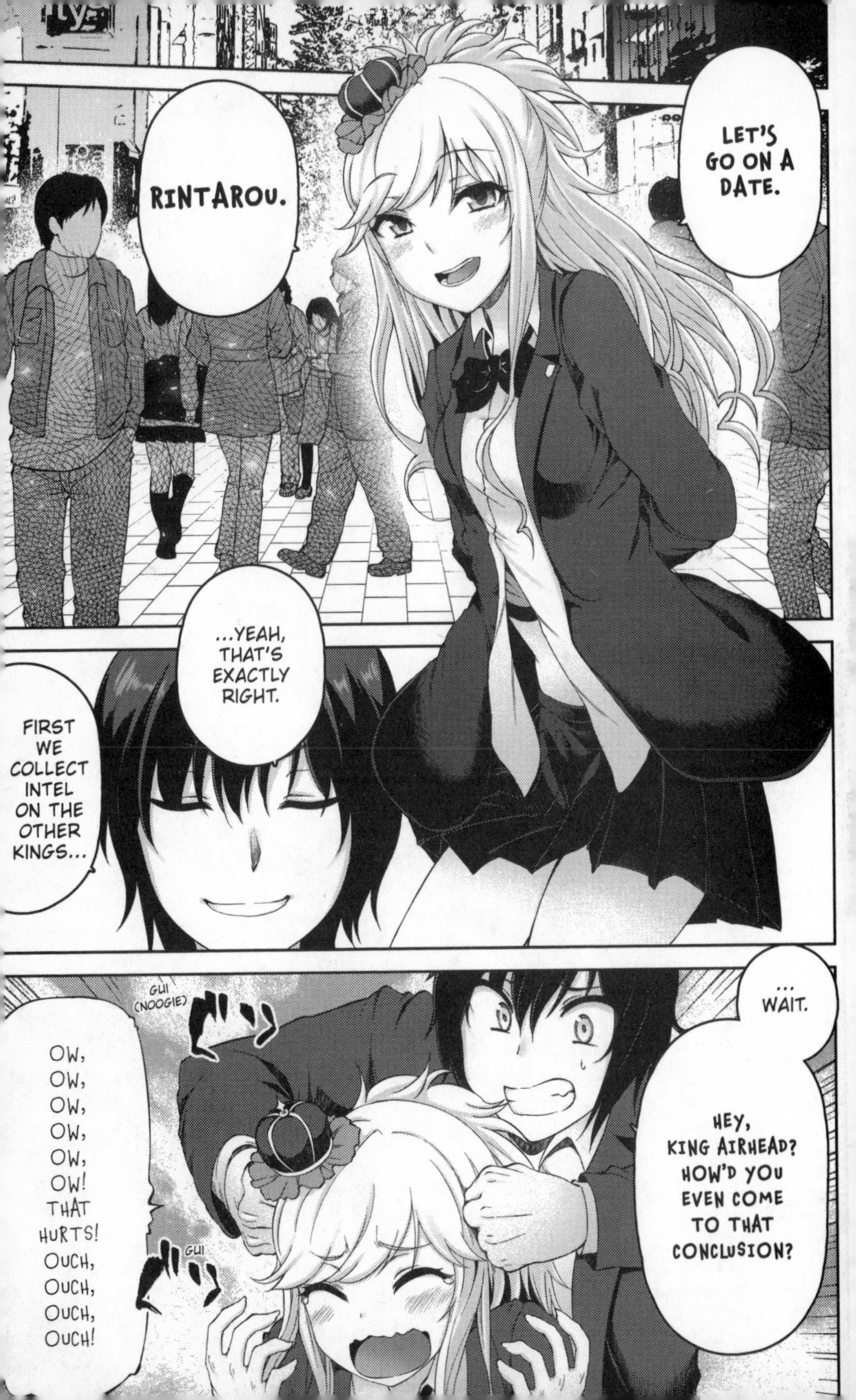
LET'S GO ON A DATE.
RINTAROU.
...YEAH, THAT'S EXACTLY RIGHT.
FIRST WE COLLECT INTEL ON THE OTHER KINGS...
... WAIT.
HEY, KING AIRHEAD? HOW'D YOU EVEN COME TO THAT CONCLUSION?
GUI (NOOGIE)
OW, OW, OW, OW, OW, OW! THAT HURTS! OUCH, OUCH, OUCH, OUCH!
GUI

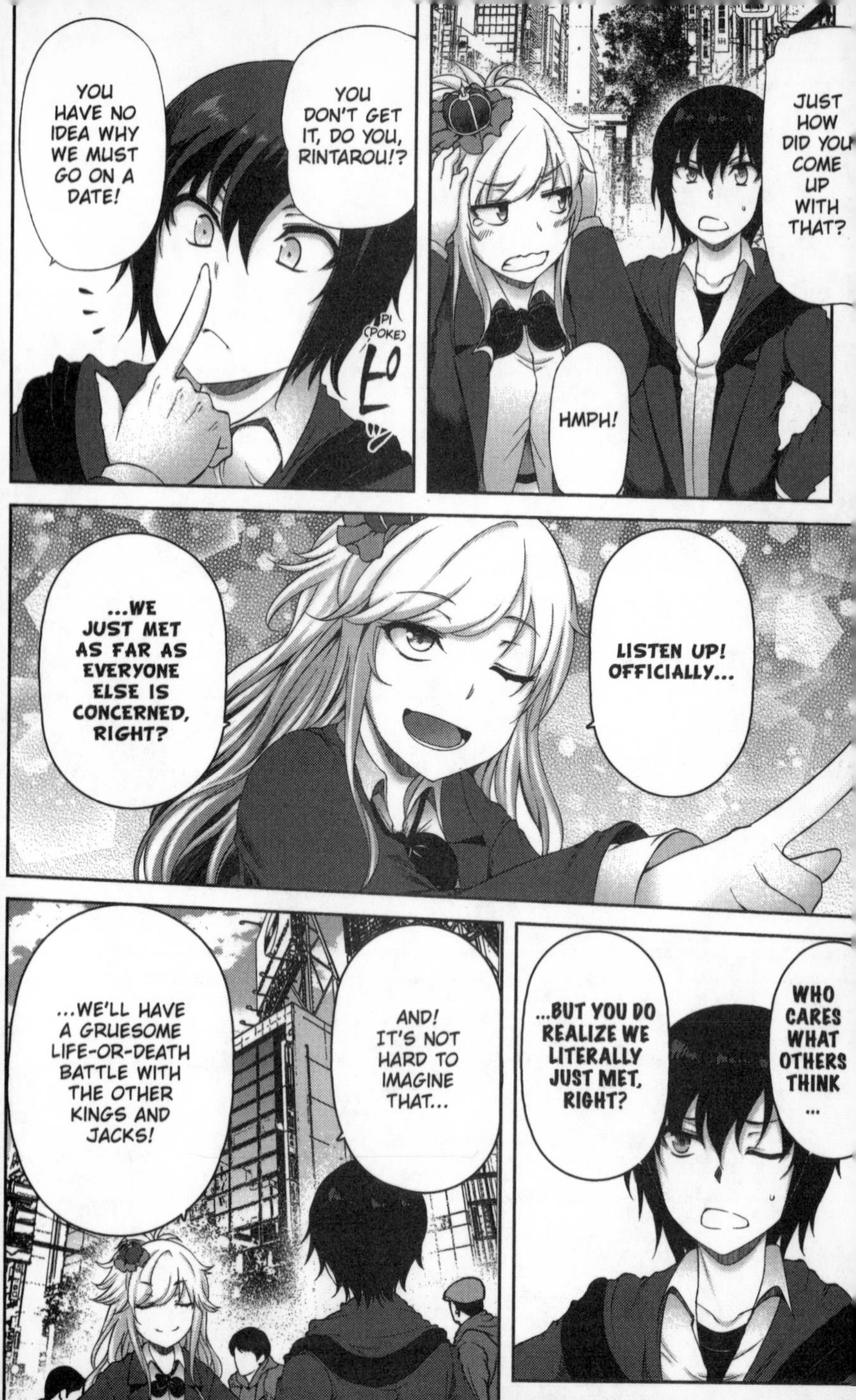
JUST HOW DID YOU COME UP WITH THAT?
HMPH!
YOU DON'T GET IT, DO YOU, RINTAROU!?
YOU HAVE NO IDEA WHY WE MUST GO ON A DATE!
PI (POKE)
LISTEN UP! OFFICIALLY...
...WE JUST MET AS FAR AS EVERYONE ELSE IS CONCERNED, RIGHT?
WHO CARES WHAT OTHERS THINK...
...BUT YOU DO REALIZE WE LITERALLY JUST MET, RIGHT?
AND! IT'S NOT HARD TO IMAGINE THAT...
...WE'LL HAVE A GRUESOME LIFE-OR-DEATH BATTLE WITH THE OTHER KINGS AND JACKS!

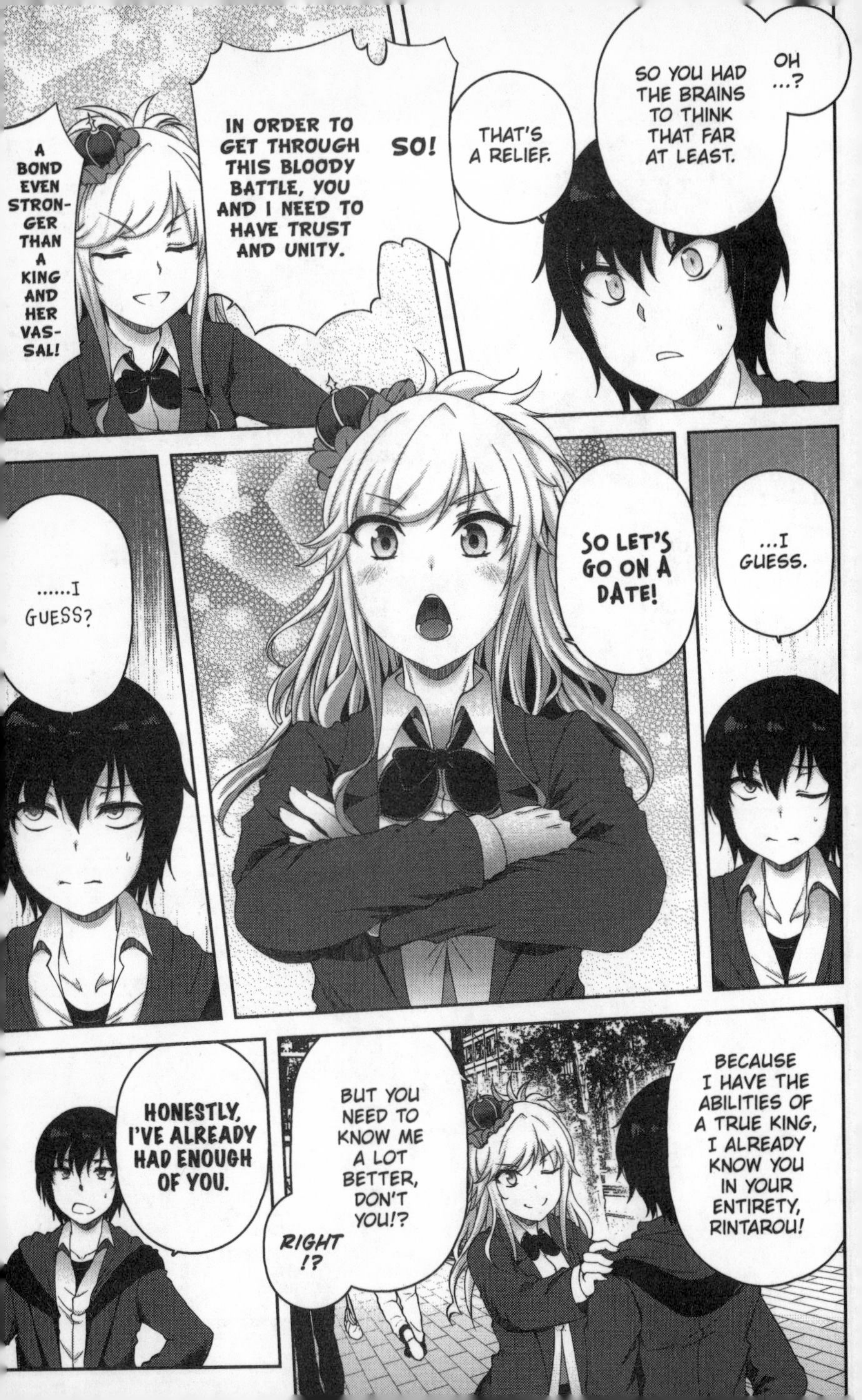
OH ...?
SO YOU HAD THE BRAINS TO THINK THAT FAR AT LEAST.
THAT'S A RELIEF.
SO!
IN ORDER TO GET THROUGH THIS BLOODY BATTLE, YOU AND I NEED TO HAVE TRUST AND UNITY.
A BOND EVEN STRONGER THAN A KING AND HER VASSAL!
...I GUESS.
SO LET'S GO ON A DATE!
......I GUESS?
BECAUSE I HAVE THE ABILITIES OF A TRUE KING, I ALREADY KNOW YOU IN YOUR ENTIRETY, RINTAROU!
BUT YOU NEED TO KNOW ME A LOT BETTER, DON'T YOU!?
RIGHT!?
HONESTLY, I'VE ALREADY HAD ENOUGH OF YOU.

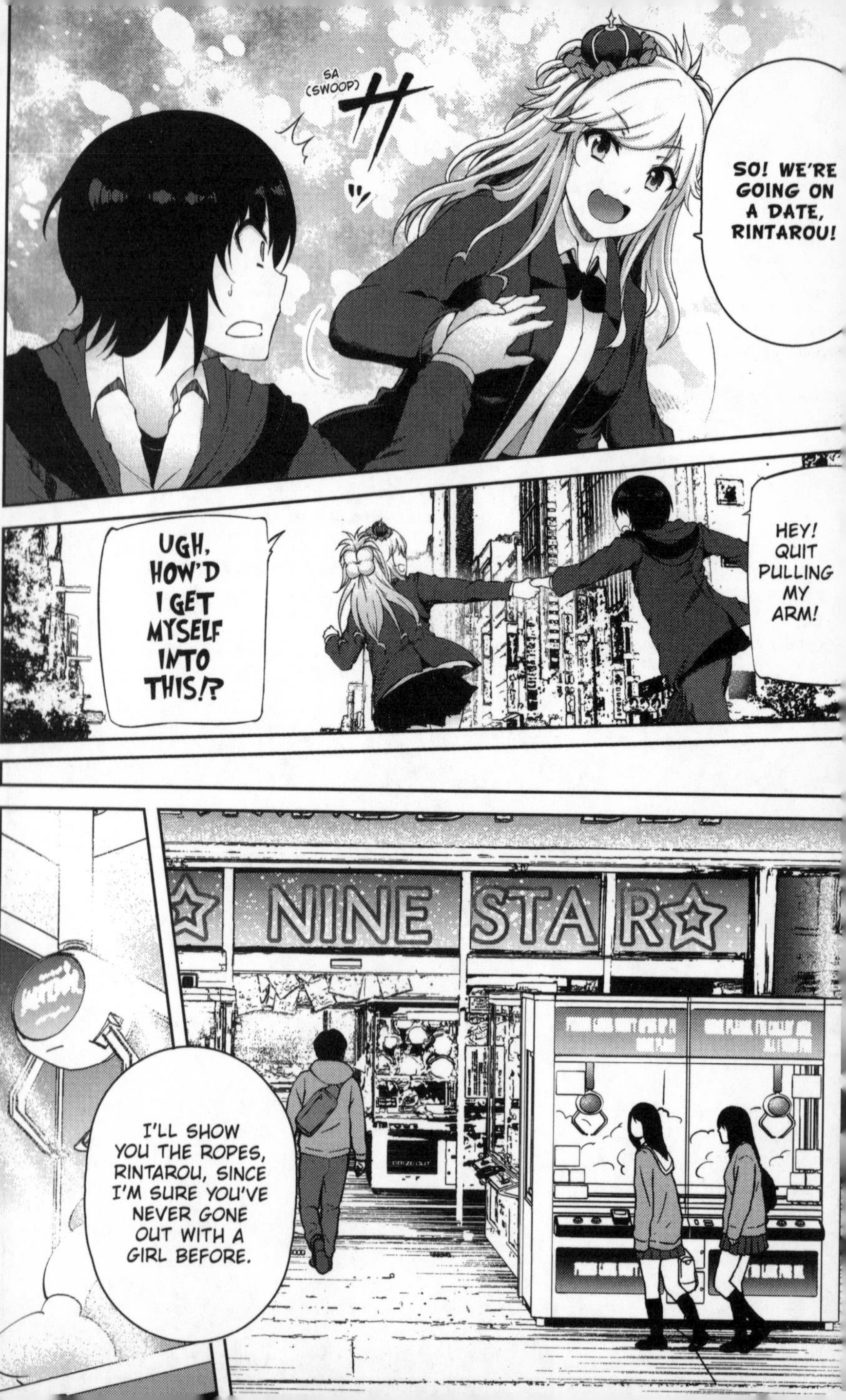
SO! WE'RE GOING ON A DATE, RINTAROU!
SA (SWOOP)
HEY! QUIT PULLING MY ARM!
UGH, HOW'D I GET MYSELF INTO THIS!?
NINE STAR
I'LL SHOW YOU THE ROPES, RINTAROU, SINCE I'M SURE YOU'VE NEVER GONE OUT WITH A GIRL BEFORE.

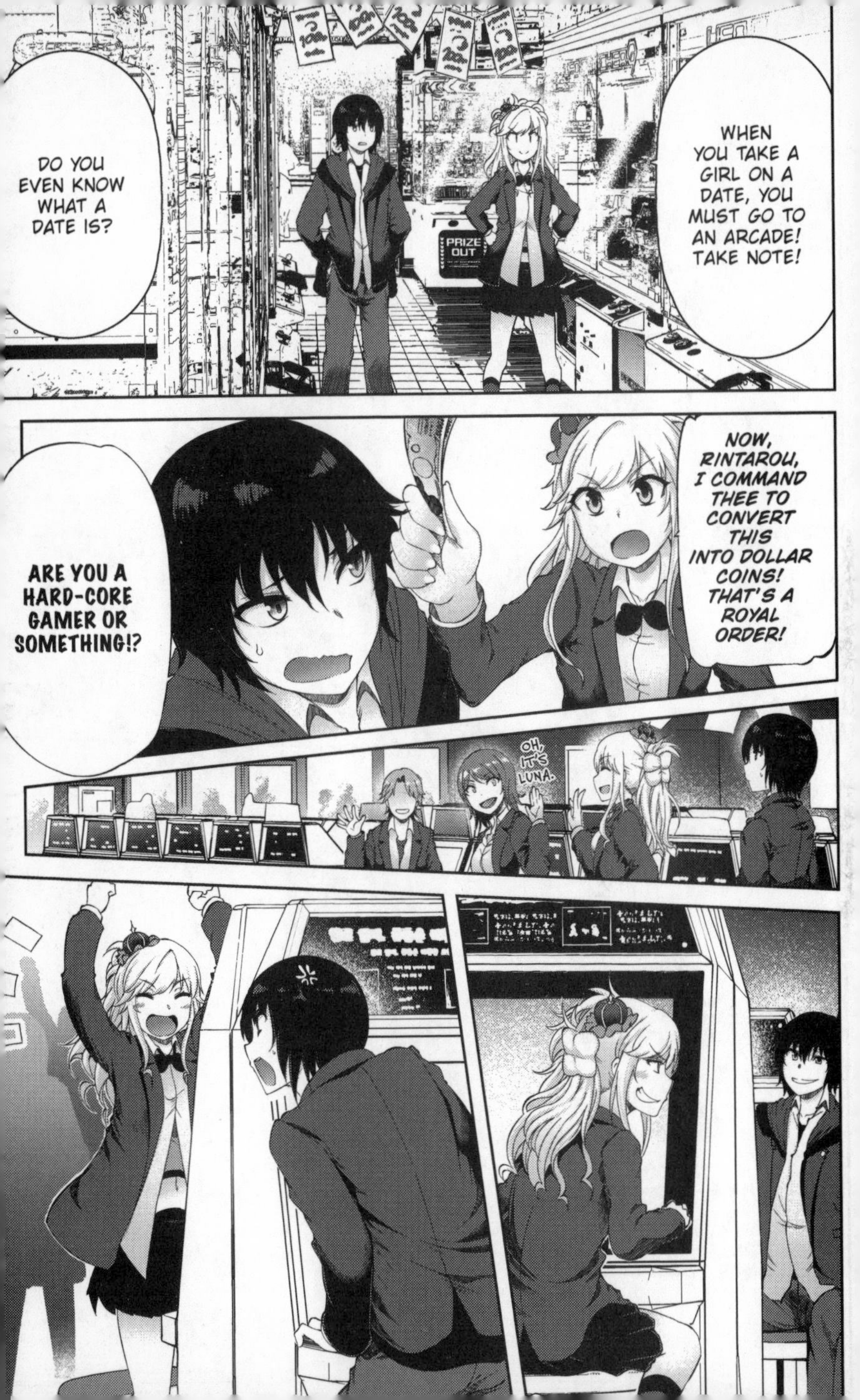
WHEN YOU TAKE A GIRL ON A DATE, YOU MUST GO TO AN ARCADE! TAKE NOTE!
PRIZE OUT
DO YOU EVEN KNOW WHAT A DATE IS?
NOW, RINTAROU, I COMMAND THEE TO CONVERT THIS INTO DOLLAR COINS! THAT'S A ROYAL ORDER!
ARE YOU A HARD-CORE GAMER OR SOMETHING!?
OH, IT'S LUNA.

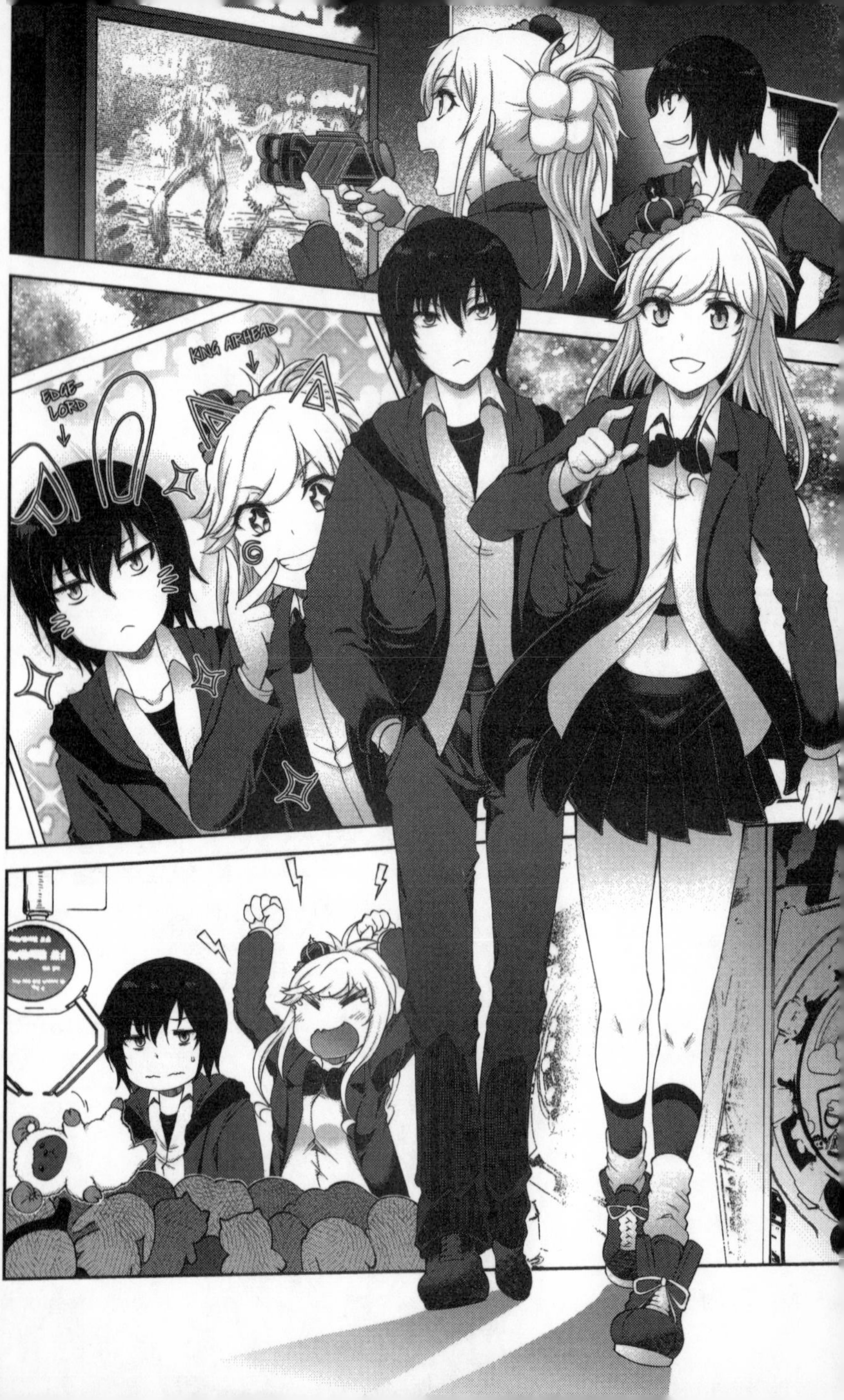
KING AIRHEAD
EDGE-LORD

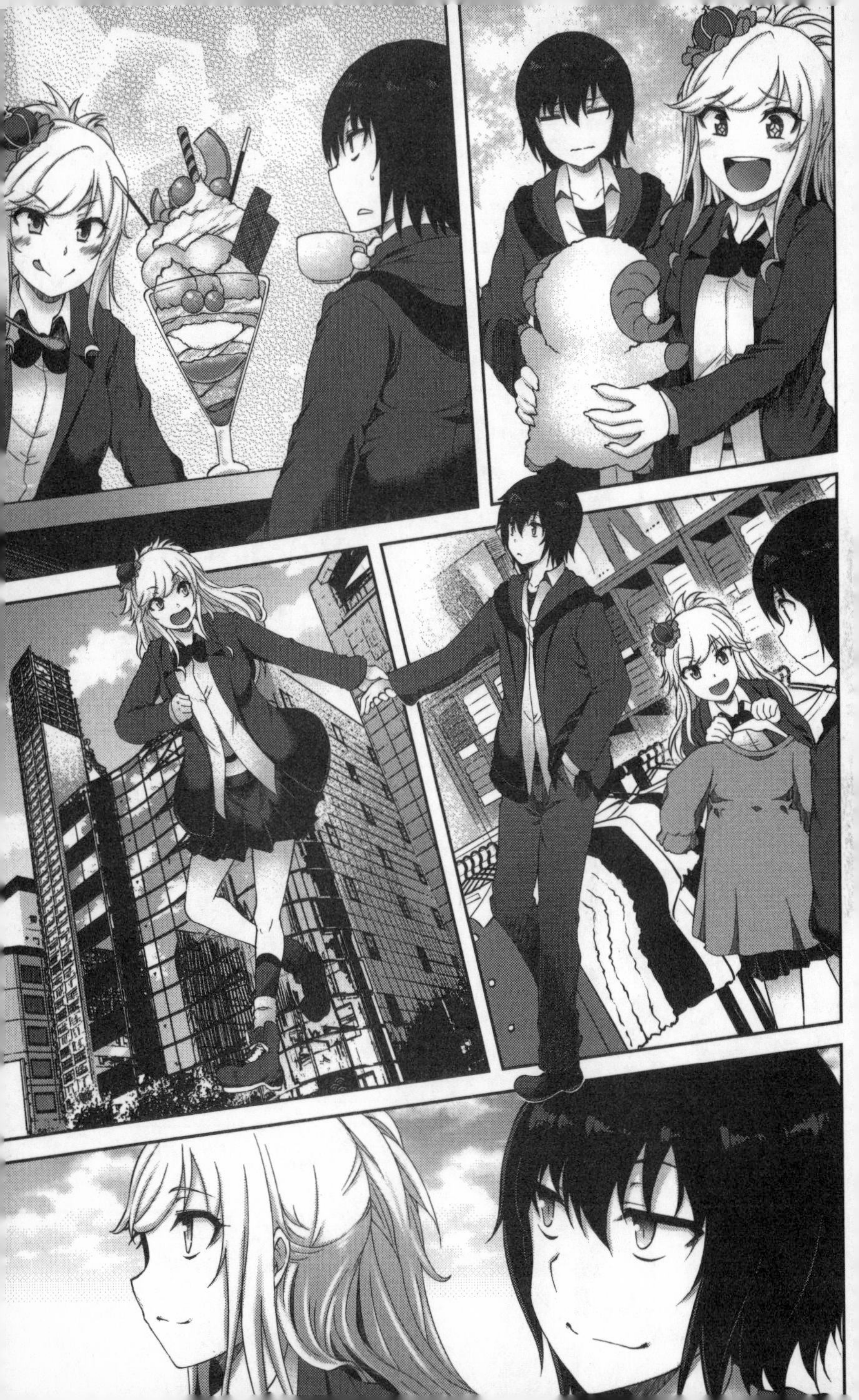

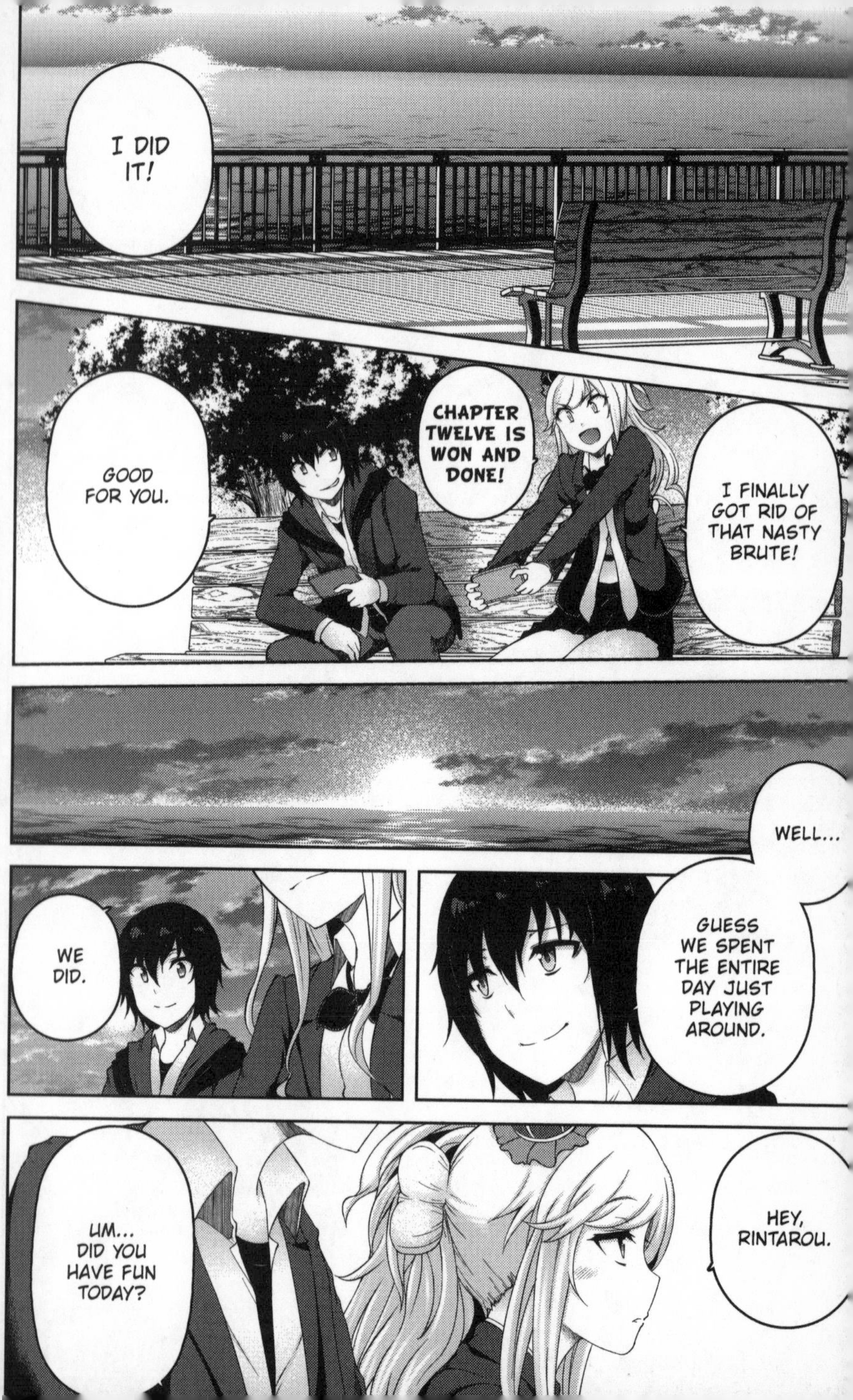
I DID IT!
I FINALLY GOT RID OF THAT NASTY BRUTE!
CHAPTER TWELVE IS WON AND DONE!
GOOD FOR YOU.
WELL...
GUESS WE SPENT THE ENTIRE DAY JUST PLAYING AROUND.
WE DID.
HEY, RINTAROU.
UM... DID YOU HAVE FUN TODAY?

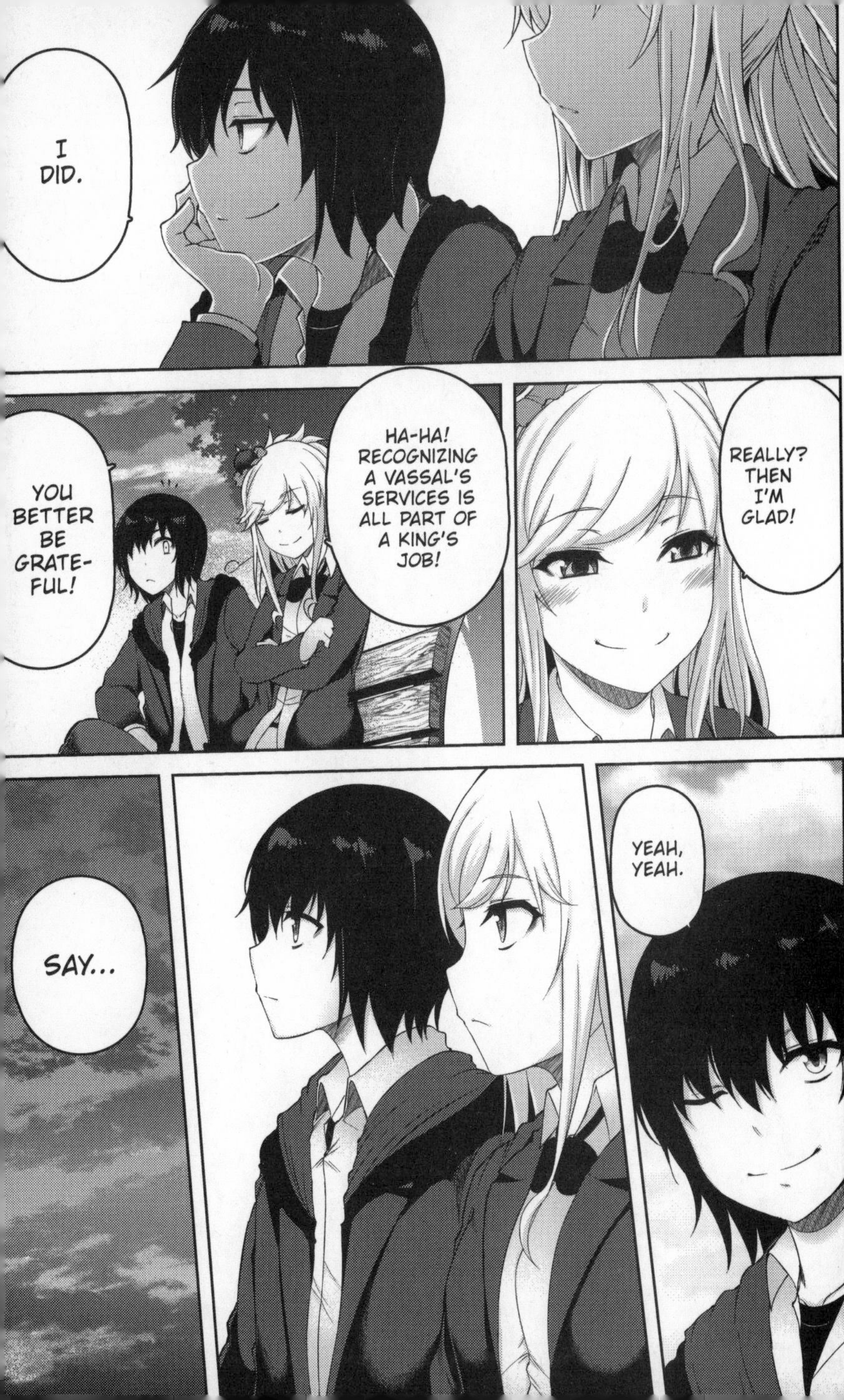
I DID.
REALLY? THEN I'M GLAD!
HA-HA! RECOGNIZING A VASSAL'S SERVICES IS ALL PART OF A KING'S JOB!
YOU BETTER BE GRATE-FUL!
YEAH, YEAH.
SAY...

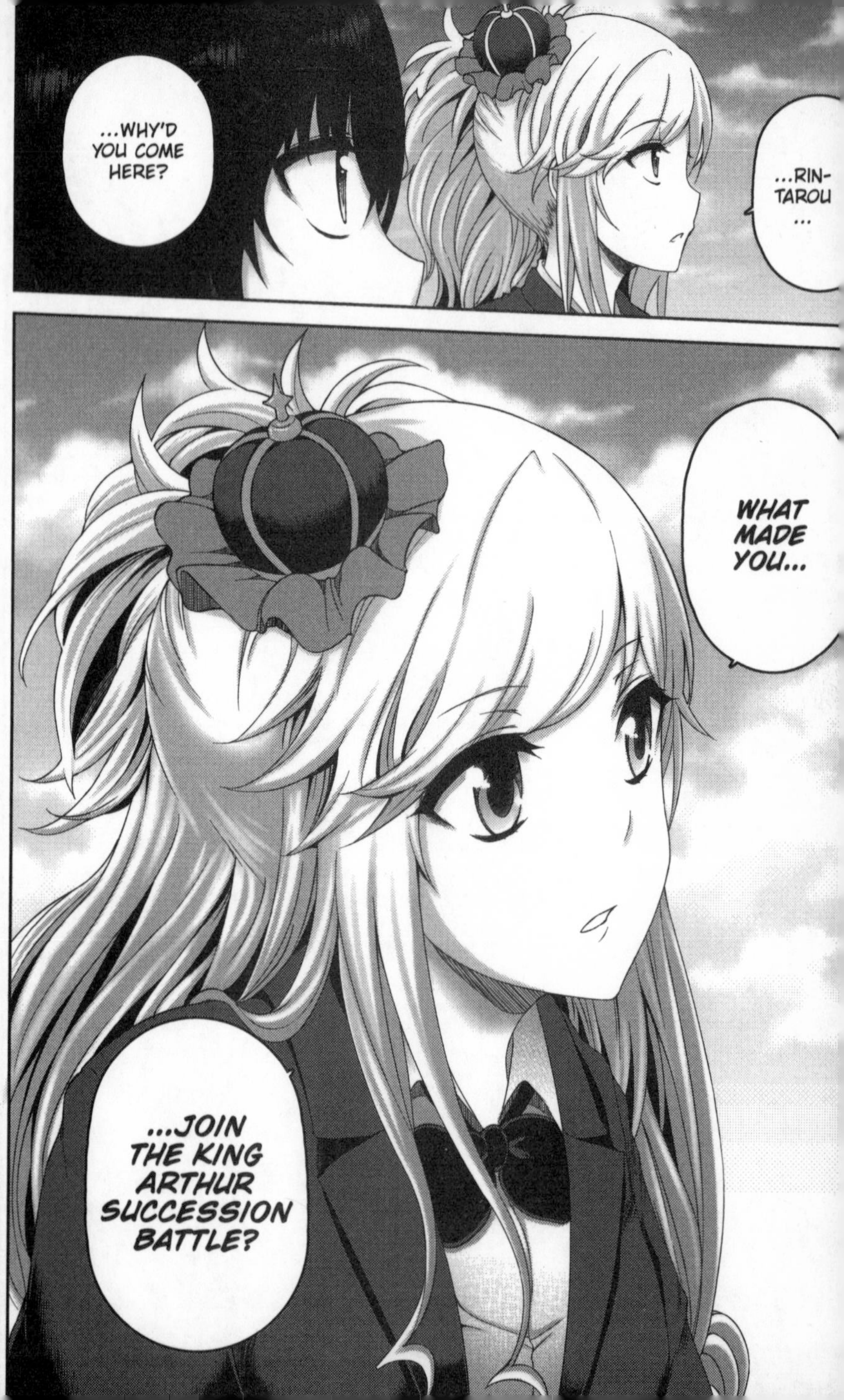
...RIN-TAROU...
...WHY'D YOU COME HERE?
WHAT MADE YOU...
...JOIN THE KING ARTHUR SUCCESSION BATTLE?

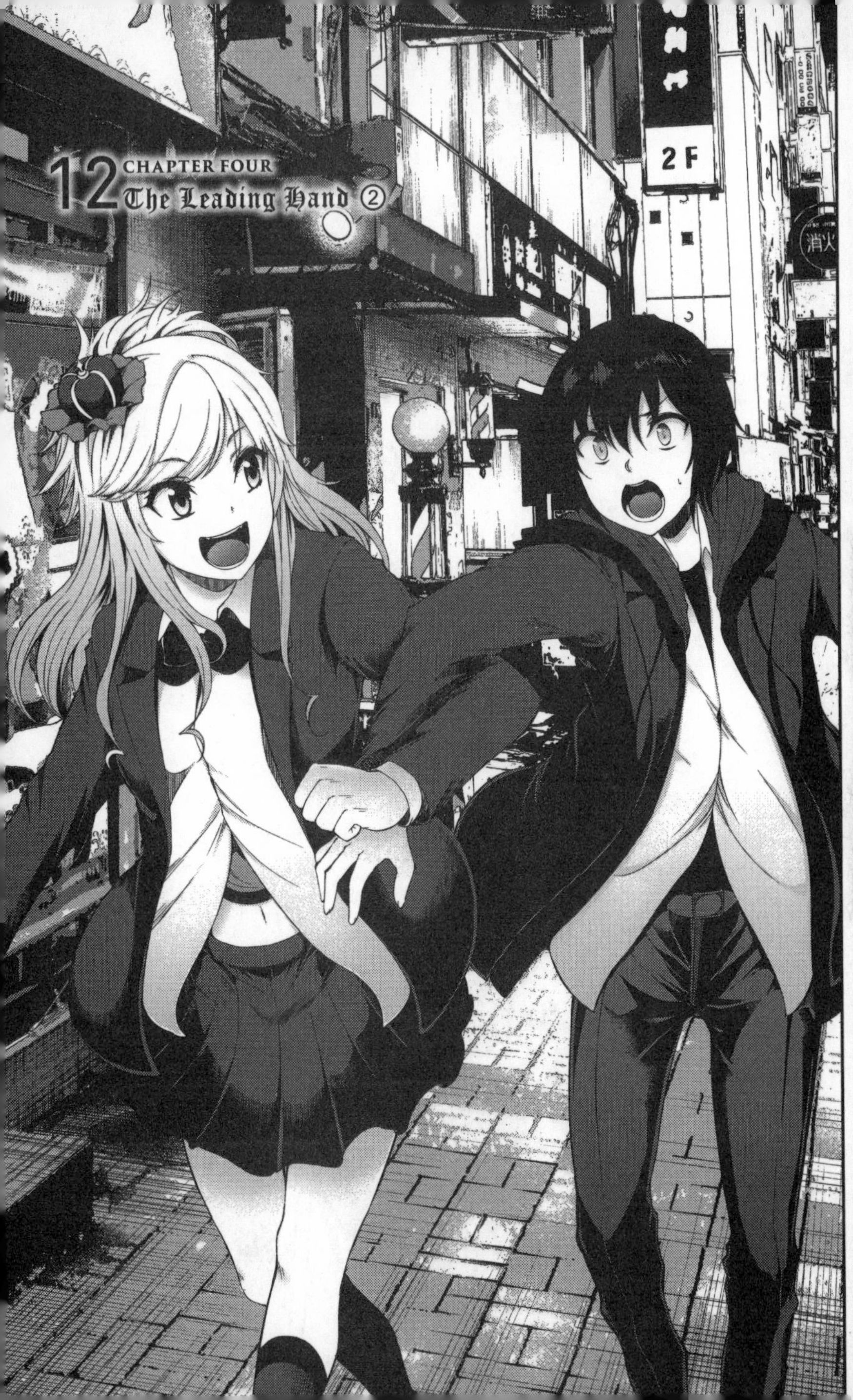
12 CHAPTER FOUR
The Leading Hand ②
2F
消火

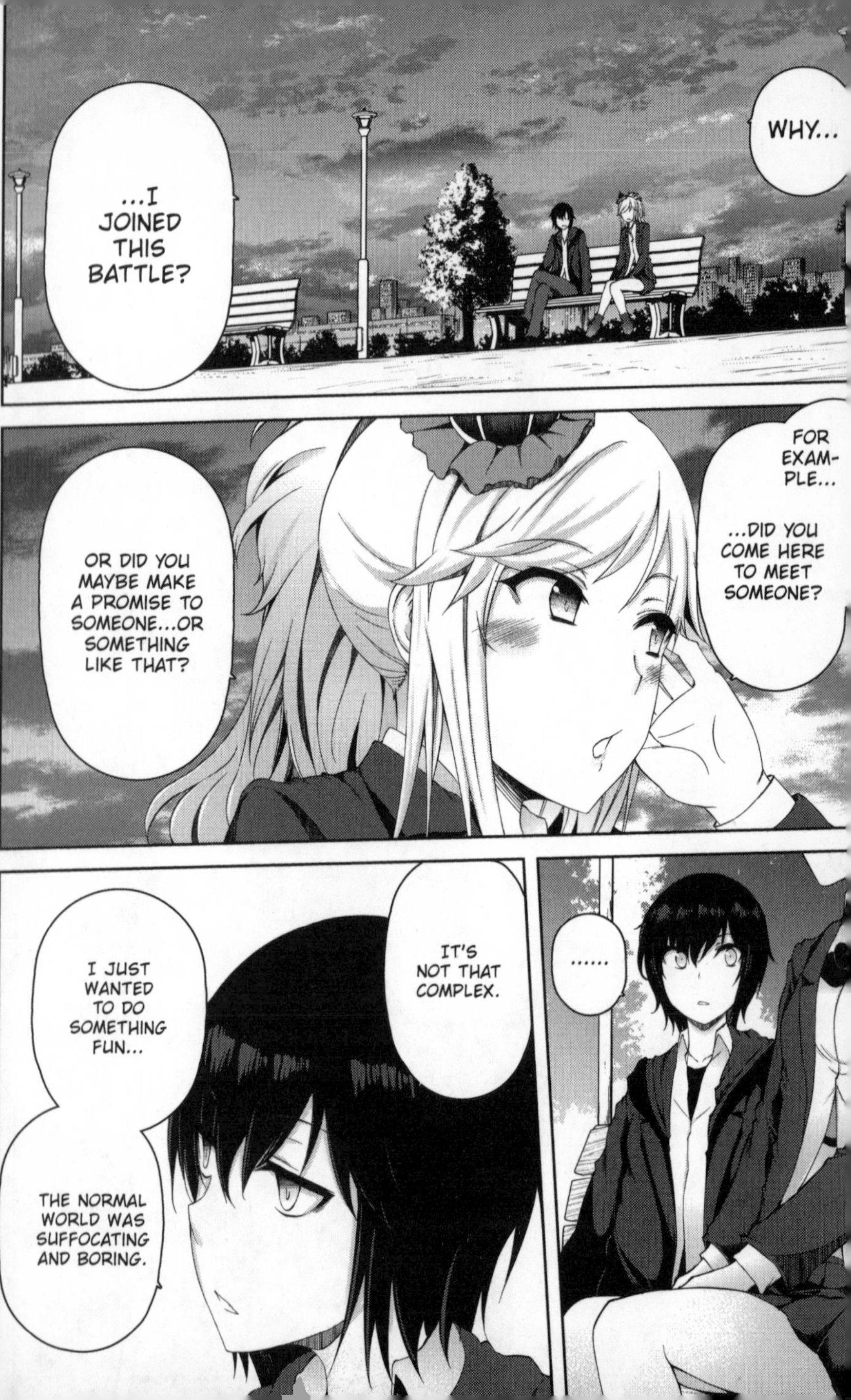
WHY...
...I JOINED THIS BATTLE?
FOR EXAMPLE...
...DID YOU COME HERE TO MEET SOMEONE?
OR DID YOU MAYBE MAKE A PROMISE TO SOMEONE...OR SOMETHING LIKE THAT?
......
IT'S NOT THAT COMPLEX.
I JUST WANTED TO DO SOMETHING FUN...
THE NORMAL WORLD WAS SUFFOCATING AND BORING.

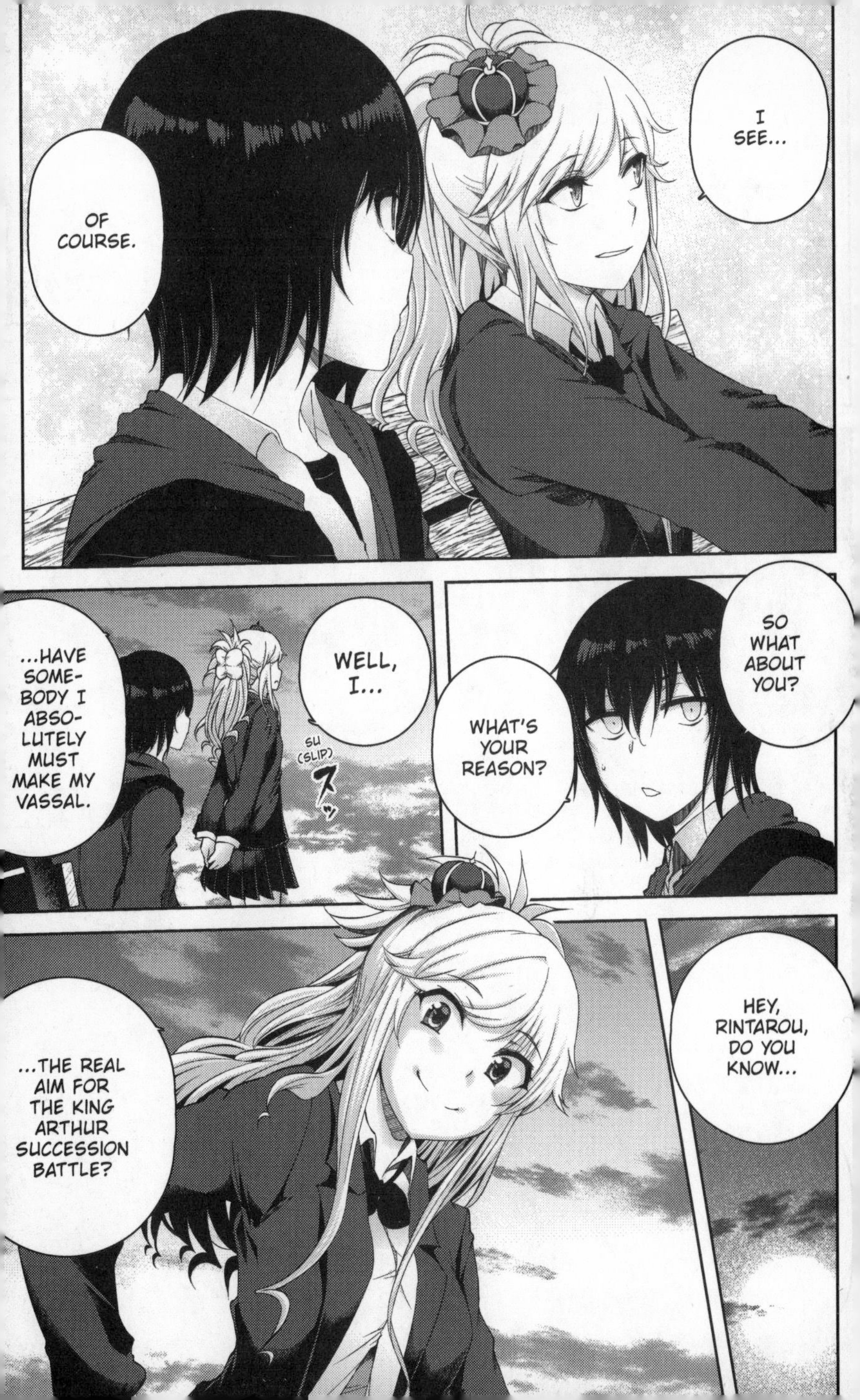
I SEE...
OF COURSE.
SO WHAT ABOUT YOU?
WHAT'S YOUR REASON?
WELL, I...
SU (SLIP)
...HAVE SOMEBODY I ABSOLUTELY MUST MAKE MY VASSAL.
HEY, RINTAROU, DO YOU KNOW...
...THE REAL AIM FOR THE KING ARTHUR SUCCESSION BATTLE?

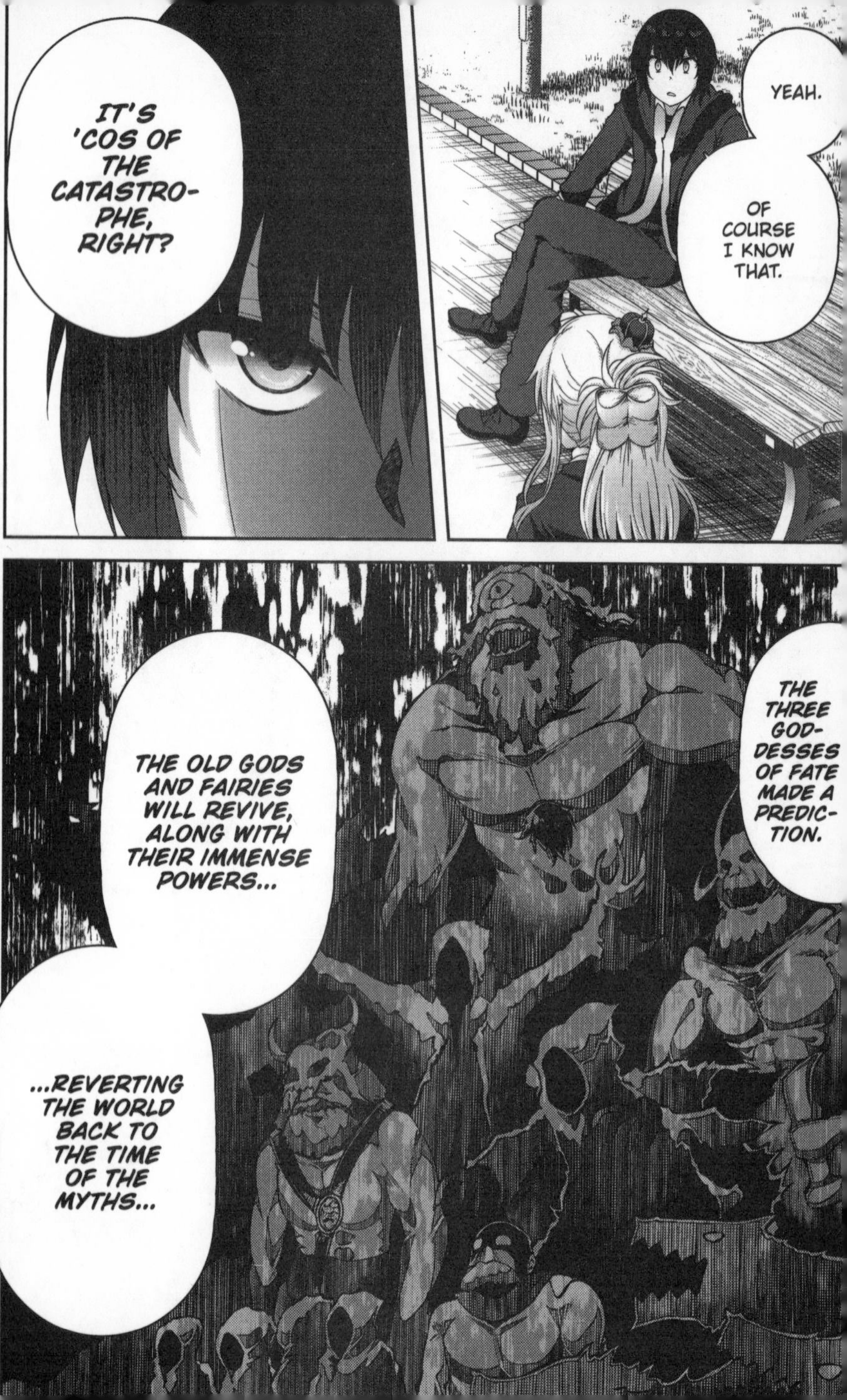
YEAH.
OF COURSE I KNOW THAT.
IT'S 'COS OF THE CATASTROPHE, RIGHT?
THE THREE GODDESSES OF FATE MADE A PREDICTION.
THE OLD GODS AND FAIRIES WILL REVIVE, ALONG WITH THEIR IMMENSE POWERS...
...REVERTING THE WORLD BACK TO THE TIME OF THE MYTHS...

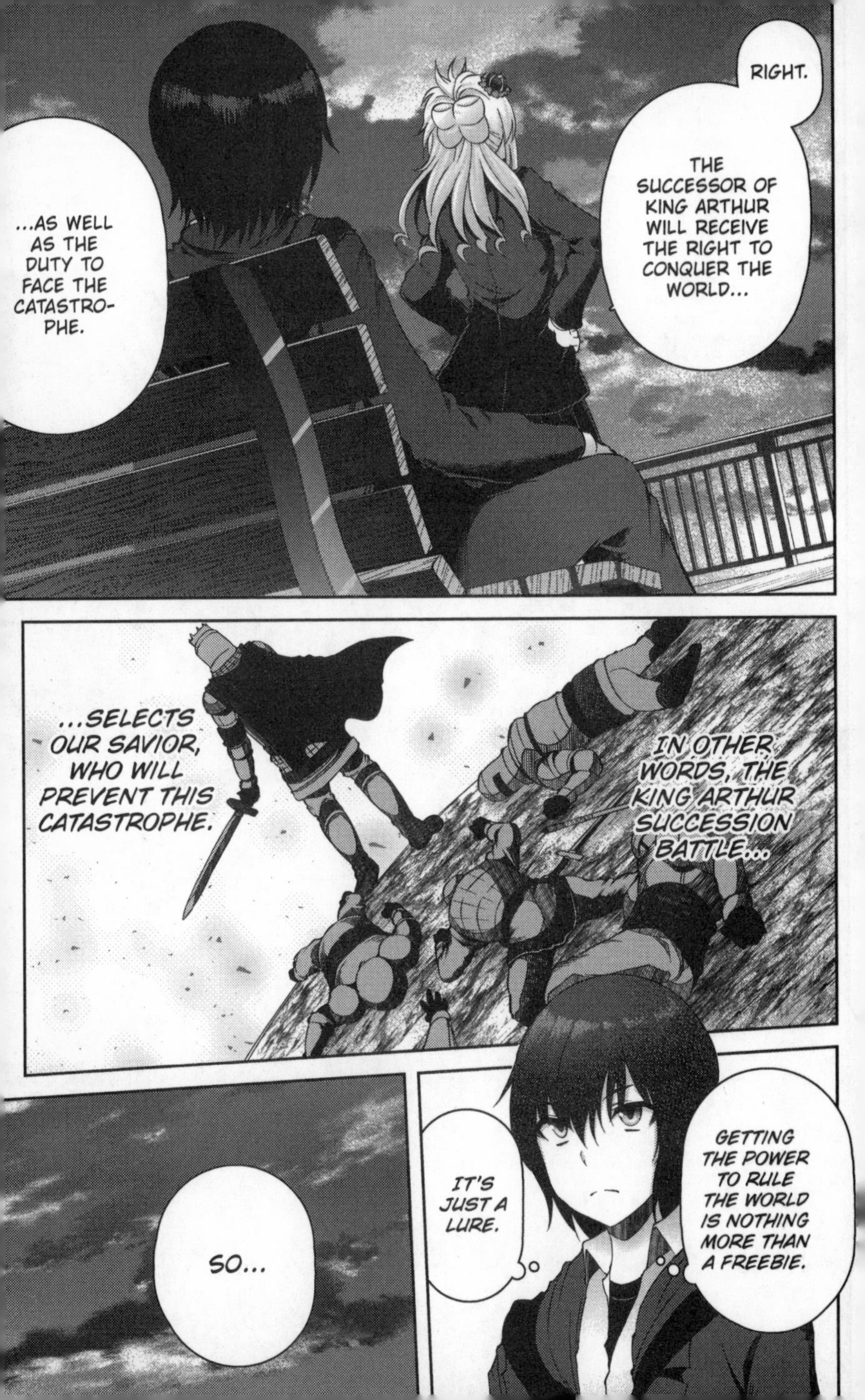
RIGHT.
THE SUCCESSOR OF KING ARTHUR WILL RECEIVE THE RIGHT TO CONQUER THE WORLD...
...AS WELL AS THE DUTY TO FACE THE CATASTRO-PHE.
IN OTHER WORDS, THE KING ARTHUR SUCCESSION BATTLE...
...SELECTS OUR SAVIOR, WHO WILL PREVENT THIS CATASTROPHE.
GETTING THE POWER TO RULE THE WORLD IS NOTHING MORE THAN A FREEBIE.
IT'S JUST A LURE.
SO...

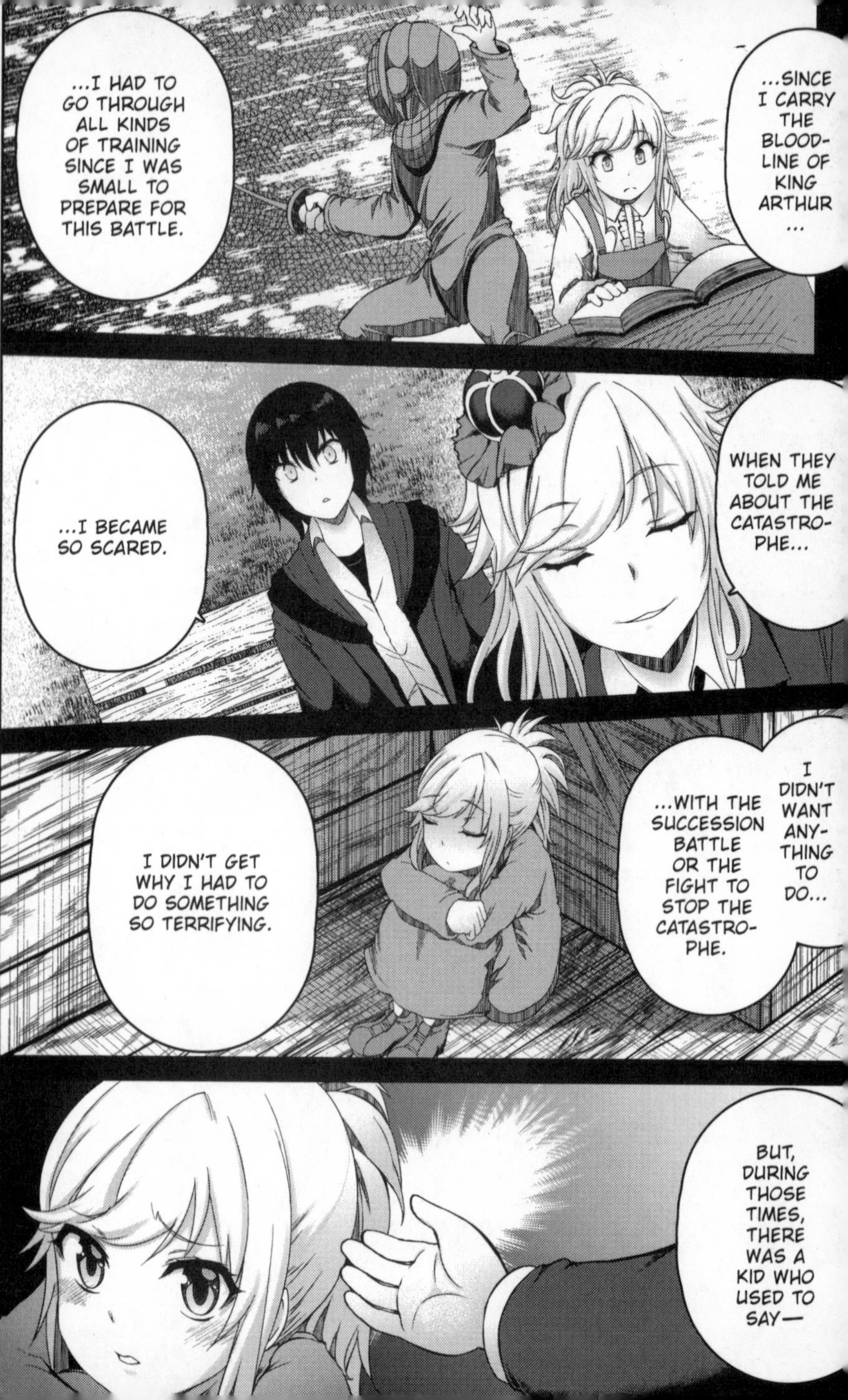
...SINCE I CARRY THE BLOODLINE OF KING ARTHUR...
...I HAD TO GO THROUGH ALL KINDS OF TRAINING SINCE I WAS SMALL TO PREPARE FOR THIS BATTLE.
WHEN THEY TOLD ME ABOUT THE CATASTROPHE...
...I BECAME SO SCARED.
I DIDN'T WANT ANYTHING TO DO...
...WITH THE SUCCESSION BATTLE OR THE FIGHT TO STOP THE CATASTROPHE.
I DIDN'T GET WHY I HAD TO DO SOMETHING SO TERRIFYING.
BUT, DURING THOSE TIMES, THERE WAS A KID WHO USED TO SAY—

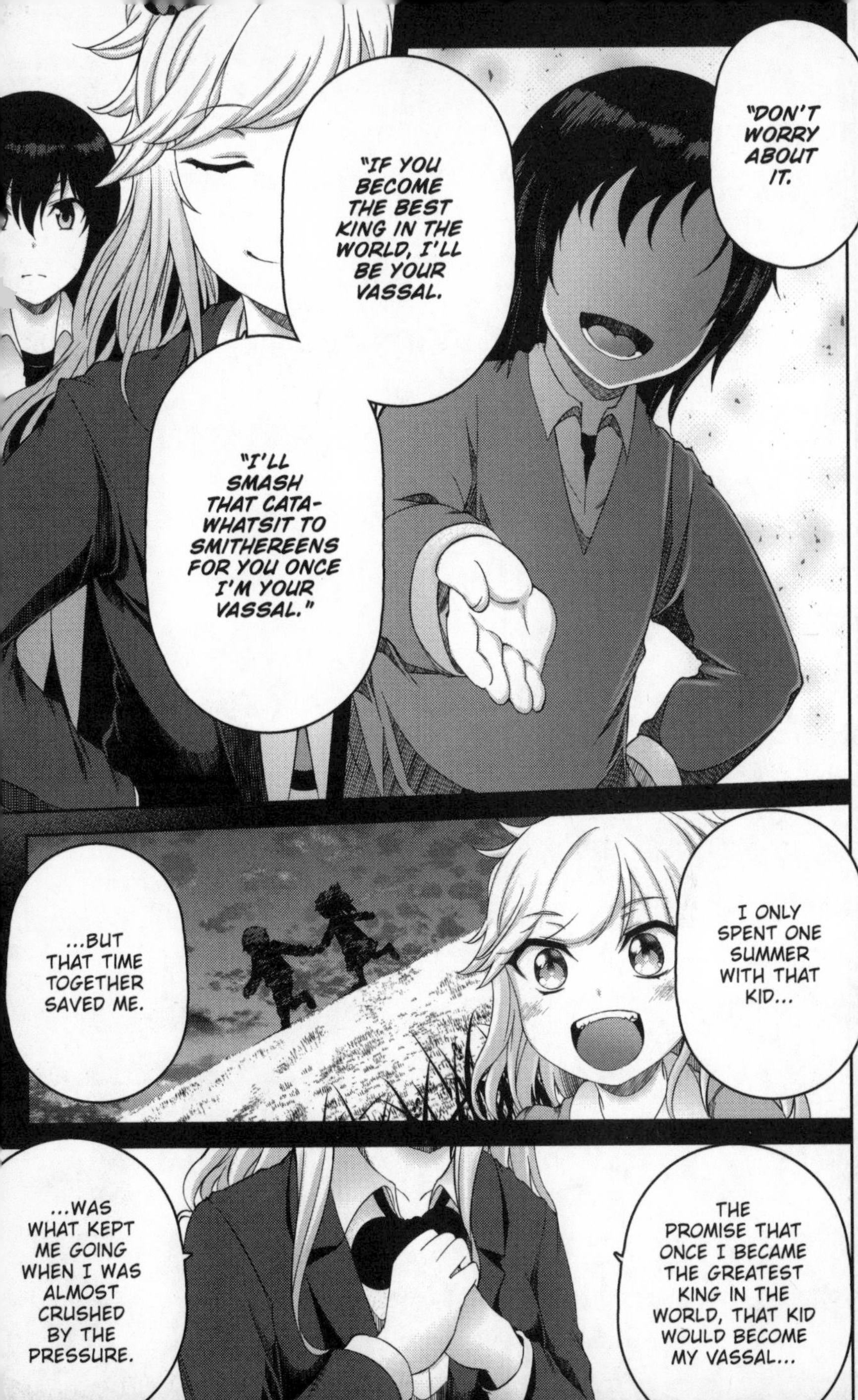
"DON'T WORRY ABOUT IT.
"IF YOU BECOME THE BEST KING IN THE WORLD, I'LL BE YOUR VASSAL.
"I'LL SMASH THAT CATA-WHATSIT TO SMITHEREENS FOR YOU ONCE I'M YOUR VASSAL."
I ONLY SPENT ONE SUMMER WITH THAT KID...
...BUT THAT TIME TOGETHER SAVED ME.
THE PROMISE THAT ONCE I BECAME THE GREATEST KING IN THE WORLD, THAT KID WOULD BECOME MY VASSAL...
...WAS WHAT KEPT ME GOING WHEN I WAS ALMOST CRUSHED BY THE PRESSURE.

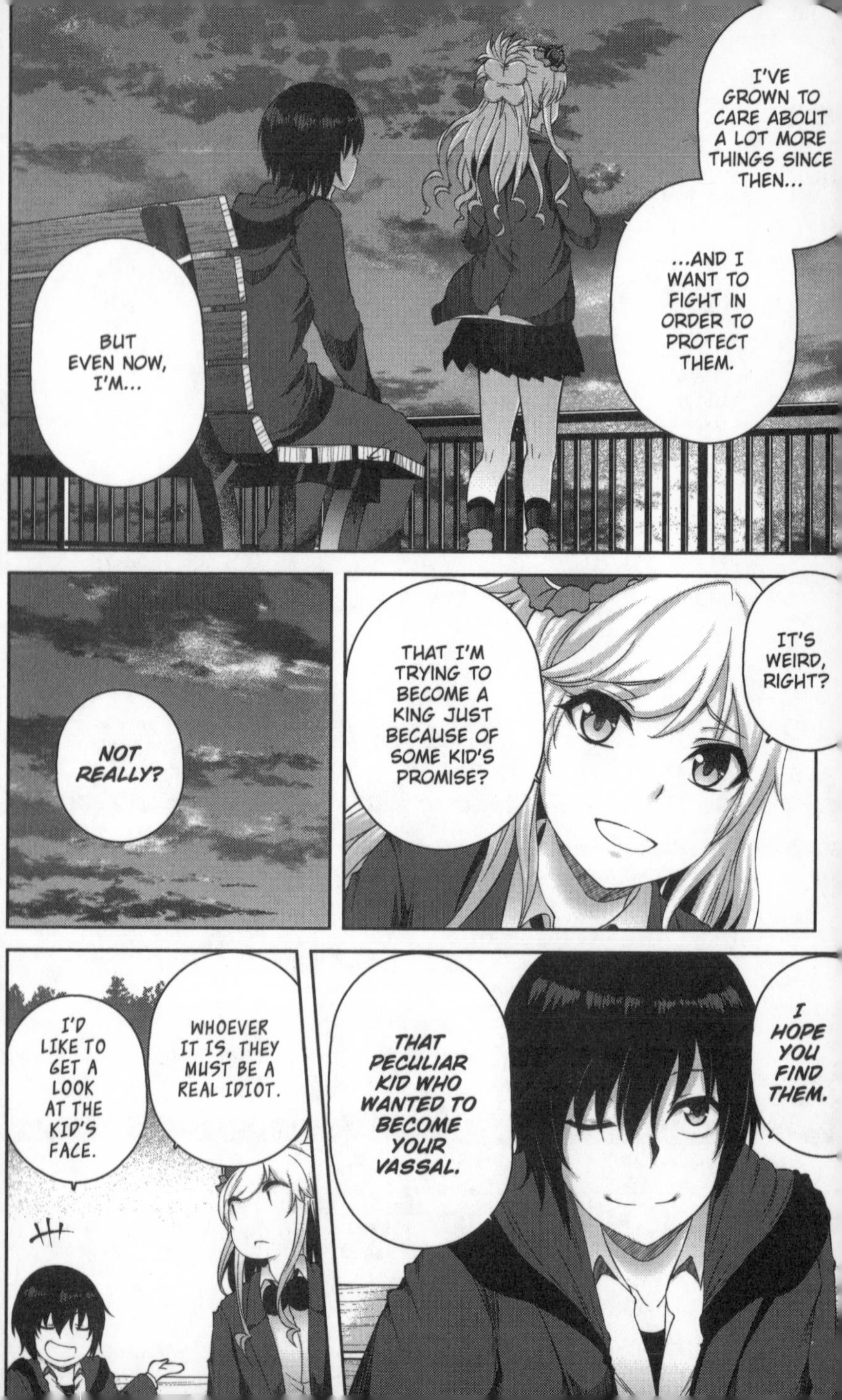
I'VE GROWN TO CARE ABOUT A LOT MORE THINGS SINCE THEN...
...AND I WANT TO FIGHT IN ORDER TO PROTECT THEM.
BUT EVEN NOW, I'M...
IT'S WEIRD, RIGHT?
THAT I'M TRYING TO BECOME A KING JUST BECAUSE OF SOME KID'S PROMISE?
NOT REALLY?
I HOPE YOU FIND THEM.
THAT PECULIAR KID WHO WANTED TO BECOME YOUR VASSAL.
WHOEVER IT IS, THEY MUST BE A REAL IDIOT.
I'D LIKE TO GET A LOOK AT THE KID'S FACE.

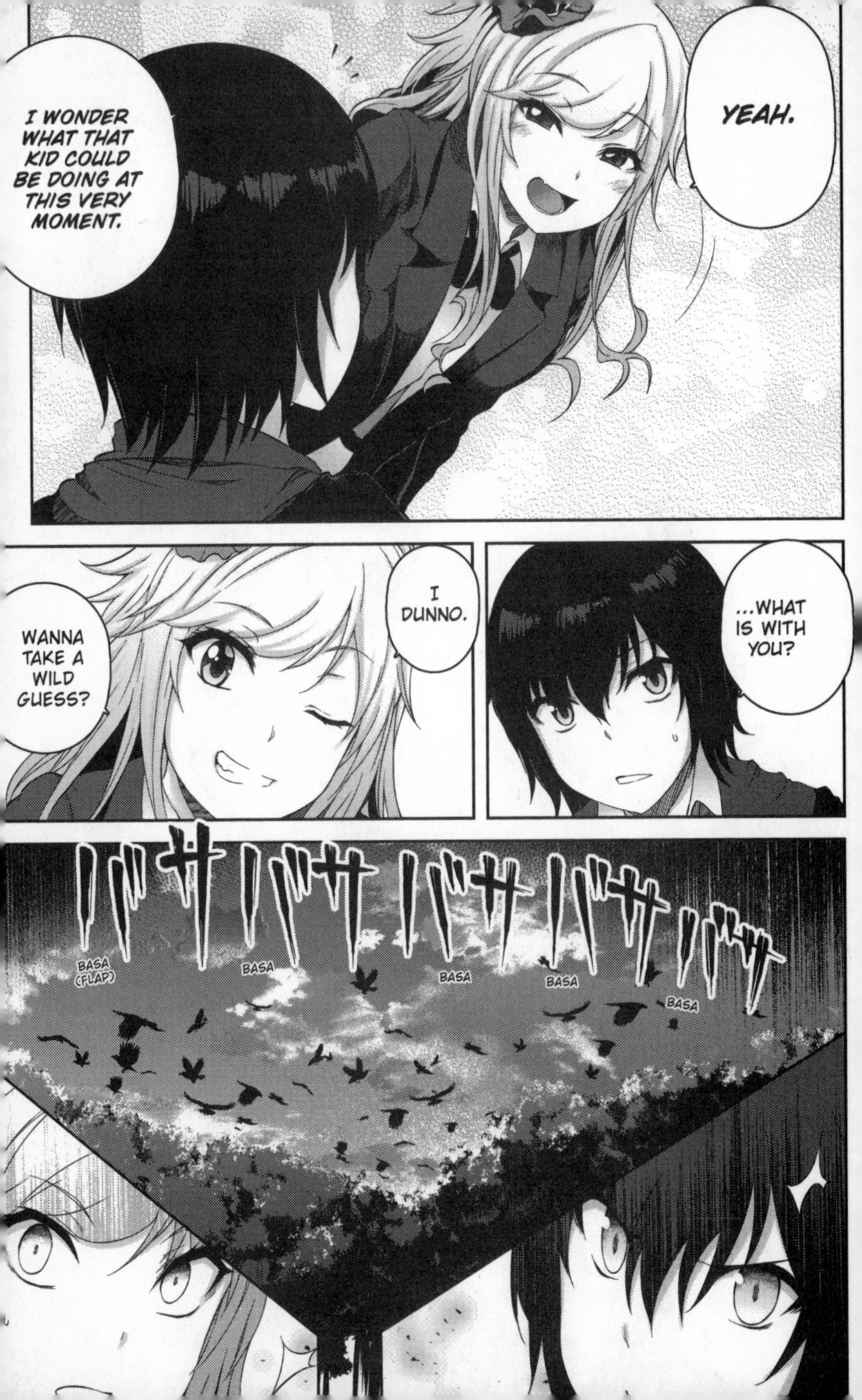
YEAH.
I WONDER WHAT THAT KID COULD BE DOING AT THIS VERY MOMENT.
...WHAT IS WITH YOU?
I DUNNO.
WANNA TAKE A WILD GUESS?
BASA
BASA
BASA
BASA
BASA (FLAP)

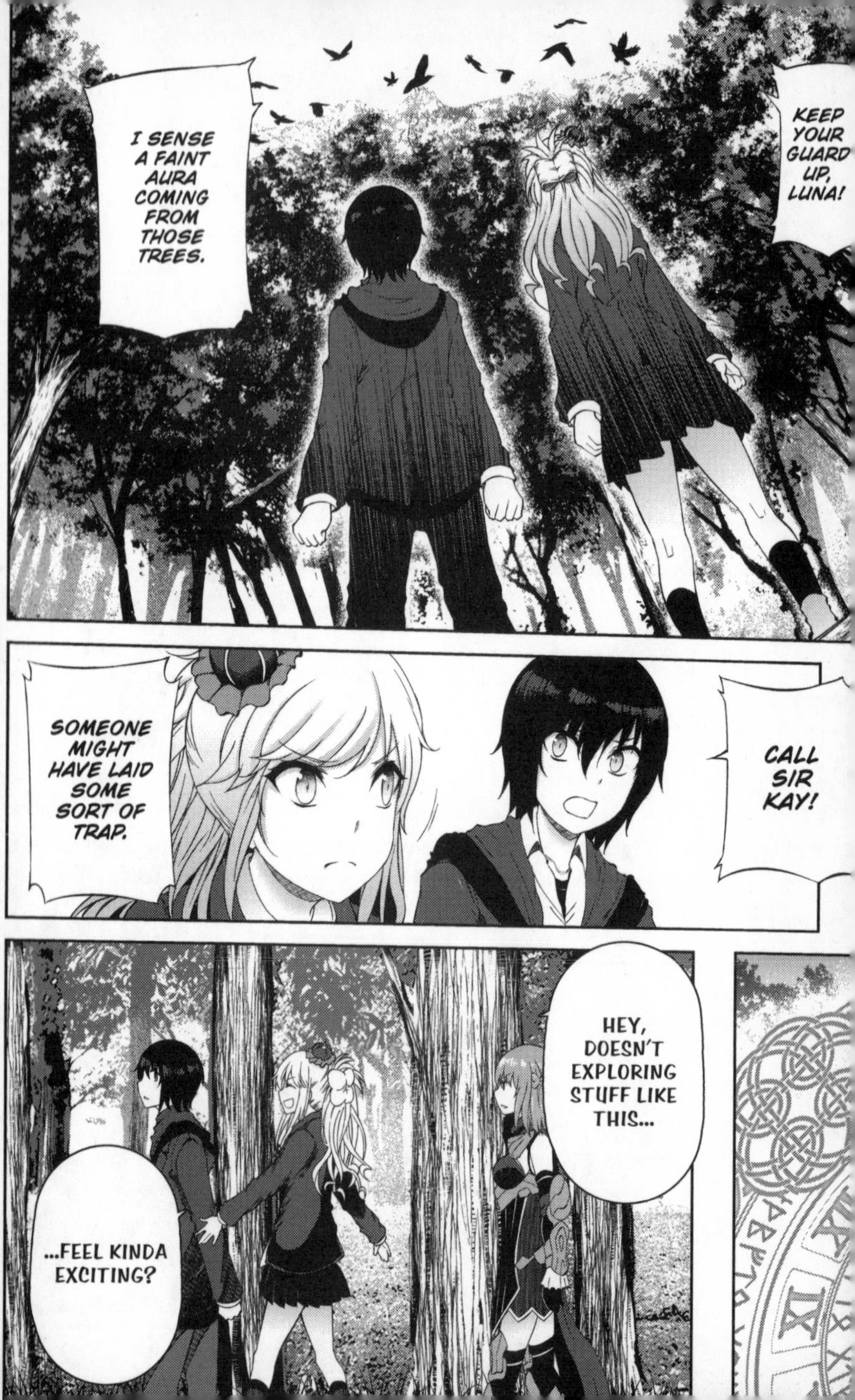
KEEP YOUR GUARD UP, LUNA!
I SENSE A FAINT AURA COMING FROM THOSE TREES.
CALL SIR KAY!
SOMEONE MIGHT HAVE LAID SOME SORT OF TRAP.
HEY, DOESN'T EXPLORING STUFF LIKE THIS...
...FEEL KINDA EXCITING?

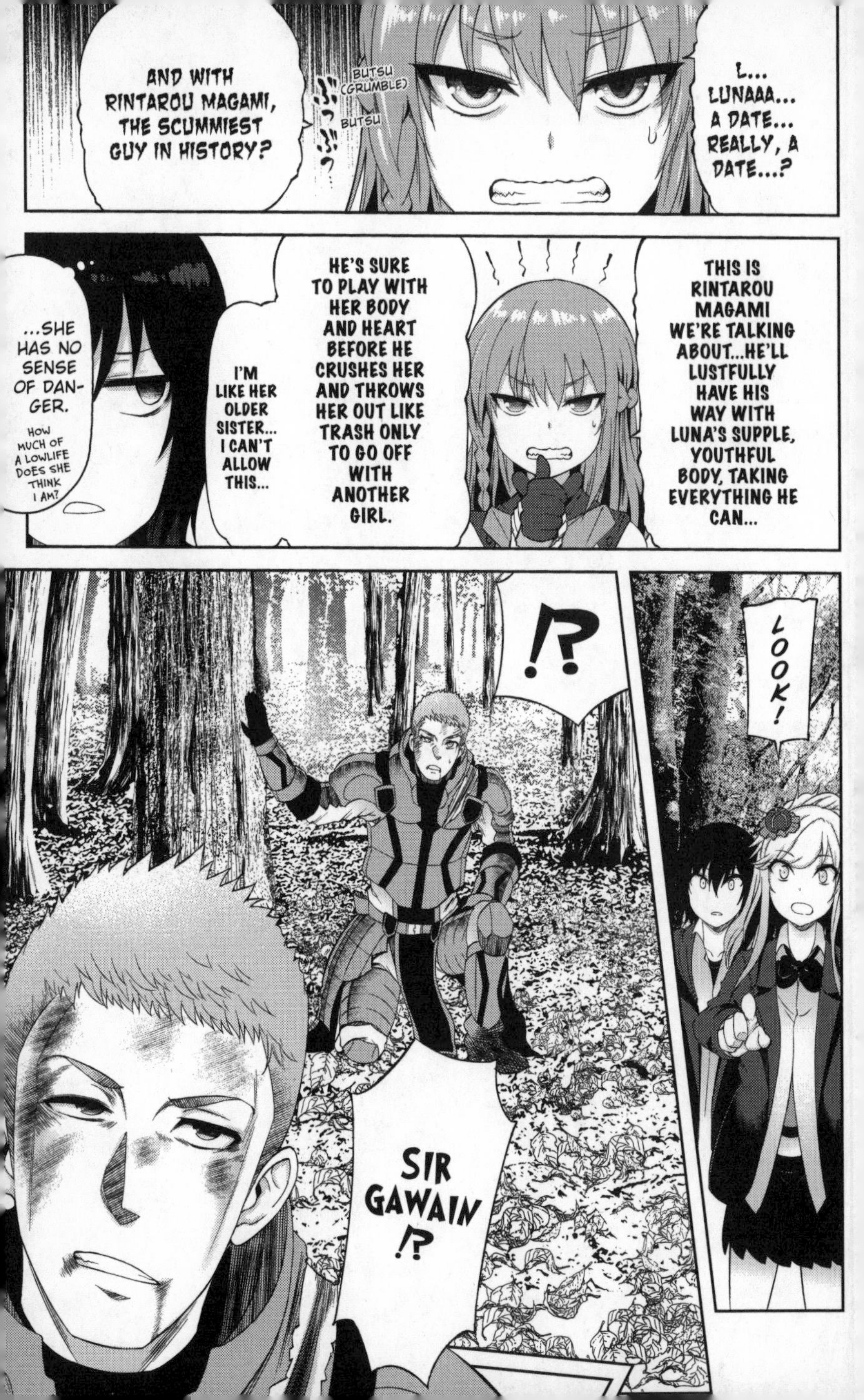
L... LUNAAA... A DATE... REALLY, A DATE...?
BUTSU (GRUMBLE) BUTSU
AND WITH RINTAROU MAGAMI, THE SCUMMIEST GUY IN HISTORY?
THIS IS RINTAROU MAGAMI WE'RE TALKING ABOUT...HE'LL LUSTFULLY HAVE HIS WAY WITH LUNA'S SUPPLE, YOUTHFUL BODY, TAKING EVERYTHING HE CAN...
HE'S SURE TO PLAY WITH HER BODY AND HEART BEFORE HE CRUSHES HER AND THROWS HER OUT LIKE TRASH ONLY TO GO OFF WITH ANOTHER GIRL.
I'M LIKE HER OLDER SISTER... I CAN'T ALLOW THIS...
...SHE HAS NO SENSE OF DAN-GER.
HOW MUCH OF A LOWLIFE DOES SHE THINK I AM?
LOOK!
!?
SIR GAWAIN !?

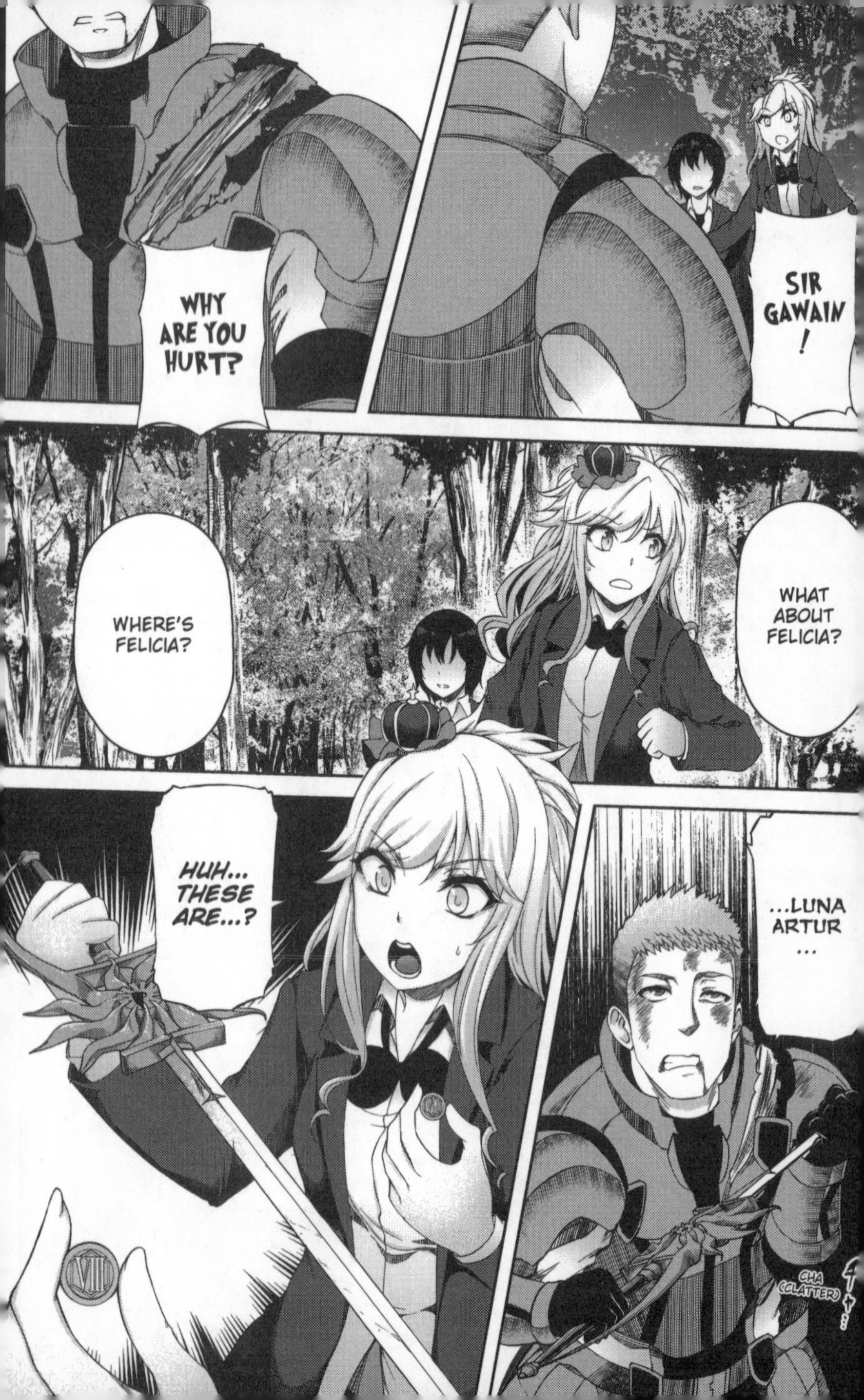
SIR GAWAIN!
WHY ARE YOU HURT?
WHAT ABOUT FELICIA?
WHERE'S FELICIA?
...LUNA ARTUR...
CHA (CLATTER)
HUH... THESE ARE...?

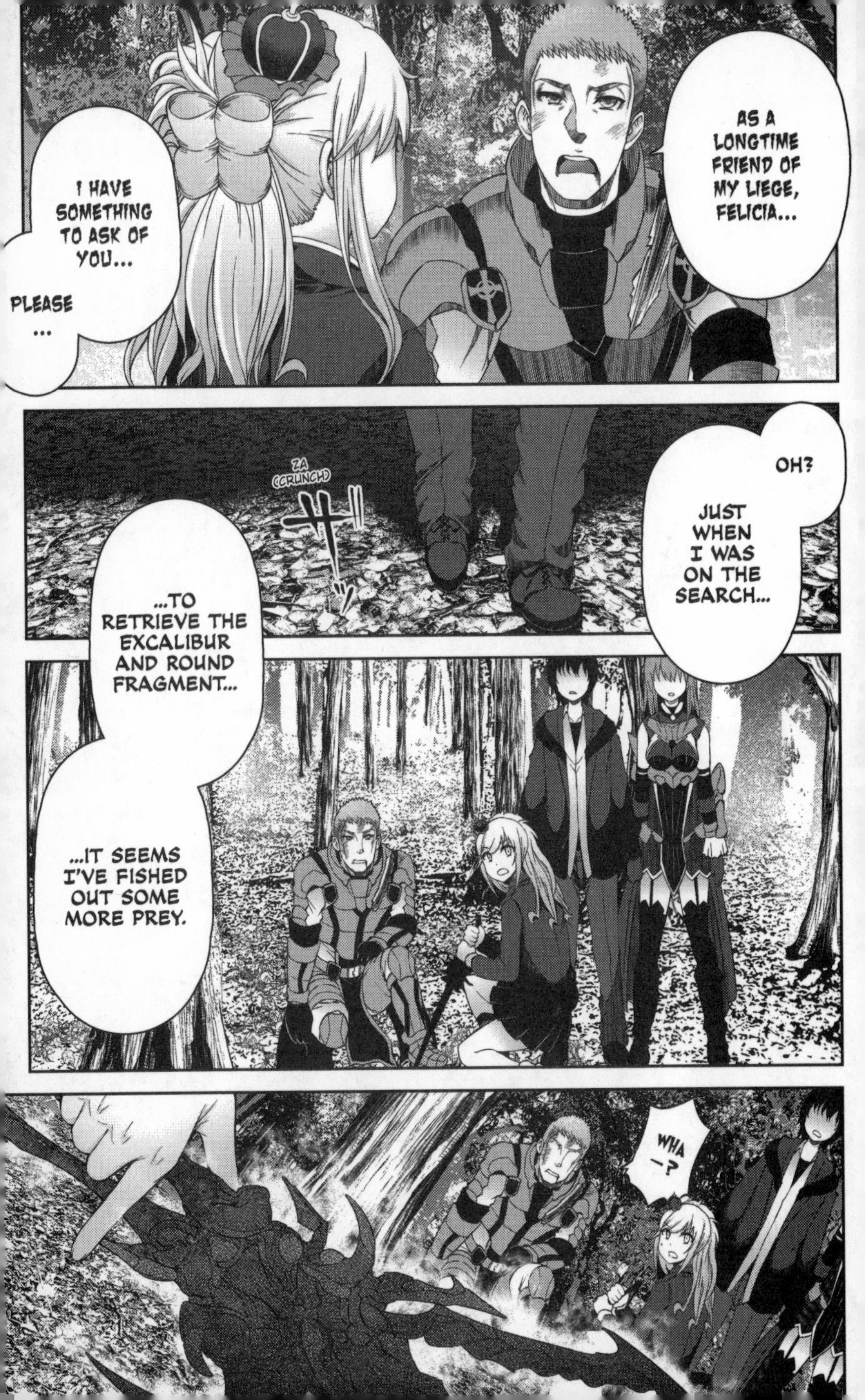
AS A LONGTIME FRIEND OF MY LIEGE, FELICIA...
I HAVE SOMETHING TO ASK OF YOU...
PLEASE ...
OH?
JUST WHEN I WAS ON THE SEARCH...
ZA (CRUNCH)
...TO RETRIEVE THE EXCALIBUR AND ROUND FRAGMENT...
...IT SEEMS I'VE FISHED OUT SOME MORE PREY.
WHA—?

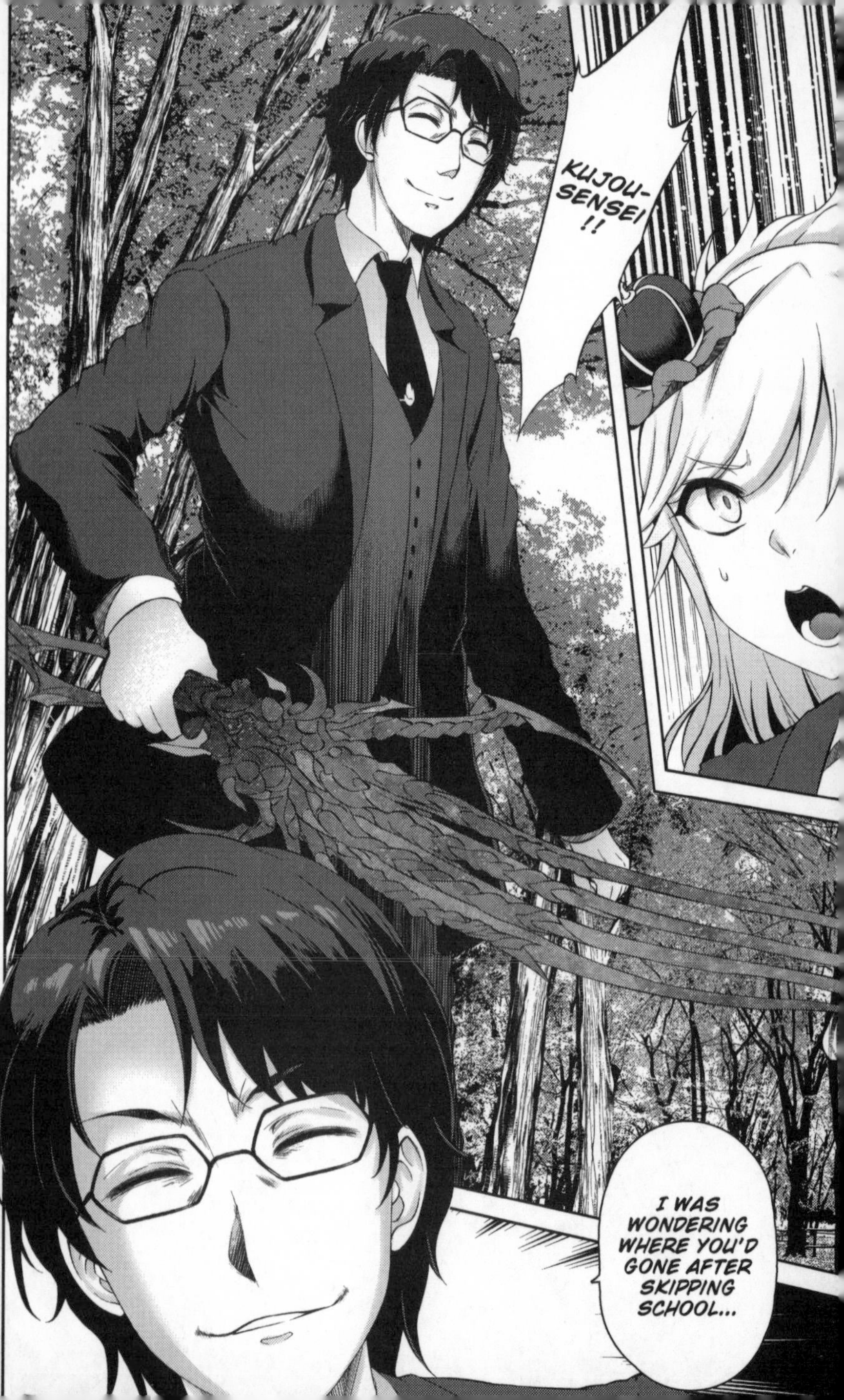
KUJOU-SENSEI!!
I WAS WONDERING WHERE YOU'D GONE AFTER SKIPPING SCHOOL...

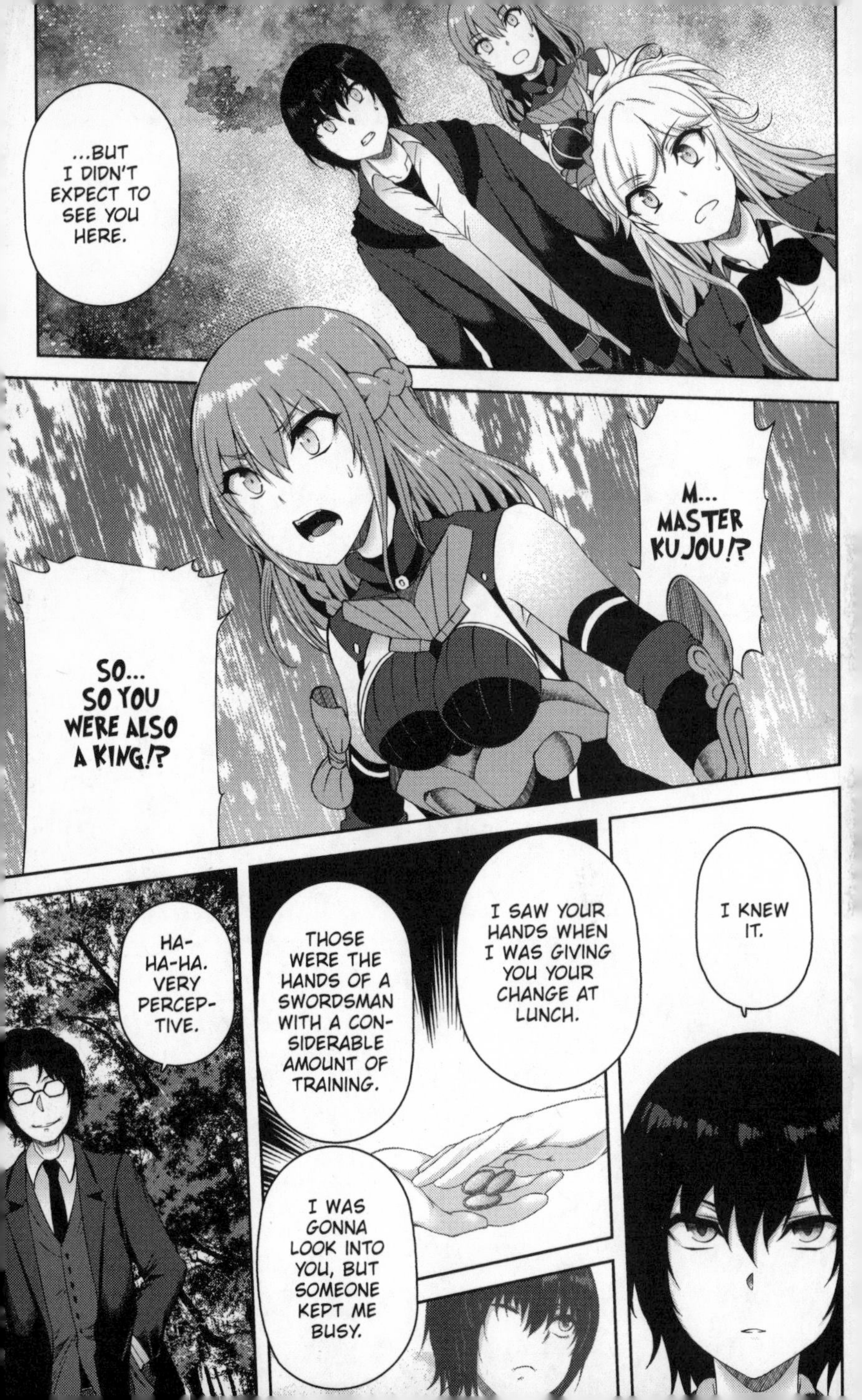
...BUT I DIDN'T EXPECT TO SEE YOU HERE.
M... MASTER KUJOU!?
SO... SO YOU WERE ALSO A KING!?
I KNEW IT.
I SAW YOUR HANDS WHEN I WAS GIVING YOU YOUR CHANGE AT LUNCH.
THOSE WERE THE HANDS OF A SWORDSMAN WITH A CONSIDERABLE AMOUNT OF TRAINING.
I WAS GONNA LOOK INTO YOU, BUT SOMEONE KEPT ME BUSY.
HA-HA-HA. VERY PERCEPTIVE.

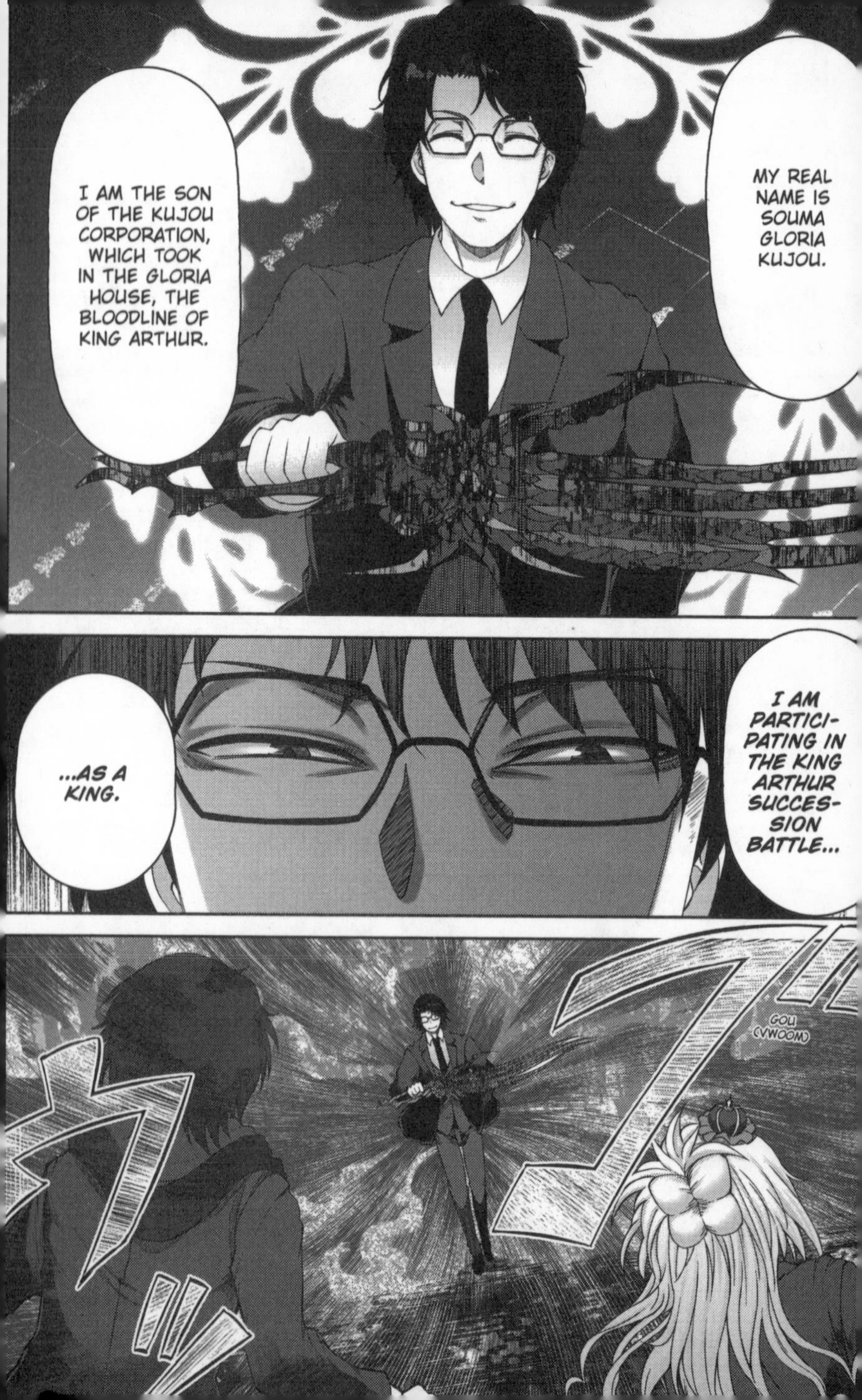
MY REAL NAME IS SOUMA GLORIA KUJOU.
I AM THE SON OF THE KUJOU CORPORATION, WHICH TOOK IN THE GLORIA HOUSE, THE BLOODLINE OF KING ARTHUR.
I AM PARTICIPATING IN THE KING ARTHUR SUCCESSION BATTLE...
...AS A KING.
GOU (VWOOM)

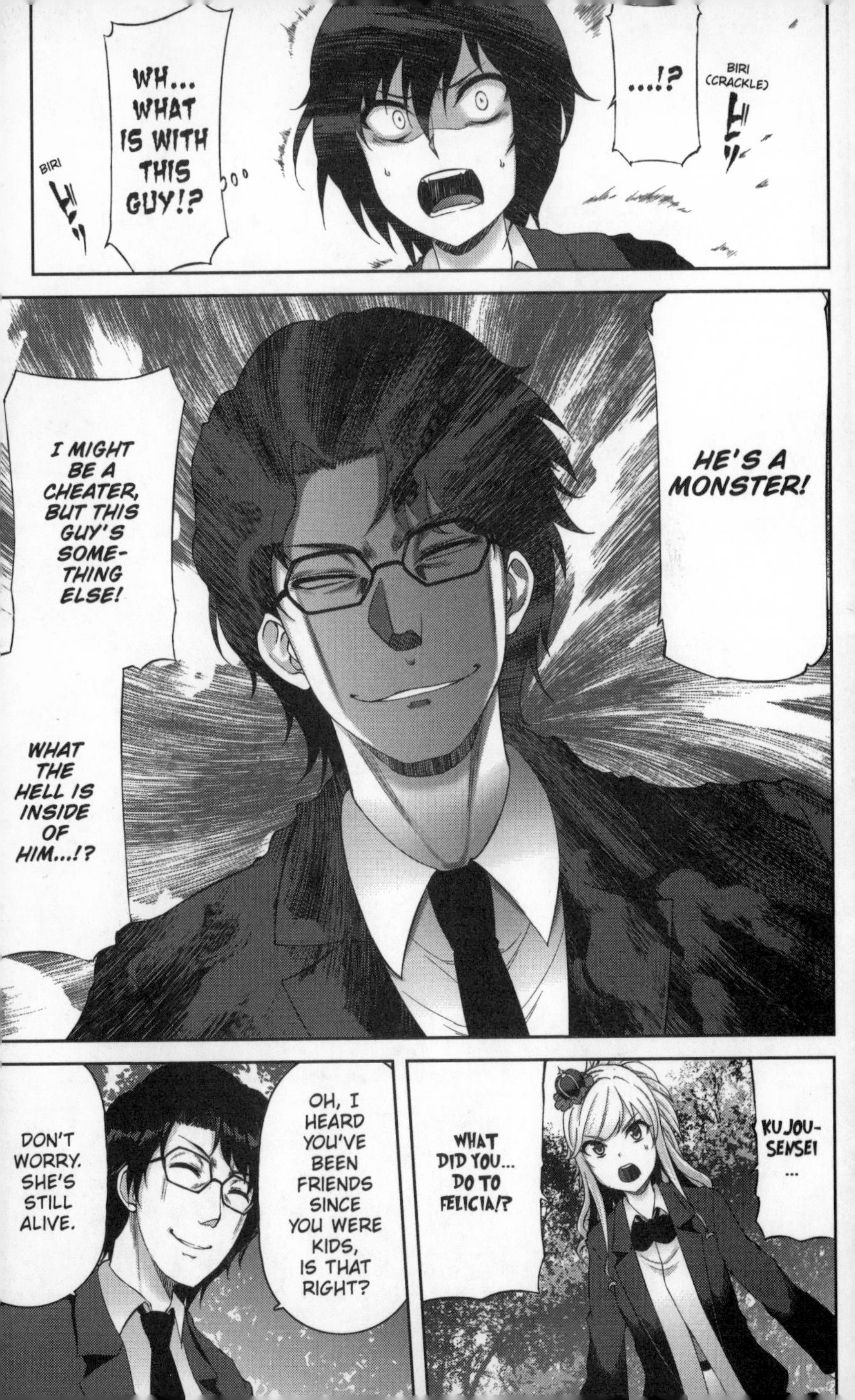
...!?
BIRI (CRACKLE)
WH... WHAT IS WITH THIS GUY!?
BIRI
HE'S A MONSTER!
I MIGHT BE A CHEATER, BUT THIS GUY'S SOME-THING ELSE!
WHAT THE HELL IS INSIDE OF HIM...!?
KUJOU-SENSEI ...
WHAT DID YOU... DO TO FELICIA!?
OH, I HEARD YOU'VE BEEN FRIENDS SINCE YOU WERE KIDS, IS THAT RIGHT?
DON'T WORRY. SHE'S STILL ALIVE.

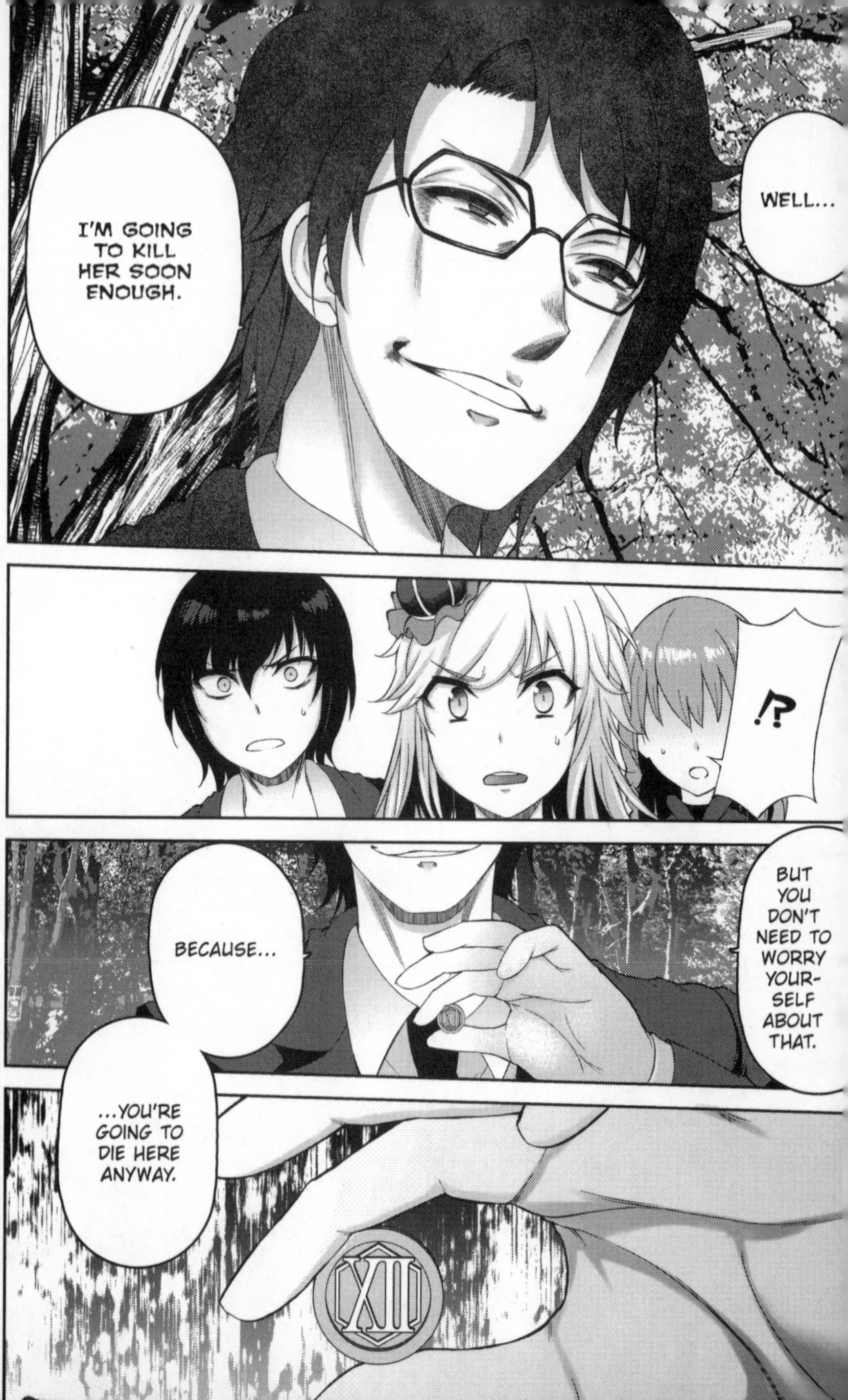
WELL...
I'M GOING TO KILL HER SOON ENOUGH.
!?
BUT YOU DON'T NEED TO WORRY YOURSELF ABOUT THAT.
BECAUSE...
...YOU'RE GOING TO DIE HERE ANYWAY.
XII

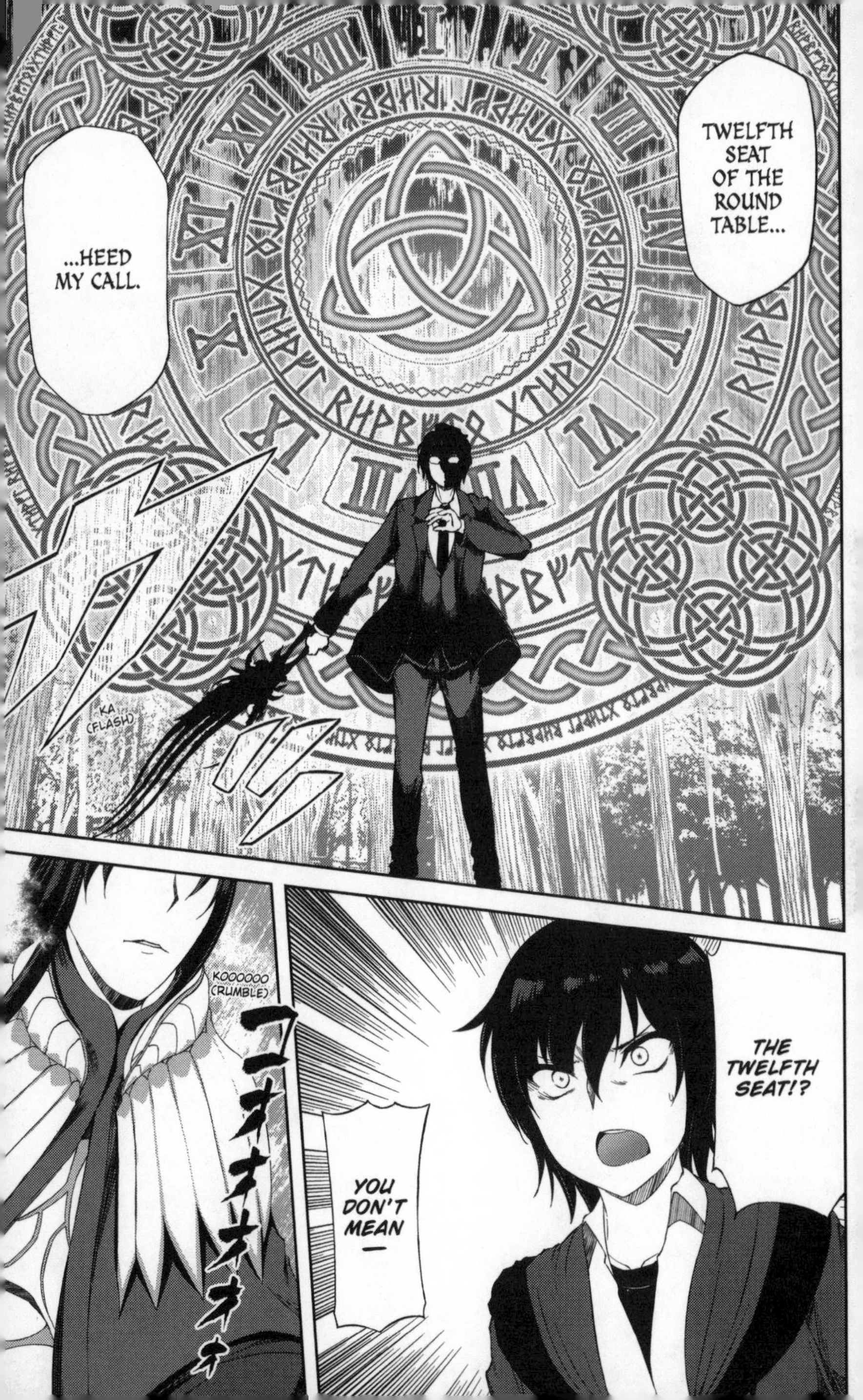
TWELFTH SEAT OF THE ROUND TABLE...
...HEED MY CALL.
KA (FLASH)
THE TWELFTH SEAT!?
YOU DON'T MEAN—
KOOOOOO (RUMBLE)

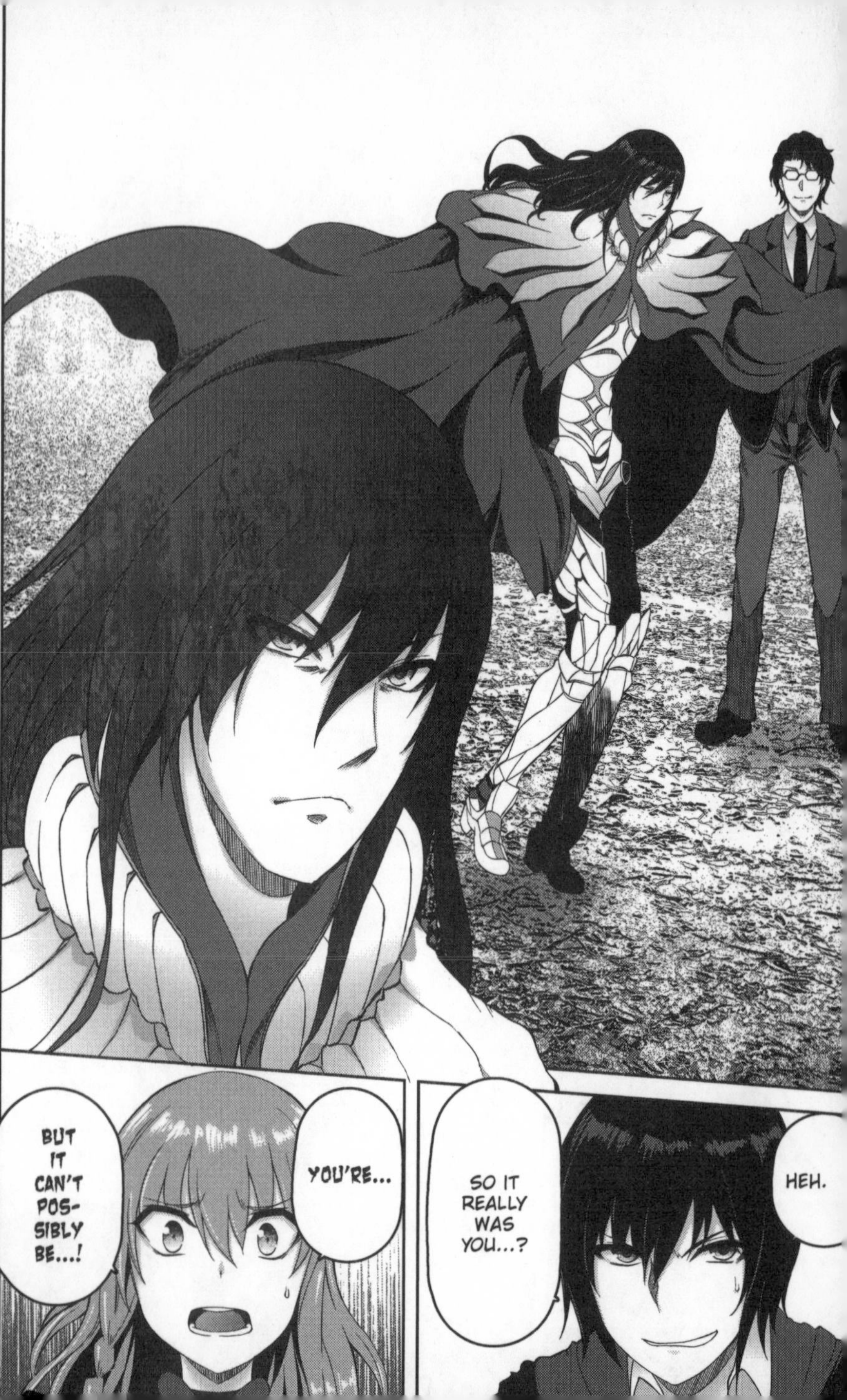
HEH.
SO IT REALLY WAS YOU...?
YOU'RE...
BUT IT CAN'T POS-SIBLY BE...!

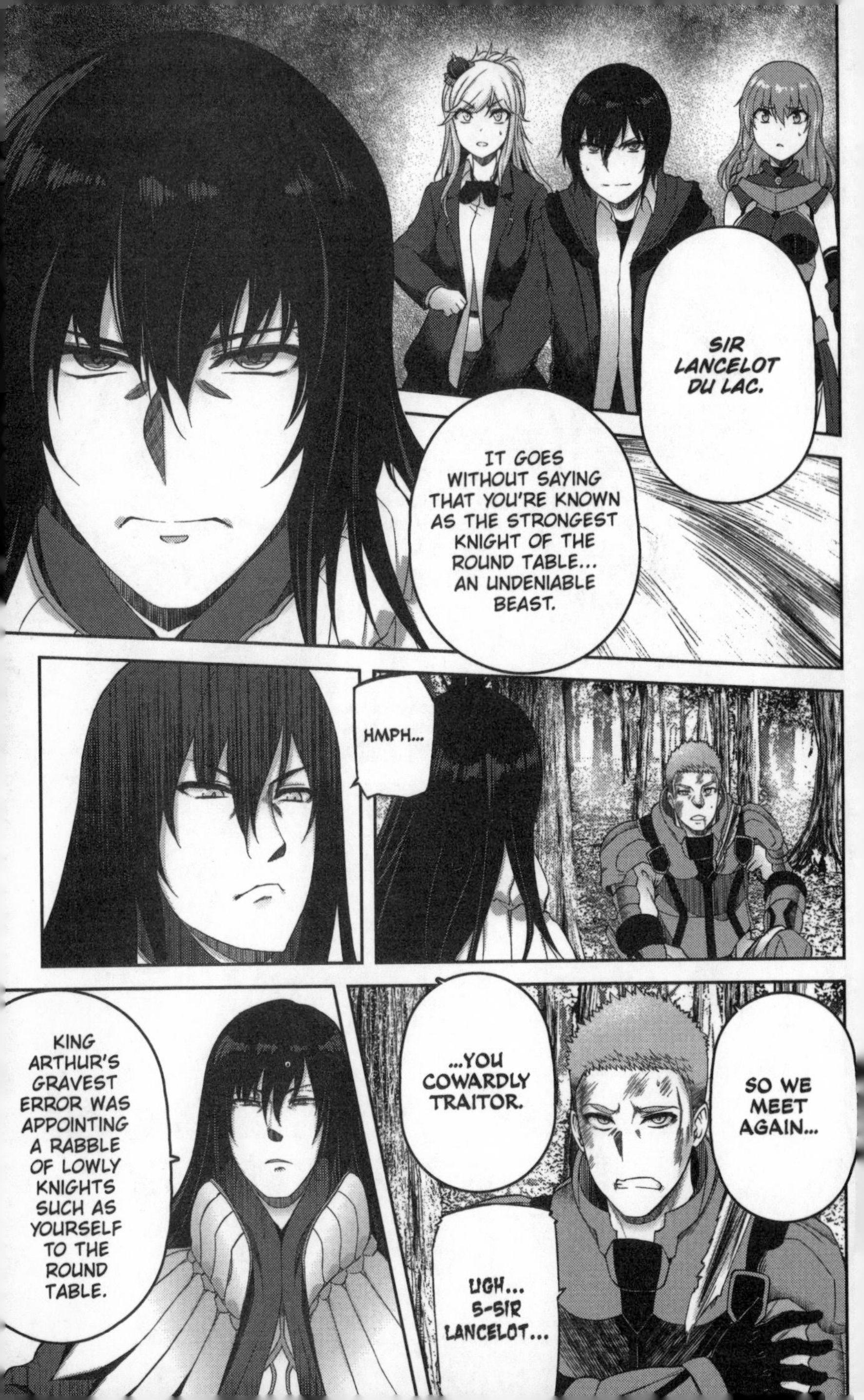

SIR LANCELOT DU LAC.
IT GOES WITHOUT SAYING THAT YOU'RE KNOWN AS THE STRONGEST KNIGHT OF THE ROUND TABLE... AN UNDENIABLE BEAST.
HMPH...
SO WE MEET AGAIN...
...YOU COWARDLY TRAITOR.
UGH... S-SIR LANCELOT...
KING ARTHUR'S GRAVEST ERROR WAS APPOINTING A RABBLE OF LOWLY KNIGHTS SUCH AS YOURSELF TO THE ROUND TABLE.

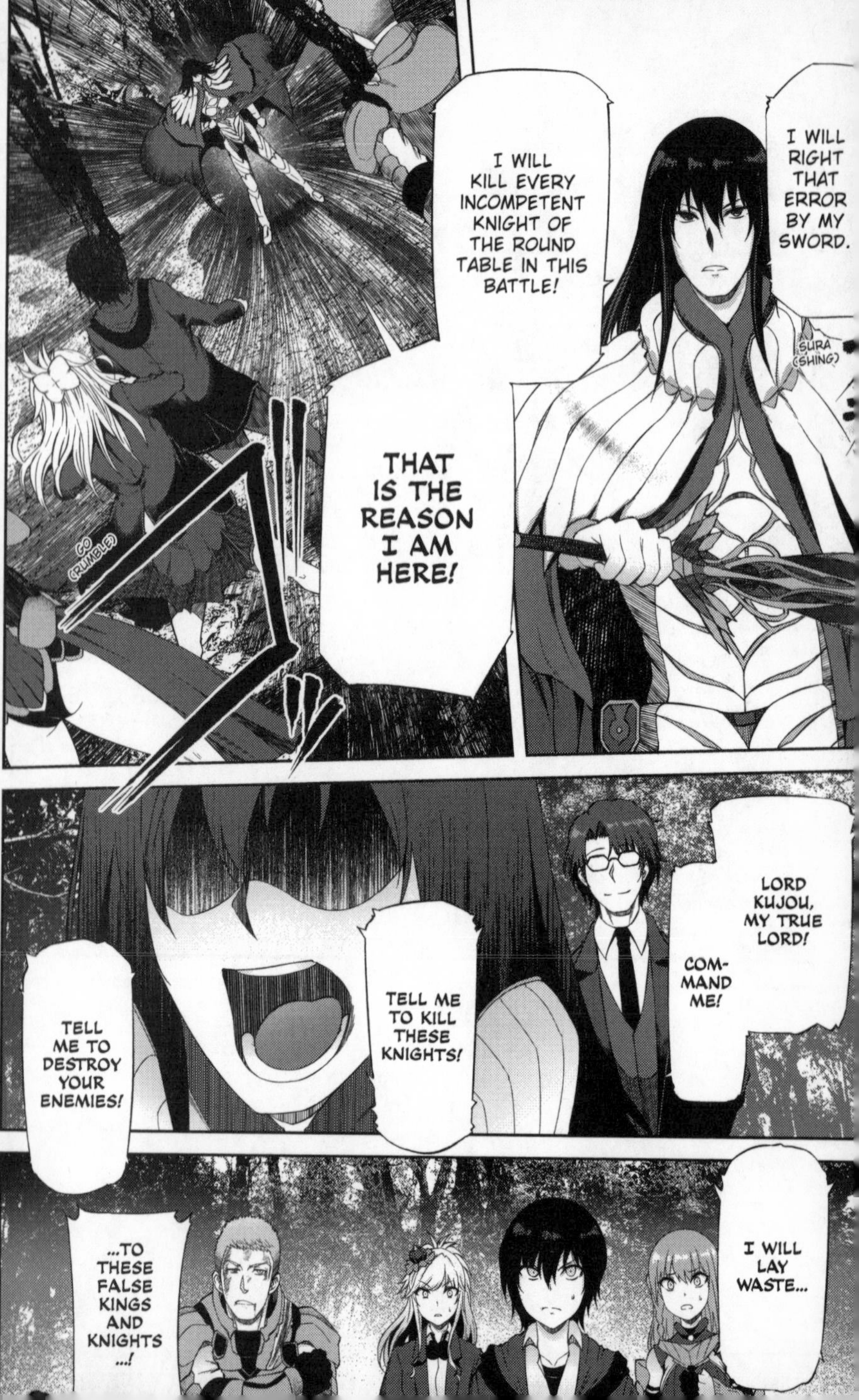
I WILL RIGHT THAT ERROR BY MY SWORD.
I WILL KILL EVERY INCOMPETENT KNIGHT OF THE ROUND TABLE IN THIS BATTLE!
SURA (SHING)
THAT IS THE REASON I AM HERE!
GO (RUMBLE)
LORD KUJOU, MY TRUE LORD!
COM-MAND ME!
TELL ME TO KILL THESE KNIGHTS!
TELL ME TO DESTROY YOUR ENEMIES!
I WILL LAY WASTE...
...TO THESE FALSE KINGS AND KNIGHTS...!

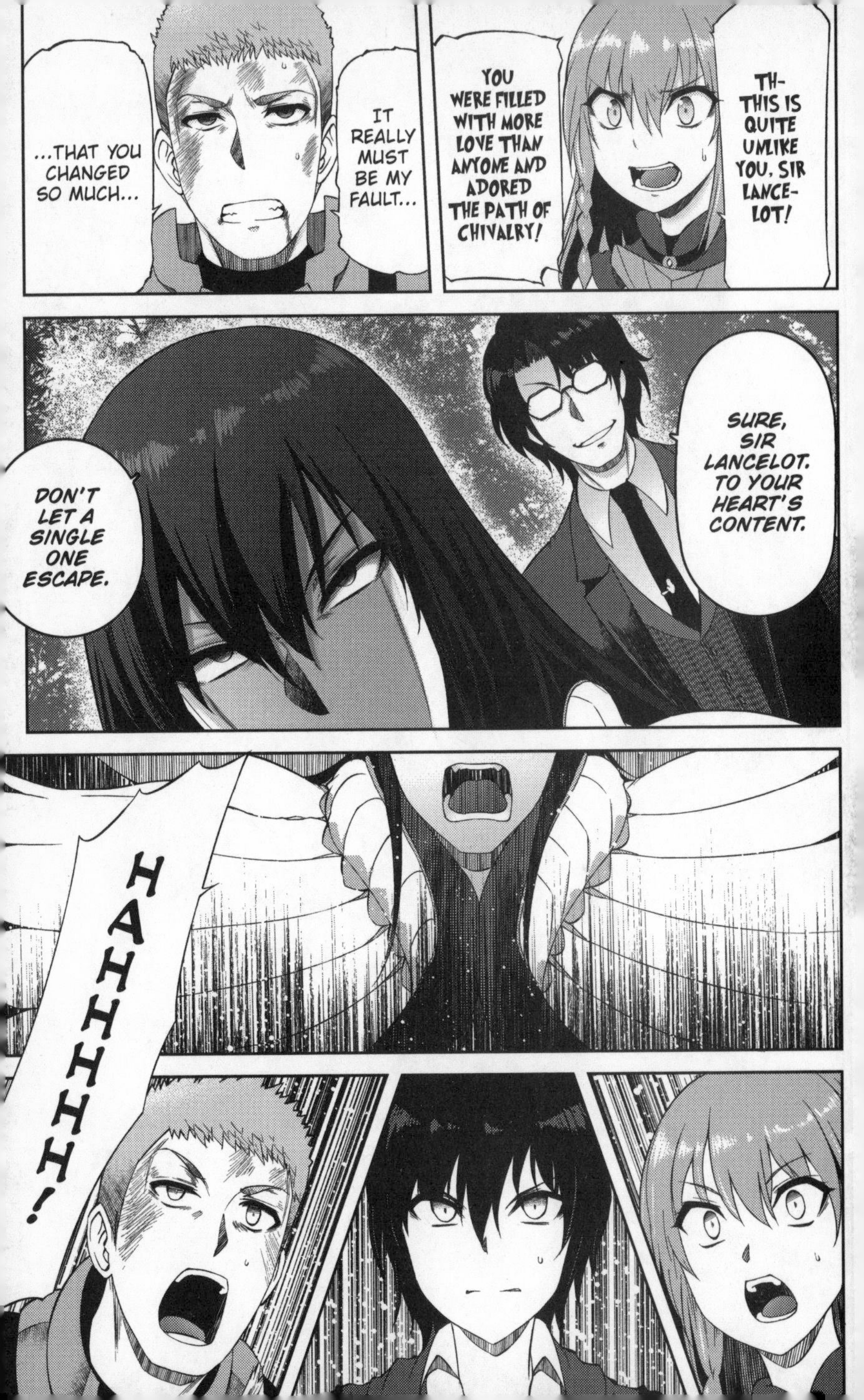
TH- THIS IS QUITE UNLIKE YOU, SIR LANCELOT!
YOU WERE FILLED WITH MORE LOVE THAN ANYONE AND ADORED THE PATH OF CHIVALRY!
IT REALLY MUST BE MY FAULT...
...THAT YOU CHANGED SO MUCH...
SURE, SIR LANCELOT. TO YOUR HEART'S CONTENT.
DON'T LET A SINGLE ONE ESCAPE.
HAHHHHHH!

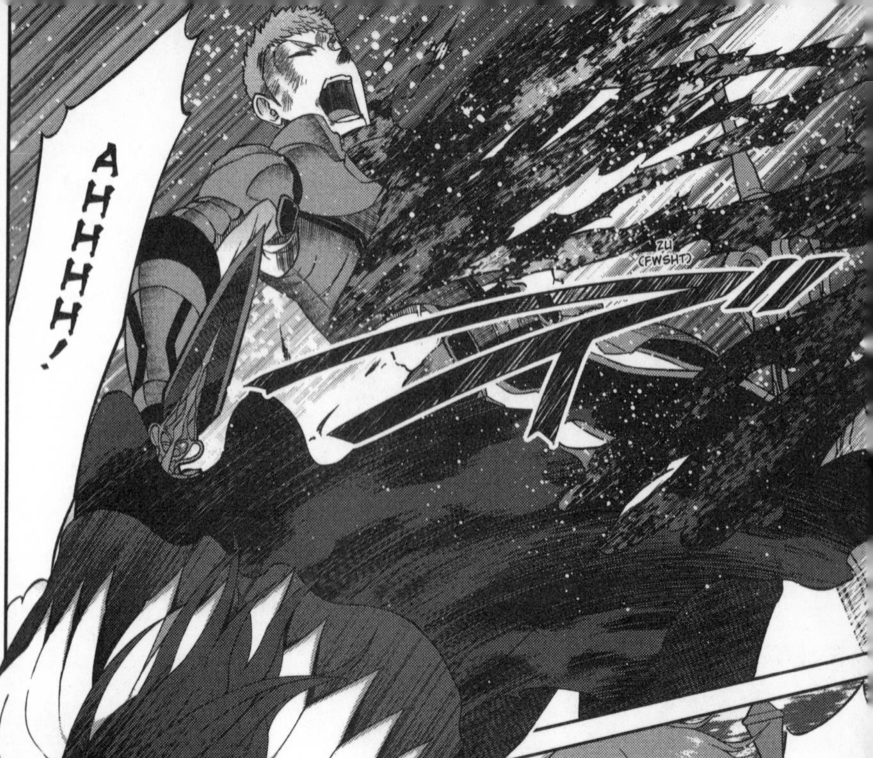
AHHHHH!
ZU (FWSHT)
GUUUUUH!
BA (BWOOSH)
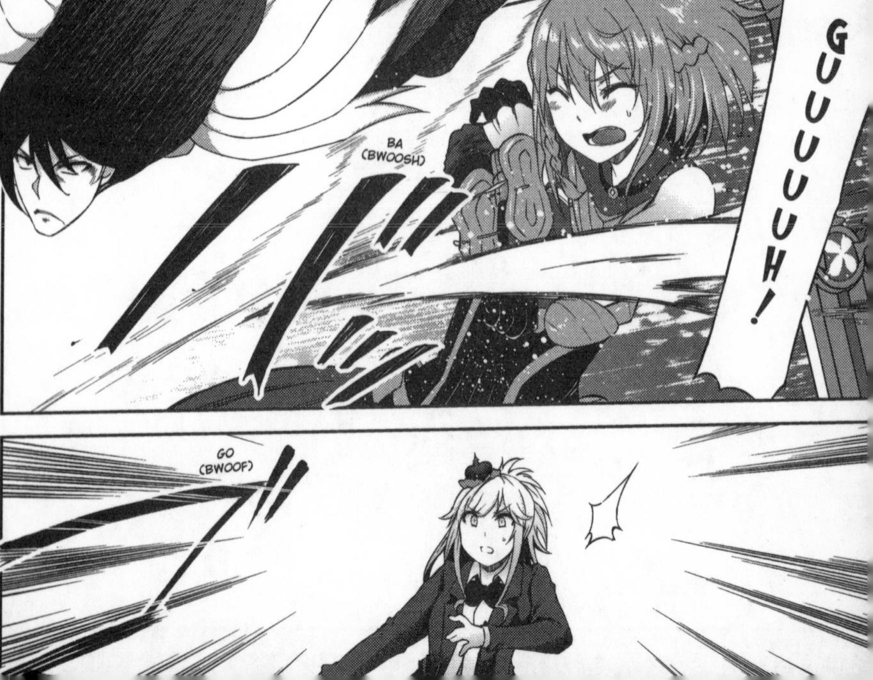
GO (BWOOF)

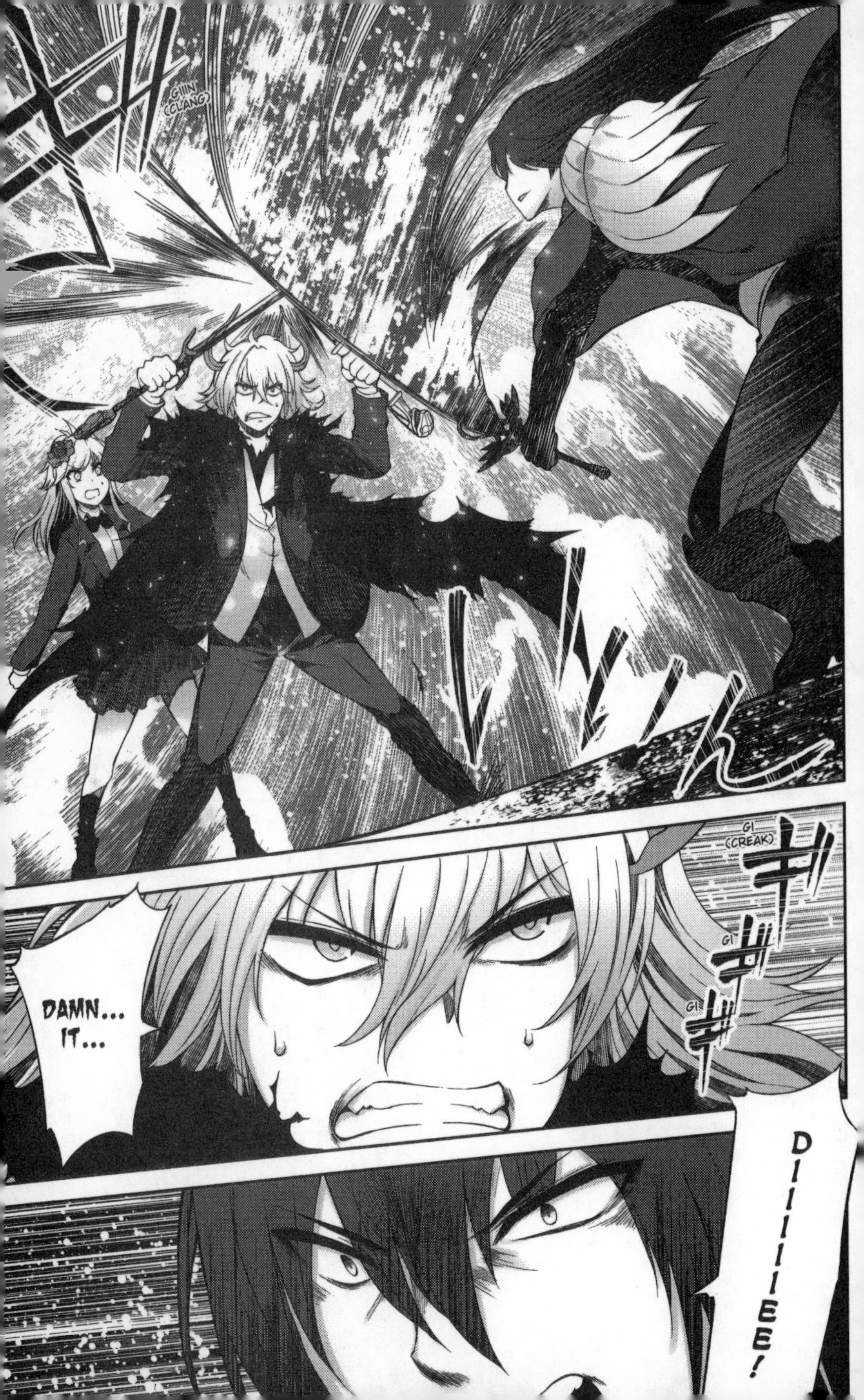
GIIN (CLANG)
GI (CREAK)
GI
GI
DAMN... IT...
DIIIIIEE!

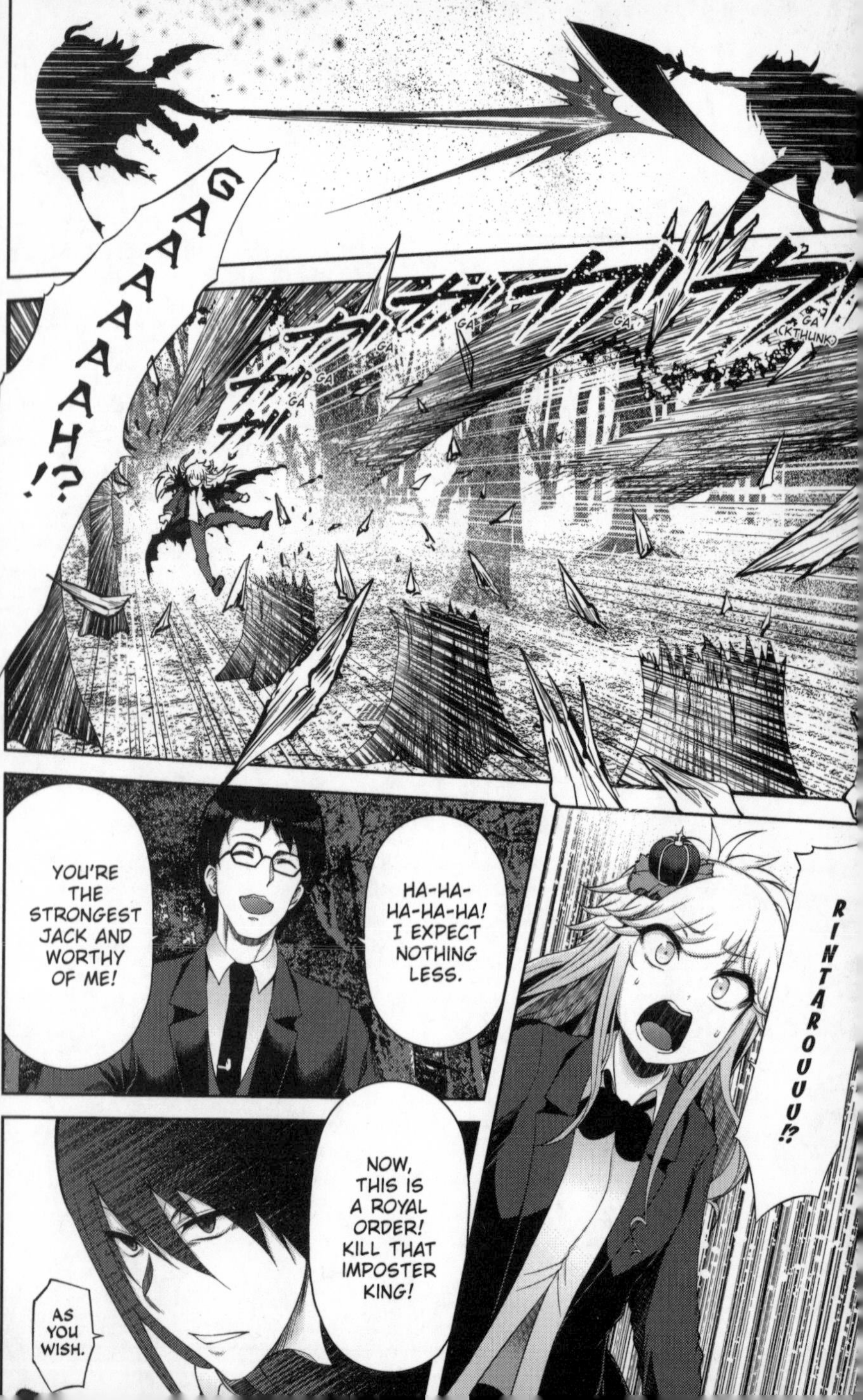
GAAAAAAAH!?
GA
GA
GA
GA
GA (KTHUNK)
RINTAROUUUU!?
HA-HA-HA-HA-HA! I EXPECT NOTHING LESS.
YOU'RE THE STRONGEST JACK AND WORTHY OF ME!
NOW, THIS IS A ROYAL ORDER! KILL THAT IMPOSTER KING!
AS YOU WISH.

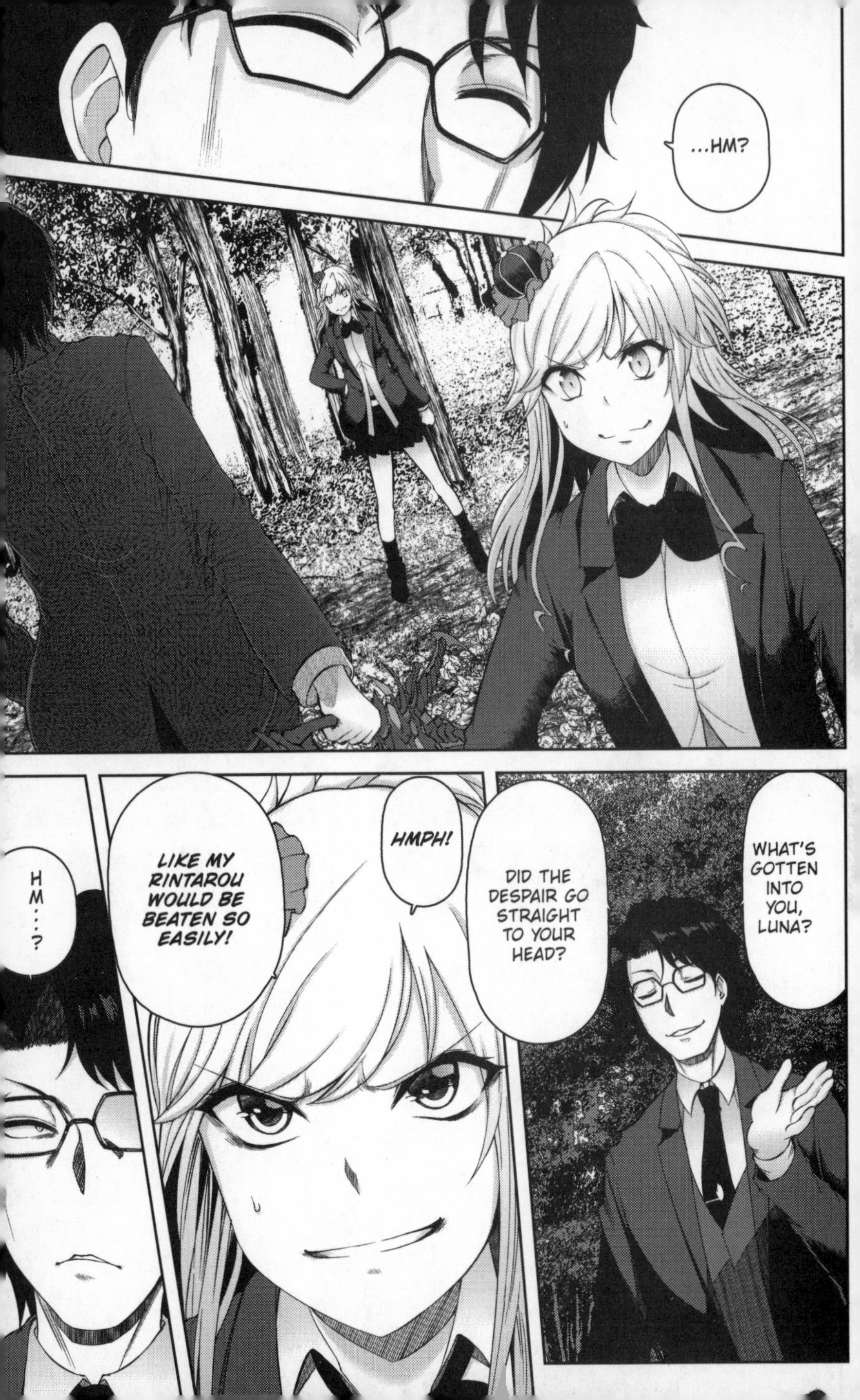
...HM?
WHAT'S GOTTEN INTO YOU, LUNA?
DID THE DESPAIR GO STRAIGHT TO YOUR HEAD?
HMPH!
LIKE MY RINTAROU WOULD BE BEATEN SO EASILY!
HM...?

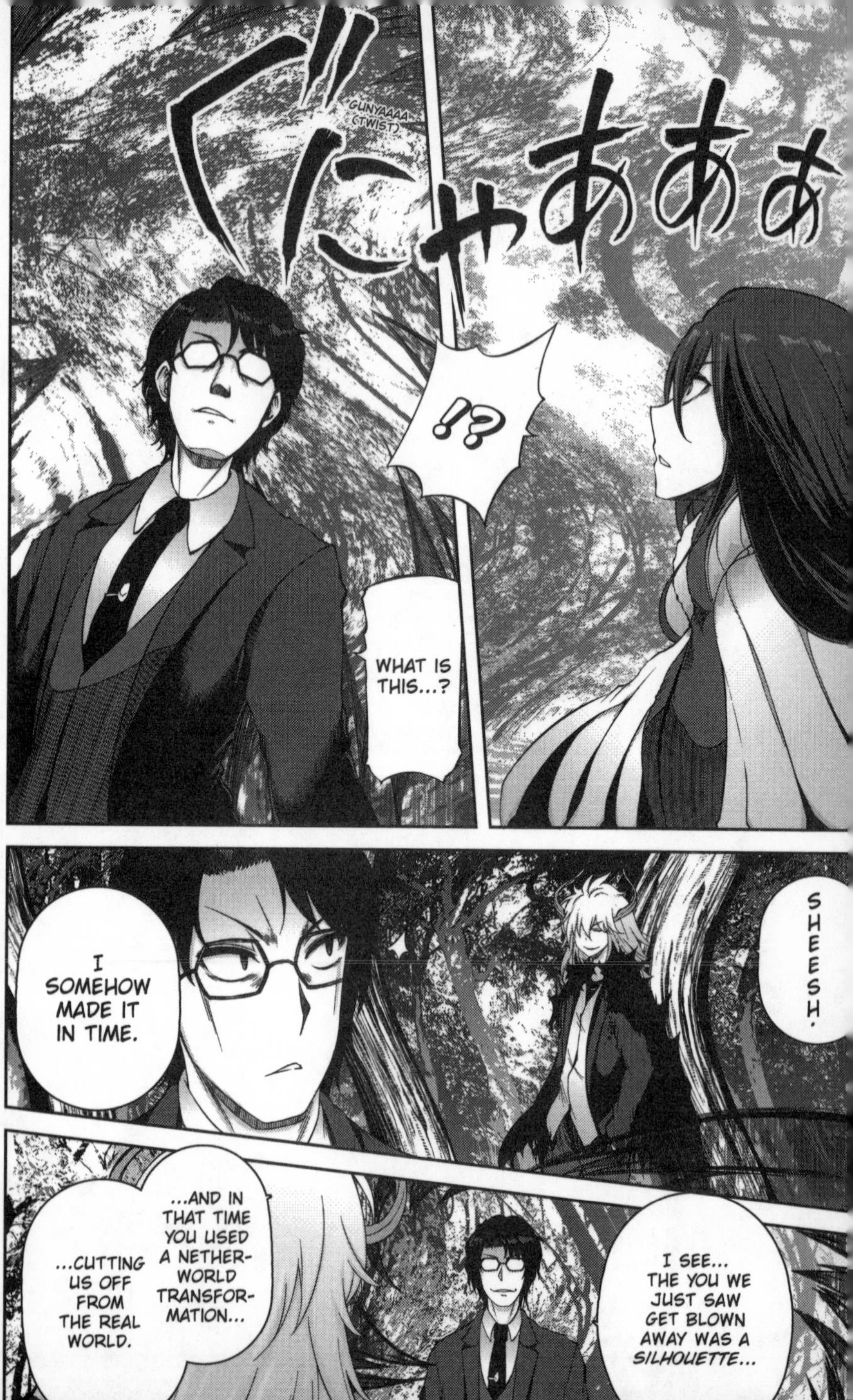
ぐにゃあああぁ
GUNYAAAA (TWIST)
!?
WHAT IS THIS...?
SHEESH.
I SOMEHOW MADE IT IN TIME.
I SEE... THE YOU WE JUST SAW GET BLOWN AWAY WAS A SILHOUETTE...
...AND IN THAT TIME YOU USED A NETHER-WORLD TRANSFORMATION...
...CUTTING US OFF FROM THE REAL WORLD.

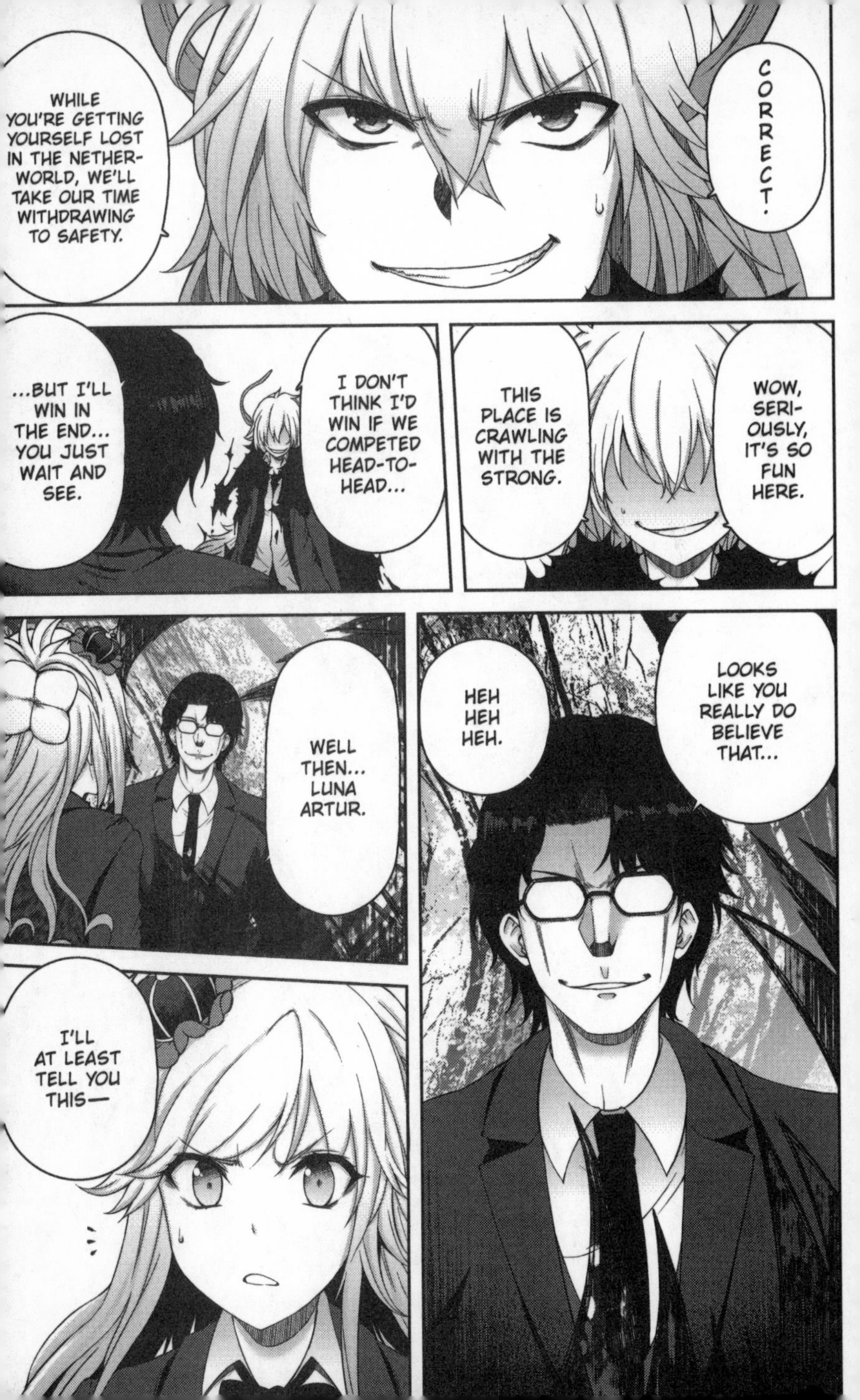
CORRECT.
WHILE YOU'RE GETTING YOURSELF LOST IN THE NETHER-WORLD, WE'LL TAKE OUR TIME WITHDRAWING TO SAFETY.
WOW, SERI-OUSLY, IT'S SO FUN HERE.
THIS PLACE IS CRAWLING WITH THE STRONG.
I DON'T THINK I'D WIN IF WE COMPETED HEAD-TO-HEAD...
...BUT I'LL WIN IN THE END... YOU JUST WAIT AND SEE.
LOOKS LIKE YOU REALLY DO BELIEVE THAT...
HEH HEH HEH.
WELL THEN... LUNA ARTUR.
I'LL AT LEAST TELL YOU THIS—

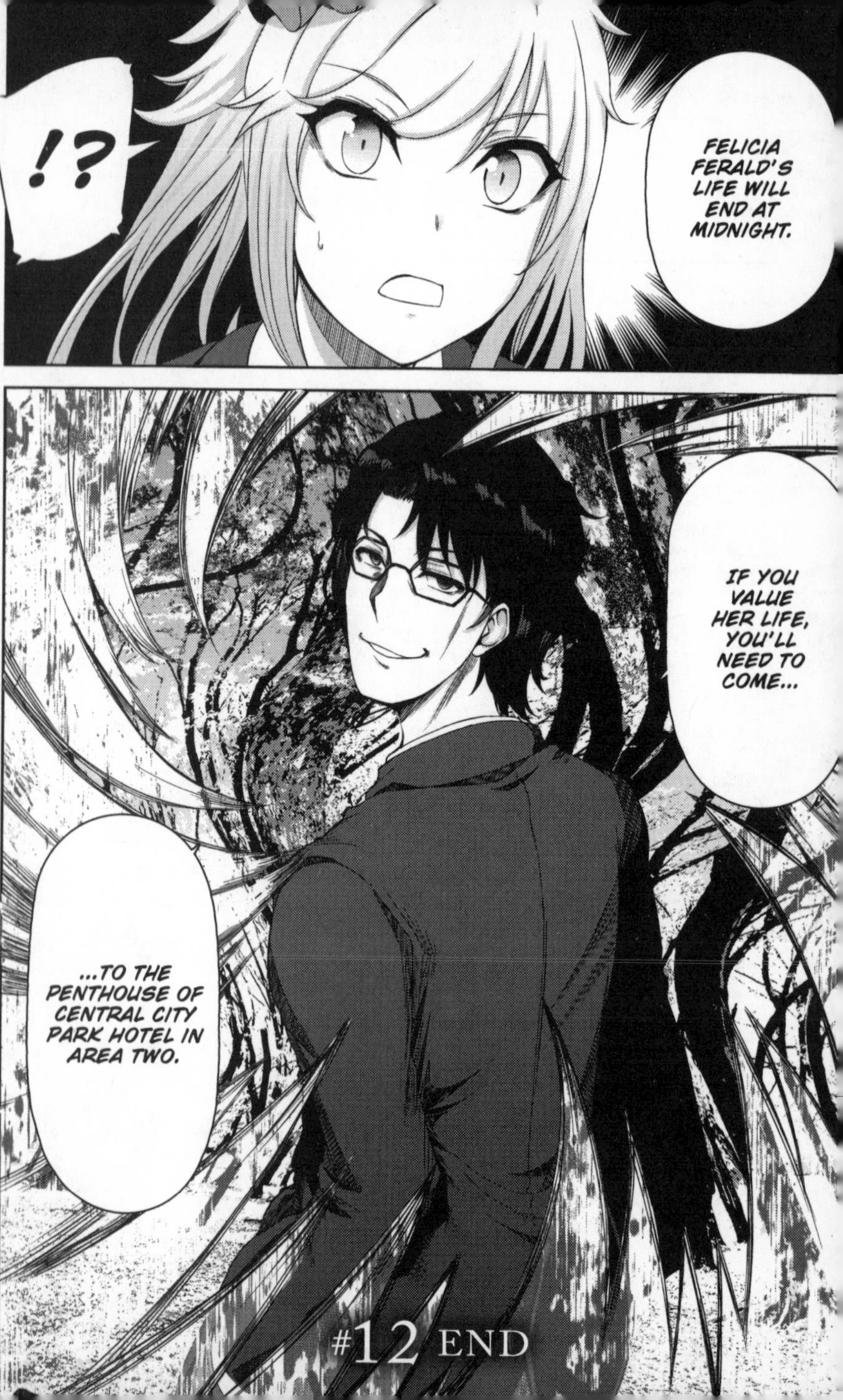
FELICIA FERALD'S LIFE WILL END AT MIDNIGHT.
!?
IF YOU VALUE HER LIFE, YOU'LL NEED TO COME...
...TO THE PENTHOUSE OF CENTRAL CITY PARK HOTEL IN AREA TWO.
#12 END

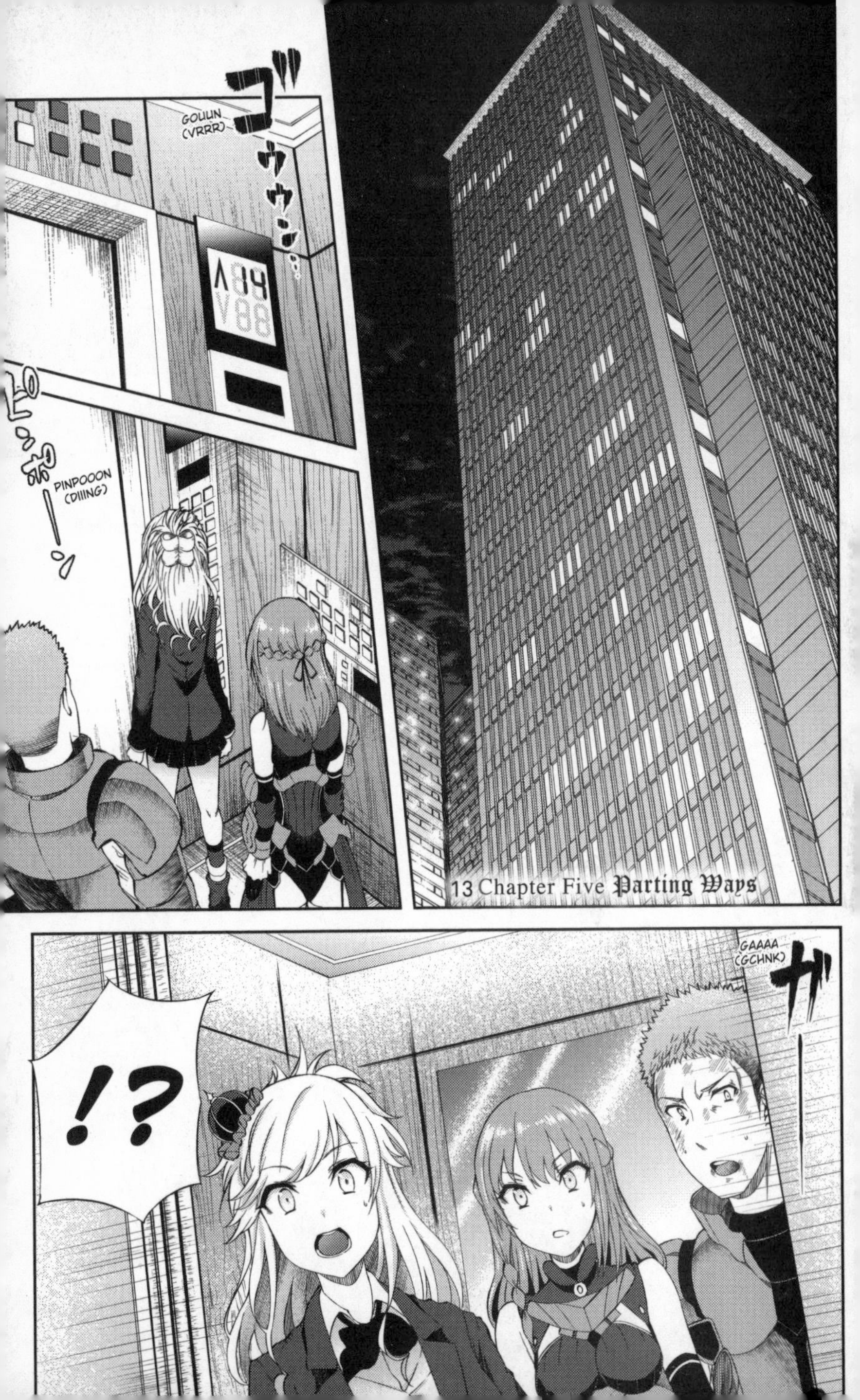
13 Chapter Five Parting Ways
GOUUN (VRRR)
PINPOOON (DIIING)
GAAAA (GCHNK)
!?

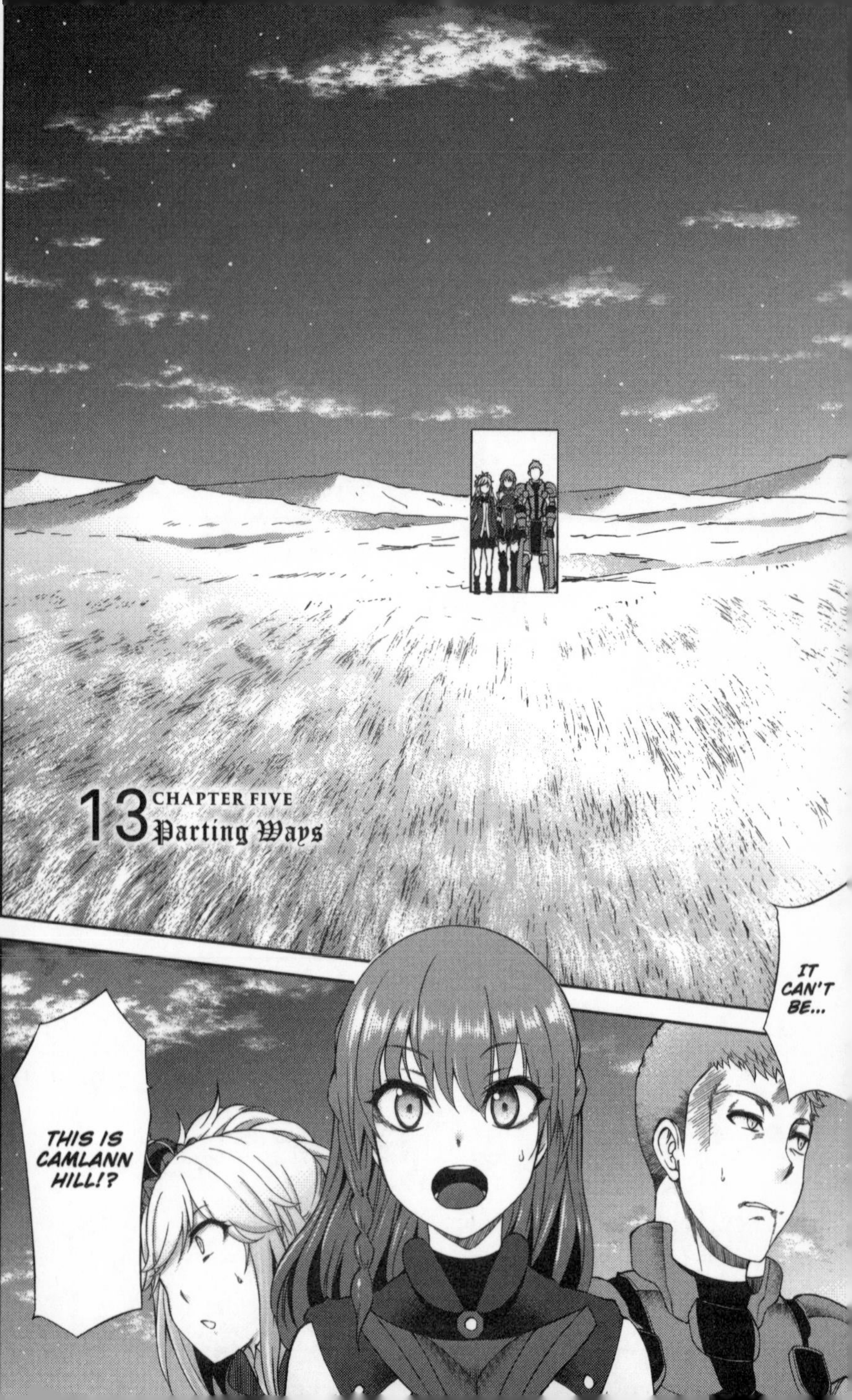
13 CHAPTER FIVE
Parting Ways
IT CAN'T BE...
THIS IS CAMLANN HILL!?

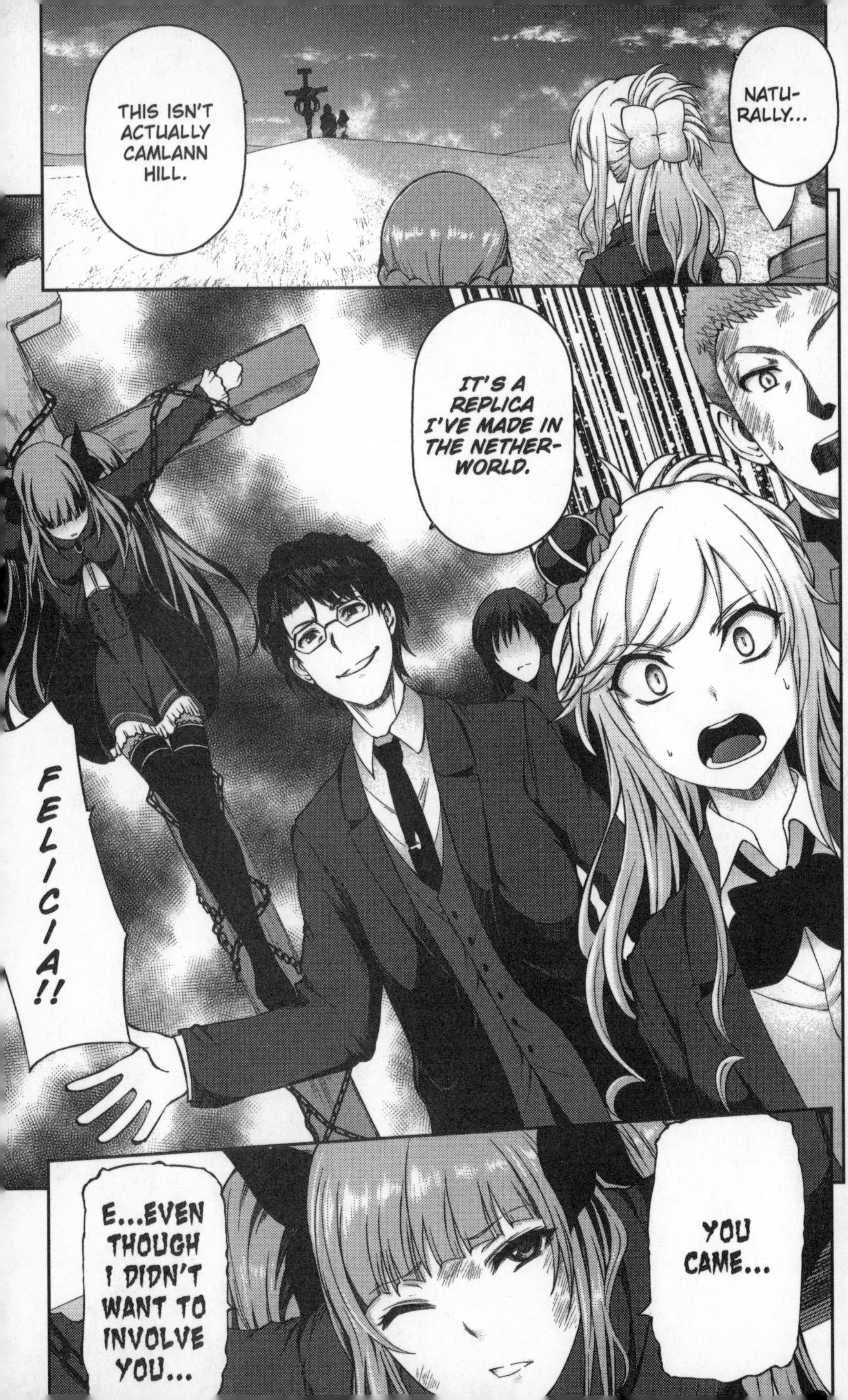
NATU-RALLY...
THIS ISN'T ACTUALLY CAMLANN HILL.
IT'S A REPLICA I'VE MADE IN THE NETHER-WORLD.
FELICIA!!
YOU CAME...
E...EVEN THOUGH I DIDN'T WANT TO INVOLVE YOU...

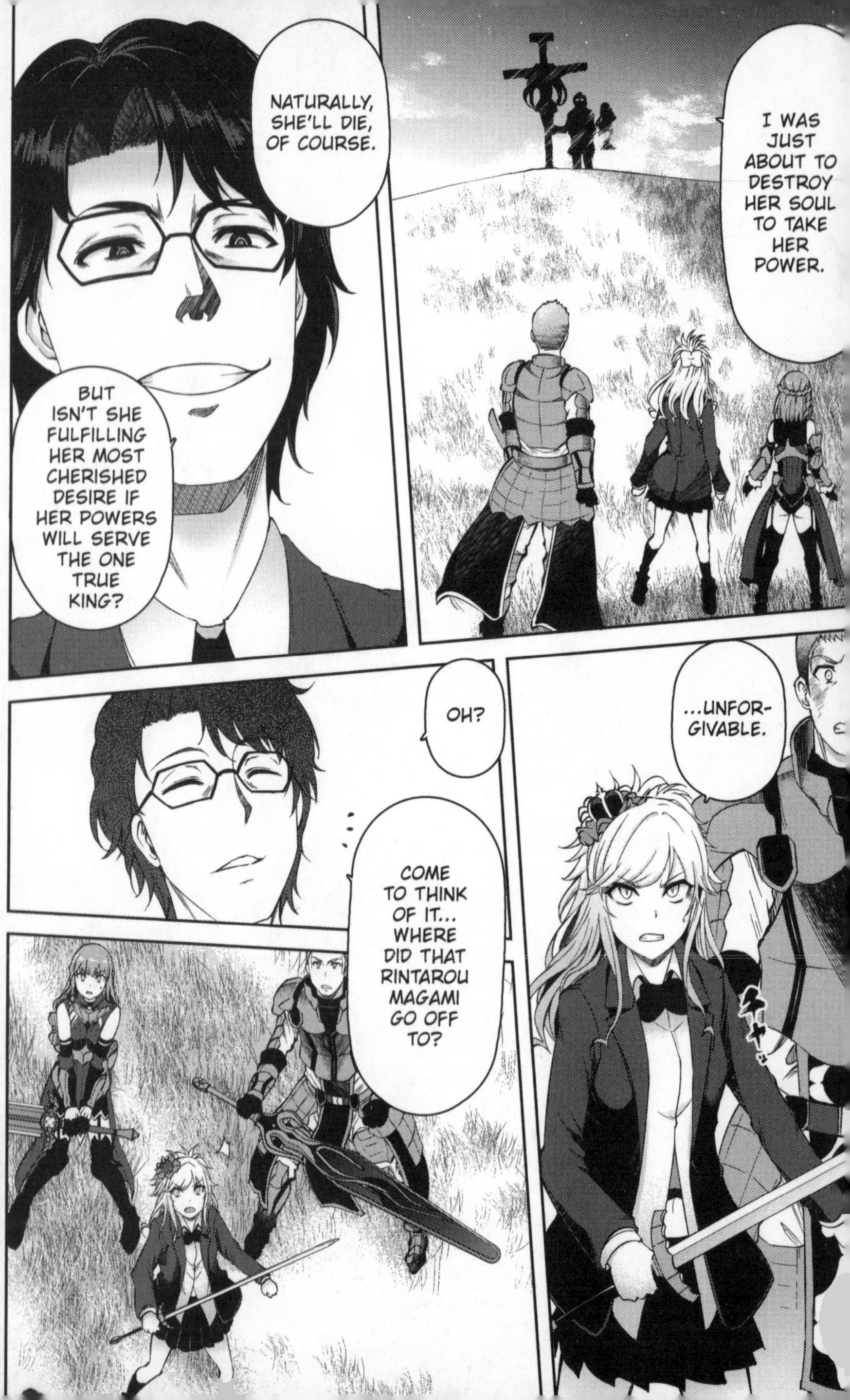
I WAS JUST ABOUT TO DESTROY HER SOUL TO TAKE HER POWER.
NATURALLY, SHE'LL DIE, OF COURSE.
BUT ISN'T SHE FULFILLING HER MOST CHERISHED DESIRE IF HER POWERS WILL SERVE THE ONE TRUE KING?
...UNFOR-GIVABLE.
OH?
...
COME TO THINK OF IT... WHERE DID THAT RINTAROU MAGAMI GO OFF TO?

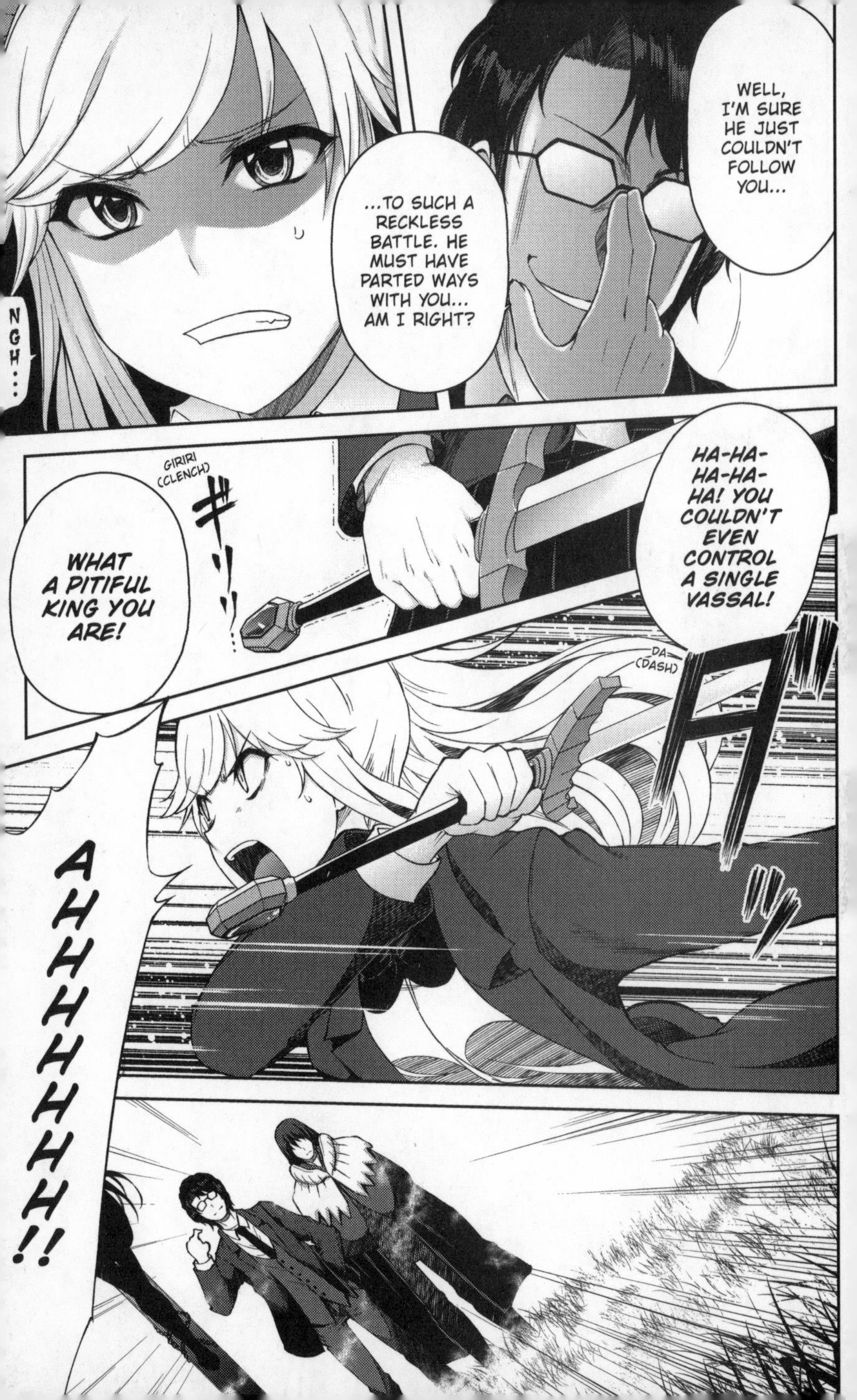
WELL, I'M SURE HE JUST COULDN'T FOLLOW YOU...
...TO SUCH A RECKLESS BATTLE. HE MUST HAVE PARTED WAYS WITH YOU... AM I RIGHT?
NGH...
HA-HA-HA-HA-HA! YOU COULDN'T EVEN CONTROL A SINGLE VASSAL!
GIRIRI (CLENCH)
WHAT A PITIFUL KING YOU ARE!
DA (DASH)
AHHHHHHHH!!

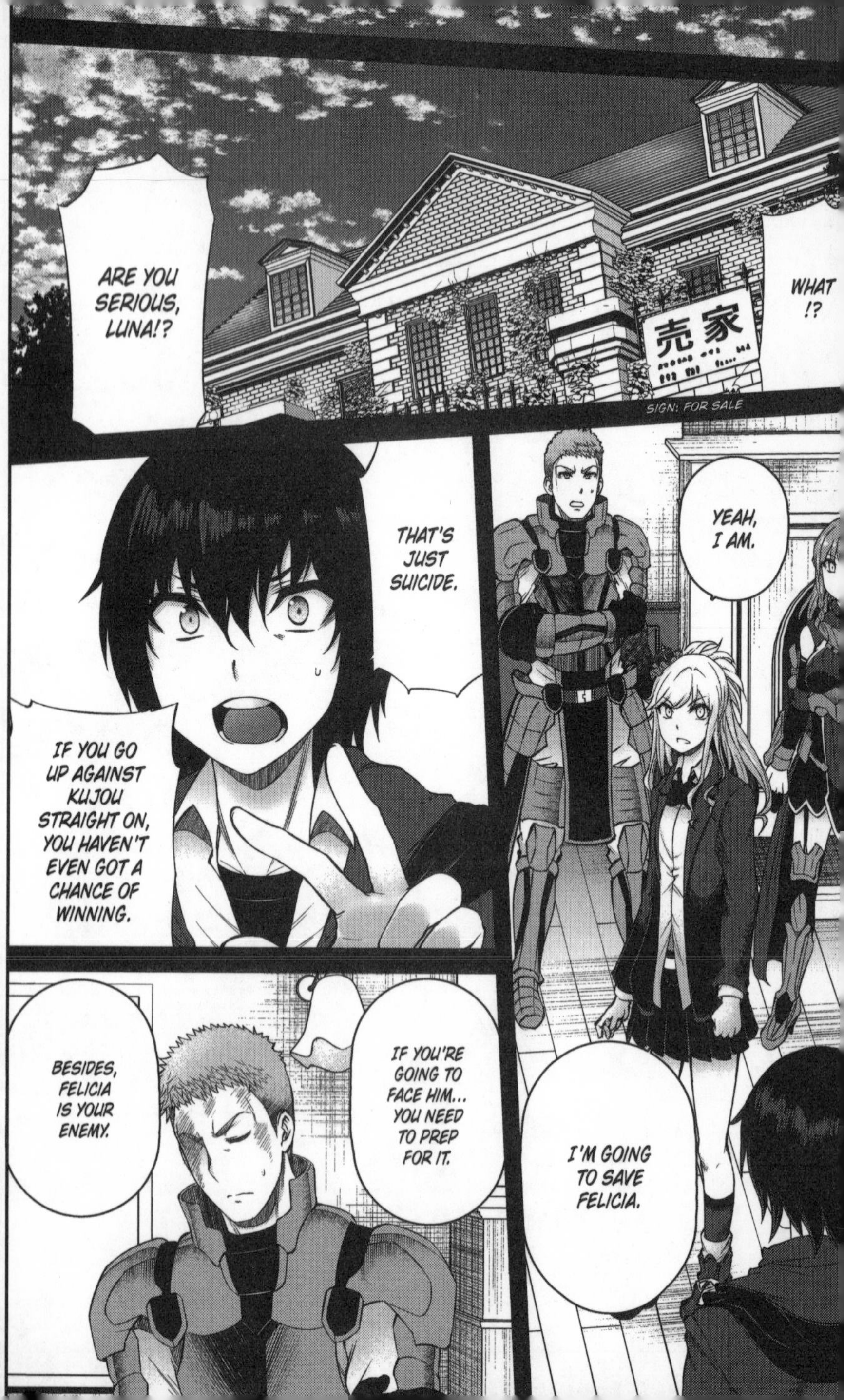
WHAT !?
ARE YOU SERIOUS, LUNA!?
売家
SIGN: FOR SALE
YEAH, I AM.
I'M GOING TO SAVE FELICIA.
THAT'S JUST SUICIDE.
IF YOU GO UP AGAINST KUJOU STRAIGHT ON, YOU HAVEN'T EVEN GOT A CHANCE OF WINNING.
IF YOU'RE GOING TO FACE HIM... YOU NEED TO PREP FOR IT.
BESIDES, FELICIA IS YOUR ENEMY.

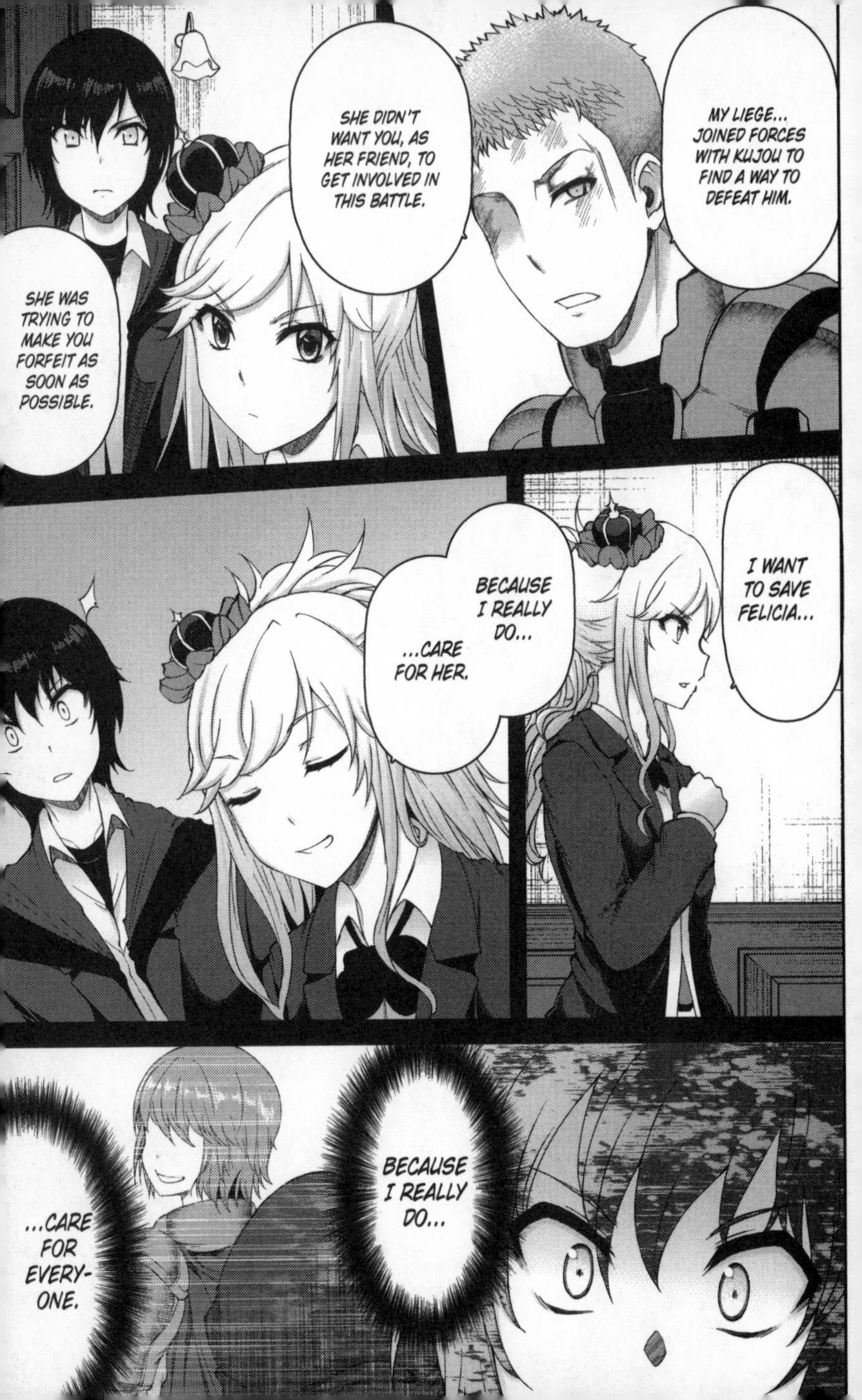
MY LIEGE... JOINED FORCES WITH KUJOU TO FIND A WAY TO DEFEAT HIM.
SHE DIDN'T WANT YOU, AS HER FRIEND, TO GET INVOLVED IN THIS BATTLE.
SHE WAS TRYING TO MAKE YOU FORFEIT AS SOON AS POSSIBLE.
I WANT TO SAVE FELICIA...
BECAUSE I REALLY DO...
...CARE FOR HER.
BECAUSE I REALLY DO...
...CARE FOR EVERY-ONE.

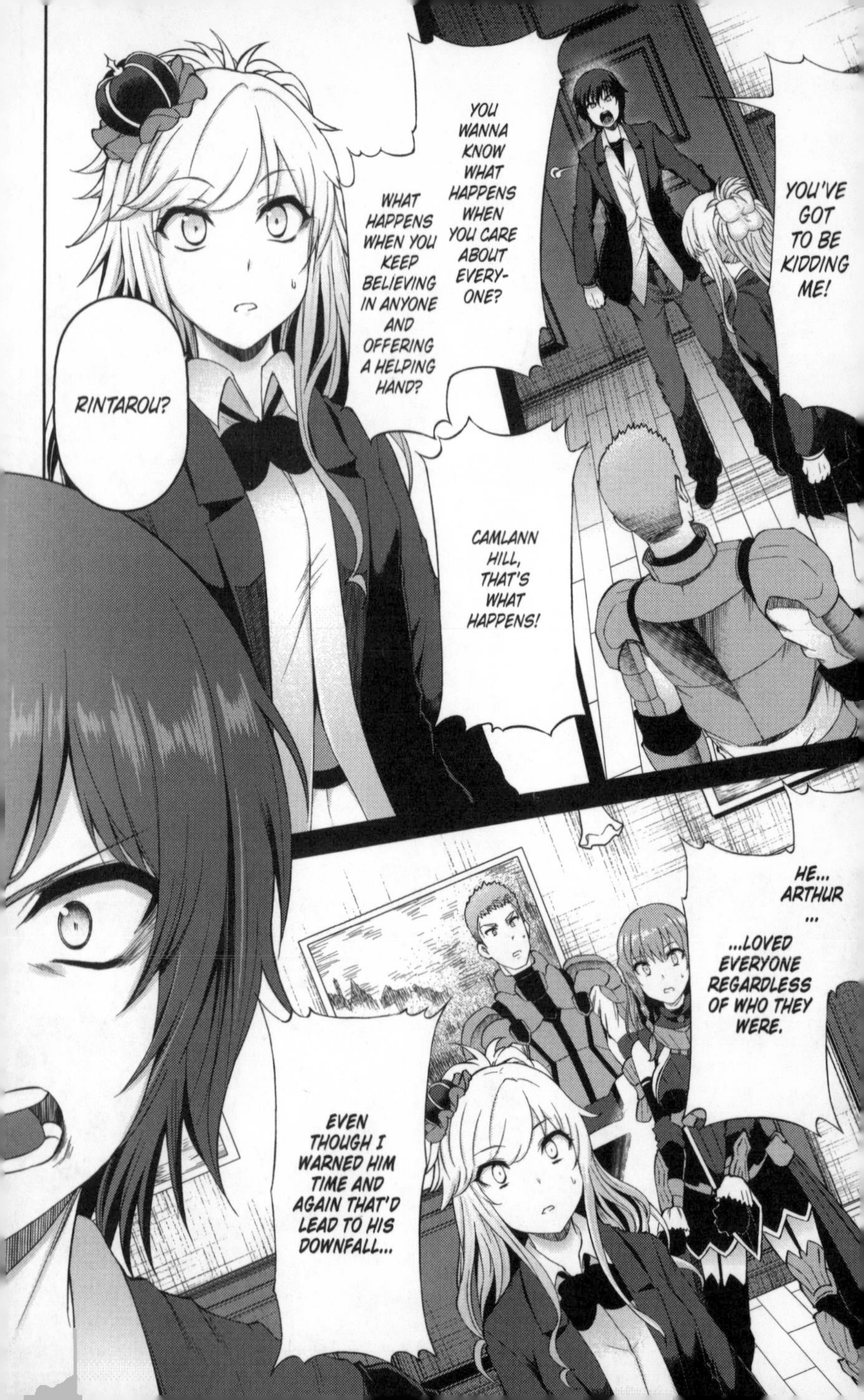
YOU'VE GOT TO BE KIDDING ME!
YOU WANNA KNOW WHAT HAPPENS WHEN YOU CARE ABOUT EVERY-ONE?
WHAT HAPPENS WHEN YOU KEEP BELIEVING IN ANYONE AND OFFERING A HELPING HAND?
CAMLANN HILL, THAT'S WHAT HAPPENS!
RINTAROU?
HE... ARTHUR ...
...LOVED EVERYONE REGARDLESS OF WHO THEY WERE.
EVEN THOUGH I WARNED HIM TIME AND AGAIN THAT'D LEAD TO HIS DOWNFALL...

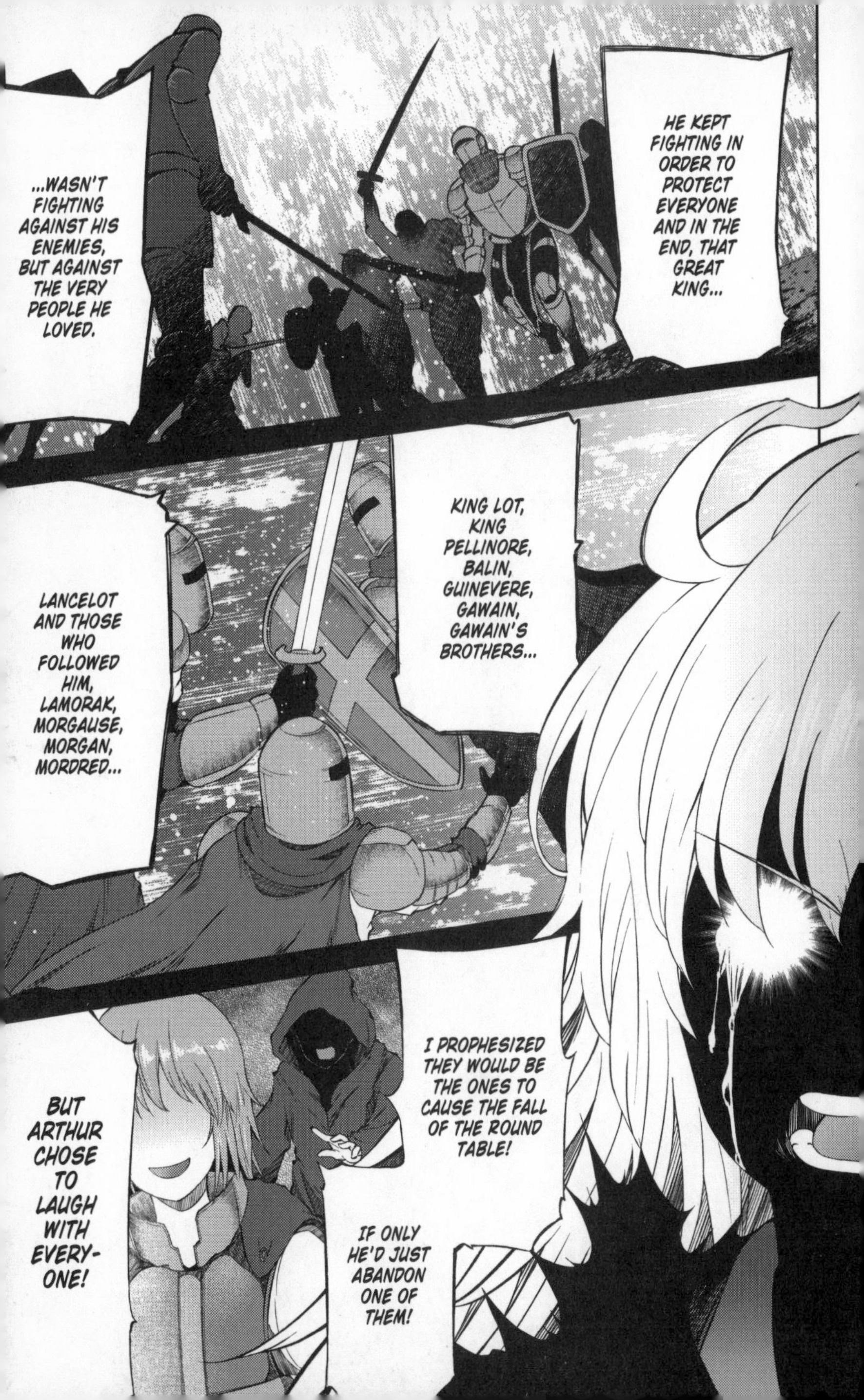
HE KEPT FIGHTING IN ORDER TO PROTECT EVERYONE AND IN THE END, THAT GREAT KING...
...WASN'T FIGHTING AGAINST HIS ENEMIES, BUT AGAINST THE VERY PEOPLE HE LOVED.
KING LOT, KING PELLINORE, BALIN, GUINEVERE, GAWAIN, GAWAIN'S BROTHERS...
LANCELOT AND THOSE WHO FOLLOWED HIM, LAMORAK, MORGAUSE, MORGAN, MORDRED...
I PROPHESIZED THEY WOULD BE THE ONES TO CAUSE THE FALL OF THE ROUND TABLE!
BUT ARTHUR CHOSE TO LAUGH WITH EVERY-ONE!
IF ONLY HE'D JUST ABANDON ONE OF THEM!

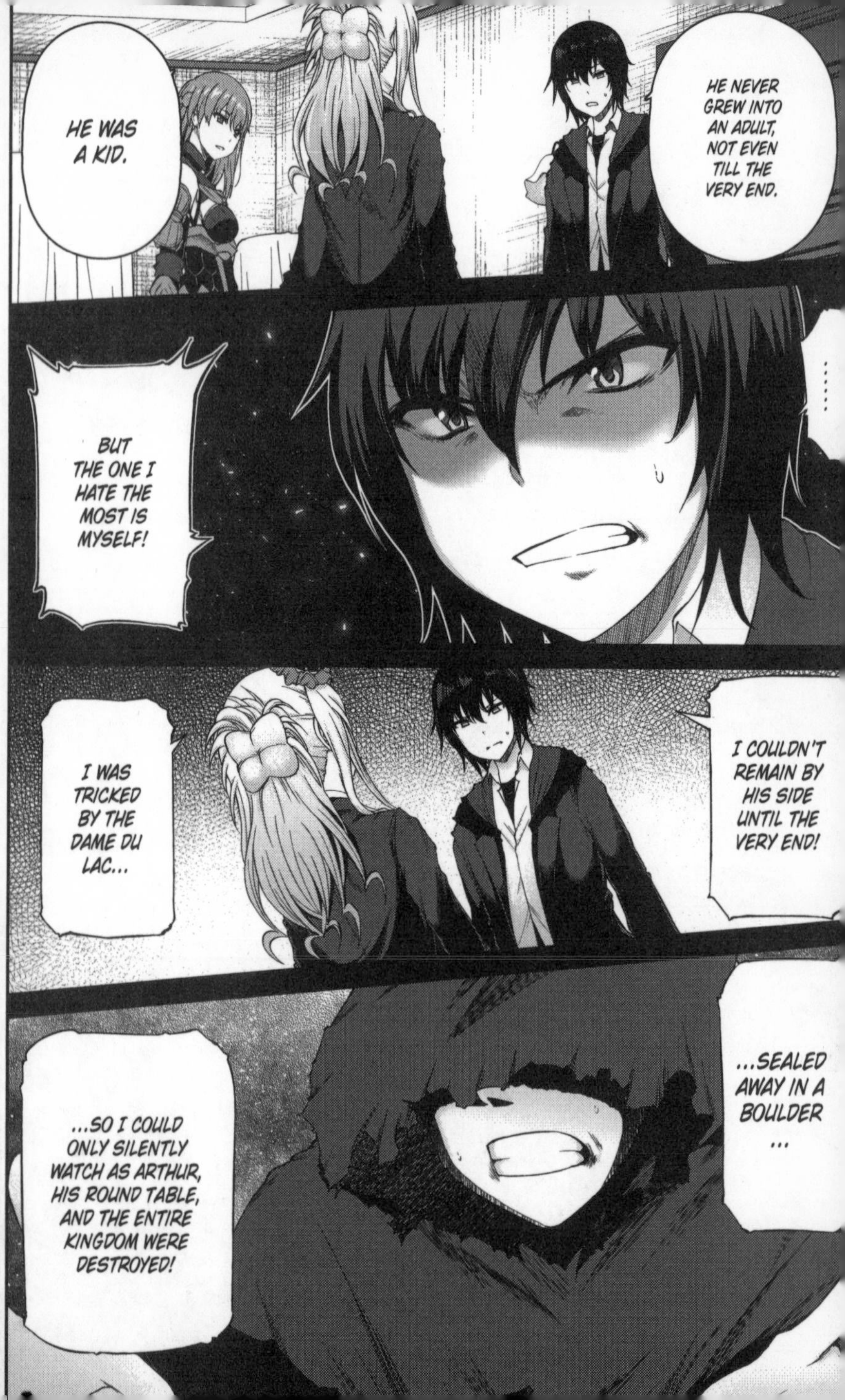
HE NEVER GREW INTO AN ADULT, NOT EVEN TILL THE VERY END.
HE WAS A KID.
......
BUT THE ONE I HATE THE MOST IS MYSELF!
I COULDN'T REMAIN BY HIS SIDE UNTIL THE VERY END!
I WAS TRICKED BY THE DAME DU LAC...
...SEALED AWAY IN A BOULDER ...
...SO I COULD ONLY SILENTLY WATCH AS ARTHUR, HIS ROUND TABLE, AND THE ENTIRE KINGDOM WERE DESTROYED!

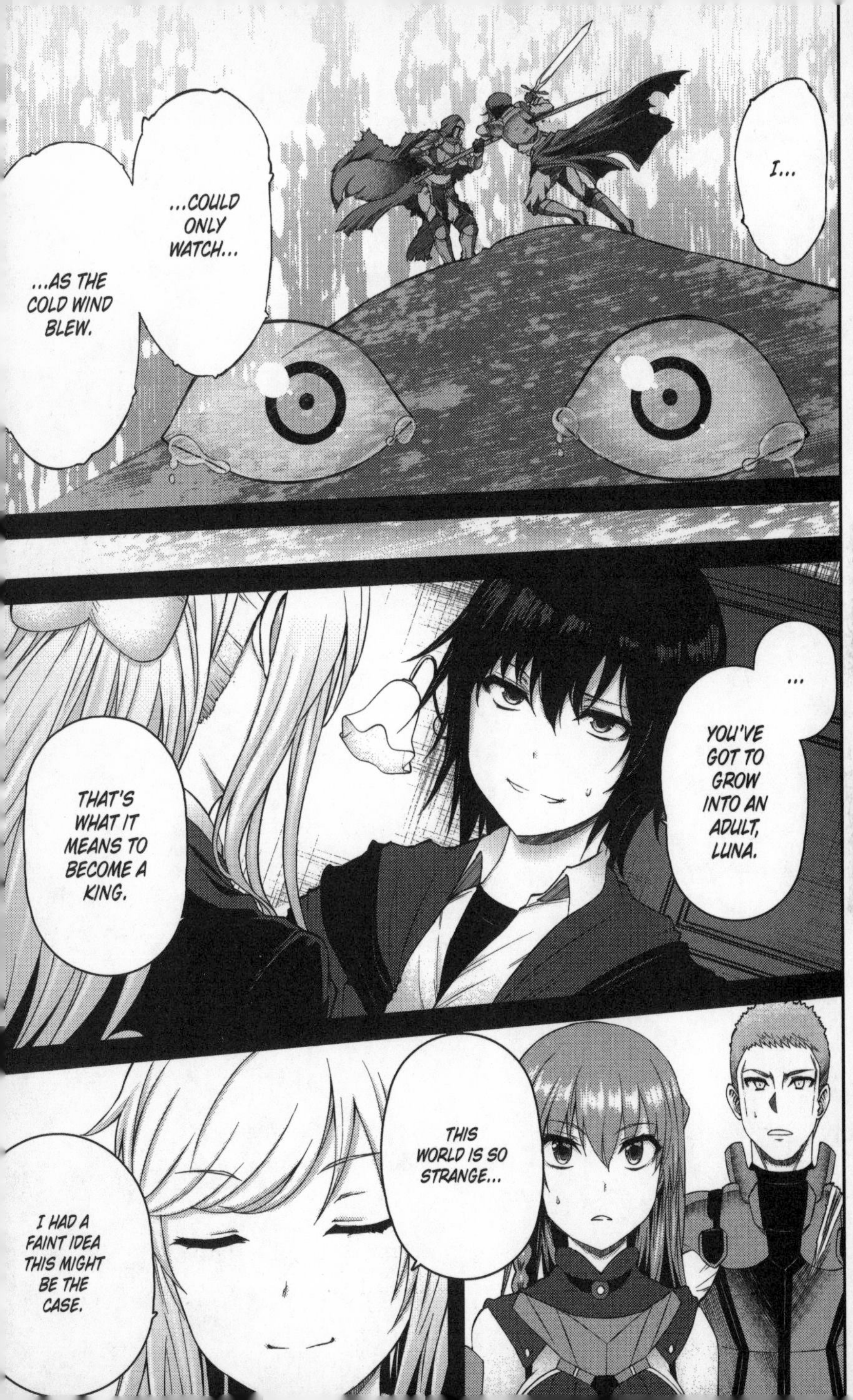
I...
...COULD ONLY WATCH...
...AS THE COLD WIND BLEW.
...
YOU'VE GOT TO GROW INTO AN ADULT, LUNA.
THAT'S WHAT IT MEANS TO BECOME A KING.
THIS WORLD IS SO STRANGE...
I HAD A FAINT IDEA THIS MIGHT BE THE CASE.

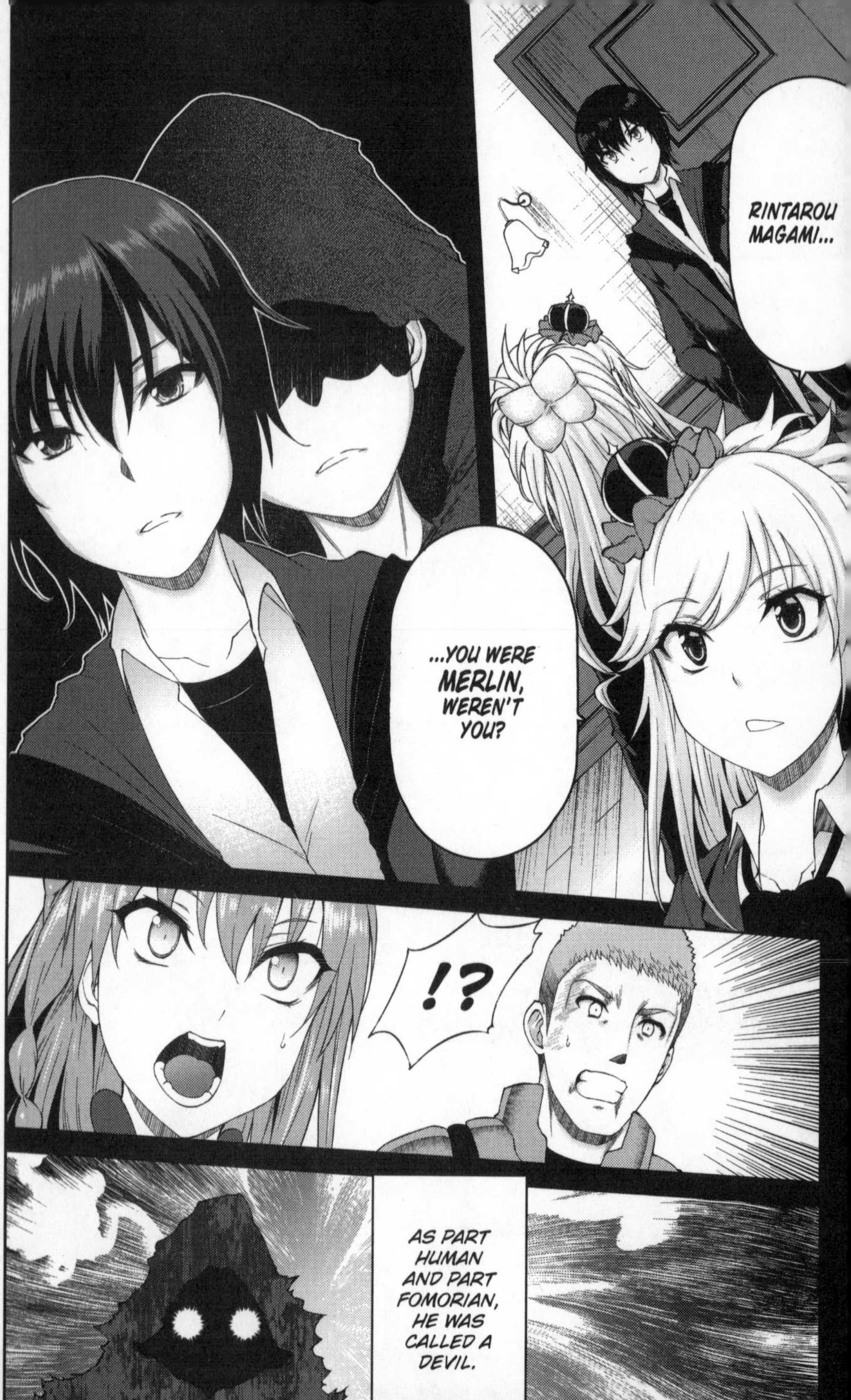
RINTAROU MAGAMI...
...YOU WERE MERLIN, WEREN'T YOU?
!?
AS PART HUMAN AND PART FOMORIAN, HE WAS CALLED A DEVIL.

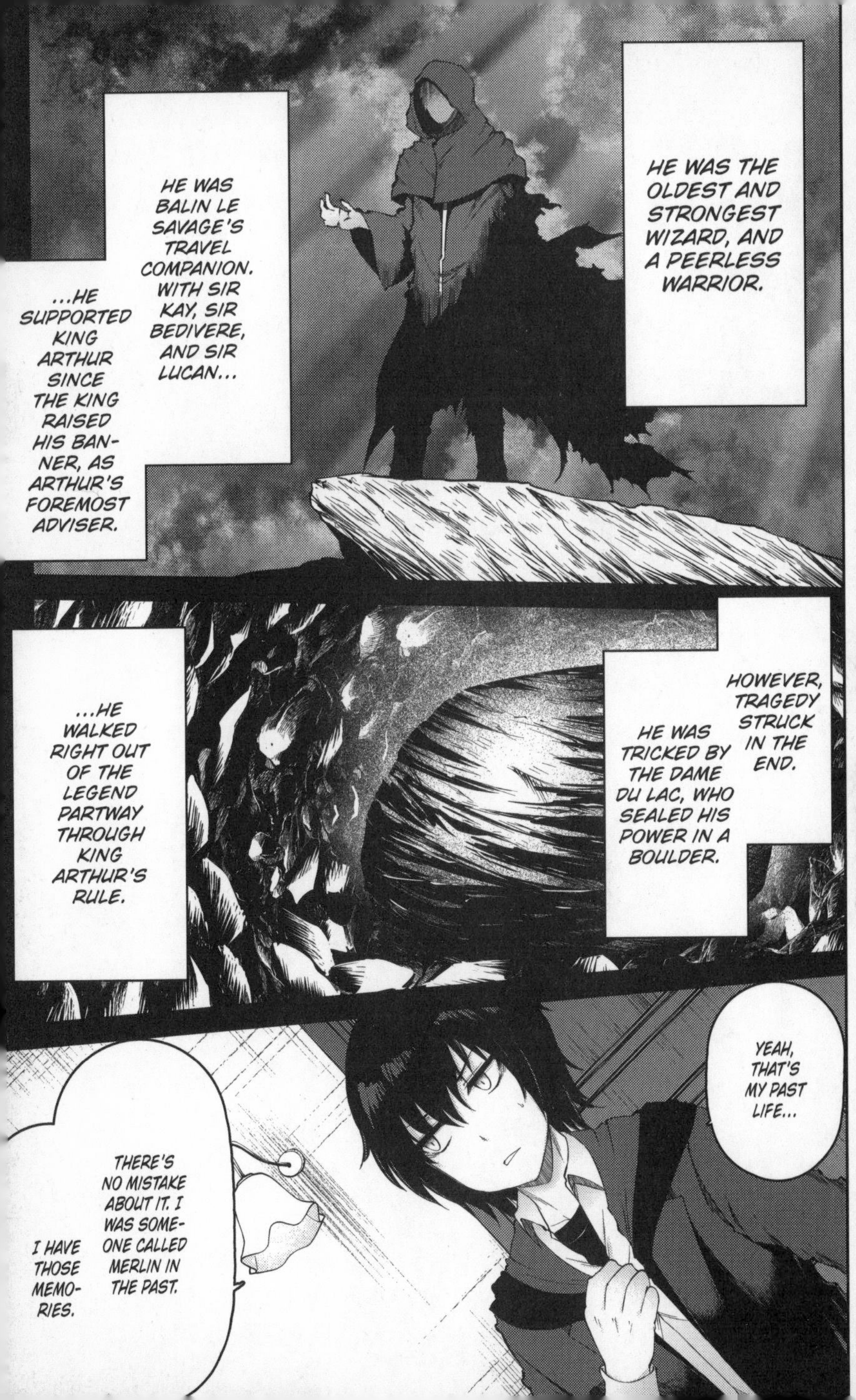
HE WAS THE OLDEST AND STRONGEST WIZARD, AND A PEERLESS WARRIOR.
HE WAS BALIN LE SAVAGE'S TRAVEL COMPANION. WITH SIR KAY, SIR BEDIVERE, AND SIR LUCAN...
...HE SUPPORTED KING ARTHUR SINCE THE KING RAISED HIS BANNER, AS ARTHUR'S FOREMOST ADVISER.
HOWEVER, TRAGEDY STRUCK IN THE END.
HE WAS TRICKED BY THE DAME DU LAC, WHO SEALED HIS POWER IN A BOULDER.
...HE WALKED RIGHT OUT OF THE LEGEND PARTWAY THROUGH KING ARTHUR'S RULE.
YEAH, THAT'S MY PAST LIFE...
THERE'S NO MISTAKE ABOUT IT. I WAS SOMEONE CALLED MERLIN IN THE PAST.
I HAVE THOSE MEMORIES.

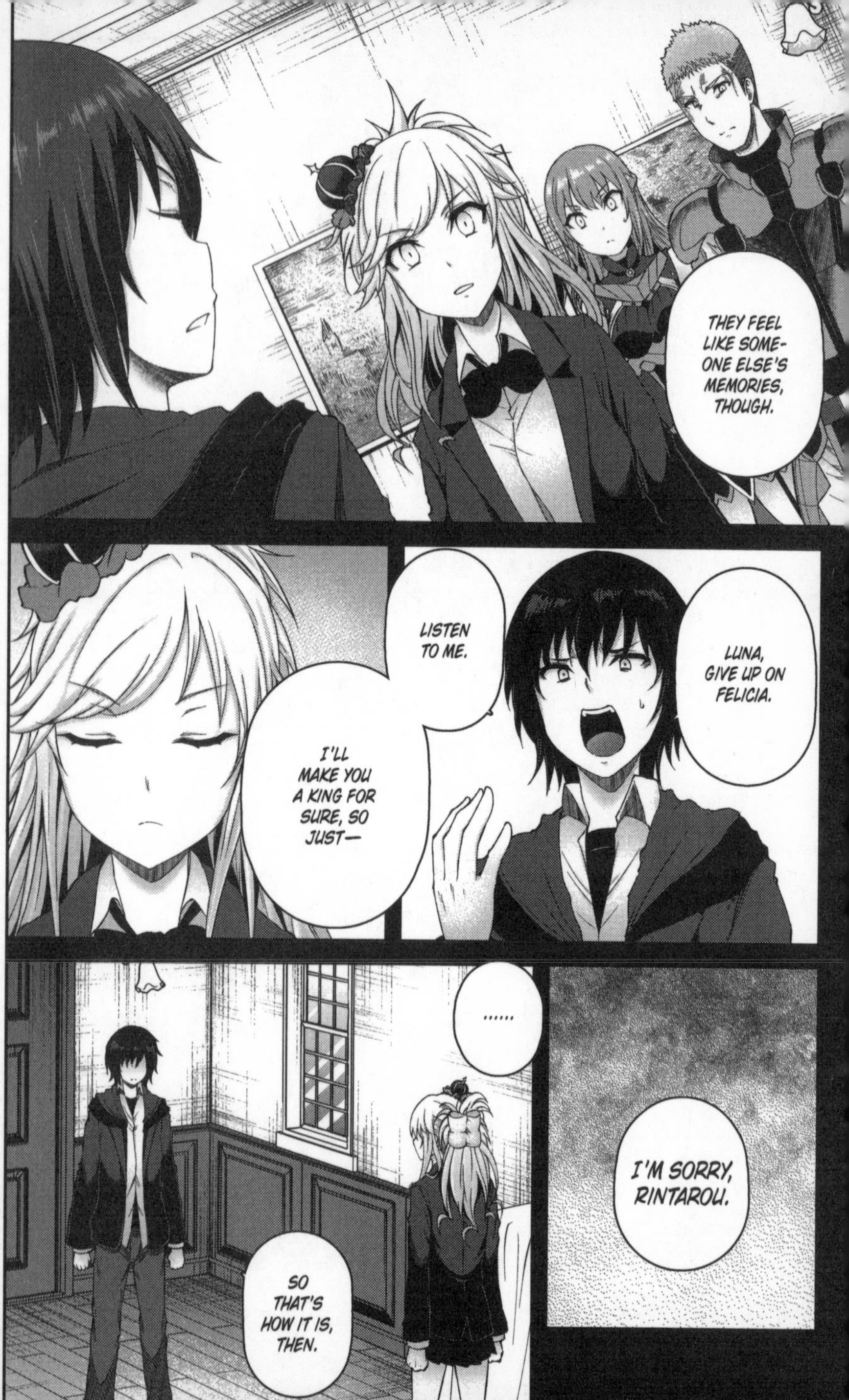
THEY FEEL LIKE SOME-ONE ELSE'S MEMORIES, THOUGH.
LUNA, GIVE UP ON FELICIA.
LISTEN TO ME.
I'LL MAKE YOU A KING FOR SURE, SO JUST—
I'M SORRY, RINTAROU.
......
SO THAT'S HOW IT IS, THEN.

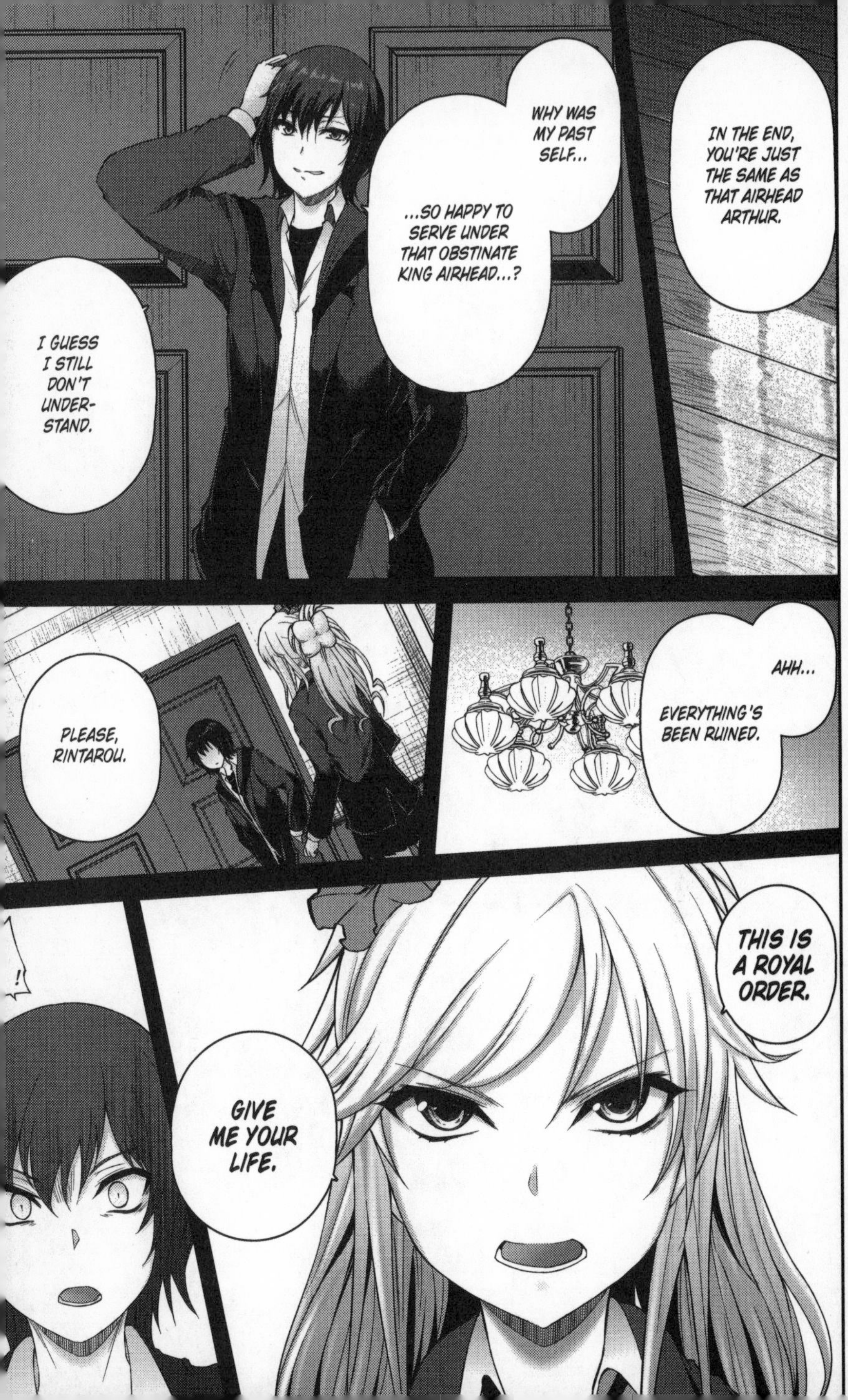
IN THE END, YOU'RE JUST THE SAME AS THAT AIRHEAD ARTHUR.
WHY WAS MY PAST SELF...
...SO HAPPY TO SERVE UNDER THAT OBSTINATE KING AIRHEAD...?
I GUESS I STILL DON'T UNDER-STAND.
AHH...
EVERYTHING'S BEEN RUINED.
PLEASE, RINTAROU.
THIS IS A ROYAL ORDER.
GIVE ME YOUR LIFE.
!

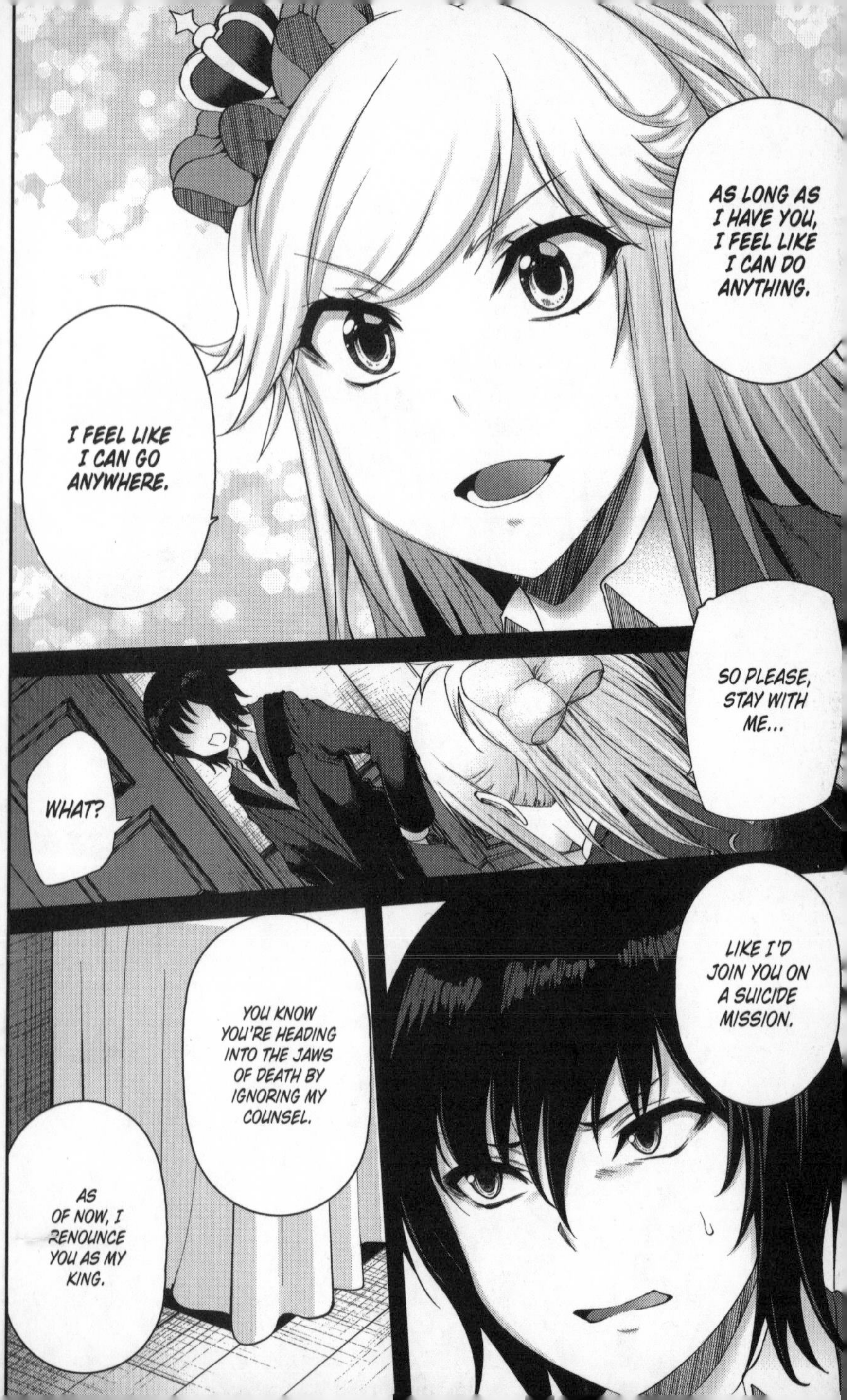
AS LONG AS I HAVE YOU, I FEEL LIKE I CAN DO ANYTHING.
I FEEL LIKE I CAN GO ANYWHERE.
SO PLEASE, STAY WITH ME...
WHAT?
LIKE I'D JOIN YOU ON A SUICIDE MISSION.
YOU KNOW YOU'RE HEADING INTO THE JAWS OF DEATH BY IGNORING MY COUNSEL.
AS OF NOW, I RENOUNCE YOU AS MY KING.

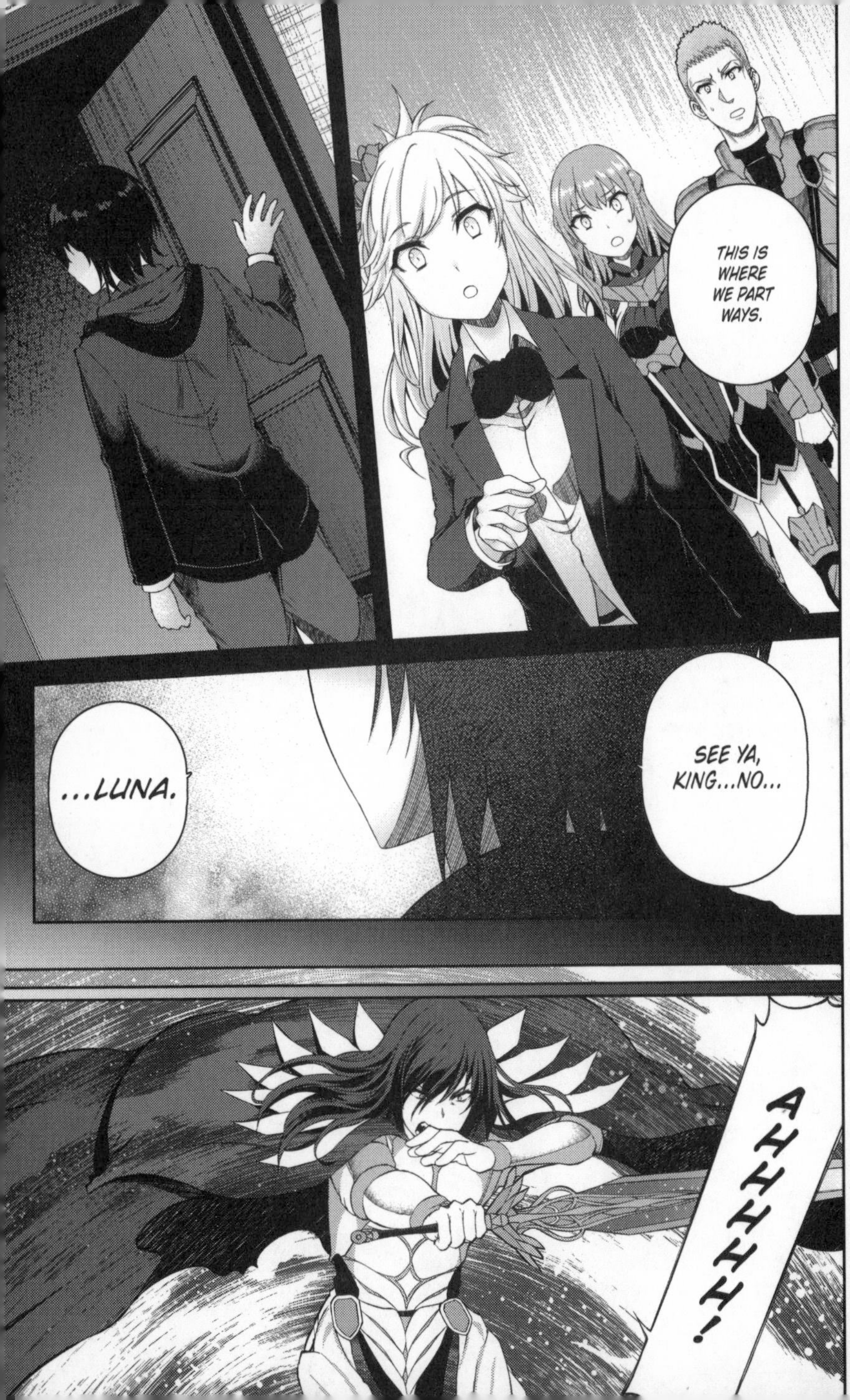
THIS IS WHERE WE PART WAYS.
SEE YA, KING...NO...
...LUNA.
AHHHHHH!

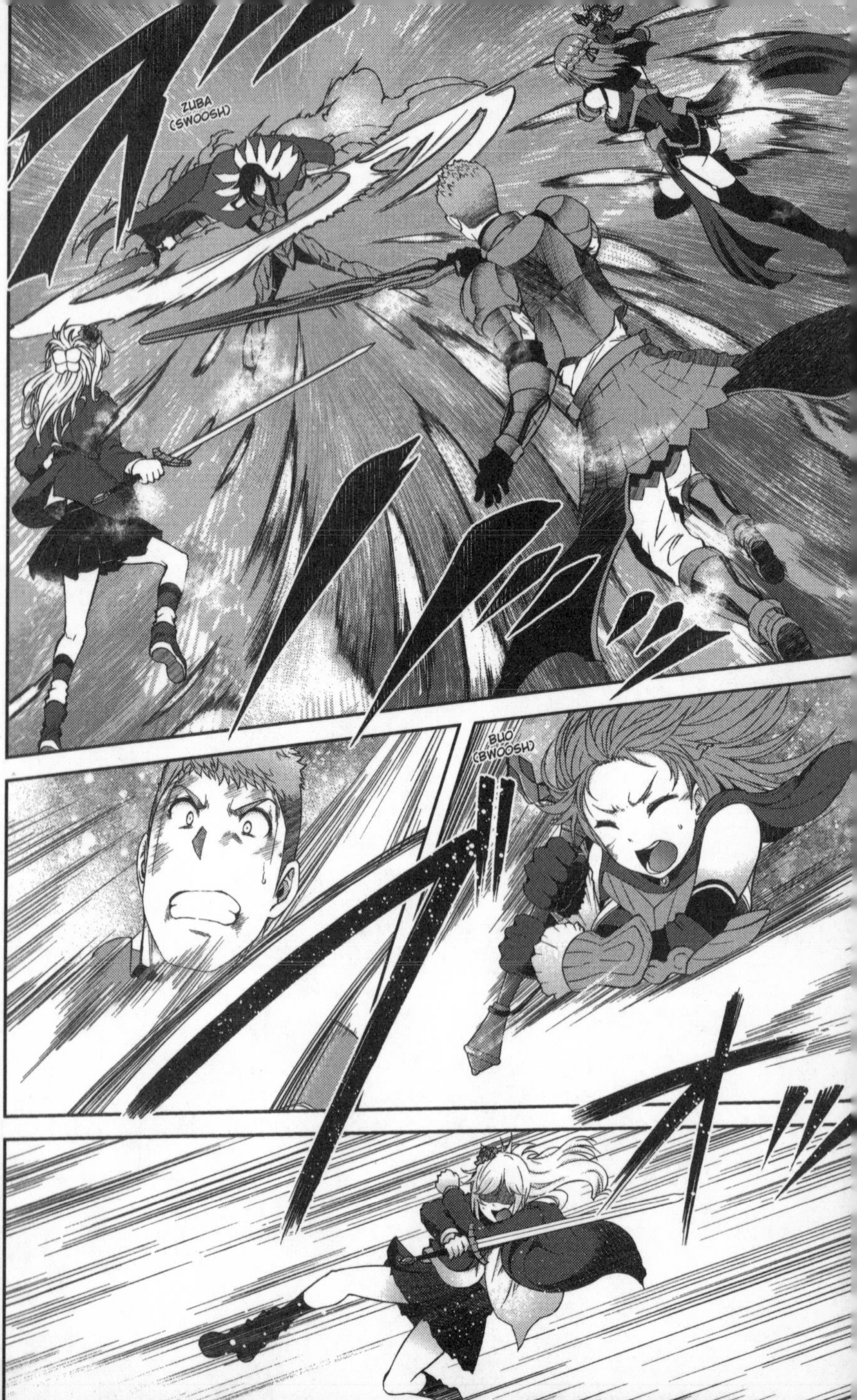
ZUBA (SWOOSH)
BUO (BWOOSH)

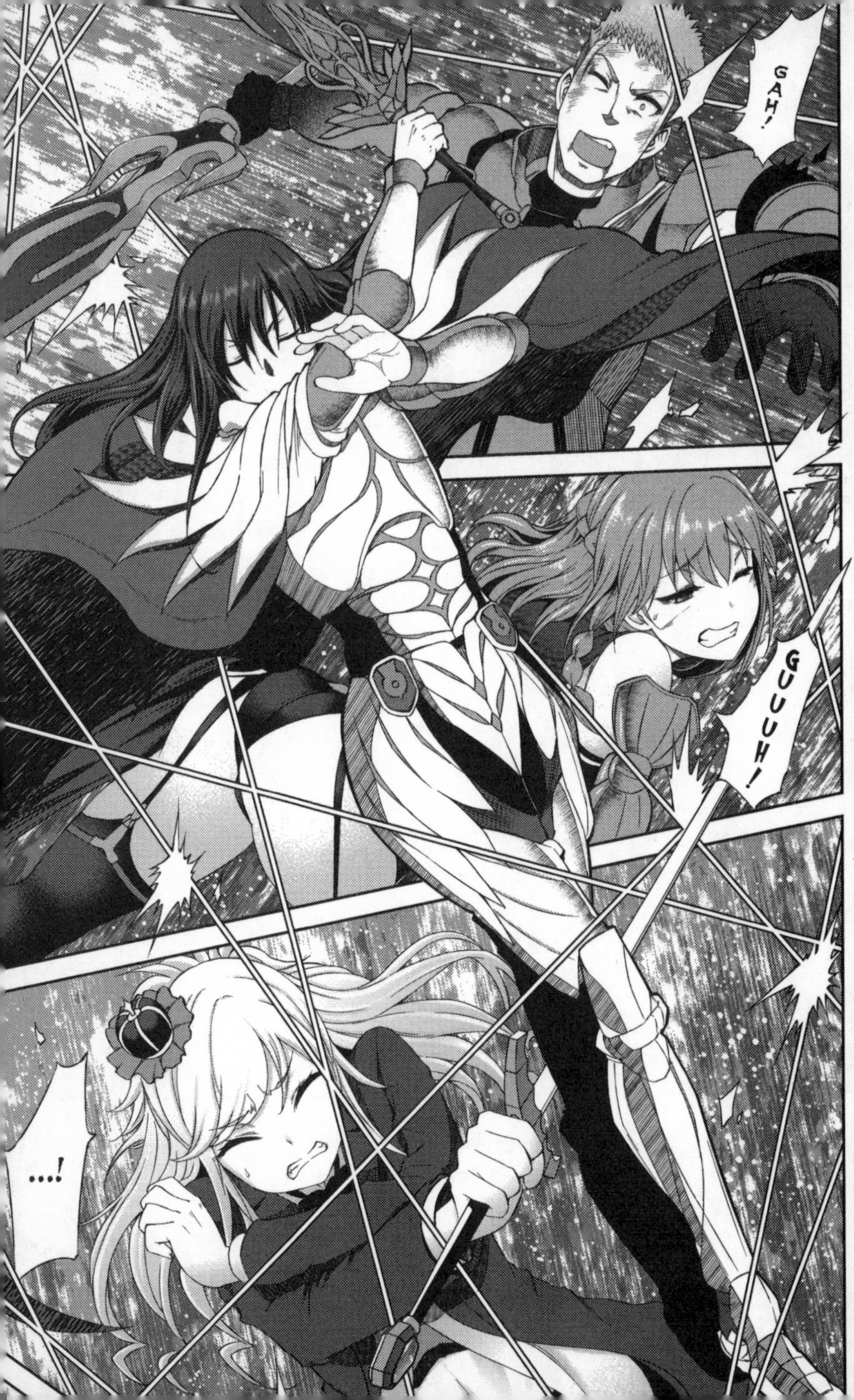
GAH!
GUUUH!
...!

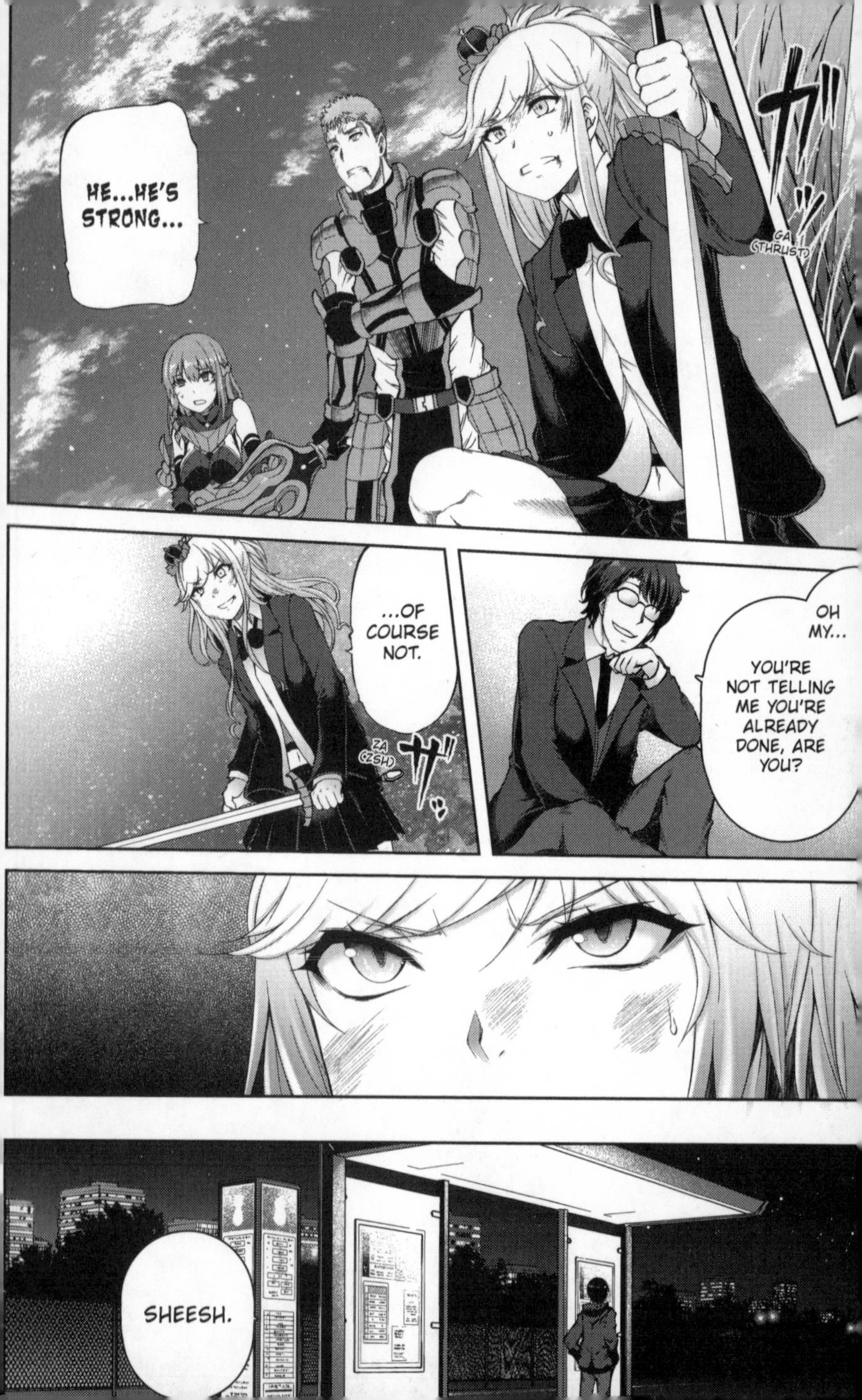
GA (THRUST)
HE...HE'S STRONG...
OH MY...
YOU'RE NOT TELLING ME YOU'RE ALREADY DONE, ARE YOU?
...OF COURSE NOT.
ZA (ZSH)
SHEESH.

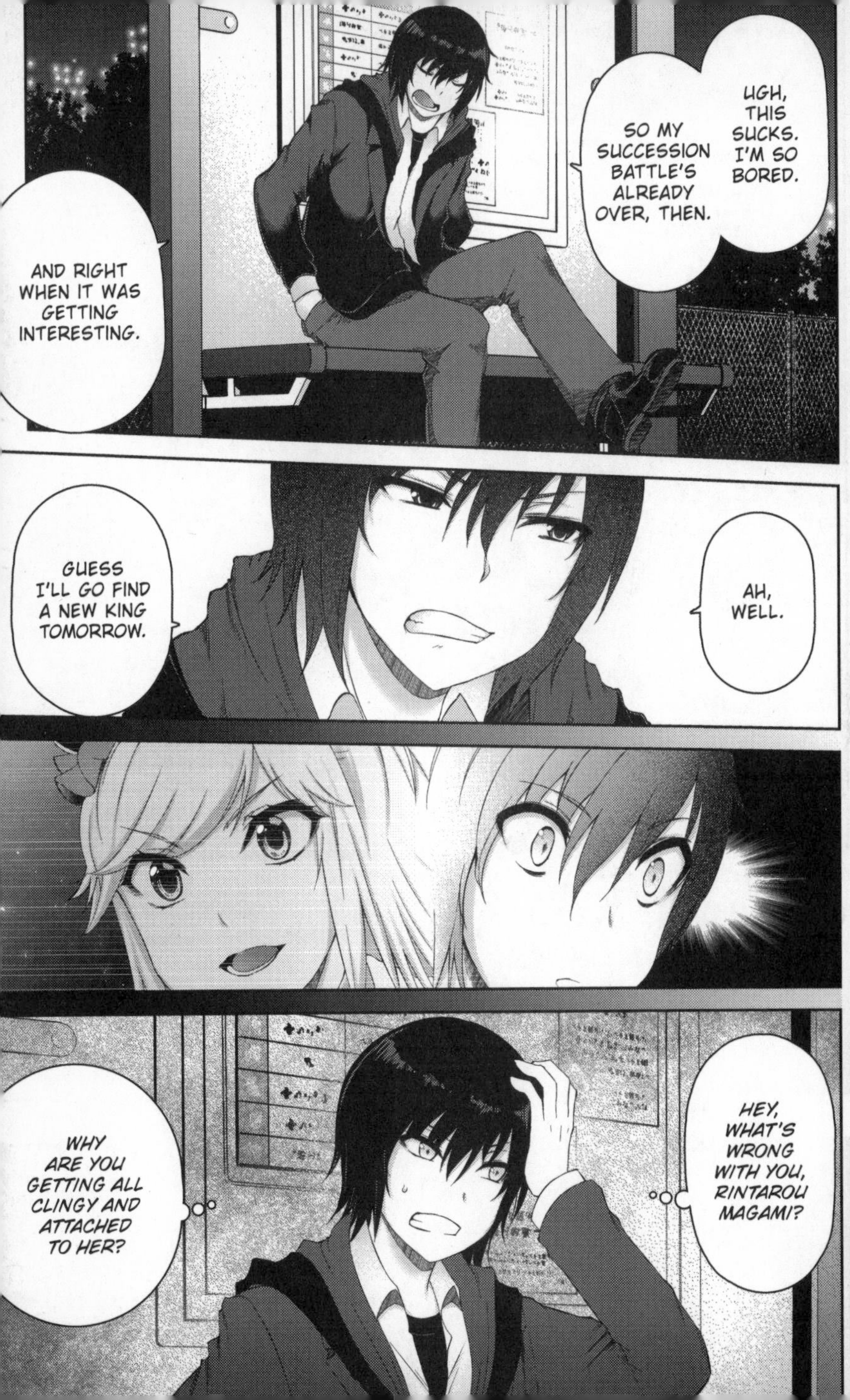
UGH, THIS SUCKS. I'M SO BORED.
SO MY SUCCESSION BATTLE'S ALREADY OVER, THEN.
AND RIGHT WHEN IT WAS GETTING INTERESTING.
AH, WELL.
GUESS I'LL GO FIND A NEW KING TOMORROW.
HEY, WHAT'S WRONG WITH YOU, RINTAROU MAGAMI?
WHY ARE YOU GETTING ALL CLINGY AND ATTACHED TO HER?

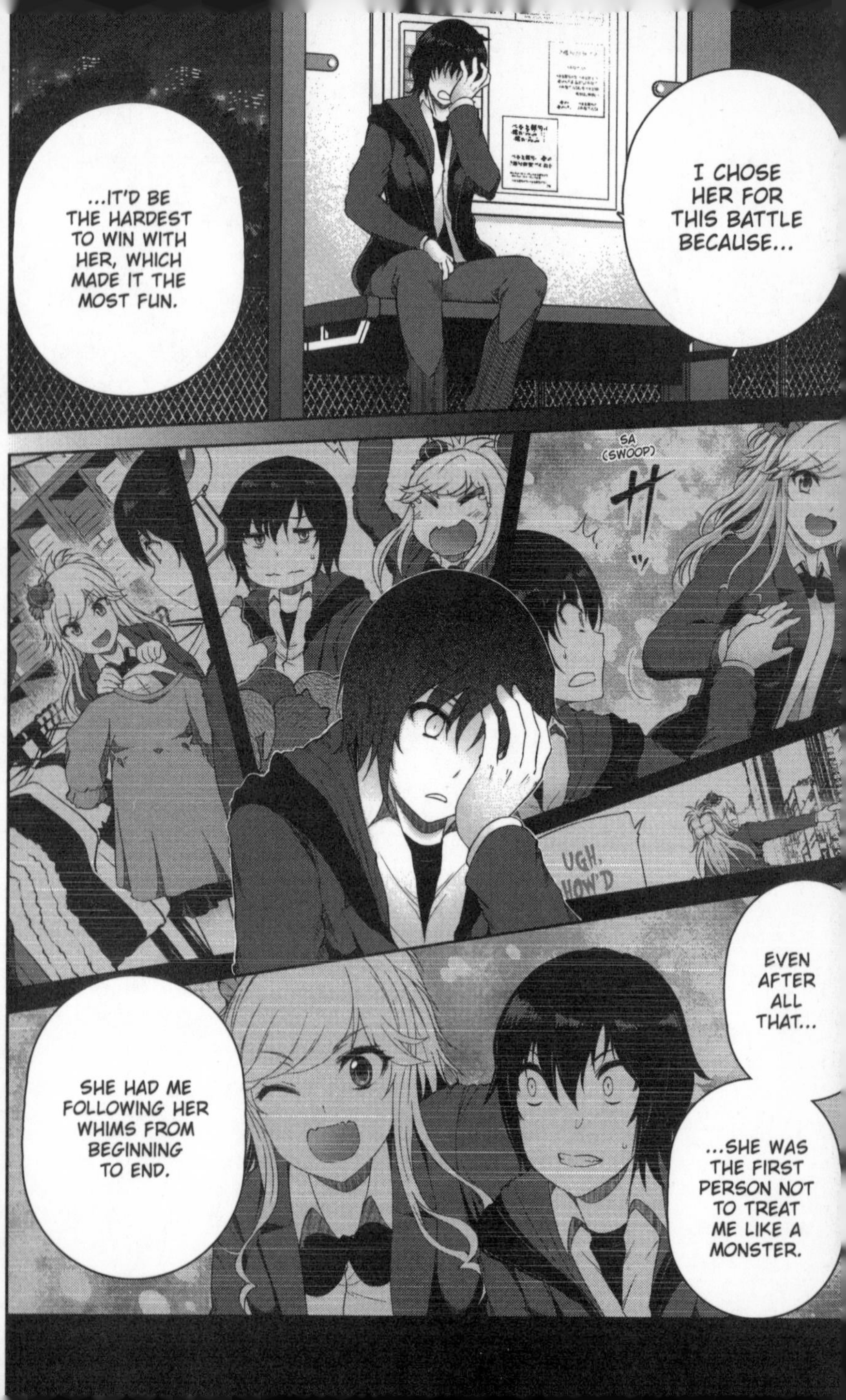
I CHOSE HER FOR THIS BATTLE BECAUSE...
...IT'D BE THE HARDEST TO WIN WITH HER, WHICH MADE IT THE MOST FUN.
SA (SWOOP)
UGH, HOW'D
EVEN AFTER ALL THAT...
...SHE WAS THE FIRST PERSON NOT TO TREAT ME LIKE A MONSTER.
SHE HAD ME FOLLOWING HER WHIMS FROM BEGINNING TO END.

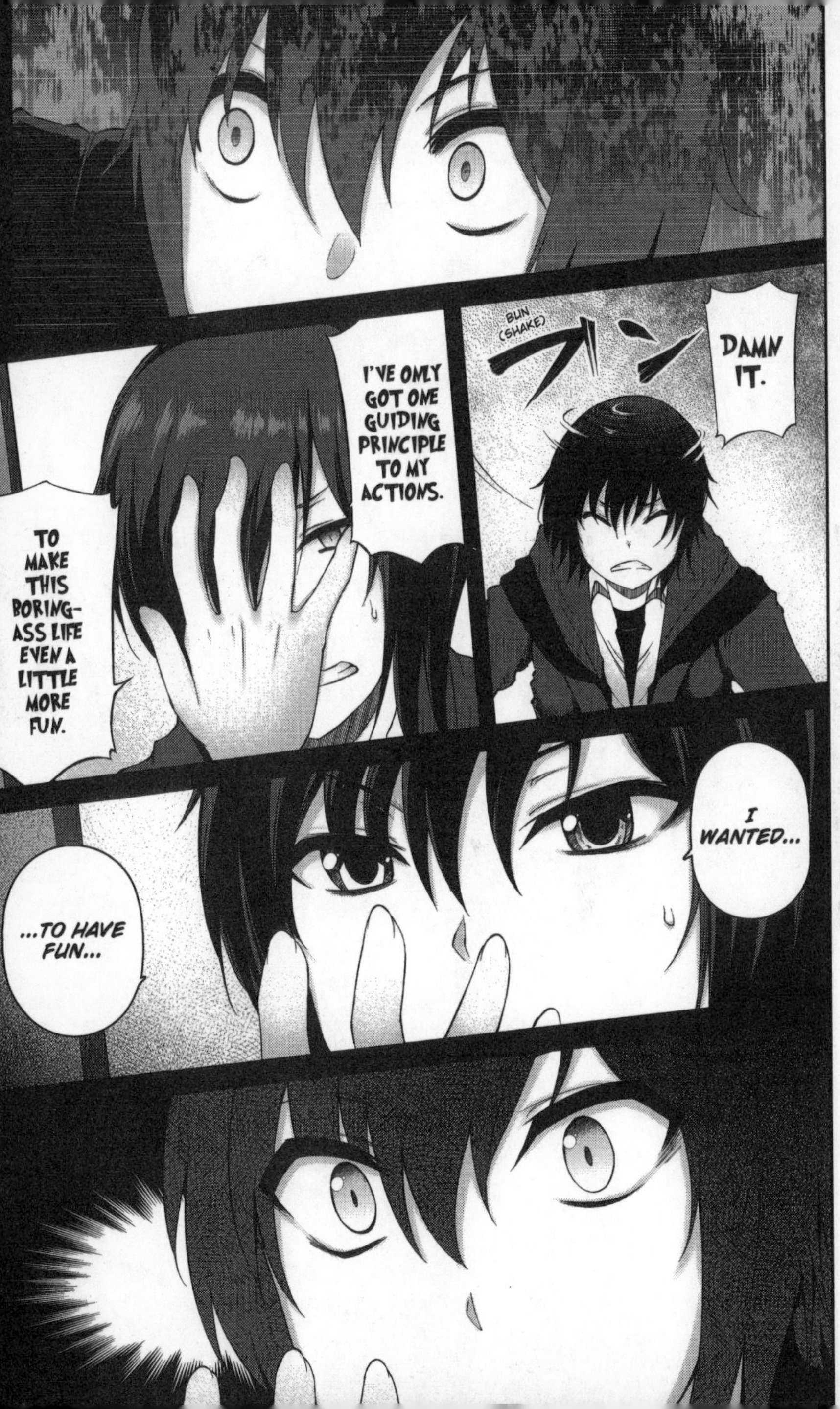
BUN (SHAKE)
DAMN IT.
I'VE ONLY GOT ONE GUIDING PRINCIPLE TO MY ACTIONS.
TO MAKE THIS BORING-ASS LIFE EVEN A LITTLE MORE FUN.
I WANTED...
...TO HAVE FUN...

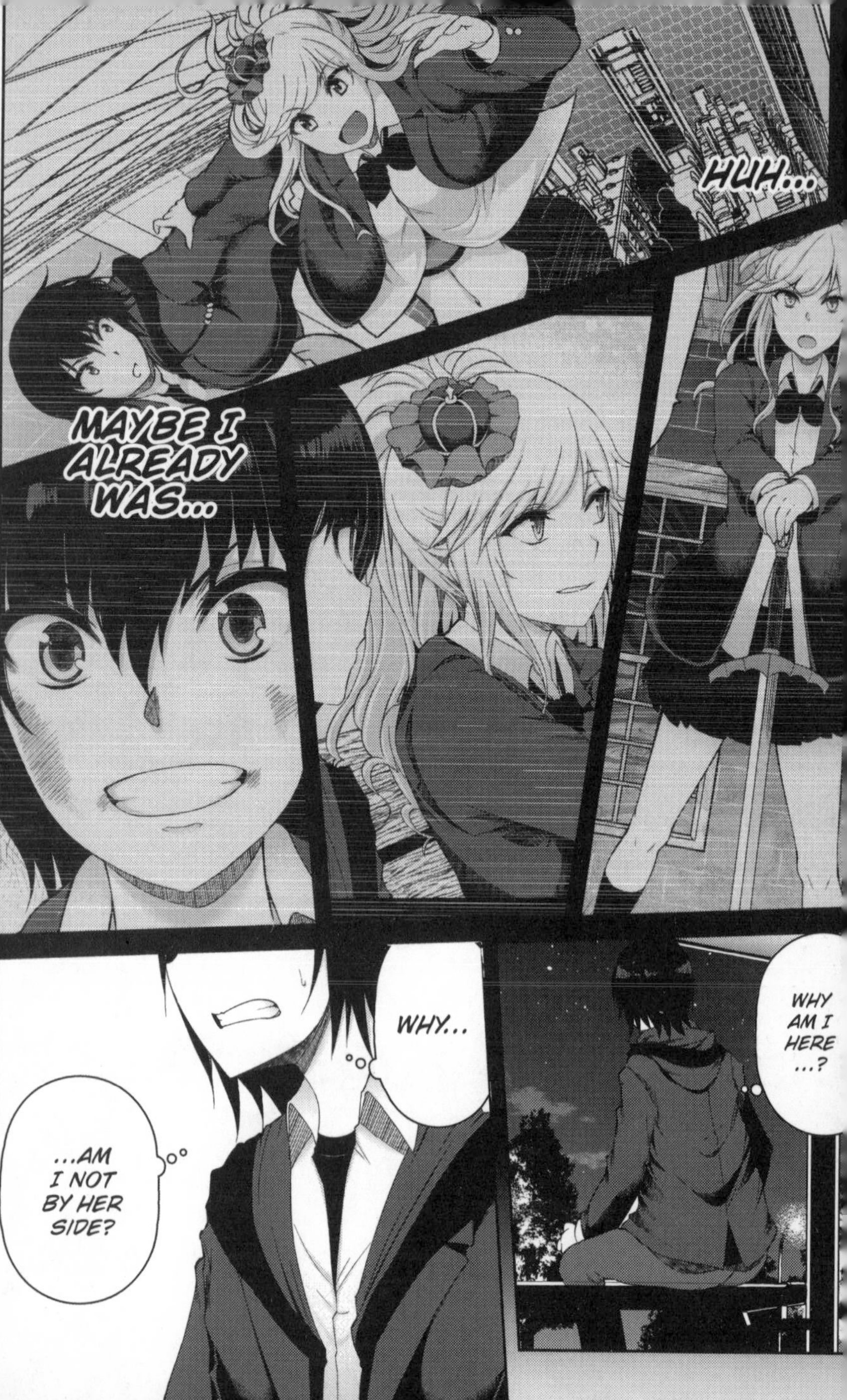
HUH...
MAYBE I ALREADY WAS...
WHY AM I HERE ...?
WHY...
...AM I NOT BY HER SIDE?

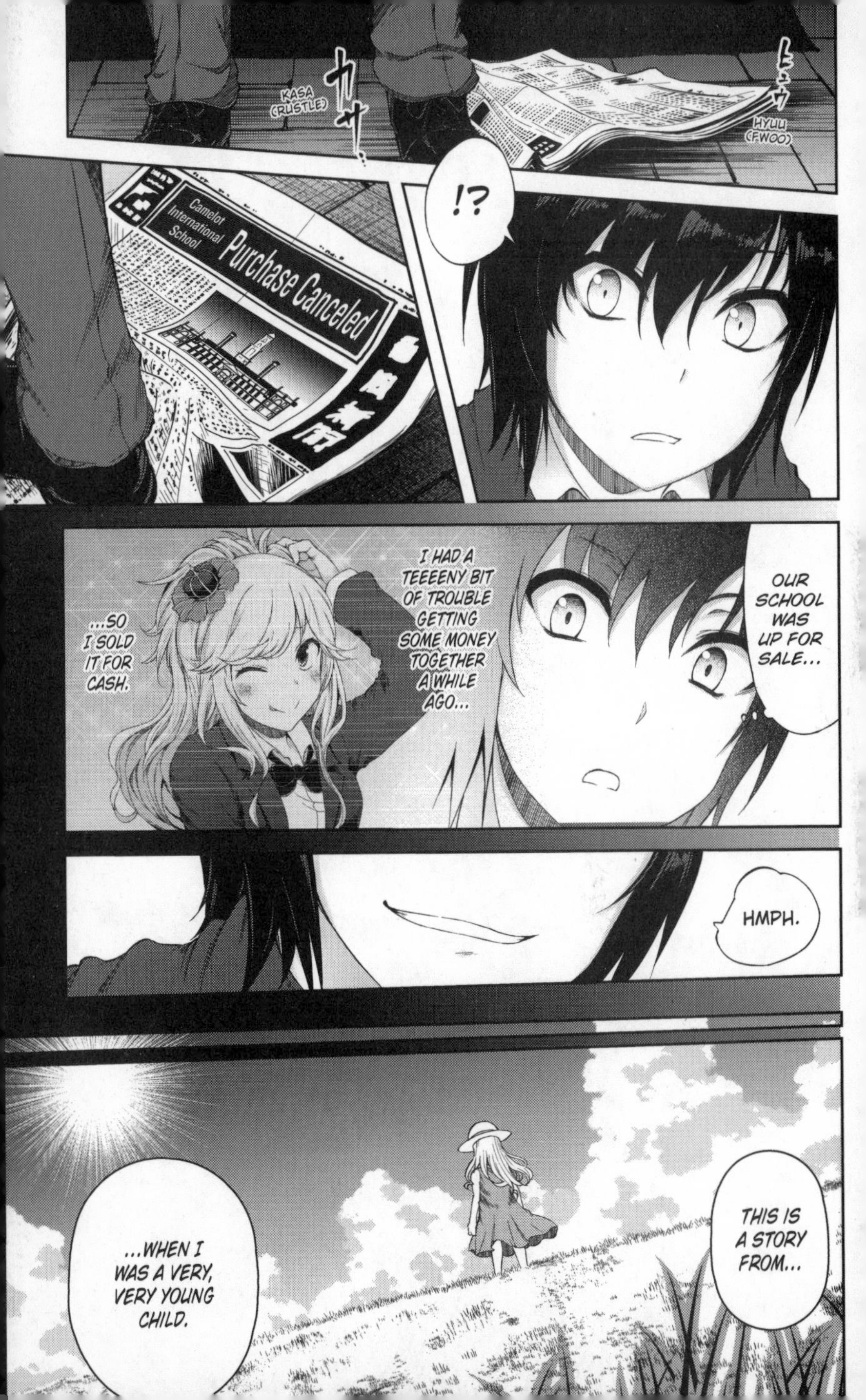
HYUU (FWOO)
KASA (RUSTLE)
!?
Camelot International School
Purchase Canceled
OUR SCHOOL WAS UP FOR SALE...
I HAD A TEEEENY BIT OF TROUBLE GETTING SOME MONEY TOGETHER A WHILE AGO...
...SO I SOLD IT FOR CASH.
HMPH.
THIS IS A STORY FROM...
...WHEN I WAS A VERY, VERY YOUNG CHILD.

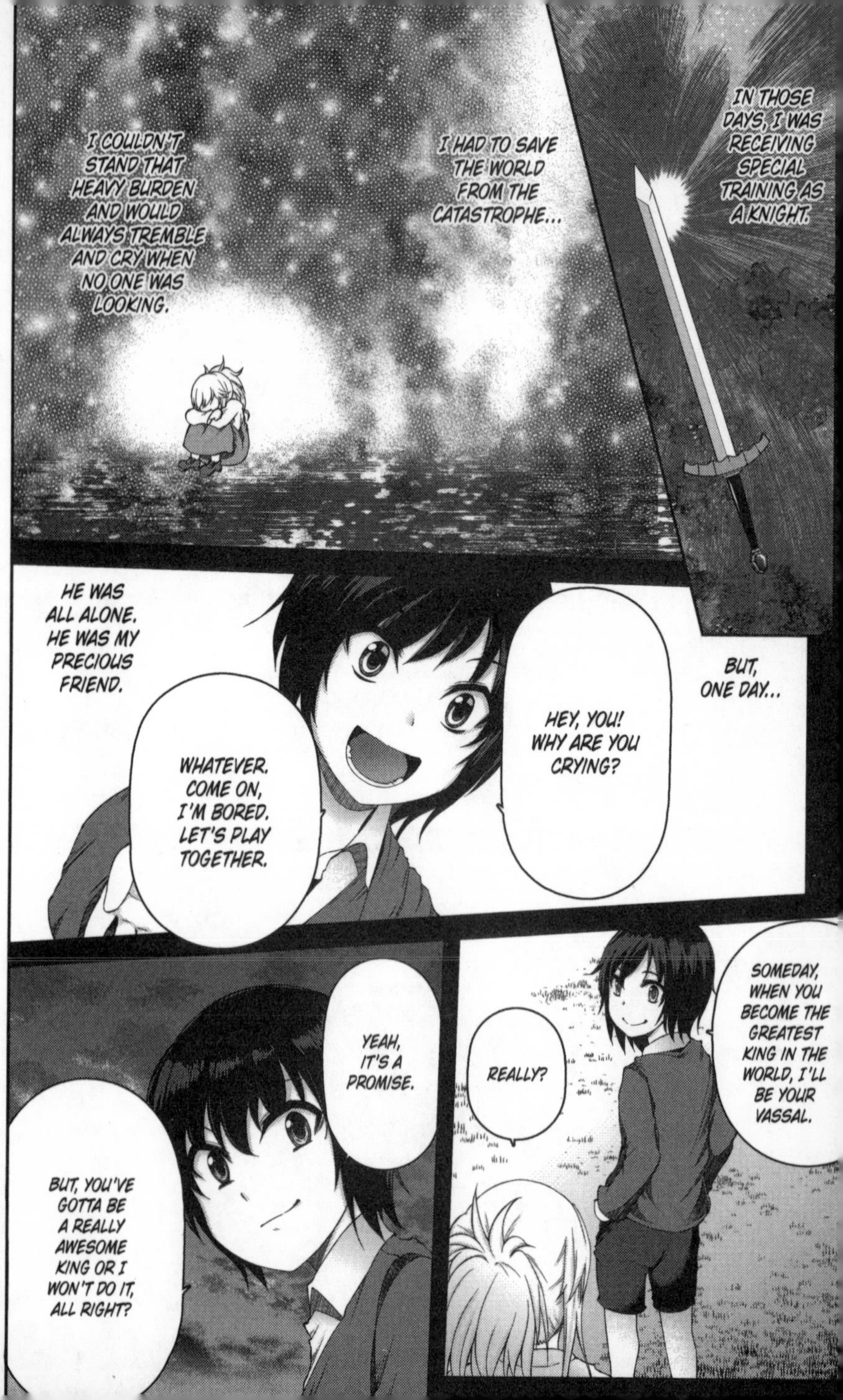
IN THOSE DAYS, I WAS RECEIVING SPECIAL TRAINING AS A KNIGHT.
I HAD TO SAVE THE WORLD FROM THE CATASTROPHE...
I COULDN'T STAND THAT HEAVY BURDEN AND WOULD ALWAYS TREMBLE AND CRY WHEN NO ONE WAS LOOKING.
BUT, ONE DAY...
HEY, YOU! WHY ARE YOU CRYING?
WHATEVER. COME ON, I'M BORED. LET'S PLAY TOGETHER.
HE WAS ALL ALONE. HE WAS MY PRECIOUS FRIEND.
SOMEDAY, WHEN YOU BECOME THE GREATEST KING IN THE WORLD, I'LL BE YOUR VASSAL.
REALLY?
YEAH, IT'S A PROMISE.
BUT, YOU'VE GOTTA BE A REALLY AWESOME KING OR I WON'T DO IT, ALL RIGHT?

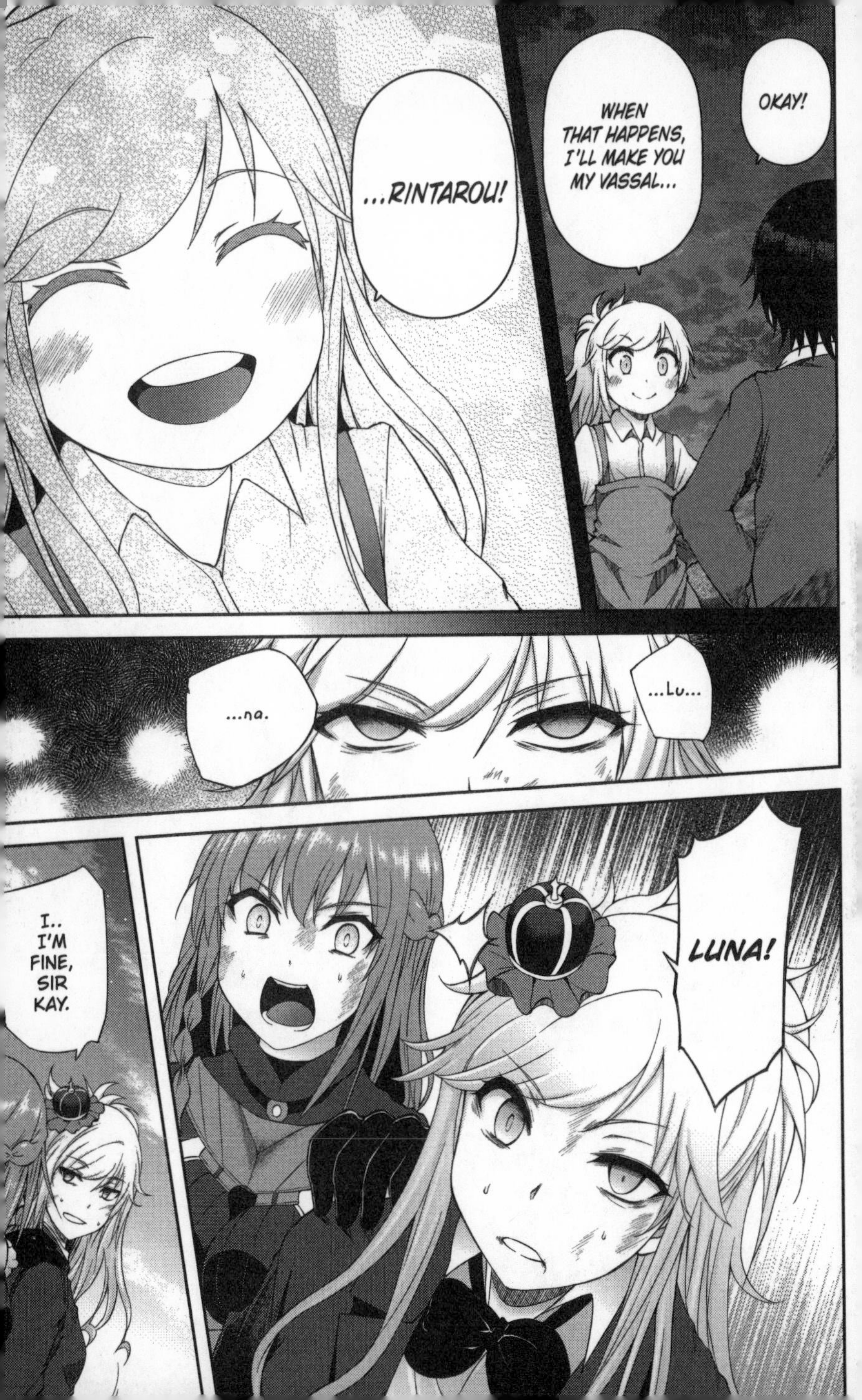
OKAY!
WHEN THAT HAPPENS, I'LL MAKE YOU MY VASSAL...
...RINTAROU!
...Lu...
...na.
LUNA!
I.. I'M FINE, SIR KAY.

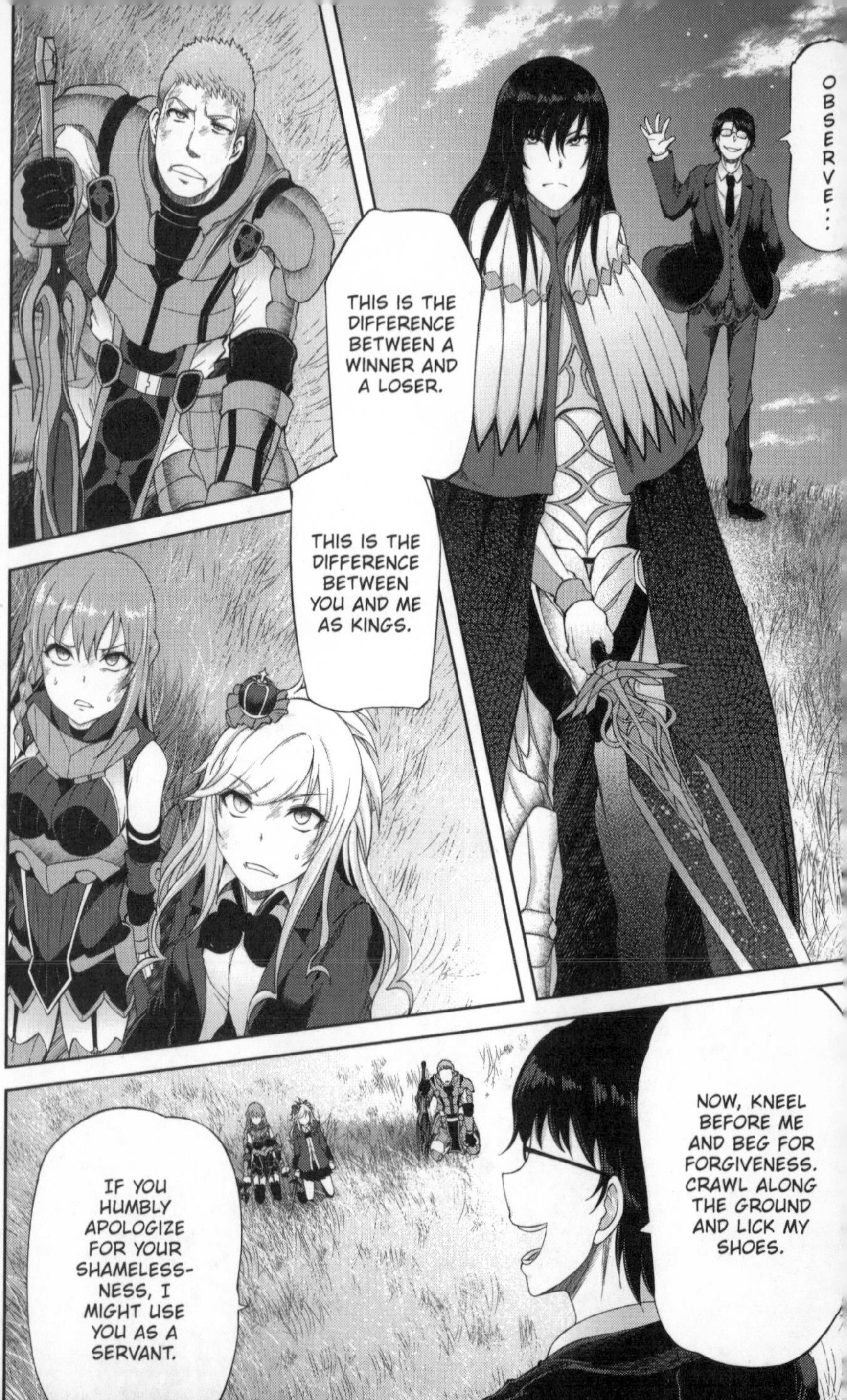
OBSERVE...
THIS IS THE DIFFERENCE BETWEEN A WINNER AND A LOSER.
THIS IS THE DIFFERENCE BETWEEN YOU AND ME AS KINGS.
NOW, KNEEL BEFORE ME AND BEG FOR FORGIVENESS. CRAWL ALONG THE GROUND AND LICK MY SHOES.
IF YOU HUMBLY APOLOGIZE FOR YOUR SHAMELESS-NESS, I MIGHT USE YOU AS A SERVANT.

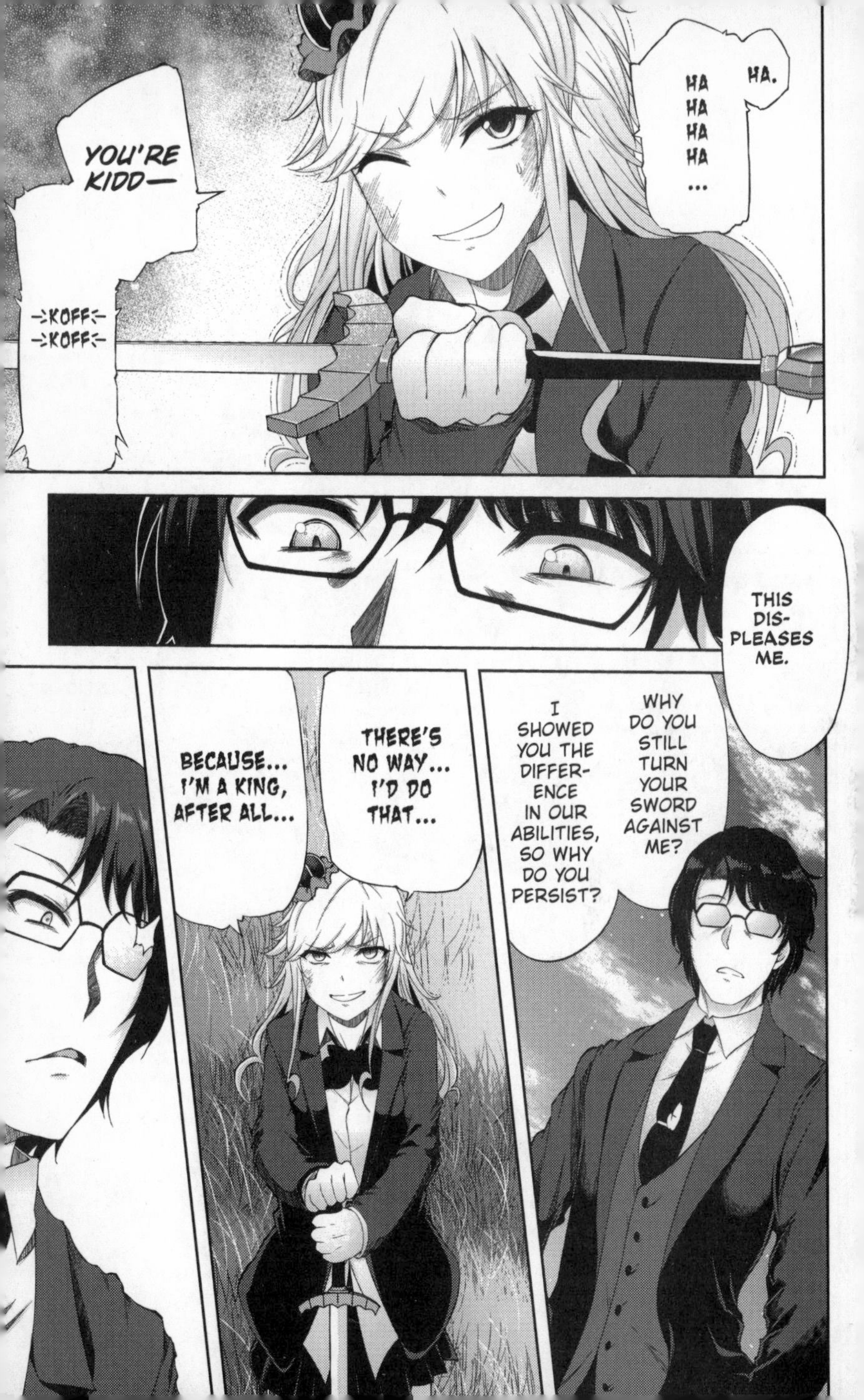
HA HA HA HA ... HA.
YOU'RE KIDD—
-KOFF- -KOFF-
THIS DIS-PLEASES ME.
WHY DO YOU STILL TURN YOUR SWORD AGAINST ME?
I SHOWED YOU THE DIFFER-ENCE IN OUR ABILITIES, SO WHY DO YOU PERSIST?
THERE'S NO WAY... I'D DO THAT...
BECAUSE... I'M A KING, AFTER ALL...

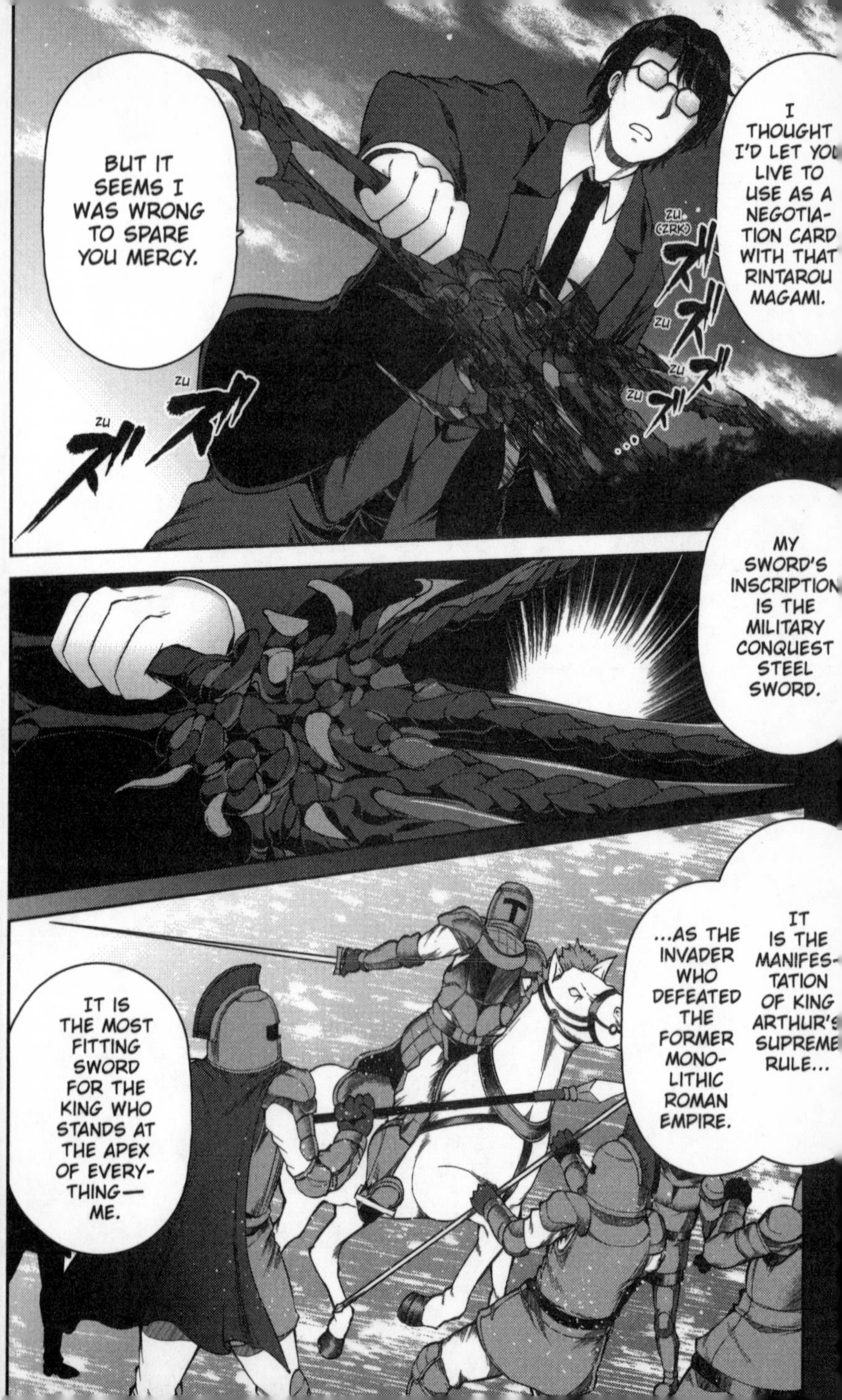

I THOUGHT I'D LET YOU LIVE TO USE AS A NEGOTIATION CARD WITH THAT RINTAROU MAGAMI.
ZU (ZRK)
ZU
ZU
ZU
...
BUT IT SEEMS I WAS WRONG TO SPARE YOU MERCY.
ZU
ZU
MY SWORD'S INSCRIPTION IS THE MILITARY CONQUEST STEEL SWORD.
IT IS THE MANIFESTATION OF KING ARTHUR'S SUPREME RULE...
...AS THE INVADER WHO DEFEATED THE FORMER MONOLITHIC ROMAN EMPIRE.
IT IS THE MOST FITTING SWORD FOR THE KING WHO STANDS AT THE APEX OF EVERYTHING— ME.

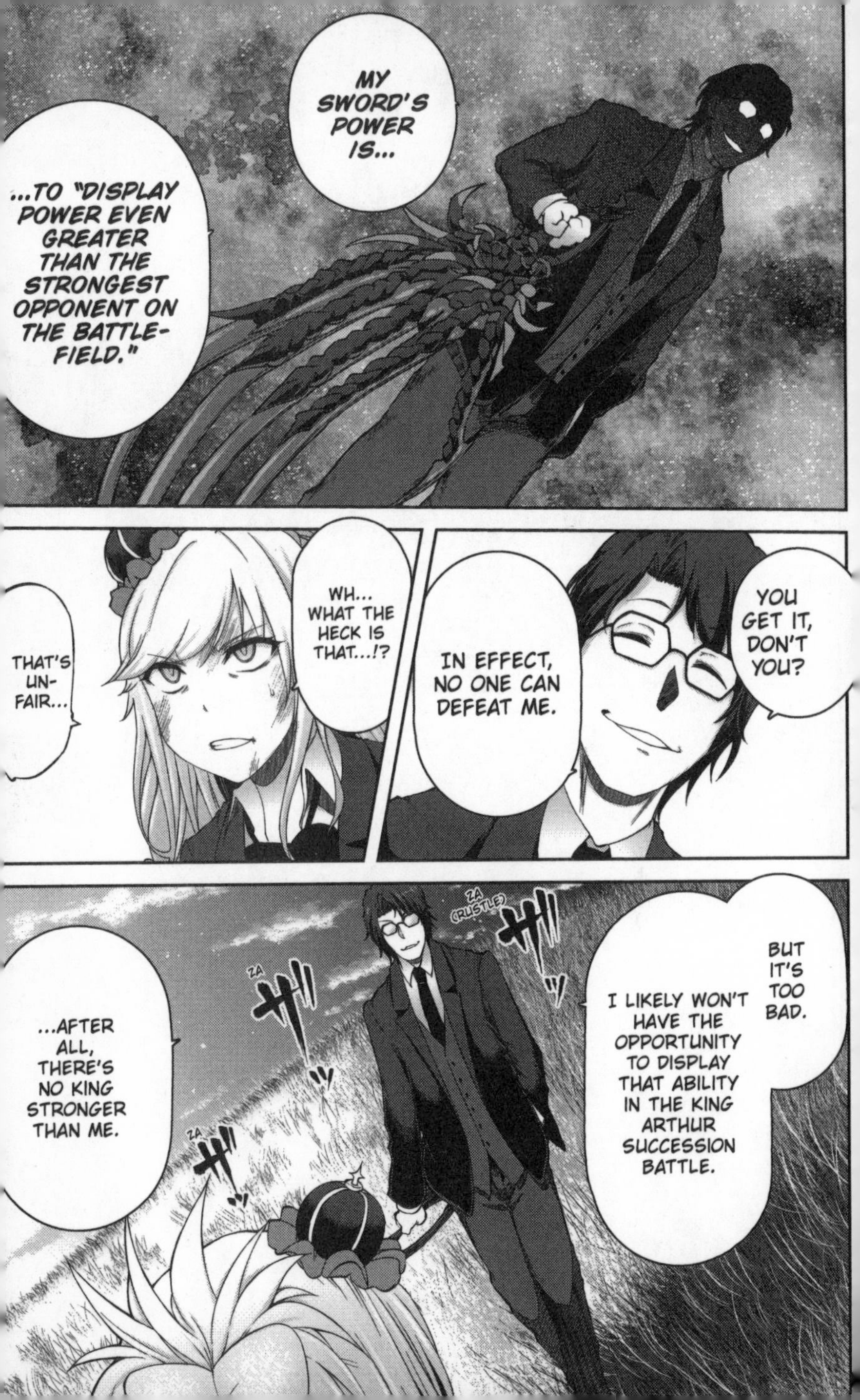
MY SWORD'S POWER IS...
...TO "DISPLAY POWER EVEN GREATER THAN THE STRONGEST OPPONENT ON THE BATTLE-FIELD."
YOU GET IT, DON'T YOU?
IN EFFECT, NO ONE CAN DEFEAT ME.
WH... WHAT THE HECK IS THAT...!?
THAT'S UN-FAIR...
BUT IT'S TOO BAD.
I LIKELY WON'T HAVE THE OPPORTUNITY TO DISPLAY THAT ABILITY IN THE KING ARTHUR SUCCESSION BATTLE.
ZA (RUSTLE)
ZA
ZA
...AFTER ALL, THERE'S NO KING STRONGER THAN ME.

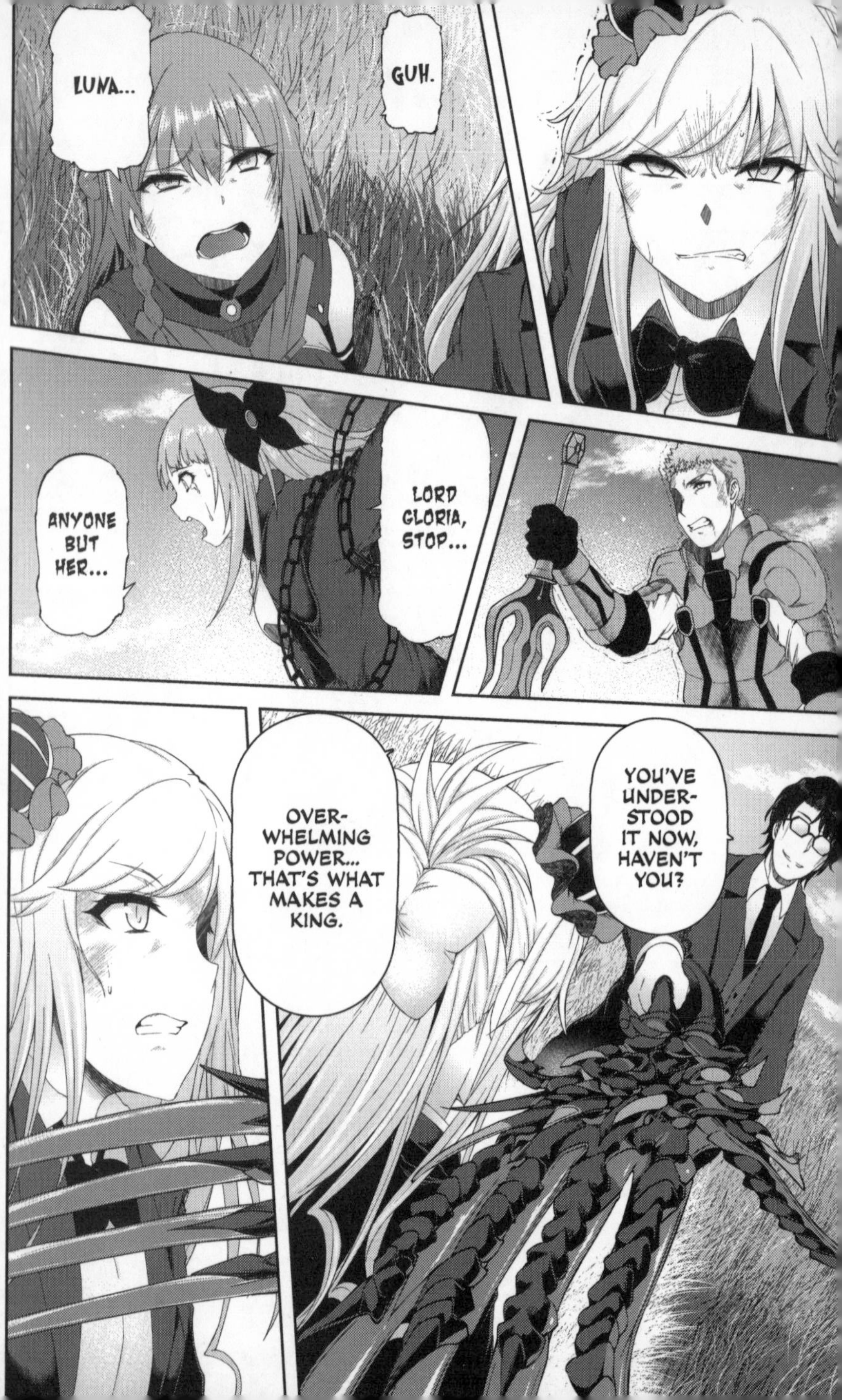
GUH.
LUNA...
LORD GLORIA, STOP...
ANYONE BUT HER...
YOU'VE UNDER-STOOD IT NOW, HAVEN'T YOU?
OVER-WHELMING POWER... THAT'S WHAT MAKES A KING.

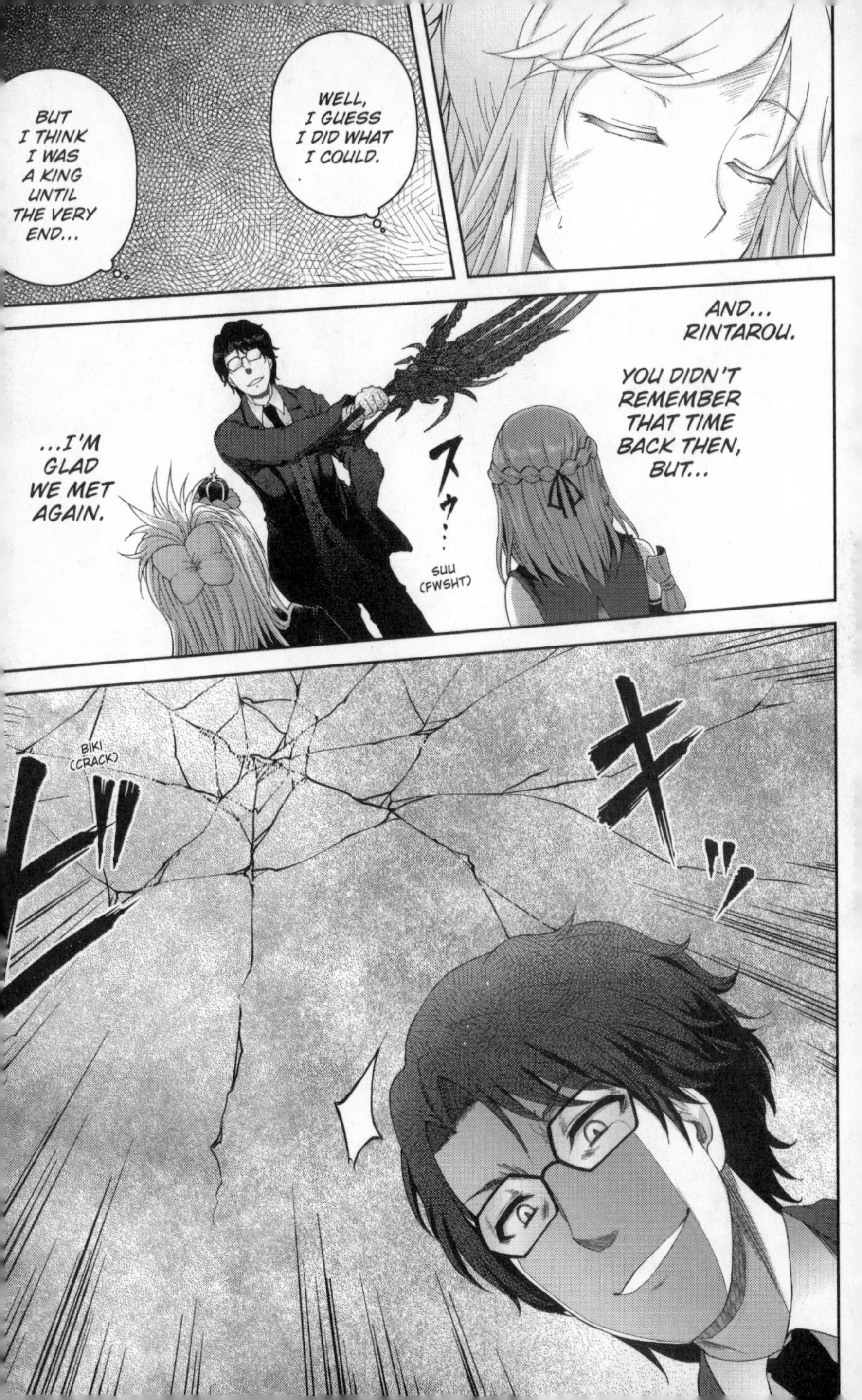
WELL, I GUESS I DID WHAT I COULD.
BUT I THINK I WAS A KING UNTIL THE VERY END...
AND... RINTAROU.
YOU DIDN'T REMEMBER THAT TIME BACK THEN, BUT...
スゥ
SUU (FWSHT)
...I'M GLAD WE MET AGAIN.
キッ
BIKI (CRACK)

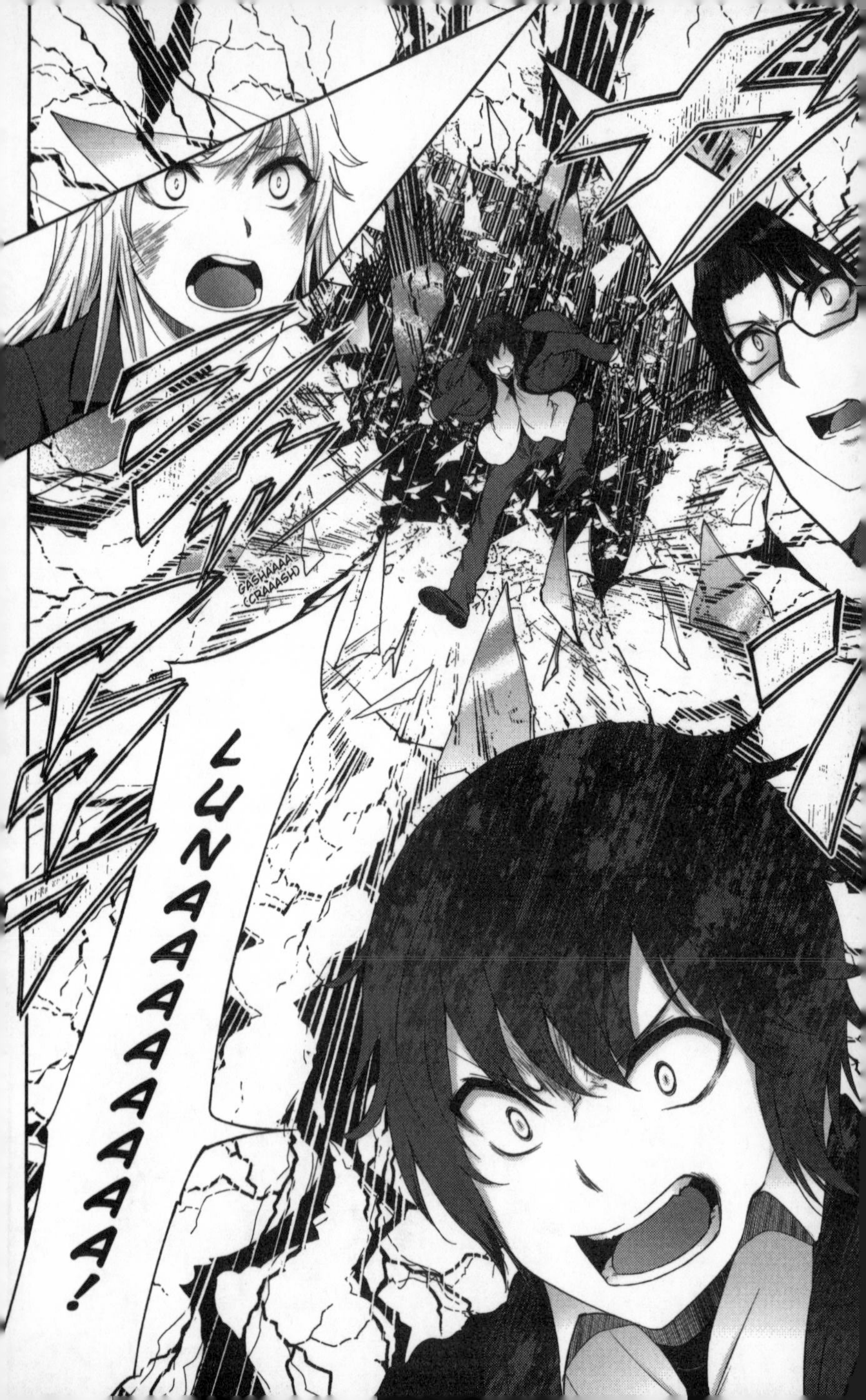
GASHAAAA (CRAAASH)
LUNAAAAAAAAAAA!

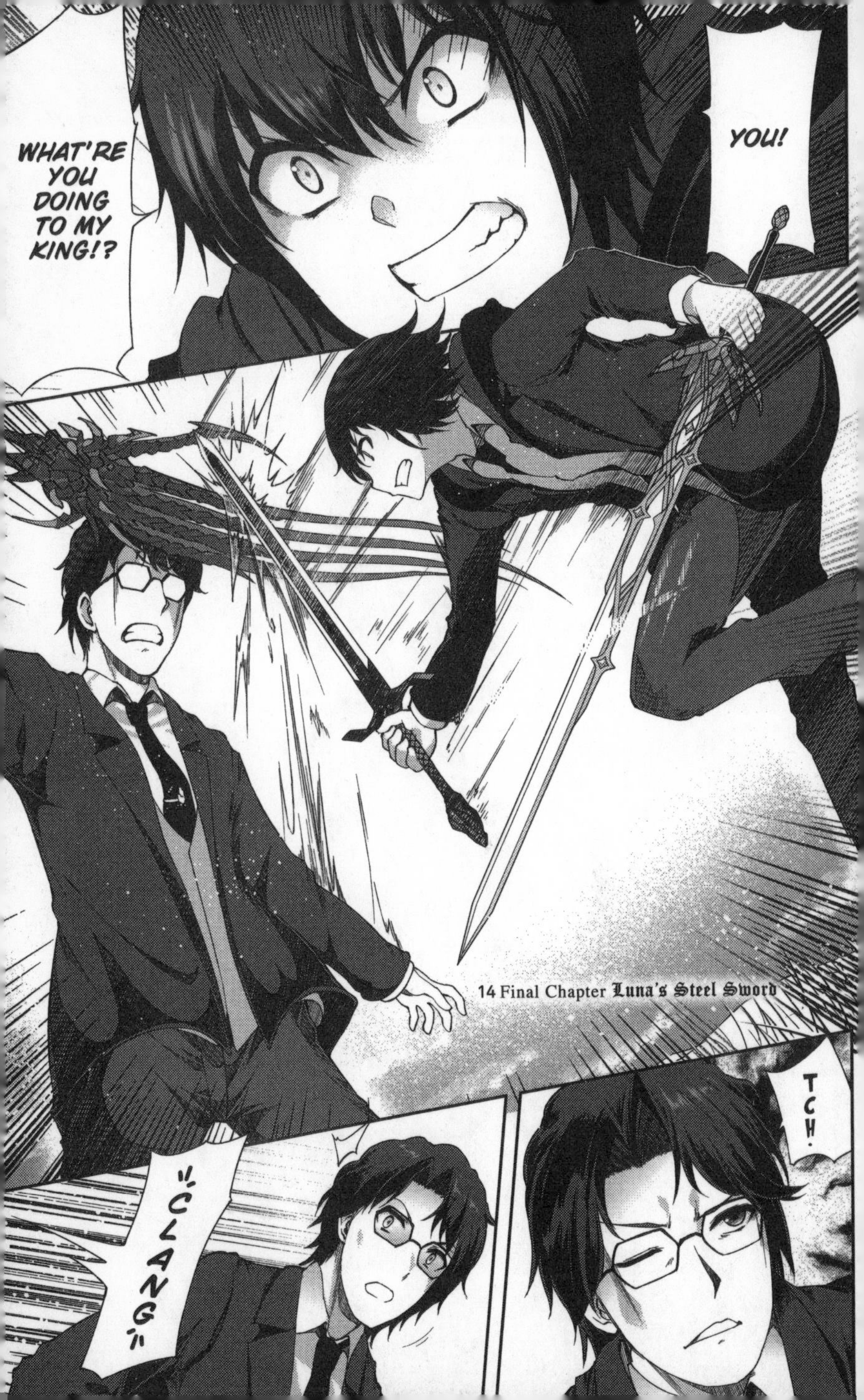
YOU!
WHAT'RE YOU DOING TO MY KING!?
14 Final Chapter Luna's Steel Sword
TCH!
CLANG!!

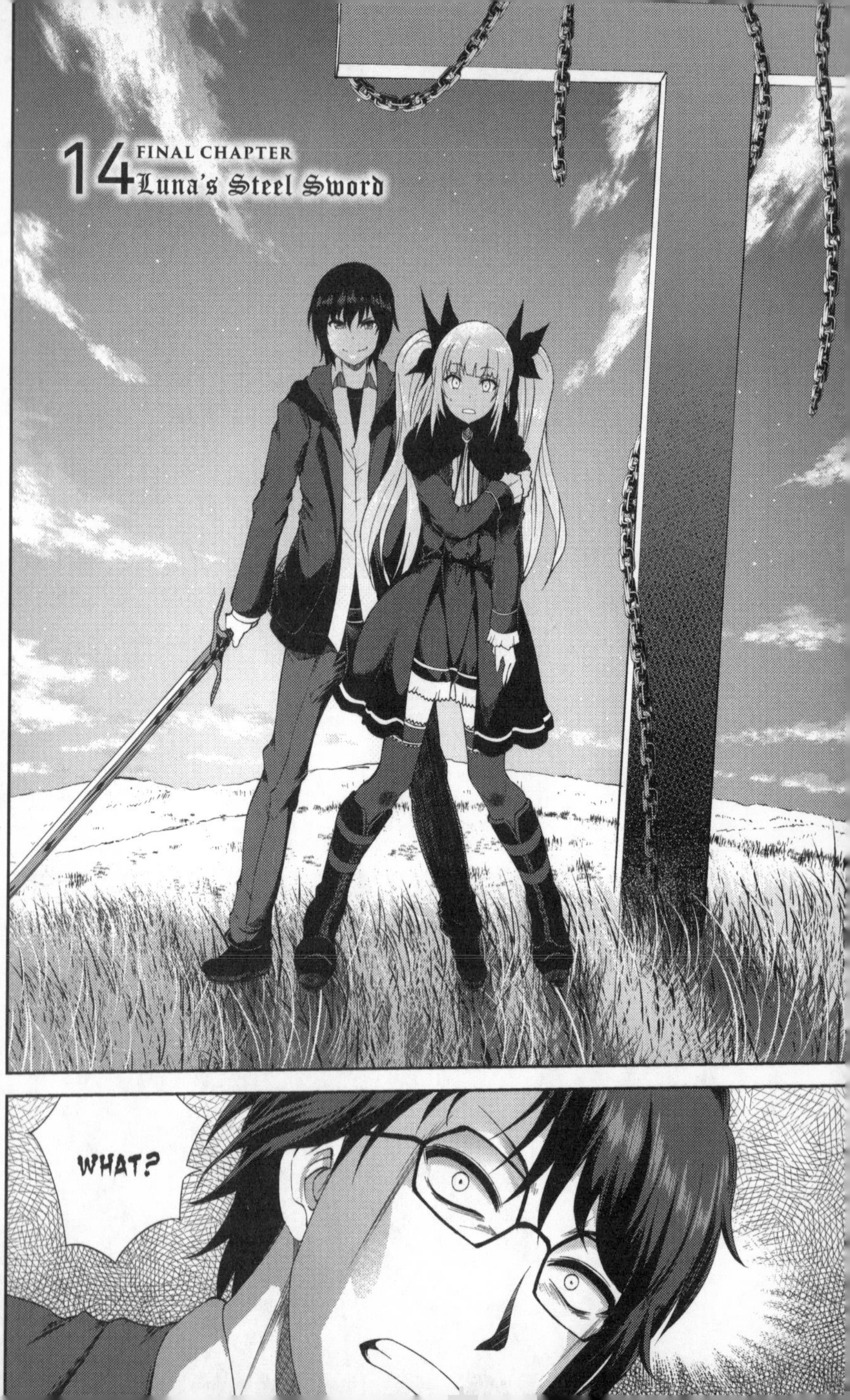
14 FINAL CHAPTER
Luna's Steel Sword
WHAT?

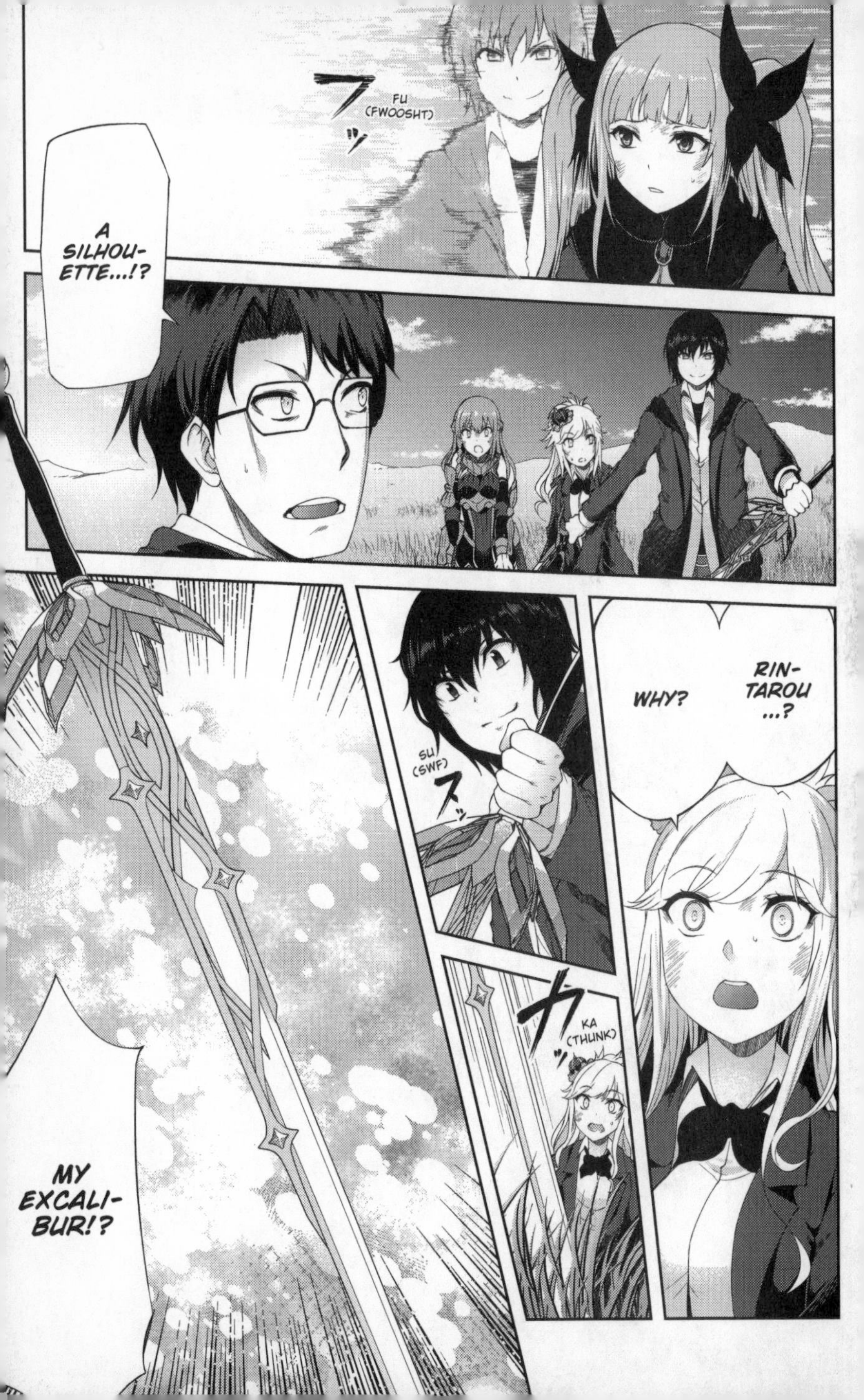
FU (FWOOSHT)
A SILHOU-ETTE...!?
RIN-TAROU ...?
WHY?
SU (SWF)
KA (THUNK)
MY EXCALI-BUR!?

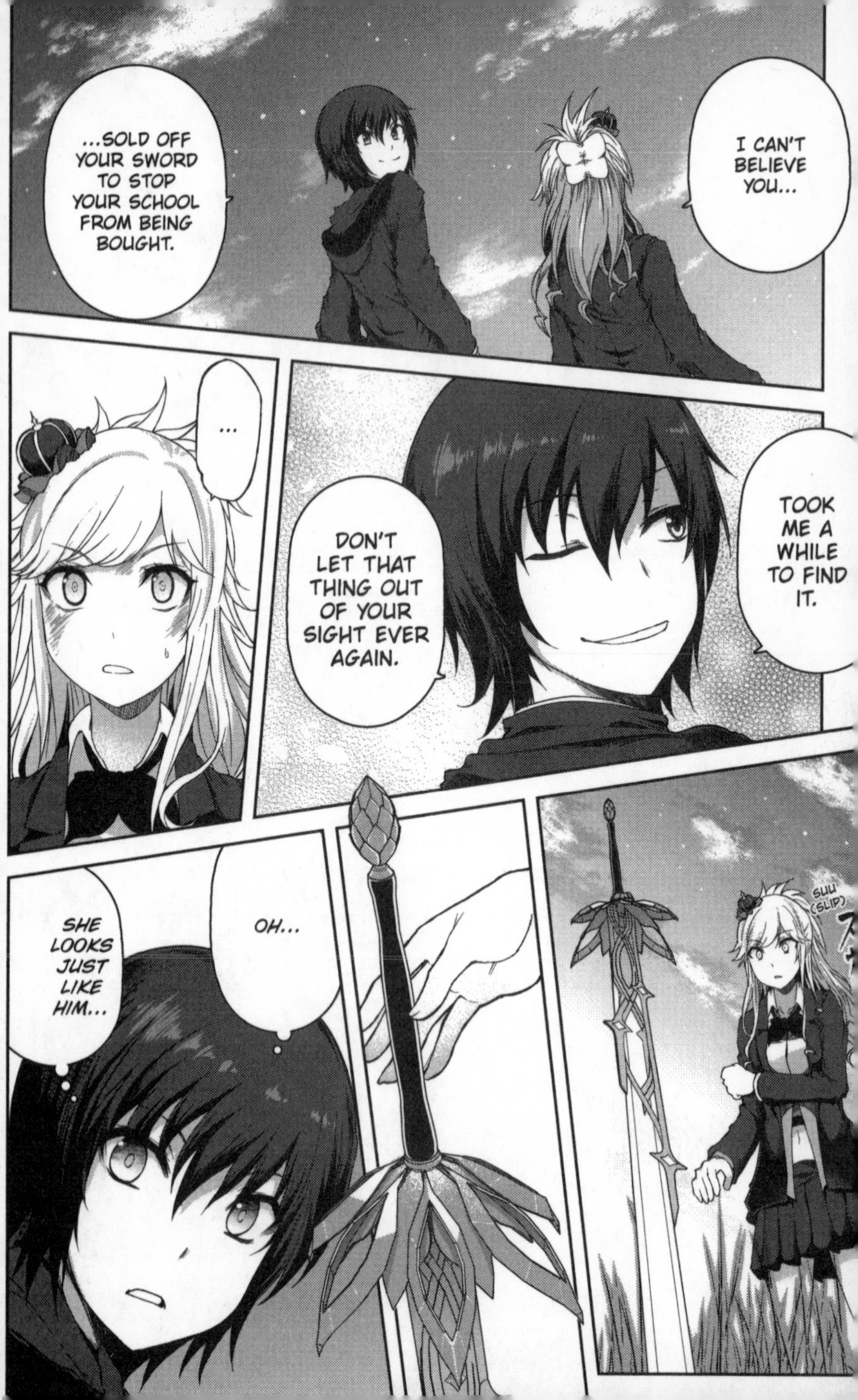
I CAN'T BELIEVE YOU...
...SOLD OFF YOUR SWORD TO STOP YOUR SCHOOL FROM BEING BOUGHT.
TOOK ME A WHILE TO FIND IT.
DON'T LET THAT THING OUT OF YOUR SIGHT EVER AGAIN.
...
SUU (SLIP)
OH...
SHE LOOKS JUST LIKE HIM...

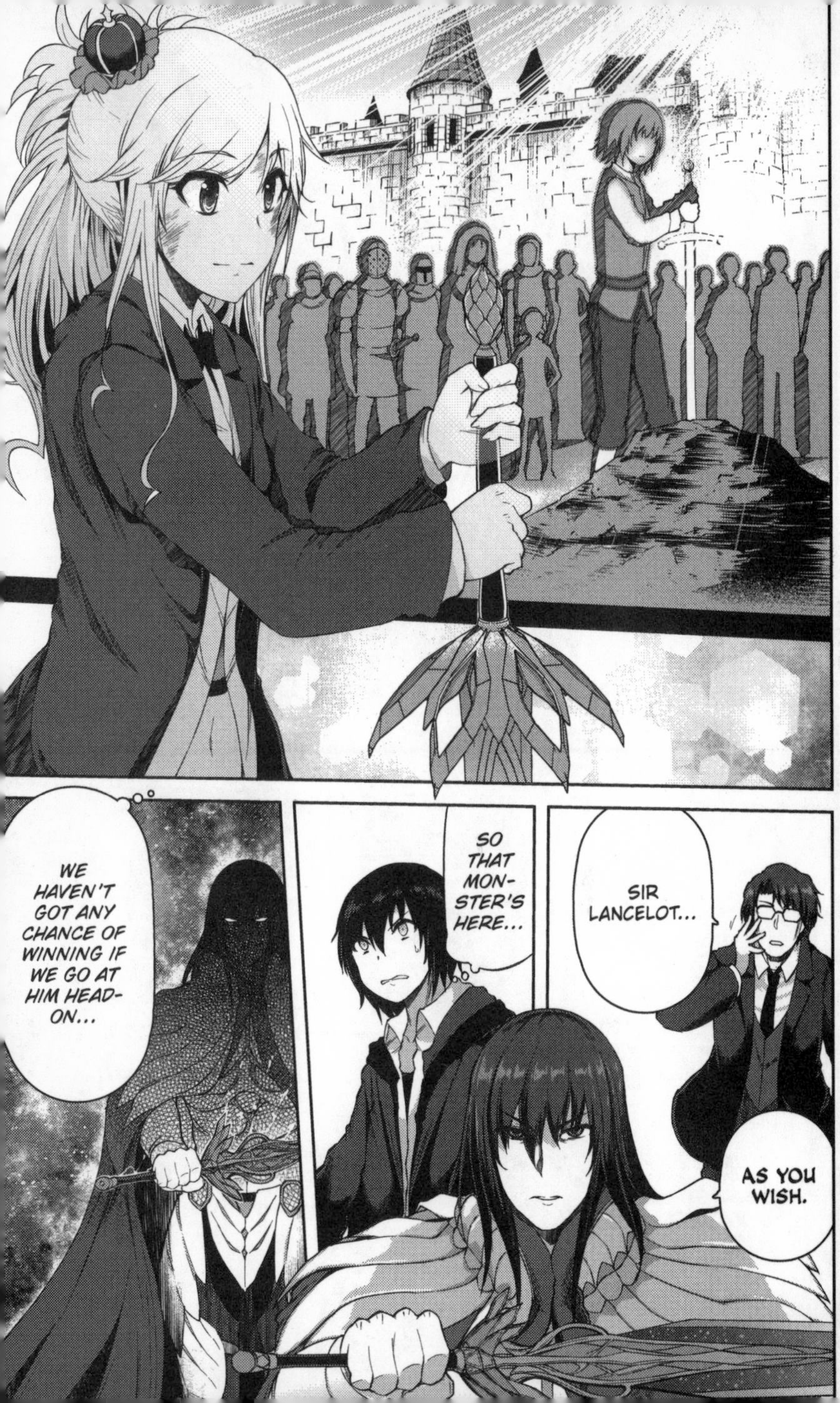
SIR LANCELOT...
AS YOU WISH.
SO THAT MONSTER'S HERE...
WE HAVEN'T GOT ANY CHANCE OF WINNING IF WE GO AT HIM HEAD-ON...

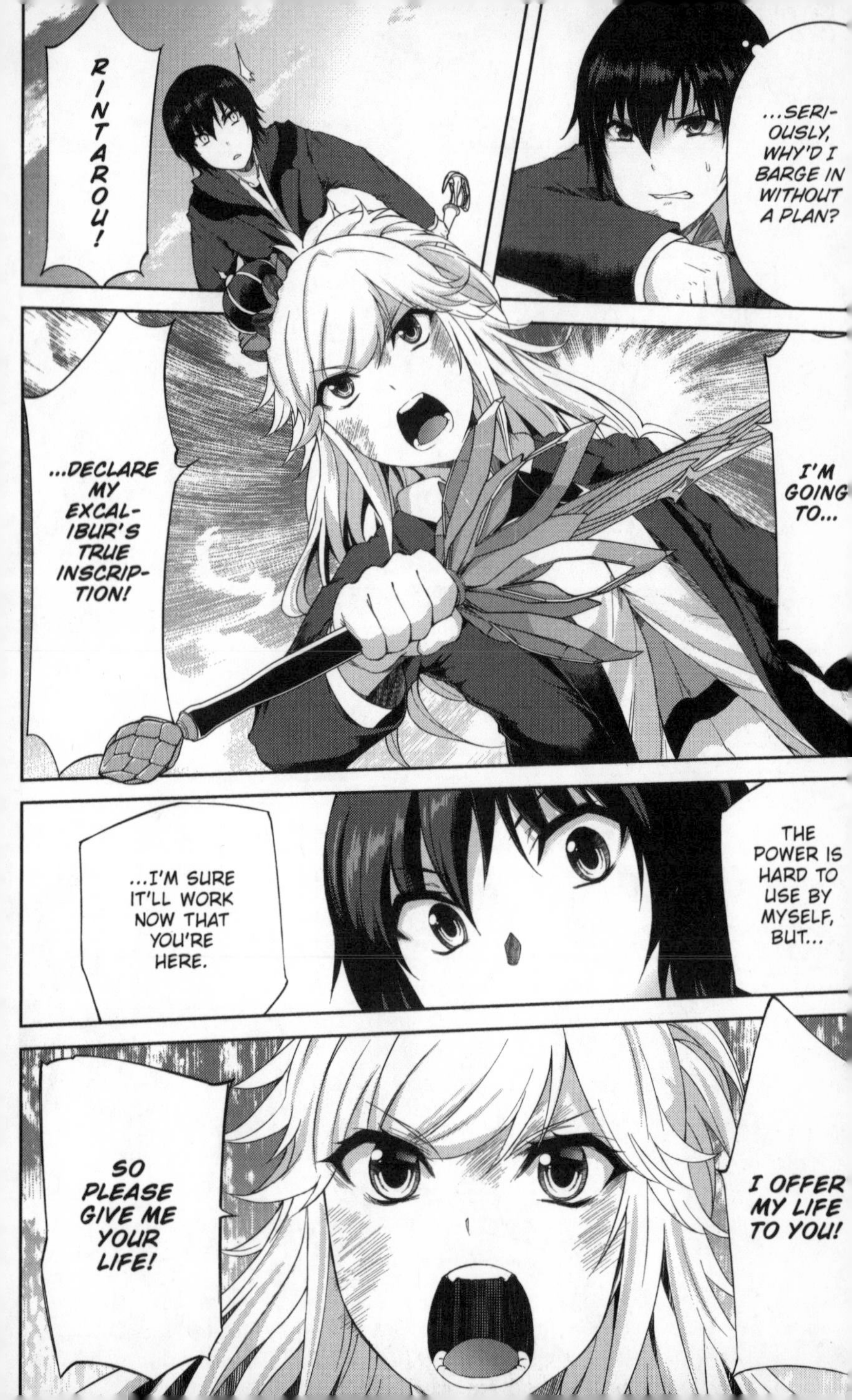
...SERIOUSLY, WHY'D I BARGE IN WITHOUT A PLAN?
RINTAROU!
I'M GOING TO...
...DECLARE MY EXCALIBUR'S TRUE INSCRIPTION!
THE POWER IS HARD TO USE BY MYSELF, BUT...
...I'M SURE IT'LL WORK NOW THAT YOU'RE HERE.
I OFFER MY LIFE TO YOU!
SO PLEASE GIVE ME YOUR LIFE!

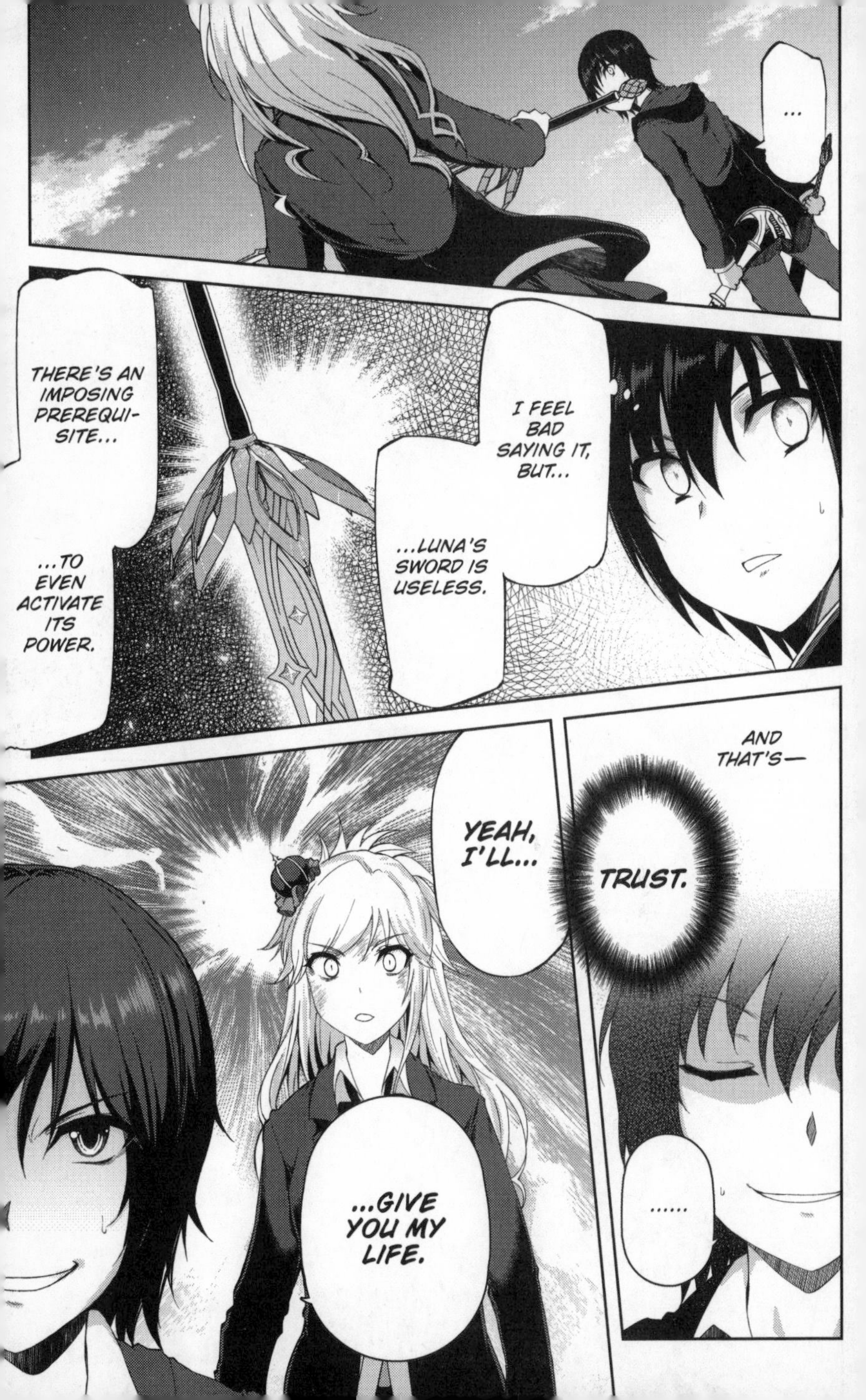
...
I FEEL BAD SAYING IT, BUT...
...LUNA'S SWORD IS USELESS.
THERE'S AN IMPOSING PREREQUI-SITE...
...TO EVEN ACTIVATE ITS POWER.
AND THAT'S—
TRUST.
......
YEAH, I'LL...
...GIVE YOU MY LIFE.

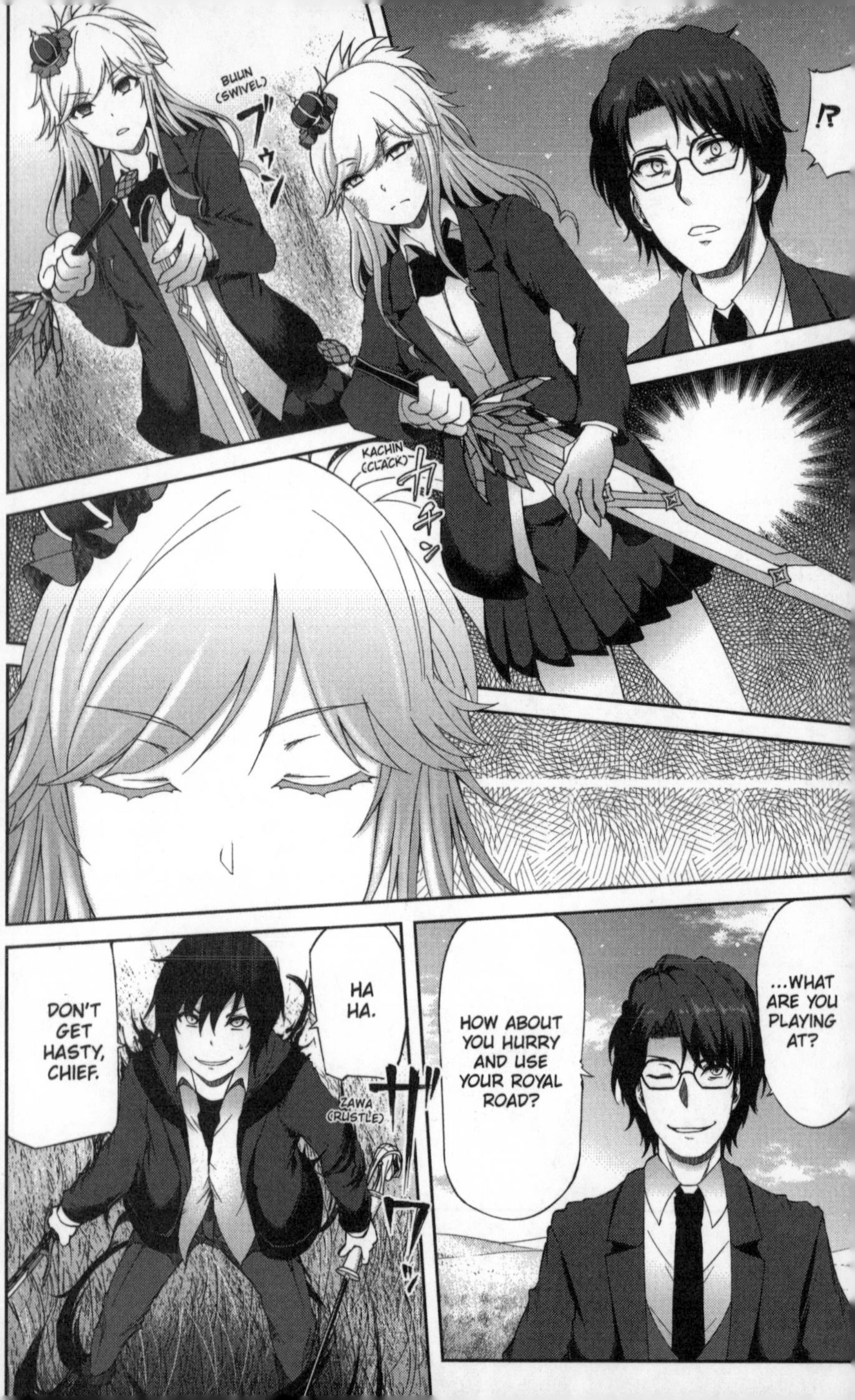
!?
BUUN (SWIVEL)
KACHIN (CLACK)
...WHAT ARE YOU PLAYING AT?
HOW ABOUT YOU HURRY AND USE YOUR ROYAL ROAD?
HA HA.
ZAWA (RUSTLE)
DON'T GET HASTY, CHIEF.

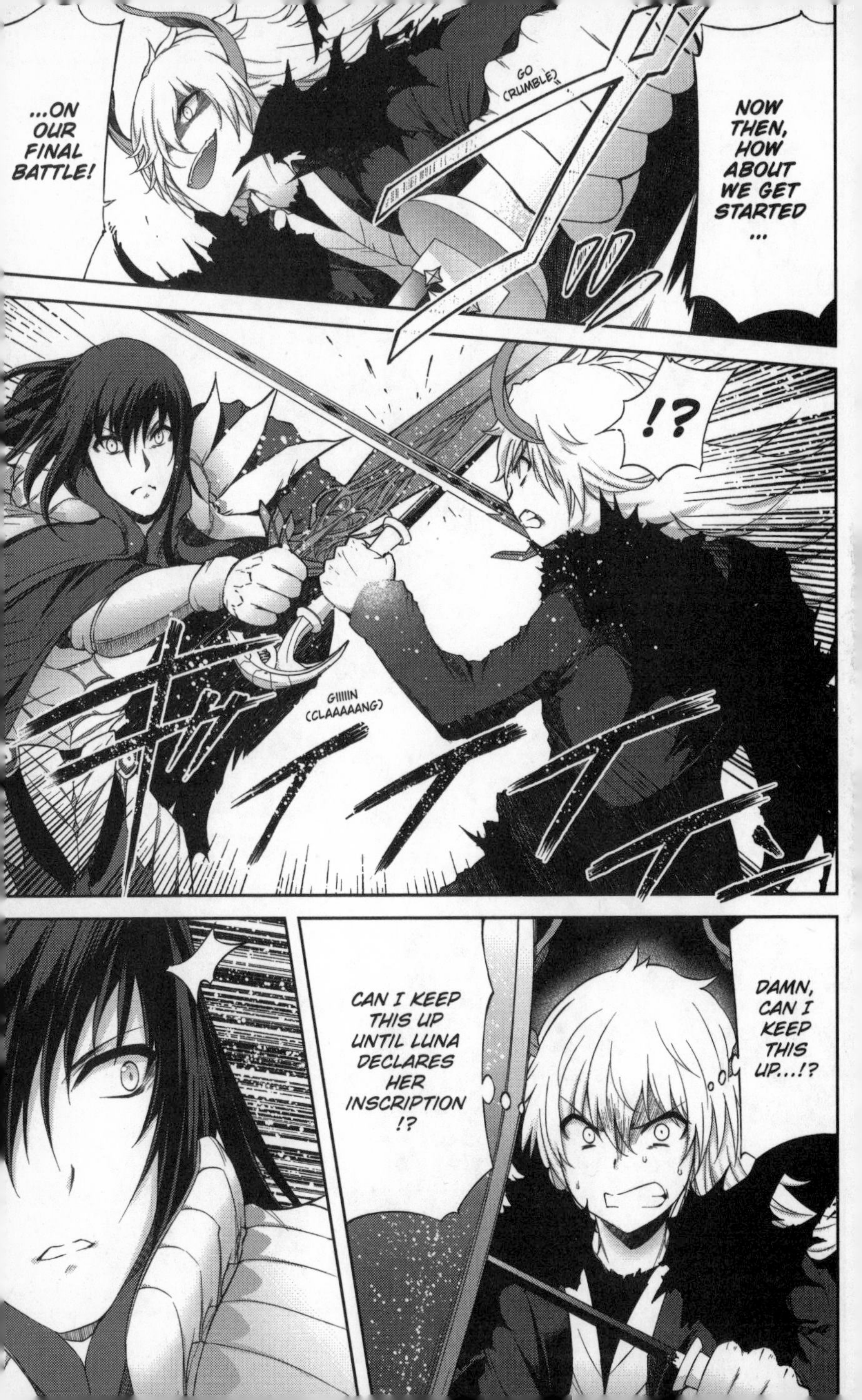
NOW THEN, HOW ABOUT WE GET STARTED ...
GO (RUMBLE)
...ON OUR FINAL BATTLE!
!?
GIIIIN (CLAAAAANG)
DAMN, CAN I KEEP THIS UP...!?
CAN I KEEP THIS UP UNTIL LUNA DECLARES HER INSCRIPTION !?

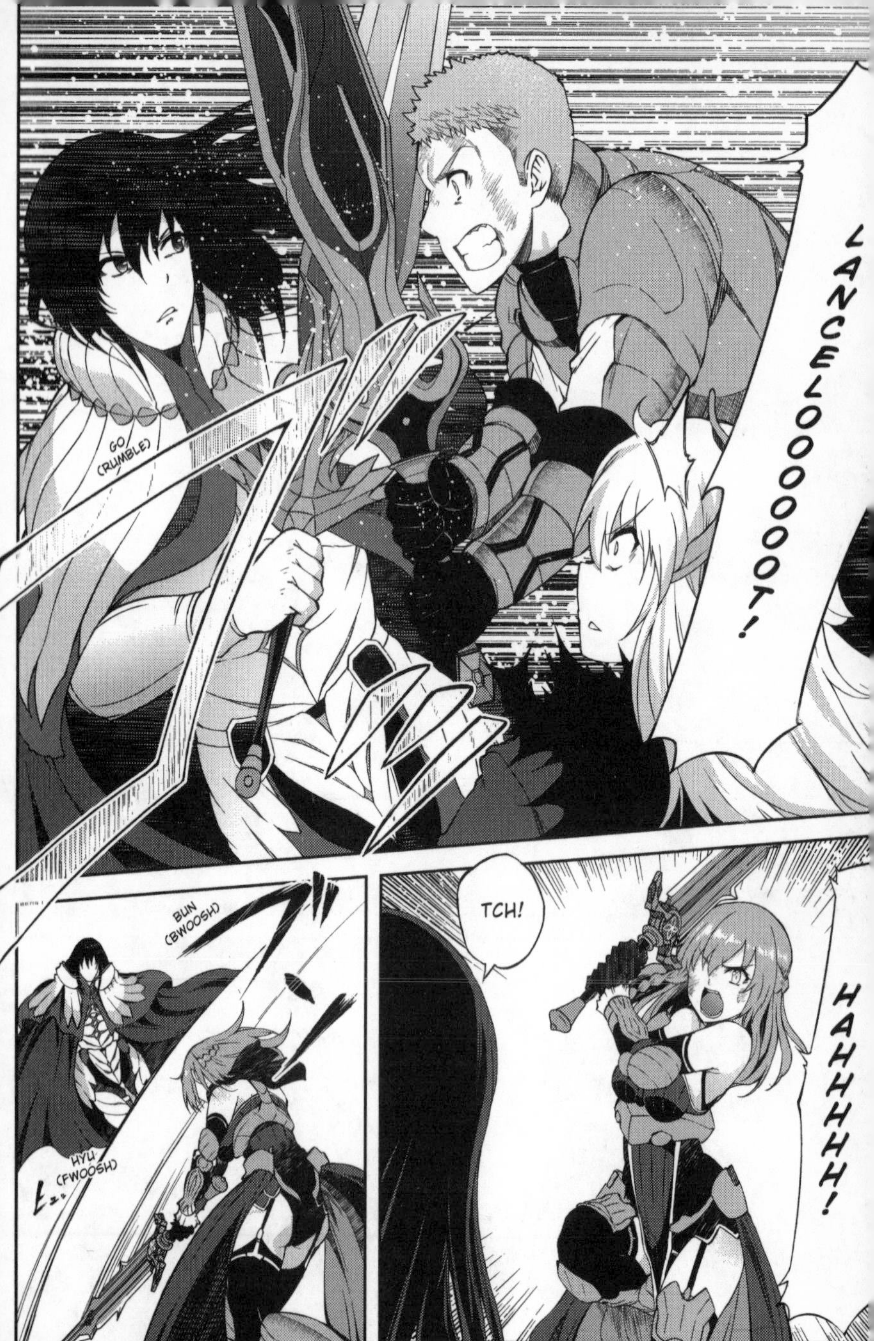
LANCELOOOOOOOT!
GO (RUMBLE)
HAHHHHHH!
TCH!
BUN (BWOOSH)
HYU (FWOOSH)

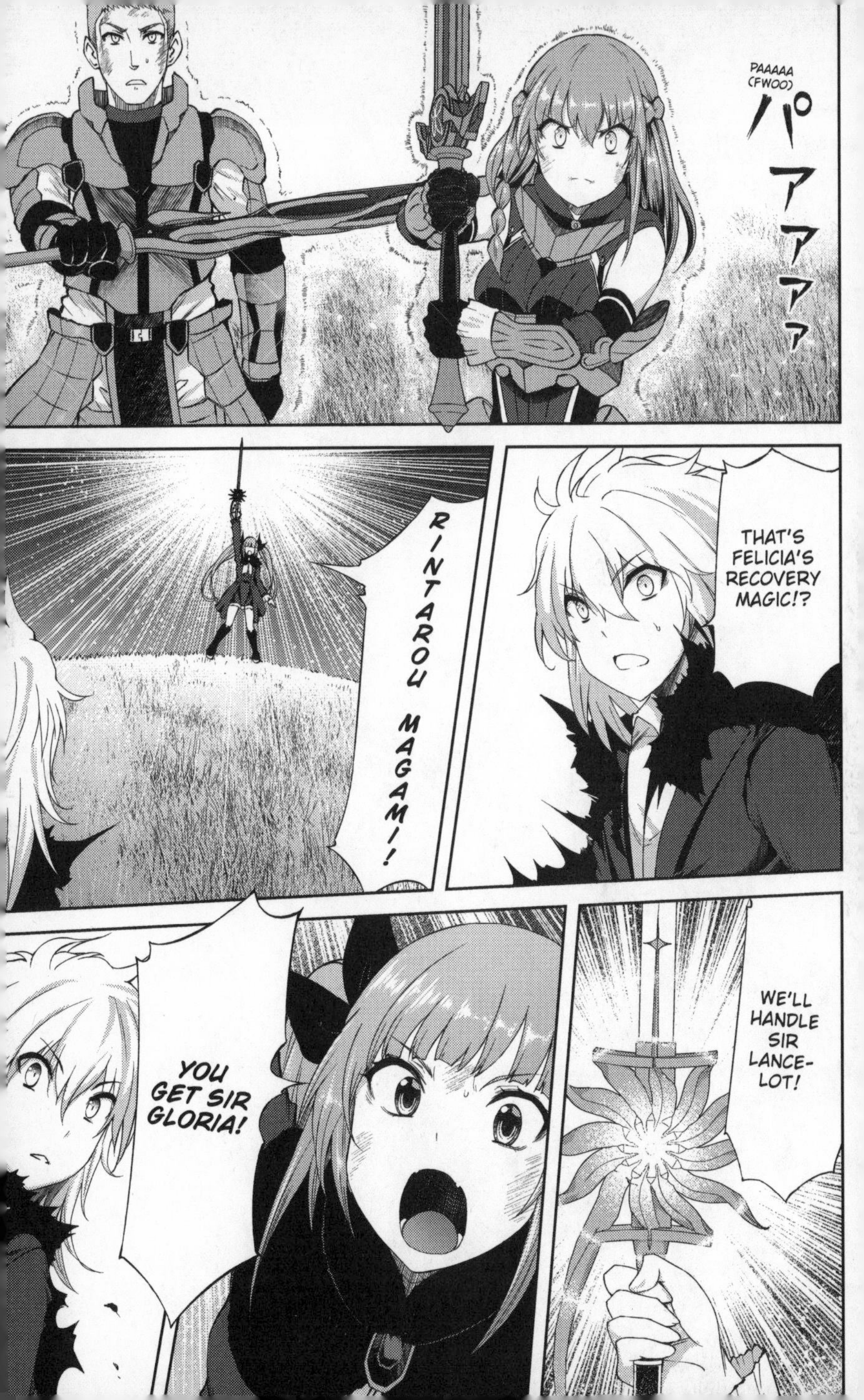
PAAAAA (FWOO)
パアアァァ
THAT'S FELICIA'S RECOVERY MAGIC!?
RINTAROU MAGAMI!!
WE'LL HANDLE SIR LANCE-LOT!
YOU GET SIR GLORIA!

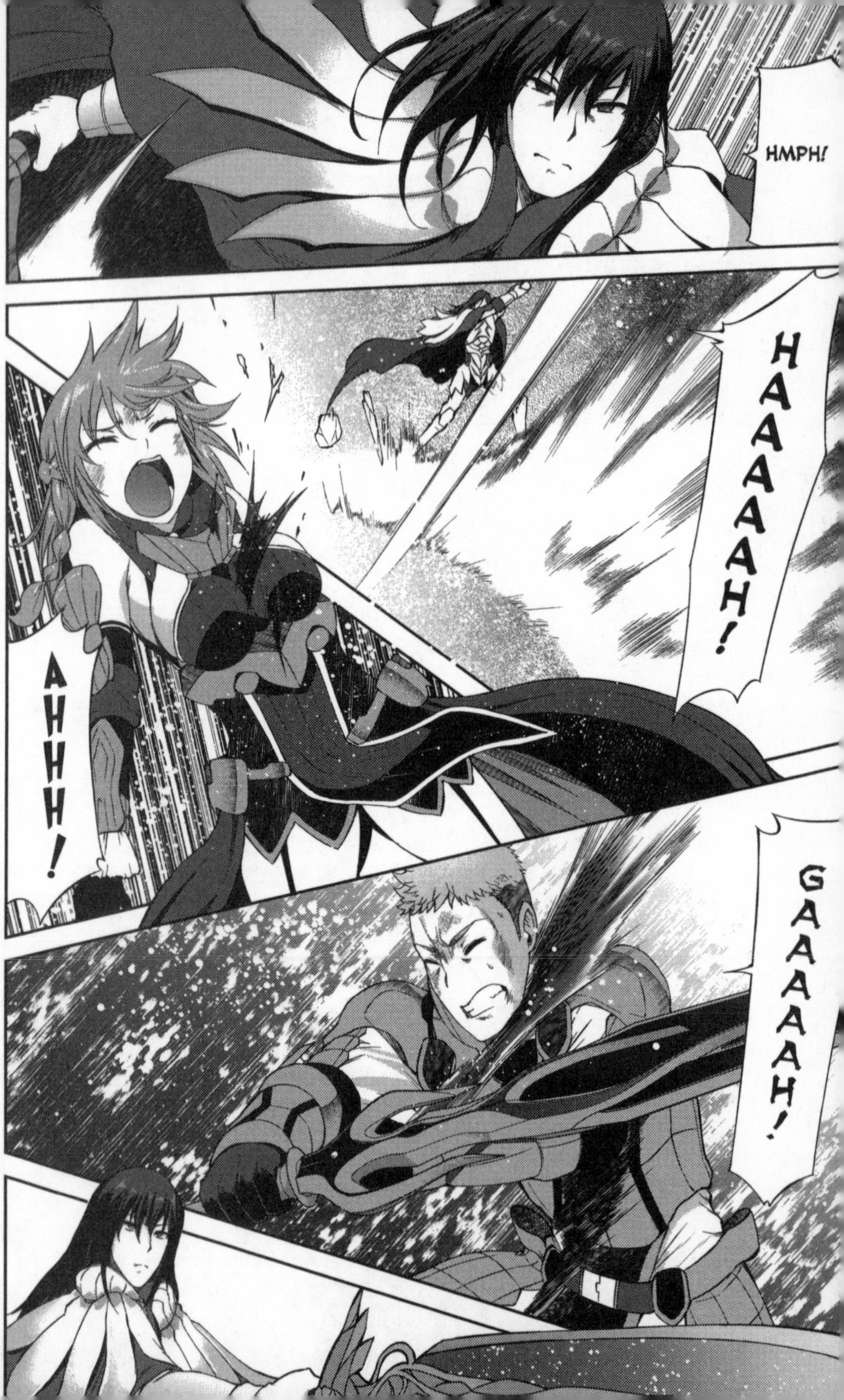
HMPH!
HAAAAAH!
AHHHH!
GAAAAAH!

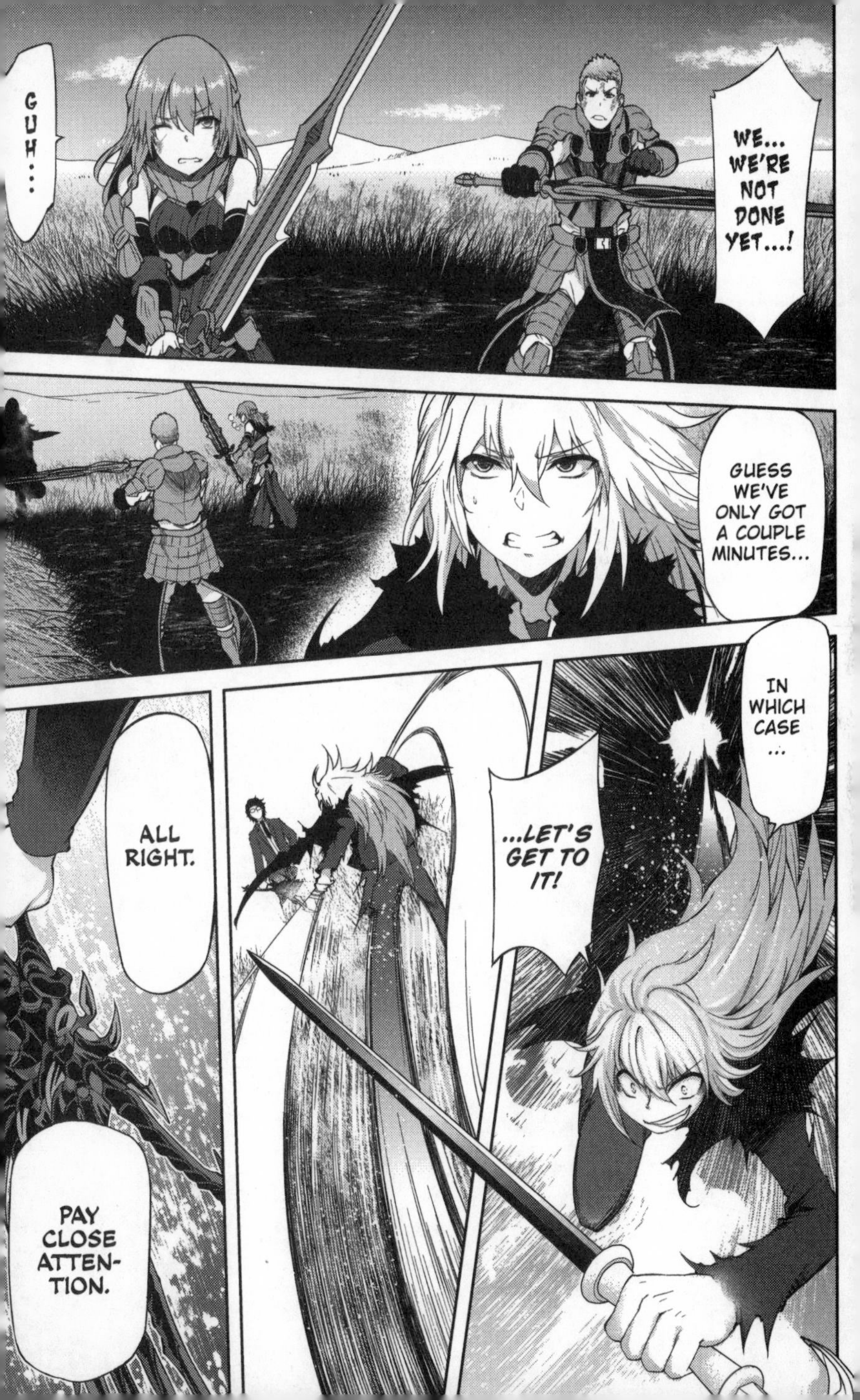
WE... WE'RE NOT DONE YET...!
GUH...
GUESS WE'VE ONLY GOT A COUPLE MINUTES...
IN WHICH CASE ...
...LET'S GET TO IT!
ALL RIGHT.
PAY CLOSE ATTENTION.

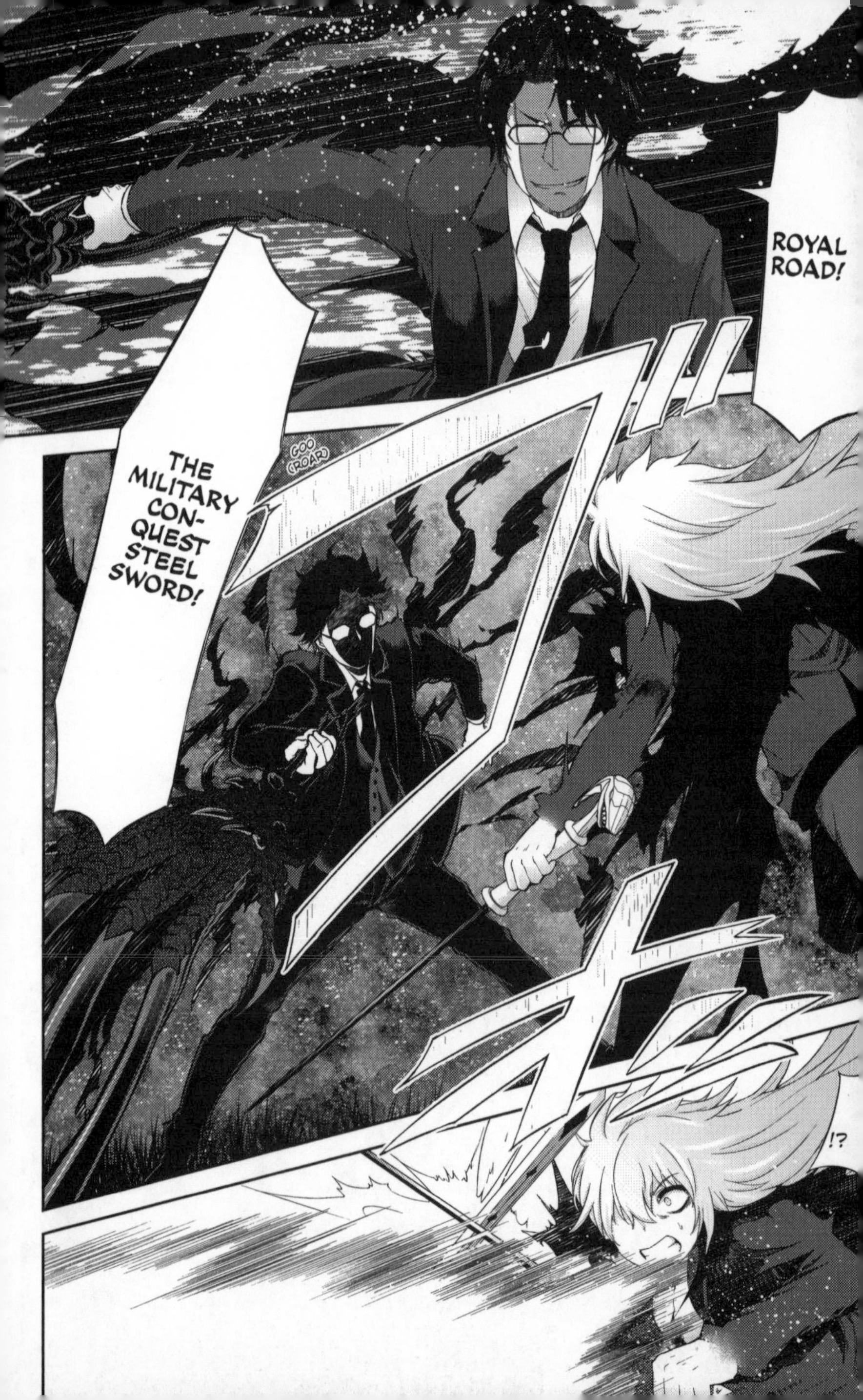
ROYAL ROAD!
THE MILITARY CON-QUEST STEEL SWORD!
GOO (ROAR)
!?

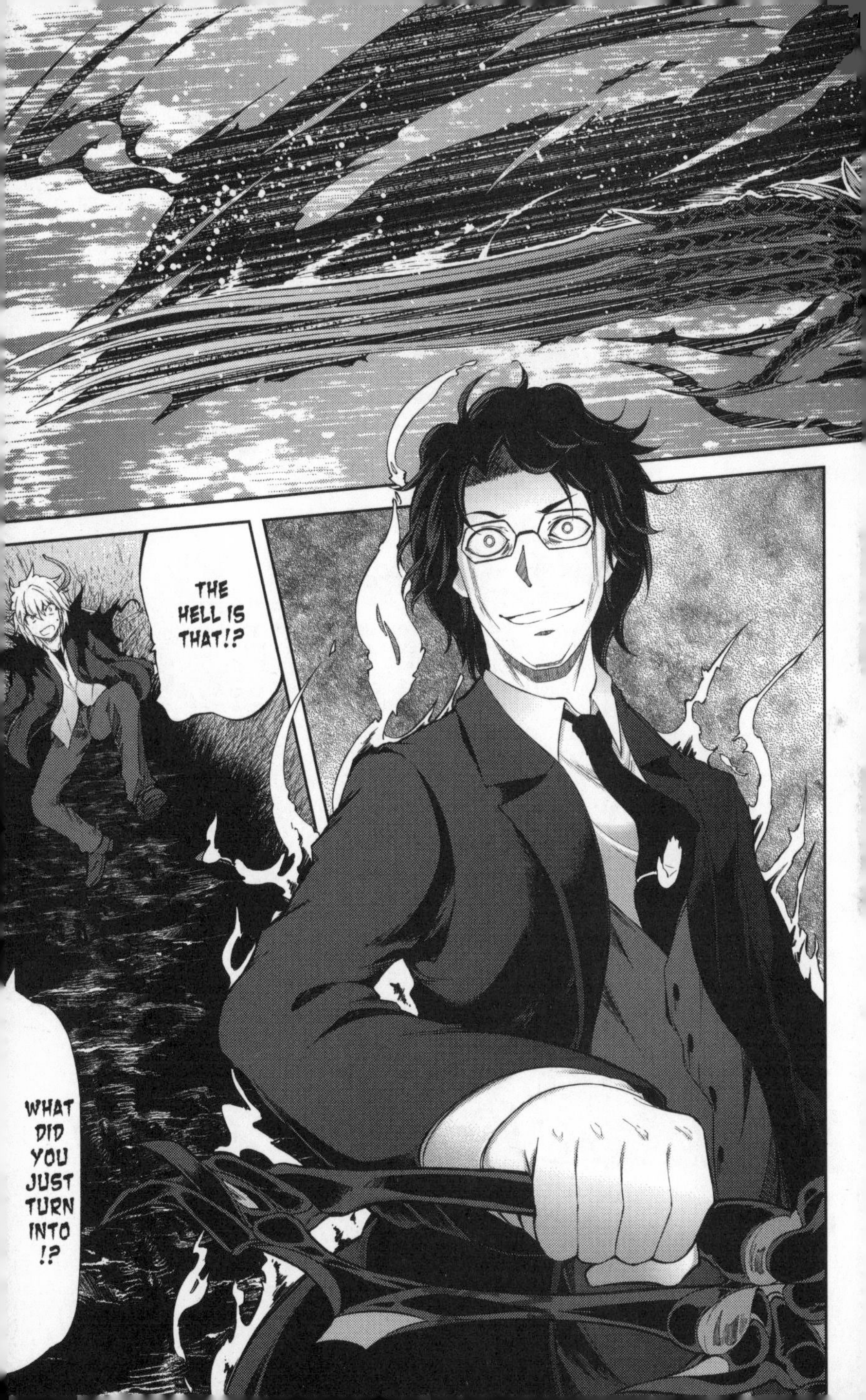
THE HELL IS THAT!?
WHAT DID YOU JUST TURN INTO !?

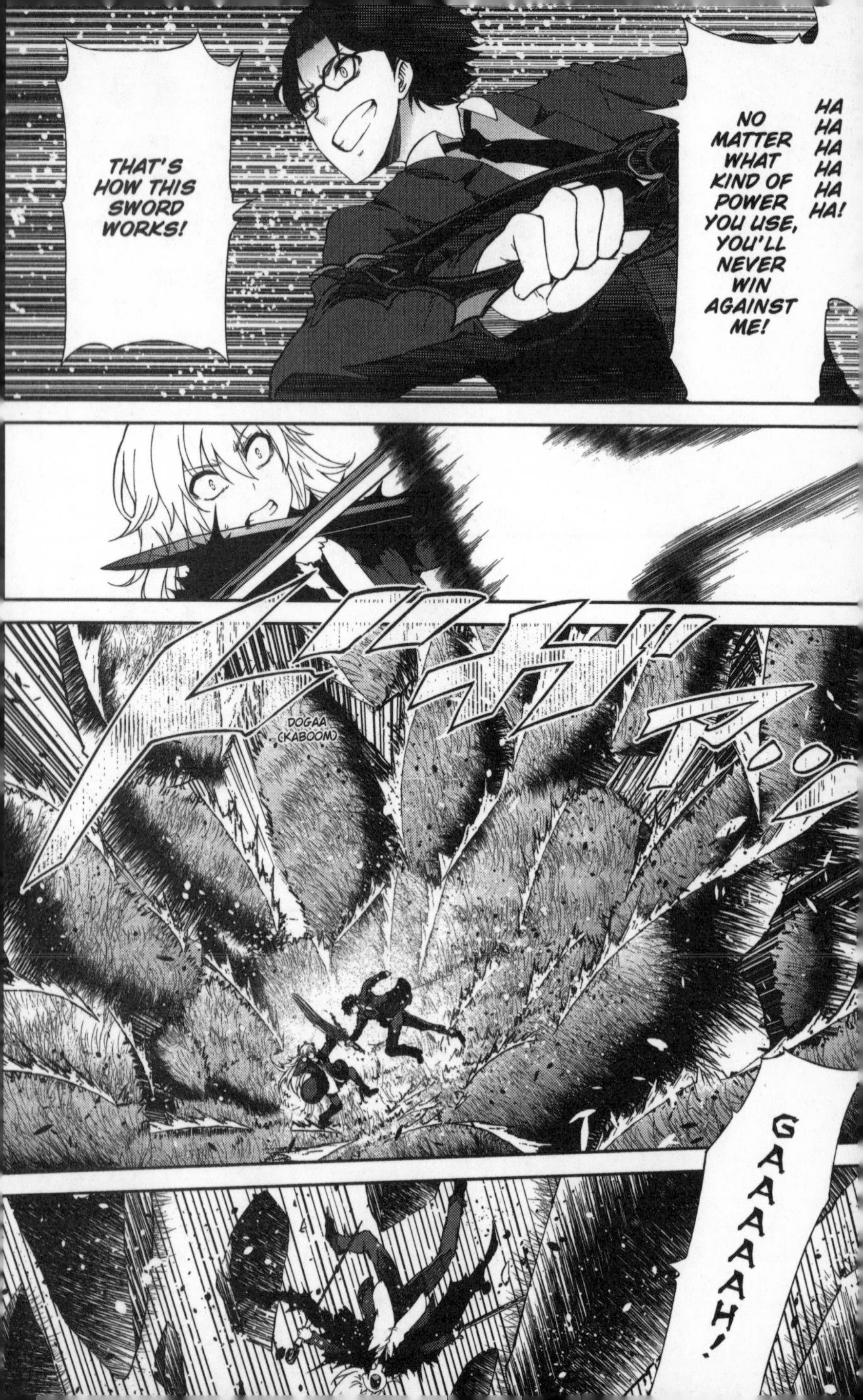
HA HA HA HA HA HA!
NO MATTER WHAT KIND OF POWER YOU USE, YOU'LL NEVER WIN AGAINST ME!
THAT'S HOW THIS SWORD WORKS!
DOGAA (KABOOM)
GAAAAAH!

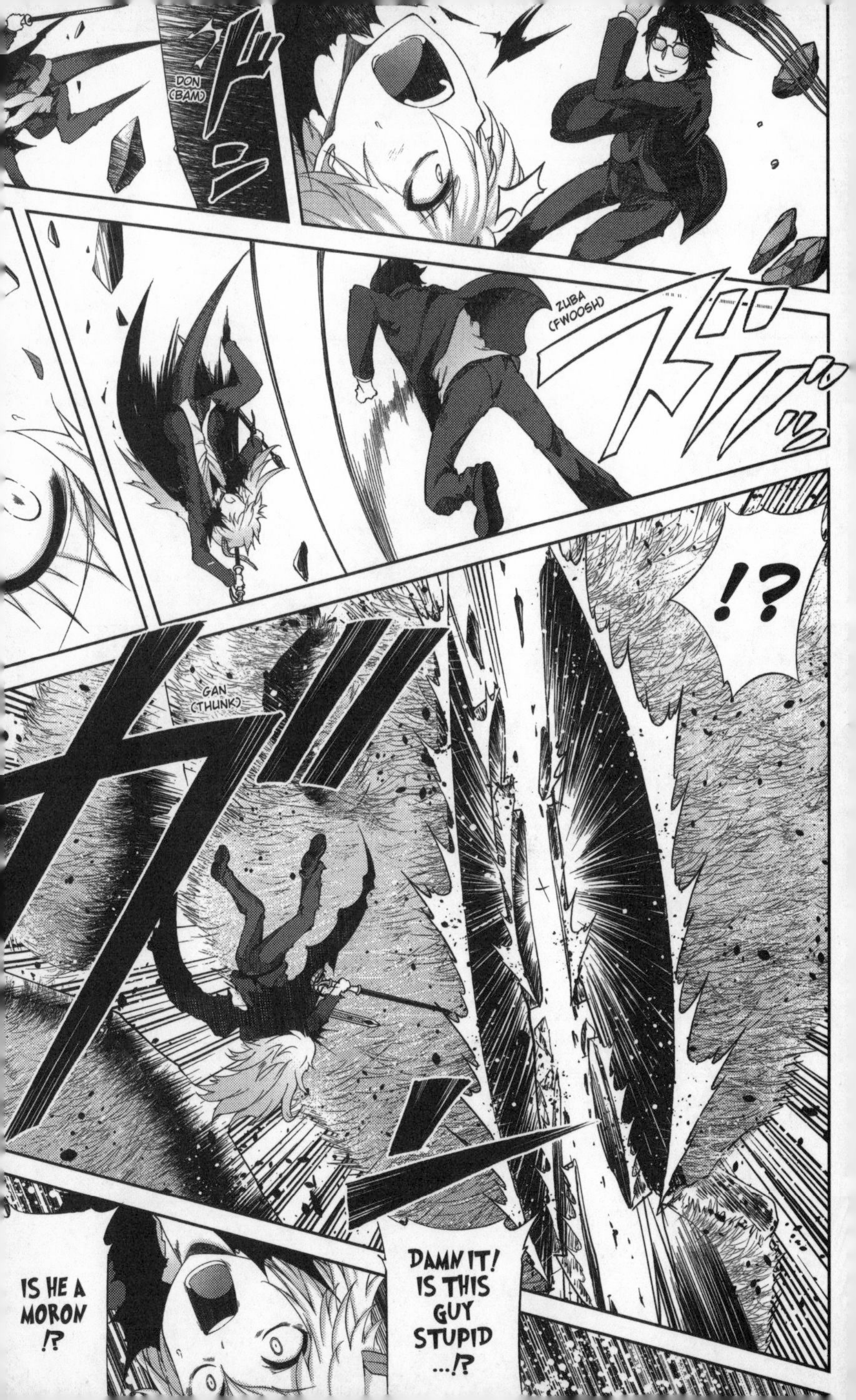
DON
(BAM)
ZUBA
(FWOOSH)
!?
GAN
(THUNK)
DAMN IT! IS THIS GUY STUPID ...!?
IS HE A MORON !?

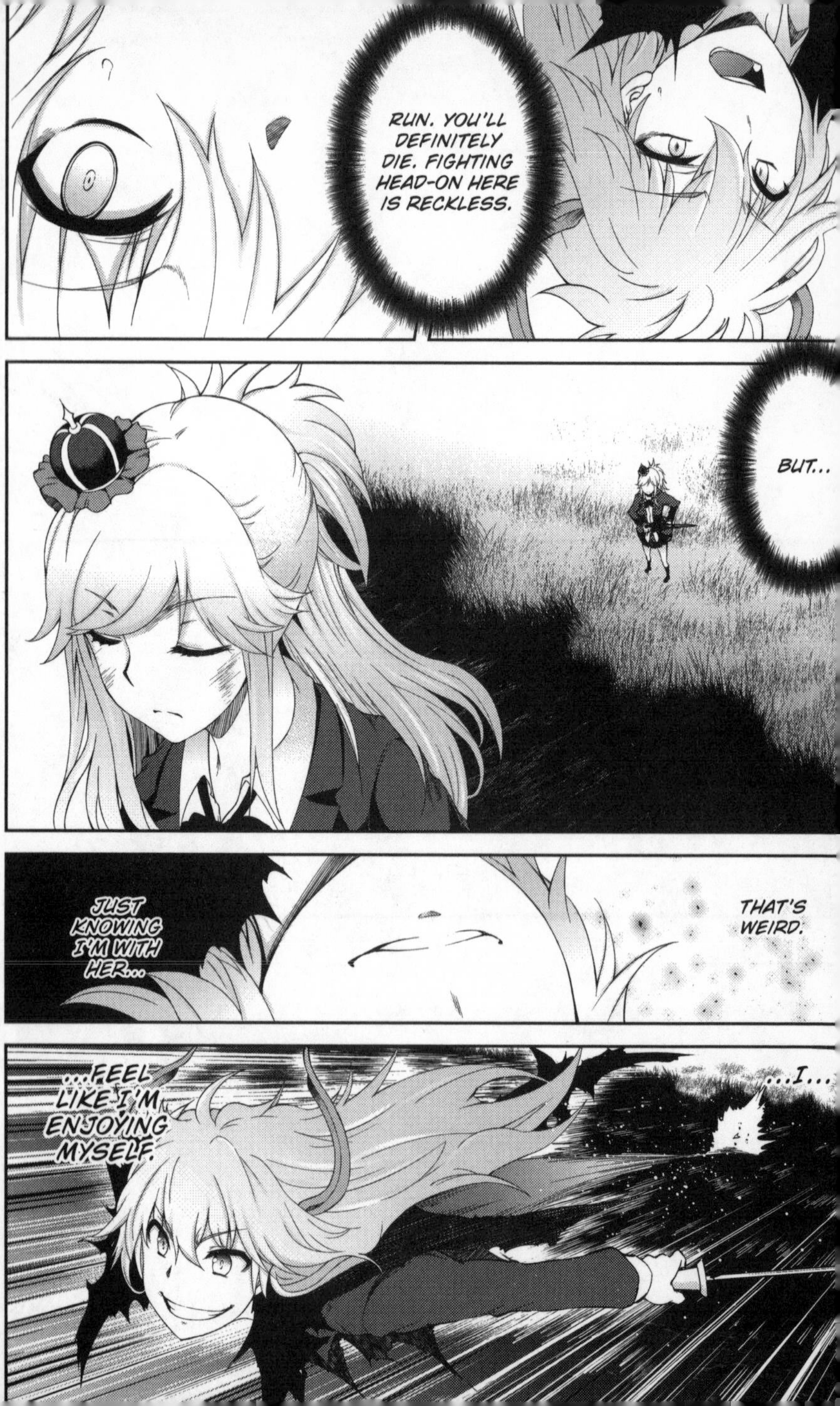
?
RUN. YOU'LL DEFINITELY DIE. FIGHTING HEAD-ON HERE IS RECKLESS.
BUT...
THAT'S WEIRD.
JUST KNOWING I'M WITH HER...
...I...
...FEEL LIKE I'M ENJOYING MYSELF.

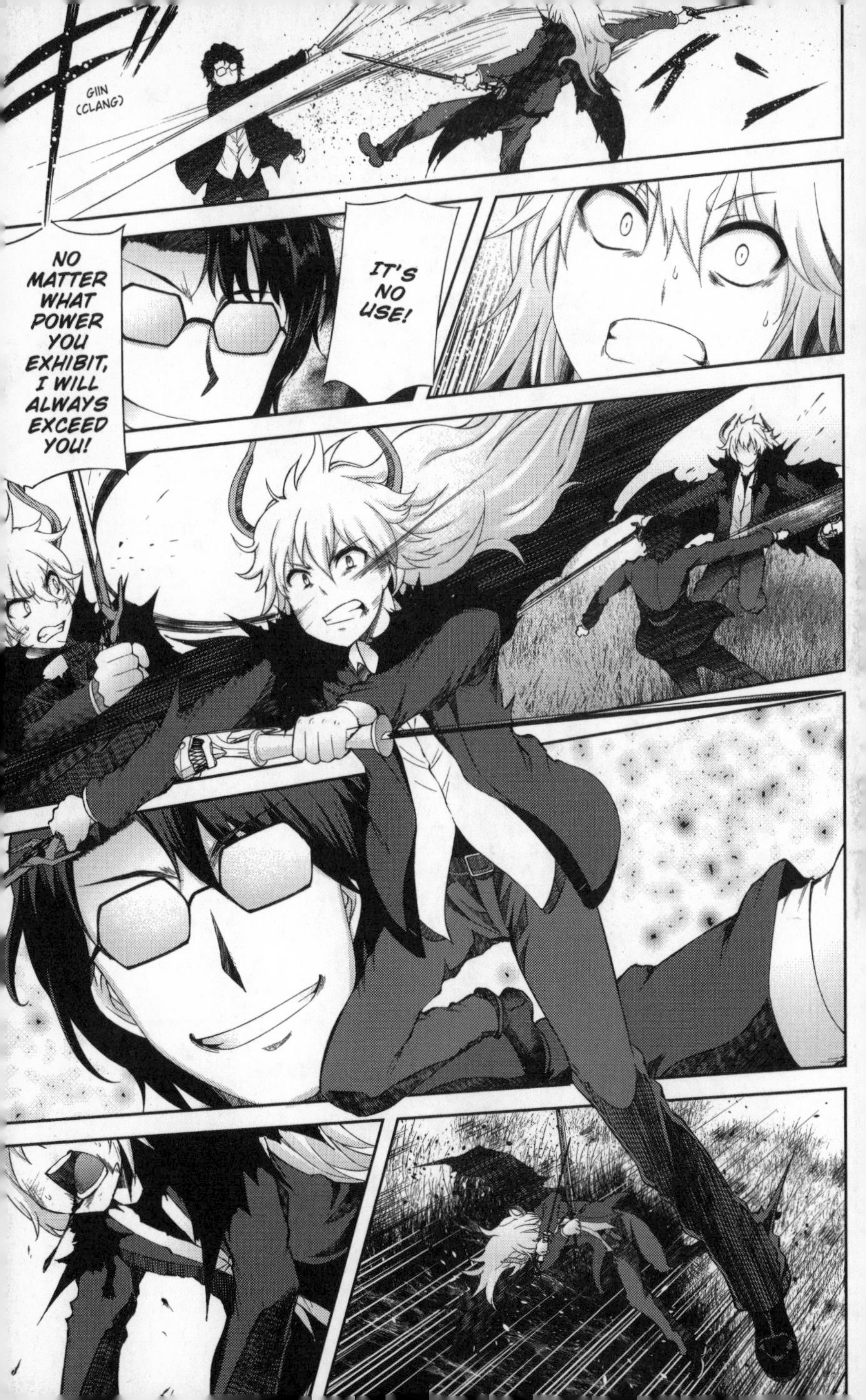
GIIN (CLANG)
IT'S NO USE!
NO MATTER WHAT POWER YOU EXHIBIT, I WILL ALWAYS EXCEED YOU!

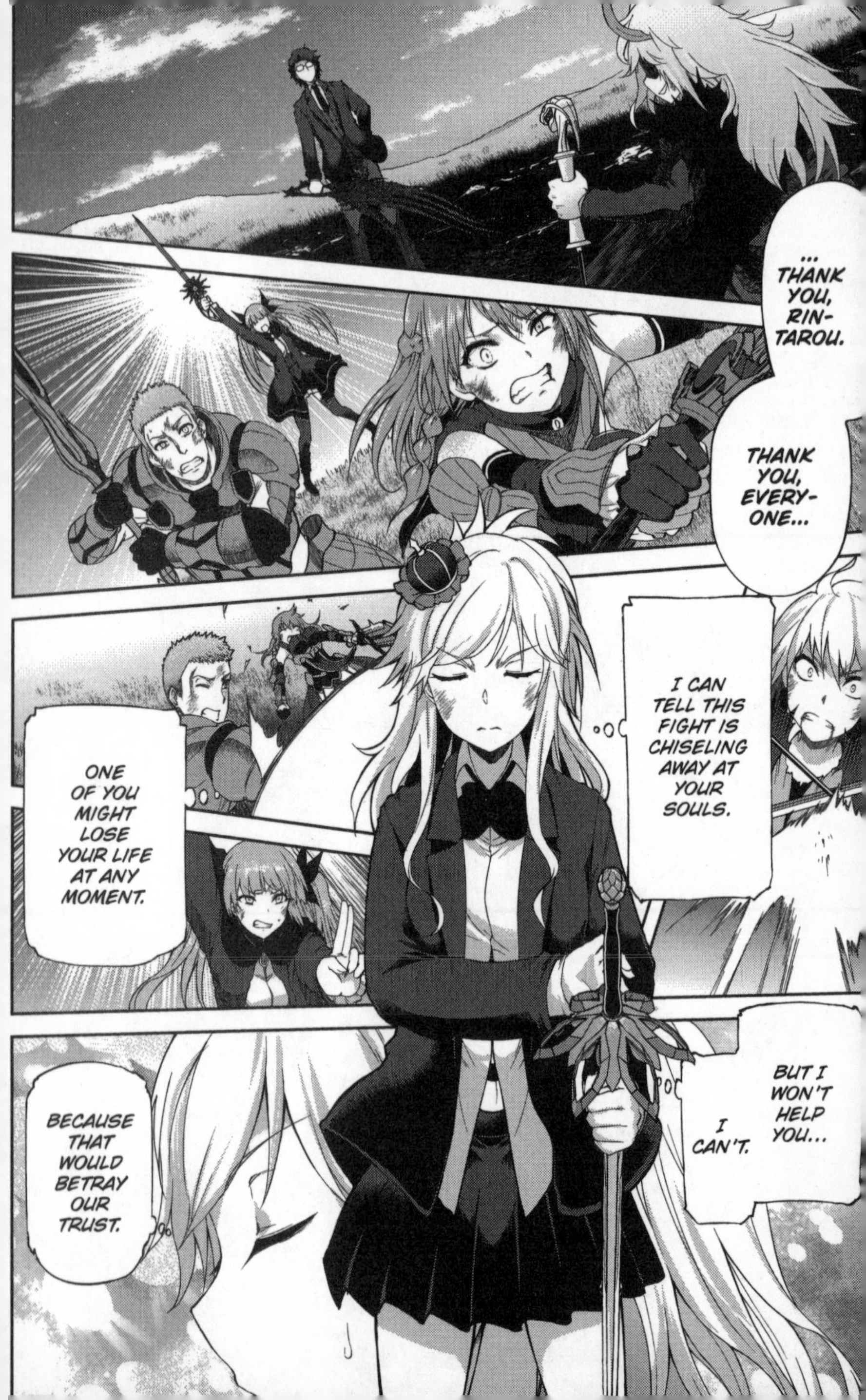

... THANK YOU, RIN-TAROU.
THANK YOU, EVERY-ONE...
I CAN TELL THIS FIGHT IS CHISELING AWAY AT YOUR SOULS.
ONE OF YOU MIGHT LOSE YOUR LIFE AT ANY MOMENT.
BUT I WON'T HELP YOU...
I CAN'T.
BECAUSE THAT WOULD BETRAY OUR TRUST.

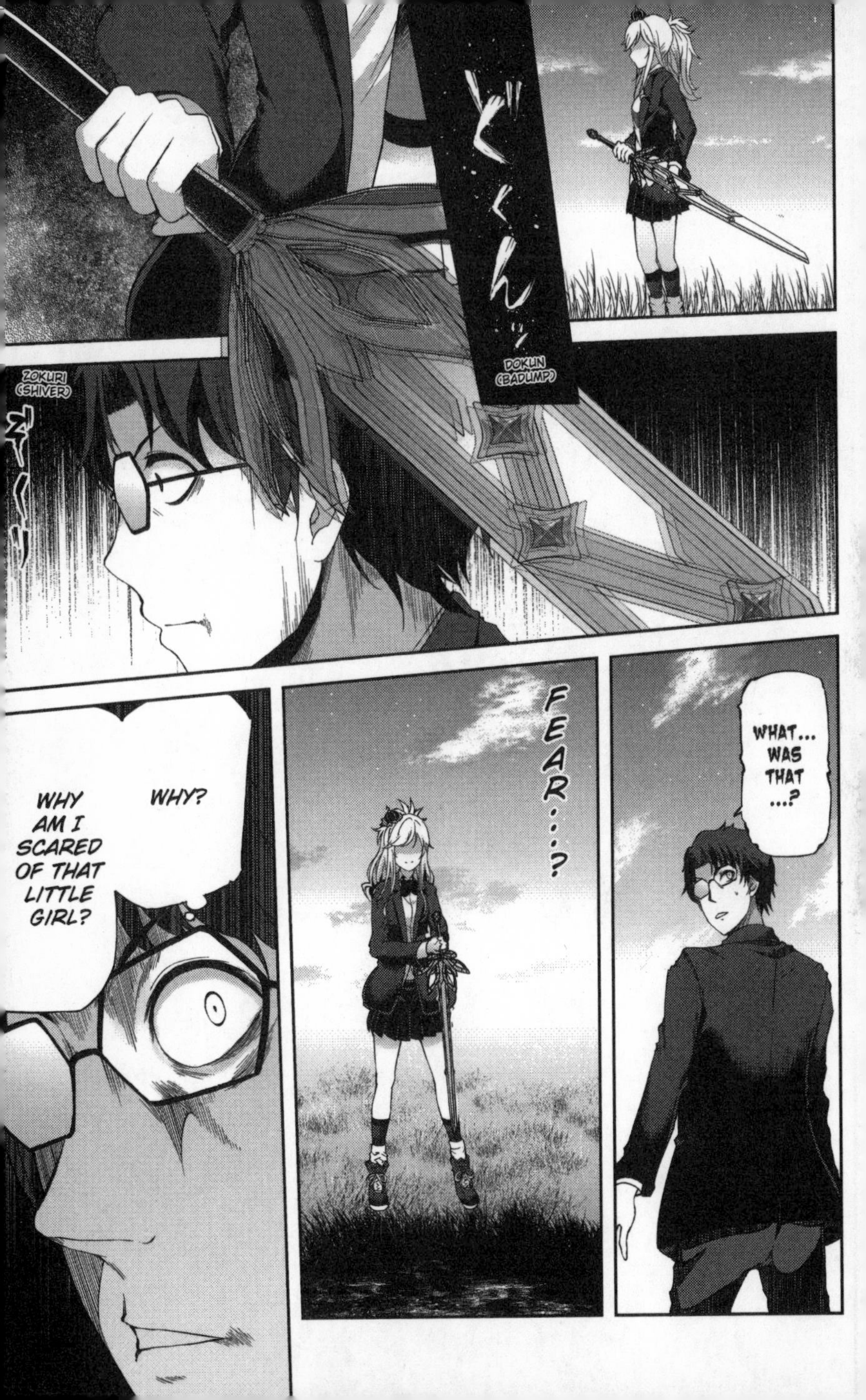

どくんッ!
DOKUN (BADUMP)
ZOKURI (SHIVER)
WHAT... WAS THAT ...?
FEAR...?
WHY?
WHY AM I SCARED OF THAT LITTLE GIRL?

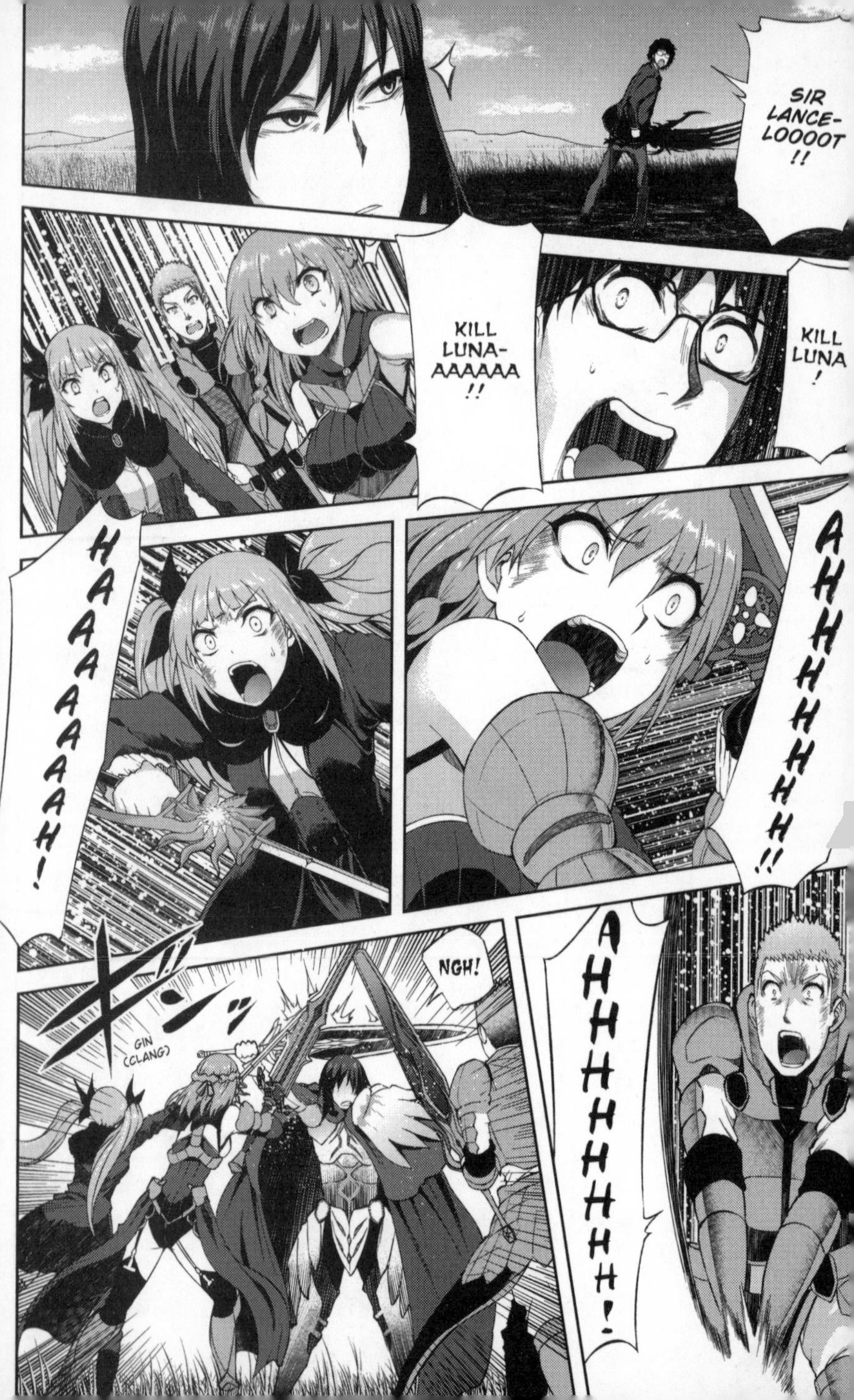
SIR LANCE-LOOOOT!!
KILL LUNA!
KILL LUNA-AAAAAA!!
AHHHHHHHH!!
HAAAAAAAH!
AHHHHHHHH!
NGH!
GIN (CLANG)

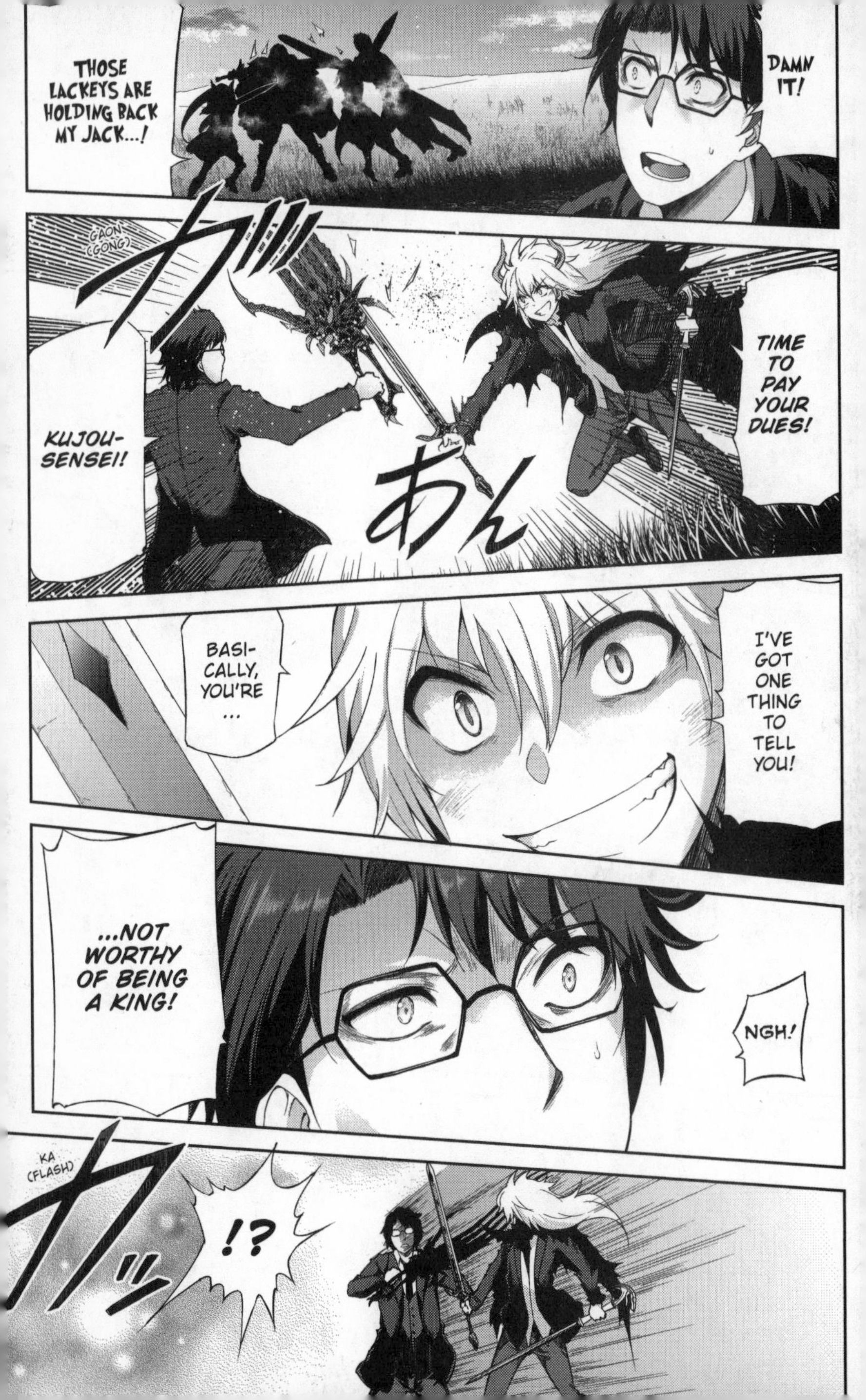
DAMN IT!
THOSE LACKEYS ARE HOLDING BACK MY JACK...!
TIME TO PAY YOUR DUES!
GAON (GONG)
ガあん
KUJOU-SENSEI!
I'VE GOT ONE THING TO TELL YOU!
BASI-CALLY, YOU'RE ...
...NOT WORTHY OF BEING A KING!
NGH!
!?
KA (FLASH)
カッ

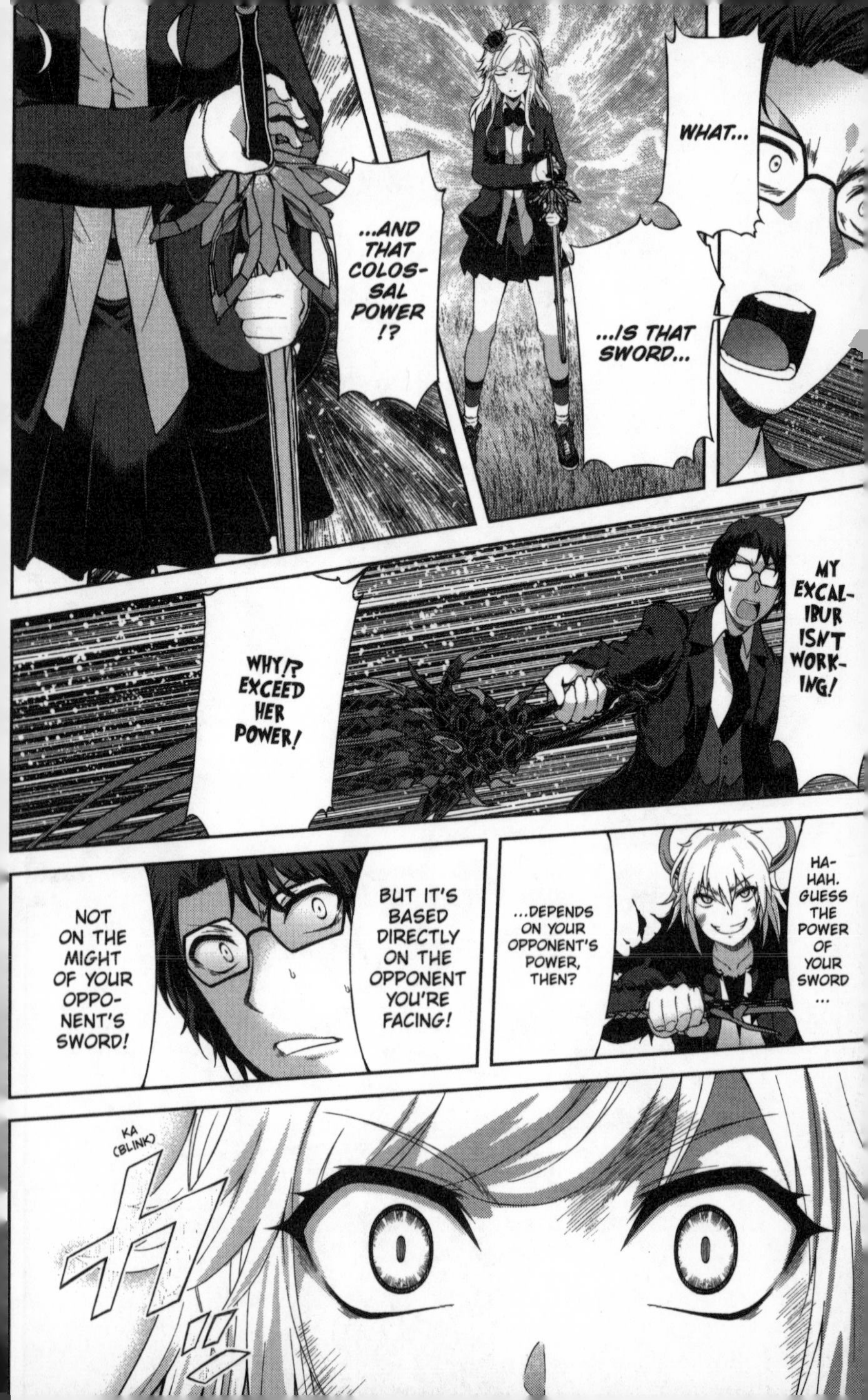
WHAT...
...IS THAT SWORD...
...AND THAT COLOSSAL POWER!?
MY EXCALIBUR ISN'T WORKING!
WHY!? EXCEED HER POWER!
HAHAH. GUESS THE POWER OF YOUR SWORD...
...DEPENDS ON YOUR OPPONENT'S POWER, THEN?
BUT IT'S BASED DIRECTLY ON THE OPPONENT YOU'RE FACING!
NOT ON THE MIGHT OF YOUR OPPONENT'S SWORD!
KA (BLINK)

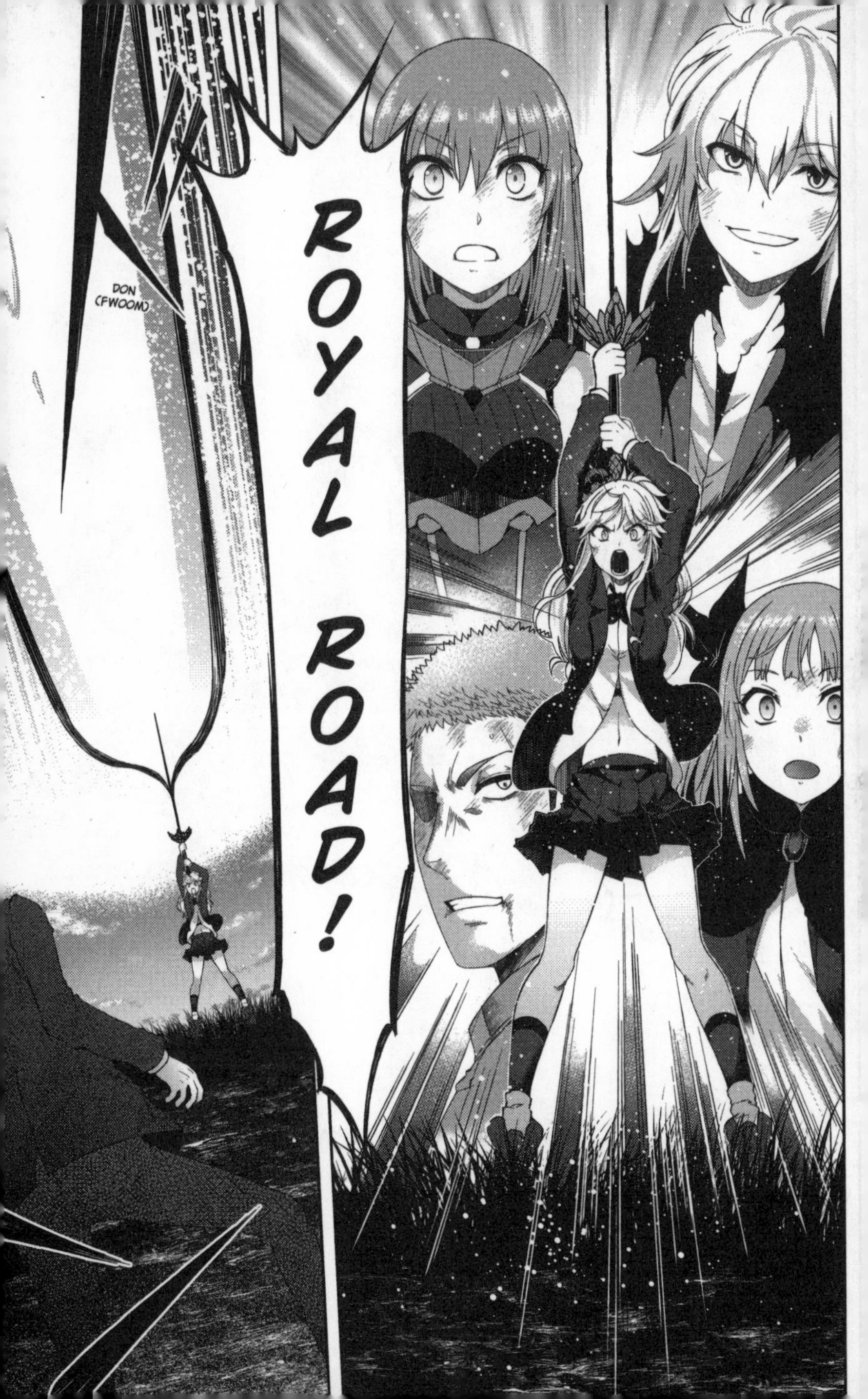
ROYAL ROAD!
DON
(FWOOM)

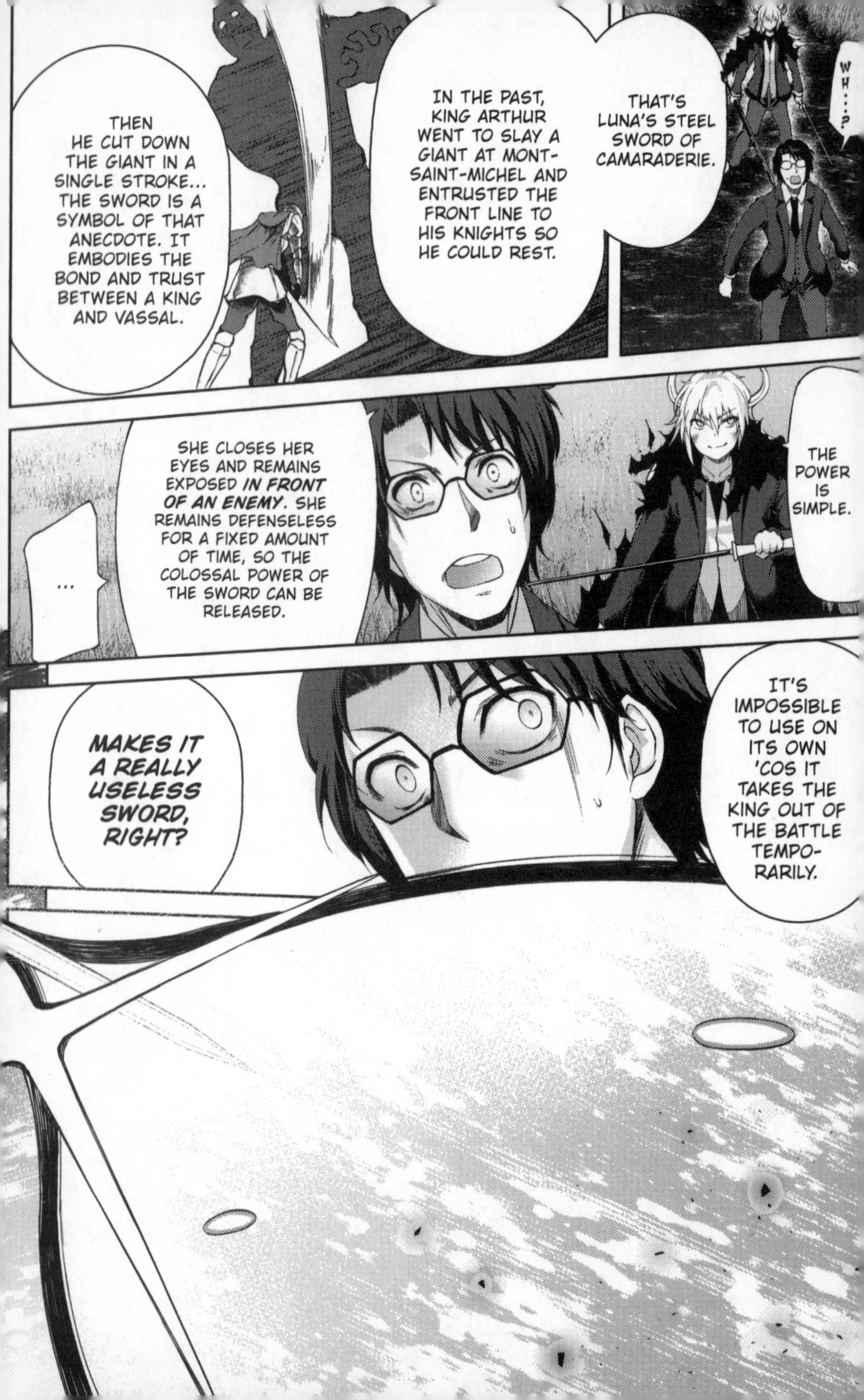
WH...?
THAT'S LUNA'S STEEL SWORD OF CAMARADERIE.
IN THE PAST, KING ARTHUR WENT TO SLAY A GIANT AT MONT-SAINT-MICHEL AND ENTRUSTED THE FRONT LINE TO HIS KNIGHTS SO HE COULD REST.
THEN HE CUT DOWN THE GIANT IN A SINGLE STROKE... THE SWORD IS A SYMBOL OF THAT ANECDOTE. IT EMBODIES THE BOND AND TRUST BETWEEN A KING AND VASSAL.
THE POWER IS SIMPLE.
SHE CLOSES HER EYES AND REMAINS EXPOSED *IN FRONT OF AN ENEMY*. SHE REMAINS DEFENSELESS FOR A FIXED AMOUNT OF TIME, SO THE COLOSSAL POWER OF THE SWORD CAN BE RELEASED.
...
IT'S IMPOSSIBLE TO USE ON ITS OWN 'COS IT TAKES THE KING OUT OF THE BATTLE TEMPO-RARILY.
MAKES IT A REALLY USELESS SWORD, RIGHT?

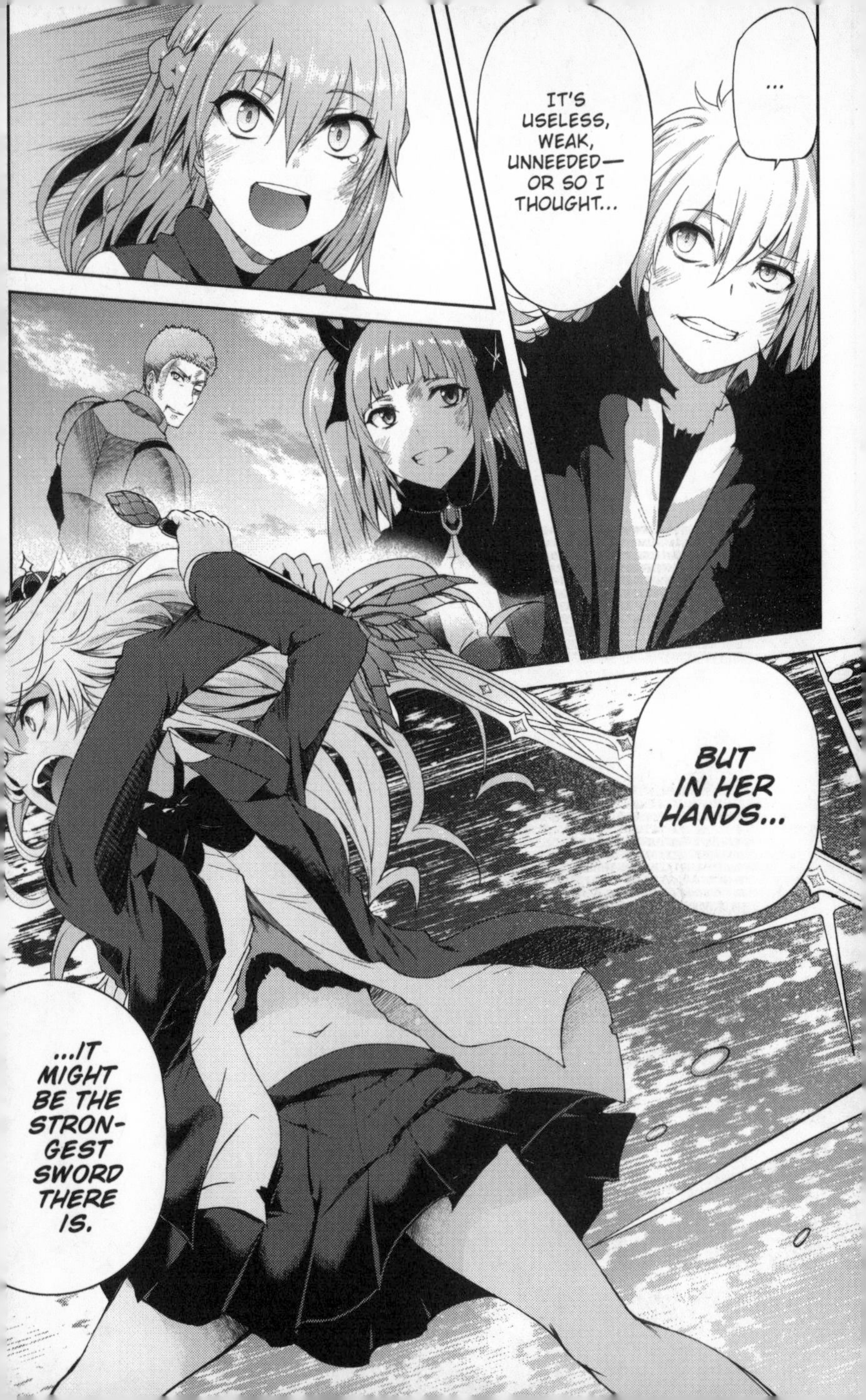
...
IT'S USELESS, WEAK, UNNEEDED—OR SO I THOUGHT...
BUT IN HER HANDS...
...IT MIGHT BE THE STRON-GEST SWORD THERE IS.

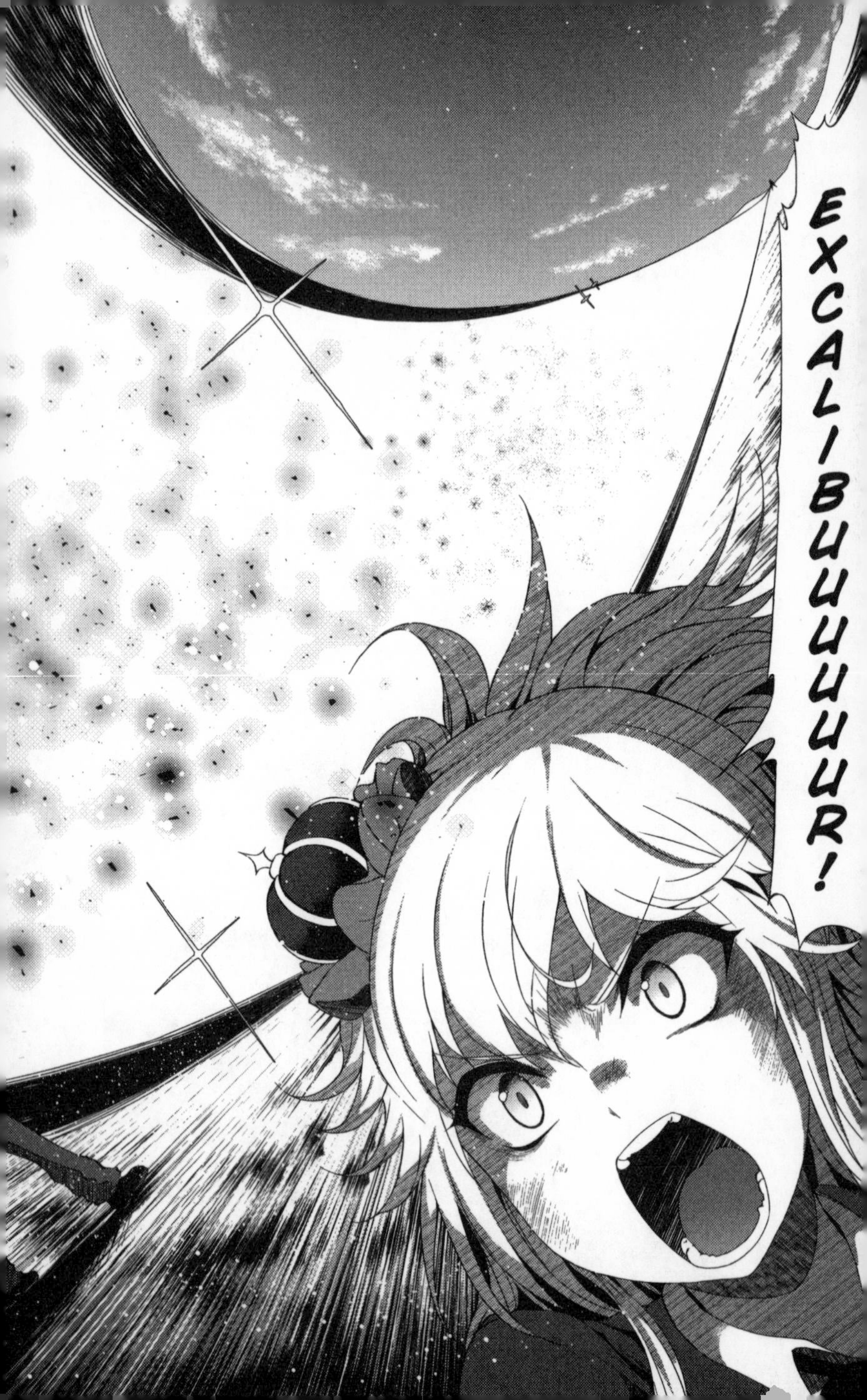
EXCALIBUUUUUR!

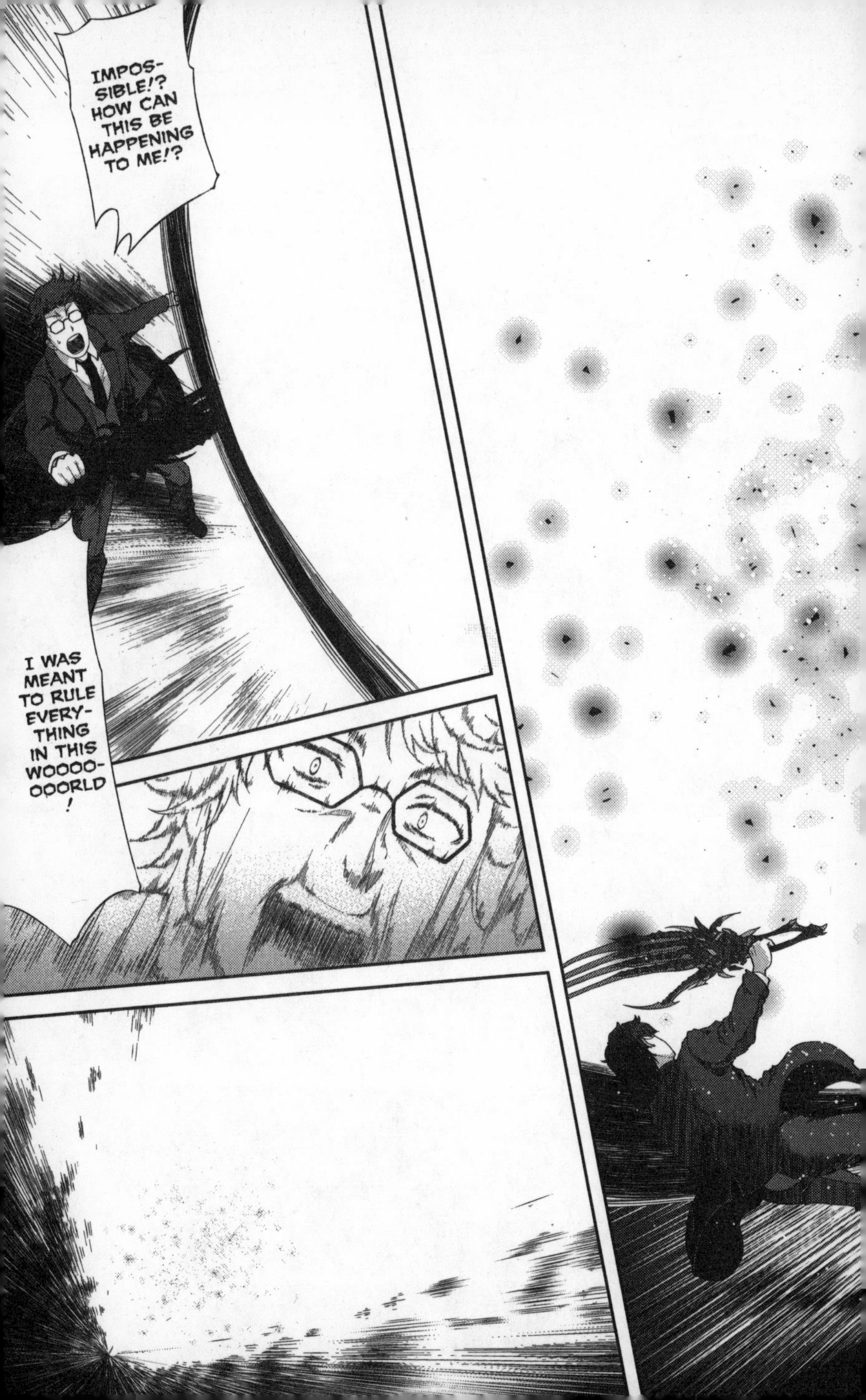
IMPOS-SIBLE!? HOW CAN THIS BE HAPPENING TO ME!?
I WAS MEANT TO RULE EVERY-THING IN THIS WOOOO-OOORLD!

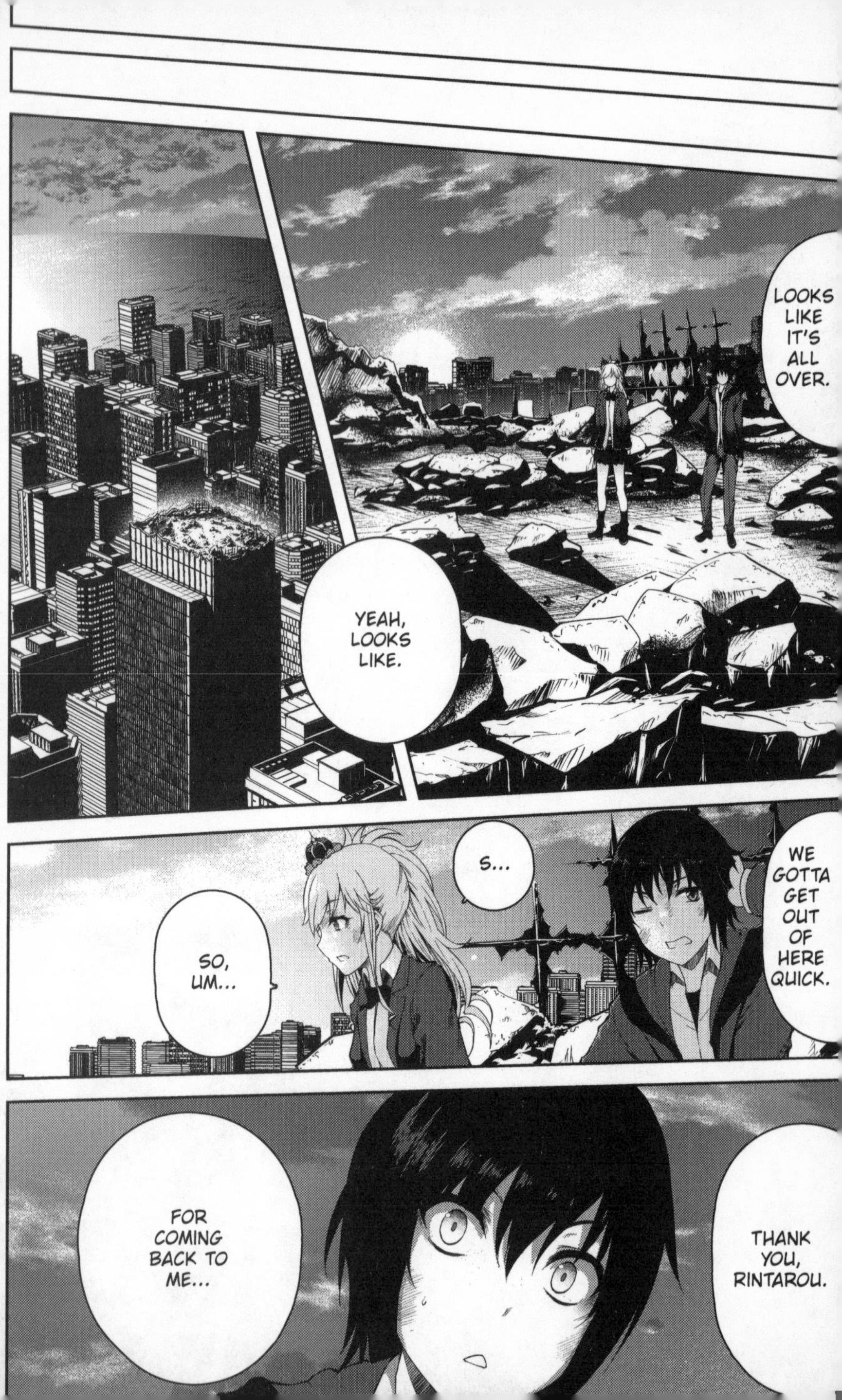
LOOKS LIKE IT'S ALL OVER.
YEAH, LOOKS LIKE.
WE GOTTA GET OUT OF HERE QUICK.
S...
SO, UM...
THANK YOU, RINTAROU.
FOR COMING BACK TO ME...

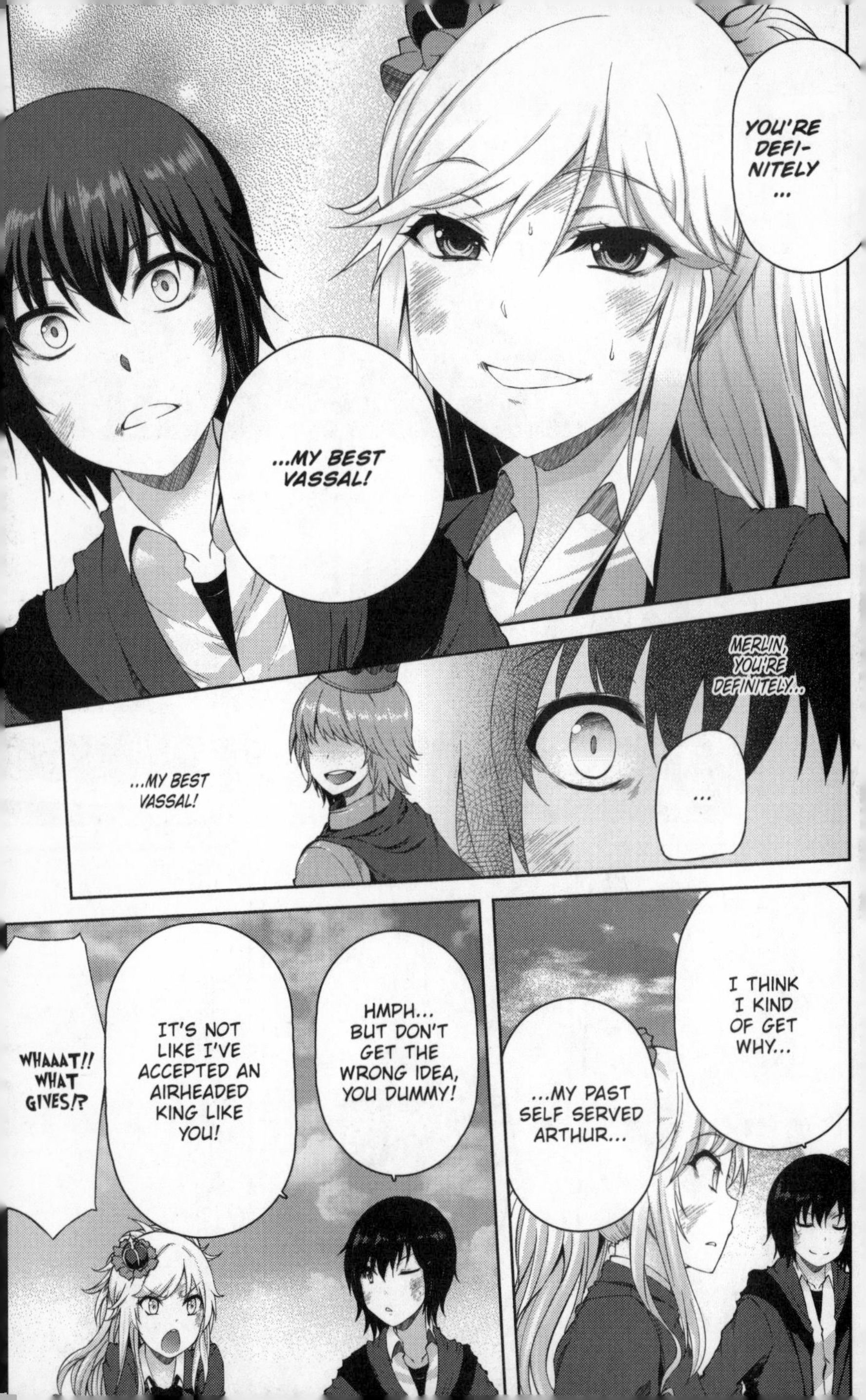
YOU'RE DEFINITELY...
...MY BEST VASSAL!
MERLIN, YOU'RE DEFINITELY...
...
...MY BEST VASSAL!
I THINK I KIND OF GET WHY...
...MY PAST SELF SERVED ARTHUR...
HMPH... BUT DON'T GET THE WRONG IDEA, YOU DUMMY!
IT'S NOT LIKE I'VE ACCEPTED AN AIRHEADED KING LIKE YOU!
WHAAAT!! WHAT GIVES!?

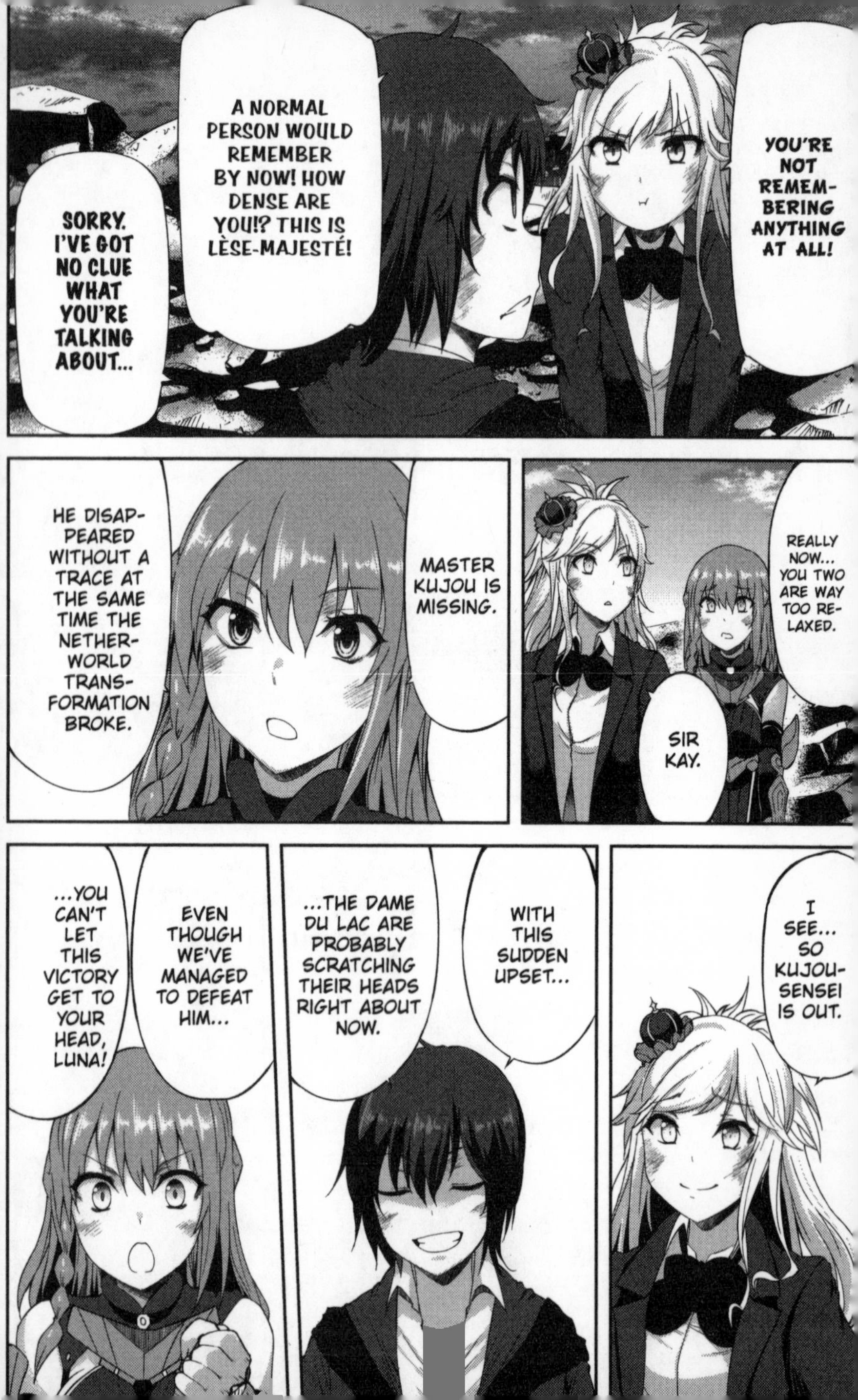
YOU'RE NOT REMEMBERING ANYTHING AT ALL!
A NORMAL PERSON WOULD REMEMBER BY NOW! HOW DENSE ARE YOU!? THIS IS LÈSE-MAJESTÉ!
SORRY. I'VE GOT NO CLUE WHAT YOU'RE TALKING ABOUT...
REALLY NOW... YOU TWO ARE WAY TOO RELAXED.
SIR KAY.
MASTER KUJOU IS MISSING.
HE DISAPPEARED WITHOUT A TRACE AT THE SAME TIME THE NETHERWORLD TRANSFORMATION BROKE.
I SEE... SO KUJOU-SENSEI IS OUT.
WITH THIS SUDDEN UPSET...
...THE DAME DU LAC ARE PROBABLY SCRATCHING THEIR HEADS RIGHT ABOUT NOW.
EVEN THOUGH WE'VE MANAGED TO DEFEAT HIM...
...YOU CAN'T LET THIS VICTORY GET TO YOUR HEAD, LUNA!

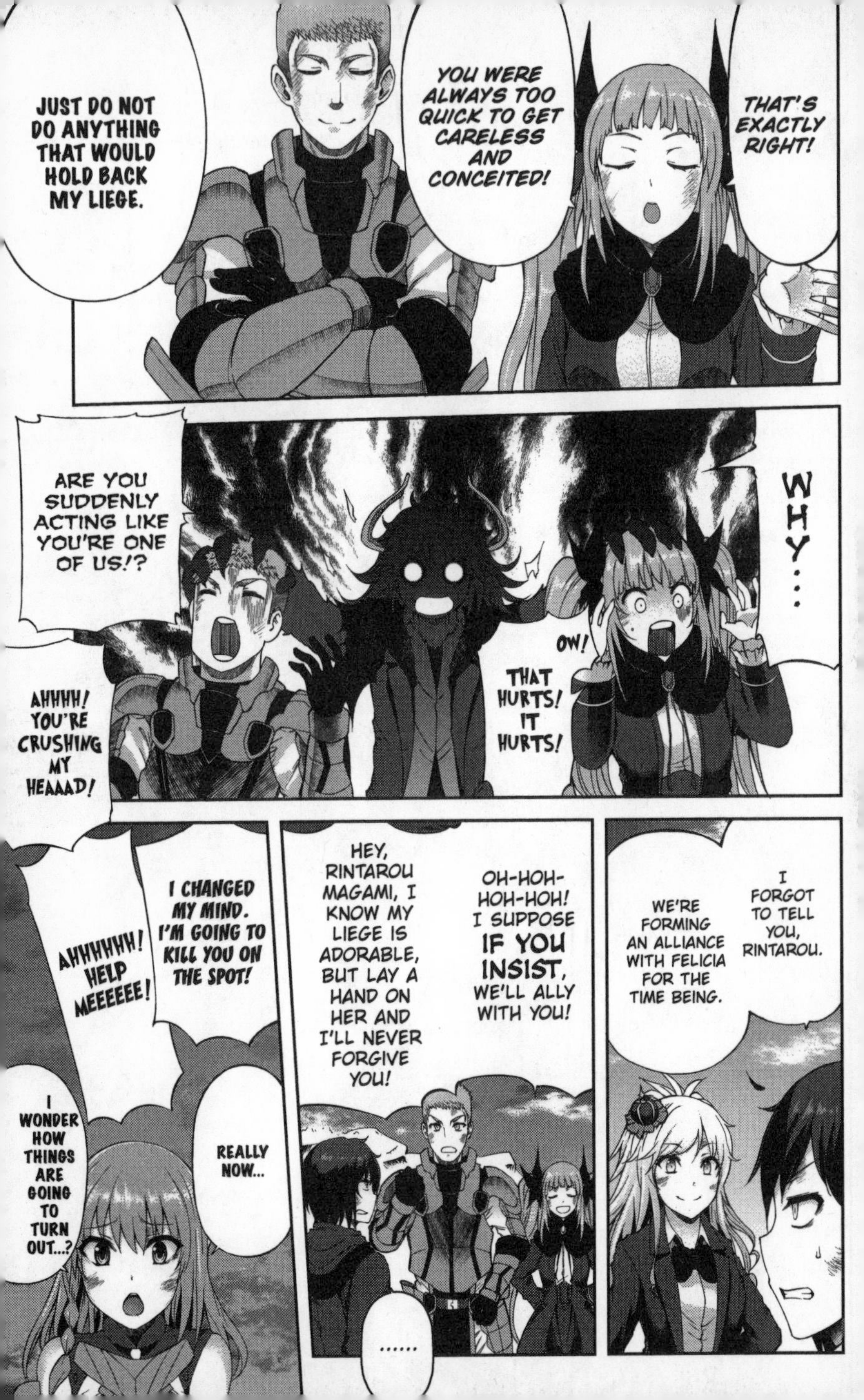
THAT'S EXACTLY RIGHT!
YOU WERE ALWAYS TOO QUICK TO GET CARELESS AND CONCEITED!
JUST DO NOT DO ANYTHING THAT WOULD HOLD BACK MY LIEGE.
WHY...
ARE YOU SUDDENLY ACTING LIKE YOU'RE ONE OF US!?
OW!
THAT HURTS! IT HURTS!
AHHHH! YOU'RE CRUSHING MY HEAAAD!
I FORGOT TO TELL YOU, RINTAROU.
WE'RE FORMING AN ALLIANCE WITH FELICIA FOR THE TIME BEING.
OH-HOH-HOH-HOH! I SUPPOSE IF YOU INSIST, WE'LL ALLY WITH YOU!
HEY, RINTAROU MAGAMI, I KNOW MY LIEGE IS ADORABLE, BUT LAY A HAND ON HER AND I'LL NEVER FORGIVE YOU!
......
I CHANGED MY MIND. I'M GOING TO KILL YOU ON THE SPOT!
AHHHHHH! HELP MEEEEEE!
REALLY NOW...
I WONDER HOW THINGS ARE GOING TO TURN OUT...?

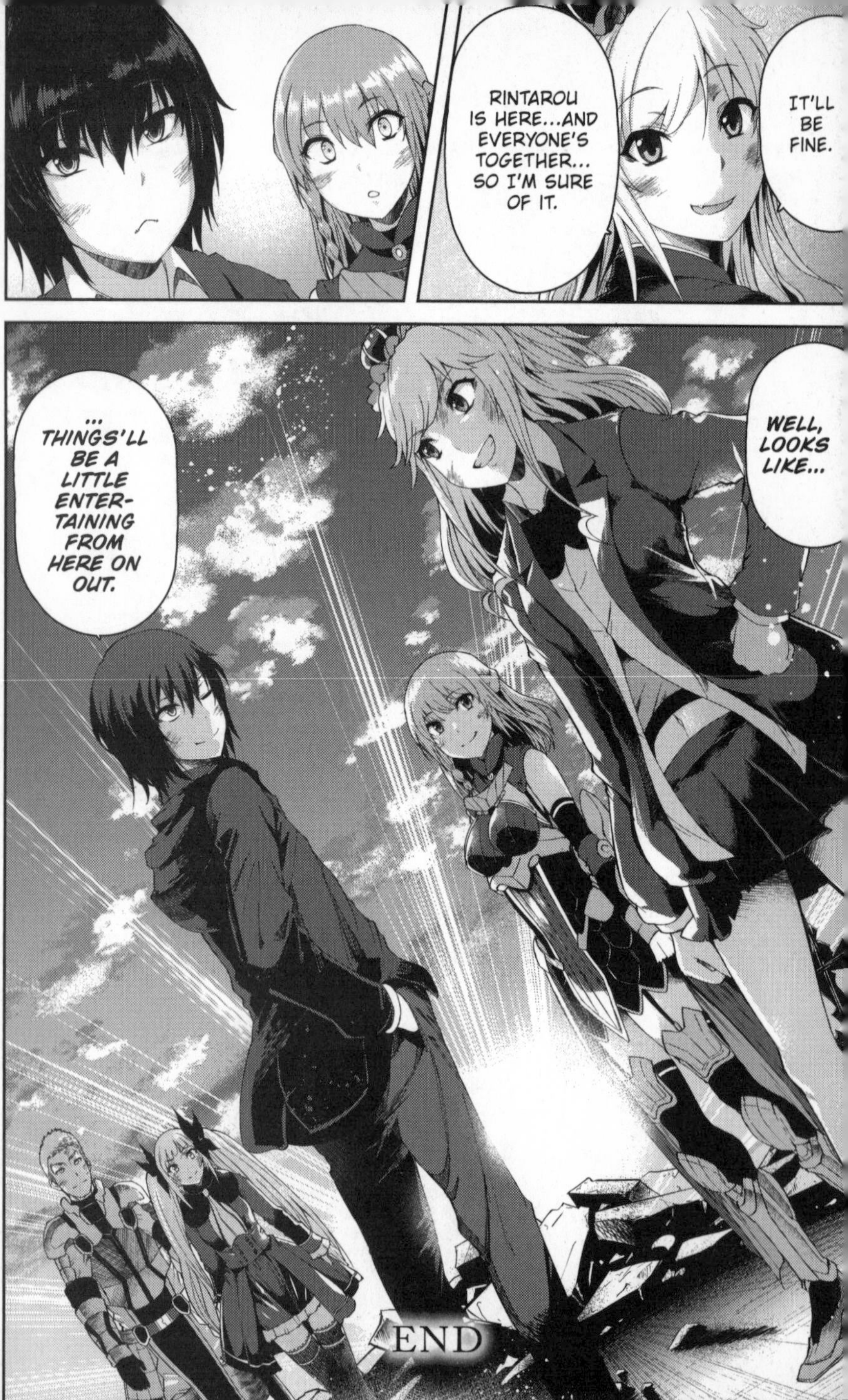
IT'LL BE FINE.
RINTAROU IS HERE...AND EVERYONE'S TOGETHER... SO I'M SURE OF IT.
WELL, LOOKS LIKE...
...THINGS'LL BE A LITTLE ENTERTAINING FROM HERE ON OUT.
END

STAFF LIST

Art
Yuzuriha

Assistant
Minoru Suto

3D & Special Thanks
Kyoujyu Issei

Cover Design
Tsuyoshi Kusano Design Office

LAST ROUND ARTHURS

LAST ROUND Arthurs

2

ORIGINAL STORY
Taro Hitsuji

ART
Yuzuriha

CHARACTER DESIGN
Kiyotaka Haimura

STORYBOARDS
Taisuke Umeki

Translation: JAN MITSUKO CASH ◆ Lettering: PHIL CHRISTIE

This book is a work of fiction. Names, characters, places, and incidents are the product of the author's imagination or are used fictitiously. Any resemblance to actual events, locales, or persons, living or dead, is coincidental.

LAST ROUND ARTHURS
©Taro Hitsuji 2020
©Yuzuriha 2020
©Kiyotaka Haimura 2020
©Taisuke Umeki 2020
First published in Japan in 2020 by KADOKAWA CORPORATION, Tokyo. English translation right arranged with KADOKAWA CORPORATION, Tokyo through Tuttle-Mori Agency, Inc.

English translation © 2021 by Yen Press, LLC

Yen Press
150 West 30th Street, 19th Floor
New York, NY 10001

Visit us at yenpress.com ◆ facebook.com/yenpress ◆ twitter.com/yenpress ◆ yenpress.tumblr.com ◆ instagram.com/yenpress

First Yen Press Edition: March 2021

Yen Press is an imprint of Yen Press, LLC.
The Yen Press name and logo are trademarks of Yen Press, LLC.

The publisher is not responsible for websites (or their content) that are not owned by the publisher.

Library of Congress Control Number: 2020938734

ISBN: 978-1-9753-2096-6 (paperback)
978-1-9753-2097-3 (ebook)

10 9 8 7 6 5 4 3 2 1

WOR

Printed in the United States of America